P9-CTA-580

COSTA RICA

Where to Stay and Eat
for All Budgets

Must-See Sights
and Local Secrets

Ratings You Can Trust

Fodor's Travel Publications   New York, Toronto, London, Sydney, Auckland
www.fodors.com

FODOR'S COSTA RICA 2007
Editor: Margaret Kelly, Shannon M. Kelly

Editorial Production: Linda K. Schmidt
Editorial Contributors: Yolanda Hernandez, Dorothy MacKinnon, Joy Rothke, Ryan Sarsfield, Suzanna Starcevic, Jeffrey Van Fleet
Maps: David Lindroth, *cartographer;* Bob Blake and Rebecca Baer, *map editors;* additional cartography provided by Henry Colomb, Mark Stroud, and Ali Baird, Moon Street Cartography
Design: Fabrizio La Rocca, *creative director;* Chie Ushio, Guido Caroti, Siobhan O'Hare, Tina Malaney, Brian Ponto
Photography: Melanie Marin, *senior picture editor*
Production/Manufacturing: Angela McLean
Cover Photo (red-eyed tree frog): ©Turco

ISBN-10: 1–4000–1686–X

ISBN-13: 978–1–4000–1686–0

ISSN: 1522–6131

SPECIAL SALES
This book is available for special discounts for bulk purchases for sales promotions or premiums. Special editions, including personalized covers, excerpts of existing books, and corporate imprints, can be created in large quantities for special needs. For more information, write to Special Markets/Premium Sales, 1745 Broadway, MD 6-2, New York, New York 10019, or e-mail specialmarkets@randomhouse.com.

AN IMPORTANT TIP & AN INVITATION
Although all prices, opening times, and other details in this book are based on information supplied to us at press time, changes occur all the time in the travel world, and Fodor's cannot accept responsibility for facts that become outdated or for inadvertent errors or omissions. So **always confirm information when it matters,** especially if you're making a detour to visit a specific place. Your experiences—positive and negative—matter to us. If we have missed or misstated something, **please write to us.** We follow up on all suggestions. Contact the Costa Rica editor at editors@fodors.com or c/o Fodor's at 1745 Broadway, New York, NY 10019.

PRINTED IN THE UNITED STATES OF AMERICA

10 9 8 7 6 5 4 3 2 1

Be a Fodor's Correspondent

Your opinion matters. It matters to us. It matters to your fellow Fodor's travelers, too. And we'd like to hear it. In fact, we *need* to hear it.

When you share your experiences and opinions, you become an active member of the Fodor's community. That means we'll not only use your feedback to make our books better, but we'll publish your names and comments whenever possible. Throughout our guides, look for "Word of Mouth," excerpts of your unvarnished feedback.

Here's how you can help improve Fodor's for all of us.

Tell us when we're right. We rely on local writers to give you an insider's perspective. But our writers and staff editors—who are the best in the business—depend on you. Your positive feedback is a vote to renew our recommendations for the next edition.

Tell us when we're wrong. We're proud that we update most of our guides every year. But we're not perfect. Things change. Hotels cut services. Museums change hours. Charming cafés lose charm. If our writer didn't quite capture the essence of a place, tell us how you'd do it differently. If any of our descriptions are inaccurate or inadequate, we'll incorporate your changes in the next edition and will correct factual errors at fodors.com *immediately.*

Tell us what to include. You probably have had fantastic travel experiences that aren't yet in Fodor's. Why not share them with a community of like-minded travelers? Maybe you chanced upon a beach or bistro or B&B that you don't want to keep to yourself. Tell us why we should include it. And share your discoveries and experiences with everyone directly at fodors.com. Your input may lead us to add a new listing or highlight a place we cover with a "Highly Recommended" star or with our highest rating, "Fodor's Choice."

Give us your opinion instantly at our feedback center at www.fodors.com/feedback. You may also e-mail editors@fodors.com with the subject line "Costa Rica Editor." Or send your nominations, comments, and complaints by mail to Costa Rica Editor, Fodor's, 1745 Broadway, New York, NY 10019.

You and travelers like you are the heart of the Fodor's community. Make our community richer by sharing your experiences. Be a Fodor's correspondent.

Bon voyage!

Tim Jarrell, Publisher

CONTENTS

PLANNING YOUR TRIP

Be a Fodor's Correspondent 3
About This Book 6
What's Where 7
Quintessential Costa Rica 12
When to Go 15
If You Like 16
Great Itineraries 19

REGIONS

1 SAN JOSÉ 23
Exploring San José 28
Where to Eat .40
Where to Stay 49
Nightlife & the Arts 56
Shopping 60
San José Essentials 63

2 THE CENTRAL VALLEY 67
West of San José 72
North of San José 81
Cartago and Irazú Volcano 94
The Turrialba Region 103
Central Valley Essentials 109

3 THE NORTHERN PLAINS 111
Northwest of San José 116
The Arenal Volcano Area 122
Monteverde Cloud Forest Area 135
Caño Negro Refuge Area 152
The Puerto Viejo Loop 154
Northern Plains Essentials 166

4 NORTH PACIFIC 169
Far Northern Guanacaste 174
The Nicoya Coast 188
The Tempisque River Basin 238
North Pacific Essentials 243

5 CENTRAL PACIFIC 247
The Southern Nicoya Tip 252
Inland 266
The Coast 270
Central Pacific Essentials 305

6 SOUTH PACIFIC 307
The Central Highlands 312
Valle de El General Region 317
The Coast 325
The Golfo Dulce 334
The Osa Peninsula 345
South Pacific Essentials 364

7 CARIBBEAN 367
The Northern Lowlands 372
The Northern Caribbean Coast 377
Coastal Talamanca 389
Caribbean Essentials 411

8 ECOTOURISM
COSTA RICA–STYLE 415

UNDERSTANDING COSTA RICA

Costa Rica at a Glance 428
A Brief History 430
Wildlife & Plant Glossary 432
Menu Guide .438
Vocabulary 441

SMART TRAVEL TIPS 445

INDEX 478

ABOUT OUR WRITERS 496

CLOSE-UPS

Where the Streets Have No Name 33
Teatro Nacional 36
Missing History 39
Speaking Costa Rican 73

COSTA RICA IN FOCUS

A National Hero 82
Coffee, the Golden Bean 92
La Negrita 95
White-Water Thrills 104
Certificate of Sustainable Tourism . . .121
What Is a Cloud Forest? 136
Bird Country 144
A Biological Superpower 153
More Texan than Tropical 179
Guanacaste National Park 182
The Ecological Blue Flag 194
Making a Difference 198
Understanding Costa Rica's Climate . .243
A Darker Side of Tourism 257
Diving the Deep at Coco Island 271
Catch the Wave 278
Getting Married in Costa Rica 298
A Mosaic of Forests 319
La Amistad National Park 325
Going Fishing? 335
Where Have All the Forests Gone? . .348
Wildlife-Watching Tips 351
Snorkelers' Paradise 363
Rain Forest Aerial Tram 376
A Province Apart 384
Caribbean Carnaval 391
The Old Atlantic Railroad 393
Reefs at Risk 399
Afro-Caribbean Heritage 403

THE CENTRAL VALLEY
Driving the Orosi Valley Loop 97
THE NORTHERN PLAINS
Arenal Volcano .126
Canopy Tours 138
NORTH PACIFIC
Choosing a Beach 189
CENTRAL PACIFIC
Manuel Antonio National Park 291
SOUTH PACIFIC
Corcovado National Park 357
CARIBBEAN
Tortuguero National Park 380

The Orosi Valley Loop 98
The Northern Plains 118–119
La Fortuna 124
Monteverde & Santa Elena 142
The North Pacific 176–177
Liberia 185
North Pacific Beaches 190–192
Tamarindo & Playa Langosta 212
The Central Pacific 254–255
Jacó 276
Quepos & Manuel Antonio 287
Manuel Antonio National Park 293
The South Pacific 314
Corcovado National Park 360
The Caribbean Coast 374–375
Tortuguero .378
Cahuita 395
Puerto Viejo de Talamanca 401

MAPS

Costa Rica .10–11
Downtown San José 30–31
Where to Stay & Eat in San José . .42–413
The Central Valley 74–75
Alajuela 84

ABOUT THIS BOOK

Our Ratings

Sometimes you find terrific travel experiences and sometimes they just find you. But usually the burden is on you to select the right combination of experiences. That's where our ratings come in.

As travelers we've all discovered a place so wonderful that its worthiness is obvious. And sometimes that place is so experiential that superlatives don't do it justice: you just have to be there to know. These sights, properties, and experiences get our highest rating, **Fodor's Choice,** indicated by orange stars throughout this book.

Black stars highlight sights and properties we deem **Highly Recommended,** places that our writers, editors, and readers praise again and again for consistency and excellence.

By default, there's another category: any place we include in this book is by definition worth your time, unless we say otherwise. And we will.

Disagree with any of our choices? Care to nominate a place or suggest that we rate one more highly? Visit our feedback center at www.fodors.com/feedback.

Budget Well

Hotel and restaurant price categories from ¢ to $$$$ are defined in the opening pages of each chapter. For attractions, we always give standard adult admission fees; reductions are usually available for children, students, and senior citizens. Want to pay with plastic? **AE, D, DC, MC, V** following restaurant and hotel listings indicate whether American Express, Discover, Diners Club, MasterCard, and Visa are accepted.

Restaurants

Unless we state otherwise, restaurants are open for lunch and dinner daily. We mention dress only when there's a specific requirement and reservations only when they're essential or not accepted—it's always best to book ahead.

Hotels

Hotels have private bath, phone, TV, and air-conditioning and operate on the European Plan (aka EP, meaning without meals), unless we specify that they use the Continental Plan (CP, with a Continental breakfast), Breakfast Plan (BP, with a full breakfast), or Modified American Plan (MAP, with breakfast and dinner) or are all-inclusive (including all meals and most activities). We always

list facilities but not whether you'll be charged an extra fee to use them, so when pricing accommodations, find out what's included.

Many Listings
★	Fodor's Choice
★	Highly recommended
✉	Physical address
⊹	Directions
🏠	Mailing address
☎	Telephone
🖷	Fax
⊕	On the Web
✍	E-mail
🎟	Admission fee
⊙	Open/closed times
►	Start of walk/itinerary
Ⓜ	Metro stations
▭	Credit cards

Hotels & Restaurants
🏨	Hotel
🛏	Number of rooms
⚴	Facilities
⯊⊙⯊	Meal plans
✕	Restaurant
⚱	Reservations
🏛	Dress code
⤢	Smoking
🆒	BYOB
✕🏨	Hotel with restaurant that warrants a visit

Outdoors
🏌	Golf
⛺	Camping

Other
☺	Family-friendly
🔢	Contact information
⇨	See also
✉	Branch address
☞	Take note

WHAT'S WHERE

SAN JOSÉ	This is not the Costa Rica of the postcards and travel brochures, and you should not sacrifice precious rain-forest and beach days for time in the sprawling, congested capital of San José. It is the political, economic, and cultural center of the country, the font from which all things emanate and hub to which all roads lead. To liken the city to New York or London is grossly unfair; it can't compare. But to the Costa Rican out in the provinces, it is the Big Apple . . . well, maybe "Big Pineapple." San José is also an amazingly friendly city, and while you should keep your wits about you, it is safer than many other Latin American capitals. No place in Costa Rica can top the city for restaurants, culture, and nightlife, and after a week of slogging through the rain forest, your body may crave a dose of civilization.
THE CENTRAL VALLEY	San José is smack dab in the center of this tidy, prosperous mountain valley with numerous day-trip possibilities. The valley's many beautiful inns are alternatives to staying in the capital on your first and last nights in Costa Rica. And in fact, the international airport is not in San José, but in the Central Valley, in Alajuela. The metro area's urban sprawl is spreading to the Central Valley in some spots, as is evidenced by the shopping-malled, office-towered, fast-food-ed highway entrances to Escazú and Santa Ana, but a few kilometers away, oxcarts bearing sugarcane bound for the local mill or coffee beans destined for the local processor trundle down gravel roads. Three provincial capitals—Alajuela, Cartago, and Heredia—pinpoint the valley; all are quieter versions of what San José once was and never will be again. Farther afield lie the country's two most accessible active volcanoes (Poás and Irazú), the historic Orosi Valley, and the agricultural community of Turrialba, fast becoming Costa Rica's white-water capital.
THE NORTHERN PLAINS	It's tough to pigeonhole the vast region that Costa Ricans call the Zona Norte (Northern Zone). Suffice it to say, if you can't find something in the Northern Plains that interests you, you should consider turning in your passport. Monteverde Cloud Forest, a cooler tropical forest, is the place to fly through the forest on a canopy tour—this is the region that gave birth to the concept of zipping along cables (while securely harnessed) between treetop platforms. Nearby, Lake Arenal beckons windsurfers, and Arenal Volcano, one of the world's 10 most

WHAT'S
WHERE

active, spits fire and warms the waters of the Tabacón Hot Springs. Two overlooked and underrated destinations with eco-appeal are the Sarapiquí region, whose many eco-lodges deserve more popularity, and the wetland Caño Negro Reserve near the Nicaraguan border.

THE NORTH PACIFIC

Guanacaste Province, the country's most touristed region, manages to combine beaches and bovines without missing a beat. The dry, grassland interior of the Nicoya Peninsula remains the domain of cowboys and cattle, the folkloric image most associated with Costa Rica, although the rest of the country has happily embraced it as its own. A chain of enormously popular beaches lines the coast, and this is the North Pacific of the tourist brochures. Each beach has traits that confer on it a unique personality: Flamingo's quiet refinement is a respite for the well-to-do; Tamarindo's nightlife is legendary; Avellanas's strong swells draw the surfers; Ostional's nesting sea turtles continue a millennia-old cycle of life; and the Papagayo Peninsula's all-inclusive resorts envelop you in creature comforts. And here's a region with its own small-but-growing international airport, in Liberia. So if your travels are concentrated here, there's no reason to fly in and out of San José at all.

THE CENTRAL PACIFIC

Costa Rica's Central Pacific coast mixes sophistication and funkiness, sometimes right down the street from each other. The port city of Puntarenas, once the country's favorite beach destination (but no longer), anchors the region. The beaches south of there are some of the nearest to San José, hours closer than those on the North Pacific coast, and undeniably popular because of their easy access. This is Costa Rica's "party hearty" region, with funky surf towns Jacó and Malpaís and somewhat more refined, but still lively, twin communities Quepos and Manuel Antonio. You need not be a 19-year-old "spring breaker" to enjoy the Central Pacific. Plenty of grown-up and family-friendly activities are available between the dens of revelry, and we've found the best selection of restaurants outside San José on this section of the coast. Some of the strands of beach get downright isolated–just you, the macaws, and the monkeys. And calmer beach towns like New Agey Montezuma are just a ferry ride away, across the gulf on Nicoya Peninsula's southern tip.

THE SOUTH PACIFIC	The South rarely sees first-time visitors. In fact, many second- and third-timers have never ventured south of Cartago. But inevitably, once they do, they kick themselves for waiting so long. Terms get bandied about to describe the region: "the Amazon of Costa Rica" or "the most biodiverse place on the planet." Clichéd though they sound, they're true. Corcovado National Park conjures up the Tarzan-movie jungle images you've seen. Lodges in its Osa Peninsula accommodate those who wish to bond with nature but don't wish to sleep *directly* in it. But not all is jungle down here: the region takes in Chirripó, Costa Rica's highest peak, a long hike of moderate difficulty. And Dominical, Zancudo, and Pavones, three of our favorite beach towns, ones rarely mentioned in the fun-in-the-sun pantheon, are here in the South Pacific. Access (or lack thereof) means everything here, and roads can be atrocious even by Costa Rican standards, making it essential to travel by 4WD vehicle or fly.
THE CARIBBEAN	Despite its name, Costa Rica's Caribbean is no St. Lucia. It doesn't have miles of white-sand beaches or crystal-blue waters. There is a similar English-speaking, Afro-Caribbean population here, but mixed with indigenous, Asian, and the dominant Latino culture. What this version of the Caribbean (also called "the Atlantics") *does* have is nature galore, with dense forests, coral reefs, and lumbering turtles engaging in age-old nesting rituals. Long the province of European backpackers, the region is less known in North American circles. Many Costa Ricans write it off as all reggae, rain, and robbery. Yes to the first. Mostly yes to the second: it does rain more here than elsewhere in the country, which is why it's so green. But no to the third: crime is no more prevalent here than anywhere else in the country. If you seek luxury resorts, look elsewhere. Instead, the Caribbean has a wide price range in everything from backpackers' digs to trendy bed-and-breakfasts at a fraction of Pacific-coast prices.

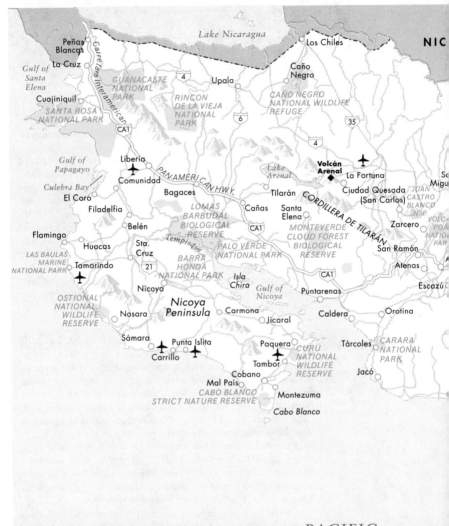

Peñas Blancas
La Cruz
Gulf of Santa Elena
Cuajiniquil
SANTA ROSA NATIONAL PARK
Gulf of Papagayo
Liberia
Comunidad
Culebra Bay
El Coro
Filadelfia
Flamingo
LAS BAULAS MARINE NATIONAL PARK
Huacas
Tamarindo
OSTIONAL NATIONAL WILDLIFE RESERVE
Nicoya
Nosara
Sámara
Carrillo
Punta Islita

Lake Nicaragua
Los Chiles
Caño Negro
Upala
CAÑO NEGRO NATIONAL WILDLIFE REFUGE
GUANACASTE NATIONAL PARK
RINCON DE LA VIEJA NATIONAL PARK
Bagaces
LOMAS BARBUDAL BIOLOGICAL RESERVE
Belén
Sta. Cruz
Tempisque
BARRA HONDA NATIONAL PARK
PALO VERDE NATIONAL PARK
Nicoya Peninsula
Carmona
Jicaral
Isla Chira
Cañas
Santa Elena
Tilarán
Lake Arenal
Volcán Arenal
La Fortuna
Ciudad Quesada (San Carlos)
CORDILLERA DE TILARÁN
MONTEVERDE CLOUD FOREST BIOLOGICAL RESERVE
San Ramón
Atenas
CAT
Gulf of Nicoya
Puntarenas
Caldera
Paquera
Tambor
CURÚ NATIONAL WILDLIFE RESERVE
Cobano
Mal País
CABO BLANCO STRICT NATURE RESERVE
Montezuma
Cabo Blanco
Tárcoles
CARARA NATIONAL PARK
Jacó
Orotina
Escazú
Zarcero
JUAN CASTRO BLANCO N.P.

PAN-AMERICAN HWY.
Carretera Interamericana

NIC

PACIFIC OCEAN

TO ISLA DEL COCO

0   30 miles
0   45 km

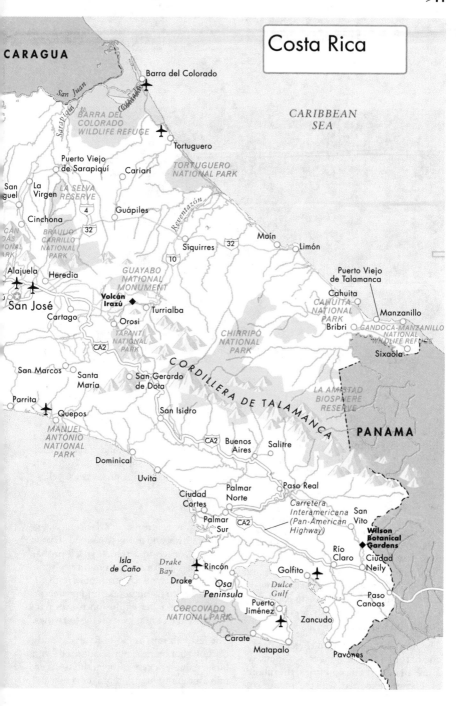

Costa Rica

CARAGUA

San Juan

Barra del Colorado

CARIBBEAN SEA

BARRA DEL COLORADO WILDLIFE REFUGE

Tortuguero

Puerto Viejo de Sarapiquí

Cariari

TORTUGUERO NATIONAL PARK

San guel

La Virgen

LA SELVA RESERVE

Guápiles

Cinchona

Moín

4

BRAULIO CARRILLO NATIONAL PARK

32

CAN DÁS IONAL RK

Siquirres

32

Limón

10

Alajuela

Heredia

GUAYABO NATIONAL MONUMENT

Puerto Viejo de Talamanca

Cahuita

Volcán Irazú ◆

Turrialba

CAHUITA NATIONAL PARK

Manzanillo

San José

Cartago

Orosi

Bribri

GANDOCA-MANZANILLO NATIONAL WILDLIFE REFUGE

TAPANTÍ NATIONAL PARK

CHIRRIPÓ NATIONAL PARK

Sixaola

CA2

San Marcos

Santa María

San Gerardo de Dota

C O R D I L L E R A   D E   T A L A M A N C A

LA AMISTAD BIOSPHERE RESERVE

Parrita

Quepos

San Isidro

PANAMA

MANUEL ANTONIO NATIONAL PARK

Dominical

CA2

Buenos Aires

Salitre

Uvita

Palmar Norte

Paso Real

Ciudad Cortés

Carretera Interamericana (Pan-American Highway)

San Vito

Palmar Sur

CA2

Wilson Botanical Gardens ◆

Río Claro

Ciudad Neily

Isla de Caño

Drake Bay

Rincón

Golfito

Drake

Osa Peninsula

Dulce Gulf

Paso Canoas

CORCOVADO NATIONAL PARK

Puerto Jiménez

Zancudo

Carate

Matapalo

Pavones

QUINTESSENTIAL COSTA RICA

Coffee

Call any Costa Rican business office to speak to someone around 3 PM and you'll probably end up leaving a message; odds are the person you're calling is on a coffee break. Here in Costa Rica there's no shame in prioritizing coffee over afternoon calls.

If nearby Honduras was the original "Banana Republic," 19th-century Costa Rica was a "Coffee Republic," with coffee barons holding enormous sway over the era's affairs. Coffee remains inexorably entwined with the country, with economists paying close attention to world prices and kids in rural areas still taking class time off to help with the harvest. Costa Rica takes its coffee drinking seriously, and even very young children partake.

The irony is that it's hard to get a decent cup of the stuff here. True to economic realities of developing countries, the quality product gets exported, with the inferior cof-

fee staying behind for the local market. (The same is true of bananas, Costa Rica's other signature agricultural product.) The best places to get a cup of high-quality Costa Rican coffee are upscale restaurants and hotels. Owners understand foreign tastes and have export-quality coffee on hand. Gift shops sell the superior product as well.

Festivals

Every day is a patron saint's day somewhere in Costa Rica, and unless you spend all your time ensconced in a resort, you'll probably see a sign for some community's annual *festejo patronal* (patron-saint festival), in homage to its namesake and protector. A loud firecracker explosion rouses participants at dawn to kick off the festivities.

The festivals mirror Costa Rica: devoutly Catholic but increasingly secularized, with bingo games, rickety carnival rides—a certain amount of luck and prayer is in order

You need to scratch below the surface to experience Tico culture—it doesn't hit you like a ton of bricks the way nearby Guatemala's does. The rituals of daily life are quiet, subdued, and peaceful. Costa Ricans wouldn't have it any other way.

there—horse parades, and amateurish bull-fights. (The bull is not killed in Costa Rica.) The Imperial—Costa Rica's most popular brand of beer—flows copiously. But it is still a religious tradition, and an important part of the day is a mass and parade where the saint's figure is carried through the streets. Visitors are always welcome: "¡Venga!" you'll be told if you stand tentatively at the edge of crowd. "Come, join us!"

Celebrating Smallness

In a bigger-is-better world it's refreshing to find a country that revels in its smallness. The ostentatious monuments glittering with gold common elsewhere in Latin America are nowhere to be found here. A nation whose first settlers were not conquistadors but hardworking farmers would have none of that. Streets and sidewalks seem a little narrower in Costa Rica, and

beds and doorways are a little shorter, too. Even the name Costa Ricans give to themselves, Ticos, comes from their peculiar way of forming the diminutive of nouns. Other Spanish speakers add the suffix *-ito* to denote something small (*un momentito*), but Costa Ricans say *un momentico*. (Whether or not it will be just a little moment is another story.) And no phrase brings a sparkle to a Costa Rican's eye like "*Mi país muy chiquitico*" (My very tiny little country).

Oxcarts

The oxcart is the folkloric symbol of Costa Rica and a common subject for local artisans. The western Central Valley town of Sarchí is the best place to buy these souvenirs, which can take the form of objects as small as paper-clip holders, ashtrays, and earrings; larger items like salad bowls and planters; or full-size oxcarts–turned–cof-

QUINTESSENTIAL COSTA RICA

fee tables. (The larger works can be disassembled and shipped home.) Oxcarts do still lumber along rural roads ferrying coffee and sugarcane (and sometimes passengers) to and fro. But in the 21st century they are more likely to do parade duty; San José holds a large oxcart festival the last weekend in November. The brightly painted carts look anything but utilitarian, with wheels rotating in kaleidoscopic colors.

Mom & Pop Places

Some 75 percent of the properties in Costa Rica are small, independently owned lodgings with fewer than 30 rooms, even in San José. An individual style imprints each of those lodgings, from scruffy hostels to fashionable inns. What these places lack in a concierge and business center they more than make up for in style and memorable experience. The chain hotels are beginning to take hold in Costa Rica, es-

pecially on the North Pacific coast. But the fly-'em-in, fly-'em-out mass tourism, fine-tuned in Mexico and the Caribbean Islands, remains in its infancy here. That can make a visit to Costa Rica a bit pricier, since you are usually purchasing your lodging, airfare, transportation, and tours à la carte. But it also keeps tourism here more small-scale and exclusive.

WHEN TO GO

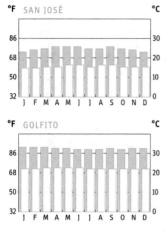

Costa Rica has an astounding number of microclimates, dictated by its many forests and changes in altitude, so the weather varies dramatically for such a small country. For information about specific regions, *see* "When to Go" at the front of each chapter.

The sunniest, driest season in most of the country occurs from roughly mid-December through April, which is the busiest tourist season. For you, that means more advance planning, some flexibility in choosing a hotel, and higher prices. Afternoon showers kick in by May and last through November most everywhere, with a brief dry season in June and July. The Caribbean coast flies in the face of these norms with rains spread out fairly evenly throughout the year, with brief *drier* seasons February through April and September through October. Costa Rica promotes the rainy season as the "green season," touting lush vegetation, smaller crowds, and lower prices. Showers interrupt your afternoon beach time and remote roads can be washed out during the worst of the rains.

Temperatures generally range between 70°F (20°C) and 85°F (30°C). It's the humidity, not the heat, that causes you discomfort, especially in the dense forest of the Caribbean coast, the northern lowlands, and the Osa Peninsula. The arid North Pacific is Costa Rica's hottest region, with temperatures frequently exceeding 90°F (33°C) in the dry season.

One final point: We typically hear, "I didn't realize the rain forest would be so . . . *rainy.*" Well, you heard it here: it rains often and heartily in the rain forest. The dense foliage and elaborate root systems rely on frequent showers year-round.

Climate

⚡ Forecasts **Weather Channel Connection** ⊕ www.weather.com.

San José's average temperatures are typical of other highland towns; and Golfito's are similar to those of most coastal and lowland towns.

IF YOU LIKE

Beaches

Costa Rica has 1,290 km (799 mi) of coastline to choose from, most of it lined with beaches which are, by law, all public. Most are not the picture-postcard white strands of the Caribbean Islands or Mexico; the dark sand here is of volcanic origin and waters tend to be rough, not crystal-blue. Note that beaches near population centers get strewn with trash quite quickly. It's one of the great ironies of Costa Rica that a country renowned for its environmental achievements litters with such laissez-faire. Limited access tends to make for more scenic beaches. The following are some of our favorites.

- **Dominical, South Pacific.** This is a hopping surfer town which does enhance the experience, and in that regard we recommend this as a great beach in a great beach town.

- **Malpaís, Central Pacific.** Accessed via a steep gravel road, Malpaís is a quiet strand ripe for beachcombing and sunning.

- **Playa Flamingo, North Pacific.** Though not very isolated, Flamingo is an example of how environmentally conscious communities can make their beaches sparkle.

- **Playa Grande, North Pacific.** Conservationists have kept this beach pristine for nesting leatherback turtles.

- **Playa Pavones, South Pacific.** The surfing is good at remote Pavones, a stunning combination of black sand, tropical forest, and glistening waters.

- **Punta Uva, Caribbean.** The farthest from town of the Puerto Viejo de Talamanca beaches, and the most pristine.

- **Tortuguero, Caribbean.** The turtle population here makes this isolated beach one of the world's top naturalist draws.

Bird-Watching

As part of the narrow isthmus connecting the Americas, Costa Rica is a natural biological melting pot. With less than 0.03% of the planet's surface, it is home to some 875 bird species, more than the United States and Canada combined. Some stay year-round; others come and go with winter migration.

- **Caño Negro, Northern Plains.** Waterfowl, such as jabiru and snail kites, are abundant.

- **Carara National Park, Central Pacific.** Scarlet macaws are reliable sightings, as are great egrets, boat-billed herons, anhingas, and trogons.

- **Cerro de La Muerte, South Pacific.** This is probably the best place in the country to spot a resplendent quetzal.

- **Corcovado National Park, South Pacific.** The largest population of (endangered) scarlet macaws in the country lives here.

- **La Selva Biological Station, Northern Plains.** If you're interested in (but totally clueless about) bird-watching, sign up in advance for the Birdwatching 101 course. Scientists have tallied nearly 500 species here.

- **Monteverde Cloud Forest, Northern Plains.** The resplendent quetzal, the blue-crowned motmot, the orange-bellied trogon, and the emerald toucanet are just some of the 400 species that have been logged here.

- **Tortuguero National Park, Caribbean.** The bare-throated tiger heron, the sungrebe, and the agami heron are some of Tortuguero's many waterfowl species.

Rain Forests

Costa Rica has set aside some 15 percent of its territory for national parks and reserves. Yet deforestation takes place at an alarming rate, its old-growth forests falling victim to illegal logging, aided by a scarcity of resources to enforce environmental laws and the pressures of development. That said, Costa Rica's existing rain forests thrive. A typical hectare (2½ acres) of forest might be home to nearly 100 species of trees. (Contrast that with a mere 30 in the richest forests of North America.) Go with a guide, both for your safety and the information they can provide. We forever marvel at their ability to spot a sloth at a hundred paces.

- **Braulio Carrillo National Park, Northern Plains.** Though it's the closest rain forest to San José, this primary swath of jungle is difficult to access, with dense flora and tough trails. But determination yields impressive mammals, birds, and plants.

- **Corcovado National Park, South Pacific.** If you don't mind the mud, you'll love the wild and wooly primary forests here.

- **La Selva Biological Station, Northern Plains.** One of the best opportunities to see lots of wildlife without roughing it.

- **Manuel Antonio National Park, Central Pacific.** Even a quick jaunt along the trails lets you see squirrel monkeys, white-faced coatis, and iguanas.

- **Monteverde Cloud Forest Reserve, Northern Plains.** The most famous of Costa Rica's cloud-forest reserves.

Surfing

Deliciously warm water, year-round waves, and two coasts add up to one of the world's best-known surfing destinations. There's even better news: that popularity hasn't yet translated into overcrowding. Most surfers bring their own boards, as evidenced by the crowds that get off the plane and make a beeline for the oversize luggage carousel, but you'll find plenty of places to rent equipment if you're not quite that hardcore.

- **Jacó, Central Pacific.** Easily accessible Jacó draws the many surfers who come here as much for the partying as the waves.

- **Pavones, South Pacific.** It's a long trip here, but your reward is one of the world's longest left-breaking waves.

- **Puerto Viejo de Talamanca, Caribbean.** One of the world's best (and toughest) waves, Salsa Brava, laps right offshore in town.

- **Tamarindo, North Pacific.** The north coast's consummate surfing town and a good place for beginners; the stretch of shoreline north to Playa Grande and south to Playa Negra satisfies experts.

IF YOU LIKE

Volcanoes

Of Costa Rica's 300 or so volcanoes, some 230 are underwater and extinct. Of the 70 on dry land, 5 are active (listed below), 15 have been labeled "dormant"—projected to spring back to life at some undetermined future date—and the rest are extinct. Volcán Irazú got its second wind in 1963 after 30 years of inactivity. No one was more surprised than John F. Kennedy, who was here on a visit at the time and was sprinkled with ash like everyone else. Over four decades later, prediction is still an imprecise science.

- **Arenal, Northern Plains.** The most famous volcano in Costa Rica, Arenal has a classic cone that forms an iconic backdrop to the town of La Fortuna. On clear nights you can see red-hot lava spitting from its summit.

- **Irazú, Central Valley.** A cinch to visit as a day trip from San José, here you can walk right up to the edge of steaming craters.

- **Poás, Northern Plains.** Like Irazú, at Poás you can get close to the crater, and it is also close to San José. We find Poás, with its beautiful crater lake, a bit more impressive.

- **Rincón de la Vieja, North Pacific.** This moonlike landscape of steaming craters and fizzing fumaroles is worth the rugged drive and rough hike.

- **Turrialba, Central Valley.** The least-visited of the active volcanoes, Turrialba rises 3,330 meters (10,910 feet) above sea level. You can see the Pacific on a clear day.

White-Water Adventures

Insanely steep hills and heavy rainfall make the country a mecca for white-water sports, and there's a level of ease or difficulty to match anyone's expertise (or lack thereof). Have fun, but be brutally frank with yourself about your abilities and fears before setting out on any rafting or kayaking excursion. (*See* CloseUp box "White-Water Thrills" *in* Chapter 2 for more guidelines.) Base yourself in these places to find whitewater outfitters.

- **La Fortuna, Northern Plains.** Trips on the Toro, Balsa, San Carlos, and Sarapiquí rivers are offered out of La Fortuna.

- **Puerto Viejo de Sarapiquí, Northern Plains.** Outfitters based here can take you on similar excursions to those offered from La Fortuna.

- **Quepos, Central Pacific.** Head here for action on the Savegre and Naranjo rivers.

- **San José.** You might not guess it, but San José is a major rafting center; the Reventazón and Pacuare rivers are close enough that you can be back in time for dinner. The Pacuare, El General, and Corobicí rivers lend themselves to overnight or multiday trips.

- **Turrialba, Central Valley.** Many outfitters congregate in Turrialba, arguably the country's white-water capital, and close to the action.

GREAT ITINERARIES

BEACHES, RAIN FORESTS, AND VOLCANOES

Day 1: Arrival

Arrive in San José (most arrivals are in the evening) and head straight to one of the small luxury hotels north of the city in the Central Valley. A favorite of ours is Finca Rosa Blanca, a fairy-tale retreat overlooking miles of coffee farms.

Logistics: Brace yourself for long lines at immigration if you arrive in the evening along with all the other large flights from North America. Try to get a seat near the front of the plane and don't dawdle when disembarking.

Day 2: Poás Volcano and Tabacón Hot Springs

Volcán Poás, where you can peer over the edge of a crater, lies nearby. Fortify yourself with the fruits, jellies, and chocolates sold by vendors on the road up to the summit. A scenic drive takes you to the La Fortuna/Arenal Volcano area. Drop your luggage at one of many fantastic hotels (Montaña de Fuego is our pick for fabulous volcano views), and go directly to Tabacón Hot Springs & Resort. Take a zipline or hanging bridges tour through the forest canopy and then pamper yourself with a spa treatment. Finish the day by sinking into a volcanically heated mineral bath with a cocktail at your side as the sun sets behind fiery Arenal.

Logistics: Get an early start to get the best views of Poás. Shuttle vans (⇨ Bus Travel *in* Smart Travel Tips A to Z) can get you to Arenal and have hotel-to-hotel service.

Day 3: Caño Negro Wildlife Refuge

Spend your entire day in the Caño Negro Wildlife Refuge, a lowland forest reserve replete with waterfowl near the Nicaraguan border.

Logistics: Book your trip the night before; tour operators in La Fortuna keep evening hours for exactly that reason. All transport will be included.

Day 4: Scenic Drive to the Central Pacific

Today's a traveling day—a chance to really see the country's famous landscape and infamous roads. (Believe us, they get a lot worse than this route.) A few hours' drive from Arenal takes you to fabled Manuel Antonio on the Central Pacific coast. Beyond-beautiful hotels are the norm here, and you have your choice of seaside villas or tree-shrouded jungle lodges. We like the hillside La Mariposa, which has commanding views.

Logistics: Hotel-to-hotel shuttle-van services (⇨ Bus Travel *in* Smart Travel Tips A to Z) can get you to Manuel Antonio. If you drive instead, start out as early as possible. You'll pass through two mountainous stretches (between La Fortuna and San Ramón, and between Atenas and the coast) that fog over by midafternoon.

Day 5: Manuel Antonio National Park

Manuel Antonio is Costa Rica's most famous national park for a reason: it has beaches, lush rain forest, mangrove swamps, and rocky coves with abundant marine life. You can—and should—spend an entire day exploring the park, home to capuchin monkeys, sloths, agoutis, and 200 species of birds. It's also one of two locales in the country where you'll see squirrel monkeys.

Logistics: Almost all Manuel Antonio hotels have transport to the park. If yours doesn't, taxis are plentiful and cheap.

Day 6: Beach Yourself

Days 1 through 5 were "on the go" days. Reward yourself today with lots of relaxation. Manuel Antonio means beaches, and there are several to choose from. Manuel Antonio and neighboring Quepos mean restaurants, too, the best selection of any beach community in the country.

Logistics: Most everything you need here strings along the 5-km (3-mi) road between Quepos and Manuel Antonio National Park. It's practically impossible to get lost.

Day 7: San José

A morning drive back to San José gives you time to spend the afternoon in the city. We like the cozy, classy Hotel Le Bergerac. Visit the Teatro Nacional, the capital's must-see sight, and save time for late-afternoon shopping. An evening dinner caps off your trip before you turn in early to get ready for tomorrow morning's departure.

Logistics: As the number of visitors to Costa Rica grows, so does the number of passengers using Juan Santamaría Airport. We recommend you check in three hours before your flight. Better safe than sorry.

MORE BEACHES, RAIN FORESTS, AND VOLCANOES

Day 1: Arrival

Most arrivals to Liberia, Costa Rica's second international airport, are in early afternoon. You can't go wrong with any North Pacific beach, but we like Playa Hermosa for its pivotal location, one that lets you use it as a base for visiting area attractions. Check out small, personal, breezy Hotel Playa Hermosa/Bosque del Mar, the perfect antidote to the mega-resorts that lie not too far away.

Logistics: The big all-inclusives up here have their own minivans to whisk you in air-conditioned comfort from airport to resort. Smaller lodgings such as Hotel Playa Hermosa/Bosque del Mar can arrange to have transport waiting, with advance notice.

Day 2: Playa Hermosa

Morning is a great time to laze on the beach in this part of Costa Rica. The breezes are refreshingly cool and the sun hasn't started to beat down. After lunch, explore Playa Hermosa's metropolis, the small town of Playas del Coco. Quite frankly Coco is our least favorite beach up here. But we like the town for its little souvenir shops, restaurants, and local color.

Logistics: Taxis are the easiest way to travel between Playa Hermosa and Coco, about 10 minutes away. Have your hotel call one, and flag one down on the street in town when it's time to return.

Day 3: Rincón de la Vieja Volcano

The top of Rincón de la Vieja Volcano with its steaming, bubbling, oozing fumaroles lies about 90 minutes from Hermosa. Lather on the sunscreen and head for the Hacienda Guachipelín and its vol-cano-viewing hikes, canopy tours, rappelling, horse riding, mountain biking, and river tubing. Cap off the day with a spa treatment, complete with thermal mud bath.

Logistics: If you don't have a rental car, book a private driver for the day, which can usually be arranged through your hotel.

Day 4: Golf or Diving

Golf is big up here. The 18-hole Garra de León course at the Paradisus Playa Conchal resort is about 45 minutes from Hermosa. The other popular, slightly pricey, sport here is scuba diving. Dive operators are based in nearby Playas del Coco or Playa Panamá. A daylong course gives you a taste of the deep.

Logistics: The resort will arrange transport to and from the golf course, and dive operators will pick you up from and return you to your hotel.

Day 5: Palo Verde National Park

We like the morning guided tours at Palo Verde National Park, one of the last remaining dry tropical forests in Central America. The Organization for Tropical Studies, which operates the biological station there, has terrific guides. Spend the afternoon observing nature in a more relaxed fashion with a float down the nearby Río Corobicí. (These are not the screaming rapids so famed in white-water circles.)

Logistics: This excursion is a bit round-about, so this is the day your own vehicle would come in handiest. But you can also hire a private driver (arranged through your hotel). Bring water to drink: it gets hot here.

Day 6: Sailing

Make your final day a relaxing one with a few hours on the waves. Many sailboats operate out from this section of coast. Our choice is the 52-foot *Samonique III* (⇨ Chapter 4), which sails out of Playa Flamingo most afternoons at 2. A four-hour excursion includes sandwiches, appetizers, and an open bar. Legendary Pacific sunsets are tossed in at no extra charge.

Logistics: The *Samonique III* folks can arrange transport from hotel to boat and back again.

Day 7: Departure

Grab a last dip in the ocean this morning, because your flight departs from Liberia in the early afternoon.

Logistics: The advent of international flights to Liberia has fueled this region's meteoric rise to fame, but the airport's size has not kept pace with the number of passengers. Expansion is eventually on the way, but presently, lines can be long. Allow yourself plenty of time for check-in.

TIPS

❶ Fly into Liberia. While it's logical to think "San José" when planning flights to Costa Rica, it makes no sense if you plan to spend your entire time in the North Pacific.

❷ A car is ideal for this itinerary, yet many area attractions and tour operators provide transport to and from area lodging if you aren't too far afield. (One of the reasons we like Playa Hermosa.)

❸ All-inclusive resorts do a good job of organizing local excursions with local operators, so if you're staying at one, take advantage of them.

❹ Beach to beach often requires travel back inland. There is no real (i.e., navigable) coastal road.

❺ If ever there were a case for an off-season vacation, this is it. This driest, hottest part of the country gets very dry and hot from January through April. The rains green everything up, and frankly, we prefer the region during the low season.

San José

Post Office, San José

WORD OF MOUTH

"Are you interested in San Jose? Some people would say 'Don't do it—there's nothing there,' but we have found it interesting to walk around town, see the Gold Museum, the Jade Museum, the Teatro Nacional, the Plaza de la Cultura, the Mercado Central."

—shillmac

WELCOME TO SAN JOSÉ

City view

TOP 5
Reasons to Go

1 **Historic Barrios Amón and Otoya:** quiet tree-lined streets and century-old houses turned trendy hotels and restaurants.

2 **Gold and Jade museums:** They're not the Louvre or the Smithsonian, but still fascinating and worth a visit.

3 **Eating out:** the only place in Costa Rica with such a variety of cuisines.

4 **Nightlife:** the hottest scene in the country for dance clubs, bars, and chilled-out late-night cafés.

5 **Location, location, location:** From the capital's pivotal position you can be on a coffee tour, at the base of a giant volcano, or riding river rapids in just 30 minutes.

TO INTERNATIONAL AIRPORT (16 km /10 mi)

Terminal Atlántico Norte

Terminal Coca-Cola

Mercado Central

La Sabana Park

Museum of Costa Rican Art

Avenida Central

HOSPITAL

LA ME

Avenida to San Martín

Calle 14

Calle 8

Terminal de Puntarenas

The primarily residential neighborhoods West of Downtown are anchored by large La Sabana Park. There is also the Museum of Costa Rican Art.

| 0 | | 500 yards |
| 0 | | 500 meters |

Spices at Mercado Central   Parque Central

Getting Oriented

In a high valley, 3,809 feet above sea level, San José lies just 9 degrees north of the equator, but the altitude keeps things refreshingly temperate year round. The metropolitan area holds more than 1 million residents, but the city proper is small, with some 300,000 people living in its 44 square km (17 square mi). Most of the sights are concentrated in three downtown neighborhoods, La Soledad, La Merced, and El Carmen, named for their anchor churches. The borders of the city are fuzzy: San José melts into its suburbs with nary a sign to denote where one community ends and another begins.

Historic barrios Amón and Otoya and the Children's Museum are a few of the attractions North of Downtown.

Downtown holds San José's historic and commercial districts and most of its tourist attractions, including the Jade and Gold museums, the Mercado Central, and the Teatro Nacional, the city's most impressive building.

East of Downtown, a number of good restaurants and hotels, along with the University of Costa Rica, are ensconced in the suburb of San Pedro.

Teatro Nacional

SAN JOSÉ PLANNER

When to Go

San José is pleasant year-round, with highs of 26–28°C (79–83°F) and lows of 17–19°C (65–68°F). December and February are the coolest months. In March and April the heat picks up noticeably. May–November, the pattern is usually: sunny mornings, brief afternoon showers, and clear brisk evenings. September and October are waterlogged, and it can rain nonstop for days at a time.

The Kindness of Strangers

In a 2003 *Scientific American* study called "Simple Acts of Kindness" (a take on the famous Blanche DuBois line in Tennessee Williams's play *A Streetcar Named Desire*), Costa Rica's capital was rated the second friendliest city among 58 worldwide. Here the kindness of strangers doesn't stop at giving you directions; locals will often lead you to where you want to go.

Do It in a Day

If you have only a day in the city, the must-see stops are the National Theater and the Gold Museum, both on the same block. We recommend the guided tour of the theater. If you have more time, take in the Museo del Jade (Jade Museum) and Museo Nacional (National Museum) as well. Or pay a visit to the Museo para la Paz (Peace Museum). The Museo de Niños (Children's Museum), north of downtown, is a popular kid-pleaser. Our Good Walk (⇨ p. 12) takes you past the top sights, giving you a taste of the city in just an hour.

■ TIP→→ Within San José, taxis are inexpensive and much faster than city buses

Play It Safe

San José is safer than most other Latin American capitals; the biggest problem is theft. But standard precautions apply:

■ Exchange money only at banks.

■ Select ATMs in well-lighted areas, and conceal cash immediately.

■ Use only licensed red taxis, with yellow triangles on the front doors.

■ Park in guarded, well-lighted lots.

■ Never leave anything in sight in your parked vehicle.

City Tours

Grayline Tours Costa Rica (☎ 220–2126 ⊕ www.graylinecostarica.com) operates a half-day sightseeing-and-shopping tour.

The **Instituto Costarricense de Turismo** (⇨ San José Essentials, *below*)

gives out a brochure outlining a self-guided historical walk through downtown.

Real Town Tour (☎ 221–5443 or 396–3033) gives two-hour English-language tours of typical neighborhoods southeast of downtown.

Tren Tico (Tico Train; ☎ 226–1346), really a truck pulling a string of wagons, picks you up at the Gran Hotel Costa Rica for a 25-minute city tour without commentary, from 10 to 4 on Sunday and holidays.

Day Trips from the Capital

Some of these attractions provide pickup service in San José. Alternatively, tour operators include many of these attractions on their itineraries. (⇨ *Central Valley Planner* in Chapter 2 and *Northern Plains Planner* in Chapter 3 for tour-operator contacts.)

DESTINATION	FROM SAN JOSÉ (BY CAR)	
Butterfly Farm	45 min west	⇨ p. 83
Café Britt	30 min north	⇨ p. 91
Carara Biological Reserve	2 hrs southwest	⇨ p. 268
Doka Estate	1 hr west	⇨ p. 85
Guayabo National Monument	2 hrs southeast 4WD necessary	⇨ p. 106
INBioparque	10 min north	⇨ p. 89
Irazú Volcano	60 min east	⇨ p. 96
La Paz Waterfall Gardens	2 hrs north	⇨ p. 155
Orosi Valley	60 min southeast	⇨ p. 97
Poás Volcano	60 min northwest	⇨ p. 154
Rain Forest Aerial Tram	45 min north	⇨ p. 376
River Rafting	2–2½ hrs	⇨ p. 104
Sarchí	60 min northwest 30 min by car from Poás	⇨ p. 117
Tortuga Island	3 hrs west	⇨ p. 258

■ TIP➡➡ When you head back to town from a day trip, browse the souvenir shops that congregate around Parque Morazán or in the northeastern suburb of Moravia.

Prices

WHAT IT COSTS in Dollars

	$$$$	$$$	$$	$	¢
Restaurants	over $25	$15–$25	$10–$15	$5–$10	under $5
Hotels	over $250	$150–$250	$75–$150	$50–$75	under $50

Restaurant prices are per-person for a main course at dinner. Hotel prices are for two people in a standard double room in high season, excluding service and tax (16.4%).

EXPLORING SAN JOSÉ

Downtown

By Jeffrey Van Fleet

It's a trend seen the world over: businesses and residents flee city centers for the ample space, blissful quiet, and lower-priced real estate of the suburbs. Costa Rica's burgeoning capital is no exception to that rule, but downtown San José still remains the historic and vibrant (if noisy and congested) heart of the city. Government offices have largely stayed put downtown—actually, the presidency is the only public institution to have moved its headquarters to the 'burbs—as have the majority of tourist attractions. If you spend any time here sightseeing, you'll find yourself in the center of San José.

Make no mistake: the city's traffic is overwhelming, and the narrow downtown streets, laid out in the days of the oxcart, barely handle the daily influx of vehicles. Pedestrians have the right of way here, but no driver seems to know or care about that little annoyance in Costa Rican traffic law. You can take refuge along the several blocks of Avenida Central and Calles 2 and 17 that have been converted into pedestrian malls, and take heart that more of those traffic-free streets are on city planners' drawing boards.

What to See

⓮ **Catedral Metropolitana** (Metropolitan Cathedral). Built in 1871, and completely refurbished in the late 1990s to repair earthquake damage, this neoclassic structure east of the park with a corrugated tin dome is not terribly interesting outside, but inside are patterned floor tiles, stained-glass windows depicting various saints and apostles, and framed polychrome bas-reliefs illustrating the 14 Stations of the Cross. The renovation did away with one small time-honored tradition: rather than purchase and light a votive candle, the faithful now deposit a 50-colón coin illuminating a bulb in a row of tiny electric candles. The interior of the small Capilla del Santísimo (Chapel of the Host) on the cathedral's north side evokes ornate old Catholicism, much more so than the cathedral itself, and is a place for quiet reflection and prayer. Masses are held throughout the day on Sunday starting at 7 AM, with one in English each Saturday at 4 PM. ✉ *C. Central, between Avdas. 2 and 4, Barrio La Merced* ☎ *221–3820* ☉ *Weekdays 6–6, Sun. 6 AM–9 PM.*

⓲ **Centro Nacional de la Cultura** (National Cultural Center). Costa Rica cherishes its state enterprises. Here the government is your light and water utility, your phone company, your Internet service provider, your bank, your insurance agent, and your hospital. It is also your distillery, and this complex served as the headquarters of the Fábrica Nacional de Licores (FANAL, or National Liquor Factory) until 1981, when it moved to a modern facility west of Alajuela. In a heartwarming ex-

CAUTION

Don't drive in the city if you can avoid it. The streets are narrow and congested, and many drivers treat traffic regulations as suggestions rather than laws.

A GOOD WALK

1

All visitors manage to find their way to the **Plaza de la Cultura** ❶, a favorite meeting spot in the heart of the city, and it makes a good kick-off point for a walk. The ornate **Teatro Nacional** ❷ sits on the south side of the plaza. Pop in and buy a ticket for an evening performance, and/or grab a cup of coffee at the lobby café. The **Museo del Oro Precolombino** ❸ lies under the plaza. The gold collection could easily captivate for an hour or two. From here, head two blocks north on Calle 5 to **Parque Morazán** ❹, whose centerpiece Templo de Música is the symbol of the city. Traffic is particularly dangerous here, so take heed. The Edificio Metállico, a metal building that serves as a school, fronts the park's north side. Continue just east of the park on Avenida 3 to the small **Parque España** ❺, one of the city's most pleasant green spaces. The ornate building on the park's north side is the Andrew Carnegie–funded Casa Amarilla. At Avenida 7 is the modern Instituto Nacional Segoros

(INS) building, whose 11th-floor **Museo del Jade** ❻ has an extensive American jade collection and great city views. The Ministry of Culture complex, the **Centro Nacional de la Cultura** ❼ fronts the park's east side. From Parque España, walk one long block east to the **Parque Nacional** ❾. Two blocks south on Calle 17 is a pleasant pedestrian mall. Pass the Asamblea Legislativa, where Costa Rica's congress meets, and come to the **Museo Nacional** ⓫. Loop around to the museum's west side to one of the higher levels on the Plaza de la Democracia, a great vantage point for sunsets—but otherwise just an expanse of concrete. Avenida Central fronts the plaza's north side. Head back downhill, into the hustle and bustle of the city center. The avenue becomes a lively pedestrian mall at Calle 9, and two blocks later you return to the Plaza de la Cultura. ☉ TIMING TIPS→→ **The walk takes about an hour at a stroll. If you take a more leisurely approach, lingering at the parks or museums, the walk could take hours.**

ception to the usual "tear it down" mentality so prevalent in San José, the Ministry of Culture converted the sloped-surface, double-block 1853 factory into a 14,000-square-meter center of its own offices, two theaters, and a museum. The metal **Teatro FANAL** (☎ 222–2974), once the fermentation area, now hosts frequent theater and music performances. The clay-brick **Teatro 1887** (☎ 222–2974) served as the factory's personnel office, and today dedicates itself to performances by the National Dance Company. What is now the theater's lobby was once the chemical testing lab. The stone-block storage depot next to the water towers at the southeast side of the complex became the **Museo de Arte y Diseño Contemporáneo** (⇨ below). A stone gate and sun clock grace the entrance nearest the museum. ⊠ *C. 13 between Avdas. 3 and 5, Barrio Otoya* ☎ *257–5524* ☉ *Weekdays 8–5, Sat. 10–5.*

❶⓱ **Correos de Costa Rica** (Central Post Office). The handsome, carved seagreen exterior of the post office, dating from 1917, is hard to miss among

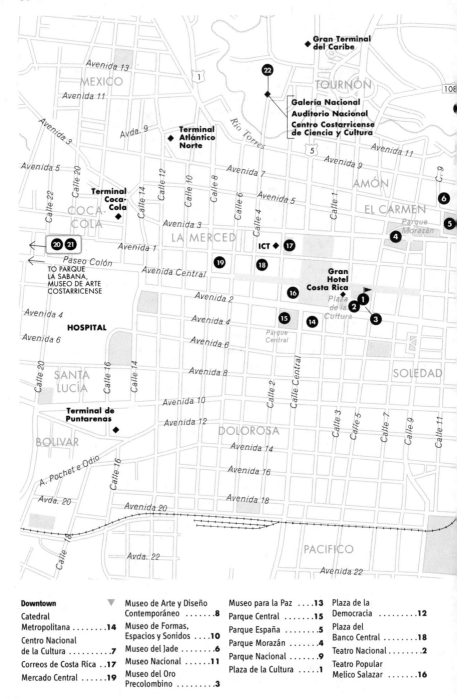

Downtown

Catedral
Metropolitana **14**

Centro Nacional
de la Cultura **7**

Correos de Costa Rica ..**17**

Mercado Central **19**

Museo de Arte y Diseño
Contemporáneo **8**

Museo de Formas,
Espacios y Sonidos **10**

Museo del Jade **6**

Museo Nacional **11**

Museo del Oro
Precolombino **3**

Museo para la Paz **13**

Parque Central **15**

Parque España **5**

Parque Morazán **4**

Parque Nacional **9**

Plaza de la Cultura **1**

Plaza de la
Democracia **12**

Plaza del
Banco Central **18**

Teatro Nacional **2**

Teatro Popular
Melico Salazar **16**

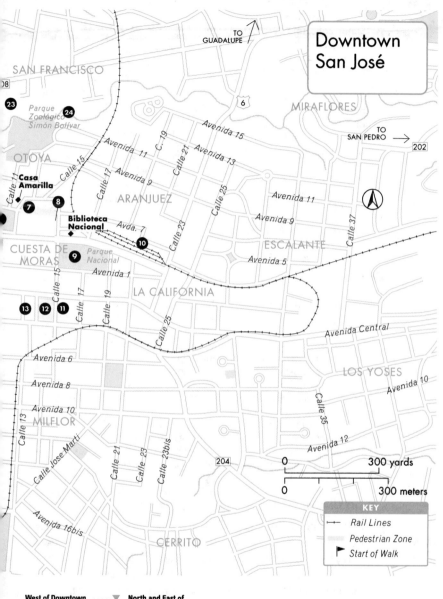

Downtown San José

TO
GUADALUPE

SAN FRANCISCO

08

23

Parque Zoológico Simón Bolívar **24**

MIRAFLORES

6

OTOYA

Avenida 15

C. 19

Avenida 11

Calle 21

Avenida 13

Avenida 15

TO
SAN PEDRO →

202

Calle 15

Avenida 17

Avenida 9

Calle 25

Avenida 11

Casa Amarilla

Calle 1

ARANJUEZ

Avenida 9

7   **8**

Calle 37

Biblioteca Nacional

Avda. 7

Calle 23

ESCALANTE

10

CUESTA DE MORAS

9 *Parque Nacional*

Avenida 5

Avenida 1

Calle 15

LA CALIFORNIA

Calle 17

Calle 19

13 **12** **11**

Calle 25

Avenida Central

Avenida 6

LOS YOSES

Avenida 8

Avenida 10

Calle 35

Avenida 10

Calle 13

MILFLOR

Calle Jose Marti

Avenida 12

Calle 21

Calle 23

Calle 23bis

204

0   300 yards

0   300 meters

Avenida 16bis

CERRITO

KEY

+—+   *Rail Lines*

        Pedestrian Zone

▶   *Start of Walk*

West of Downtown . . . . . ▼

Museo de
Arte Costarricense **20**

Parque Metropolitano
La Sabana **21**

North and East of Downtown . . . . ▼

Jardín de
Mariposas Spyrogyra . . **23**

Museo de los Niños . . . **22**

Parque Zoológico
Simón Bolívar **24**

the bland buildings surrounding it. Stamp collectors should stop at the **Museo Filatélico** (Philatelic Museum; ☎ 223–6918), to the left as you face the stamp windows, for its display of first-day stamp issues. Early-20th-century telegraphs and telephones are also on display. The museum is open weekdays 8–5; admission is free. From the second-floor balcony you can see the loading of *apartados* (post-office boxes) going on below: Ticos (which is what Costa Ricans call themselves) covet these hard-to-get boxes, as the city's lack of street addresses makes mail delivery a challenge. ✉ *C. 2, between Avdas. 1 and 3, Barrio La Merced* ⊗ *Weekdays 7:30–6, Sat. 7:30–noon.*

⑲ **Mercado Central** (Central Market). This block-long melting pot is a warren of dark, narrow passages flanked by stalls packed with spices (some purported to have medicinal value), fish, fruit, flowers, pets, and wood and leather crafts. But the 1880 structure is a kinder, gentler introduction to a Central American market; there are no pigs or chickens or their accompanying smells to be found here. A few stands selling tourist souvenirs congregate near the entrances, but this is primarily a place where the average Costa Rican comes to shop. There are also dozens of cheap restaurants and snack stalls, including the country's first ice-cream vendor. Be warned: the concentration of shoppers makes this a hot spot for pickpockets, purse snatchers, and backpack slitters. Enter and exit at the southeast corner of the building (Avda. Central at C. 6). The green-and-white SALIDA signs direct you to other exits, but they spill onto slightly less safe streets. Use the image of the Sacred Heart of Jesus, the market's patron and protector, near the center of the building, as your guide; it faces that safer corner by which you should exit. (Things probably weren't planned that way.) ✉ *Bordered by Avdas. Central and 1 and Cs. 6 and 8, Barrio La Merced* ⊗ *Mon.–Sat. 6–6.*

NEED A BREAK?

Pop's. Here's the place to get the crème de la crème of locally made Costa Rican ice cream. Mango is a favorite flavor. After a long walk on crowded sidewalks, it may just save your sanity. This prolific chain is everywhere, and you'll find three outlets downtown. ✉ *Avda. Central, between Cs. 1 and 3* ✉ *Avda. Central, between Cs. 7 and 9* ✉ *Calle 4, between Avdas. Central and 1.*

❽ **Museo de Arte y Diseño Contemporáneo** (Museum of Contemporary Art and Design). This wonderfully minimalist space is perfect for serving as the country's premier modern-art venue. The MADC, as it is known around town, hosts changing exhibits of work by artists and designers from all over Latin America. You can arrange for a guided visit with a couple of

Where the Streets Have No Name

ADMITTEDLY, SOME OF THE streets in San José do have names, but no one seems to know or use them. Streets in the center of the capital are laid out in a grid, with *avenidas* (avenues) running east and west, and *calles* (streets), north and south. Odd-numbered avenues increase in number north of Avenida Central; even-numbered avenues, south. Streets east of Calle Central have odd numbers; those to the west are even. The farther you get from downtown, the scarcer street signs become. Costa Ricans rely instead on a charming and exasperating system of designating addresses by the distance from well-known landmarks, as in "100 meters north and 50 meters west of the school." Another quirk: "100 meters" always refers to one city block, regardless of how long it actually is. Likewise, "200 meters" is two blocks, and so on. Historically, the reference point was the church, but these days it might be anything from a bar to a Burger King, or even a landmark that no longer exists: the eastern suburb of San Pedro uses the *higuerón*, a fig tree that was felled long ago, but lives on in the hearts of Costa Ricans. It's no wonder that those who can afford it opt to have their mail delivered to a post-office box. Your best bet is to follow the time-honored practice and *ir y preguntar:* keep walking and keep asking.

days' advance notice. ⊠ *C. 15, between Avdas. 3 and 5, Barrio Otoya* ☎ *257-7202* ⊕ *www.madc.ac.cr* ⊠ *$1.50* ⊙ *Tues.–Sat. 10–5.*

🔟 **Museo de Formas, Espacios y Sonidos** (Museum of Forms, Spaces and Sounds). The 1871 Atlantic Railway Station, which once bustled with passengers leaving and arriving on trains to and from Limón, has been converted into an interactive sound and space museum. Exhibits are labeled in Spanish; you wouldn't get much out of them without a knowledge of the language. In back are a couple of former trains that once served the Caribbean route. A bust outside honors Tomás Guardia, one of the few dictators in this peaceful country's history. He launched construction of the railroad. ⊠ *Avda. 3, between Cs. 19 and 21, Barrio La California* ☎ *223-4173* ⊠ *$1* ⊙ *Mon.–Fri. 9:30–3.*

★ ❻ **Museo del Jade** (Jade Museum). This is the world's largest collection of American jade—that's "American" in the hemispheric sense. Nearly all the items on display were produced in pre-Columbian times, and most of the jade (pronounced *hah*-day in Spanish) dates from 300 BC to AD 700. In the spectacular Jade Room, pieces are illuminated from behind so you can appreciate their translucency. A series of drawings explains how this extremely hard stone was cut using string saws with quartz-and-sand abrasive. Jade was sometimes used in jewelry designs, but it was most often carved into oblong pendants. The museum also has other pre-Columbian artifacts, such as polychrome vases and three-legged *metates* (small stone tables for grinding corn), and a gallery of modern art. The final room on the tour has a startling display of ceramic fertility symbols. A photo-filled, glossy guide to the museum in English sells for $17; the Spanish version is only $4. ⊠ *INS building, Avda. 7, between Cs. 9 and 11, 11th fl., Barrio El Carmen* ☎ *287–6034* ⊕ *portal.ins-cr.com/social/MuseoJade/* ⬚ *$2* ⊙ *Weekdays7:30–3:30.*

⓫ Museo Nacional (National Museum). In the whitewashed Bellavista Fortress, which dates from 1870, the National Museum gives you a quick and insightful lesson in English and Spanish on Costa Rican culture from pre-Columbian times to the present. Glass cases display pre-Columbian artifacts, period dress, colonial furniture, religious art, and photographs. Some of the country's foremost ethnographers and anthropologists are on the museum's staff. Outside are a veranda and a pleasant, manicured courtyard garden. A former army headquarters, this now-tranquil building saw fierce fighting during a 1931 army mutiny and during the 1948 revolution, as the bullet holes pocking its turrets attest. But it was also here that three-time president José "Don Pepe" Figueres abolished the country's military in 1949. ⊠ *C. 17, between Avdas. Central and 2, Barrio La Soledad* ☎ *257–1433* ⊕ *www.geocities.com/Athens/Agora/9751/* ⬚ *$4* ⊙ *Tues.–Sat. 8:30–4, Sun. 9–4.*

★ ❸ Museo del Oro Precolombino (Pre-Columbian Gold Museum). The dazzling, modern museum of gold, in a three-story underground structure beneath the Plaza de la Cultura, contains the largest collection of pre-Columbian gold jewelry in Central America—20,000 troy ounces in more than 1,600 individual pieces—all owned by the Banco Central, and displayed attractively in low-lit, bilingual exhibits. Many pieces are in the form of frogs and eagles, two animals perceived by the region's pre-Columbian cultures to have great spiritual significance. Most spectacular are the varied shaman figurines, which represent the human connection to animal deities. One of the halls houses the **Museo Numismática** (Coin Museum; admission included with Gold Museum), a repository of historic coins and bills and other objects used as monetary units throughout the country's history. Rotating art exhibitions live on another level of the complex. ⊠ *Eastern end of Plaza de la Cultura, C. 5, between Avdas. Central and 2, Barrio La Soledad* ☎ *243–4202* ⊕ *www.museosdelbancocentral.org* ⬚ *$6* ⊙ *Daily 9:30–4:30.*

⓭ Museo para la Paz (Peace Museum). Former president Oscar Arias won the 1987 Nobel peace prize for his tireless efforts to bring reconciliation to a war-torn Central America, and today he remains a vocal force for international peace and social justice. His Arias Foundation operates this museum, with bilingual exhibits documenting the isthmus's turbulent history and promoting the cause for peace. Messages from other Nobel laureates—the Dalai Lama, Lech Walesa, Rigoberta Menchú, Jimmy Carter, and Henry Kissinger among them—adorn one room. Begin your visit in the auditorium watching a 12-minute video in English, *The Dividends of Peace.* There's also an hour-long video that delves into the topic if you have the time. The museum may not appear to be open when you walk by. Knock on the gate or, better yet, call and let the attendant know you're coming. ⊠ *Avda. 2 and C. 13, Barrio La Soledad* ☎ *223–4664* ⬚ *Free* ⊙ *Weekdays 8–noon and 1:30–4:30.*

⓯ Parque Central (Central Park). At the city's nucleus, this simple tree-planted square—it's more a plaza than a park—has a gurgling fountain and concrete benches, and a life-size bronze statue of a street sweeper cleaning up some bronze litter. In the center of the park is a spiderlike, mango-color gazebo donated by former Nicaraguan dictator Anastasio Somoza. Several years ago a referendum was held to decide whether to demolish the despot's gift, but Ticos voted to preserve the bandstand for posterity. ⊠ *Bordered by Avdas. 2 and 4 and Cs.2 and Central, Barrio La Merced.*

❺ **Parque España.** One of our favorite spots in the capital is this shady little park. A bronze statue of Costa Rica's Spanish founder, Juan Vásquez de Coronado, overlooks an elevated fountain on its southwest corner; the opposite corner has a lovely tiled guardhouse. A bust of Queen Isabella of Castile stares at the yellow compound to the east of the park, the Centro Nacional de la Cultura (National Center of Culture). Just west of the park is a two-story, metal-sided school made in Belgium and shipped to Costa Rica in pieces more than a century ago. Local lore holds that the intended destination was really Chile, but that Costa Rica decided to keep the mistakenly shipped building components. The yellow colonial-style building to the east of the modern INS building is the 1912 **Casa Amarilla,** home of Costa Rica's Foreign Ministry. The massive ceiba tree in front, planted by John F. Kennedy and the presidents of all the Central American nations in 1963, gives you an idea of how quickly things grow in the tropics. The building is not open to the public. A garden around the corner on Calle 13 contains a 2-meter-wide section of the Berlin Wall donated by Germany's Foreign Ministry after reunification. Ask the guard to let you into the garden if you want a closer look. ⊠ *Bordered by Avdas. 7 and 3 and Cs. 11 and 17, Barrio El Carmen* ☏ *257–7202.*

❹ **Parque Morazán.** Anchored by the 1920 Templo de Música (Temple of Music), a neoclassic bandstand that has become the symbol of the city, the largest park in downtown San José is somewhat barren, though the Pink and Golden Trumpet trees on its northwest corner brighten things up when they bloom in the dry months. The park is named for Honduran general Francisco Morazán, whose dream for a united Central America failed in the 1830s. Avoid the park late at night, when a rough crowd and occasional muggers appear. ⊠ *Avda. 3, between Cs. 5 and 9, Barrio El Carmen.*

❾ **Parque Nacional** (National Park). A bronze monument commemorating Central America's battles against American invader William Walker in 1856 forms the centerpiece of this large and leafy park. Five Amazons, representing the five nations of the isthmus, attack Walker, who shields his face from the onslaught. Costa Rica maintains the lead and shelters a veiled Nicaragua, the country most devastated by the war. Guatemala, Honduras, and El Salvador might dispute this version of events, but this is how Costa Rica chose to commission the work by French sculptor Louis Carrier Belleuse, a student of Rodins, in 1895. Bas-relief murals on the monument's pedestal depict key battles in the war against the Americans.

❶ **Plaza de la Cultura.** The crowds of people, vendors, and street entertainers at the Plaza de la Cultura—it's a favored spot for local marimba bands, clowns, jugglers, and colorfully dressed South Americans playing Andean music—hide the fact that the expanse is really just a mass of con-

Teatro Nacional

THE NATIONAL THEATER is easily the most enchanting building in Costa Rica, and San José's don't-miss sight. Chagrined that touring prima donna Adelina Patti bypassed San José in 1890, wealthy coffee merchants raised import taxes to hire Belgian architects to design this building, lavish with cast iron and Italian marble. The theater was inaugurated in 1897 with a performance of Gounod's *Faust,* featuring an international cast. The sandstone exterior is marked by Italianate arched windows, marble columns with bronze capitals, and statues of strange bedfellows Ludwig van Beethoven (1770–1827) and 17th-century Spanish golden-age playwright Pedro Calderón de la Barca (1600–81). The Muses of Dance, Music, and Fame are silhouetted in front of an iron cupola. Given the provenance of the building funds, it's not surprising that frescoes on the stairway inside depict coffee and banana production. Note Italian painter Aleardo Villa's famous ceiling mural *Alegoría del Café y Banano* (*Allegory of Coffee and Bananas*), a joyful harvest scene that appeared on Costa Rica's old five-colón note. (The now-defunct bill is prized by collectors and by tourists as a souvenir, and is often sold by vendors in the plaza between the theater and the Gran Hotel Costa Rica next door. The sumptuous neo-Baroque interior sparkles thanks to an ongoing restoration project. And what's an old theater without its resident ghost? Patrons have claimed to see moving figures in the second-floor paintings in the Teatro Nacional.

The best way to see the theater's interior is to attend one of the performances, which take place several nights a week; intermission gives you a chance to nose around. Stop at the *boletería* (box office) in the lobby and see what strikes your fancy. (Don't worry if you left your tuxedo or evening gown back home; as long as you don't show up for a performance wearing shorts, jeans, or a T-shirt, no one will care.) Alternatively, a nominal admission fee gets you in beyond the lobby for an informative guided daytime visit. Tours in English are given at 9, 10, and 11 AM, and 1, 2, and 3 PM. The theater is sometimes closed for rehearsals, so call before you go. ✉ *Plaza de la Cultura, Barrio La Soledad* ☎ *221-1329* ⊕ *www. teatronacional.go.cr* ✑ *$3* ◷ *Mon.–Sat. 9–4.*

❷ crete. The ornate **Teatro Nacional,** one of San José's signature buildings, dominates the plaza's southern half. Pop in and buy a ticket for an evening performance—the prices are amazingly reasonable. The Museo de Oro Precolombino, with its highly visited exhibits of gold, lies under the plaza. The plaza's western edge is defined by the Gran Hotel Costa Rica, with its 24-hour Café 1930. ✉ *Bordered by Avdas. Central and 2 and Cs. 3 and 5, Barrio La Soledad.*

⓬ Plaza de la Democracia. President Oscar Arias built this terraced open space west of the Museo Nacional to mark 100 years of democracy and to receive dignitaries during the 1989 hemispheric summit. The view west toward the dark-green Cerros de Escazú is nice in the morning and fabulous at sunset. The plaza is dominated by a statue of José "Don Pepe"

Figueres, three-time president and leader of the 1948 revolution. Jewelry, T-shirts, and crafts from Costa Rica, Guatemala, and South America are sold in a string of stalls along the western edge. ⊠ *Bordered by Avdas. Central and 2 and Cs. 13 and 15, Barrio La Soledad.*

NEED A BREAK?

Duck into the **Café del Teatro Nacional** (⊠ Plaza de la Cultura, Barrio La Soledad 🕾 221–3262), beside the theater, to sit at a marble table and sip a hazelnut mocha beneath frescoed ceilings. The frescoes are part of an allegory of seminude figures celebrating the 1897 opening of the theater. Coffees run from $1 to $2, depending on how much alcohol or ice cream is added. Sandwiches and cakes are $3 to $4. The place follows the standard practice of having a TV on at all times, albeit softly in this case. The café keeps the same hours as the theater, but is open until curtain time on performance nights, and during intermission.

⓭ Plaza del Banco Central (Central Bank). An extension of Avenida Central, the plaza is popular with hawkers, money changers, and retired men and can be a good place to get a shoe shine and listen to street musicians. Outside the western end of Costa Rica's modern federal reserve bank building, don't miss Fernando Calvo's *Presentes,* 10 sculpted, smaller-than-life figures of bedraggled *campesinos* (peasants). A bronze 500-kg (1,100-lb) statue by Manuel Vargas of a buxom rural woman resides at sidewalk level on the small, shady plaza south of the bank. It's public art at its best. Beware: the money changers here are notorious for circulating counterfeit bills and using doctored calculators to shortchange unwitting tourists. Instead, change money at banks or through cash machines, where you get the best rate. In fact, you can stop by a money-exchange kiosk right here operated by Banco Nacional, one of the state banks, and open seven days a week. ⊠ *Bordered by Avdas. Central and 1 and Cs. 2 and 4, Barrio La Merced.*

⓰ Teatro Popular Melico Salazar (Melico Salazar Theater). Across Avenida 2 on the north side of Parque Central stands San José's second major performance hall (after the Teatro Nacional). The 1928 building is on the site of a former 19th-century military barracks felled by an earthquake. The venue was later named for Costa Rican operatic tenor Manuel "Melico" Salazar (1887–1950). It was constructed specifically to provide a less highbrow alternative to the Teatro Nacional. But these days the Melico is plenty cultured and provides the capital with a steady diet of music and dance performances. ⊠ *Avda. 2 and C. 2, Barrio La Merced* 🕾 *221–4952.*

West of Downtown

Paseo Colón, one of San José's major boulevards, heads due west from downtown and leads to the vast La Sabana park, the largest parcel of green space in the city. La Sabana anchors the vast west side of the city. A block or two off its exhaust-ridden avenues are quiet residential streets, and you'll find the U.S., Canadian, and British embassies here.

What to See

⓴ Museo de Arte Costarricense (Museum of Costa Rican Art). A splendid collection of 19th- and 20th-century Costa Rican art, labeled in Spanish and English, is housed in 12 exhibition halls here. Be sure to visit the top-floor Salón Dorado to see the stucco, bronze-plated bas-relief mural depicting Costa Rican history, created by French sculptor Louis Feron. Wan-

CAUTION

The ubiquitous TOURIST INFORMATION signs you see around downtown are really private travel agencies looking to sell you tours rather than provide unbiased information. The ICT (⇨ San José Essentials) is the official tourist office.

der the sculpture garden in back and take in Jorge Jiménez's 7-meter-tall *Imagen Cósmica,* which depicts pre-Columbian traditions. ⊠ C. 42 and Paseo Colón, Paseo Colón ☎ 222–7155 ⊕ www.musarco.go.cr ☜ $5, free Sun. ⊘ Tues.–Fri. 10–6, weekends 10–4.

㉑ Parque Metropolitano La Sabana. Though it isn't centrally located, La Sabana (the savannah) comes the closest of San José's green spaces to achieving the same function and spirit as New York's Central Park. A statue of 1930s president León Cortes greets you at the park's principal entrance at the west end of Paseo Colón. Behind the statue a 5-meter-tall menorah serves as a gathering place for San José's small Jewish community during Hanukkah. La Sabana was once San José's airport, and the whitewashed Museo de Arte Costarricense, just south of the Cortes statue, served as terminal and control tower. The round Gimnasio Nacional (National Gymnasium) sits at the southeast corner of the park and hosts sporting events and the occasional concert. The Estadio Nacional (National Stadium) near the park's northwest corner is the site of important soccer matches, and is one of the country's major outdoor concert venues. In between are acres of space for soccer, basketball, tennis, swimming, jogging, picnicking, and kite flying. The park hums with activity on weekend days. You're welcome to join in the early-morning, outdoor aerobics classes on Saturday and Sunday. Like most of San José's green spaces, La Sabana should be avoided at night. ⊠ Bordered by C. 42, Avda. de las Américas, and Autopista Próspero Fernández, Paseo Colón.

North and East of Downtown

Immediately northeast of downtown lie the splendid historic neighborhoods of Barrio Amón and Barrio Otoya. Both are repositories of historic houses that have escaped the wrecking ball, and many now serve as hotels, restaurants, and offices. (And a few actually are private residences as well.) Barrio Escalante, to the east, is not quite as gentrified, but fast becoming a fashionable address.

The sprawling suburb of San Pedro begins several blocks east of downtown San José. The town is home to the University of Costa Rica and all the intellect and cheap eats and nightlife that a student or student-wannabe could desire. But away from the heart of the university, San Pedro is also awash in the consumerism of shopping malls, fast-food

CLOSE UP

Missing History

1

BLAME IT ON THE EARTHQUAKES. Costa Ricans are quick to attribute the scarcity of historic architecture in San José and around the country to a history of earth tremors. Indeed, major earthquakes have struck various locales around Costa Rica 10 times since the mid-18th century (6 times in the 20th century), felling untold numbers of historical structures.

But blame it on the wrecking ball, too, says architect Gabriela Sáenz, who works with the Ministry of Culture's Center for Research and Conservation of Cultural Patrimony. The tear-it-down approach really began to take its toll in the 1970s, an era when boxy, concrete buildings were in vogue around the world, Sáenz says. Costa Rica didn't establish its first school of architecture until 1972, staffed by faculty from Mexico, England, and Brazil. "It was hard for a real Costa Rican tradition to take hold," she explains. Mix that with a lack of government regulation and what Sáenz calls a typical Tico do-your-own-thing penchant, and the result is

the San José, chock-full of squat buildings, you see today.

The tide began to turn in 1995 with the passage of the Law of Historic and Architectural Patrimony. Over 300 historic structures in the country are presently protected under the legislation, and new buildings are added to the registry each year. But legal protection is no guarantee of funding necessary to actually restore a historic landmark.

You need to look hard, but San José really does have several diamonds in the rough. The National Theater and Post Office remain the two most visited examples of historic architecture in the capital. But the National Museum; the Museum of Forms, Spaces and Sounds; the National Center of Culture; and several small hostelries and restaurants around town—especially in Barrios Amón and Otoya—all are modern transformations and restorations of structures with past histories.

---

restaurants, and car dealerships, but also manages to mix in stately districts such as the stylish Los Yoses for good measure. To get to San Pedro, take a $2 taxi ride from downtown and get off in front of Banco Nacional, just beyond the rotunda with the fountain at its center.

What to See

★ ☾ ㉓ **Jardín de Mariposas Spyrogyra** (Spyrogyra Butterfly Garden). An hour or two at this magical garden is entertaining and educational for nature lovers of all ages. Self-guided tours enlighten you on butterfly ecology and give you a chance to see the winged creatures close up. After an 18-minute video introduction, you're free to wander screened-in gardens along a numbered trail. Some 30 species of colorful butterflies flutter about, accompanied by 6 types of hummingbirds. Try to come when it's sunny, as butterflies are most active then. A small, moderately priced café borders the garden and serves sandwiches and Tico fare. Spyrogyra abuts the northern edge of Parque Zoológico Simón Bolívar, but you enter on the outskirts of Barrio Tournón, near El Pueblo Shopping Center. ✉ *50 m east and 150 m south of main entrance to El Pueblo, Barrio Tournón* ☎ *222–2937* ✉ *$5; $3, children under 12* ⊘ *Daily 8–4.*

🌤 ㉒ **Museo de los Niños.** San José's Children's Museum is housed in a former jail, and big kids may want to check it out just to marvel at the castlelike architecture and the old cells that have been preserved in an exhibit about prison life. Three halls in the complex are filled with eye-catching seasonal exhibits for kids, ranging in subject from local ecology to outer space. The exhibits are annotated in Spanish, but most are interactive, so language shouldn't be

much of a problem. The museum's most popular resident is the Egyptian exhibit's sarcophagus; the mummy draws the "oohs" and "ewws." Officially, the complex is called the Centro Costarricense de Ciencia y Cultura (Costa Rican Center of Science and Culture), and that will be the sign that greets you on the front of the building. The **Galería Nacional,** adjoining the main building, is more popular with adults; it usually shows fine art by Costa Rican artists free of charge. Also adjoining the museum is the classical music venue **Auditorio Nacional.** ✉ *North end of C. 4, Barrio El Carmen* ☎ *258–4929* ⊕ *www.museocr.com* ✉ *$2, $1 for children under 12* ⊘ *Tues.–Fri. 8–4:30, weekends 9:30–5.*

🌤 ㉔ **Parque Zoológico Simón Bolívar.** Considering Costa Rica's mind-boggling diversity of wildlife, San José's zoo is rather modest in scope, and gets mixed reviews for some of its cramped exhibition spaces. It does, however, provide an introduction to some of the animals you might see in the jungle. The park is set in a forested ravine in historical Barrio Amón, offering soothing green space in the heart of the city. ✉ *Avda. 11 and C. 11, Barrio Amón* ☎ *233–6701* ✉ *$2; children under 6, $2.50* ⊘ *Weekdays 8:30–4, weekends 9–4:30.*

┌─
│ **NEED A**
BREAK?
└─
We have to admit that Costa Rican baked goods tend toward the dry-as-dust end of the spectrum. But Italian-style bakery **Giacomín** (✉ Next to Automercado, Los Yoses, San Pedro ☎ 234–2551 ✉ C. 2, between Avdas. 3 and 5, Barrio La Merced ☎ 221–5652), near the University of Costa Rica, is an exception—it seems that a touch of liqueur added to the batter makes all the difference. Stand, European-style, at the downstairs espresso bar, or take your goodies to the tables and chairs on the upstairs balcony. Both branches close from noon to 2.

WHERE TO EAT

Wherever you eat in San José, be it a small *soda* (informal eatery) or a sophisticated restaurant, dress is casual. Meals tend to be taken earlier than in other Latin American countries; few restaurants serve past 10

PM. Local cafés usually open for breakfast at 7 AM and remain open until 7 or 9 in the evening. Restaurants serving international cuisine are usually open from 11 AM to 9 PM. Some cafés that serve mainly San José office workers are closed Sunday. Restaurants that do open on Sunday do a brisk business: it's the traditional family day out (and the maid's day off). Casino restaurants in downtown San José are open 24 hours.

San José

AMERICAN
$–$$

✕ **JR Ribs.** Frederic Remington meets Barrio Amón in this restaurant made to look like an Old West saloon that happens to butt up against a ravine near the zoo entrance. Texas-style ribs are still enough of a novelty cuisine in Costa Rica that the diners have fun here—there always seems to be someone's birthday lunch or dinner going on here—even if they haven't mastered the art of not getting the tangy barbecue sauce on their ties and blouses and all over the plastic faux-rawhide tablecloths. For the less adventurous, an upstairs dining room serves Costa Rican food buffet-style weekdays for lunch. Stay downstairs; it's much more entertaining. ✉ *Avda. 11 and C. 11, Barrio Amón* ☎ *223–0523* ⊟ *AE, DC, MC, V* ⊘ *No dinner Sun.*

$–$$

✕ **News Café.** Pounce on one of the six streetside tables if they're free when you enter. The passing parade on Avenida Central is yours for the price of a cup of coffee. (They probably won't be available: a regular expat crowd holds court here.) Breakfast and dinner fare is hearty, but the café is most popular at lunchtime and cocktail hour. You can get a Caesar salad and other American dishes here. Inside, the wrought-iron chairs, wood beams, and brick walls give the place an old-town tavern feel— framed newspaper front pages hang on the wall trumpeting D-Day, Pearl Harbor, and John Glenn's first space mission. The café is on the first floor of the 1960s landmark Hotel Presidente. ✉ *Avda. Central and C. 7, Barrio La Soledad* ☎ *222–3022* ⊟ *AE, DC, MC, V* ⊘ *Breakfast served.*

CAFÉS
$–$$$
Fodor$Choice
★

✕ **Café Mundo.** You could easily walk by this corner restaurant without noticing its tiny sign behind the foliage. The upstairs café serves meals on the porch, on a garden patio, or in two dining rooms. The soup of the day and fresh-baked bread start you out; main courses include shrimp in a vegetable cream sauce or *lomito en salsa de vino tinto* (tenderloin in a red-wine sauce). Save room for the best chocolate cake in town, drizzled with homemade blackberry sauce. Café Mundo is a popular, low-key gay hangout that draws a mixed gay-straight clientele. This is one of the few center-city restaurants with its own parking lot. ✉ *C. 15 and Avda. 9, Barrio Otoya* ☎ *222–6190* ⊟ *AE, MC, V* ⊘ *Closed Sun. No lunch Sat.*

¢–$

✕ **Café de la Posada.** The lack of alfresco dining in this tropical city is disappointing, but this café's terrace with tables fronting the Calle 17 pedestrian mall is a pleasant exception. The owners of this small café come from Argentina, and they know how to make a great cappuccino. Salads, quiches, and empanadas are the food specialties. The best bargains are the four rotating *platos del día* (daily specials), with entrée, salad, beverage, and dessert for $4. If you opt for dinner, make it an early one: the place closes at 7 on weeknights. ✉ *C. 17, between Avdas. 2 and 4, Barrio La Soledad* ☎ *258–1027* ⊟ *AE, DC, MC, V* ⊘ *Closed Sun., no dinner Sat.*

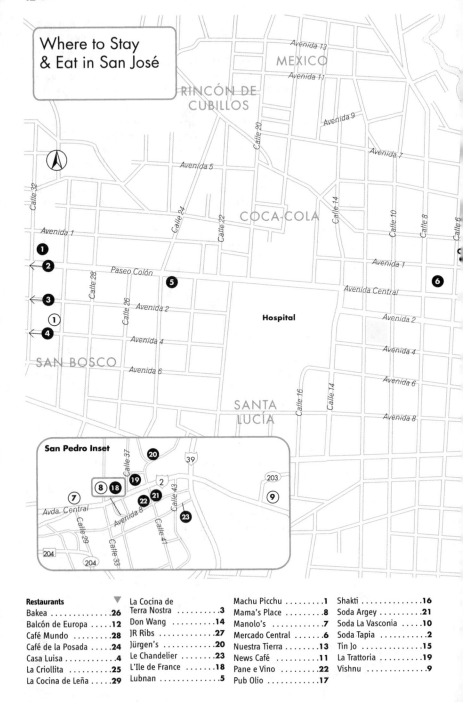

Where to Stay & Eat in San José

Restaurants ▼

Bakea **26**
Balcón de Europa **12**
Café Mundo **28**
Café de la Posada **24**
Casa Luisa **4**
La Criollita **25**
La Cocina de Leña **29**

La Cocina de
Terra Nostra **3**
Don Wang **14**
JR Ribs **27**
Jürgen's **20**
Le Chandelier **23**
L'Ile de France **18**
Lubnan **5**

Machu Picchu **1**
Mama's Place **8**
Manolo's **7**
Mercado Central **6**
Nuestra Tierra **13**
News Café **11**
Pane e Vino **22**
Pub Olio **17**

Shakti **16**
Soda Argey **21**
Soda La Vasconia **10**
Soda Tapia **2**
Tin Jo **15**
La Trattoria **19**
Vishnu **9**

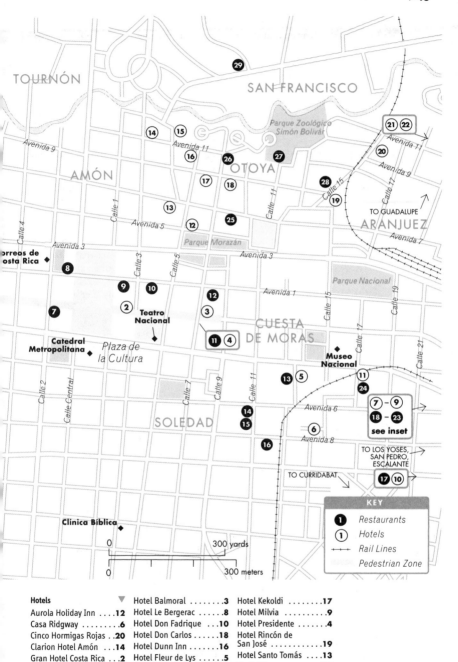

Hotels ▼		
Aurola Holiday Inn **12**	Hotel Balmoral **3**	Hotel Kekoldi **17**
Casa Ridgway **6**	Hotel Le Bergerac **8**	Hotel Milvia **9**
Cinco Hormigas Rojas ..**20**	Hotel Don Fadrique ...**10**	Hotel Presidente **4**
Clarion Hotel Amón ...**14**	Hotel Don Carlos **18**	Hotel Rincón de
Gran Hotel Costa Rica ...**2**	Hotel Dunn Inn **16**	San José **19**
Hostal Toruma **7**	Hotel Fleur de Lys **5**	Hotel Santo Tomás **13**
Hotel Aranjuez **21**	Hotel Grano de Oro **1**	Kap's Place **22**
Hotel Kekoldi	Hotel Inca Real **15**	Posada del Museo **11**

CHINESE
$–$$

✕ **Don Wang.** In a country where "Chinese cuisine" often means rice and vegetables bearing a suspicious resemblance to *gallo pinto* ("spotted rooster," a typical Costa Rican dish of black beans and rice), Don Wang's authenticity comes as a real treat. Cantonese cuisine is the mainstay here—the owner comes from that region of China—but these folks will Szechuan it up a bit if you ask. Mornings give way to the immensely popular dim sum, called *desayuno chino*, literally "Chinese breakfast." You can order dim sum all day, but the $5 specials last only until 11 AM. The dining area is built around a stone garden and small waterfall. There's no television blaring here, a refreshing change from many Costa Rican restaurants. ⊠ *C. 11, between Avdas. 6 and 8, Barrio Le Soledad* ☎ *233–6484 or 223–5925* ▤ *AE, DC, MC, V* ☺ *Breakfast served.*

COSTA RICAN
★ $–$$

✕ **La Cocina de Leña.** The name translates literally as "firewood kitchen," and it evokes the age-old Tico style of cooking. Indeed, you'll see bundles of wood as well as old tools and straw bags hung on walls to make you feel like you're down on the farm, but rustic this place is not. Popular Tico dishes such as black-bean soup, ceviche, tamales, oxtail with cassava, and plantains are served, and the restaurant has live marimba music several nights a week during high season. Although the kitchen closes at 11, you're welcome to stay as long as the band keeps playing. It is one of the few places that doesn't close during Holy Week. ⊠ *Centro Comercial El Pueblo, Avda. 0, Barrio Tournón* ☎ *223–3704* ▤ *AE, DC, MC, V.*

¢–$

✕ **La Criollita.** Kick off your day with breakfast at this emerald-green restaurant. Mornings are the perfect time to snag one of the precious tables in the back garden, an unexpected refuge from the noise and traffic of the city. Choose from the *americano*, with pancakes and toast; the *tico*, with bread, fried bananas, and *natilla* (sour cream); or the huge *criollita*, with ham or pork chops; all have eggs on the side. Workers from nearby government office buildings begin to pour in late in the morning, and the lunchtime decibel level increases appreciably. (This is the one time of day we recommend avoiding the place.) They filter out about 2 PM and once again you have a quiet place for coffee and dessert. ⊠ *Avda. 7, between Cs. 7 and 9 Barrio Amón* ☎ *256–6511* ▤ *AE, DC, MC, V* ☺ *Closed Sun. No dinner Sat. Breakfast served.*

¢–$

✕ **Mama's Place.** Mama's is a Costa Rican restaurant with a difference: the owners are Italian, so in addition to corvina *al ajillo* (sautéed with garlic) and other staple Tico fare, they serve homemade seafood chowder, traditional Italian pastas, and meat dishes with delicate wine sauces. The brightly decorated coffee shop opens onto busy Avenida 1; the more subdued dining room upstairs accommodates the overflow crowd. (You'll see former Chicago Bears football coach Mike Ditka's autographed picture up there.) At lunchtime, it's usually packed with business types drawn to the delicious and inexpensive daily specials—choose from the rotating *platos del día* (daily specials) with pasta, meat, fish, or poultry—all to the accompaniment of ample focaccia. Mama's closes at 7 PM on weeknights. ⊠ *Avda. 1, between Cs. Central and 2, Barrio El Carmen* ☎ *223–2270 or 256–5601* ▤ *AE, DC, MC, V* ☺ *Closed Sun. No dinner Sat.*

¢–$

✕ **Manolo's.** For any San José dweller, a mention of Manolo's brings their signature menu item *churros con chocolate* (fried dough with hot fudge sauce) to mind. But this 24-hour eatery is also known for its great sandwiches and espressos. Its location on the bustling Avenida Central pedestrian thoroughfare and its outdoor tables allow for some of the city's best people-watching. Inside, however, the place feels more like a diner than a café, down to its plastic-coated menu and its promise of breakfast food at any hour. The owner always prepares a few Spanish favorites in addition to the typical Tico fare, such as *tortilla española* (a thick potato-and-onion omelet). ☒ *Avda. Central, between Cs. Central and 2, Barrio La Merced* ☎ *221–2041* ▭ *AE, DC, MC, V* ☽ *Breakfast served.*

¢–$ ╳ **Nuestra Tierra.** But for the traffic zipping by on one of San José's busiest thoroughfares—and on that note, opt for a table on the side facing less busy Calle 15—you might think you're out in rural Santa Ana. Bunches of onions and peppers dangle from the ceiling, recalling a provincial Tico ranch. The generous homemade meals are delicious, and the incredibly friendly wait staff, who epitomize Costa Rican hospitality and dress in traditional folkloric clothing, prepare your coffee filtered through the traditional cloth *chorreador*. The place is open 24 hours, just in case *gallo pinto* pangs hit at 3 AM. Some disparage the place as "too touristy." Perhaps it is, but it's also fun. ☒ *Avda. 2 and C. 15, Barrio La Soledad* ☎ *258–6500* ▭ *No credit cards* ☽ *Breakfast served.*

ECLECTIC ╳ **Jürgen's.** Jürgen's is a common haunt for *politicos,* and San José's elites
$$–$$$ meet to eat here. Decorated in gold and terra-cotta with leather and wood accents, the dining room of this contemporary restaurant feels more like a lounge than a fine restaurant. In fact, the classy bar, with a large selection of good wine and good cigars, is a prominent feature. The inventive menu, with such delicacies as medallions of roast duck and tuna fillet encrusted with sesame seeds, sets this place apart from the city's more traditional venues. ☒ *250 m north of the Subaru dealership, on Blvd. Barrio Dent, Barrio Dent* ☎ *283–2239* ▭ *AE, DC, MC, V* ☽ *Closed Sun. No lunch Sat.*

$–$$$ ╳ **Bakea.** Trendy, right down to its small art gallery and whimsical rest-
Fodor'sChoice rooms, this restaurant in a restored Barrio Amón mansion is the place
★ to see and be seen, and is one of the few upscale places in town to grab a very late night bite. The term "fusion cuisine" really does apply here: Le Cordon Bleu–trained chef Camille Ratton-Pérez takes French and Costa Rican cuisine and spices it with Thai and Middle Eastern influences. Top off your meal with a *Cahuita caramelo,* a scrumptious chocolate-banana-butterscotch concoction or *tarte tatin* (carmelized apple tart). If you can't decide, go for the *paleta Bakea,* a dessert sampler platter. ☒ *C. 7 and Avda. 11, Barrio Amón* ☎ *248–0303 or 221–1051* ▭ *AE, DC, MC, V* ☽ *Closed Sun. No dinner Mon. No lunch Sat.*

FRENCH ╳ **Le Chandelier.** San José does not get classier than this restaurant,
$$–$$$$ where formal service and traditional sauce-heavy French dishes are part of the experience. The dining room is elegant, with wicker chairs, a tile floor, and original paintings. The Swiss chef, Claude Dubuis, might start you off with saffron ravioli stuffed with ricotta cheese and walnuts. His main courses include such unique dishes as corvina in a *pejibaye* (peach palm) sauce, hearts of palm and veal chops glazed in a sweet port-wine sauce, and the more familiar *pato a la naranja* (duck à l'orange), or for a tropical twist on that classic dish, try Dubuis's *pato a la maracuyá* (duck

in passion fruit). ⊠ *50 m west and 100 m south of ICE building, San Pedro* ☎ *225–3980 or 253–3241* ⊟ *AE, DC, MC, V* ⊘ *Closed Sun. No lunch Sat.*

$–$$$ ✕ **L'Ile de France.** Long one of San José's most popular restaurants, L'Ile de France, in the Hotel Le Bergerac—it's technically a separate business—has dining in a tropical garden courtyard. The fairly traditional French menu has some interesting innovations. Start with the classic onion soup or with *pâté de lapin* (rabbit liver pâté); then sink your teeth into a pepper steak, broiled lamb with seasoned potatoes, or corvina in a spinach sauce. Save room for the profiteroles filled with vanilla ice cream and smothered in chocolate sauce. L'Ile de France blends exactly the right level of intimacy, grace, and style, giving it an edge over the sophisticated Chandelier. ⊠ *Hotel Le Bergerac, C. 35, between Avdas. Central and 2, first Los Yoses entrance, San Pedro* ☎ *283–5812* ⌂ *Reservations essential* ⊟ *AE, DC, MC, V* ⊘ *Closed Sun. No lunch.*

FodorsChoice ★

ITALIAN ✕ **Balcón de Europa.** With old sepia photos and a strolling guitarist who

$–$$$ seems to have been working the room for years, Balcón de Europa transports you to the year of its inception, 1909. Pasta specialties such as the *plato mixto* (mixed plate with lasagna, tortellini, and ravioli) are so popular that they haven't changed much either. (Why tamper with success?) For something lighter, try the scrumptious heart-of-palm salad or sautéed corvina. Grab a table away from the door (i.e., from the noise of the bus stop across the street). FYI, old-timers refer to the place as Balcón de Franco; Late, legendary chef Franco Piatti was the restaurant's guiding light for years. ⊠ *Avda. Central and C. 9, Barrio La Soledad* ☎ *221–4841* ⊟ *AE, DC, MC, V* ⊘ *Closed Sat.*

$ ✕ **La Trattoria.** The green and gold here might make a Green Bay Packers fan feel right at home, but it's the excellent, reasonably priced homemade pasta dishes that make this popular lunch spot worth the stop. Begin your meal with fresh bread and any number of excellent antipasti, continuing on with your favorite pasta dish. And for dessert, who can resist tiramisu? ⊠ *Behind Automercado, Barrio Dent, San Pedro* ☎ *224–7065* ⊟ *AE, DC, MC, V* ⊘ *No dinner Sun.*

$ ✕ **Pane e Vino.** Look closely at the extensive menu here: there are 40 varieties of the capital's best thin-crust pizza, and no one will rush you if you spend too much time pondering what you want. This lively two-level restaurant—it's a small chain, but this was the first location—rounds out its offerings with a complete selection of pastas. You can dine until midnight daily, expect on Sunday, when you'll have to finish dinner by 10 PM. The Pizza Allessandre, topped with prosciutto, mozzarella, and olives, is the most popular dish, and for good reason. ⊠ *50 m west and 15 m south of Más X Menos, San Pedro* ☎ *280–2869* ⊟ *AE, MC, V.*

MEDITERRANEAN ✕ **Pub Olio.** Although this combination pub and restaurant serves the

$ full contingent of Mediterranean cuisine, we like to visit the place for drinks and Spanish-style *tapas* (appetizers). The century-old redbrick house with stained-glass windows draws everybody from tie-clad businessmen to university students who have money to spend on something more upscale than run-of-the-mill campus-area bars. Groups liven up the large front room—the quieter, smaller back rooms maintain a bit more romance—and the staff hauls umbrella-covered tables out to the sidewalk

1

on warm evenings. ✉ *200 m north of Bagelmen's, Barrio Escalante* ☎ *281–0541* 🖃 *AE, DC, MC, V* ☺ *Closed Sun; no lunch Sat.*

MIDDLE EASTERN ✕ **Lubnan.** Negotiate the quirky wrought-iron-and-burlap revolving door
$–$$ at the entrance, and you've made it into one of San José's few Middle Eastern restaurants. The Lebanese owners serve a wide variety of dishes from their native region, so if you can't decide, the *mezza* serves two people and gives you a little bit of everything. For your own individual dish, try the juicy shish kebab *de cordero* (of lamb), or if you're feeling especially adventurous, the raw ground-meat *kebbe naye* (with wheat meal) and *kafta naye* (without wheat meal). A hip bar in the back serves the same menu, but definitely eat out in the front restaurant Thursday nights for the belly dancing show. ✉ *Paseo Colón, between Cs. 22 and 24, Paseo Colón* ☎ *257–6071* 🖃 *AE, DC, MC, V* ☺ *Closed Mon. No dinner Sun.*

PAN-ASIAN ✕ **Tin Jo.** The colorful dining rooms at this converted house just south-
$–$$$ east of downtown evoke Japan, India, China, Indonesia, or Thailand.
Fodor's Choice In the Thai room an 11-meter (39-foot) mural depicts a Buddhist tem-
★ ple. You can also select from all those cuisines here, with menus to match its varied dining areas. Start with a powerful Singapore sling (brandy and fruit juices) before trying such treats as *kaeng* (Thai shrimp and pineapple curry in coconut milk), *mu shu* (a beef, chicken, or veggie stir-fry with crepes), samosas (stuffed Indian pastries), and sushi rolls. The vegetarian menu is extensive, too. Tin Jo stands out with always exceptional food, attention to detail, and attentive service that make it, hands down, the country's top Asian restaurant. ✉ *C. 11, between Avdas. 6 and 8, Barrio La Soledad* ☎ *257–3622 or 221–7605* 🖃 *AE, DC, MC, V.*

PERUVIAN ✕ **Machu Picchu.** A few travel posters and a fishnet holding crab and lob-
★ **$–$$$** ster shells are the only props used to evoke Peru, but no matter: the food is anything but plain, and the seafood is excellent at both the east- and west-side branches of this mainstay. The *pique especial de mariscos* (special seafood platter), big enough for two, presents you with shrimp, conch, and squid cooked four ways. The ceviche here is quite different from and better than that served in the rest of the country. A blazing Peruvian hot sauce served on the side adds zip to any dish, but be careful—apply it by the drop. Oh, and one more warning: the pisco sours go down very easily. ✉ *C. 32, 130 m north of KFC, Paseo Colón* ☎ *222–7384* ✉ *150 m south of Ferretería El Mar, San Pedro* ☎ *283–3679* 🖃 *AE, DC, MC, V* ☺ *Paseo Colón location closed Sun.*

SODAS ✕ **Soda Tapia.** One of San José's most popular restaurants fronts the east
¢–$ side of La Sabana park. You can dine outdoors here, but you'll contend with the traffic noise and the sight of the guard flagging cars in and out of the tiny parking lot. The place stays open until 2 AM, and around the clock on weekends. ✉ *Sabana Este* ☎ *222–6734* 🖃 *AE, DC, MC, V* ☺ *Breakfast served.*

¢ ✕ **Mercado Central.** A slew of unnamed sodas populate the heart of the central market. Grab a quick bite while you shop, and you just might find yourself rubbing elbows with the president. (He's been known to dine here.) ✉ *Bordered by Avdas. Central and 1 and Cs. 6 and 8, Barrio La Merced* ☎ *No phone* 🖃 *No credit cards* ☺ *No dinner; closed Sun.*

¢ ✕ **Soda Argey.** It's really a bit too upscale to qualify as a typical soda, but you'll find standard Costa Rican fare here and a rotating selection of casados. And these folks even deliver. ⊠ *200 m south and 100 m west of Automercado, Los Yoses, San Pedro* ☎ *280–1183* ▭ *No credit cards* ⊙ *Closed Sun. No dinner Sat.*

¢ ✕ **Soda La Vasconia.** Hundreds of sports photos plaster the wall here in what the owner calls his *museo futbolístico* (soccer museum), and the place draws crowds for that reason as well as the hearty food. It's one of the few downtown San José sodas to keep late-night hours. ⊠ *Avda. 1, between Cs. 3 and 5, Barrio El Carmen* ☎ *223–4857* ▭ *No credit cards.*

SPANISH ✕ **La Cocina de Terra Nostra.** You can get by without reservations at most
$$–$$$ San José restaurants, but not at this small, traditional, and very formal west-side Spanish restaurant. The dining room follows the Spanish theme with a tile floor, wood beams, white tablecloths, leather-and-wood Castilian-style chairs, and red, green, and yellow walls. *Champiñones al ajillo* (mushrooms sautéed with garlic and parsley) make a fine appetizer; *camarones Catalana* (shrimp in a tomato-and-garlic cream sauce) is a standout entrée. You'll find one of the city's most extensive wine lists here, strongest in varieties from France and Spain. ⊠ *100 m east and 130 m north of ICE, Sabana Norte* ☎ *296–3528* ⌕ *Reservations essential* ▭ *AE, DC, MC, V* ⊙ *No dinner Sun.*

$–$$$ ✕ **Casa Luisa.** A big open window looking into the kitchen—where chef
Fodor'sChoice María Luisa Esparducer and her staff proudly show off their trade—is
★ the first thing you encounter as you're shown to your table in this homey, upscale Catalan restaurant. The place is eclectic, with wood floors, arresting artwork, soft lighting, and flamenco music in the background. Start the meal with gazpacho or eggplant pâté, accompanied by a glass of top Spanish wine. The excellent main dishes include rosemary lamb chops, suckling pig, and grilled lobster. Finish with a platter of nuts, dates, and figs drizzled with a wine sauce or the decadent *crema catalana* with a *brûlée* glaze. Though Cocine de Terra Nostra is wonderfully elegant, we give Casa Luisa the nod in the Spanish-restaurant stakes for its combination of style and coziness. ⊠ *400 m south and 40 m east of the Contraloría, Sabana Sur* ☎ *296–1917* ▭ *AE, DC, MC, V* ⊙ *Closed Sun.*

VEGETARIAN ✕ **Shakti.** The baskets of fruit and vegetables at the entrance and the wall
¢–$ of herbal teas, health-food books, and fresh herbs for sale by the register tell you you're in a vegetarian-friendly joint. The bright and airy restaurant—much homier than Vishnu, its major veggie competition—serves breakfast, lunch, and an early dinner, closing at 7 PM each day. Homemade bread, soy burgers, pita sandwiches (veggie or, for carnivorous dining companions, chicken), macrobiotic fruit shakes, and a hearty plato del día that comes with soup, green salad, and a fruit beverage fill out the menu. The *ensalada mixta* is a meal in itself, packed with root vegetables native to Costa Rica. ⊠ *Avda. 8 and C. 13, Barrio La Soledad* ☎ *222–4475* ⌕ *Reservations not accepted* ▭ *AE, DC, MC, V* ⊙ *Closed Sun. Breakfast served.*

¢ ✕ **Vishnu.** HACIENDO UN NUEVO MUNDO proudly proclaims the sign at the door. "Making a new world" might be a bit ambitious for a restaurant goal, but Vishnu takes its vegetarian offerings seriously. The dining area looks institutional—you'll sit at a sterile booth with Formica tables and gaze at posters of fruit on the walls—but the attraction is the inexpensive food. A yummy, good-value bet is usually the plato del día, which includes soup, beverage, and dessert, but the menu also includes soy burgers, salads, fresh fruit juices, and a yogurt smoothie called *morir soñando* (literally, "to die dreaming"). ⊠ *Avda. 1, west of C. 3, Barrio El Carmen* ☎ *233–9976* ⌨ *Reservations not accepted* ⊟ *AE, DC, MC, V* ☺ *Breakfast served.*

WHERE TO STAY

Downtown

Staying in the downtown area allows you to travel around the city as most Ticos do: on foot. Stroll the city's parks, museums, and shops, and then retire to one of many small or historic hotels that have plenty in the way of character.

$$ ▦ **Aurola Holiday Inn.** The upper floors of this veritable skyscraper in a city of low-lying buildings give you commanding vistas of the surrounding mountains—day views are the best, since San José doesn't glitter quite like New York at night. The good restaurant and casino are also on the top floor, making full use of their vantage points. Inside, however, you could just as well be in Ohio, as the interior decoration betrays no local influence. The high-ceiling lobby is modern and airy, with lots of shiny marble, and the place has all the facilities a business traveler's heart could desire. ■ TIP➔ You'll get the hotel's best rates—a 30-percent discount—by walking in or reserving in advance via the local Costa Rican number. ⊠ *Avda. 5 and C. 5, Barrio El Carmen* ⊙ *Apdo. 7802–1000* ☎ *222–2424, 800/ 465–4329 in U.S.* 🖷 *255–1171* ⊕ *www.aurola-holidayinn.com* ⇥ *188 rooms, 12 suites* ⌨ *2 restaurants, a/c, in-room safes, minibars, cable TV, indoor pool, hot tub, gym, sauna, spa, bar, casino, laundry service, concierge, in-room data ports, Internet room, business services, meeting rooms, airport shuttle, car rental, free parking; no-smoking floors* ⊟ *AE, DC, MC, V* ❙◎❙ *BP.*

★ **$$** ▦ **Hotel Fleur de Lys.** We walked by this three-floor Victorian house with the hot-pink-and-lavender exterior dozens of times without ever peeking inside, assuming that a place so brassy on the outside couldn't offer anything of interest beyond its front doors. How wrong we were. A quiet elegance that you'd never imagine lies inside this 80-year-old home, with garden restaurant and art gallery, on a block-long street that gets little traffic. Unsurprisingly, given the name of the place, rooms are tagged with names of flowers rather than numbers. We like the suites, which have raised bathtubs—two of them have whirlpool tubs as well—and their dramatic glassed-in balcony entrances. ⊠ *C. 13 between Avdas. 2 and 6, Barrio La Soledad* ⊙ *Apdo. 10736–1000* ☎ *223–1206 or 257–2621* 🖷 *221–6310* ⊕*www.hotelfleurdelys.com* ⇥*31 rooms, 6 suites* ⌨*Restaurant, fans, in-room safes, cable TV, bar, Internet room, meeting room, free parking, no-smoking rooms; no a/c* ⊟ *AE, MC, V* ❙◎❙ *BP.*

$$ ▦ **Hotel Presidente.** The *presidente* referred to here is John F. Kennedy, who walked by during his 1963 visit as the hotel was under construction. You're looking at standard, medium-priced, business-class accommodation here. Each of the comfortable rooms has one double and one single bed. The hotel draws a large contingent of business and leisure-travel guests. The rooftop terrace with hot tub has one of those secret great views of the city that no one knows about. ⊠ *Avda. Central and C. 7, Barrio La Soledad* ✆ *Apdo. 2922–1000* 📠 *222–3022* 🖳 *221–1205* 🌐 *www.hotel-presidente.com* ☞ *88 rooms, 12 suites* ⌂ *Restaurant, room service, a/c, fans, cable TV, hot tub, gym, sauna, bar, casino, laundry service, Internet room, business services, free parking* 🖃 *AE, MC, V* ⊙ *BP.*

$–$$ 🏨 **Gran Hotel Costa Rica.** The one-time grande dame of San José lodgings has reclaimed that "Gran" title once again thanks to an extensive, and much appreciated, remodeling, redecorating, and retooling. A formal dining room and grand piano just off the lobby evoke the hotel's 1930s heyday. Rooms are large and bright with small windows and tubs in the tiled baths. This center-city landmark is a good deal for the money and a first choice of travelers who want to be where the action is. Even if you don't stay here, the arcaded Café 1930 that fronts the hotel is a pleasant stop for a bite any time of the day or night—it's open 24 hours. ⊠ *Avda. 2 and C. 3, Barrio La Soledad* ✆ *Apdo. 527–1000* 📠 *221–4000, 800/949–0592 in U.S.* 🖳 *255–0139* 🌐 *www. grandhotelcostarica.com* ☞ *110 rooms, 1 suite* ⌂ *3 restaurants, room service, fans, in-room data ports, in-room safes, minibars, refrigerators, cable TV, gym, massage, bar, casino, shop, babysitting, dry cleaning, laundry service, concierge, Internet room, business services, meeting rooms, no-smoking floors* 🖃 *AE, MC, V* ⊙ *CP.*

$ 🏨 **Hotel Balmoral.** You're just as likely to hear Japanese spoken in the Balmoral's lobby as you are Spanish and English; the place is quite popular with Asian visitors. As in the Presidente across the street, you'll find all the standard amenities of a medium-priced business-class hotel here, and like the Presidente, the Balmoral draws a huge number of leisure travelers, too. But we prefer the dark wood and plush, older feel here that's lacking across the street. ⊠ *Avda. Central and C. 7, Barrio La Soledad* 📠 *222–5022, 800/691–4865 in U.S.* 🖳 *221–7826* 🌐 *www.balmoral.co.cr* ☞ *102 rooms, 10 suites* ⌂ *Restaurant, a/c, fans, in-room safes, gym, massage, sauna, cable TV, bar, laundry service, Internet room, business services, meeting rooms, free parking* 🖃 *AE, DC, MC, V* ⊙ *BP.*

$ 🏨 **Posada del Museo.** This green Victorian wooden 1928 house is a great place to stay if you're bound for San José's museums; hence the name. It sits diagonally across the street from the Museo Nacional. The friendly Argentine owners live on-site. Each room is different. In the restoration, the owners have maintained the original tiles, wooden double doors, and artfully painted ceilings. The hallway on the second floor overlooks the two-story lobby from what the owners call their "Romeo and Juliet balcony." The Internet-ready data ports in each room are a rarity in a lodging of this size. ⊠ *Avda. 2 and C. 17, Barrio La Soledad* 📠 *258–1027* 🖳 *257–9414* 🌐 *www.hotelposadadelmuseo.com* ☞ *8 rooms, 2 suites* ⌂ *Restaurant, fans, cable TV, laundry service, in-room data ports, free parking; no a/c* 🖃 *AE, DC, MC, V* ⊙ *BP.*

¢ 🏨 **Casa Ridgway.** If you prefer lodgings with a social conscience, this is the place for you. (And even if you don't, it's a great budget find.) Affiliated with the Quaker Peace Center next door, Casa Ridgway draws travelers concerned about peace, the environment, and social issues, and the knowledgeable staff can give you the scoop on what's going on in those areas. In an old house on a quiet street, the bright premises include a planted terrace, a lending reference library, and a kitchen where you can cook your own food. Rooms are pretty basic and offer the option of bunk, single, or double beds. The dorm-style rooms sleep four, six, or eight. ⊠ *Avda. 6 Bis and C. 15, Barrio La Soledad* ☎ *Apdo. 1507–1000* ☎ *222–1400* ☎☎ *233–6168* ⊕ *www.amigosparalapaz. org* ⤴ *8 dorm-style rooms with shared bath, 1 double room* ⚒ *Fans, library, laundry service, Internet, meeting room, free parking; no a/c, no room phones, no room TVs* ⊟ *No credit cards* ⦿ *BP.*

¢ ⊞ **Hotel Aranjuez.** Several 1940s-era houses with extensive gardens and lively common areas with visitors swapping travel advice constitute this family-run B&B. Each room is different; some have private gardens or small sitting rooms. The Aranjuez is a short walk from most San José attractions and has discount tour services. The complimentary breakfast buffet is an amazing spread of eggs, pastries, tropical fruit, good Costa Rican coffee, and more, served on a marvelous, palm-shaded garden patio. And, a rarity in the heart of the city, this place walks the eco-walk, too, with solar-heating panels for hot water, composted gardens, and recycling. Luxurious it is not, but this is deservedly one of San José's most popular budget lodgings; reserve well in advance during the high season. ⚠ **Be sure to confirm your reservation 48 hours before you arrive and, if possible, on the day of your arrival, giving an estimated arrival time. If you don't, you might find yourself without a room when you arrive, despite your reservation.** You'll get a small discount if you pay in cash. ⊠ *C. 19, between Avdas. 11 and 13, Barrio Aranjuez* ☎ *256–1825, 877/898–8663 in U.S.* ☎ *223–3528* ⊕ *www.hotelaranjuez.com* ⤴ *35 rooms, 30 with bath* ⚒ *Dining room, fans, in-room safes, cable TV, babysitting, laundry service, Internet room, free parking, no-smoking rooms; no a/c* ⊟ *DC, MC, V* ⦿ *BP.*

★ ¢ ⊞ **Kap's Place.** This lodging literally sprawls around the neighborhood: one of the three annexes is almost two blocks away from the main building. (And if you drive by too quickly, you'll likely miss that main building with its unassuming sign and white metal door.) Inside are bright, tropical rooms with lots of tile and wood; coffee and tea are brewing all the time in the reception area, and you can use the shared kitchen. You'll be asked to sign a two-page agreement when you register attesting that you'll keep the noise down and won't bring unregistered guests to your room. The owners are anxious to maintain a family atmosphere here. ⊠ *C. 19, between Avdas. 11 and 13, 200 m west, 50 m north of Shell station, Barrio Aranjuez* ☎ *221–1169 or 257–0432* ☎ *256–4850* ⊕ *www. kapsplace.com* ⤴ *22 rooms, 20*

¿DONDE ESTA EL HO-JO?

Don't play it safe at a chain hotel, other than the few we recommend. They're all here in the city, but most provide you with the exact sameness you'd find in Cleveland. Smaller hotels and their Tico hospitality (although many are owned by foreigners) are quintessentially Costa Rica.

with bath ⚏ *Fans, Internet room, no-smoking rooms; no a/c, no TV in some rooms* ▤ *AE, DC, MC, V* ⦿ *EP.*

Barrios Amón and Otoya

Just north of downtown, old homes converted into small lodgings populate Barrios Amón and Otoya, two of the capital's most historic neighborhoods. While we generally eschew the big hotel franchises, our favorite San José chain lodging is here.

$$
Fodor'sChoice
★

⊡ **Clarion Hotel Amón.** The pink Amón Plaza achieves everything we like in a business-class hotel. It transcends its chain status and provides you with all the services and amenities you need without being a cookie-cutter high-rise. Though large for a Barrio Amón lodging, the low-rise hotel doesn't overpower the surrounding neighborhood, and takes pride in the fact that each of its 80-plus rooms is slightly different. (One common feature: there's nothing mini about the minibars.) The price of the suites (but not the double rooms) includes all international calls and shuttle transport to anywhere in the metro area. Friday night sees cocktails and a buffet dinner at the hotel's open-air Cafetal de la Luz to the accompaniment of light music, but the café makes for a pleasant stop any time, any day, whether you stay here or not. ⊠ *Avda. 11 and C. 3 Bis, Barrio Amón* ☎ *257–0191, 257–8686, 877/424–6423 in North America* 🖷 *223–4176* ⊕ *www.choicehotels.com* ⇰ *60 rooms, 27 suites* ⚏ *2 restaurants, room service, a/c, fans, in-room safes, minibars, some refrigerators, in-room broadband, gym, hot tub, massage, sauna, spa, bar, casino, shop, babysitting, dry cleaning, laundry service, Wi-Fi, business services, meeting rooms, airport shuttle, free parking, no-smoking rooms* ▤ *AE, DC, MC, V* ⦿ *BP.*

★ **$$**
⊡ **Hotel Santo Tomás.** Don't be put off by the fact that the front of this century-old former coffee-plantation house butts up against the sidewalk on a busy street; close the front door behind you and you'll find the lobby and rooms are set back away from the traffic noise. On the fringe of Barrio Amón, the hotel has spacious rooms with wood or tile floors and lots of deep, varnished-wood furnishings. Some of the tiled bathrooms have skylights. A bright breakfast room adjoins an interior patio, and if you keep traveling back into the interior of the building, you'll find a small outdoor pool, a rarity in a hotel of this size in the capital. Rates include 30 minutes of free Internet access per day, and the especially friendly, helpful staff makes this a real find. ⊠ *Avda. 7, between Cs. 3 and 5, Barrio Amón* ☎ *255–0448* 🖷 *222–3950* ⊕ *www.hotelsantotomas. com* ⇰ *19 rooms* ⚏ *Restaurant, fans, cable TV, pool, hot tub, gym, bar, Internet room, parking (fee); no a/c* ▤ *AE, MC, V* ⦿ *BP.*

★ **$**
⊡ **Hotel Don Carlos.** One of the city's first guesthouses (technically it's three different houses), the Don Carlos has been in the same family for four generations. But the spirit of Carlos Bálser, the hotel's Liechtenstein-born founder—painter, geologist, archaeologist, and general jack-of-all-trades—lives on. Most rooms in the rambling old coffee-baron house have ceiling fans and big windows. Those in the Colonial Wing have a bit more personality, and several newer rooms on the third floor have views of the Irazú and Barva volcanoes. Orchids and pre-Columbian statues adorn the abundant public areas, and the 272-tile mural in the lobby depicts the history of San José. Even if you don't stay here, the

Don Carlos has arguably the best hotel gift shop in the country, well worth a stop. ⊠ *C. 9 and Avda. 9, Barrio Amón* ✆ *Box 025216, Dept. 1686, Miami, FL 33102-5216* ☎ *221–6707, 866/675–9259 in North America* 🖷 *258–1152* ⊕ *www.doncarloshotel.com* ↶ *33 rooms* ⌣ *Restaurant, room service, fans, in-room safes, cable TV, outdoor hot tub, dry cleaning, laundry service, Internet room, airport shuttle, free parking; no a/c in some rooms* ☰ *AE, DC, MC, V* �‖ *BP.*

$ 🖽 **Hotel Dunn Inn.** Adjoining 1926 and 1933 houses fuse to create the cozy Barrio Amón experience at bargain prices, so the Dunn Inn is justifiably immensely popular. (Reserve well in advance.) Pinewood dominates in one section; brick in the other. Sun-filled rooms bear indigenous Bribri names. One room has a balcony, and a few do not have street-facing windows but look onto an interior courtyard. All have terra-cotta floors and little touches such as fresh flowers. The delightful, skylight-covered central patio serves as a bar and breakfast room. ⊠ *Avda. 11 at C. 5, Barrio Amón* ☎ *222–3232 or 222–3426* 🖷 *221–4596* ⊕ *www.hoteldunninn.com* ↶ *24 rooms* ⌣ *Restaurant, fans, no a/c, cable TV, minibars, bar, Internet room, business services, parking (fee)* ☰ *AE, DC, MC, V* �‖ *EP.*

$ 🖽 **Hotel Kekoldi.** You'd think you were in Miami Beach with all the pastels, but the art-deco, pink-and-white Kekoldi sits right in the heart of Barrio Amón. The secluded interior garden with umbrella-covered tables is a pleasant respite from the hustle and bustle of the city. The enormous, so-called "master queen" room overlooks that garden. The drapes, spreads, and pillows in all rooms echo the bright tropical prints throughout the hotel. Rooms contain in-room safes with a rental cost of $3 per night. Parking here is a scant two spaces, making this place a better option if you don't have a vehicle. ⊠ *Avda. 9, between Cs. 5 and 7, Barrio Amón* ☎ *248–0804* 🖷 *248–0767* ⊕ *www.kekoldi.com* ↶ *10 rooms* ⌣ *Fans, in-room safes, no a/c, cable TV, laundry service, Internet room, free parking* ☰ *AE, MC, V* �‖ *BP.*

$ 🖽 **Hotel Rincón de San José.** Never mind that the interior looks more European than Latin American. (It was once called the Hotel Edelweiss, and everyone still refers to it by its old name.) This elegant little inn has comfortable rooms in a charming area near the Parque España. Rooms have carved doors, custom-made furniture, and small bathrooms. Most have hardwood window frames and floors; several have bathtubs. Complimentary breakfast is served in the garden courtyard, which doubles as a bar. ⊠ *Avda. 9 and C. 15, Barrio Otoya* ☎ *221–9702* 🖷 *222–7184* ⊕ *www. hotelrincondesanjose.com* ↶ *29 rooms* ⌣ *Fans, in-room safes, cable TV, bar, laundry service, parking (fee); no a/c* ☰ *AE, DC, MC, V* �‖ *CP.*

★ ¢ 🖽 **Cinco Hormigas Rojas.** The name of this whimsical little lodge translates as "five red ants." Behind the

> **WORD OF MOUTH**
>
> "We stayed (and ate) at the Hotel Grano de Oro in San José. We had wonderful meals there. It's not big, but they have a quaint dining area, great menu, great service, and an outdoor garden patio. . . . Dinner for two of us with salad, wine and meal and dessert, tax/tip ran under $50 (expensive by CR standards, but not by our Boston, MA standards). And very good."
>
> –april0404

wall of vines that obscures it from the street is a wild garden—it's an unexpected urban bird-watching venue—leading to an interior space filled with original artwork. The largest, newest room (the Hoja Dansante, or Dancing Leaf) overlooks the minijungle that is the front entrance. Color abounds, from the bright hues on the walls right down to the toilet seats. Sure enough, the resident owner is an artist—Mayra Güell turned the 80-year-old house she inherited from her grandmother into San José's most original B&B–cum–art gallery. She tosses in thoughtful touches such as a healthful boxed breakfast if you're heading out on an early-morning excursion, and coffee and tea 24/7. If you cherish the sameness and predictability of a chain hotel, look elsewhere, but if there's an artistic bent to your personality, this is your place. ⊠ *C. 15, between Avdas. 9 and 11, Barrio Otoya* ☎ *255–3412* 🖷 *257–8581* ⊕ *www. crtimes.com/tourism/cincohormigasrojas/maincinco.htm* 🛏 *4 rooms, 1 with bath* △ *Fans, laundry service, parking (fee); no a/c in some rooms, no room phones, no TV in some rooms* ▭ *AE, MC, V* ⧦ *BP.*

¢ ▦ **Hotel Inca Real.** The Ecuadorian owners have constructed a modern Spanish colonial–style hotel that evokes South, rather than Central, America. Rooms congregate around a bright, skylight-covered, plant-filled central patio with wrought-iron gates around the second- and third-floor passageways. All rooms are ample in size. Those on the first floor are tiled; those on the second and third floors are carpeted. Some rooms have three beds, and all have back-friendly orthopedic mattresses. ⊠ *Avda. 11, between Cs. 3 and 5, Barrio Amón* ☎ *223–8883 or 223–8991* 🖷 *221–1356* ⊕ *www.hotelincareal.com* 🛏 *33 rooms* △ *Fans, in-room safes, cable TV, bar, laundry service, Internet room, car rental, travel services, free parking; no a/c* ▭ *V* ⧦ *CP.*

West of Downtown

San José's vast west side contains only a smattering of lodgings, but you'll find one of the city's best here.

$$ ▦ **Hotel Grano de Oro.** Two wooden houses on San José's west side—
Fodor'sChoice one dates from the turn of the 20th century, and the other from the
★ 1950s—have been melded together and converted into one of the city's most charming inns, decorated throughout with old photos of the capital and paintings by local artists. Each room in the place is different, and although you can't go wrong with any of them, the older house's rooms are the nicest, especially the Garden Suite, with hardwood floors, high ceilings, and private garden. A modest restaurant, run by a French-trained chef, is surrounded by a lovely indoor patio and bromeliad-filled gardens. The hotel's sundeck has a view of both the city and the far-off volcanoes. ⊠ *C. 30, between Avdas. 2 and 4, Paseo Colón* ⌖ *1701 N. W. 97th Ave., SJO 36, Box 025216, Miami, FL 33102-5216* ☎ *255–3322* 🖷 *221–2782* ⊕ *www.hotelgranodeoro.com* 🛏 *32 rooms, 3 suites* △ *Restaurant, room service, fans, in-room safes, cable TV, outdoor hot tub, laundry service, Internet room, free parking, no-smoking rooms; no a/c* ▭ *AE, DC, MC, V* ⧦ *EP.*

East of Downtown

The small properties beyond downtown, toward the university, offer personalized service and lots of peace and quiet. Plenty of restaurants and bars are within easy reach, and downtown San José is just a 10-minute cab ride away.

$$ ✕❏ **Hotel Le Bergerac.** Any other lodging of this caliber would be content to live off its reputation, and we'd never begrudge Le Bergerac if it did rest on its well-established laurels as one of San José's great hotels. But these folks are always tweaking and remodeling, and each time you return you'll likely discover something new. (What *doesn't* change much is the rates; they've kept pretty constant over time.) The hotel occupies two former private homes and is furnished with antiques. All rooms have custom-made wood-and-stone dressers and writing tables; deluxe rooms have two beds, private garden terraces or balconies, and large bathrooms. The location on a steep hill might disorient you; you could walk upstairs to your room, fling open the terrace doors, expecting to walk out onto a balcony, and find instead a ground-level patio and mountain view. The hotel's restaurant, L'Ile de France (⇨ Where to Eat), is one of the city's best, so dinner reservations are essential, even for guests. Breakfast is served on a garden patio. Le Bergerac remains the cream of a crop of small, upscale San José hotels. There are many of them, but the service, attention to detail, and ample gardens set this place apart. Hands down, this is our favorite lodging in the city. ⊠ *C. 35, between Avdas. Central and 2, first entrance to Los Yoses, San Pedro* ✆ *Apdo. 1107-1002, San José* ☎ *234–7850* 🖷 *225–9103* ⊕ *www.bergerachotel.com* ↩ *27 rooms* ⚹ *Restaurant, fans, in-room safes, cable TV, bar, dry cleaning, laundry service, in-room data ports, Internet room, meeting room, airport shuttle, free parking, no-smoking rooms; no a/c* 🖃 *AE, DC, MC, V* ¶◎¶ *BP.*

Fodor's Choice ★

$ ❏ **Hotel Don Fadrique.** This tranquil, family-run B&B on the outskirts of San José was named after Fadrique Guttiérez, an illustrious great-uncle of the owners who constructed the Fortín in Heredia. A collection of original Costa Rican art decorates the lobby and rooms, most of which have hardwood floors, peach walls, and pastel bedspreads. Several carpeted rooms downstairs open onto lots of lush garden space. There are also an enclosed garden patio and an adjoining small art gallery where meals are served. Parking is free, but on the street, with a guard present 24/7. ⊠ *C. 37 at Avda. 8, Los Yoses, San Pedro* ✆ *Apdo. 1754-2050, San Pedro* ☎ *225–8186 or 225–7050* 🖷 *224–9746* ⊕ *www.hoteldonfadrique.com* ↩ *20 rooms* ⚹ *Dining room, fans, in-room safes, cable TV, laundry service, Internet room, airport shuttle, car rental; no a/c* 🖃 *AE, MC, V* ¶◎¶ *BP.*

$ ❏ **Hotel Milvia.** Apply the principles of feng shui to an old militia arms depository, and you get a charming B&B on a San Pedro backstreet. Manager Florencia Urbina belongs to a local art consortium called Bocaracá, whose motto is "Art in Society." She takes that maxim seriously: the group's lush tropical paintings adorn the lobby, breakfast salon, small bar, and common areas. Your room will be decorated with lovely hand-painted tiles and classic Tico furniture, and you pass through a Zen meditation garden each time you enter and exit the building. The Milvia is a great value, and makes for a charming, artsy respite from the noise of the city. Julia Roberts and Susan Sarandon are a couple of celebrities who have stayed here. ✉ *100 m east, 100 m north, and 100 m east of Centro Comercial Muñoz y Nanne, San Pedro* ✆ *Apdo. 1660-2050, San Pedro* ☎ *225–4543 or 283–9548* 🖷 *225–7801* ⊕ *www.novanet. co.cr/milvia/* ⇨ *9 rooms* ⚴ *Fans, in-room safes, cable TV, bar, laundry service, Internet room, free parking, no-smoking rooms; no a/c* ▭ *AE, DC, MC, V* ⦿ *BP.*

¢ ▦ **Hostal Toruma.** The headquarters of RECAJ, Costa Rica's active Hostelling International network, is housed in a colonial-style bunga-low, built around 1900, several blocks east of downtown. Backpackers from around the world hang out and exchange travel tales in the bright tiled lobby and veranda. The on-site information center offers dis-counted tours. Beds on the ground floor are in small compartments with doors; rooms on the second floor have standard bunks. There are also three private rooms for couples. HI cardholders receive a 20-percent dis-count. ✉ *Avda. Central, between Cs. 29 and 31, Barrio La California* ✆ *Apdo. 1355-1002, San José* ☎ *234–8186* 🖷 *224–4085* ⊕ *www. hicr.org* ⇨ *80 beds in 17 dormitory rooms with shared baths, 3 pri-vate rooms without bath* ⚴ *Fans, Internet room, free parking; no a/c, no room phones, no room TVs* ▭ *MC, V* ⦿ *CP.*

NIGHTLIFE & THE ARTS

The Arts

The best source for theater, dance, film, and arts information is the "Viva" entertainment section of the Spanish-language daily *La Nación*. The paper also publishes the "Tiempo Libre" section each Friday, highlighting what's going on over the weekend. *San José Volando* is a free monthly magazine found in many upscale hotels and restaurants, and publishes features about what's going on around town. Listings in both publica-tions are in Spanish, but are easy to decipher. The "Weekend" section of the English-language weekly *The Tico Times* lists information about arts and culture, much of it events of interest to the expatriate commu-nity. The paper comes out each Friday.

Art Galleries

San José's art galleries, public or private, museum or bohemian, keep daytime hours only, but all kick off a new show with an evening exhibit opening. They're free and open to the public, and offer a chance to rub elbows with Costa Rica's art community (and to sip wine and munch on appetizers). Listings appear in *La Nación*'s "Viva" section. Your time in the capital might coincide with one of these by happenstance. (They're rarely announced in the paper more than a day or two in advance.) Look for the term *inauguración* (opening).

Theater & Music

Broadway or the West End it isn't, but San José has an active theater scene. More than a dozen theater groups (many of which perform slapstick comedies) hold forth in smaller theaters around town. If your Spanish is up to it, call for a reservation. The curtain rises at 8 PM, Friday through Sunday, with some companies staging performances on Thursday nights, too.

There are frequent dance performances and concerts in the **Teatro FANAL** and **Teatro 1887**, both in the **Centro Nacional de la Cultura** (⊠ C. 13, between Avdas. 3 and 5, Barrio Otoya ☎ 257–5524). The **Eugene O'Neill Theater** (⊠ Centro Cultural Costarricense–Norteamericano, Avda. 1 and C. 37, Barrio Dent, San Pedro ☎ 207–7554) has chamber concerts and plays most weekend evenings. The cultural center is a great place to meet expatriate North Americans.

The **Teatro La Aduana** (⊠ C. 25, Avda. 3, Barrio La California ☎ 257–8305) holds frequent dance and stage performances, and is home to the Compañía Nacional de Teatro (National Theater Company). The baroque **Teatro Nacional** (⊠ Plaza de la Cultura, Barrio La Soledad ☎ 221–1329) is the home of the excellent National Symphony Orchestra, which performs on Friday evenings and Sunday mornings between April and November. The theater also hosts visiting musical groups and dance companies. Tickets are $4–$40. San José's second-most popular theater, the **Teatro Popular Melico Salazar** (⊠ Avda. 2, between Cs. Central and 2, Barrio La Merced ☎ 221–4952) has a full calendar of music and dance, as well as a few offbeat productions. Something goes on nearly every night of the week; tickets are $2–$20.

Nightlife

Bars

No one could accuse San José of having too few watering holes, but outside hotels there aren't many places to have a quiet drink, especially downtown—Tico bars tend to be on the lively side.

There's nothing wrong with your eyes; it's the low pinkish lighting when you walk into the ultratrendy **Bajarse al Moro** (⊠ 650 m east of church of Santa Teresita, Barrio Escalante ☎ 234–9814). The African drumbeats are a bit louder than you might need. It's much quieter in the back. Intensely and proudly bohemian **Café Expresivo** (⊠ 350 m east of church of Santa Teresita, Barrio Escalante ☎ 224–1202) hosts poetry readings and acoustic guitar concerts and serves light pastas and sandwiches. **El Observatorio** (⊠ C. 23, across from Cine Magaly Barrio La California ☎ 223–0725) strikes an unusual balance between casual and formal: it's the kind of place where an over-30 crowd goes to watch a soccer game on TV, but wears a tie or dress to do so. The capital's best live-music venue, hands-down, is the New York–style **Jazz Café** (⊠ Avda. Central next to Banco Popular, San Pedro ☎ 253–8933), which draws big crowds, especially for live jazz on Tuesday and Wednesday nights.

Costa Rica's only microbrewery, **K & S Brewery** (⊠ Centro Comercial Cristal, 600 m south of Pop's ice-cream shop, Curridabat ☎ 283–7583), serves its own pilsners and lagers—they're a refreshing change from the ubiquitous Imperial brand drunk by the masses—with bar and restaurant.

A refreshing change from the ultrayoung, ultrahip El Pueblo venues, **Los Balcones** (✉ Centro Comercial El Pueblo, Avda. 0, Barrio Tournón ☎ 256–9494) specializes in *nueva trova* music, a folk genre that grew out of Latin American protest movements. (Think Joan Baez transported to the 21st century and singing in Spanish.) An older expat crowd hangs out at **Mac's Bar** (✉ South side of La Sabana Park, next to the Tennis Club, Sabana Sur ☎ 234–3145), which gets our nod for serving the city's best burgers and usually has a sporting event playing on the television.

The dressy **Meridiano al Este** (✉ Across from La Primavera gas station, Avda. Central and C. 21, Barrio La California ☎ 221–0650) is a mixed bag with everything from rock to nueva trova. Call first to see if the evening matches your tastes.

Fill up on Spanish-style tapas at Mediterranean bar and restaurant **Pub Olio** (✉ 200 m north of Bagelmen's, Barrio Escalante ☎ 281–0541). It draws a mix of professionals and older college students. Videos from the '60s, 70's, and '80s provide the backdrop at **Vyrus** (✉ 100 m west of Spoon, San Pedro ☎ 280–5890). Inside is dark, couply, and kissy; the outdoor balcony is much more conducive to singing along with that Duran Duran song you haven't heard in ages.

Cafés and Restaurants

Partake of 26 varieties of crepes, with or without rum, with or without Grand Marnier, on the front patio of **Cocorrico Verde** (✉ 75 m south of former Banco Popular, San Pedro). It's a stone's throw, but a world away, from the commotion of the campus nightlife. Near the university, **Fezcafé** (✉ C. de la Amargura, San Pedro ☎ 280–6982) is a quiet alternative to the rowdy nightlife nearby, at least until 8 PM on weeknights. Smack-dab in the center of the campus nightlife, **Omar Khayyam** (✉ C. de la Amargura, San Pedro ☎ 253–8455) is a blissfully quiet refuge from the noise of the nearby bars. Share a jug of wine and falafel or hummus with fried yuca on the covered patio. **Saudade** (✉ C. 17, between Avdas. 2 and 6, Barrio La Soledad ☎ 233-2134) holds poetry readings many Wednesday evenings, and has live music on Fridays, all to the accompaniment of desserts and quiches.

Casinos

Ask about casino rules before you dive in and play: there are a few Costa Rican variations—for example, you don't get a bonus for blackjack, but you do for three of a kind or straights under local rules—and yet some places proudly boast that they play exactly like they do in Las Vegas. Costa Rica has become the world's preeminent offshore-betting mecca, with many casinos operating desks where you can place a wager on sporting events back home.

The term "casino" gets tossed around loosely in Costa Rica: a hotel can put a couple of video poker machines in its lobby and claim it operates a casino. The casino at the Hotel del Rey in Barrio El Carmen—arguably the city's most famous and definitely its most notorious gambling establishment—swarms with prostitutes. Avoid it.

A few of the city's larger hotels have legitimate casinos, including the Clarion Amón Plaza, the Aurola Holiday Inn (the view from the casino is breathtaking), and the Gran Hotel Costa Rica.

The 24-hour **Casino Colonial** (⊠ Avda. 1, between Cs. 9 and 11, Barrio El Carmen ☎ 258–2807) has a complete casino, bar, restaurant, and cable TV, and a betting service for major U.S. sporting events.

Dance Clubs

San José's discos attract a very young crowd. Quite frankly, you'll feel ancient if you've passed 30. Live-music halls draw dancers of all ages, but most of these populate rougher neighborhoods on the city's south side and are best avoided.

Ebony 56 (⊠ Centro Comercial El Pueblo, Avda. 0, Barrio Tournón ☎ 223–2195) does triple duty as disco, sports bar, and café and draws an under-25 crowd. **Friends** (⊠ Centro Comercial El Pueblo, Avda. 0, Barrio Tournón ☎ 233–5283) plays mostly pop and Latin music, draws a still young clientele, but slightly older than that of Ebony 56 next door. **Planet Mall** (⊠ Mall San Pedro, C. 42 and Avda. 2 ☎ 280–4693), on the top floor of the massive San Pedro Mall, bills itself as the largest disco in Central America. Dress to impress; this is one of the city's most expensive dance bars.

For a dance-hall experience in a good neighborhood, we recommend the enormous **El Tobogán** (⊠ 200 m north and 100 m east of La República, Barrio Tournón ☎ 223–8920), an alternative to the postage stamp–size floors of most discos. Live Latin bands get everyone on their feet Friday and Saturday nights.

Gay & Lesbian

San José has a few bars, restaurants, and dance places patronized primarily by a gay and lesbian clientele, although all are welcome. Another tier of businesses, exemplified by the venerable Café Mundo, draws a mixed gay-straight crowd.

DANCE FEVER

Step into a San José nightclub and you might think Costa Ricans are born dancing. They aren't, but most learn to merengue, rumba (*bolero* here), mambo, cha-cha, and *swing* as children. Play catch-up at dance school **Merecumbé** (☎ 224–3531), which has ten branches around the city. With a few days' notice you can arrange a private lesson with an English-speaking instructor and get the basics of merengue and bolero. Other steps are projects for longer stays—or for continuing back home.

The gay-and-lesbian resource center **1@10 Café Internet** (⊠ C. 3 and Avda. 7, Barrio Amón ☎ 258–4561 ⊕ www.1en10.com) can provide you with information on gay and lesbian San José. Many more establishments dot the city than the tried-and-true places we mention below. A couple we visited preferred not to be listed in a guidebook. Others cater to tastes not quite so conventional. The popularity of still others waxes and wanes with changing fashions. The good folks at 1@10 can clue you in on what's hot and what's not.

Al Despiste (⊠ Across from Mudanzas Mundiales, Zapote ☎ 283–7164) is a gay bar that serves light bocas. A gay and lesbian crowd frequents **La Avispa** (⊠ C. 1, between Avdas. 8 and 10, Barrio La Soledad ☎ 223–5343), which has two dance floors with videos and karaoke, and a quieter upstairs bar with pool tables. The last Wednesday of each month is ladies' night.

El Bochinche (⊠ C. 11, between Avdas. 10 and 12, Barrio La Soledad ☎ 221–0500) is a gay bar that doubles as a Mexican restaurant. **Déjà Vu** (⊠ C. 2, between Avdas. 14 and 16A, Barrio El Pacífico ☎ 223–3758) is a mostly gay, techno-heavy disco with two dance floors and weekly drag shows. Take a taxi to and from here; the neighborhood's sketchy. Restaurant and bar **.G** (⊠ 50 m southeast of the higuerón [fig tree], San Pedro ☎ 280–3726) draws a primarily gay and lesbian clientele. Pronounce the name *pun-to hay*.

SHOPPING

Specialty Stores

Crafts

The arts-and-crafts tradition in Costa Rica is not as strong as in, say, Guatemala or Peru, and at first glance you might be disenchanted with what you see in the run-of-the-mill souvenir shops around town. Keep your disappointment in check until you visit two of San José's outstanding purveyors of fine artisan work.

Fodor'sChoice ★ Downtown San José's must-stop shop is **Galería Namu** (⊠ Avda. 7, between Cs. 5 and 7, behind Aurola Holiday Inn, Barrio Amón ☎ 256–3412), which sells Costa Rican folkloric art and the best indigenous crafts in town. Its inventory brims with colorful creations by the Guaymí, Boruca, Bribri, Chorotega, Huetar, and Maleku peoples—all Costa Rican indigenous groups. You can also find ex-

> **TALKING SHOP**
>
> Shopping in Costa Rica will seem blissfully low-key, especially if you've earned your stripes in places with high-pressure sales pestering, such as Mexico and Jamaica. Vendors will ask, "*¿En qué puedo servirle?*" ("How can I help you?"), as you walk by their stands, but if you're just looking, a simple "*No gracias*" ("No, thank you") reply suffices to be left alone. Prices are fixed, but fair. There's no haggling here.

EDIBLE SOUVENIRS

Costa Rica's foremost product is its foremost souvenir: Café Rey, Café Volio, and the ubiquitous Café Britt are superior brands of arabica **coffee,** and you'll find their foil-wrapped export-quality packages in supermarkets—which have the best prices—or souvenir shops. Their labels read *grano entero* (whole bean) or *molido* (ground); and *tostado claro* (light roast) or *tostado oscuro* (dark roast). The good ground stuff will also say *puro* (pure), and will not be mixed with sugar the way that Costa Ricans drink it. Britt is the only one that offers you the more sedate *descafeinado* (decaffeinated) option. And while you're at it, pick up a *chorreador,* too. Most gift shops sell the small stands with a cloth through which you can brew coffee the time-honored Tico way. (It's more tedious than Mr. Coffee, but is guaranteed to generate more conversation among your guests back home.)

Costa Rica's best **rum** is the aged Centenario—pick up a bottle for about $10. In addition to *añejo* (aged), it also comes *blanco* (white), and *conmemorativo* (commemorative), a premium aged, limited-production edition. There are several brands of **coffee liqueurs** (*licor de café*), including Café Rica and Golden Cream, but Britt makes the best one (although the Don Braulio–brand hand-painted bottles add visual pizzazz to your home bar). Buy these at any of San José's abundant supermarkets and liquor stores. FANAL, the government distillery, bottles Cacique-brand **guaro,** a 60-proof sugarcane liquor. "Firewater" might be a better description for it; try it only if you dare.

Any self-respecting Tico home or restaurant keeps a bottle of **Salsa Lizano,** one of the country's signature food products, on hand. Its tang brightens up meat, vegetable, and rice dishes, and a bottle fits nicely into your carry-on.

All these edibles can be found at **Más X Menos** (pronounced "Más *por* Menos") supermarkets throughout the country. It beats souvenir stores' prices for coffee, food, liquor, and other beverages. The main San José branch is at Avenida Central, between Calles 11 and 13.

quisitely carved ivory-nut "Tagua" figurines made by Wounan Indians from Panama's Darién region. Take note of carved balsa masks, woven cotton blankets, and hand-painted ceramics. The store looks expensive when you first walk in—and indeed, the sky is the limit in prices—but if your budget is not so flush, say so: the good folks here can help you find something in the $10–$20 range that will make a more cherished souvenir of your trip than a *Pura Vida* T-shirt. And as an added bonus you'll get an information sheet describing your work's creator and art style. Namu has a reputation for fair prices for customers, and for fair pay to artists or artisans.

★ The staff and selection at **Kaltak Artesanías** (⊠ 50 m north of Colegio María Inmaculada, Moravia ☎ 297-2736) make it a real standout from all the Moravia shops. Walk in with some unformulated "I'm not sure what I want" notions, and the folks here will help you find that perfect souvenir or gift from among the selection of ceramics (Pefi and Osenbach designs are well represented), wood-and-leather rocking chairs, oxcarts of all sizes, orchids, and carvings from native *cocobolo* and *guápinol* woods and ash wood.

Music

San José's music stores stock the Latin sounds of every artist from Chayanne to Shakira, but Costa Ricans take special pride in their home-town Latin-fusion group, the Grammy award–winning Editus.

Tunes waft outside from branches of **Music Box** (⊠ Avda. Central and C. 5, Barrio La Soledad ☎ 258–1359 ⊠ Avda. Central and C. 2, Barrio La Merced ☎ 256–4922), a small chain. The staff is always happy to offer recommendations. In addition to selling everything else imaginable, downtown department store **Universal** (⊠ Avda. Central, between Cs. Central and 1, Barrio El Carmen ☎ 222–2222) stocks a good selection of Latin CDs in its first-floor music department.

Souvenirs

Hotel gift shop **Boutique Annemarie** (⊠ Hotel Don Carlos, C. 9 and Avda. 9, Barrio Amón ☎ 221–6063) has a huge selection of popular souvenirs and CDs of Costa Rican musicians. Café Britt operates souvenir shops **Casa Tica** and **El Cafetal** in the **Aeropuerto Internacional Juan Santamaría** (⊠ 16 km [10 mi] northwest of downtown San José, just outside Alajuela) for those last-minute purchases. Choose from Britt coffee ($5 per pound)—the only brand sold here—and a terrific selection of good-quality merchandise, such as hand-carved bowls and jewelry, aromatherapy candles, banana-paper stationery, and Costa Rica travel books. There's nary another store in the country carrying such a variety all in one place. The catch is that the shop charges U.S. prices for this luxury.

Some 100 souvenir vendors congregate in the block-long covered walkway known as the **Calle Nacional de Artesanía y Pintura.** (⊠ C. 13, between Avdas Central and 2, western side of Plaza de la Democracia), and offer some real bargains in hammocks, wood carvings, and clothing. Dozens of souvenir vendors set up shop on the two floors of **La Casona** (⊠ C. 2, between Avdas. Central and 1, Barrio El Carmen ☎ 222–7999), in a rickety old downtown mansion. It's much like a flea market, and it's a fun place to browse. **Mercado Central** (⊠ Bordered by Avdas. Central and 1 and Cs. 6 and 8, Barrio La Merced) doesn't bill itself for souvenir shopping—the maze of passageways is where the average Costa Rican comes to stock up on day-to-day necessities—but a few stalls of interest to tourists congregate near the entrances. The tour buses always find their way to **Plaza Esmeralda** (⊠ 800 m west of Jacks, Pavas ☎ 296–0312 ⊕ www.plaza-esmeralda.com), and the place hums with all the activity of a port when a cruise ship is docked. Quality is high and you can watch your souvenir being created in front of you. Jewelry is a mainstay here, and there's even a replica of an emerald mine.

SAN JOSÉ ESSENTIALS

1

Transportation

BY AIR

ARRIVING & DEPARTING Two airports serve San José. Aeropuerto Internacional Juan Santamaría is the destination for all international flights as well as those of domestic airline SANSA in a terminal a couple of blocks away. Domestic NatureAir flights depart from Aeropuerto Internacional Tobías Bolaños. Arrival and departure at the tiny Tobías Bolaños Airport is very informal. For in-depth information about arriving at Juan Santamaría airport, getting to and from the airport, and airlines *see* Air Travel *in* Smart Travel Tips A to Z.

🛪 Airports **Aeropuerto Internacional Juan Santamaría (SJO)** ⊠ 16 km/10 mi northwest of downtown San José, just outside Alajuela ☎ 437–2400. **Aeropuerto Internacional Tobías Bolaños (SYQ)** ⊠ 3 km/2 mi west of the city center, Pavas ☎ 232–2820.

BY BUS

ARRIVING & DEPARTING San José has no central bus terminal, and buses to many destinations depart from street corners. The four largest bus stations—the Gran Terminal del Caribe, the Terminal Atlántico Norte, the Terminal de Puntarenas, and the so-called Terminal Coca-Cola (the former Coke bottling plant)—are all in dicey neighborhoods. Always take a taxi to and from the bus station, and at the Coca-Cola never take your eyes off your belongings. Call your individual bus line for information about schedules rather than the terminal itself. Consider the comfort of a shuttle-van service in an air-conditioned minivan for travel out of the capital. For bus and shuttle-van information and departure points from San José to other areas of the country, *see* Bus Travel *in* Smart Travel Tips A to Z.

🚌 Bus Terminals **Gran Terminal del Caribe** ⊠ C. Central and Avda. 13, Barrio Tournón. **Terminal Coca-Cola** ⊠ C. 16, between Avdas. 1 and 3, Barrio México. **Terminal Atlántico Norte** ⊠ C. 12 and Avda. 9, Barrio México. **Terminal de Puntarenas** ⊠ C. 16, between Avdas. 10 and 12, Barrio Cuba.

GETTING AROUND City bus service is absurdly cheap (30¢–50¢) and easy to use. For Paseo Colón and La Sabana, take buses marked SABANA–CEMENTERIO from stops at Avenida 2 between Calles 5 and 7, or on Avenida 3 next to the *correos* (post office). For the suburbs of Los Yoses and San Pedro near the university, take ones marked SAN PEDRO from Avenida Central, between Calles 9 and 11.

BY CAR

ARRIVING & DEPARTING San José is the hub of the national road system. Paved roads fan out from Paseo Colón west to Escazú and northwest to the airport and Heredia. For the Pacific coast, Guanacaste, and Nicaragua, take the Carretera Interamericana (Pan-American Highway) north (CA1), which continues beyond the airport. Calle 3 runs north into the highway to Guápiles, Limón, and the Atlantic coast through Braulio Carrillo National Park, with a turnoff to the Sarapiquí region. If you follow Avenida Central or 2 east through San Pedro, you'll enter the Pan-American Highway south (CA2), which has a turnoff for Cartago, Volcán Irazú, and Turrialba before it heads southeast over the mountains toward Panama. For car-rental information, *see* Car Rental *in* Smart Travel Tips A to Z.

GETTING AROUND　Almost every street in downtown San José is one-way. Try to avoid driving at peak hours (7–9 AM and 5–6:30 PM), as traffic gets horribly congested. Parking lots, scattered throughout the city, charge around $1 an hour. Outside the city center you can park on the street, where *guachimen* ("watchmen" or car guards) usually offer to watch your car for a 500-colón tip, more if you're going to be away from the car for a few hours. Even so, never leave shopping bags or valuables inside your parked car. For car-rental information, *see* Car Rental *in* Smart Travel Tips A to Z.

BY TAXI

GETTING AROUND　Taxis are a good deal within the city. You can hail one on the street (all licensed taxis are red with a gold triangle on the front doors) or have your hotel or restaurant call one for you, as cabbies tend to speak only Spanish and addresses are complicated. (A good way to avoid getting lost is to have someone write down the address to show to the driver.) A 3-km (2-mi) ride costs around $2, and tipping is not the custom. Taxis parked in front of expensive hotels charge about twice the normal rate. By law, all cabbies must use their meters—called *marías*—when operating within the metropolitan area; if one refuses, negotiate a price before setting off, or hail another. ■ TIP→ **The surest way to antagonize a driver is to slam the door; be gentle.** Cab companies include Alfaro, San Jorge, Coopetaxi, and if you need to go to the airport, the orange Taxis Unidos. Many unofficial taxis (*piratas*) ply the streets as well. They might be red cars with a margarine container on the dashboard painted to resemble a taxi sign. Some locals use them, but they have no meters, are illegal and often unsafe, and carry no insurance in the event of an accident.

🗗 Taxi Companies **Alfaro** ☎221-8466. **Coopetaxi** ☎235-9966. **San Jorge** ☎221-3434. **Taxis Unidos** ☎ 221-6865.

Contacts & Resources

Banks and emergency contacts follow each town listed in the chapter.

BANKS & EXCHANGING SERVICES

Get all the cash you need before you head out of San José. Outside the capital there are fewer banks and ATMs, making it more difficult to change money (although the situation is improving). It is virtually impossible to change currency other than U.S. dollars or traveler's checks outside of San José. Euros and Canadian dollars are becoming easier to exchange at banks in San José, but we recommend playing it safe and bringing U.S. dollars. Lines at the state banks—Banco Nacional, Banco de Costa Rica (BCR), Bancrédito (BCAC), and Banco Popular—move *very* slowly, but you can change dollars and cash traveler's checks. The private Scotiabank and BAC San José (formerly Banco San José) perform the same services with more palatable lines, but they have many fewer outlets. (Though a branch of the Canadian bank of the same name, Scotiabank here provides no access to your accounts back home, other than with your ATM card.) You can get local currency using your MasterCard or Visa at the Juan Santamaría Airport: there are machines in the check-in area, near Gate 4 of the boarding area, and near the baggage-claim carousels. The ATH (A Toda Hora) and Red Total networks accept Plus- and Cirrus-affiliated cards. A few—very few—Red Total machines give cash against American Express and Diners Club cards as well. Ask at your hotel for the location of the nearest bank or *cajero automático* (ATM), and specify whether you need a MasterCard- or Visa-friendly machine.

🏦 Banks **BAC San José** ✉ Avda. 2, between Cs. Central and 1, Barrio El Carmen ☎ 295-9797. **Banco de Costa Rica** ✉ Avda. Central between Cs. 4 and 6 ☎ 287-9008. **Banco Nacional** ✉ Avda. 1, between Cs. 2 and 4, Barrio La Merced ☎ 212-2000. **Bancrédito** ✉ Avda. 4, between Cs. Central and 2 ☎ 212-7000. **Scotiabank** ✉ Avda. 1, between Cs. Central and 2, Barrio La Merced ☎ 287-8700.

EMERGENCIES

🏥 Hospitals The private Clínica Bíblica and Clínica Católica hospitals are superior (if more expensive) alternatives to San José's state hospitals. Both have English-speaking staff. **Clínica Bíblica** ✉ Avda. 14, between Cs. Central and 1, Barrio El Pacífico ☎ 522-1000 ⊕ www.clinicabiblica.com. **Clínica Católica** ✉ Attached to San Antonio Church on C. Esquivel Bonilla, Guadalupe ☎ 246-3000 ⊕ www.clinicacatolica.com.

💊 Late-Night Pharmacies **Fischel Pharmacy** ✉ Clínica Católica, attached to San Antonio Church on C. Esquivel Bonilla, Guadalupe ☎ 283-6616 ✉ Across from Banco Popular, San Pedro ☎ 295-7694.

The Central Valley

Pacuare River

WORD OF MOUTH

"In Cartago we visited . . . the most awesome church: the Basilica de Nuestra Senora de los Angeles—a must-see. Lankester Gardens was a very pleasant stop. The orchids are obviously beautiful, but so are all of their gardens. (Bug spray is a good idea.) Then onto the Orosi Valley—oh my gosh! What a spectacular view! Coming down the mountain, you get glimpses of the valley, just beautiful."

—dfarmer

WELCOME TO THE CENTRAL VALLEY

View from Irazú Volcano

TOP 5
Reasons to Go

1 Coffee: Get up close and personal with harvesting and processing on coffee tours at two of the valley's many plantations: Café Britt and Doka Estate.

2 The Orosi Valley: Spectacular views and quiet, bucolic towns make this area a great day trip or overnight from San José.

3 Rafting the Pacuare River: Brave the rapids as you descend through tropical forest on one of the best rivers in Central America.

4 The views: Ascend the volcanic slopes that border the valley, meeting superb views almost anywhere you go.

5 Avian adventures: Flock to Tapantí National Park to see emerald toucanets, resplendent quetzals, and nearly every species of Costa Rican hummingbird. Rancho Naturalista is the bird-lovers' hotel of choice.

The areas North and West of San José are dominated by coffee farms and small valley towns whose beautiful hotels attract lots of tourists on their first and last nights in the country. Café Britt and Doka Estate are both here, as is the international airport, near Alajuela.

Coffee beans   Guayabo National Monument

Getting Oriented

The Central Valley is something of a misnomer, and its Spanish name, the *meseta central* (central plateau) isn't entirely accurate either. The two contiguous mountain ranges that run the length of the country—the Cordillera Central range (which includes Poás, Barva, Irazú, and Turrialba volcanoes) to the north and the Cordillera de Talamanca to the south—don't quite line up in the middle, leaving a trough between them. The "valley" floor is 3,000 feet above sea level. In the valley, your view toward the coasts is obstructed by the two mountain ranges. But from a hillside hotel, your view of San José and the valley can be spectacular.

In the eastern Central Valley are Cartago and Irazú Volcano. Cartago is an older city than San José, with some significant historic attractions. Irazú is Costa Rica's tallest volcano. On a clear day you can see both the Atlantic and Pacific oceans from its peak.

Rafting trips on the Pacuare and Reventazón are based in Turrialba, a bustling little town. The nearby Guayabo Ruins, of a city deserted in AD 1400, is Costa Rica's only significant archaeological site.

An often overlooked beauty is the Orosi Valley. The drive into the valley is simply gorgeous, and a tranquil way to spend a day. Birding destination Tapantí National Park is at the southern edge of the valley.

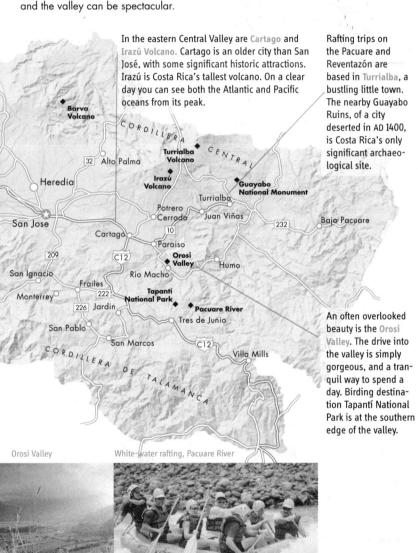

Orosi Valley

White-water rafting, Pacuare River

CENTRAL VALLEY PLANNER

When to Go

Known for its "eternal spring," the Central Valley lacks the oppressive seasonal heat and rain of other parts of the country and is almost always suitable for a visit. Average highs are 24–27°C (75–80°F). Afternoon downpours are common from mid-May to December (with a slight drop-off around July), but the amount of rain is modest compared to the Caribbean coast and the southern Pacific. Don't rule out the rainy season—fewer travelers mean you won't need reservations, rain is usually during afternoon siesta hours, and the valley is swathed in green after a few months of moisture. Holy Week (the week before Easter) and the last two weeks of the year are prime vacation times for Ticos, so reserve cars and hotel rooms in advance.

Choosing a Place to Stay

For getting away from it all and still being close to the country's primary transportation hub, the lodges around San José are ideal. Rustic *cabinas* (cottages), sprawling coffee plantations, nature lodges, and hilltop villas with expansive views are some of your options. The large chains are here as well, but the real gems are the so-called "boutique" hotels, many of which have unique designs that take advantage of exceptional countryside locations. Tropical gardens are the norm, rather than the exception, and air conditioning is usually not necessary.

Getting There

The region has an extensive network of paved roads in relatively good shape. The Pan-American Highway runs east–west through the valley and the center of San José. Mountains ring the valley, so most trips to or from the lowlands require a drive up in elevation then back down. The bus network is good, but since sights tend to be spread out it's less time-consuming to travel by car. Consider taking taxis. They're plentiful, they know the roads (most of the time), and the prices are reasonable. Even several $10 taxi rides per day—and $10 gets you quite a ways—are cheaper than a rental car.

■ TIP→→ Navigating the winding roads around the Central Valley is difficult at best, and absurd at its worst. Call ahead for directions, and don't hesitate to ask a local for assistance along the way.

How Much Time?

You could spend an entire week in the Central Valley without getting bored, but if you have only a week or two in Costa Rica, we recommend a maximum of two days before heading to rain forests and beaches in other parts of the country. Spending a day after you arrive, then another day or two before you fly out gives you a taste of the region, breaks up the travel time, and makes your last day interesting, rather than spent in transit back to San José. The drive between just about any two points in the Central Valley is two hours or less, so it's ideal for short trips. In a day you can explore the Orosi Valley and Cartago, raft the Pacuare River, or hop from the Butterfly Farm to a coffee plantation.

■ TIP→→ Bring a jacket—it can get chilly at night in any of the Central Valley towns, and downright cold at higher elevations.

2

Recommended Tour Operators

These San José–based tour operators arrange transport from some hotels (generally those in San José and around the airport). Costa Rica Sun Tours, Costa Rica's Temptations, Grayline, and Swiss Travel have myriad tour options:

■ **Costa Rica Sun Tours** (☎ 296-7757 ⊕ www.crsuntours. com).

■ **Costa Rica's Temptations** (☎ 239-9999 ⊕ www.crtinfo.com).

■ **Grayline Tours Costa Rica** (☎ 220-2126 ⊕ www. graylinecostarica. com).

■ **Horizontes** (☎ 222-2022 ⊕ www.horizontes. com) has countrywide natural-history and adventure trips

■ **Swiss Travel** (☎ 282-4898 ⊕ www. swisstravelcr.com).

Crowned Woodnymph

WHITE-WATER OUTFITTERS

Most outfitters are based in San José. Tico's River, Costa Rica Ríos, and Rainforest World are in Turrialba. Many have both rafting and kayaking.

■ **Costa Rica Expeditions** (☎ 257-0766 ⊕ www. costaricaexpeditions. com).

■ **Costa Rica Nature Adventures** (☎ 225-3939 or 224-0505, 800/235-6150 in North America ⊕ www.crna.co.cr).

■ **Costa Rica Ríos** (☎ 556-9617 ⊕ www. costaricarios.com).

■ **Exploradores Outdoors** (☎ 222-6262 ⊕ www. exploradoresoutdoors. com).

■ **Rainforest World** (☎ 556-0014 or 357-7250 ⊕ www. rforestw.com).

■ **Ríos Tropicales** (☎ 233-6455 ⊕ www.riostropicales. com).

■ **Tico's River** (☎ 556-1231 or 394-4479 ⊕ www. ticoriver.com).

Rafting, Pacuare River

Price Categories

WHAT IT COSTS in Dollars					
	$$$$	**$$$**	**$$**	**$**	**¢**
Restaurants	over $25	$15–$25	$10–$15	$5–$10	under $5
Hotels	over $250	$150–$250	$75–$150	$50–$75	under $50

Restaurant prices are per-person for a main course at dinner. Hotel prices are for two people in a standard double room in high season, excluding service and tax (16.4%).

WEST OF SAN JOSÉ

Updated by
Suzanna
Starcevic

As you drive north or west out of San José, the city's suburbs and industrial zones quickly give way to arable land, most of which is occupied by coffee farms. Within Costa Rica's coffee heartland are plenty of tranquil agricultural towns and two provincial capitals, Alajuela and Heredia. Both cities owe their relative prosperity to the coffee beans cultivated on the fertile lower slopes of the Poás and Barva volcanoes. The upper slopes, too cold for coffee crops, are dedicated to dairy cattle, strawberries, ferns, and flowers, making for markedly different and thoroughly enchanting landscapes along the periphery of the national parks. Since the hills above these quaint valley towns have some excellent restaurants and lodgings, rural overnights are an excellent alternative to staying in San José.

Escazú

❶ Once a traditional coffee-farming town at the foot of a small mountain range (the Cordillera de Escazú), Escazú is now primarily a bedroom community for San José. As you exit the highway and crest the first gentle hill, you might think you made a wrong turn and ended up in southern California—strip malls, fast food, Persian rugs for sale—basically nothing to indicate that you're in Costa Rica. There's even a bagel shop! But farther up you return to small-town Central America. Narrow roads wind their way up the steep slopes of the *cordillera* (mountain range), past postage-stamp coffee fields and lengths of shoulder-to-shoulder, modest houses with tidy gardens and the occasional oxcart parked in the yard. Unfortunately, the area's stream of new developments and high-rises have steadily chipped away at the rural areas—each year you have to climb higher to find the kind of scene that captured the attention of many a Costa Rican painter in the early 20th century. In their place are plenty of fancy homes and condos, especially in the San Antonio and San Rafael neighborhoods. Escazú's historic church faces a small plaza, surrounded in part by weathered adobe homes. The town center is several blocks north of the busy road to Santa Ana, which is lined with a growing selection of restaurants, bars, and shops.

Exploring

High in the hills above Escazú stands the tiny community of **San Antonio de Escazú,** famous for its annual oxcart festival held the second Sunday of March. The view from here—of nearby San José and distant volcanoes—is impressive by both day and night. If you head higher than San Antonio de Escazú, brace yourself for virtually vertical roads that wind up into the mountains toward **Pico Blanco,** the highest point in the Escazú Cordillera, which is a half-day hike to ascend (drive to The White House and ask for directions). Our preference is **San Miguel,** one peak east (ask for directions at Valle Azul Restaurant, 2 km/1.5 mi north of San Antonio de Escazú). The latter takes you past three large crosses and spectacular scenery, and there's less risk of getting lost.

Speaking Costa Rican

CLOSE UP

2

SPANISH IN COSTA RICA TENDS TO BE localized and has many of its own peculiarities. Costa Rica is a land where eloquent speech and creative verbal expression are highly valued. For example, here the response to a "thank you" is the gracious, uniquely Tico *"Con mucho gusto"* ("With much pleasure") instead of *"De nada"* ("It's nothing"), which is used in much of Latin America. In other cases, informality is preferred: the conventional *Señor* and *Señora*, for example, are eschewed in favor of the more egalitarian *Don* and *Doña*, used preceding a first name. Even President Abel Pacheco is called "Don Abel." Exercise caution when selecting from the list below. While young Costa Rican men address everyone as *maje* (dude), you might get a withering look if you, a visitor, follow suit.

adios	good-bye; but also used as "hello" in rural areas
agarrar de maje	to pull someone's leg
birra	beer
brete	work
cachos	shoes
chunche	any thingamajig
clavar el pico	to fall asleep
estar de chicha	to be angry
estar de goma	have a hangover
harina	money
jupa	head
macho, macha	a person with blonde hair
matar la culebra	waste time
maje	buddy, dude, mate
mamá de Tarzán	know-it-all
maría	a woman's name; also a taxi meter
montón	a lot
paño	towel
pelo de gato	cat hair; or fine, misty rain that falls during December
peso	colón

pinche	a tight-fisted person
ponerse hasta la mecha	get drunk
porfa	please
pura vida	fantastic, great
rojo	red; also a 1,000-colón note
soda	an inexpensive local restaurant
torta	a big mistake or error
tuanis	cool
tucán	toucan; also a 5,000-colón note
upe	anyone home?

Common phrases

Con mucho gusto	used in response to "thank you" instead of "de nada"
Muy bien, gracias a Dios	very well, thank goodness
Muy bien, por dicha	very well, luckily
Si Dios quiere	God willing

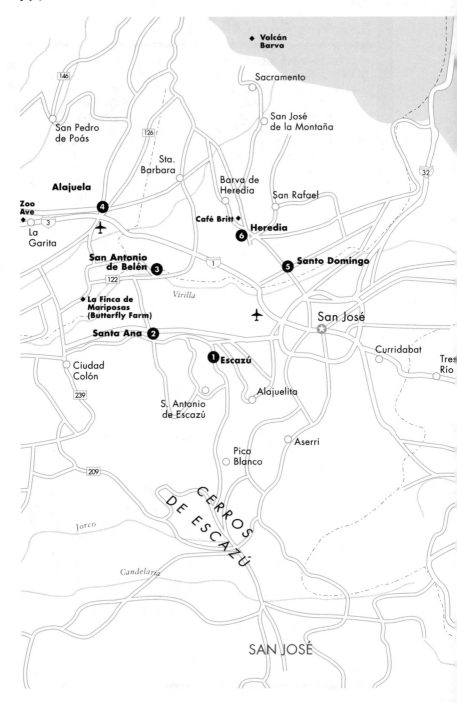

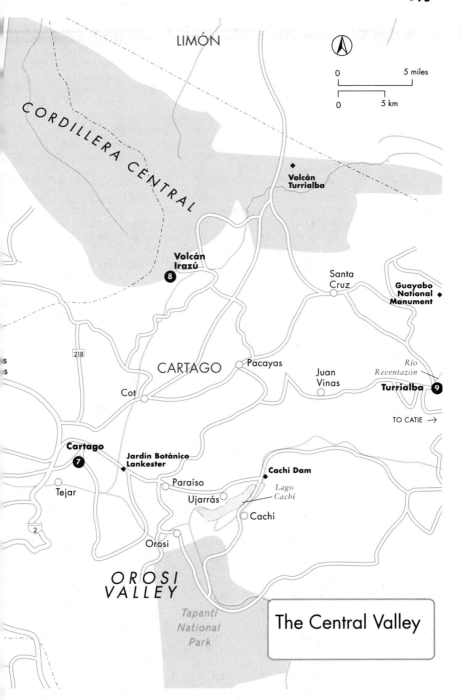

Where to Stay & Eat

$$–$$$$ ✕ **Le Monastère.** This monastery-themed formal restaurant high in the San Rafael hills has a great view of the Central Valley. The dining room is dressed up in antiques, with tables set for a five-course meal; waiters don short friar tunics over their standard black pants and white shirts, which makes the atmosphere too theatrical for some tastes, but the classic French dishes are outstanding. La Cava, the bar beneath the dining room, has live music Monday through Saturday and is open into the wee hours. ✉ *1.5 km/1 mi southwest of the Paco Shopping Center in San Rafael de Escazú; take old road west to Santa Ana, turn left at Paco and follow signs, always bearing right* ☎ *289–4404* ⊕ *www.monastere-restaurant.com* ▭ *AE, DC, MC, V* ☉ *Closed Sun. No lunch.*

$$–$$$ ✕ **Taj Mahal.** This burst of Northern Indian flavor is such a rarity in Central America that we can overlook the slightly less-than-factual claim that the restaurant is the isthmus's only such option. The suburban mansion went through a few dining incarnations before Taj Mahal became a hit in 2003. Richly swathed in warm fuchsias, red ochres, and golds, the dining area sprawls through a handful of small, intimate rooms out to an outdoor gazebo in the tree-covered backyard. The price-to-portion size is a little high, particularly for North Americans used to good, cheap Indian food, but the sharp Tandoori dishes, curries, and biryanis are a welcome vacation from ubiquitous European and American fare. ✉ *1 km/³⁄₄ mi west of the Paco mall on the old road to Santa Ana* ☎ *228–0980* ▭ *AE, DC, MC, V* ☉ *Closed Mon.*

$–$$ ✕ **Barbecue Los Anonos.** Established in 1960, Los Anonos expanded from its original rustic collection of deep booths with wooden benches in 2003, adding a more elegant room decorated with historic photos. It is a popular spot with Costa Rican families on weekend nights, and businesspeople on weekdays, who come for the economical three-course lunches. The best bet is the grilled meat, and there is plenty to choose from, including imported U.S. beef and less expensive Tico cuts. Fresh fish, shrimp, and half a dozen salads are other choices. ✉ *400 m west of Los Anonos Bridge* ☎ *228–0180* ▭ *AE, DC, MC, V* ☉ *Closed Mon.*

¢–$ ✕ **Cerros.** This San Antonio hills favorite combines smoky thin-crust pizza with the essence of the Central Valley—simple and sincere. Pull up a chair to the gingham-covered tables on the semi-enclosed patio, and you have the perfect view of a Costa Rican microcosm. The valley drops down just behind the soccer field and the green trimmed church across the street, revealing the shimmering panorama of Escazú, Alajuela, and Heredi. The bar, dotted with framed posters of past oxcart-driver festivals, is a safe and lively place to hang out and mix with the locals. ✉ *South side of*

HOCUS POCUS

During colonial days, Escazú was dubbed the City of Witches because many native healers lived in the area. Locals say that Escazú is still home to witches who will tell your fortune or concoct a love potion for a small fee, but you'd be hard-pressed to spot them in the town's busy commercial district. Try a soccer field instead; the city's team is christened *Las Brujas* (The Witches).

the soccer field, San Antonio de Escazú ☎*228–1831* ▭*Cash only* ☉*Dinner only weekdays.*

$$$$ ✕▣ **White House Hotel.** Formerly the Tara Resort Hotel, this luxurious little inn and spa near the top of Pico Blanco reopened in December 2004 after a renovation with a White House theme, and it appears that the transition from the Old South to Pennsylvania Avenue has been successful. Most rooms are named for a president, so fans of Clinton, Ford, or say, Warren G. Harding, are in luck. You can even come and go in a limo or helicopter if you so desire. The restaurant, The Capital Grill ($$–$$$$), features American-style surf and turf dishes like filet mignon, prime rib, and swordfish, and the glass walls do the view justice. Upscale, adrenaline-fueled diversions include the new casino—added in early 2006—and Harley-Davidson rentals and tours ($150/day). ⊠ *½ km/ ¼ mi south of the cemetery of San Antonio de Escazú* ☎ *288–6362* 🖷 *288–6365* ⊕ *www.whitehousecostarica.com* ⇔ *4 rooms, 10 suites, 2 bungalows* ⚄ *Restaurant, room service, fans, in-room safes, cable TV (plasma), pool, whirlpool tub, fitness room, massage, sauna, spa, bar, casino, laundry service, Internet, airport pickup, helipad; no a/c, no kids under 12* ▭ *AE, DC, MC, V* ▢⦶ *CP.*

$$ ▣ **Posada El Quijote.** Perched on a hill in the Bello Horizonte neighborhood, with a great view of the city, this bed-and-breakfast strikes the right balance between a small inn and a private residence. Being here feels like visiting a friend, albeit a friend with great taste. The best view is from the sundeck, just off the spacious living room, which has a couch, a fireplace, and lots of modern art. The apartments and the two "deluxe" rooms have comparable views. Smaller "standard" rooms overlook the surrounding gardens, and aren't nearly as nice. The staff is extremely helpful. It's a bit hard to find, so you may want to take a taxi, or call for directions. ⊠ *Bello Horizonte de Escazú, first street west of Anonos Bridge, 1 km/½ mi uphill* ☎ *289–8401* 🖷 *289–8729* ⊕ *www.quijote. co.cr* ⇔ *8 rooms, 2 apartments* ⚄ *Fans, cable TV, travel services, laundry service, Wi-Fi, Internet, some pets allowed, airport pickup; no a/c in some rooms* ▭ *AE, DC, MC, V* ▢⦶ *BP.*

$ ▣ **Casa de las Tías.** The name means "The Aunts' House," which is appropriate for this yellow house with a front porch and picket fence at the end of short road in San Rafael de Escazú. A few simple antiques and old photos of the aunts themselves complete the effect. The rooms and furnishings feel slightly aged, but make up for it in charm, and the large backyard and gardens give the illusion of being much farther than a mere 150 m from a major commercial street. ⊠ *100 m south and 150 m east of the Cruce Escazú (turn east just south of Restaurante Cerutti)* ☎ *289–5517* 🖷 *289–7353* ⊕ *www.hotels.co.cr/casatias.html* ⇔ *5 rooms* ⚄ *Fans, laundry service, no-smoking rooms, airport pickup; no a/c, no kids under 12* ▭ *AE, MC, V* ▢⦶ *BP.*

$ ▣ **Costa Verde Inn.** Rooms at this large and quiet B&B on the outskirts of Escazú make nice use of local hardwoods, and their white walls display traditional Peruvian art. South American art also adorns the main building, where a large sitting area has comfortable chairs and a fireplace. The inn is surrounded by gardens, and at night you can see the lights of San José twinkling to the east, though just three of the rooms take advantage of the view. The inn is at the end of a narrow driveway with an unassuming gate, but you'll see a sign if you've found the right place—ring the bell. ⊠ *From southeast corner of second cemetery (the farthest west), 300 m south* ☎ *228–4080* 🖷 *289–8591* ⊕ *www. costaverdeinn.com* 🛏 *11 rooms, 3 apartments, 3 studios* ⚲ *Fans, refrigerators, cable TV, pool, whirlpool tub, airport pickup; no a/c, no room phones* 🖃 *AE, MC, V* |⊖| *BP.*

Nightlife

Escazú is the Central Valley's hot spot for nightlife—many Josefinos head here for the restaurants, bars, and dance clubs that cater to a young, cell phone–toting crowd. The highest concentration of nightspots is in the **Trejos Montealegre shopping center** (⊠ The first strip on your left as you enter Escaź, just off the highway between San José and Ciudad Colón).

One of the more popular watering holes with the under-30 set is **Henry's** (⊠ 500 m west of El Cruce, Plaza San Rafael, 2nd fl. ☎ 289–6250), which features TV sports by day, varied music by night, and a pseudo-"islands" decor, with beach paintings and surfboards. Costa Ricans refer to this style bar as an "American Bar," which is fairly accurate.

Toku (⊠ 100 m northeast of El Cruce, San Rafael ☎ 228–4091) added a more upscale alternative for nightlife seekers when it opened in early 2005. The ample food menu has received mixed reviews, but the bar/restaurant is best known for eclectic live music, from local up-and-comers to yesterday's international headliners. Dining, bar, and concert areas are separate.

Shopping

If you get the shopping bug and absolutely must visit a mall while on vacation, Escazú is the place to do it. **Multiplaza,** on the south side of the Autopista Próspero Fernández, approximately 5 km (3 mi) west of San José, is a big one; high-end **Itskatzu,** 1 km (½ mi) east of Multiplaza has a much higher restaurant-to-retail ratio.

★ You can watch local craftsmen ply their trade at **Biesanz Woodworks** (⊠ Bello Horizonte, 800 m south of the Escuela Bello Horizonte; follow signs ☎ 289–4337), where expat artist Barry Biesanz creates unique items from Costa Rican hardwoods, which are carved on-site. It's difficult to find, so take a taxi or call for directions from your hotel.

To & from Escazú

5 km/3 mi (15 min) southwest of San José.

To drive to Escazú from San José, turn left at the western end of Paseo Colón, which ends at the Parque La Sabana. Take the first right, and get off the highway at the second exit. The off-ramp curves sharply left; follow it about 1 km (½ mi), sticking to the main road, to El Cruce at the bottom of the hill (marked by a large Scotiabank). Continue through the traffic light for San Rafael addresses; turn right for the old road to Santa Ana. Buses for Escazú leave from San José (along the west side of the Coca Cola) continuously. Green-and-white buses to Santa Ana leave from the Coca Cola every 10 mins; for places along the Autopista

Próspero Fernández or Piedades, take buses marked "Pista" or "Multiplaza"; those marked "Calle Vieja" pass through Escaź on the old road.

Escazú Essentials

Bank/ATM Banco Nacional ⊠ Southwest side of Parque Central ☎ 228-0009. **Banco de Costa Rica ATM** ⊠ North side of church ☎ 288-3902.

Hospital Hospital CIMA ⊠ Next to PriceSmart, just off the highway to Santa Ana, 12 km/7½ mi (15 mins) west of downtown San José ☎ 208-1000.

Pharmacy Farmacia San Miguel ⊠ North side of Parque Central ☎ 228-2339.

Taxis Coopetaxi ☎ 224-7979.

Santa Ana

This once-tranquil agricultural community on the opposite side of the *cordillera* (mountain range) from Escazú is in the midst of a boom, and shopping malls and housing developments are popping up along its periphery. But the town center, with its rugged stone church surrounded by homes and businesses, has changed little in the past decade. The church, which was built between 1870 and 1880, has a Spanish-tile roof, carved wooden doors, and two pre-Columbian stone spheres flanking its entrance. Its rustic interior—bare wooden pillars and beams and black iron lamps—seems appropriate for an area with a tradition of ranching. Because it is warmer and drier than the towns to the east, Santa Ana is one of the few Central Valley towns that doesn't have a good climate for coffee, and is instead surrounded by pastures and patches of forest—it isn't unusual to see men on horseback here.

Where to Stay & Eat

$–$$ ✕ **Bacchus.** Take a Peruvian chef trained in France and a Italian owner and you get Bacchus, a welcome addition to the local dining scene. The cuisine is a mix of French and Italian dishes such as duck breast in a port sauce, baked mushroom-and-polenta ragout, and a variety of pizzas. Modern art decorates the simple but elegant interior, and outdoor seating is available. An extensive wine list and reasonable prices make it a great pick for dinner. ⊠ *200 m east and 100 m north of church* ☎ *282-5441* ▤ *AE, DC, MC, V.*

$–$$ ✕ **Tex Mex.** This Gringo favorite serves a fairly standard Mexican menu—tacos, burritos, quesadillas, and so on—plus a few grilled meat items, such as the Argentinean *churrasco* (a thick tenderloin cut), complete with *salsa chimichuri* (diced garlic and parsley in olive oil). There are about two dozen *bocas* (appetizers, or snacks), which are mostly smaller versions of entrée items. The enchiladas may not be as good as what you find in San Antonio, but the setting is pleasant, with a yard shaded by massive trees. Seating is on a covered brick patio

WORD OF MOUTH

"We spent our first night in CR at [Xandari] and I was very impressed. . . . They upgraded our room since it was my birthday and the room and view were fabulous. I've traveled quite a bit and this was one of the nicest rooms I have ever stayed in—very clean, comfortable bed, huge private patio area, beautiful grounds, and a great dinner. . . . Loved it!"

–ltilson

or in an adjacent dining area enclosed by windows, for cool nights. A few simple, inexpensive rooms are available for rent in an attached house. ⊠ *50 m northeast of Catholic church* ☎ *282–6342* ⊟ *AE, DC, MC, V* ☺ *Closed Mon.*

★ $$$ ✕⌂ **Alta.** The view from this Iberian-style hotel perched on a hillside above Santa Ana is impressive, but then, so is the hotel. The sloping stairway entrance lined with tall columns and greenery is reminiscent of a narrow street in southern Spain, an effect reinforced by the barrel-tile roof and ocher-stucco walls; the narrow hallways feel like an old castle. Guest rooms are hardly spacious, but are nicely done in earth tones, with colonial-style furniture and bathrooms with hand-painted tiles. The restaurant, La Luz ($$), has a hardwood floor, a beamed ceiling, and plenty of windows for admiring the distant hills and the pool and gardens below. The eclectic and unusual menu includes spaetzle, curry, shrimp flambé, marinated lamb chops, and Moroccan chicken. ⊠ *2½ km/1½ mi west of Paco shopping center, on the old road between Santa Ana and Escazú, Alto de las Palomas* ☎ *282–4160, 888/388–2582 in U.S.* 🖷 *282–4162* ⊕ *www.thealtahotel.com* ⤳ *18 rooms, 5 suites* ⌂ *Restaurant, in-room safes, minibars, cable TV, pool, gym, whirlpool tub, sauna, laundry service, Internet, airport pickup* ⊟ *AE, MC, V* ⏀ *CP.*

$ ⌂ **Hotel Posada Canal Grande.** This small hotel tucked in the hills to the west of Santa Ana is a great value. Each room is different, and most have unique wicker beds. The second-floor rooms open to the balcony over the pool and have the view, but the first floor isn't bad either. Two fourposter beds are placed in the shade by the pool, just to lounge on. On a clear day you can see the Gulf of Nicoya to the west. ⊠ *20 km/13 mi (25 min) west of downtown San José on the Próspero Fernández highway to Ciudad Colón; 500 m north of the Piedades de Santa Ana Bus Terminal (where the highway narrows).* ☎ *282–4089 or 282–4101* 🖷 *282–5733* ⊕ *www.hotelcanalgrande.com* ⤳ *12 rooms* ⌂ *Restaurant, cable TV, pool, sauna, bar, laundry service, Internet, airport pickup; no a/c* ⊟ *AE, DC, MC, V* ⏀ *BP.*

Shopping

Large, glazed pots with ornate decorations that range from traditional
★ patterns to modern motifs are the specialties at **Cerámica Las Palomas** (⊠ Old road to Santa Ana, opposite Alta Hotel ☎ 282–7001). Flowerpots and lamps are also common works, and the staff will eagerly show you the production process, from raw clay to art.

To & from Santa Ana

17 km/10 mi (25 min) southwest of San José.

From San José, turn left at the western end of Paseo Colón, which ends at the Parque La Sabana. Take the first right, and get on the highway. Get off at the 6th exit; bear left at the flashing red lights, winding past roadside ceramics and vegetable stands before hitting the town center, about 2 km (1 mi) from the highway. Buses leave San José for Santa Ana every 10 mins (highway route) and 20 mins (old-road route) from 5 AM to 11 PM. A steady stream of buses for Escazú run from several stops around the Coca-Cola terminal (Av. 1/3, Ca. 14/16).

Santa Ana Essentials
🏦 Bank/ATM **Banco de Costa Rica** ✉ 100 m west of church ☎ 203-4281. **Banco Popular** ✉ Southwest corner of church ☎ 203-7970. **Banco Nacional** ✉ Northwest corner of church ☎ 282-2479.

🏦 Pharmacy **Farmacia Sucre** ✉ 25 m south of church ☎ 282-1296.

NORTH OF SAN JOSÉ

As you set out from San José or the international airport to explore the towns to the north, you're first faced with pavement, hotels, and malls—not especially scenic. It's only when you reach the centers of these small towns that you feel you've arrived in Central America. Santo Domingo and San Antonio de Belén blend into the outskirts of San José. Farther north, Alajuela and Heredia are bustling provincial capitals with charismatic central parks. Throughout this area, tucked into the urban scenery and lining volcanic slopes, are fields of that great Costa Rican staple, coffee.

San Antonio de Belén

❸ San Antonio de Belén has little to offer visitors but its rural charm and proximity to the international airport. The latter led developers to build several of the San José area's biggest hotels here. The town also lies on the route of entry for Alajuela's Butterfly Garden. It's also a convenient departure point for trips to the western Central Valley, Pacific coast, and northern region. If you stay at the Marriott, you likely won't even see the town, just the busy highway between San José and Alajuela.

Where to Stay & Eat

$$ ✕🖼 **El Rodeo.** This quiet hotel has spacious rooms with polished hardwood floors, high ceilings, and narrow balconies overlooking small gardens and rooms in the adjacent building. It bills itself as a "country hotel," though this is more in image than fact. An open-air lounge on the second floor has a pool table and wicker furniture. Breakfast is served on a porch overlooking the pool, which gets very little use, since most of the guests are business travelers. The large wooden restaurant ($–$$) in front of the hotel is quite popular with Ticos, who pack it on weekends. Decorated with saddles, steer skulls, and other ranching paraphernalia, the restaurant serves an array of grilled meats, from the Argentinean churrascos to T-bones, as well as several fish and shrimp dishes. ✉ *Road to Santa Ana, 2 km/1 mi east of Parque Central* ☎ *293-3909* 🖨 *239-3464* ⊕ *www.hotelelrodeocostarica.com* ↪ *20 rooms, 9 suites* ♂ *Restaurant, in-room safes, minibars, cable TV, tennis court, pool, whirlpool tub, sauna, laundry service, Wi-Fi, Internet, meeting rooms, travel services* 🖃 *AE, DC, MC, V* ⏹ *BP.*

★ ♻ **$$$$** 🖼 **Marriott Costa Rica Hotel.** Towering over a coffee plantation west of San José, the stately Marriott's thick columns, wide arches, and central courtyard are re-creations straight out of the 17th century, and hand-painted tiles and abundant antiques complete the historic appearance. Guest rooms are more contemporary, but they're elegant enough, with hardwood furniture and sliding glass doors that open onto tiny balconies. The service is comprehensive; if, for instance, you would like ballboys

A National Hero

WHEN THE COSTA RICANS DROVE invader Walker's army from their country in 1857, they chased his troops to Rivas, Nicaragua. The filibusters took refuge in a wooden fort. Juan Santamaría, a poor, 25-year-old drummer with a militia from Alajuela, offered to burn it down to drive them out. Legend says that Santamaría ran toward the fort carrying a torch, and that although he was shot repeatedly, he managed to throw it and to burn the fort down. His bravery wasn't recognized at the time, probably because of his modest origins, but in 1891 a statue depicting a strong and handsome soldier carrying a torch was placed in Alajuela, thus immortalizing Santamaría. For this occasion, Ruben Darío, the great Nicaraguan writer, dedicated a poem to him. The entire account may be apocryphal; some historians doubt there ever *was* such a person. But don't tell that to the average Tico. April 11 is now a national holiday in Costa Rica, called Juan Santamaría Day, which celebrates the Costa Rican victory at the Battle of Rivas.

to help you fine-tune your tennis game, then this may be your place. ⊠ *¾ km/½ mi west of Firestone, off Autopista General Cañas, San Antonio de Belén* ☎ *298–0000, 800/228–9290 in U.S.* 📠 *298–0011* ⊕ *www.marriott.com* 🛏 *244 rooms, 7 suites* ⚅ *2 restaurants, café, bar, in-room safes, in-room data ports, driving range, putting green, 3 tennis courts, 2 pools, gym, health club, hair salon, sauna, executive lounge, shop, babysitting, dry cleaning, laundry service, concierge, business services, meeting rooms, airport shuttle, car rental, travel services, free parking* ⊟ *AE, DC, MC, V.*

To & from San Antonio de Belén
17 km/10 mi (20 min) northwest of San José.

From San José, turn right at the west end of Paseo Colón onto the Pan-American Highway (Carretera General Cañas). The San Antonio de Belén exit is at an overpass 6 km/4 mi west of the Heredia exit, by the Real Cariari Mall. Turn left at the first intersection, cross over the highway, continue 2½ km/1½ mi, turn left at a large soccer field, driving 1½ km/1 mi to the center of town. San Antonio is only 10 minutes from the airport.

San Antonio de Belén Essentials
🏧 Bank/ATM **Banco de Costa Rica** ⊠ 50 m north of rear of church ☎ 293-0247. **BAC San José ATM** ⊠ 200 m west of soccer field.
🏧 **DHL** ⊠ 600 m east of the Real Cariari Mall ☎ 210-3939 or 209-6000 ⊕ www.dhl.com.
🏧 Taxis **Asotaxis Belén** ☎ 293-4712.

Alajuela

❹ Because of its proximity to the international airport (5–10 minutes away) many travelers spend their first or last night in Alajuela, but the beauty of the surrounding countryside persuades some to stay longer. Alajuela is Costa Rica's third-most-populated city (50,000), and a mere

2

30-minute bus ride from the capital, but it has a decidedly provincial air. Architecturally it differs little from the bulk of Costa Rican towns: it's a grid of low-rise structures painted in pastel colors.

Exploring

Royal palms and massive mango trees fill the **Parque Central** (⊠ C. Central, between Avdas. 1 and Central), which also has a lovely fountain imported from Glasgow and concrete benches where locals gather to chat. Surrounding the plaza is an odd mix of charming old buildings and sterile concrete boxes, including a somewhat incongruous McDonald's.

The large, neoclassic **Catedral** (⊠ C. Central, between Avdas. 1 and Central ☎ 443–2928) has interesting capitals decorated with local agricultural motifs and a striking red metal dome. The interior is spacious but rather plain, except for the ornate cupola above the altar. It's open daily 7–6.

Alajuela was the birthplace of Juan Santamaría, the national hero who lost his life in a battle against the mercenary army of U.S. adventurer William Walker when the latter invaded Costa Rica in 1856. The **Parque Juan Santamaría** (⊠ C. Central and Avda. 2.) has a statue of the young Santamaría. After a restoration in early 2005, Juan should keep his youthful good looks for years to come—which, sadly, is more than we can say for the abandoned-looking, weedy concrete lot he stands on.

Juan Santamaría's heroic deeds are celebrated in the **Museo Juan Santamaría,** housed in the **old jail,** one block north of Parque Central. It's worth a look, but not a linger, which is too bad because Santamaría's story is an interesting one. The orchid collection is impressive. ⊠ *Avda. 3, C. Central/2* ☎ *441–4775* ▦ *Free* ☉ *Tues.–Sun. 10–5:30.*

☾ Spread over the lush grounds of **Zoo Ave** is a collection of large cages holding toucans, hawks, parrots, and even two quetzals (the macaws range free), not to mention crocodiles, turtles, monkeys, wild cats, and other interesting critters. The zoo, the best in Costa Rica, runs a breeding project for rare and endangered birds, all of which are destined for eventual release. It has a total of 120 bird species, including such rare ones as the quetzal, fiery-billed aracari, several types of eagles, and even ostriches. An impressive mural at the back of the facility shows Costa Rica's 850 bird species painted to scale. ⊠ *La Garita de Alajuela; head west from Alajuela center past cemetery, turn left after stone church in Barrio San José, continue on 2 km/1 mi; or head west of Pan-American Hwy. to Atenas exit, then turn right* ☎ *433–8989* ⊕ *www. zooave.com* ▦ *$15* ☉ *Daily 9–5.*

★ ☾ Observe and photograph butterflies up close at the **The Butterfly Farm** (La Finca de Mariposas), in the suburb of La Guácima. The farm's several microclimates keep comfortable some 40 species of tropical butterflies. Come when it's sunny if you can—that's when butterflies are most active. This is the original butterfly farm, but there are other butterfly gardens near Volcán Poás at La Paz Waterfall Gardens and in Monteverde. In 2004 the museum launched an annual mural contest, turning not only its own buildings but surrounding corner stores and houses into canvases for talented Costa Rican artists. It's well worth a drive around—

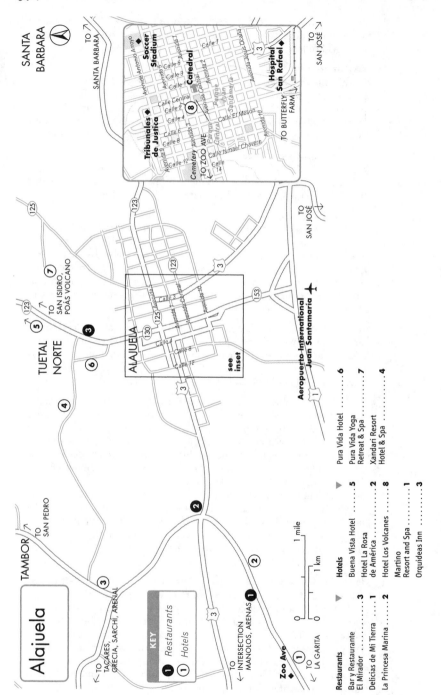

Alajuela

KEY
1 *Restaurants*
① *Hotels*

Restaurants ▶

Bar y Restaurante
El Mirador **3**
Delicias de Mi Tierra **1**
La Princesa Marina **2**

Hotels ▶

Buena Vista Hotel **5**
Hotel La Rosa
de América **2**
Hotel Los Volcanes **8**
Martino
Resort and Spa **1**
Orquideas Inn **3**
Pura Vida Hotel **6**
Pura Vida Yoga
Retreat & Spa **7**
Xandari Resort
Hotel & Spa **4**

TUETAL NORTE

TAMBOR

ALAJUELA

see inset

Aeropuerto Internacional
Juan Santamaría

SANTA BARBARA

Tribunales de Justicia ♦

Soccer Stadium

Catedral ♦

Hospital San Rafael ♦

Cemetery

Parque Central

TO ZOO AVE

Zoo Ave ♦

TO LA GARITA

TO TACARES, GRECIA, SARCHÍ, ARENAL

TO SAN PEDRO

TO SAN ISIDRO, POÁS VOLCANO

TO INTERSECCIÓN MANOLOS, ARENAS

TO SANTA BARBARA

TO SAN JOSÉ

TO BUTTERFLY FARM

0   1 mile
0   1 km

the farm's ticket office has a rudimentary catalogue of the paintings. ⊠ *From San José, turn south (left) at the intersection just past Real Cariari Mall, turn right at church of San Antonio de Belén, left at the corner, then follow the butterfly signs* ☎ *438–0400* ⊕ *www.butterflyfarm. co.cr* ⧆ *$15, $25 with transportation from San José* ☉ *Daily 8:30–5.*

★ Considering the amount of coffee you'll drive past in the Central Valley, you might want to dedicate 60 minutes of your vacation to learning about the crop's production. **Doka Estate,** a working coffee plantation with more than 70 years in the business, offers a comprehensive tour that takes you through the fields, shows you how the fruit is processed and the beans are dried, and lets you sample the local brew. The best time to take this tour is during the October-to-February picking season. ⊠ *10 km/6 mi north of Alajuela's Tribunales de Justicia, turn left at San Isidro and follow signs, San Luis de Sabanilla* ☎ *449–5152* 🖷 *449–6427* ⊕ *www. dokaestate.com* ⧆ *$16, $30 with transportation (4-person minimum) from San José, Alajuela, Heredia, Escazú, or San Antonio* ☉ *Tours daily at 9, 10, 11, 1:30, 2:30, and 3:30; Sat. and Sun. last tour at 2:30.*

EN ROUTE If you head straight through Alajuela, with the Parque Central on your right, you'll be on the road to Poás Volcano; you should pass the Tribunales de Justicia (the county courthouse) on your right as you leave town. If you turn left upon reaching the Parque Central, and pass the town cemetery on your right, you'll be on the old road to Grecia. About 3 km (2 mi) northwest of town on that road, you'll come upon an old concrete church on the right, which marks your arrival in Barrio San José, a satellite community of Alajuela. A left turn after the church will take you to a lovely rural area called **La Garita** (the Guardhouse), from where the road continues west to Atenas and the Central Pacific beaches. La Garita is a popular weekend destination for Tico families, who head there for the abundant restaurants

Where to Stay & Eat

$–$$ ✕ **Bar y Restaurante El Mirador.** Perched on a ridge several miles north of town, El Mirador has a sweeping view of the Central Valley that is impressive by day but more beautiful at dusk and night when the basin is filled with twinkling lights. Get a window table in the dining room, or one on the adjacent porch if it isn't too cool. The menu, which includes *lomito* (tenderloin) and corvina served with various sauces, and several shrimp or chicken dishes, plays second fiddle to the view. You could just stop in around sunset for drinks and appetizers. Free transportation from most Alajuela hotels is sometimes available. There are at least two other restaurants nearby with similar names and views—this one is on the main road, close to the Buena Vista Hotel. ⊠ *Road to Poás, 5 km/3 mi north of Tribunales de Justicia* ☎ *441–9347* ⊟ *AE, DC, MC, V* ⧄ *Reservations essential on weekends.*

¢–$ ✕ **Delicias de Mi Tierra.** The name translates as "Delicacies of my Land," and tasty and traditional Tico favorites are in fact served here: arroz con pollo, *pozol* (corn and pork soup), *casado campesino* (stewed beef with rice, beans, corn, potatoes, and plantains), and *chorreada con natilla* (a corn-bread pancake with sour cream). Long wooden tables and benches are surrounded by cane walls, decorative oxcart wheels, dried gourds, and tropical plants—the kind of decor trying so hard to be traditional that it's anything but. Ordering a few *entraditas* (appetizers) is a good way to sample dishes, as is the *parrillada de campo* (country barbecue), a platter with grilled chicken, beef, pork, rice, beans, fried plantains, and salad, or the larger *fiesta de gallos*, a mixed platter of corn tortillas with various fillings. Closing time is 8 PM. ⊠ *1½ km/1 mi west of the Barrio San José church* ☎ *433–8536* ▤ *AE, DC, MC, V.*

¢–$ ✕ **La Princesa Marina.** This large open-air eatery (part of a chain) at the intersection of the old Alajuela-Grecia road and the road to La Garita is popular with Ticos, who pack it on weekends to feast on inexpensive seafood. The selection is vast, with 10 types of fish, shrimp, or octopus ceviche, fish fillets served with various sauces, three sizes of shrimp prepared a dozen ways, whole fried fish, lobster tails, and several *mariscadas* (mixed seafood plates). Pastas, rice dishes, beef, and chicken are some other choices, but the seafood is your best bet here. The decor is utilitarian—bare tables, ceiling fans, and dividers of potted plants separating the sections, but you avoid that feeling of being in a contrived tourist venue. ⊠ *Barrio San José, west of church* ☎ *433–7117* ▤ *AE, DC, MC, V.*

$–$$ ✕▦ **Orquideas Inn.** This friendly and spirited hotel has a colorful, Spanish-style main building, a bar dedicated to Marilyn Monroe, and tropical gardens. Deluxe rooms, on a hill with a view of three volcanoes, are spacious, with bamboo furniture. Smaller rooms have terra-cotta tile floors and Guatemalan fabrics; those on the garden side are quieter, and worth the extra $10. A sumptuous breakfast buffet is served on the bar's patio. The restaurant's ($–$$) eclectic selection ranges from Costa Rican *casados* (plates of rice, beans, fried plantains, salad, and meat, chicken, or fish) to unusual dishes, like tilapia in a shrimp-and-corn sauce. The over-the-top presentation (ceviche served in a half-coconut adorned with plantains, for one) has to be seen to be believed, and it tastes as good as it looks. ⊠ *2½ km/1½ mi northwest of the Princesa Marina* ➬ *26 rooms, 4 suites* ☎ *433–9346* 🖷 *433–9740* ⊕ *www.orquideasinn.com* 🛇 *Restaurant, fans, cable TV, pool, whirlpool tub, massage, bar, shop, laundry service, dial-up Internet, meeting room, airport pickup, travel services; no room phones* ▤ *AE, MC, V* ⌾I *BP.*

$$$–$$$$ ▦ **Pura Vida Yoga Retreat & Spa.** Yoga workshops are an integral part of your stay here, and you should have at least some interest in the discipline to fully enjoy your stay. The spa has the full range of traditional offerings, as well as cutting-edge treatments like *watsu* (water shiatsu) and hot-stone massage. The variety of rooms ranges from large suites to carpeted and furnished tents; all are quite nice, if not super-luxurious. Most of the bamboo-filled rooms have large windows and look out over the valley or tropical gardens. The weekly rate includes yoga classes, full-day rafting and two other eco-adventure tours, airport transfers, three healthful meals per day, and one $70 massage. You can drop in for any number of days, but the experience is structured around the five- to seven-day "Mind, Body & Spirit" package. Credit cards accepted for bookings from the U.S., but only cash and traveler's checks are accepted at the hotel. ⊠ *7 km/4 mi northeast of stadium; make a sharp left at the Apolo 15 Bar, continue ½ km/¼ mi to cream-colored*

gate, *Pavas de Carrizal* ☎ *483–0033 or 483–1128 in Costa Rica, 888/ 515–4580 in U.S.* 🖨 *483–0041* ⊕ *www.puravidaspa.com* ⤳ *30 rooms, 12 tent bungalows, 4 suites* ⚐ *Dining room, spa, airport shuttle; no a/c, no room phones, no room TVs* ▭ *MC, V* ⦿ *FAP.*

$$$–$$$$ 🏨 **Xandari Resort Hotel & Spa.** The tranquil and colorful Xandari is a
Fodor's Choice strikingly original inn and spa. Its bold design is the brainchild of a tal-
★ ented couple—he's an architect, she's an artist. Contemporary pueblo-
esque villas along a ridge overlooking Alajuela and San José are spacious,
with plenty of windows, colorful paintings, large terraces, and secluded
lanais (sunbathing patios). It's the kind of place that makes you want
to take pictures of your hotel room. Some villas stand alone and some
share a building, but nearly all of them have spectacular views. So does
the restaurant, which serves tasty, often organic, low-fat food. A 4-km
(3-mi) trail through the hotel's forest reserve winds past five waterfalls.
✉ *5 km/3 mi north of Tribunales de Justicia, turn left after small bridge, follow signs, Apdo. 1485–4050* ☎ *443–2020, 800/686–7879 in U.S.* 🖨 *442–4847* ⊕ *www.xandari.com* ⤳ *22 villas* ⚐ *Restaurant, some fans, in-room safes, minibars, 2 pools, whirlpool tub, spa, bar, shop, art stu-dio, laundry service, dial-up Internet, airport shuttle, travel services, no-smoking rooms; no a/c, no room TVs* ▭ *AE, MC, V* ⦿ *CP.*

$$$ 🏨 **Martino Resort and Spa.** This relatively small Italian-style resort hotel
has a casino, spa, and spacious grounds, with the occasional classical
sculpture to catch your eye. It's a small step below the international luxury chains in both quality and price, but still a good value. The rear of
the main building is gorgeous, with a restaurant balcony that looks over
the pool. The rooms have terraces, wood furnishings, and carved wooden
doors, and the restaurant, which is well regarded locally, serves pastas
and Italian-style meat and seafood dishes. ✉ *Across from Zoo Ave on the road to La Garita* ☎ *433–8382* 🖨 *433–9052* ⊕ *www.hotelmartino. com* ⤳ *34 junior suites, 3 standard, 4 deluxe suites, and 1 villa* ⚐ *Restau-rant, room service, bar, cable TV, pool, beauty salon, gym, spa, travel services, nature trails, casino, laundry service, Wi-Fi, Internet, meeting rooms, no-smoking rooms* ▭ *AE, DC, MC, V* ⦿ *BP.*

$–$$ 🏨 **Buena Vista Hotel.** Perched high above Alajuela, this hotel does have
the "good view" it is named for, but few of its rooms share in that vista,
which is best appreciated from the back lawn. Three balcony rooms on
the second floor in back have decent views of the Central Valley, but
even better are the views of Poás Volcano from the three rooms above
the lobby. Most rooms, however, overlook the lawns, or pool area. They
are fairly standard—carpeted and sparsely decorated, with small baths
and TVs—with none of the pizzazz of similarly priced options. The staff
are superb, and the restaurant behind the lobby serves international dishes
and grilled items. ✉ *6 km/4 mi north of Alajuela's Tribunales de Jus-ticia on road to Poás* ☎ *442–8595, 800/506–2304 in U.S.* 🖨 *442–8701* ⊕ *www.hotelbuenavistacr.com* ⤳ *19 rooms, 4 junior suites* ⚐ *Restau-rant, fans, cable TV, pool, bar, shop, dial-up Internet, airport shuttle, travel services, no-smoking rooms, handicapped accessible; no a/c, no room phones* ▭ *AE, DC, MC, V* ⦿ *CP.*

★ **$–$$** 🏨 **Pura Vida Hotel.** Thanks to its location on a ridge north of town, sev-
eral of this hotel's rooms have views of Poás Volcano, and all of them
offer tranquility and abundant birdsong. The two rooms in the main

house have the best views, but *casitas* (little houses) scattered around the large garden offer more privacy. Some of these bright and cheery bungalows have separate bedrooms, and most of them have small terraces with chairs. Continental breakfasts and delicious dinners (by reservation) are served on a covered terrace behind the house. The helpful owners and proximity to the airport (15 minutes) make this a good place to begin and end a trip. ⊠ *Tuetal, 2 km/1 mi north of Tribunales de Justicia, veer left at Y* 🏠🏠 *430–2929* ⊕ *www.puravidahotel.com* ✆ *2 rooms, 4 bungalows* ⚅ *Restaurant, fans, Internet, laundry service, airport shuttle, travel services, no-smoking rooms; no a/c, no phones in some rooms, no room TVs* ☰ *AE, MC, V* ⦿ *CP.*

$ ▦ **Hotel La Rosa de América.** This small hotel tucked off the road to La Garita is a simple and relaxed place to unwind. There are six buildings, most divided into two units, arranged around the pool and gardens. The white-walled rooms are simple, but it's a quiet place to sleep. Calling ahead for directions is a good idea, but once you're there, you'll have easy access to nearby restaurants and Zoo Ave. ⊠ *2½ km/1½ mi from La Princesa Marina, on the left; look for the small sign* 🏠🏠 *433–2741 or 433–2455* ⊕ *www.larosadeamerica.com* ✆ *12 rooms* ⚅ *Fans, in-room safes, cable TV, pool, laundry service, Internet, no smoking rooms; no a/c, no room phones* ☰ *AE, DC, MC, V* ⦿ *BP.*

$ ▦ **Hotel Los Volcanes.** Descendents of the Catalan family that thrived in this heritage house in 1920 still lives next door. Historic photos of the mansion in its heyday line the earthy-toned walls. Its incarnation as a hotel began in 2000. Spacious rooms with low-slung, wide beds make the ceilings seem sky high. Private and shared bath options make this oasis accessible to budget travelers as well—but avoid the room next to the washer and dryer. Breakfast is served in a fig-tree shaded courtyard. Plenty of restaurants are within walking distance, the airport is a 10-minute taxi ride away, and just a few blocks away is the bus stop for La Garita, Poás, and most destinations in central and northwest Costa Rica. ⊠ *100 m north, 25 m east of the northwest corner of Parque Central, across from the Juan Santamaría museum.* ☎ *441–0525* 🖨 *440–8006* ✆ *7 rooms with private bath, 4 with shared bath* ⚅ *Fans, cable Internet, laundry service, travel services; no a/c, no room phones* ☰ *V* ⦿ *BP.*

To & from Alajuela
20 km/13 mi northwest of San José.

To reach Alajuela, follow directions to San Antonio de Belén (⇨ above). Continue west on the highway past the San Antonio turnoff and turn right at the airport. Buses travel between San José (Av. 2, Ca. 12/14, opposite the north side of Parque La Merced), the airport, and Alajuela, and run every 5 minutes from 4:40 AM to 11 PM. The bus stop in Alajuela is 400 m west, 25 m north of the central park (C. 3 and Av. 1). Buses leave San José for Zoo Ave from La Merced church (C. 14/ Ave. 4) Saturdays and Sundays at 8, 9, 10, 11 AM, and noon, returning on the hour from 10 AM to 3 PM.

Alajuela Essentials
🏧 Bank/ATM **Banco de Costa Rica** ⊠ Southwest corner of Parque Central ☎ 440–9039. **Banco Nacional** ⊠ West side of Parque Central ☎ 441–0373.

🏥 Hospital **Hospital San Rafael** ⊠1 km/½ mi northeast of the airport, on the main road to Alajuela. ☎ 436-1001.

🏥 Pharmacy **Farmacia Chavarría** ⊠ Southwest corner of Parque Central ☎ 441-1231. **Farmacia Catedral** ⊠ Northeast corner of Parque Central ☎ 441-3555.

🚕 Taxis **Cootaxa** ☎443-3030 or 442-3030.

COFFEE'S MELTING POT

Coffee is touted as a quintessential part of Costa Rica's history and culture; paradoxically, the majority of coffee-plantation workers in the country today are Nicaraguan.

2

Santo Domingo

❺ Between Heredia and San José, the town of Santo Domingo de Heredia has plenty of traditional architecture and a level of tranquility that belies its proximity to the capital, a mere 15-minute drive away. Established in the early 19th century, Santo Domingo is surrounded by coffee farms and several smaller, even quieter communities. It has two Catholic churches, including one of the country's two basilicas. The Iglesia del Rosario, which faces the town's sparsely planted Parque Central, was built in the 1840s and is open for mass every morning from 7 to 10. The larger Basilica de Santo Domingo, which stands across from a soccer field on the north end of town, is open for evening mass from 5 to 7, and is as a venue for classical music concerts throughout the year, including the July-to-August International Music Festival.

Exploring

🏛 Santo Domingo's main attraction is **INBioparque,** which does a good job of exhibiting the country's various ecosystems. It's a useful, if slightly expensive, primer before you head out to the hinterlands. Wander trails through climate-controlled wetlands and out to tropical dry forest. The forests may not look much different, but your English-speaking guide will explain the subtleties. Along the way, stop at the butterfly farm, snake and insect exhibits, and bromeliad garden. The tour is packed with information—perhaps too much—but if you're visiting Costa Rica for its ecology, it's a worthwhile lesson. Kids will love the world's only bullet-ant farm, and the Base CA-05 exhibit opened in late 2005—a virtual aerial flyover of Central America introduced by astronaut Franklin Chang (on video). A restaurant serves typical Costa Rican fare, and the gift shop has souvenirs and books on natural history. ⊠ *Road between Santo Domingo and Heredia, 400 m north and 200 m west of Shell gas station; follow the signs—you can't miss it* ☎ *507-8107* ⊕ *www. inbioparque.com.* 🎫 *$15 adults, $8 kids* ☉ *Tues.–Sun., 8–4. Tours at 9, 11 and 1, reservations recommended.*

Where to Stay & Eat

★ **$$** ⨉🏨 **Hotel Bougainvillea.** You might forget that you're only 15 minutes from San José on the Bougainvillea's extensive grounds, which bump up against coffee farms. The spacious and carpeted but otherwise unremarkable rooms are furnished with local hardwoods. Rooms on the second and third floors have large balconies; get one with a view of the gardens behind the hotel. The gardens, which are shaded by large trees, hold an extensive bromeliad collection, and have ample open areas for kids, are so big that they have their own brochure. Pre-Columbian pottery and paintings by Costa Rican artists decorate the lobby and restaurant ($–$$), which serves a small but excellent selection of Continental cuisine. An hourly shuttle takes you to the Hotel Villa Tournón in San José. ⊠ *2 km/1 mi east of Santo Domingo de Heredia, Santo Tomas* ☎ *244–1414* 🖶 *244–1313* ⊕ *www.hb.co.cr* 🛏 *77 rooms, 4 suites* ⚹ *Restaurant, fans, cable TV, tennis court, pool, sauna, bar, shop, laundry service, meeting rooms, Wi-Fi, Internet, travel services, no-smoking rooms; no a/c* ⊟ *AE, DC, MC, V.*

To & from Santo Domingo

18 km/11 mi (30 mins) northeast of Escazú, 7 km/4 mi (15 mins) northwest of San José.

From downtown San José, head north on C. Central 4 km/3 mi to the central park in Tibas; continue 100 m and turn left. Follow this road another 2½ km/1½ mi to Santo Domingo. From the west end of Paseo Colón, turn right onto the Pan-American Highway (aka the Carretera General Cañas), then right off the highway just before it heads onto an overpass, after the Hotel Irazú (on the right). Keep to this road for about 2 km/1½ mi to the first intersection after it becomes one-way. Turn right at the lights, continue 3 km/1½ mi (past INBioparque) until the road Ts; a left here brings you into town. *See* Heredia *for* bus information.

Heredia

❻ With a population of around 22,000, Heredia is the capital of one of Costa Rica's most important coffee provinces, with some of the country's best-preserved colonial towns. Founded in 1706, the city bears witness to how difficult preservation can be in an earthquake-prone country; most of its colonial structures have been destroyed by the tremors and tropical climate. Still, the city and neighboring towns retain a certain historic feel, with old adobe buildings scattered amid the concrete structures. The nearby villages of Barva and Santo Domingo de Heredia have more colonial and adobe buildings, and the roads that wind through the hills above those towns pass through charming scenery and rural enclaves, making them excellent routes for exploration.

Exploring

Heredia proper is centered around a tree-studded **Parque Central**, which is surrounded by a few historic buildings. The park has a cast-iron fountain imported from England in 1879 and a simple kiosk where the municipal band plays Sunday-morning and Thursday-night concerts. ⊠ *C. Central and Avda. Central.*

The impressive **Iglesia de la Inmaculada Concepción** is a whitewashed stone church built between 1797 and 1804 to replace an adobe temple dating from the early 1700s. Its thick stone walls, small windows, and squat buttresses have kept it intact through two centuries of quakes and tremors. It has a pale interior with marble floors and stained-glass windows, and is flanked by tidy gardens. ⊠ *Eastern end of Parque Central* ☎ *237–0779* ☉ *Daily 6–6.*

To the north of the Parque Central stands a strange, decorative tower called the **Fortín** (Little Fort), which was built as a military post in the 1880s by the local oligarch Fadrique Gutiérrez. It never did see action, and now serves as a symbol of the province. It's worth a walk by, but is closed to the public. The old brick building next to the Fortín is the Palacio Municipal (Town Hall). ⊠ *C. Central and Avda. Central* ☎ *No phone* ☒ *Free.*

Two blocks south of the Parque Central is Heredia's **Mercado Viejo** (Old Market), which has fewer souvenirs for sale than San José's Mercado Central but is less cramped and safer. On the next block to the southeast is the **Mercado Nuevo** (New Market), which holds dozens of *sodas* (simple restaurants). ⊠ *C. Central and Avda. 6* ☉ *Mon.–Sat., 7–6.*

At the edge of a middle-class neighborhood between Heredia and Barva is the **Museo de Cultura Popular** (Museum of Popular Culture), which preserves a farmhouse built in 1885 with an adobelike technique called *bahareque*. Run by the National University, the museum is furnished with antiques and surrounded by a small garden and coffee fields. An adjacent open-air restaurant serves inexpensive Costa Rican lunches on weekends. Just walking around the museum is fine, but calling ahead to reserve a hands-on cultural tour (such as tortilla-making) really makes it worth the trip. ⊠ *Between Heredia and Barva; from the Musmanni in Santa Lucia de Barva, 100 m north, 1 km/½ mi east (follow signs)* ☎ *260–1619* ⊕ *www.ilam.org/cr/museoculturapopular* ☒ *$1* ☉ *Mon.–Fri. 8–4; Sat. and Sun. 10–4.*

★ The producer of Costa Rica's most popular export-quality coffee, **Café Britt,** gives a lively tour that highlights Costa Rica's history of coffee cultivation through a theatrical presentation that is admittedly a bit hokey. From the get-go, your "tour guides" are professional actors, but good actors to be sure, and if you don't mind the song and dance, it's fun. Take a short walk through the coffee farm and processing plant, and learn how professional coffee tasters distinguish a fine cup of java. One major difference between this tour and that of Doka Estate in Alajuela is that Doka takes you through the processing (mill). Britt, ever the innovators, provides a similar tour add-on by request. ⊠ *From Heredia, take road to Barva; follow signs* ☎ *800/462–7488 from U.S. and Canada, 277–1500 in Costa Rica* ⊕ *www.cafebritt.com* ☒ *$20 tour only, $27 with transportation, $35 with transportation and lunch* ☉ *Tours Dec.–May, daily at 9, 11, and 3; and June–Nov., daily at 11.*

Where to Stay and Eat

$–$$ ✕ **Oky Grill & Cafe.** Barva's main draw is strong Costa Rican flavor, so you may be inclined to pass by the clean white and green lines of Oky

Coffee, the Golden Bean

WHEN COSTA RICA'S FIRST elected head of state, Juan Mora Fernández, began encouraging his compatriots to cultivate coffee back in 1830, he could hardly have imagined how profound an impact the crop would have on his country. Over the last 100 years coffee has transformed Costa Rica from a colonial backwater into a relatively affluent and cosmopolitan republic.

It was the "golden bean" that financed the construction of most of the nation's landmarks. Lured by plantation jobs, tens of thousands of immigrant families from Europe and elsewhere in the Americas moved to Costa Rica in the 1800s and early 1900s, and were given land in exchange for cutting down the forest and planting coffee. They formed the backbone of a middle-class majority that has long distinguished Costa Rica from most of the rest of Latin America.

Thanks to its altitude and mineral-rich volcanic soil, the Central Valley is ideal for growing coffee, and the crop covers nearly every arable acre of this region. But coffee is not actually native to Costa Rica: plants first arrived in Costa Rica from the Caribbean in 1791.

The coffee-growing cycle begins in April/May, when rains make the dark-green bushes explode into a flurry of white blossoms. By November the fruit starts to ripen, turning from green to red, and the busy harvest begins as farmers race to get picked "cherries" to *beneficios* (processing plants), where the beans—two per fruit—are removed, washed, dried by machine, and packed in burlap sacks for export. Costa Rica's crop is consistently among the world's best, and most of the high-grade exports wind up in Europe and the United States.

Traditionally, coffee bushes are grown in the shade of trees. Recently, however, many farmers have switched to sun-resistant varieties, cutting down shade trees to pack in more coffee bushes, and destroying habitats for migratory birds in the process. Environmentalists and many farmers are promoting a return to the old system by labeling shade coffee ECO-OK. (And shade coffee *does* actually taste better.) Though coffee prices have declined sharply since 2000, the crop still remains king in the Central Valley.

Ticos are fueled by lots of coffee, and generally make it in a *chorreador*, a wooden stand with a cloth filter—which makes a strong cup of java. Sadly, many Ticos drink the low-grade stuff, often mixed with molasses, peanuts, or corn for bulk. Most of the good stuff is exported. Reliable brands are Café Rey's Tarrazú, Café Britt, Volio, and Montaña.

Café on the way to or from the Museum of Culture. But if you're hungry, that would be a shame. The large wall canvases and dark wood tables and chairs give off a European ambience—as does the food, overseen by the café's namesake and owner, Oky María Numez. If you're not up for the German-style steak or anything in a heavy sauce, asparagus crepes and an assortment of light sandwiches are delicious alternatives. There are a generous dessert selection and an extensive list of shakes and iced

2

coffees. ⊠ *From the Automercado in Barva de Heredia, 500 m north, 200 m east* ☎ *263–6632* ▭ *AE, DC, MC, V.*

$ ✕ **L'Antica Roma.** The food here more than makes up for the less-than-tasteful red curtains, gold walls and faded images of the Coliseum. The ample menu offers close to 30 pizza varieties, all baked in a wood burning oven, and homemade fresh pasta, such as three-mushroom ravioli. Two TVs with sports are suspended indoors, so the handful of tables on the wrought-iron enclosed outdoor patio lend themselves better to conversation. ⊠ *Across from the Hotel Valladolid, downtown Heredia (C. 7 and Av. 7)* ☎ *262–9073* ▭ *AE, DC, MC, V.*

$$$–$$$$
Fodor's Choice
★

Finca Rosa Blanca Country Inn. There's nothing common about this luxurious little B&B overlooking coffee farms; you need only step through the front door of the Gaudí-esque main building to marvel at its soaring ceiling, white-stucco arches, and polished wood. Each guest room is different, but all have original art, local hardwoods, and colorful fabrics. The spacious two-story suite is out of a fairy tale, with a spiral staircase leading up to a window-lined tower bedroom. On the grounds, which are planted with tropical flowers and shaded by massive fig trees, are two two-bedroom villas. The owners work very hard to make the hotel as eco-friendly as possible, using composting, solar panels, and other methods—the hotel is one of only two in the country to receive five green leaves—the ICT's highest Certificate of Sustainable Tourism ranking. Four-course dinners are available. ⊠ *1 km/½ mi east and 800 m north of Café Britt Distribution Center in Santa Barbara de Heredia, Barrio Jesus* ☎ *269–9392* 🖷 *269–9555* ⊕ *www. fincarosablanca.com* ↩ *7 rooms, 2 villas* ♧ *Dining room, fans, in-room safes, pool, whirlpool tub, horseback riding, laundry service, Wi-Fi, cable Internet, airport shuttle, travel services; no a/c, no room TVs* ▭ *AE, MC, V* ⫮ *BP.*

$ **Hotel Valladolid.** This is hands down the best hotel in downtown Heredia. The tall (for Heredia) and narrow building with a rooftop terrace has just 11 modern rooms, designed for business travelers and visiting professors at the nearby National University. The tile floors and white walls aren't exactly inspired, but are just fine for a night's sleep. ⊠ *400 m north and 100 m west of the main entrance of La Universidad Nacional (C. 7 and Avda. 7)* ☎ *260–2905* 🖷 *260–2912* ⊕ *www. hotelvalladolid.net* ↩ *11 rooms* ♧ *In-room safes, microwave, refrigerator, cable TV, whirlpool tub, sauna, bar, laundry service, dial-up Internet* ▭ *AE, DC, MC, V* ⫮ *CP.*

¢   **Hotel Ceos.** Occupying an old wooden home a block north of the Parque Central, the Hotel Ceos has basic accommodations for travelers on a tight budget. Historic photos decorate the ground floor, and the rooms are painted pastels, but are small and time-worn. The large balcony on the second floor, furnished with a sofa and chairs is perfect for shooting the breeze with a beer. The downstairs soda serves inexpensive breakfasts and light meals. ⊠ *Avda. 1 and C. Central (100 m north and 100 m west of the Central Park)* ☎ *262–2628* 🖷 *262–2639* ⊕ *www. hamerica.net* ↩ *10 rooms* ♧ *Restaurant, fans, cable TV; no a/c* ▭ *AE, MC, V* ⫮ *EP.*

To & from Heredia

4 km/3 mi north of Santo Domingo, 11 km/6 mi (25 mins) northwest of San José.

The narrow routes to Heredia are notoriously clogged at almost all times; avoid them during rush hours if possible. Turn right at the west end of Paseo Colón. Follow Pan-American Highway 2 km/1¼ mi; take the second exit, just before the highway heads onto an overpass, and just after the Hotel Irazú (on the right). To get to the center of Heredia, follow that road for 5½ km/3½ mi, then turn left at the Universidad Nacional; continue straight on this road to reach the Britt Coffee Tour, Museo de Cultura Popular, Sacramento, Barva, and points beyond. Yellow and red buses run between San José (Ca. 12, Av. 2, La Merced church) and Heredia every 5 to 10 minutes daily (between 5 AM and 10 PM), following the above car route. The steady stream of purple and white buses leaving from C. 1, Av. 7–9 every 3–5 minutes passing through Santo Domingo are sometimes a better bet during rush hour, particularly the directo buses that start after 4 PM; these buses also run from midnight to 4 AM on the hour. If you're without a car, taxi is the recommended method for getting to Café Britt or Barva.

Heredia Essentials

🏧 Bank/ATM **Banco Popular** ✉ 200 m east of northeast corner of Parque Central ☎ 260-9407. **Banco Nacional** ✉ Southwest corner of Parque Central ☎ 277-6900. 🏧 Pharmacy **Farmacia Chavarria** ✉ Southwest corner of Parque Central ☎ 263-4670. 🏧 Mail **Correos** ✉ Northwest corner of Parque Central.

EN ROUTE ★

At the center of **Barva de Heredia,** a small community about 3 km (2 mi) north of Heredia proper, is the Parque Central, surrounded by old adobe shops with Spanish tile roofs on three sides and a white stucco church to the east. Flanked by royal palms, the stout, handsome church dates from the late 18th century; behind it is a lovely little garden shrine to the Virgin Mary. On a clear day you can see verdant Volcán Barva (⇨ Chapter 3) towering to the north, and if you follow the road that runs in front of the church and veer left at the Y, you will wind your way up the slopes of that volcano to Vara Blanca, where you can either drive north to the La Paz Waterfall Gardens, or continue straight to Poás Volcano National Park (⇨ Chapter 3). If you veer right at the Y and drive up the steep, narrow road, you'll pass through San José de la Montaña and Paso Llano to reach Sacramento, where the road turns into a rough dirt track leading to the Barva sector of Braulio Carrillo National Park (⇨ Chapter 3). If you turn left when you reach Barva's central plaza, you'll head to San Pedro and Santa Barbara, where roads head south to Alajuela and north to Vara Blanca.

CARTAGO AND IRAZÚ VOLCANO

Cartago, due east of San José, was the country's first capital, and thus has scattered historical structures and the impressive Basílica de Los Angeles. To the north of Cartago towers massive Irazú Volcano, which is covered with farmland and topped by an impressive crater.

La Negrita

ON THE NIGHT OF AUGUST 1 and well into the early morning hours of August 2, the road to Cartago from San José clogs with worshippers, some of whom have traveled from as far away as Nicaragua to celebrate the 1635 appearance of Costa Rica's patron saint, La Negrita (the Black Virgin). At a spring behind the church, people fill bottles with water believed to have curative properties. Miraculous healing powers are attributed to the saint, and devotees have placed thousands of tiny symbolic crutches, ears, eyes, and legs next to her diminutive statue. Tour buses and school groups, along with shops selling the saint's likeness, make the scene a bit of a circus. The statue has twice been stolen, most recently in 1950 by José León Sánchez, now one of Costa Rica's best-known novelists, who spent 20 years on the prison island of San Lucas for having purloined the Madonna.

Cartago

7 Although it's a small city, Cartago was the country's first capital and held that title for almost three centuries. It's much older than San José, but earthquakes have destroyed most of its colonial structures, leaving just a few interesting buildings among the concrete boxes. Cartago became Costa Rica's second most prominent city in 1823, when the seat of government was moved to the emerging economic center of San José. You'll see some attractive old buildings as you move through town, most of them erected after the 1910 quake. The majority of the architecture in tiny Cartago is bland, with one impressive exception: the gaudy Basílica de Nuestra Señora de Los Angeles.

Most visitors see Cartago on their way to or from the Orosi Valley or Turrialba, and there is little reason to stay the night. The Orosi Valley, a short drive away, has better choices.

Exploring

Churches in some form or another have stood at the site of the present-day Parque Central since 1575, and have been knocked down by earthquakes and reconstructed many times. Undeterred by complete destruction in 1841, the citizens of Cartago began work on a Romanesque cathedral some years later, but the devastating earthquake of 1910 halted work and put an end to the last attempt at building a structure on the site. **Las Ruinas** (⊠ C. 1/2 and Avda. 2), or "the ruins" of this unfinished house of worship, now stand in a pleasant park planted with tall pines and bright impatiens. During the week, the friendly caretaker, *Don* Orlando, can let you in if the gates are locked. Among the many legends attributed to the ruins is the gruesome story of the priest of one of the earlier churches at the site, who after falling in love with his sister-in-law, was murdered by his brother. His ghost, dressed as a priest but headless, still haunts the grounds.

The **Basílica de Nuestra Señora de los Angeles** (Our Lady of the Angels Basilica; ⊠ C. 16, between Avdas. 2 and 4, 7 blocks east of central Sq. ☎ 551–0465) is a hodgepodge of architectural styles from Baroque to Byzantine, with a dash of Gothic. The interior is even more striking, with a colorful tile floor, intricately decorated wood columns, and lots of stained glass. The church is open daily 6 AM to 7 PM. The basilica is also the focus of an annual pilgrimage to celebrate the appearance of La Negrita, or the Black Virgin, Costa Rica's patron saint.

Where to Eat

Haute cuisine just doesn't exist here. Instead, Cartago gives you a fine opportunity eat some *comida típica*. On just about any street downtown you'll find a *soda* (simple café), and the women in the kitchen will serve you the same style food they cook at home for their own families. There are literally dozens of places of comparable quality. One rule of thumb: the busier the better—the locals know where to eat well.

To & from Cartago

22 km/14 mi (25 mins) southeast of San José.

From San José, drive east on Avenida 2 through San Pedro and Curridabat to the highway entrance, where you have three road options—take the middle one marked Cartago. Shortly before Cartago, a Y intersection marks the beginning of the route up Irazú, with traffic to Cartago veering right. Buses between San José and Cartago leave every 10 minutes daily (C. 5, Av. 18/20) from 5 AM to midnight; buses to Paraíso leave weekdays from the same terminal every half hour. Cartago buses to San José pick up 200 m east of the central market. Buses to Orosi leave Cartago every 15–30 minutes from 5:30 AM to 10 PM, 100 m east, 25 m south of the southwest corner of Las Ruinas.

Cartago Essentials

🏦 Bank/ATM **Banco de Costa Rica** ⊠ Av. 4 and C. 5/7 ☎ 551-4690. **ATM** ⊠ Northwest corner of Las Ruinas.

🏦 Hospital **Hospital Max Peralta Jiménez** ⊠ 200 m south, 150 m east of Las Ruinas ☎ 551-1999.

🏦 Pharmacy **Farmacia Central** ⊠ Just south of Las Ruinas ☎ 551-0698.

🏦 Taxis **Taxis El Carmen** ☎ 551-0836.

Volcán Irazú

❽ Volcán Irazú is Costa Rica's highest volcano, at 11,260 feet, and its summit has long been protected as a national park. The mountain looms to the north of Cartago, and its eruptions have dumped considerable ash on the city over the centuries. The most recent eruptive period lasted from 1963 to 1965, beginning the day John F. Kennedy arrived in Costa Rica for a presidential visit. Boulders and mud rained down on the countryside, damming rivers and causing serious floods. Although farmers who cultivate Irazú's slopes live in fear of the next eruption, they're also grateful for the soil's richness, a result of the volcanic deposits.

The road to the summit climbs past vegetable fields, pastures, and native oak forests. You pass through the villages of Potrero Cerrado and

Continued on page 103

DRIVING THE OROSI VALLEY LOOP

Gardens, Churches, and Landscapes. This classic day trip—popular with locals but still off the beaten tourist path—is not something you find in most guide books. But if you've got a day to spend near San José, we highly recommend this route past coffee plantations, small towns, and verdant landscapes, with countless breathtaking views. The region is unique because it is one of the few areas in Costa Rica that still has remnants (ruins and churches) of 17th-century Spanish colonialism. But the highlight of the tour is spending at least a couple of hours in Tapantí National Park tracking the resplendent quetzal or marveling at the many orchid species.

■ TIP➔➔Traffic jams are rarely a problem, but expect company on weekends from fellow motorists—and mountain bikes. (Costa Rica's Olympic cycling team trains here.)

The Drive

Start from Cartago, 22 km (14 mi) southeast of San José. At the basílica in the center of town turn left onto the busy road to Paraíso and Orosi. After 6 km (4 mi), a blue sign on the right marks the short road to the lush gardens of the **Jardín Botánico Lankester** (☎ 552–3247 💌 $5 ⊙ Daily 8:30–4:30), one of the world's foremost orchid collections, with more than 1,100 native and introduced species of orchids. Bromeliads, heliconias, and aroids also abound, along with 80 species of trees, including rare palms. The best time to come is January through April, when the most orchids are in bloom. The garden's gift shop is one of the few places in Costa Rica to buy orchids that you can take home legally. (They come

in small bottles and don't flower for four years, so you'll need some serious patience.) Admission is $5; the garden is open daily 8:30–4:30.

Head east toward Paraíso and then into the town itself. Hang a right at the central park. Some 2 km (1 mi) beyond is the **Sanchiri Mirador,** one of the valley's best *miradores* (lookout points). But our favorite vantage point is at a point on the road just beyond Sanchiri where the earth appears to drop away, and the valley comes into view as you make the steep descent to the town of Orosi. Here's a case for letting someone else do the driving.

Many a visitor has wondered, upon first seeing dreary Paraíso, with its concrete-block buildings and crowded

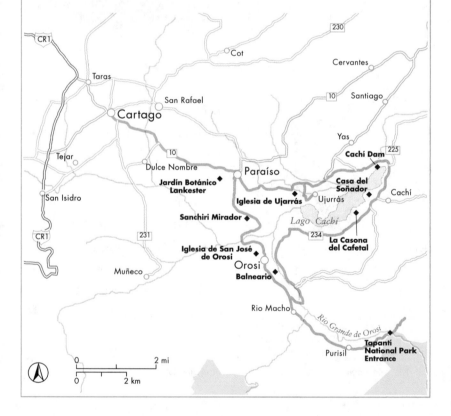

Orosi church

roads, how it ended up with so prodigious a name as "Paradise." But you need merely drive a couple of kilometers south from the central park and gaze down at the vast Orosi Valley to understand what inspired the town's founders. For travelers, Paraíso is on the map for only two reasons: it is the gateway to Orosi, and it has one of the country's best botanical gardens.

The town of Orosi, in the heart of the valley, has but one major attraction: the beautifully restored 1743 **Iglesia de San José de Orosi** (⌂ Across from soccer field, center of town ☏ 533–3051). It's the country's oldest church still in use, and one of the only structures still remaining from the colonial era. It has a low-slung whitewashed facade; the roof is made of cane overlaid with terracotta barrel tiles. Inside are an antique wooden altar and ancient paintings of the stations of the cross and the Virgin of Guadalupe, all brought to Costa Rica from Mexico. If you can find someone to open it for you, also take a look inside the religious-art museum next door. Admission to the museum is 50¢ and hours vary. The church is open Tuesday–Sunday 9–noon and 1–5.

It's not a must-do stop, but if you're craving relaxation, the **Balneario** (Thermal Baths; ⌂ South of Orosi on road to Orosi Lodge), fed by a hot spring, are open to the public for a nominal fee (less than $1) Wednesday through Monday, 7:30–4.

South from Orosi, the road becomes a rugged track following the Río Grande de Orosi past coffee plantations, elegant *fincas* (farmhouses), and seasonal barracks for coffee pickers before it's hemmed in by the steep slopes of thick jungle. At the bottom of the loop road, deviate (follow signs) to enter **Tapantí**

Resplendent quetzal

National Park (⊠ 14 km/8 mi south of Orosi ☎ 200–0090). Though it's worth the trip for just an hour or two of exploring, you could easily fill a day in the park. Stretching from the southern corner of the Orosi Valley up into the Talamanca Mountains, Parque Nacional Tapantí encompasses 47 square km (18 square mi) of largely pristine, remote cloud forest. It provides refuge for more than 400 bird species, including the emerald toucanet, violaceous trogon, and most of the country's hummingbirds.

The rangers' office and visitor center are on the right just after the park entrance. You can leave your vehicle at a parking area 1½ km (1 mi) up the road. From here loop trails head off into the woods on both sides. One trail passes a picnic area and several swimming holes with (cold) emerald waters. The other trail is along a forested hillside. About 1½ km (1 mi) up from the parking area is an entrance to the La Pava Trail on the right, leading down a steep hill to the riverbank. If you continue

¼ mi past the trailhead you arrive at a 300-foot stair trail leading to a lookout. Since the park clouds up in the afternoon, it's best to get an early start. Admission to the park is $7; it's open daily 8–4.

Amid coffee farms on the eastern end of the Orosi Valley, the village of Cachí survives on two industries: coffee and electricity. In the 1960s the national power company, ICE, dammed the Reventazón River near Cachí to create a reservoir for what was once the country's biggest hydroelectric project. The Represa de Cachí (Cachí Dam) is the closest thing the town has to a tourist attraction, and is worth stopping at for the view of the reservoir and narrow Reventazón Valley, but most people stop here to eat at the Casona del Cafetal, just south of the dam, and to shop for crafts at the Casa del Soñador.

Head back to the loop road and drive 15 km (9 mi) north, past the town of Cachí. Just before the Cachí Dam lies the immensely popular restaurant **La Casona del Cafetal** (⇨ Where to Eat *in* Cachí). It is touristy, but great fun, and well worth a stop for a late lunch. You'll have lots of company on a Sunday, the traditional maid's day off in Tico homes. Stop in at the unique artisan shop **Casa del Soñador** (House of the Dreamer; ⊠ 2 km/1¼ mi south of the Cachí Dam ☎ 577–1186 or 577–1983), established by local wood sculptor Macedonio Quesada. Though Macedonio died years ago, his sons Miguel and Hermes and a former apprentice are still here, carving interesting, often comical little statues out of coffee roots. You can learn about the carving process through a day-long apprenticeship, free of charge. The shop is open daily 8–6.

Continue past the dam into the small hamlet of Ujarrás, then follow the signs

2

to the site of the ruins of Costa Rica's first church, **Iglesia de Ujarrás** (✉ In a small park, 1 km/½ mi from Restaurante Típico Ujarrás, Ujarrás ☎ 574–7376). Built between 1681 and 1693 in honor of the Virgin of Ujarrás, the church, together with the surrounding village, was abandoned in 1833 after a series of earthquakes and floods wreaked havoc here, at the lowest point of the Orosi Valley. An unlikely Spanish victory in 1666 over a superior force of invading British pirates was attributed to a prayer stop here. The site is open daily 2–6. A final 6-km (3½-mi) drive to Paraíso from Ujarrás completes the loop.

Logistics

Renting a car in San José is the best way to go. Public transportation is a partial option only; buses run clockwise from Paraíso to Cachí or counterclockwise to Orosi, but neither route completes the loop. Several San José tour operators offer this excursion as a guided day trip from the capital. One such company

Coffee Fields

is **Lava Tours** (☎ 278–2558, 888/862–2424 in the U.S. ☐ 413/410–2583 in U.S. ⊕ www.lava-tours.com), whose loop tour around Cachí Lake is $85.

WHERE TO STAY AND EAT

PARAÍSO

$–$$ ✕ ⊡ **Sanchirí Mirador.** The greatest asset of this rustic place is its amazing view, from a hillside high above the valley. The large open-air restaurant ($–$$), partially enclosed by windows, has simple wooden chairs, flowery tablecloths, and a menu dominated by Costa Rican standards such as *arroz con pollo* (rice with chicken). Twelve modern rooms were built in early 2005 to go with 10 older wooden cabins. All of the new rooms have the view, but only 3 of the cabins do. The rooms themselves are nothing spectacular, but waking up to the view is well worth the modest price. ✉ 2 km/1 mi south of Parque Central ☎ 574–5454 ☐ 574–8586 ⊕ www.sanchiri.com ↩ 20 rooms ☐ Restaurant, bar, playground, laundry services, cable, Internet; no a/c in some rooms ☐ AE, DC, MC, V ⏐◯⏐ BP.

CACHÍ

★ **$–$$** ✕ **La Casona del Cafetal.** The valley's best lunch stop is on a coffee plantation overlooking the Cachí Reservoir. It's firmly on the beaten path, which means frequent visits from tour groups. The spacious brick building has a high barrel-tile roof, with tables indoors and on a tiled portico on the lake side. Casados and other Costa Rican staples accompany inventive dishes such as *arroz* *tucurrique* (baked rice with cheese and heart of palm) and corvina *guarumos* (stuffed with mushrooms). After lunch, take a stroll down to the lake. The **gift shop** sells similar sculptures to those fashioned at Casa del Soñador. But unless you'll be at the restaurant anyway, go directly to the latter shop for crafts—it's far superior. ⊠ *2 km/1 mi south of Cachí Dam* ☎ *577–1414* ⊟ *AE, DC, MC, V* ☾ *No dinner.*

¢–$ ✕ **Soda El Chilito Mexicano.** A great alternative to the touristy La Casona is this little café with some vaguely Mexican choices on the menu, but prepared Tico-style. This is where the locals eat, and it's good. ⊠ *Northwest side of the soccer field* ☎ *577–1664.*

OROSI

¢–$ ✕ **Bar y Restaurante Coto.** This place has good food and a location right on the plaza. Options range from sandwiches to seafood dishes, and tenderloin in a "secret" *Orosi* sauce. Works by local artists are for sale. ⊠ *North side of Plaza de Deportes (soccer field)* ☎ *533–3032* ⊟ *AE, DC, MC, V.*

¢–$ ✕ **Gecko's.** This textbook backpacker hangout is the latest venture of Dutch and Canadian partners Toine and Sara Verkuijlen, who also run a Spanish school and hostel in Orosi. The café is bright and open, with groovy music and free-spirited clothes for sale. The creative menu ranges from traditional Costa Rican food to Kroket (deep-fried meat roll on a bun) and shish kebab. Helpful staff run a tourist-information desk inside. ⊠ *400 yds south of church* ☎ *533–3640* ⊟ *No credit cards.*

$$–$$$$ ⊡ **Hotel Rio Perlas Spa & Resort.** Thermal springs fill one of the pools at this hotel squeezed into a small valley. The place has a condo community feeling, with a driveway running the length of the property and the rooms divided among many smaller buildings. Rooms are nice, but not especially luxurious; they have dark tile floors and wood furniture. There is a replica of the Orosi church on the property. ⊠ *6 km/3½ mi south of Paraíso, turn right at bridge, then 2 ½ km/1½ mi; look for large sign* ☎ *533–3341 or 533–2543* ⊟ *533–3085* ⊕ *www.hotelrioperlas.com.*

$ ⊡ **Orosi Lodge.** Run by a German couple who have built a warm rapport with the community, the little lodge blends in with Orosi's pretty, old-town architecture: whitewashed walls are trimmed in blue, ceilings are high, and natural wood is used throughout. Some furnishings, such as the clay lamps in the rooms, are done by local artisans. Common areas are colorful, with paintings and sculpture by local artists. Double beds have two twin-size comforters. Second-floor rooms have views of the Orosi Valley and Irazú Volcano. The hip coffee shop brews a great cup of joe, and Latin music usually plays from a 1960s' jukebox in the foyer. ⊠ *350 yds south, 100 yds west of the soccer field* ☎ *533–3578* ⊕ *www.orosilodge.com.*

NEAR TAPANTÍ NATIONAL PARK

$ ⊡ **Kiri Mountain Lodge.** This small, family-run hotel has easy access to the park and its own 70-hectare private reserve with waterfalls and most of the same wildlife seen at Tapantí. The number of bird species in the lodge's gardens alone is impressive, especially hummingbirds. Rooms are small and simple, with tile floors and tiny bathrooms, but their porches have views of a jungle-laden hillside. The restaurant serves a small selection of Costa Rican food; fresh trout, raised in nearby ponds, is the best option. You can also catch your own trout and have them cook it for you. ⊠ *Turnoff 2 km/1¼ mi before Tapantí park entrance* ☎ *533–2272* ⊕ *www.kirilodge.com.*

San Juan de Chicuá before reaching the summit's bleak but beautiful **crater.** Irazú is considered active, but the gases and steam that billow from fumaroles on the northwestern slope are rarely visible from the peak above the crater lookouts.
■ TIP➜ Set out as early in the morning as possible—before the summit is enveloped in clouds—and wear warm, waterproof clothing. When conditions are clear, you can see the chartreuse crater lake and, if you're lucky, views of nearby mountains and either the Pacific or Caribbean in the distance. There are no trails at the summit, but a paved road leads all the way to the top, where a small coffee shop sells hot beverages.

Where to Eat

¢–$ ╳ **Restaurant 1910.** Decorated with vintage photos of turn-of-the-20th-century buildings and landscapes, this restaurant documents the disastrous 1910 earthquake that rocked this area and all but destroyed the colonial capital of Cartago. The menu is predominantly Costa Rican, with such traditional specialties as *pozol* (corn and pork soup) and arroz con pollo. One of the less common dishes is corvina fillet with béarnaise sauce. ⊠ *Road to Parque Nacional Volcán Irazú; 300 m north of Cot–Pacayas turnoff* ☎ 536–6063 ▤ AE, MC, V.

¢–$ ╳ **Restaurante Noche Buena.** If you've raced up Irazú to catch the clear early-morning views, a late breakfast or early lunch at this bright roadside stop is a great excuse to linger in the area. Sample typical gallo pinto, homemade desserts such as tres leches, and—not to be missed—the best fried yuca around. The pale wood floors and walls have a studied rustic charm, but the ample, bougainvillea-draped patio is a fresher option; neither have particularly impressive views. The Costa Rican owner has added a 3-km (2-mi) trail to waterfalls, and construction is under way for a museum dedicated to the volcano. ⊠ *At Km 21, road to Parque Nacional Volcán Irazú* ☎ 530–8013 ▤ AE, DC, MC, V.

To & from Volcán Irazú

31 km/19 mi (45 mins) northeast of Cartago, 50 km/31 mi (1½ hrs) east of San José.

Follow directions to Cartago (➪ *above*), but shortly before the city a Y intersection marks the beginning of the road up Irazú; traffic to Cartago veers right, then left immediately past the first lights. From downtown Cartago, take the road to Irazú at the northeast corner of the Basilica. Signs from Cartago lead you to the park. Buses head to Volcán Irazú from San José (C. 1/3, Av. 2) weekends at 8 AM and return at 12:30 PM.

Paraíso Essentials

🔋 Pharmacies **Farmacia Guadalajara** ⊠ 200 m west of central park ☎ 574-7286.
🔋 Post Office **Correos** ⊠ 100 m north of central park.
🔋 Taxis **Servitransporte Paraíso** ☎ 574-7228.

Orosi Essentials

🅿 Pharmacies **Farmacia Tabor** ✉ Southeast corner of soccer field.

🚕 Taxis **Luis Arce** ☎ 379-3993. **Hector Mata** ☎ 388-1608.

THE TURRIALBA REGION

The agricultural center of Turrialba and the nearby Guayabo ruins lie considerably lower than the Central Valley, so they enjoy a more tropical climate. There are two ways to reach this area from San José, both of which pass spectacular scenery. The more direct route, accessible by heading east through both Cartago and Paraíso, winds through coffee and sugar plantations before descending abruptly into Turrialba. For the second route, turn off the road between Cartago and the summit of Irazú near the town of Cot. That narrow route twists along the slopes of Irazú and Turrialba volcanoes past some stunning scenery—stately pollarded trees lining the road, riotous patches of tropical flowers, and metal-girder bridges across crashing streams. From Santa Cruz, a hiking trail leads up to the 10,900-foot summit of Volcán Turrialba. As you begin the descent to Turrialba town, the temperature rises and sugarcane alternates with fields of neat rows of coffee bushes.

Turrialba

9 The relatively well-to-do agricultural center of Turrialba (population 30,000) suffered when the main San José–Puerto Limón route was diverted through Guápiles in the late 1970s. The demise of the famous Jungle Train that connected these two cities was an additional blow. But today, because of the beautiful scenery and a handful of upscale nature lodges, ecotourism is increasingly the focus of the town's efforts. The damming of the Reventazón River has cut down on the number of tourists, but significant numbers of kayakers and rafters flock here to run the Pacuare. Turrialba has two major factories: Conair, which you'll see on the road to Siquirres, and a Rawlings factory, which makes all the baseballs used in the Major Leagues. Though pleasant enough and with a youthful vibe from the nearby university and the white-water folk, Turrialba doesn't have much to offer, but the surrounding countryside hides some spectacular scenery and patches of rain forest. Finally, there's Volcán Turrialba, which you can ascend on foot or horseback, and it's well worth the effort.

> **CORRUPTION CRACKDOWN**
>
> Long a proponent of do-as-I-say, not-as-I-do anticorruption policies, Costa Rica got tough on bigwigs in 2004. Three former presidents were taken into custody for allegedly accepting bribes in a telecommunications deal. One—Miguel Ángel Rodríguez—was forced to step down two weeks after taking over the presidency of the Organization of American States (OAS). The sight of former leaders being led away in handcuffs has shaken many Costa Ricans' faith in their democracy, but others see it as a positive sign that no one is above the law.

White-Water Thrills

YOU'RE STRUGGLING TO HANG on and paddle, you can't hear a thing over the roar, and you were just slammed with a mighty wall of water. Sound like fun? Then you're in the right place. The **Río Pacuare** and the **Río Reventazón** draw rafters and kayakers from all over the world to Turrialba. Right next to Turrialba, the Reventazón has Class II, III, and IV rapids. The Pacuare, farther from Turrialba, has a spectacular 22-km (14-mi) run with a series of Class III and IV rapids. The scenery includes lush canyons where waterfalls plummet into the river and expanses of rain forest.

Nearly every outfitter has day trips, but some also have multiday trips that include jungle hikes. Nature Adventures and Ríos Tropicales (⇨ *Central Valley Planner* at the beginning of this chapter) even have their own lodges on the river. Age requirements for children vary by outfitter. The typical trip starts with a van ride to the put-in; including a breakfast stop, it usually takes about 2½ hours from hotel to river. After the first half of the run, guides flip one of the rafts over to form a crude lunch table. Then you continue up the river to Siquirres, and pile back in the van for the ride home.

It would be unwise to choose your company based merely on price: those with bargain rates are probably skimping somewhere. Good outfitters require you to wear life vests and helmets, have CPR-certified river guides with near-fluent English skills, and have kayakers accompany the rafts in case of emergencies. A 5:1 guest-to-guide ration is good, 10:1 is not. Local Turrialba companies have better prices and allow you to book a trip at the last minute. Hotels and travel agencies book trips with larger outfitters, who can pick you up from nearly anywhere in the Central Valley. Prices range from about $70 to $100.

Falling out of the raft happens all the time, and is no big deal. The worst-case scenario is getting caught underwater or under the raft, but surprisingly, most fatalities are heart-attack victims, so don't participate if you're high-risk. You should also be able to swim. Almost every long-standing company has had a death—it is simply the reality of the business. Don't hesitate to ask about safety records. The vast majority of trips, however, are pure exhilarating fun.

While temporarily stalled, plans are still in the works to dam the Pacuare. This would be the last nail in the coffin for the rafting industry (the Reventazón was dammed in the 1960s) and would destroy one of nature's real gems. Locals will surely put up a fight, but run it now while you can.

Exploring

Although you can't easily drive up to its summit as you can at Poás and Irazú, **Volcán Turrialba** is still worth visiting. The easiest way to arrange the excursion is to call the **Volcán Turrialba Lodge** (☏ 273–4335) and request a guide. You can ascend the 6 km (4 mi) from the lodge on foot or horseback in 1 to 2 hours (allow 5 hours for the round trip, including exploring), and at 3,329 m (10,920 feet) with luck you'll see clear down to the Caribbean coast. On the road that runs from Pacayas to Turrialba through Santa Cruz there is a signed turnoff at La Pastora, west of Santa Cruz, that leads up the mountain. The drive up is 15 km (9 mi) and starts paved, but the road gets worse the higher you go.

> **WORD OF MOUTH**
>
> There really isn't much in Turrialba. Probably why I want to live there.   –Suzie2

In most cases you'll need a 4WD to make the last section before the trailhead, which is in a very small community called La Central de Turrialba. The road veers left toward the Volcán Turrialba Lodge, while a very washed out road leads right toward the summit. If you want to take the latter route, you can park on the left just after the school; usually someone is around to charge you a few dollars for the privilege, but like elsewhere in the country, it in no way guarantees your car's safety. We recommend parking at Volcán Turrialba Lodge—they don't charge, will point you on the way, and you can rest up with some snacks and hot chocolate at the restaurant when you're done. Get an early start and dress for the weather—it can get chilly up there even during the day. A park employee hangs out at the top to collect the $1 entrance fee and hand out maps. For general National Park information, dial 192 in Costa Rica. A 4WD vehicle can make it up the "road" to the summit in the dry season.

OFF THE BEATEN PATH

A good place for bird-watching, the **CENTRO AGRONÓMICO TROPICAL DE INVESTIGACIÓN Y ENSEÑANZA** (Center for Tropical Agricultural Research and Education), better known by its acronym, CATIE, is one of the leading tropical research centers in Latin America. You might catch sight of the yellow-winged northern jacana or the purple gallinule in the lagoon near the main building. The 8-square-km (3-square-mi) property includes landscaped grounds, seed-conservation chambers, greenhouses, orchards, experimental agricultural projects, a large swath of rain forest, labs and offices, and lodging for students and teachers. Behind the administration building lies the lake that once was rapids on the Reventazón River. The CATIE staff are working to improve visitor access; 2-hour guided tours (call ahead to reserve) of the impressive Botanical Garden have been added, and forest trails are planned for the future. ⊠ *3 km/2 mi outside Turrialba, on the road to Siquirres* ☎ *558–2000 or 556–6431* ⊕ *www.catie.ac.cr* ⊠ *$5, $15 with guide, $10 for groups of more than 5* ☉ *Weekdays 7–4.*

On the slopes of Turrialba Volcano is **Guayabo National Monument,** Costa Rica's most significant archaeological site. It's interesting, but definitely no Chichén Itzá. Records mentioning the ruins go back to the mid-1800s, but systematic investigations didn't begin until 1968, when a local landowner out walking her dogs discovered what she thought was a tomb. A friend, archaeologist Carlos Piedra, began excavating the site and unearthed the base wall of a chief's house in what eventually turned out to be the ruins of a large community (around 10,000 inhabitants) covering 49 acres, 10 of which have been excavated. The city was abandoned in AD 1400, probably because of disease or war. A guided tour in Spanish takes you through the rain forest to a *mirador* (lookout) from which you can see the layout of the excavated circular buildings. Only the raised foundations survive, since the conical houses themselves were built of wood. As you descend into the ruins, notice the well-engineered surface and covered aqueducts leading to a trough of drinking water that still functions today. Next you'll pass the end of an 8-km (5-mi) paved walkway used to transport the massive

KEEPING COOL

Central Valley's climate is often a great surprise to first-time visitors—it's not at all the steamy tropics you've imagined. It's usually cool enough at night to go without air-conditioning, so don't be surprised if many hotels don't have it.

building stones; the abstract patterns carved on the stones continue to baffle archaeologists, but some clearly depict jaguars, which were revered by Indians as deities. The hillside jungle is captivating, and the trip is further enhanced by bird-watching possibilities: 180 species have been recorded. If you arrive from the east via the Santa Teresita (Lajas) route, you can make it in any car; but via the alternative Santa Cruz route you'll need a four-wheel-drive vehicle to get here. ⊠ *Drive through the center of Turrialba to a girded bridge; take road northeast 16 km/10 mi (20 mins); take a left at the well-marked turn-off, continue another 3 km/2 mi on rough road to the monument. If you've taken the scenic Irazú foothills route to Turrialba and have a 4X4, the Santa Cruz route—11 km/7 mi (35 mins)—is an option. Turn left on rough road from Santa Cruz; climb 5 km, past the Escuela de Guayabo; turn right at the sign for the monument; the road descends 6 km/4 mi to the site* ☎ 559–1220, 192 in Costa Rica ☜ $4 ☉ Daily 8–3:30.

Outdoor Activities

Foot and horseback are the best ways to reach the summit of Turrialba Volcano. **Volcán Turrialba Lodge** (☎☎ 273–4335) arranges guided horseback and hiking trips.

Where to Stay & Eat

¢–$ ✕ **La Garza Bar y Restaurante.** Similar to La Feria in scope but slightly more atmospheric and with a bar, La Garza also runs the gamut from hamburgers to chicken, but has a better seafood selection. (Sorry vegetarians, "beetsteak" is a misprint.) ⊠ *Northwest corner of the park* ☎ 556–1073 ☴ AE, DC, MC, V.

¢–$ ✕ **Restaurante La Feria.** This family-style restaurant has the usual midscale Costa Rican fare, ranging from fast food to "filet mignon." Casados and gallo pinto compete with more familiar chicken and seafood dishes. Even spaghetti is on the menu. A permanent exhibition of national art and a useful Turrialba-info corner make this a worthwhile stop. ⊠ *Just west of Hotel Wagelia, at the entrance to town* ☎ 556–0386 ☴ AE, DC, MC, V ☉ Tues. lunch only.

$$$$ ▦ **Rancho Naturalista.** Customized guided bird-watching and horseback tours within a 150-acre private nature reserve are the reasons to stay here. The ranch is a birder's paradise and the narrow focus may be too much for nonbird-watchers not interested in riding horses. More than 400 species of birds and thousands of different kinds of moths and butterflies live

on the reserve and nearby sites, and a resident ornithologist helps you see and learn as much as you want. The two-story lodge is upscale modern with rustic touches, as are the separate cabins. Good home cooking is served in the indoor and outdoor dining rooms, both of which have beautiful views of Volcán Irazú and Turrialba Valley. Guided tours, meals, and your birding guide are all included in the price. ⊠ *20 km/12 mi southeast of Turrialba, 1½ km/1 mi along a semipaved road from Tuís* ☎ *433–8278 for reservations, 554–8100 for directions* 🖷 *433–4925* ⊕ *www.ranchonaturalista.net* ➪ *15 rooms, 12 with bath* ⌂ *Dining room, horseback riding, dial-up Internet, airport pickup; no a/c, no room phones, no room TVs, no smoking* ▭ *No credit cards* ¶⦶ *FAP.*

★ **$$$** 🖸 **Casa Turire.** Set near sugar plantations and overlooking an artificial lake, this timeless hotel looks like a manor house that has survived mysteriously intact from the turn of the 20th century. In fact, it's the product of more recent imaginations. From the royal palms that line the driveway to the tall columns and tile floors, Casa Turire is an exercise in elegance and attention to detail. High-ceiling guest rooms have hardwood floors and furniture, small balconies, and bright bathrooms with tubs. The central courtyard is a civilized spot in which to relax after a day's adventure, and the restaurant serves reasonably priced international cuisine. The master suite is exceptional, built on two floors with a huge wraparound balcony. ⊠ *8 km/5 mi south on Carretera a la Suiza from Turrialba, Apdo. 303–7150* ☎ *531–1111* 🖷 *531–1075* ⊕ *www. hotelcasaturire.com* ➪ *12 rooms, 4 suites* ⌂ *Restaurant, room service, fans, in-room safes, satellite TV, pool, whirlpool tub, massage, bike rental, canoeing, bar, shop, laundry service, Internet, meeting rooms, transport services; no a/c in some rooms* ▭ *AE, MC, V* ¶⦶ *BP.*

$ 🖸 **Turrialtico.** Dramatically positioned on a hill overlooking the valley east of Turrialba, this hotel has impressive views of the surrounding countryside. An open-sided restaurant occupies the ground floor, above which are handsome rooms with hardwood floors. Ask for one on the west side—these have dazzling views of Turrialba and, if there are no clouds, Volcán Irazú. The restaurant serves a small selection of authentic Costa Rican dishes. The only problem is that the rustic wooden construction makes the rooms anything but soundproof. ⊠ *8 km/5 mi east of Turrialba on road to Siquirres* ☎ *538–1111 or 538–1415* 🖷 *538–1575* ⊕ *www.turrialtico.com* ➪ *18 rooms* ⌂ *Restaurant, bar, fans, shop, laundry service, horseback riding; no a/c, no room phones, no room TVs* ▭ *AE, MC, V* ¶⦶ *BP.*

$ 🖸 **Volcán Turrialba Lodge.** On the slope of the volcano, usually accessible only by 4WD (which the lodge will arrange for a fee), the lodge has simple but comfortable rooms, most with a wood-burning stove. You'll eat well, too: the proprietors serve healthful Costa Rican food. Even more compelling are the tours, one of which goes deep into the Turrialba crater. Mountain-biking and horseback-riding trips can be arranged, as well as a 10-hour trek from the Volcán Turrialba to Guápiles via Braulio Carrillo National Park. This place is not for everyone—it gets chilly up here over 10,000 feet, but it's a unique mountain escape and a great value. ▪ TIP➔ **Day-trippers are welcome.** ⊠ *20 km/12 mi east of Cot, turn right at Pacayas on the road to Volcán Turrialba, 4 km/2½ mi on dirt rd.* ☎☎ *273–4335* 🖷 *273–0703* ⊕ *www.volcanturrialbalodge.com* ➪ *27 rooms* ⌂ *Dining room,*

bar, handicapped accessible rooms; no a/c, no room phones, no room TVs
🖭 *AE, DC, MC, V* 🍽 *FAP.*

To & from Turrialba

58 km/36 mi (1½ hrs) east of San José.

The road through Cartago continues east through Paraíso, where you turn left at the northeast corner of the central park to pick up the road to Turrialba. Marked by signs, this road leads north to Guayabo National Monument. Buses between San José and Turrialba leave hourly (5:15 AM to 7 PM) from C. 13, Av. 6, just northeast of the downtown court buildings. Buses depart the Turrialba terminal (200 m west of central park) every half hour to Cartago, every hour to San José, and every two hours to Limón.

Turrialba Essentials

🔋 Bank/ATM **Banco Nacional** ⊠ C. 1 at Avda. Central 🕿 556-1211. **Banco de Costa Rica** ⊠ C. 3 at Avda. Central 🕿 556-2619.

🔋 Hospital **Hospital Dr. William Allen** ⊠ Avda. 2, 100 m west of C. 4 🕿 556-4343.

🔋 Pharmacy **Farmacia San Buen Aventura** ⊠ 50 m south of west side of central park 🕿 556-0379.

🔋 Internet **Internet Dimensión** ⊠ East side of central park 🕿 556-1586.

🔋 Post Office **Correos** ⊠ Avda. 8 at C. Central (50 m north of central park).

🔋 Taxi **Transgalo** 🕿 556-9393.

CENTRAL VALLEY ESSENTIALS

Transportation

BY AIR

There is no regional air travel within the Central Valley.

ARRIVING & DEPARTING The Juan Santamaría International Airport (10 km/6 mi) is just outside Alajuela. You can get taxis from the airport to any point in the Central Valley for $8 to $50. Immediately outside the terminal, you'll see a booth where you can hire a taxi. Some hotels arrange pickup. For more information, *see* Air Travel *in* Smart Travel Tips A to Z.

BY BUS

ARRIVING & DEPARTING Buses leave the international airport for Alajuela several times an hour; from Alajuela you can catch buses to Grecia, Sarchí, and San Ramón. Less frequent buses (one to three per hour) serve Heredia. For travel between the airports and Escazú, Cartago, or Turrialba, you have to change buses in San José, which usually necessitates a taxi ride between bus terminals. All buses heading toward San José from Alajuela can drop you off at the airport, but you need to ask the driver when you board, and then remind him again as you draw near to the stop, *"Aeropuerto, por favor"* ("Airport, please"). For more detailed information, *see* Bus Travel *in* Smart Travel Tips A to Z.

GETTING AROUND Many visitors never consider taking a local bus to get around, but doing so puts you in close contact with locals—an experience you miss out on if you travel by taxi or tour bus. It's also cheap. If your Spanish and sense of direction are up to snuff and you have the time, give it a shot. Your hotel can help you get to the correct bus stop and get you a current schedule. Always opt for the taxi at night or when you're in a hurry.

BY CAR

ARRIVING & DEPARTING Nearly all points in the western Central Valley can be reached by car. For San Antonio de Belén, Heredia, Alajuela, and points north of San José, turn right at the west end of Paseo Colón onto the Pan-American Highway (Carretera General Cañas). All the attractions in the eastern Central Valley are accessible from San José by driving east on Avenida 2 through San Pedro, then following signs from the intersection to Cartago. To get to the Orosi Valley, head straight through Cartago, turn right at the Basílica de Los Angeles, and follow the signs to Paraíso. The road through Cartago and Paraíso continues east to Turrialba.

GETTING AROUND The best way to get around the Central Valley is by car. Most of the car-rental agencies in San José (⇨ Chapter 1) have offices at the airport in Alajuela. They will deliver vehicles and contracts to any of the hotels listed in this chapter, except those in Turrialba and the Orosi Valley.

BY SHUTTLE VAN

A more comfortable (air-conditioned!) and quicker alternative to regular bus service are the hotel-to-hotel shuttle services offered by Interbus and Gray Line. Both have a long list of destinations around the country. For more information, *see* Shuttle Van Services *under* Bus Travel, *in* Smart Travel Tips A to Z.

BY TAXI

All Central Valley towns have taxis, which usually wait for fares along the central parks. Taxis in Alajuela, Cartago, and Heredia can take you up to Poás, Irazú, and Barva volcanoes, but the trips are quite expensive (about $50). If you don't have a car, the only way to get to Tapantí National Park is to take a cab from Orosi (about $10 each way).

The Northern Plains

Guanacaste cowboy

WORD OF MOUTH

"I loved Tabacón and would go back to Arenal just for the hot springs. It's like a garden of Eden, very lush and green."

—vancouvergirl

"Just got back from Monteverde and I can easily say it was one of the highlights of our trip. The scenery is astounding and wildlife is amazing . . . The only negative [aspect] is the drive there, which is as unimaginably horrendous as it is beautiful."

—Skoob

WELCOME TO THE NORTHERN PLAINS

TOP 5
Reasons to Go

1. **Walk in a cloud (forest):** Explore Monteverde's misty world on SkyWalk, a series of treetop walkways up to 138 feet off the ground.

2. **Windsurfing:** Lake Arenal is one of the top windsurfing spots on earth; winds can reach 50-60 mph December through April.

3. **Arenal Volcano:** You can hear the rumblings of the world's third most active volcano for miles around, and, on clear nights, watch crimson lava ooze down its flanks.

4. **Watching wildlife:** Water birds, monkeys, turtles, crocodiles, jaguars, and sloths abound in the 25,000-acre Caño Negro National Wildlife Refuge.

5. **Walk down to the waterfall:** The reward for a tough hike down to Catarata Fortuna is a magnificent series of waterfalls.

0 _____ 10 mi
0 _____ 10 km

San Jose
Upala
Colonia Puntareno
6
4
San Rafael
Tronadora
Tilarán
Cañas
Monteverde Cloud Forest
GUANACASTE
Gotera
CR1

Home to the rainiest of cloud forests, the Monteverde Cloud Forest Area is also the canopy-tour capital of Costa Rica. Hanging bridges, treetop tram tours, and zip-lines: it's got it all. As if that's not enough, there are horseback riding, rappelling, and nature hikes.

Sky Walk, Monteverde

Getting Oriented

Geographically, the Zona Norte (Northern Zone), as it is known locally, separates neatly into two alluvial plains. The rich, lush terrain runs from the base of the Cordillera Central in the south to the Río San Juan, on the border with Nicaragua in the north. Most visitors begin their visit to Costa Rica in San José, and then head north to La Fortuna, using it as a base to explore the volcano, waterfall, and Caño Negro, and to participate in activities like sportfishing, windsurfing and kitesurfing at Lake Arenal, and rafting on the Sarapiquí River.

Egret, Caño Negro

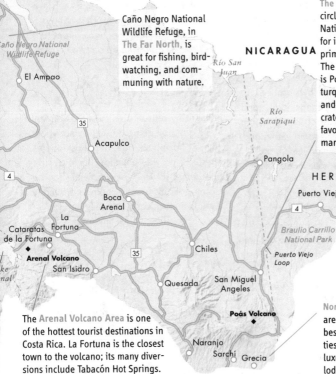

Caño Negro National Wildlife Refuge, in The Far North, is great for fishing, bird-watching, and communing with nature.

The Puerto Viejo Loop circles Braulio Carrillo National Park, rare for its easy-to-access primary rain forest. The loop's highlight is Poás Volcano; its turquoise crater lake and steaming main crater make it the favorite volcano of many a visitor.

The Arenal Volcano Area is one of the hottest tourist destinations in Costa Rica. La Fortuna is the closest town to the volcano; its many diversions include Tabacón Hot Springs. Tilarán, west of Lake Arenal, is the place to be if you're a windsurfer.

Northwest of San José are one of the country's best crafts communities, Sarchí, and some luxurious countryside lodges.

Arenal Volcano

Hiking down to La Fortuna Waterfalls

NORTHERN PLAINS PLANNER

When to Go

Late November to April is considered high season. The rainy season is July–December, but the region is always hot and humid, with frequent rain. Expect highs of 32°C (90°F) and lows of 15°C (60°F). Nights are usually cool and comfortable. At almost 5,000 feet, Monteverde has a significantly different climate: It's cool and damp most of the time, with average highs around 20°C (70°F) and lows around 13°C (55°F). Visibility changes daily (and hourly), so your chances of seeing the craters are more or less the same year-round, though you may have more luck from February to April, the hottest and driest time of the year.

Getting There

The cheapest and slowest way to get here is via public bus. The fastest and priciest is flying to La Fortuna (via NatureAir), driving yourself, or hiring a driver. A mid-range option is taking a private shuttle-bus service. Many San José–based tour companies arrange transportation and tours in the area. But La Fortuna, Arenal, and Monteverde are also full of tour companies that will arrange same-day or next-day transportation and tours for you.

Rain Forests Are . . . Rainy

There's a reason they call it the rain forest! During the rainy season it's not unusual for it to rain for several days straight. But don't curse the wet weather—it's what keeps the forests green and gorgeous. Just bring a poncho or rain jacket and waterproof footwear so you don't end up cursing yourself.

The Early Bird Catches the Sun

In the rainy season it's almost a given that you'll get a bit damp on your canopy tour, hike, or horseback ride, and most tour operators provide ponchos. But to avoid a thorough soaking, plan activities for the morning. Rains usually begin at around 2 PM, like clockwork, from July through December. The clearest time of day is before 8 AM.

What to Do

ACTIVITY	WHERE TO DO IT
Bungee Jumping	Colorado River (Grecia)
Canopy Tours	La Fortuna, Monteverde
Fishing	Lake Arenal
Hiking	Lake Arenal, Tilarán, La Fortuna
Horseback Riding	La Fortuna, Monteverde
Rafting	La Fortuna, Puerto Viejo de Sarapiquí
Rappelling	La Fortuna
Wildlife-viewing	La Fortuna, Caño Negro, Monteverde
Windsurfing	Lake Arenal

How Much Time?

If your visit is limited to two or three days, make La Fortuna your base. Don't miss the volcano, the Tabacón Hot Springs, or Caño Negro Wildlife Reserve. Most tour operators who have volcano hikes end the day at the hot springs. "Half-day" tours to Caño Negro actually take most of a day, from around 7:30 AM to 4 PM. A week in the Northern Plains is more than enough time to experience a great deal of this area—especially if you're longing to get out and get moving. Give yourself four days in La Fortuna/Arenal for rafting trips on the Sarapiquí, horseback rides, and kitesurfing or windsurfing on Lake Arenal. Devote the rest of your week to Monteverde Cloud Forest.

Choosing a Place to Stay

The La Fortuna/Arenal area has luxury resorts, mid-priced hotels, budget places, and campsites. While no longer as cheap as it was, hotel rates are low compared to American prices. If you plan to raft, hike, and go to the hot springs, a simple and comfortable cabina ($20–$40) in or around La Fortuna allows easy access to tours, restaurants, and buses—a good choice if you don't have a car. For privacy, quiet, luxury, and a volcano view, try the resorts west of Fortuna ($75–$185), closer to the volcano.

Pack Right

It's hot and wet here much of the year, so don't think fashion, think comfort and utility. Must-haves include walking shoes (sneakers are fine unless you're planning on serious hiking), water sandals, and clothing made of quick-drying materials. Don't forget a good hat to shield your face from the sun and rain, and sunglasses. A light rain jacket or poncho, and mini umbrella are worth the space as well.

Recommended Tour Operators

■ **Nature Adventures** (⊕ www.adventurecostarica.com) has five-day biking tours that combine Monteverde and Lake Arenal with the Central Valley.

■ **Costa Rica Expeditions** (⊕ www.costarica

expeditions.com) customize almost limitless vacations.

■ **Costa Rica Study Tours** (☎ 645-7090 ⊕ www.crstudytours.com) can fix you up with all manner of excursions around Monteverde.

■ If you don't have much time, **Ecoscape Nature Tours** (☎ 297-0664 ⊕ www.escapetours.com) has the best daylong Sarapiquí loop tour. It also has nighttime jungle tours in the Selva Verde reserve.

■ A one-week tour with **Travel Wizard Costa Rica** (☎ 415/662-2683 in the U.S. or Canada ⊕ www.travelwizard.com) includes Arenal and Monteverde.

Prices

■ TIP→→ The Web site www.monteverdeinfo.com has a wealth of information about the area.

WHAT IT COSTS in Dollars					
	$$$$	**$$$**	**$$**	**$**	**¢**
Restaurants	over $25	$15–$25	$10–$15	$5–$10	under $5
Hotels	over $250	$150–$250	$75–$150	$50–$75	under $50

Restaurant prices are per-person for a main course at dinner. Hotel prices are for two people in a standard double room in high season, excluding service and tax (16.4%).

NORTHWEST OF SAN JOSÉ

By Jeffrey
Van Fleet

The rolling countryside northwest of San José and west of Alajuela holds a mix of coffee, sugarcane, and pasture, with tropical forest filling steep river valleys and ravines. The Pan-American Highway makes a steady descent to the Pacific coast through this region, which is also traversed by older roads that wind their way between simple agricultural towns and past small farms and pastoral scenery. West of San Ramón the valley becomes narrow and precipitous as the topography slopes down to the Pacific lowlands. An even narrower valley snakes northward from San Ramón to Ciudad Quesada and the northern lowlands beyond.

Grecia

❶ Founded in 1838, the quiet farming community of Grecia is reputed to be Costa Rica's cleanest town—some enthusiastic civic boosters extend that superlative to all Latin America—but the reason most people stop here is to admire its unusual church.

Exploring

The brick-red, prefabricated iron **Iglesia de las Mercedes** (Church of Mercy) was one of two buildings in the country made from steel frames imported from Belgium in the 1890s (the other is the metal schoolhouse next to San José's Parque Morazán), when some prominent Costa Ricans decided that metal structures would better withstand the periodic earthquakes that had taken their toll on so much of the country's architecture. The frames were shipped from Antwerp to Limón, then transported by train to Alajuela—from which point the church was carried by oxcarts. ✉ *Avda. 1, between Cs. 1 and 3* ☎ *494–1616* ◷ *Daily 8–4.*

☾ On a small farm outside Grecia, the **Mundo de las Serpientes** (World of Snakes) is a good place to see some of the snakes that you are unlikely—and probably don't want—to spot in the wild. Sequestered in the safety of cages here are some 50 varieties of serpents, as well as crocodiles, iguanas, poison dart frogs, and various other cold-blooded creatures. Admission includes a 90-minute tour. ✉ *Poro, 2 km/1 mi east of Grecia, on road to Alajuela* ☎ *494–3700* ⊕ *www.snakes-costarica.com* ▦ *$11, children under 7, free* ◷ *Daily 8–4.*

Outdoor Activities

BUNGEE JUMPING   A 265-foot-tall bridge that spans a forested gorge over the Río Colorado is the perfect place to get a rush of adrenaline in a tranquil, tropical setting. Even if you aren't up for the plunge, it's worth stopping to watch a few mad souls do it. **Tropical Bungee** (✉ Pan-American Hwy., 2 km/1 mi west of turnoff for Grecia, down a dirt road on the right ☎ 248–2212, 398–8134 ⊕ www.bungee.co.cr) organizes trips to the bridge. The first jump is $60 and the second is $30. Transportation is free if you jump; $10 if you don't. Reservations are essential. If it's your last hurrah in Costa Rica, a van can take you straight to the San José airport after your jump.

Where to Stay

$$–$$$ 🖼 **Vista del Valle Plantation Inn.** Hon-
Fodor'sChoice eymooners frequent this B&B on an
★ orange and coffee plantation out-
side Grecia overlooking the canyon
of the Río Grande. Cottages are decorated in minimalist style with simple wooden furniture and sliding
doors that open onto small porches.
Each has its own personality; the
Nido, removed from the rest and
with the nicest decor, is the most romantic. The hotel's forest reserve
has an hour-long trail leading down
to a waterfall. Breakfast is served
by the pool or in the main house,
where you can relax in a spacious liv-
ing room. The food is quite good, and special dietary requests are accom-
modated with advance notice. It's a mere 20-minute drive from the airport.
⌧ *On highway, 1 km/½ mi west of Rafael Iglesia Bridge; follow signs* 🖅 *c/o
M. Bresnan, SJO–1994, Box 025216, Miami, FL 33102-5216* ☎ *450–0800*
🖷 *451–1165* 🌐 *www.vistadelvalle.com* 🛏 *2 rooms, 10 cottages* 🍴 *Restaurant, fans, pool, massage, whirlpool tub, horseback riding, tours; no a/c,
no room phones, no room TVs* 🖃 *AE, MC, V* 🍽 *BP.*

PAINTED OXCARTS
Coffee has come to symbolize the prosperity of the Central Valley and the nation; as such, this all-important cash crop has inspired a fair bit of folklore. Costa Rican artists have long venerated coffee work-ers, and the oxcart, once used to transport coffee to the coast, has become a national symbol. You can buy elaborately decorated carts in many different sizes at crafts shops throughout the Central Valley.

To & from Grecia
*26 km/16 mi (45 mins) northwest of Alajuela, 46 km/29 mi (1 hr)
northwest of San José.*

From San José continue west on the highway past the airport—the
turnoff is on the right—or head into Alajuela and turn left just before
the Alajuela cemetery. Buses traveling between San José and Ciudad Quesada make stops in Grecia. From Alajuela, buses to Grecia/Ciudad Quesada pick up on the southern edge of town (C. 4 at Avda. 10).

Grecia Essentials
🏧 Bank/ATM **Banco Nacional** ⌧ Northwest corner of Central Plaza ☎ 494–1727.

Sarchí

❷ Tranquil Sarchí is spread over a collection of hills surrounded by coffee plantations. Though many of its inhabitants are farmers, Sarchí is
also Costa Rica's premier center for crafts and carpentry. People drive
here from all over central Costa Rica to shop for furniture, and cara-
vans of tour buses regularly descend upon the souvenir shops outside
town. Local artisans work native hardwoods into bowls, boxes, toys,
platters, and even jewelry, but the area's most famous products are its
brightly painted oxcarts—replicas of those traditionally used to transport coffee and other agricultural products. Trucks and tractors have
largely replaced oxcarts on Costa Rican farms, but the little wagons retain their treasured place in Tico folklore and can be spotted everywhere
from small-town parades to trinket shops.

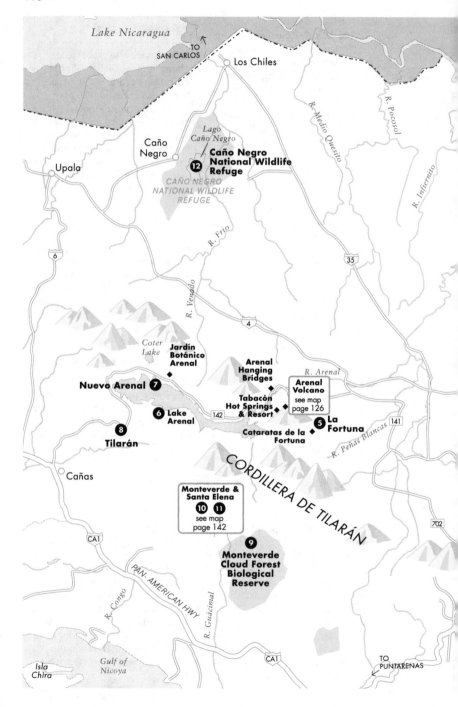

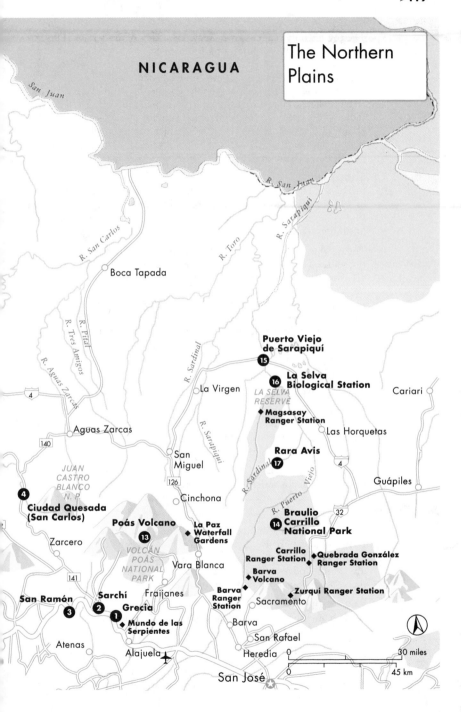

The Northern Plains

NICARAGUA

San Juan

R. San Juan

Boca Tapada

R. San Carlos

R. Toro

R. Sardinal

R. Sarapiquí

R. Pital

R. Tres Amigos

R. Aguas Zarcas

15 Puerto Viejo de Sarapiquí

16 La Selva Biological Station

Cariari

La Virgen

LA SELVA RESERVE

◆ Magsasay Ranger Station

Las Horquetas

Aguas Zarcas

San Miguel

R. Sarapiquí

17 Rara Avis

R. Sardinal

R. Puerto Viejo

4

Guápiles

JUAN CASTRO BLANCO N. P.

4 Ciudad Quesada (San Carlos)

Zarcero

141

126

Cinchona

R. Puerto Viejo

14 Braulio Carrillo National Park

32

13 Poás Volcano

◆ La Paz Waterfall Gardens

VOLCÁN POÁS NATIONAL PARK

Vara Blanca

Carrillo Ranger Station

◆ Quebrada González Ranger Station

Barva ◆ Volcano

Zurquí Ranger Station

San Ramón

3

Sarchí

2 **1**

Grecia

Fraijanes

◆ Barva Ranger Station

Sacramento

◆ Mundo de las Serpientes

Barva

Atenas

Alajuela ✈

San Rafael

Heredia

San José

0   30 miles
0   45 km

Exploring

The town's only real oxcart factory, **Taller Eloy Alfaro e Hijos** (Eloy Alfaro and Sons Workshop), was founded in 1923, and its carpentry methods have changed little since then. The two-story wooden building housing the wood shop is surrounded by trees and flowers—mostly orchids—and all the machinery on the ground floor is powered by a waterwheel at the back of the shop. Carts are painted in the back, and although the factory's main product is a genuine oxcart—which sells for about $2,000—there are also some smaller mementos that can easily be shipped home. ⊠ *200 m north of soccer field* ☎ *No phone* 🖃 *By donation* ☉ *Weekdays 8–4.*

Shopping

Sarchí is the best place in Costa Rica to buy miniature oxcarts, the larger of which are designed to serve as patio bars and can be broken down for easy transport or shipped to your home. Another popular item is a locally produced rocking chair with a leather seat and back.

Fodor's Choice
★

There's one store just north of town, and several larger complexes to the south. The nicest is the **Fábrica de Carretas Chaverri** (Chaverri Oxcart Factory) (⊠ Main road, 2 km/1 mi south of Sarchí ☎ 454–4411), and you can wander through the workshops in back to see the artisans in action. (Despite the name, much more is for sale here than oxcarts.) Chaverri is a good place to buy wooden crafts; nonwood products are cheaper in San José. Chaverri also runs a restaurant next door, **Las Carretas** (☎ 454–1633), which serves international meals all day until 6 PM and has a good lunch buffet.

To & from Sarchí

8 km/5 mi west of Grecia, 53 km/33 mi (1½ hrs) northwest of San José.

To get to Sarchí from San José, take the highway well past the airport to the turnoff for Naranjo; then veer right just as you enter Naranjo. Direct buses to Sarchí depart from Alajuela (C. 8, between Avdas. 1 and 3) every 30 minutes 6 AM–9 PM; the ride takes 90 minutes.

Sarchí Essentials

🏧 Bank/ATM **Banco Nacional** ⊠ Plaza Artesanía ☎ 454–4052.

San Ramón

❸ Having produced a number of minor bards, San Ramón is known locally as the City of Poets. San Ramón hides its real attractions in the countryside to the north, on the road to La Fortuna, where comfortable nature lodges offer access to private nature preserves. There's not much to see in San Ramón other than its church.

Exploring

Aside from the poets, the massive **Iglesia de San Ramón,** built in a mixture of the Romanesque and Gothic styles, is the city's claim to fame. In 1924 an earthquake destroyed the smaller adobe church that once stood here, and the city lost no time in creating a replacement—this great gray concrete structure took a quarter of a century to complete, from 1925 to 1954. To ensure that the second church would be earthquake-

Certificate of Sustainable Tourism

ONE TRIP TO COSTA RICA AND you'll swear everything here is eco-lodges, eco-tourism, eco-this, eco-that. But "sustainability," the buzzword in Costa Rican tourism these days, also has to do with conserving cultural, as well as natural, resources. The Certification for Sustainable Tourism (CST) program, administered jointly by the Costa Rican Tourism Institute, National Chamber of Tourism, Ministry of the Environment, and University of Costa Rica, recognizes businesses that adhere to those ideals. Those that submit to a rigorous assessment are evaluated on their employment of local people, respect for local culture, contribution to the economic and social well-being of the community, and preservation of natural resources. Businesses that rely heavily on foreign investment and whose earnings are mostly repatriated outside Costa Rica don't make the cut (but probably don't submit to an evaluation in the first place).

Instead of stars, 55 hotels have earned one to five leaves for their efforts. At this writing, Finca Rosa Blanca, north of Heredia in the Central Valley, and Lapa Ríos, at Cabo Matapalo on the South Pacific, are the only two lodgings to hold five leaves. The resort and hotels that are recognized are not all small "mom-and-pop" places: Manuel Antonio's Sí Como No and Arenal's Tabacón have been recognized as well. Nor are they only places in the middle of the rain forest: San José's large but unobtrusive Clarion Hotel Amón is among several city lodgings proudly displaying awards.

While other countries have their own rating systems for eco-friendly lodgings, many of these suffer from corrupt policies that allow ratings to be bought. The CST is one of the best and most thorough awards programs in the world. In fact, the World Tourism Organization has adopted it as its model, and countries from Mexico to Malawi now employ similar standards. You'll find a list of Costa Rican CST holders at the program's bilingual Web site, www.turismo-sostenible.co.cr.

proof, workers poured the concrete around a steel frame that was designed and forged in Germany (by Krupp). Step past the formidable facade and you'll discover a bright, elegant interior. ⊠ *Across from Parque Central* ☎ *445–5592* ☉ *Daily 6–11:30 AM and 1:30–7 PM.*

Where to Stay & Eat

$–$$ ✕ **La Colina.** This roadside diner, with its requisite plastic chairs, has an eclectic menu with some typical and some not-so-typical entrées. Start your meal with a delicious ceviche, moving on to the famous rice and chicken or, for the more adventurous, *lengua en salsa* (tongue in tomato sauce). Meals begin with complimentary chips and pickled vegetables. ⊠ *Highway to Puntarenas, 2 km/1 mi west of San Ramón* ☎ *445–4956* ▤ *AE, DC, MC, V* ☉ *Breakfast served.*

★ **$$$** ▦ **Villablanca.** This charming hotel is on a working dairy and coffee farm constructed and once owned by former Costa Rican president Rodrigo Carazo. The farmhouse contains the reception desk, bar, and restaurant;

down the hill are lovely casitas, each a replica of a traditional adobe farmhouse complete with whitewashed walls, tile floors, cane ceilings, and fireplaces. Resident guides lead nature walks through the adjacent cloud-forest reserve, which is excellent bird-watching territory. Horses are available for exploring the rest of the farm. ⊠ *20 km/12 mi north of San Ramón on road to La Fortuna* ⌖ *Apdo. 247–1250, Escazú* ☎ *461–0300* 🖷 *461–0302* ⊕ *www.villablanca-costarica.com* 🛏 *43 casitas* ⟁ *Restaurant, horseback riding, bar, theater, gift shop; no a/c, no room phones, no room TVs* ▭ *AE, DC, MC, V* ❘◉❘ *BP.*

To & from San Ramón

23 km/14 mi west of Sarchí, 59 km/37 mi (1½ hrs) northwest of San José.

San Ramón is on the Pan-American Highway west of Grecia. To reach the hotels to the north of town, head straight through San Ramón and follow the signs. Buses traveling to Ciudad Quesada from San José stop in San Ramón. From Alajuela, buses to San Ramón/Ciudad Quesada pick up on the southern edge of town (C. 4 at Avda. 10).

San Ramón Essentials

🏧 Bank/ATM **Banex** ⊠ 150 m north of Palí supermarket ☎ 445–3602.

EN ROUTE The small town of **Zarcero**, 15 km (9 mi) north of San Ramón on the road to Ciudad Quesada, looks like it was designed by Dr. Seuss. Evangelisto Blanco, a local landscape artist, modeled cypress topiaries in fanciful animal shapes—motorcycle-riding monkeys, a lightbulb-eyed elephant—that enliven the park in front of the town church. The church interior is covered with elaborate pastel stencilwork and detailed religious paintings by the late Misael Solís, a well-known local artist.

THE ARENAL VOLCANO AREA

Whether you come here from San José or Liberia, prepare yourself for some spectacular scenery—and a bumpy ride. As you bounce along on your way to Arenal, you may discover that "paved" means different things in different places, and that potholes are numerous. Any discomfort you experience is more than made up for by the swathes of misty rain forest and dramatic expanses of the Cordillera Central. Schedule at least 3½ hours for the trip.

Ciudad Quesada (San Carlos)

❹ Highway signs point you to CIUDAD QUESADA, but it's simply "San Carlos" in local parlance. Like so many other places in Costa Rica, the landscape is splendid, but what passes for architecture varies from ordinary to downright hideous. San Carlos is where everyone in the region comes to shop, take in a movie, get medical care, and generally take care of the necessities. There's also an enormous bus terminal where you can make connections to almost anywhere in the northern half of the country. If you're traveling from San José to points north, your bus will stop here (even if it's a so-called "express"). This lively mountain market town–provincial capital serves a fertile dairy region and is worth a stop for a soak in the soothing thermal waters in the area.

Exploring

Termales del Bosque lets you soak those tired muscles, as you watch the birds, for a more reasonable price than most of the hot springs in the region. ✉ *Hwy. 140, 7 km/4½ mi east of Ciudad Quesada* ☎ *460–1356* ⊕ *www.termalesdelbosque.com* ✑ *Day pass $6, children under 6, $1* ☺ *Open daily 8 AM–10 PM.*

Where to Stay

★ $ 🏨 **Laguna del Lagarto Lodge.** One of Costa Rica's smaller eco-lodges is a hideaway in a 1,250-acre rain forest near the Nicaraguan border. Most of the rustic cabin rooms come with single beds. Some 380 bird species and counting have been logged here. Buffet-style meals are served on a patio with river and forest views. Rates include one guided walk on the 10 km (6 mi) of forest trails, a tour of the butterfly garden, and use of canoes. Recommended extras include horseback riding and a boat trip up to the border on the San Carlos River. Ask about transfers available (at extra cost) from various points, including San José. ✉ *7 km/4 mi north of Boca Tapada* ☎ *289–8163* 🖶 *289–5295* ⊕ *www.lagarto-lodge-costa-rica.com* ↶ *20 rooms, 18 with bath* ⚗ *Dining room, horseback riding, bar, laundry service; no a/c, no room phones, no room TVs* 🖃 *MC, V.*

To & from Ciudad Quesada

45 km/28 mi (45 mins) northwest of Zarcero.

Ciudad Quesada is on the Pan-American Highway north of Zarcero. Buses from San José leave Terminal Atlantico Norte on the hour, from 5 AM to 7 PM. The trip takes around 2½ hours. The Ciudad Quesada bus terminal is a couple of kilometers from the center of town; taxis wait at the terminal to take you downtown or to your hotel.

Ciudad Quesada Essentials

🏦 Bank/ATM **Banco Nacional** ✉ Across from cathedral ☎ 401-2000.
🏥 Hospital **Hospital de San Carlos** ✉ 2 km/1 mi north of park ☎ 460-1176.

Arenal Volcano National Park	See Page 126

La Fortuna

❺ At the foot of massive Volcán Arenal, the small community of La Fortuna attracts visitors from around the world. Nobody comes to La Fortuna—an ever-expanding mass of hotels, tour operators, souvenir shops, and *sodas*—to see the town itself. Instead, thousands of tourists flock here each year to use it as a hub to visit the natural wonders that surround it. La Fortuna is also the best place to arrange trips to the Caño Negro National Wildlife Refuge (⇨ *below*).

After the 1968 eruption of Arenal Volcano, La Fortuna was transformed from a tiny, dusty farm town to one of Costa Rica's tourism powerhouses, where tourists converge to see the volcano in action. Volcano

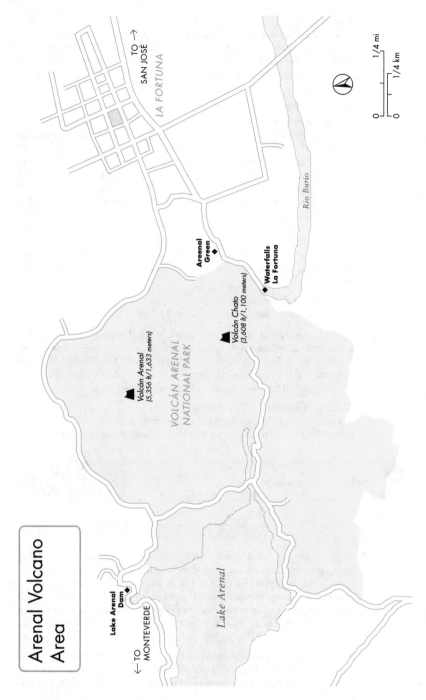

Arenal Volcano
Area

TO SAN JOSÉ →

LA FORTUNA

Río Burío

Arenal
Green ◆

Waterfalls
La Fortuna ◆

Volcán Chato
(3,608 ft/1,100 meters)

Volcán Arenal
(5,356 ft/1,633 meters)

VOLCÁN ARENAL
NATIONAL PARK

Lake Arenal
Dam ◆

← TO
MONTEVERDE

Lake Arenal

0   1/4 mi
0   1/4 km

viewing can be hit or miss, though, especially during the rainy season (May–November). One minute Arenal looms menacingly over the village; the next minute clouds shroud its cone. Early morning is always the best time to catch a longer gaze.

NAVIGATING LA FORTUNA Taxis in and around La Fortuna are relatively cheap, and public buses run throughout the day. Get a cab at the stand on the south side of Parque Central.

WORD OF MOUTH

"It would be a shame to miss seeing Arenal, but there are no guarantees [you'll] see it even if you go. [J]ust hearing that boom periodically is a treat though, and if it is heard while sitting in hot springs, all the better."

–Suzie2

3

Exploring

> Baldi Termae hot springs
> Tabacón Hot Springs
> See Page 127

The town's squat, pale, concrete **Church of San Juan Bosco,** unremarkable on its own, wins Costa Rica's most-photographed-house-of-worship award. The view of the church from across the central park, with the volcano in the background makes a great photo. ⊠ *West side of Parque Central* ☎ *No phone.*

NEED A BREAK? The semi-open-air **Café Rainforest** (⊠ 30 m south of Parque Central ☎ 365–6370) is one of the best of the American-style cafés and coffeehouses that have sprung up in La Fortuna, and is one of the few places in the country you can get a cup of decaf. Ice cream is also served.

> Arenal Hanging Bridges
> See Page 141

♻ **Ecocentro Danaus,** a small ecotourism project outside of town, exhibits 300 species of tropical plants, abundant animal life—including sloths and caimans—and butterfly and orchid gardens. It's also a great place to see Costa Rica's famed red poison dart frogs up close. (⊠ $5 ⊘ Daily 8–4. A guided evening tour ($12) should be reserved in advance. ⊠ 4 km/2½ mi east of La Fortuna ☎ 393–8437).

♻ Getting to the **Cataratas de la Fortuna** (La Fortuna Waterfall) requires a **Fodor'sChoice** strenuous walk down ¼ mi of precipitous steps, but is worth the effort. ★ Allow 25 to 50 minutes to reach the falls. Swimming in the pool under the waterfall is usually safe. Wear sturdy shoes or water sandals with traction, and bring snacks and water. You can get to the trailhead from La Fortuna by walking or taking an inexpensive taxi ride. Arranging a tour with an agency in La Fortuna is the easiest option. ⊠ *Yellow entrance sign off the main road toward the volcano, 7 km/4 mi south of La Fortuna* ⊠ *$6 ⊘ Daily 8–4.*

Continued on page 128

ARENAL VOLCANO

Costa Rica's most active volcano dominates the landscape here. Night is the best time to see it in action: on a clear evening you can see rocks spewing skyward and molten lava rolling down its sides.

Volcán Arenal, at 1,624 meters (5,328 feet), dominates the landscape here.

Volcanologists estimate Arenal's age at around 4,000 years. It lay dormant for at least 400 years until 1968. It may be local folklore, but Ticos that homesteaded this area in the 1930s and '40s referred to Arenal as "the mountain" and apparently, despite its conical shape, did not realize it was a volcano. On July 29, 1968, an earthquake shook the area, and 12 hours later Arenal blew. The village of Arenal, to the west, bore the brunt of the shock waves, poisonous gases, and falling rocks. Some 100 people were killed in three days. Since then, Arenal has been in a constant state of activity—eruptions, accompanied by thunderous rumbling sounds, are sometimes as frequent as one per hour. An enormous eruption in 1998 put the fear back into the local community, though there were no casualties, and led to the closure of

NOW YOU SEE IT, NOW YOU DON'T

The volcano is often hidden in cloud cover, so you may have to stay more than one day to get in a good viewing session. Your chances are best during the dry season (February–April), and dawn hours are the best for seeing the cone. The lava flow is most visible between midnight and pre-dawn, one reason to book a hotel on the lava side of the volcano. Tip: Wait until around 2 PM or so to see if the weather is clear, then book your afternoon volcano hike.

Route 42 and the evacuation of several nearby hotels. This earthshaking event reminded everyone what it really means to coexist with the world's third most active volcano.

The volcano is within 30,000-acre Arenal Volcano National Park, one of Costa Rica's largest parks and most popular destinations. Also in the park are Lake Arenal, the country's most important source of hydroelectric power, and Cerro Chato, an extinct volcano. Cerro Chato's collapsed crater, now an aquamarine lake, can be reached if you're up to a vigorous and steep four-hour hike. ⊠ *Turnoff to ranger station 3½ km/2 mi east of Lake Arenal, and 2 ½ km/1 ½ mi west of Tabacón* ☎ *695–5180* 💵 *$7* ☉ *Daily 8 AM–4 PM and at night with authorized guides and groups.*

Volcano Hikes

Desafío and Jacamar get you close to the action, but still a safe distance away. Afternoon tours end with an optional stop at a hot springs (for an extra fee). Transportation is included.

Desafío Adventures. ⊠ *Behind the church, La Fortuna* ☎ *479-9464* ⊕ *www. desafiocostarica.com* 💵 *$20* ☉ *Tours at 3:30 PM.*

Jacamar Naturalist Tours ⊠ *Across from Parque Central, La Fortuna* ☎*479-9767 www.arenaltours.com* 💵 *$30* ☉ *Tours at 8 AM and 3 PM.*

⚠ Never hike beyond the warning signs, even if the volcano appears to be calm. Toxic hot gases are released by even small eruptions (which are frequent), and they move faster than you can.

HOT SPRINGS

Tabacón Hot Springs & Resort

Where else can you lounge in a natural hot-springs waterfall with a volcano spitting fireballs overhead? Tabacón Resort's Tabacón Hot Springs is a busy day spa and hotel with gardens, waterfalls, hot mineral-water soaking streams, swimming pools, swim-up bars, and restaurants, all in a florid Latin interpretation of grand European baths. The best deal is the $45 zip-line canopy tour, which includes access to the waters. Make spa-treatment appointments at least one day in advance. A shuttle can bring you from central La Fortuna. ⊠ *Highway toward Nuevo Arenal, 13 km/8 mi northwest of La Fortuna* ☎ *460-2020 or 256-1500* ⊕ *www.tabacon.com* 💵 *Day pass $29, package with lunch and dinner $45, 45-min massage $55* ☉ *Daily noon-10.*

A little more economical and less crowded, Baldi Termae has 10 hot-springs-fed pools that vary in temperature and share views of Volcán Arenal. It has a swim-up bar, too. ⊠ *4 km/2½ mi west of La Fortuna* ☎ *479-9651* 💵 *$25* ☉ *Daily 10-10.*

ROOMS WITH A VIEW

Some or all rooms at the following La Fortuna–area hotels have views of the volcano.

- Tabacón Hot Springs & Resort
- Arenal Observatory Lodge
- Arenal Country Inn
- Hotel Las Cabañitas Resort
- Montaña de Fuego
- Hotel San Bosco

OFF THE BEATEN PATH

In 1945 a farmer in the mountain hamlet of Venado fell in a hole, and thus were discovered the **VENADO CAVERNS** (Cavernas de Venado). The limestone caves contain eight chambers extending about 1½ mi. Sunset Tours (Outdoor Activities, *below*) runs trips. If you're nonclaustrophobic, willing to get wet, and don't mind bats, this could be the ticket for you. (✉ 45 mins north of La Fortuna and 20 mins southeast of San Rafael ☎ 479–9415 💴 $35 ☉ Daily 7–8).

> **CAUTION**
>
> The ubiquitous OFFICIAL TOURIST INFORMATION signs around La Fortuna and Monteverde aren't "official" at all, but are merely storefront travel agencies and tour operators hoping to sell you tours.

Outdoor Activities

Fodor's Choice ★ **Desafío Adventures** (✉ Behind the church ☎ 479–9464 ⊕ www.desafiocostarica.com) can take you rafting, horseback riding, hiking, and rappelling. **Sunset Tours** (☎ 479–9800 ✉ Across from south side of church ⊕ www.sunsettourcr.com) pioneered excursions to the Caño Negro Wildlife Refuge and Venado Caverns and is one of the country's best tour operators. **Jacamar Naturalist Tours** (✉ Across from Parque Central ☎ 479–9767 ⊕ www.arenaltours.com) launches a variety of tours.

| Canopy Tours | See Page 138 |

FISHING   Lake Arenal is enormous and stocked with game fish, including tilapia, *guapote* (Central American rainbow bass), and *machaca* (Central American shad). Most tour operators and hotels can set you up with guides. Rates begin at $150. **Jacamar Naturalist Tours** (⇨ *above*) has morning and afternoon sportfishing trips to Lake Arenal.

HORSEBACK RIDING ★   If you're interested in getting up to Monteverde from the Arenal–La Fortuna area without taking the grinding four-hour drive, there's an alternative: **Desafío Adventures** (✉ Behind church ☎ 479–9464 ⊕ www.desafiocostarica.com) has a 4½-hour guided horseback trip ($65). The trip involves taxi or van service from La Fortuna to the southern shore of Lake Arenal, and from that trail's end to Monteverde, circumventing poorly maintained trails. A boat ride across Laguna de Arenal is included. You leave La Fortuna at 7:30 AM and arrive in Monteverde around 2:30 PM. You can also take the trip in reverse (⇨ Monteverde, *below*). ⚠ Many other agencies lead horseback tours between La Fortuna and

> **CAUTION**
>
> What's the newest craze in Monteverde and Arenal? Four-wheel all-terrain vehicles. Numerous businesses rent them these days, but we've heard too many reports of rollover accidents, and don't recommend them.

View of Arenal Volcano on a clear day.

(above) Manuel Antonio National Park coastline. *(opposite page, top)* Tica dancer performs at a cultural festival in San José. *(opposite page, bottom)* White-faced capuchins are the most commonly seen monkeys in Costa Rica.

(top) Digging into Class-IV rapids on the Pacuáre River. *(bottom)* Sky Walk's hanging-bridge hike in Monteverde Cloud Forest. *(opposite page)* A scarlet macaw and blue-and-gold macaw get chummy.

(top) Sun-seekers at Espadilla Beach, in Manuel Antonio National Park. *(bottom)* Black river turtles hang out in Tortuguero, Costa Rica's slowpoke central.

(top) Coffee beans must be hand-picked, because they don't all ripen at the same time. *(bottom)* Painted oxcarts are one of Costa Rica's signature crafts.

(top) The clear-blue crater lake at Poás Volcano. (bottom left) All that glitters is gold at San José's Pre-Columbian Gold Museum. (bottom right) The heliconia is found in abundance throughout Costa Rica.

Monteverde, but along treacherous trails, and some riders have returned with stories of terrified horses barely able to navigate the way. Stick with Desafío.

The ride from La Fortuna to the Fortuna Waterfall is appropriate for both novice and experienced riders. **Chaves Horse Tours** (☎ 354–9159 or 479–9023) has guided horse tours to the waterfall.

RAFTING AND KAYAKING   Several La Fortuna operators offer Class III and IV white-water trips on the Río Toro. The narrow river requires the use of special, streamlined boats that seat just four and go very fast. The easier Balsa, Peñas Blancas, Arenal, and San Carlos rivers have Class II and III rapids and are close enough to town that they can be worked into half-day excursions. **Canoa Aventura** (☎ 479–8200 ⊕ www.canoa-aventura.com) can design a canoeing trip with ample wildlife viewing on the Río Peñas Blancas and also has daylong canoe tours of the Caño Blanco Wildlife Refuge. Tours are appropriate for beginners, and instruction is provided, ★ but the folks here can tailor excursions if you're more experienced. **Desafío Adventures.** (⊠ Behind church ☎ 479–9464 ⊕ www.desafiocostarica.com) pioneered rafting trips in this region, and has day trips on the Río Toro for experienced rafters ($80), half-day rafting and kayaking outings on the nearby Arenal and Balsa rivers ($55) ideal for beginners, as well as a leisurely wildlife-viewing float on the Peñas Blancas ($45). **Ríos Tropicales** (⊠ 1 km/½ mi west of La Fortuna ☎ 479–0075 ⊕ www.flowtrips.com) does the standard trips on the Toro, Peñas Blancas, and Arenal rivers.

RAPPELLING   Rappel down five waterfalls ranging in height from 60 to 150 feet with **Pure Trek Canyoning** (☎ 461–2110, 866/569–5723 in North America ⊕ www.puretrek.com). Two guides lead small groups—10 is the maximum size—on a four-hour tour ($85) that departs at 7 AM or noon to a private farm near La Fortuna, with plenty of wildlife-watching opportunities along the way. The excursion includes transportation, all gear, breakfast (for the morning tour), and a light lunch.

Where to Eat

$-$$$ ✕ **Don Rufino.** The town's most elegant-looking restaurant is really quite informal. The L-shaped bar fronting the main street has become a popular expat and tourist hangout and lends a relaxed air to the place. No need to dress up here: this is La Fortuna, after all. The friendly waitstaff might suggest tilapia in bacon and tomato sauce or spinach ricotta to the accompaniment of coconut rice. ⊠ *Across from gas station* ☎ 479–9997 ⊗ *Breakfast served.*

$ ✕ **Rancho la Cascada.** You can't miss its tall, palm-thatch roof in the center of town. The festive up-

AS TICO AS GALLO PINTO

This is how the saying goes, but how Costa Rican is the country's signature rice-and-black bean dish? Nicaraguans also claim it as their own, and the rivalry has led to three Guinness Book of World Records bids for the largest batch. Costa Rica captured the first title in 2003, only to have Nicaragua top it a mere 12 days later. After more than a year of grumbling, in 2005 Costa Rica snatched the title back with a 5,000 pounds of rice and beans. It's now Nicaragua's serve. Stay tuned.

stairs contains a bar, with large TV, neon signs, and flashing lights. Downstairs the spacious dining room—decorated with foreign flags—serves basic, midpriced Costa Rican fare. Its location right in the center of town makes it a favorite for tour groups. ☒ *Across from northeast corner of Parque Central* ☎ 479–9145 ☰ *AE, DC, MC, V.*

¢–$ ✕ **Las Brasitas.** Chicken turns over wood on a rotisserie in a brick oven at this pleasant restaurant on the road heading out of town toward the volcano. Try the succulent chicken when it ends up in the tasty fajitas or any of the other ample-size Mexican dishes. Service is good, and you have your choice of three open-air dining areas arranged around a garden. Two are secluded and intimate; the third less so, being closer to the road. ☒ *200 m west of church* ☎ 479–9819 ☰ *MC, V.*

¢–$ ✕ **La Choza de Laurel.** Here's a case study in what tourism does to a place: tantalizing rotisserie chicken, the cloves of garlic and bunches of onions still dangle from the roof and draw in passersby to this old favorite, open-air Costa Rican–style restaurant a short walk from the center of town. But the owners have also opened a much grander, more modern installation two blocks away as well. The place opens early; it's a great place to grab a hearty breakfast on your way to the volcano. ☒ *100 m northwest of church, or 300 m northwest of church* ☎ 479–9231 ☰ *MC, V* ☺ *Breakfast served.*

¢–$ ✕ **Lava Rocks Café.** A couple of trendy steps above the average *soda* in food and atmosphere (and a bit higher in price), this open-air café has tasty *casados* (plates with rice, beans, fried plantains, and fish, chicken, or meat) and sandwiches, and we love their rich fruit *batidos* (milk shakes). ☒ *Across from south side of church* ☎ 479–8039 ☰ *MC, V.*

¢ ✕ **Soda La Parada.** La Fortuna's only 24-hour eatery is a convenient place to grab a quick and cheap meal, and to stock up on snacks for long bus rides. ☒ *Across from Parque Central and regional bus stop* ☎ 479–9547 ☰ *No credit cards* ☺ *Breakfast served.*

Where to Stay

★ $$$–$$$$ ▦ **Tabacón Resort.** Without question, Tabacón, with its impeccably landscaped gardens and hot-springs rivers at the base of Volcán Arenal, is one of Central America's most compelling resorts. The hot springs and small but lovely spa customarily draw visitors inland from the ocean with no regrets. All rooms have tile floors, a terrace or patio, and big bathrooms. Some have volcano views; others overlook the manicured gardens. The suites are some of the country's finest lodgings, with tile floors, plants, beautiful mahogany armoires and beds, and two-person whirlpool baths. The hotel's intimacy is compromised by its scale and its popularity with day-trippers, but it has some private areas—including a dining room and pool—for overnight guests only. ☒ *13 km (8 mi) northwest of La Fortuna on highway toward Nuevo Arenal* ☎ 460–2020, 519–1900 in San José, 877/277–8291 in North America ☒ 460–5724, 519–1940 in San José, 877/277–8292 in North America ☒ *Apdo. 181–1007, San José* ⊕ *www.tabacon.com* ⮒ *95 rooms, 11 suites* ⌂ *2 restaurants, dining room, cable TV, 9 pools, outdoor hot tub, spa, 3 bars, business services, meeting rooms, airport shuttle, travel services* ☰ *MC, V* ⦿ *BP.*

$$ ▦ **Chachagua Rain Forest Hotel.** At this working ranch, intersected by a brook, you can see *caballeros* (cowboys) at work, take a horseback ride into the rain forest, and look for toucans from the open-air restaurant, which serves local meat and dairy products. Each cabina has a pair of double beds and a deck with a picnic table. Large, reflective windows enclosing each cabina's shower serve a marvelous purpose: birds gather outside your window to watch their own reflections while you bathe and watch them. The lodge is 3 km/2 mi up a rough track—four-wheel drive is a must in rainy season—on the road headed south from La Fortuna to La Tigra. ⊠ *12 km/7 mi south of La Fortuna* ⊕ *Apdo. 476–4005, Ciudad Cariari* ☎ *468–1010* 🖷 *468–1020* ⊕ *www. chachaguarainforesthotel.com* 🛏 *32 cabinas* ⚹ *Restaurant, tennis court, pool, horseback riding, massage, bar, meeting rooms; no a/c, no room phones, no room TVs* ⊟ *MC, V* ⊠ *BP.*

$$ 🏨 **Montaña de Fuego.** On a manicured grassy roadside knoll, this highly

Fodor'sChoice recommended collection of cabins affords utterly spectacular views of

★ Volcán Arenal. The spacious, well-made hardwood structures have large porches, and rooms have rustic decor. The friendly management can arrange tours of the area. ⊠ *8 km/5 mi west of La Fortuna* ☎ *460–1220* 🖷 *460–1455* ⊕ *www.montanadefuego.com* 🛏 *66 cabinas* ⚹ *Restaurant, fans, minibars, cable TV, 2 pools, hot tub, sauna, spa, horseback riding, 2 bars, shop, laundry service, meeting room, travel services* ⊟ *AE, DC, MC, V* ⊠ *BP.*

$–$$ 🏨 **Arenal Observatory Lodge.** You're as close as anyone should be to an active volcano at the end of the winding road leading to the lodge—a mere 1¾ km (1 mi) away. The isolated lodge was founded by Smithsonian researchers in 1987. It's fairly rustic, emphasizing that outdoor activities are what it's all about. Rooms are comfortable and simply furnished (comforters on beds are a cozy touch), and most have stellar views. After a hike, take a dip in the infinity-edge pool or 12-person hot tub, which face tall pines on one side and the volcano on the other. The dining room, which serves tasty and hearty food, has great views of the volcano and lake. ⊠ *3 km/2 mi east of dam on Laguna de Arenal; from La Fortuna, drive to Tabacón Resort and continue 4 km/2½ mi past resort to turnoff at base of volcano; turn and continue for 9 km/5½ mi* ⊕ *Apdo. 13411–1000, San José* ☎ *692–2070, 290–7011 in San José* 🖷 *692–2074, 290–8427 in San José* ⊕ *www.arenalobservatorylodge. com* 🛏 *48 rooms, 46 with bath; 2 suites* ⚹ *Restaurant, pool, outdoor hot tub, horseback riding, bar, laundry service; no a/c, no room phones, no room TVs* ⊟ *AE, MC, V* ⊠ *BP.*

★ **$** 🏨 **Hotel San Bosco.** Covered in blue-tile mosaics, this two-story hotel is certainly the most attractive and comfortable in the main part of town. Two kitchen-equipped cabinas (which sleep 8 or 14 people) are a good deal for families. The spotlessly clean, white rooms have polished wood furniture and firm beds and are linked by a long veranda lined with benches and potted plants. ⊠ *220 m north of La Fortuna's gas station* ☎ *479–9050* 🖷 *479–9109* ⊕ *www.arenal-volcano.com* 🛏 *34 rooms, 2 cabinas* ⚹ *Pool, hot tub; no room phones, no TV in some rooms* ⊟ *AE, DC, MC, V* ⊠ *EP.*

★ ¢ 🏨 **Cabinas Oriuma.** Right in the center of town, Oriuma is a popular choice for budget travelers and tour groups. The modern rooms are sparkling clean. The second-floor balcony is a pleasant spot to relax and read, watch the happenings in the Parque Central across the street, or plan your next rain-forest adventure. ⊠ *15 m north of Parque Central* ☎ *479–9111* ✆ *oriuma@racsa.co.cr* ⤴ *20 rooms* ☙ *Fans, cable TV; no room phones* ⊟ *MC, V* ⫶◯⫶ *EP.*

¢ ⫶⊡⫶ **La Pradera.** "The Prairie" is a simple roadside hotel with comfortable guest rooms that have high ceilings, spacious bathrooms, and verandas. Two rooms have whirlpool tubs. Beef eaters should try the thatch-roof restaurant next door. The steak with jalapeño sauce is a fine, spicy dish. ⊠ *2 km/1 mi west of La Fortuna* ☎ *479–9597* 🖷 *479–9167* ⤴ *28 rooms* ☙ *Restaurant, cable TV, pool, hot tubs, bar; no a/c in some rooms, no room phones* ⊟ *MC, V* ⫶◯⫶ *BP.*

Shopping

Lunática (⊠ 350 m east of town church ☎ 479–8255) sells vibrant, colorful works by artists both known and unknown from around the country, some of them local. Charming owner Francesa Marchi knows the area's arts, from the works of the nearby indigenous Maleku groups to those from a cooperative made up of women from local villages.

★ **Toad Hall** (⊠ Road between Nuevo Arenal and La Fortuna ☎ 692–8020), open daily from 8 to 6, sells everything from indigenous art to maps to recycled paper and used books. The owners can give you the lowdown on every tour and tour operator in the area; they also run a deli-café with light snacks and views of the lake and volcano.

Nightlife

People in La Fortuna tend to turn in early, though there are a few clubs and discos for the night owls. **Volcán Look Disco** (⊠ 5 km/3 mi west of La Fortuna ☎ 479–9616), which bills itself as the largest Costa Rican disco outside San José, erupts with dancing and music on weekends. Pizzeria **Vagabundo** (⊠ 3 km/2 mi west of La Fortuna ☎ 479–9565) turns into a lively bar in the evening with foosball and billiards in the back room.

To & from La Fortuna

50 km/30 mi (45 mins) northwest of Ciudad Quesada, 17 km/11 mi east of Arenal Volcano, 190 km/118 mi (3 hrs by car; 25 mins by plane) north of San José.

NatureAir flies daily to La Fortuna (FTN); flights land at an airstrip at the hamlet of El Tanque, 7 km (4 mi) east of town. **Sunset Tours** (⊠ South side of church, La Fortuna ☎ 479–9800) serves as the local agent for NatureAir and provides transportation to and from the airstrip for $5 each way. Shuttle-van service (⇨ The Northern Plains Essentials, *below*) is a cheaper way to get to La Fortuna, and the vans will pick you up from your hotel. Buses head to La Fortuna from San José three times daily, departing in the morning. Buses make multiple stops and can take much longer than driving yourself; for example, the trip from Ciudad Quesada can take 1½ hours by bus, but is only 45 minutes by car. **Desafío Adventures** (⊠ Behind church, La Fortuna ☎ 479–9464 ⊕ www.desafiocostarica.com) provides a fast, popular three-hour transfer between Monteverde and La Fortuna via taxi, boat, then another taxi, for $21 each way.

La Fortuna Essentials

Bank/ATM **Banco de Costa Rica** ⊠ South side of church (money exchange booth). **Banco Nacional** ⊠ Central Plaza ☎ 479–9022. **Banco Popular** ⊠ 50 m east of Central Plaza ☎ 479–9422.

Medical Clinic **Seguro Social** ⊠ 300 m east of Parque Central ☎ 479–9643.

Pharmacy **FarmaTodo** ⊠ 50 m north of La Fortuna's gas station ☎ 479–8155.

Lake Arenal

6 Shimmering Lake Arenal, all 125 square km (48 square mi) of it, lies between green hills and a rumbling volcano. It's Costa Rica's largest inland body of water. Many visitors are surprised to learn it's a man-made lake, created in 1973 when a giant dam was built. A natural depression was flooded, and a 20-mile-long by 9-mi-wide lake was born. The almost constant winds from the Caribbean make this area a windsurfing mecca. Outfitters in La Fortuna, Nuevo Arenal, and Tilarán run fishing, wind-surfing, and kitesurfing trips on the lake. Desafío, an operator based in La Fortuna and Monteverde, has a half-day horseback trip between the two towns, with great views of the lake.

Nuevo Arenal

7 Much of the original town of Arenal, at one of the lowest points near Lake Arenal, was destroyed by the volcano's 1968 eruption, and the rest was destroyed in 1973, when Lake Arenal flooded the region. Nuevo Arenal, created about 30 km (19 mi) away from the site of the old town, doesn't have much to interest tourists, but is about halfway between La Fortuna and Tilarán, making it a good base.

Where to Stay

$$ 🏠 **Villa Decary.** There's everything to recommend at this hillside lodging overlooking Lake Arenal, but it all goes back to owners Jeff and Bill and their attentive service. Rooms have large picture windows and private balconies—great places to take in the ample bird-watching opportunities—and bright yellow-and-blue spreads and drapes. Higher up the hill, spacious bungalows afford an even better view. Rates include a filling breakfast of eggs, pancakes, fruits, and juices. ⊠ *2 km/1½ mi east of Nuevo Arenal* ☎ *383–3012* 🖷 *694–4330* ⊕ *www.villadecary.com* 🛏 *5 rooms, 3 bungalows* ⚭ *Restaurant, no a/c, no room phones, no room TVs* ⊟ *AE, DC, MC, V* ⋈ *BP.*

FodorsChoice ★

$ 🏠 **Chalet Nicholas.** John and Cathy Nicholas (and their resident Great Danes) have converted their hillside home into a charming bed-and-breakfast with stunning views of the lake and volcano. The two rosewood rooms downstairs have tile floors. Up a spiral staircase lies the L-shaped, all-wood double loft with three beds and a back porch that overlooks the large garden. All rooms have volcano views. Birds abound: 100 species have been cataloged on the grounds. Chat about your plans for the day with your fellow guests over one of Cathy's ample breakfasts. ⊠ *2 km/1½ mi west of Nuevo Arenal* ☎ *694–4041* ⊕ *www.chaletnicholas. com* 🛏 *3 rooms* ⚭ *Restaurant, gift shop; no a/c, no room phones, no room TVs, no smoking* ⊟ *No credit cards* ⋈ *BP.*

FodorsChoice ★

To & from Nuevo Arenal

40 km/25 mi (1 hr) west of La Fortuna.

Despite years of government promises to upgrade the major tourist route from Volcán Arenal to Nuevo Arenal, the highway around the north shore of Lake Arenal remains one of Costa Rica's most potholed (and that's saying something in a region notorious for terrible roads). Expect smooth sailing west of the Tabacón Resort as far as the Arenal Dam, after which sections of the road deteriorate badly until you arrive in Nuevo Arenal. Beware of deep, tire-wrecking washouts at all times. This stretch adds a bone-jarring hour to an otherwise lovely drive with spectacular lake and volcano views all the way. Public buses run several times daily from La Fortuna.

Nuevo Arenal Essentials

🏦 Bank/ATM **Banco Nacional** ✉ West side of church ☎ 694-4122.

Tilarán

❽ Heading west around Laguna de Arenal, you pass a couple of small villages and several charming hotels ranging from the Cretan-inspired fantasy Hotel Tilawa to the rustic Rock River Lodge. The quiet whitewashed town of Tilarán, on the southwest side of the lake—a windmill farm in the hills high above the town attests to this being the windiest place in the country—is used as a base by bronzed windsurfers. For those days when you get "skunked" (the wind fails to blow), horseback riding and mountain biking can keep you busy. A lakeside stroll is a pleasant way to while away a few hours.

Outdoor Activities

WINDSURFING & KITESURFING   Several hotels rent windsurfing equipment ($40/day). The best selection of wind- and kitesurfing equipment for rent or purchase can be found at lakefront **Tilawa Wind Surf** (✉ Hotel Tilawa, 8 km/5 mi north of Tilarán ☎ 695-5050). It's the only outfitter here open year-round. Full- and half-day lessons are also available for $150 and $100, respectively.

Where to Stay

$ ▦ **Hotel Tilawa.** This Costa Rican homage to the Palace of Knossos on Crete has neoclassical murals, columns, and plant-draped arches that somehow don't seem dramatically out of place. The large rooms have two queen-size beds with Guatemalan bedspreads and natural wood ceilings; the bathrooms are especially spacious. Sailing tours in a 39-foot catamaran, the windsurfing and kitesurfing school and shop, and the skateboarding park make this a practical place to base yourself if you want an active vacation. Packages include the use of windsurfing gear. The open-air patio restaurant dishes up steaks and seafood. ⊠ *8 km/5 mi north of Tilarán* ☎ *695–5050* 🖷 *695–5766* ⊕ *www.tilawa.com* 🖃 *Apdo. 92–5710, Tilarán* ☞ *20 rooms* ☖ *Restaurant, pool, hot tub, windsurfing, boating, mountain bikes, horseback riding, bar, laundry service; no a/c, no room TVs* ☲ *MC, V.*

To & from Tilarán
22 km/14 mi (45 mins) southwest of Nuevo Arenal, 62 km/38 mi (1½ hrs) west of La Fortuna.

The road from La Fortuna via Nuevo Arenal is treacherous, narrow, and potholed. Give yourself sufficient time—say, two hours—for the trip. Public buses travel to and from La Fortuna several times daily.

Tilarán Essentials
🏦 Bank/ATM **Banco Nacional** ⊠ Central Plaza ☎ 695–5610. **CooTilarán** ⊠ 150 m north of church.

🏥 Hospital **Clínica Tilarán** ⊠ 200 m west of Banco Nacional ☎ 695–5093.

MONTEVERDE CLOUD FOREST AREA

Monteverde is a rain forest, but you won't be in the tropics, rather in the cool, gray, misty world of the cloud forest. Almost 900 species of epiphytes, including 450 orchids, are found here; most tree trunks are covered with mosses, bromeliads, ferns, and other plants. Monteverde spans the Continental Divide, extending from about 1,500 meters (4,920 feet) on the Pacific slope and 1,350 meters (4,430 feet) on the Atlantic slope up to the highest peaks of the Tilarán Mountains at around 1,850 meters (6,070 feet).

Monteverde Cloud Forest Biological Reserve

★ ❾ In close proximity to several fine hotels, the private Reserva Biológica Bosque Nuboso Monteverde is one of Costa Rica's best-kept reserves, with well-marked trails, lush vegetation, and a cool, damp climate. The collision of moist winds with the Continental Divide here creates a constant mist whose particles provide nutrients for plants growing at the upper layers of the forest. Giant trees are enshrouded in a cascade of orchids, bromeliads, mosses, and ferns, and in those patches where sunlight penetrates, brilliantly colored flowers flourish. The sheer size of everything, especially the leaves of the trees, is striking. No less astounding is the variety: 2,500 plant species, 400 species of birds, 500 types of butterflies, and more than 100 different mammals have so far been cataloged at Monteverde. A damp and exotic mixture of shades,

CLOSE UP

What Is a Cloud Forest?

CLOUD FORESTS ARE A TYPE OF rain forest, but are very different from the hot, humid lowland forests with which most people are familiar. First of all, they're cooler. Temperatures in Monteverde Cloud Forest, for example, are in the 65°F range year-round, and feel colder due to the near-constant cool rain. Cloud forests—also known as montane forest—occur at elevations of around 6,500 to 11,500 feet. At this altitude, clouds accumulate around mountains and volcanoes, providing regular precipitation as well as shade, which in turn slows evaporation. Moisture is deposited directly onto vegetation, keeping it lush and green. The trees here, on top of high ridges and near the summits of volcanoes, are transformed by strong, steady winds that sometimes topple them and regularly break off branches. The resulting collection of small, twisted trees and bushes is known as an elfin forest. The conditions in cloud forests create unique habitats that shelter an unusually high proportion of rare species, making conservation vital. Monteverde is Costa Rica's most touristed cloud forest, but not its only one. Other cloud forests are in nearby Santa Elena Reserve, the Los Angeles Cloud Forest Reserve near San Ramón (⇨ *above*), and around San Gerardo do Dota (⇨ chapter 6).

smells, and sounds, the cloud forest is also famous for its population of quetzals, which can be spotted feeding on the *aguacatillo* (like an avocado) trees; best viewing times are early mornings from January until September, and especially during the mating season of April and May. Other forest-dwelling inhabitants include hummingbirds and multicolor frogs.

For those who don't have a lucky eye, a short-stay aquarium is in the field station; captive amphibians stay here just a week before being released back into the wild. Although the reserve limits visitors to 160 people at a time, Monteverde is one of the country's most popular destinations. Come early and allow a generous slice of time for leisurely hiking to see the forest's flora and fauna; longer hikes are made possible by some strategically placed overnight refuges along the way. At the reserve entrance you can buy self-guide pamphlets and rent rubber boots; a map is provided when you pay the entrance fee. A two-hour guided night tour starts each evening at 7:15—reservations are required—and the reserve provides transport from area hotels for an extra $2. ☎ 645–5122 ⊕ *www.cct.or.cr* ✉ *$12, plus $15 with guide services; $13 night tour* ☉ *Daily 7–4.*

To & from Monteverde Biological Reserve
10 km/6 mi (30 mins) south of Santa Elena, 35 km/22 mi (2 hrs) southeast of Tilarán, 167 km/104 mi (5 hrs) northwest of San José.

Buses from Santa Elena leave at 6 AM and 1 PM daily. Taxis from Santa Elena are $7. Buses from Tilarán leave once a day, at 1 PM. Buses from San José leave twice daily from the Terminal Atlántico Norte (C. 12 at

Avda. 9), at 6:30 AM and 1:30 PM. The roads to the park are some of the worst in the country.

Monteverde & Santa Elena

10 **11** The area's first residents were a handful of Costa Rican families fleeing the rough-and-ready life of nearby gold-mining fields during the 1940s. They were joined in the early 1950s by Quakers, conscientious objectors from Alabama fleeing conscription into the Korean War. A number of things drew them to Costa Rica: just a few years earlier it had abolished its military, and the Monteverde area offered good grazing. But it was the cloud forest that lay above their dairy farms that soon attracted the attention of ecologists. Educators and artisans followed, giving Monteverde and its "metropolis," the village of Santa Elena, a mystique all their own. Monteverde's Quakers, or more officially, the Society of Friends, no longer constitute the majority these days, but their imprint on the community remains strong.

"Monteverde" refers generally to the entire area, but officially it's the original Quaker settlement that congregates around its dairy-processing plant down the mountain from the reserve entrance. (Road signs designate it that way.)

The only way to see the area's reserves, including the Monteverde Cloud Forest, is to hike them (⇨ Hiking *in* Outdoor Activities, *below.*)

NAVIGATING MONTEVERDE & SANTA ELENA

There will be times you wish you had your own vehicle, but it's surprisingly easy to get around the Monteverde area without a car. Taxis are plentiful; it's easy to call one from your hotel, and restaurants are happy to summon a cab to take you back to your hotel after dinner. Taxis also congregate in front of the church on the main street in Santa Elena. Many tour companies will pick you up from your hotel and bring you back at the end of the day, either free or for a small fee.

Exploring

Several conservation areas that have sprung up near Monteverde make attractive day trips, particularly if the Monteverde Reserve is too busy. The **Santa Elena Reserve** just west of Monteverde is a project of the Santa Elena high school and has a series of trails (45 minutes–4 hours) that can be walked alone or with a guide. The **Camino Verde Information Center** (⊠ Main street in town) operates a shuttle service to the reserve with fixed departures and returns. Reservations are required, and the cost is $2 each way. ⊠ *6 km/4 mi north of Santa Elena* ☎ *645–5390* ⊕ *www.reservasantaelena.org* ⊠ *$10* ⊙ *Daily 7–4.*

⟳ If your time in Monteverde is limited, consider spending it at **Selvatura,** a kind of nature theme park—complete with canopy tour

> **CAUTION**
>
> Never take advice from the street "guides" who meet incoming buses in La Fortuna and Monteverde. They claim to want to help you find accommodations and tours, when in reality they receive kickbacks for sending tourists to less-than-desirable hotels or to unqualified "tour guides."

Continued on page 143

CANOPY TOURS

Why should monkeys have all the fun? Biologists have long known that much of the action in the rain forest happens off the ground, near the tops of trees. This is where the most eye-catching animals—birds and monkeys—make their homes.

What Is a Canopy Tour?

There are two basic types of canopy tours: one that gives you a chance to see treetop animals up close; and one that lets you behave like them. The former are canopy tours in the literal sense, where you walk along suspension bridges, ride along in a tram, or are hoisted up to a platform to get a closer look at birds, monkeys, and sloths. They may also be called hanging-bridges tours, sky walks, or platform tours.

The latter, and much more popular, type of canopy tour has less to do with learning about nature. Instead, it is a fast-paced and fun experience where you are attached to a zip line with a safety harness and then "fly" from one tree platform to the next. When most people say "canopy tour" they are generally referring to a zip-line tour. These tours are great fun, but don't plan on seeing the resplendent quetzal as you zip from platform to platform. (Your shouts of exhilaration will probably scare them all away.)

Tree-to-tree zip lines date back to the 19th century, and were introduced as a means for rain-forest study in Costa Rica in the 1970s by U.S. biologist Donald Perry. Darren Hreniuk, a Dutch-turned-Tico entrepreneur, opened the country's first commercial canopy tour in Monteverde in the mid-1990s. It was an almost immediate success. Within a decade, there were close to 100 canopy tours operated by various companies and individuals. Canopy tours now generate some $120 million annually, and attract a reported 200,000 tourists each year.

■ **TIP** ➔➔ If the day is overcast, save your money. All you'll see are clouds, and you can do that for free back on the ground.

Is It Safe?

Flying through the air, while undeniably cool, is also inherently dangerous. So before you strap into a harness, be certain that the safety standards are first rate. Like so much in Costa Rica, there is no government oversight of canopy tours, so you are dependent on the representations of the operators.

Since 1997 two zip-line tour deaths have been attributed to faulty equipment; one in 2000 on a San Lorenzo Canopy Tour in San Ramón, the other in 1997, at a canopy tour near La Fortuna (neither company is listed in this book). Both women plummeted to earth after their harnesses came apart. Considering that thousands of tourists enjoy the canopy tours each year, the safety record is quite good. Nevertheless, don't fall for sales pitches, and take your time to choose wisely. If anything seems "off" or makes you uncomfortable, walk away.

Just as importantly: Listen closely to the guides and follow their instructions. Don't attempt to take photos in flight and never argue with the guide when s/he is making a decision to preserve your safety. A good operator will refund your money or reschedule your tour if it's cancelled due to weather.

ZIP-LINE TOURS IN MONTEVERDE & ARENAL

Reservations are required for all zip-line tours.

The Arenal Rain Forest Reserve (⇨ *Hanging Bridges and Trams*) is a suspension-bridge and gondola tour with a zip-line option.

Aventura Canopy, the newest zip-line operater in this region, takes you over 16 cables—some extending 2,000 feet—one rappel, and one Tarzan swing on a 2½-hour tour. ⊠ *Road to Santa Elena Reserve, across from bus terminal, Santa Elena* ☎ 645–6959 ⊕ *www.aventuracanopy.com* ⊠ *$45.*

★ *Fodor's Choice* **The Original Canopy Tour** near La Fortuna has well-trained guides who send you whizzing between trees that stand about 328 feet over the streams of Tabacón. If it's a small tour, they may be able to snap a picture of you. ⊠ *Tabacón Resort, 13 km/8 mi northwest of La Fortuna on highway toward Nuevo Arenal* ☎ 460–2020 or 291–4465 ⊕ *www.canopytour.com* ⊠ *$45 (includes Tabacón Hot Springs day pass).*

★ **The Original Canopy Tour** near Santa Elena was the first zip-line tour in Costa Rica and is still one of the best, with 10 platforms in the canopy, and lasting 2½ hours. You arrive at most of the platforms using a cable-and-harness traversing system and climb 42 feet inside a strangler fig tree to reach one. ⊠ *Across from La Esperanza Supermarket, Santa Elena* ☎ 645–5243, 291–4465 in San José ⊕ *www.canopytour.com* ⊠ *$45.*

Selvatura is the only zip-line tour built entirely inside the cloud forest. It has 15 lines and 18 platforms. ⊠ *Office across from church, Santa Elena* ☎ 645–5929 ⊕ *www.selvatura.com* ⊠ *$40.*

Sky Trek has 11 cables that are longer than those of the Original Canopy Tour—the longest more than 2,500 feet. The zip lines here extend between towers above the canopy, rather than between trees, and you'll more likely notice the effects of the wind on this one. ⊠ *Across from Banco Nacional, Santa Elena* ☎ 645–5238 ⊕ *www.crskyadventures.com* ⊠ *$44, shuttle $1.*

CAN I DO IT?

You don't need any particular skills or athleticism to participate in a zip-line tour, but you do need some degree of fearlessness to allow yourself to be suspended hundreds of feet in the air. You'll also be asked to "brake" for yourself by squeezing the zip line before you get to the tree, so those with hand injuries or arthritis may have problems. Talk with the tour operator before you book. Tour operators usually have (and should have) weight and age restrictions; ask about these beforehand.

ASK BEFORE YOU BOOK:

■ How long has the company been in business, and are they insured?

■ Is the company a member of the Association of Adventure Tour Operators, and/or does it abide by the association's safety guidelines?

■ Are cables, harnesses, and other equipment manufacturer-certified?

■ Is there a second safety line that connects you to the zip line in case the main pulley gives way?

■ Are participants clipped to the zip line while on the platform? (They should be.)

■ What sort of training do the guides receive?

■ Does the tour operator give a thorough pre-tour safety briefing—in English—that addresses such issues as how much climbing and walking are involved?

■ What's the price? Costs vary from around $20 to $75. An extremely low price may indicate a second-rate operation.

HANGING BRIDGES AND TRAMS

The Natural Wonders Tram is an hour-long ride through the rain-forest canopy in a two-person carriage on an elevated track. You control the speed of your carriage. Alternatively, a 1½-km (1-mi) walk gives you a ground-level perspective. The site opens for night visits with advance reservations. ⊠ *Off main road between Santa Elena and Monteverde, on turnoff to Jardín de Mariposas* ☎ *645–5960* 🖃 *$15* ⊗ *Daily 8 AM–6 PM.*

Tree Top Walkways, at Selvatura, takes you to heights of 500 feet on a 3-km (2-mi) walk along very stable bridges, ranging from 36 to 150 feet, through the same canopy terrain as the zip-line tour. ⊠ *Office across from church, Santa Elena* ☎ *645–5929* ⊕ *www.selvatura.com* 🖃 *$20.*

Sky Walk allows you to walk along five hanging bridges, at heights of up to 138 feet, connected from tree to tree. Imposing towers, used as support, mar the landscape somewhat. Reservations are required for guided tours. ⊠ *Across from Banco Nacional, Santa Elena* ☎ *645– 5296* ⊕ *www.crskyadventures.com* 🖃 *$17, $27 tours* ⊗ *Daily 7–4.*

Arenal Hanging Bridges is actually a series of trails and bridges that form a loop through the primary rain forest of a 250-acre private reserve, with great bird-watching and volcano-viewing. Fixed and hanging bridges allow you to see the forest at different levels. It's open rain or shine, and there are things to do in both climates. Shuttle service from La Fortuna can be arranged. ⊠ *Arenal Dam, 4 km/2½ mi west of Tabacón* ☎ *479–9686 or 253–5080* ⊕ *www. hangingbridges.com* 🖃 *$20; $30 bird tour, $35 evening tour* ⊗ *Daily 7–4:30; evening tour at 5:30.*

The Arenal Rain Forest Reserve, a canopy tour–bridge walk complex near La Fortuna, is operated by the Sky Trek–Sky Walk folks in Monteverde. Alpine-style gondolas transport you to the site, from which you can descend via a zip-line canopy tour or hike through the cloud forest along a series of suspended bridges. ⊠ *12 km/7 mi west of La Fortuna, El Castillo* ☎ *479–9944* ⊕ *www. arenalreserve.com* 🖃 *$60, $50 tram only, shuttle $8* ⊗ *Daily 7–4.*

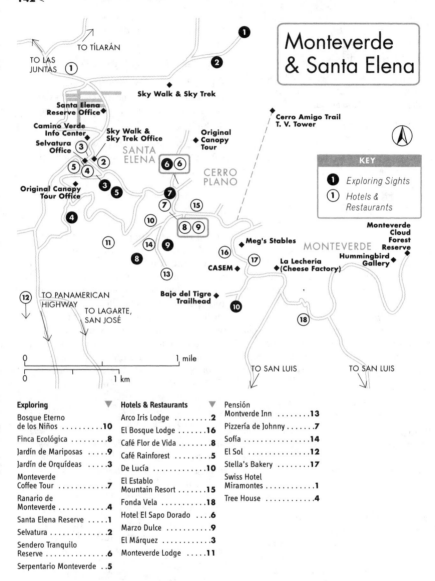

Monteverde & Santa Elena

TO TÍLARÁN

TO LAS JUNTAS ①

❶

❷

Sky Walk & Sky Trek

Santa Elena
Reserve Office ◆

Camino Verde
Info Center ◆
Selvatura
Office ③

Sky Walk &
Sky Trek Office

SANTA
ELENA ②

Original
◆ Canopy
Tour

⑤ ④

Original Canopy
Tour Office ◆

③ ❺

❹

⑪

⑫ TO PANAMERICAN
HIGHWAY

TO LAGARTE,
SAN JOSÉ

Cerro Amigo Trail
T. V. Tower

CERRO
PLANO

⑥ ⑥

❼

⑦ ⑮

⑧ ⑨

⑩

⑭ ⑨

❽

⑬

Bajo del Tigre ◆
Trailhead

❿

Meg's Stables ◆

⑯ ⑰

CASEM ◆

La Lecheria
◆(Cheese Factory)

MONTEVERDE

Monteverde
Cloud
Forest
Reserve

Hummingbird
Gallery ◆

⑱

0 _____ 1 mile
0 _____ 1 km

TO SAN LUIS

TO SAN LUIS

KEY

❶ Exploring Sights

① Hotels &
Restaurants

Exploring ▼

Bosque Eterno
de los Niños **10**

Finca Ecológica **8**

Jardín de Mariposas **9**

Jardín de Orquídeas **3**

Monteverde
Coffee Tour **7**

Ranario de
Monteverde **4**

Santa Elena Reserve **1**

Selvatura **2**

Sendero Tranquilo
Reserve **6**

Serpentario Monteverde . . **5**

Hotels & Restaurants ▼

Arco Iris Lodge **2**

El Bosque Lodge **16**

Café Flor de Vida **8**

Café Rainforest **5**

De Lucía **10**

El Establo
Mountain Resort **15**

Fonda Vela **18**

Hotel El Sapo Dorado **6**

Marzo Dulce **9**

El Márquez **3**

Monteverde Lodge **11**

Pensión
Monteverde Inn **13**

Pizzería de Johnny **7**

Sofía **14**

El Sol **12**

Stella's Bakery **17**

Swiss Hotel
Miramontes **1**

Tree House **4**

and bridge walks—just outside the Santa Elena Reserve. A 100-bird hummingbird garden and an enormous enclosed 50-species *mariposario* (butterfly garden) sit near the visitor center. Not to be missed is the world's largest private insect collection. As if that weren't enough, a *herpetario* (frog and reptile house) opened in 2005. Transportation from area hotels is included in the price. You can choose from numerous mix-and-match packages, depending on which activities interest you, or take it all in, with lunch included, for $78. ✉ *Office across from church, Santa Elena* ☎ *645–5929* ⊕ *www.selvatura.com* 🖃 *Prices vary, depending on package* ☉ *Daily 8:30–4:30.*

Only in Monteverde would visitors groove to the nightlife at an exhibition of 20 species of frogs, toads, and other amphibians. Bilingual biologist-guides take you through a 45-minute tour of the terrariums in the **Ranario de Monteverde**, just outside Santa Elena. For the best show, come around dusk and stay well into the evening, when the critters become more active and much more vocal. (Your ticket entitles you to a second visit.) There's a small frog-and-toad-theme gift shop. ✉ *½ km/¼ mi southeast of Supermercado La Esperanza, Santa Elena* ☎ *645–6320* ⊕ *www.ranario.com* 🖃 *$9* ☉ *Daily 9–8:30.*

At the **Serpentario Monteverde**, greet 40 species of live Costa Rican reptiles and amphibians with glass safely between you and them. Guided tours in English or Spanish are included in your admission price. ✉ *Just outside Santa Elena on road to Monteverde* ☎ *645–6002* ⊕ *www.snaketour. com* 🖃 *$8; $3, children 8–12; free, children under 8* ☉ *Daily 9–8.*

The 200-acre **Sendero Tranquilo Reserve** is managed by the Hotel Sapo Dorado and bordered by the Monteverde Cloud Forest Biological Reserve and the Guacimal River. Narrow trails are designed to have as little impact on the forest as possible (only groups of two to six are allowed). A guide leads you through primary and secondary forest and a deforested area. Because of the emphasis on minimal environmental impact, animals here tend to be more timid than at some other reserves. ✉ *3 km/2 mi north of Monteverde Reserve entrance, Cerro Plano* ☎ *645–5010* 🖃 *$22* ☉ *Tours depart daily at 7:30 AM and 1 PM; reservations required.*

Bite your tongue before requesting Costa Rica's ubiquitous Café Britt up here. Export-quality Café Monteverde is the locally grown product. The **Monteverde Coffee Tour** lets you see the process up close from start to finish, from shade growing on the area's Turín plantation, 7 km (4 mi) north of Santa Elena; transport to the *beneficio*, the processing mill where the beans are washed and dried; and finally to the roaster. Reservations are required, and pickup is from area hotels. ☎ *645–7090* ⊕ *www.crstudytours.com* 🖃 *$25* ☉ *Tours at 8 AM and 1 PM.*

Finca Ecológica is a private wildlife refuge with four trails on its 75-acre Ecological Farm, plus birds, sloths, agoutis, coatimundis, two waterfalls, and a coffee plantation. If you can't make it all the way up to the Monteverde Reserve for the evening hike, there's a top-notch guided, two-hour twilight walk that begins each evening at 5:30. Reservations are required. ✉ *Turnoff to Jardín de Mariposas, off main road between Santa*

Bird Country

NEARLY 850 BIRD SPECIES have been identified in Costa Rica, more than in the United States and Canada combined, and all in an area about half the size of Kentucky. Consequently, bird-watchers flock here by the thousands. The big attractions tend to be eye-catching species like the keel-billed toucan, but it is the diversity of shape, size, coloration, and behavior that makes bird-watching in Costa Rica so fascinating.

Tropical superstars: Parrots, parakeets, and macaws; toucans and toucanets; and the elusive but legendary resplendent quetzal are a thrill for those of us who don't see them every day.

In supporting roles: Lesser known but equally impressive species include motmots, with their distinctive racket tails; oropéndolas, which build remarkable hanging nests; and an amazing array of hawks, kites, and falcons.

Color me red, blue, yellow . . . : Two of the most striking species are the showy scarlet macaw and the quirky purple gallinule; tanagers, euphonias, manakins, cotingas, and trogons are some of the country's loveliest plumed creatures, but none of them matches the iridescence of the hummingbirds (⇨ below).

Singing in the rain: The relatively inconspicuous and seemingly ubiquitous clay-colored robin is Costa Rica's national bird. It may look plain, but its song is melodious, and since the males sing almost constantly toward the end of the dry season—the beginning of their mating season—local legend has it that they call the rains.

The big and the small of it: The scintillant hummingbird is a mere 2½ inches tall and weighs just over 2 grams, while the jabiru, a long-legged stork, can grow to more than 4 feet tall and can weigh up to 14 pounds.

Hummingbirds: Costa Rica hosts 51 members of the hummingbird family, compared with just one species for all of the United States east of the Rocky Mountains. Time spent near a hummingbird feeder will treat you to an unforgettable display of accelerated aerial antics and general pugnacity.

"Snow birds": If you're here between October and April, don't be surprised if some feathered friends from home made similar vacation plans. When northern birds fly south for the winter, they don't all head to Miami. Seasonal visitors like the Kentucky warbler make up about a quarter of the amazing avian panorama in Costa Rica.

Bird-watching can be done everywhere in the country—all you need is a pair of binoculars and a copy of *A Guide to the Birds of Costa Rica*, the excellent field guide by Gary Stiles and the late Alexander Skutch. And don't let the rainy season deter you: seasonal *lagunas* (lagoons) such as Caño Negro and the swamps of Palo Verde National Park, which disappear during the dry months, are excellent places to see birds. For more information, *see* the Wildlife Glossary *in* the Understanding Costa Rica chapter.

Elena and Monteverde ☎ *645–5869* ⊕ *www.fincaecologicamonteverde. com* ✉ *$9, twilight walk $15* ⊘ *Daily 7–5.*

Forty species of butterflies flit about in four enclosed botanical gardens at the **Jardín de Mariposas** (Butterfly Garden). Morning visits are best, since the butterflies are most active early in the day. ✉ *Near Pensión Monteverde Inn; take right-hand turnoff 4 km/2½ mi past Santa Elena on road to Monteverde, continue for 2 km/1 mi* ☎ *645–5512* ⊕ *www. best.com/~mariposa* ✉ *$8; children 3–12; free, children under 3* ⊘ *Daily 9:30–4.*

The **Jardín de Orquídeas** (Orchid Garden) showcases more than 400 species of orchids, including two unnamed, one of which is the world's smallest. The Monteverde Orchid Investigation Project manages the gardens. ✉ *150 m south of Banco Nacional* ☎ *645–5308* ✉ *$7; $3, children 7–12; free, children under 7* ⊘ *Daily 8–5.*

The 54,000-acre **Bosque Eterno de los Niños** (Children's Eternal Rain Forest) dwarfs the Monteverde and Santa Elena reserves. It began life as a school project in Sweden and blossomed into a fundraising effort in 44 countries. Much of it is not open to the public but the Monteverde Conservation League offers stays at San Gerardo and Poco Sol, two remote field stations within the forest. The $34 packages include dormitory accommodation and meals. Hiking tours of the forest are available (⇨ Hiking, *below*). ✉ *100 m south of CASEM* ☎ *645–5305* ✉ *Forest $7, children under 12, free; transportation from area hotels $2* ⊘ *Daily 8–4:30.*

<table>
<tr><td>**NEED A BREAK?**</td><td>Long before tourists flocked up here, dairy farming was the foundation of Monteverde's economy. Quakers still operate what is locally referred to as the Cheese Factory, or **La Lechería** (✉ ½ km/¼ mi south of CASEM, halfway between Santa Elena and Monteverde Reserve ☎ 645-2850, 645-7090 tours). The factory store sells local cheeses and ice cream. Stop in for a cone. It's open Monday–Saturday 7:30–5 and Sunday 7:30–4. If you have more time, take a two-hour tour of the operation Monday–Saturday at 9 or 2. Tours are $8 and wind up with a cheese-sampling session. Reserve in advance.</td></tr>
</table>

Canopy Tours   See Page 138

HIKING   The Monteverde Conservation League's (MCL's) **Bajo del Tigre trail** in the Bosque Eterno de los Niños rain forest (⇨ Exploring, *above*) makes for a gentle, self-guided 1½-km (1-mi) hike through secondary forest. Along the trail are 27 points of interpretation, many with lessons geared toward kids. A separate guided twilight walk ($15) begins at 5:30 PM and lasts two hours, affording the chance to see the nocturnal side of the cloud forest; reservations are required. The trail is open daily 8 to 4:30; admission to the forest ($7, children under 12, free) applies.

The 75-acre private wildlife refuge **Finca Ecológica** (⇨ Exploring, *above*) has four trails ranging from 1 to 3 km and a two-hour guided twilight walk ($14) each evening at 5:30. Reservations are required. The 1.4-km Youth Challenge Trail at **Santa Elena Reserve** (⇨ Exploring, *above*) takes about 45 minutes to an hour to negotiate; you can stop at an observation platform with views as far away as the Arenal Volcano—that is, if the clouds clear. If you're feeling hardy, try the 5-km (3-mi) Caño Negro Trail, clocking in at around 4 hours.

Hike 200 acres through four different stages of cloud forest at the **Sendero Tranquilo Reserve** (⇨ Exploring, *above*), including one area illustrating the results of cloud-forest devastation. Tours are arranged through Hotel El Sapo Dorado (⇨ Where to Stay & Eat, *below*) and require a two-person minimum and six-person limit.

HORSEBACK RIDING ★ Long-established **Desafío Adventures** (⊠ Across from La Esperanza supermarket, Santa Elena ☎645–5874 ⊕www.monteverdetours.com) leads four-hour horseback tours to the San Luis Waterfall, an area not often taken in by Monteverde visitors, and also has shorter excursions on farms around Santa Elena. For the Monteverde–La Fortuna trip ($65), you travel by car and boat, with a three-hour horseback ride on a flat trail along Lake Arenal. Farms for resting the animals are at each end. It's infinitely more humane for the horses (and you) than the muddy, treacherous mountain trails used by dozens of other individuals who'll offer to take you to Arenal. Tour prices range from $25 to $48.

⚠ The ride from Monteverde to La Fortuna can be dangerous with outfitters that take inexperienced riders along steep trails. Desafío should be your only choice for getting from Monteverde to La Fortuna on horseback.

Escorted half-day horseback-riding tours ($40) with **Caballeriza El Rodeo** (⊠ West entrance of town of Santa Elena, at tollbooth ☎ 645–5764) are on a private farm. Excursions are for everyone from beginner to experienced rider. A two-hour sunset tour ($25) begins at 4 PM. Family-operated **El Palomino** (⊠ Just outside of Santa Elena ☎ 645–5479) gives escorted afternoon half-day horseback-riding tours ($25) on farm areas around Santa Elena. Transportation from your hotel is included.

On a horseback tour with **Gold Tours** (⊠ Monteverde Homestay, 150 m northeast of school, Cerro Plano ☎ 645–6914) you visit a 1920s gold mine. The excursion ($40) includes a demonstration of the panning methods used during those heady days, and on the trip back a visit to a *trapiche,* a traditional sugarcane mill. Everyone from small children to seasoned experts can participate on these guided horseback-riding trips ($15–$50) with **Meg's Stables** (⊠ Main road, across from CASEM ☎ 645–5419). Reservations are a good idea in high season, and essential if you want an English-speaking guide. A tour to the San Luis waterfalls is geared toward experienced riders.

■ TIP→ Book horseback trips in the morning during rainy season (July–December). Rains usually begin at around 2 PM.

Where to Stay & Eat

$-$$$ ╳ **De Lucía.** Cordial Chilean owner José Belmar is the walking, talking (in five languages) menu at this elegant restaurant, always on hand to chat with guests. All entrées are served with grilled vegetables and fried plantains, and include sea bass with garlic sauce and orange chicken. The handsome wooden restaurant with red mahogany tables is given a distinct South American flavor by an array of Andean tapestries and ceramics. An excellent dessert choice is *tres leches* (three milks), a richer-than-rich cake made with condensed, whole, and evaporated milk. ⊠ *Turnoff to Jardín de Mariposas, off main road between Santa Elena and Monteverde, Cerro Plano* ☎ 645–5337 ⊟ *AE, MC, V.*

$-$$ ╳ **Pizzería de Johnny.** Everyone makes it to this stylish but informal place with candles and white tablecloths. The Monteverde pizza, with the works, is the most popular dish, and pastas, sandwiches, and a decent wine selection round out the menu. ⊠ *Road to Monteverde Reserve, 1½ km/1 mi southeast of Santa Elena* ☎ 645–5066 ⊟ *MC, V.*

$-$$ ╳ **Sofía.** One of the area's newest restaurants is giving nearby De Lucía a run for the title of "Monteverde's most stylish restaurant." (This is still Monteverde, so you can leave your eveningwear at home.) Waiters in crisp black aprons scurry attentively around the three dining rooms with ample window space. We like Sofía for its variety of about a dozen main courses, a mix of chicken, beef, pork, seafood and vegetarian entrees. Try the chimichanga with corvina and shrimp and a side of coconut rice. There's an extensive wine and cocktail selection, too. ⊠ *Turnoff to Jardín de Mariposas, off main road between Santa Elena and Monteverde, Cerro Plano* ☎ 645–7017 ⊟ *MC, V.*

$-$$ ╳ **Tree House.** The name describes the place: this two-story restaurant on Santa Elena's main street is built around a 60-year-old fig tree. Tree branches shelter first-floor tables from the afternoon mist, but not entirely. If that's a problem, grab a table on the upper floor. The menu mixes pastas and seafood with Costa Rican cuisine. For a taste of everything, try the *típico* platter. ⊠ *Across from AyA, Santa Elena* ☎ 645–5751 ⊟ *MC, V* ☺ *Breakfast served.*

$ ╳ **Cafe Flor de Vida.** This popular vegetarian restaurant has a menu that includes chili, a huge veggie burger, sandwiches, soups, salads, bagels, and plenty of desserts. ⊠ *Road to Monteverde Reserve, 1½ km/1 mi southeast of Santa Elena* ☎ 645–6328 ⊟ *AE, DC, MC, V* ☺ *Breakfast served.*

$ ╳ **El Márquez.** Seafood is an unexpected treat up here in the mountains, and it's fresh: the owner gets shipments up from Puntarenas several times weekly. The place is nothing fancy; expect plastic tables and chairs, with lots of local flavor. Portions are big, but prices aren't. You could have trouble finishing the generous mixed seafood platter with shrimp, crab, and octopus in a white-wine sauce, or the jumbo shrimp with a sauce of mushrooms and heart of palm. ⊠ *Across from Banco Nacional, next to Suárez veterinary clinic, Santa Elena* ☎ 645–5918 ⊟ *MC, V* ☺ *Closed Sun.*

¢-$ ╳ **Café Rainforest.** Here's a great, trendy place to warm up with a cup of coffee on a chilly evening, and there are plenty of those up here. If it's not too cold, check out the open-air second-floor balcony that overlooks the street. ⊠ *Across from AyA, Santa Elena* ☎ 645–5841 ⊟ *MC, V* ☺ *Breakfast served.*

¢–$ ✕ **Marzo Dulce.** A tiny place with a small menu, but what this place does, it does well. The everchanging blackboard menu might offer skewered chicken with cilantro or mixed greens with passion fruit dressing. Marzo Dulce—with its orange walls, white tile floors, and wood ceiling—makes a good afternoon break from your nature trekking, a good place to warm up

with one of the café's gourmet coffee drinks. Be sure to grab a pastry or baked good on your way out. ⊠ *100 m north of Cerro Plano school, Cerro Plano* ☎ 645–6568 ▭ *No credit cards* ☾ *Breakfast served.*

¢–$ ✕ **Stella's Bakery.** This local institution is one of the few spots that open at 6 AM. It's a good place to get an early-morning fix before heading to the Monteverde Reserve. Pastries, rolls, muffins, natural juices, and coffee are standard breakfast fare. Take them with you if you're running short of time. Lunch consists of light sandwiches, soups, and pastas. ⊠ *Across from CASEM, Monteverde* ☎ 645–5560 ▭ *V* ☾ *Breakfast served. No dinner.*

$$ ✕▨ **Fonda Vela.** Owned by the Smith brothers, whose family was among
Fodor'sChoice the first American arrivals in the 1950s, these steep-roof chalets have
★ large bedrooms with white-stucco walls, wood floors, and huge windows. Some have better views of the wooded grounds; others, of the far-off Gulf of Nicoya. The most innovatively designed of Monteverde's hotels is also one of the closest to the reserve entrance. Both restaurants ($$) prepare local and international recipes with flair, served indoors or on the veranda. ⊠ *1½ km/1 mi northwest of Monteverde Reserve entrance, Monteverde* ☎ 645–5125, 257–1413 in San José ▤ 645–5119, 257–1416 in San José ⊕ *www.fondavela.com* ⊙ *Apdo. 70060–1000, San José* ↪ *40 rooms* ♢ *2 restaurants, minibars, refrigerators, cable TV, horseback riding, bar, laundry service, Internet room, meeting room; no a/c* ▭ *AE, DC, MC, V* †◯| *EP.*

$$ ✕▨ **Hotel El Sapo Dorado.** After beginning its life as a nightclub, the "Golden Toad" became a popular restaurant and then graduated into a very pleasant hotel. Geovanny Arguedas's family arrived here to farm 10 years before the Quakers did, and he and his wife, Hannah Lowther, have built secluded hillside cabins with polished paneling, tables, fireplaces, and rocking chairs. The restaurant ($$) is well known for its pastas, pizza, vegetarian dishes, and sailfish from Puntarenas. ⊠ *6 km/4 mi northwest of Monteverde Reserve entrance, Monteverde* ☎ 645–5010 ▤ 645–5180 ⊕ *www.sapodorado.com* ⊙ *Apdo. 9–5655, Monteverde* ↪ *30 rooms* ♢ *Restaurant, massage, bar; no a/c, no room phones, refrigerators, no room TVs* ▭ *V* †◯| *EP.*

$$–$$$$ ▨ **Monteverde Lodge.** The well-established Costa Rica Expeditions op-
Fodor'sChoice erates this longtime favorite close to Santa Elena. Rooms have vaulted
★ ceilings, bathtubs—an amenity rarely seen here—and great views. A table abuts the angled bay window overlooking the 15 acres of grounds, a perfect place to have a cup of coffee and bird-watch from indoors. The restaurant and bar congregate around an enormous but cozy lobby fire-

place. Relax in the whirlpool tub in the enormous solarium, a perfect place to unwind after a day of tromping through the reserves. Or take in the evening slide presentation, showcasing cloud-forest life. ⊠ *200 m south of Ranario de Monteverde, Santa Elena* 🏠 *Apdo. 6941–1000, San José* ☎ *645–5057, 257–0766, or 222–0333* 🖷 *257–1165, 800/886–2609 from U.S.* ⊕ *www.costaricaexpeditions.com* 🛏 *27 rooms* 🍴 *Restaurant, whirlpool tub, bar, gift shop, Internet, meeting room, tours; no a/c, no room TVs* 🟰 *AE, DC, MC, V* ⟟⟨ *EP, MAP, FAP.*

$–$$$ 🏨 **El Establo Mountain Resort.** Mixing old and new, "The Stable" began life as just that, a stable near the road, remodeled and apportioned into comfortable rooms with basic furnishings. A newer pink building perches on the hill above with large suites with wood-and-stone walls. Some contain lofts; all come with amenities rarely seen up here, such as bathtubs, phones, and enormous windows with views of the Gulf of Nicoya. The newest building, higher on the hill, has rooms with hot tubs, private balconies, and even more commanding views. ⊠ *3½ km/2 mi northwest of Monteverde* ☎ *645–5110* 🖷 *645–5041* ⊕ *www. hotelelestablo.com* 🛏 *120 rooms* 🍴 *Restaurant, snack bar, cable TV, pool, spa, whirlpool tub, massage, bar, tours; no a/c, no TV in some rooms* 🟰 *AE, DC, MC, V* ⟟⟨ *BP.*

$$ 🏨 **El Sol.** A charming Spanish-German family tends to guests at one of
FodorsChoice those quintessential get-away-from-it-all places just 10 minutes down
★ the mountain from—and a noticeable few degrees warmer than—Santa Elena. Two fully furnished *ojoche*-wood cabins perch on the mountainside on the 25-acre farm. Every vantage point in the cabins—the living area, the bed, the desk, the shower, and even the toilet—has stupendous views. The property has 3 km (2 mi) of trails, a stone-walled pool, and a Finnish sauna. Meals can be arranged and taken in the main house or brought to your cabin. ⊠ *4 km/2½ mi southwest of Santa Elena* ☎ *645–5838* 🖷 *645–5042* ⊕ *www.elsolnuestro.com* 🛏 *2 cabins* 🍴 *Restaurant, pool, sauna, horseback riding; no a/c, no room phones, no room TVs* 🟰 *No credit cards* ⟟⟨ *EP.*

$ 🏨 **Swiss Hotel Miramontes.** Switzerland meets the cloud forest at this Swiss-owned and -operated small inn. Each room has a private porch. Guests have access to a private orchid garden with over 300 varieties. If you're tired of rice and beans, the restaurant serves a variety of Swiss, Austrian, Italian, and French dishes. ⊠ *1 km south of Santa Elena* ☎ *645–5152* 🖷 *645–5297* ⊕ *www.swisshotelmiramontes.com* 🛏 *8 rooms, 2 chalets* 🍴 *Restaurant, fans, tours; no a/c* 🟰 *MC, V* ⟟⟨ *BP.*

★ ¢–$ 🏨 **Arco Iris Lodge.** Just outside the center of town, this tranquil spot has cozy cabins set on 4 acres of birding trails. Cabin decor ranges from rustic to plush, but all lodgings come with porches. Start your day with a delicious breakfast buffet, including homemade bread and granola. The laid-back German management can provide good advice about how to spend your time in the area. ⊠ *70 m south of Banco Nacional, Santa Elena* ☎ *645–5067* 🖷 *645–5022* ⊕ *www.arcoirislodge.com* 🛏 *18 cabins* 🍴 *Horseback riding, laundry service; no a/c, no room phones, no room TVs* 🟰 *AE, MC, V* ⟟⟨ *EP.*

¢ 🏨 **El Bosque Lodge.** Convenient to the Bajo del Tigre nature trail and Meg's Stables, El Bosque's quiet, simple rooms are grouped around a central camping area. A bridge crosses a stream and leads to the hotel.

Brick-oven pizzas are served on the veranda. ⊠ *2½ km/1½ mi southeast of Santa Elena on road to Monteverde Reserve, Monteverde* ☎ *645–5318* 📠 *645–5129* ⊕ *www.bosquelodge.com* ✉ *Apdo. 5655, Santa Elena* 🛏 *29 rooms* ⚬ *Restaurant, bar, laundry service, Internet room; no a/c, no room TVs* ▭ *AE, DC, MC, V* ¶◎ *EP.*

¢ 🖾 **Pensión Monteverde Inn.** One of the cheapest inns in the area is quite far from the Monteverde Reserve entrance, on a 28-acre private preserve. The bedrooms are basic, but they have stunning views of the Gulf of Nicoya as well as hardwood floors, firm beds, and powerful, hot showers. Home cooking is served by the chatty David and María Savage and family. ⊠ *5 km/3 mi past Butterfly Garden on turnoff road, Cerro Plano* ☎📠 *645–5156* 🛏 *10 rooms* ⚬ *Dining room; no a/c, no room phones, no room TVs* ▭ *No credit cards* ¶◎ *BP.*

Shopping

Arts & Crafts Part gallery, part workshop, **Art House** (⊠ 1½ km/1 mi southeast of Santa Elena on road to Monteverde Reserve ☎ 645–5275) has five rooms of colorful, locally made carvings, masks, wall hangings, and hammocks. **Atmosphera** (⊠ Turnoff to Jardín de Mariposas, Cerro Plano ☎ 645–6555) specializes in locally made primitivist wood carvings.

Bromelia's (⊠ 100 m east of CASEM, Monteverde ☎ 645–6272) bills itself as a bookstore, but sells colorful batiks, masks, and jewelry, too. The **Cooperativa de Artesanía de Santa Elena y Monteverde** (CASEM; ⊠ Next to El Bosque hotel, Monteverde ☎ 645–5190) artisans' cooperative sells locally made crafts, mostly by women. The prices are much higher than at most other places. **Coopesanta Elena** (⊠ Next to CASEM ☎ 645–5901) is the distributor for packages of the area's gourmet Café Monteverde coffee and accoutrements.

The **Community Art Center** (⊠ 50 m southwest of Cheese Factory ☎ 645–6121) exhibits and sells the works of local artists and artisans.

The **Hummingbird Gallery** (⊠ Just outside entrance to Monteverde Reserve ☎ 645–5030) sells books, gifts, T-shirts, great Costa Rican coffee, prints, and slides by nature specialists Michael and Patricia Fogden, as well as watercolors by nature artist Sarah Dowell.

Nightlife

"Wild nightlife" takes on a particular meaning here. You can still get up close with nature after the sun has gone down. Several of the reserves have guided evening walks—advance reservations and separate admission are required—and the Ranario and Serpentario keep evening hours. Noted area biologist Richard LaVal presents a slide show

---

THE UBIQUITOUS SODA

In Costa Rica the word *soda* has nothing to do with a carbonated beverage. (That's a *gaseosa* here.) Instead a soda is a small, often family-run restaurant frequented by locals that you'll find in every town and city. Don't expect anything as fancy as a menu. A board usually lists specials of the day. The lunchtime *casado* (literally, "married")—a "marriage" of chicken, pork, or beef with rice, beans, cabbage salad, and natural fruit drink—sets you back about $2. Just pay the cashier when you're done.

called **Sounds and Scenes of the Cloud Forest** at the Monteverde Lodge nightly at 6:15 ($5). Advance reservations are required.

The area now has a splendid concert venue, the **Anfiteatro Monteverde** (Monteverde Amphitheater) (✉100 m east of CASEM, Monteverde ☎ 645–6272), which opened in

2005. The semi-open-air facility adjoins the Moon Shiva restaurant—your ticket stub entitles you to a dinner discount there—and resembles a giant cocoon with 200 concrete terraced seats. Dress warmly: evenings get chilly here.

To & from Monteverde & Santa Elena

Monteverde is 167 km/104 mi (5 hrs) northwest of San José. Santa Elena is 6 km/4 mi (30 mins) north of Monteverde and 35 km/22 mi (2 hrs) southeast of Tilarán.

Getting here means negotiating some of the country's legendarily rough roads, but don't let that deter you from a visit. Years of promises to pave the way up here have collided with politics and scarce funds, but many residents remain just as happy to keep Monteverde out of the reach of tour buses and day-trippers. Your own vehicle gives you the greatest flexibility, but a burgeoning number of shuttle-van services connect Monteverde with San José and other tourist destinations throughout the country. And once you're here, if without wheels, the community's rugged taxis can get you from hotel to restaurant to reserve. **Desafío Adventures** (✉ Across from Supermercado La Esperanza ☎ 645–5874 ⊕ www.desafiocostarica.com) provides a fast, popular three-hour transfer between Monteverde and La Fortuna. The taxi-boat-taxi service costs $21 one-way.

If your bones can take it, a very rough track leads from Tilarán via Cabeceras to Santa Elena, near the Monteverde Cloud Forest Biological Reserve, doing away with the need to cut across to the Pan-American Highway. You need a 4WD vehicle and you should inquire locally about the current condition of the road. The views of Nicoya Peninsula, Lake Arenal, and Volcán Arenal reward those willing to bump around a bit. Note, too, that you don't really save much time—on a good day, it takes about 2½ hours as opposed to the 3 required via Cañas and Río Lagarto on the highway.

Monteverde & Santa Elena Essentials

🏧 Bank/ATM **Banco Nacional** ✉ 50 m north of bus station, Santa Elena ☎ 645–5610.
🏥 Medical Clinic **Seguro Social** ✉150 m south of soccer field, Santa Elena ☎645–5076.
💊 Pharmacy **Farmacia Vitosi** ✉ Across from La Esperanza supermarket, Santa Elena ☎ 645–5004.
ℹ️ Tourist Information **InfoMonteverde** ✉ Across from La Esperanza Supermarket, Santa Elena ☎ 645–6565.

CAÑO NEGRO REFUGE AREA

Long a favorite among fishing enthusiasts and bird watchers, this remote area is off the beaten track and may be difficult to get to if your time in Costa Rica is short. You can cross into Nicaragua via Los Chiles here but it is not easy, and in light of the recent border disputes with Nicaragua, we do not recommend it.

Caño Negro National Wildlife Refuge

12

Fodor'sChoice
★

A lowland rain-forest reserve in the far northern reaches of Costa Rica near the Nicaraguan border, Refugio Nacional de Vida Silvestre Caño Negro covers 98 square km (38 square mi). Caño Negro has suffered severe deforestation over the years, but most of the Río Frío is still lined with trees, and the park's vast lake is an excellent place to watch such waterfowl as jabiru, anhinga, and the roseate spoonbill, as well as a host of resident exotic animals. In the dry season, you can ride horses, but the visit here chiefly entails a wildlife-spotting boat tour. Caño Negro can be reached from the Nuevo Arenal–La Fortuna area, or you can approach via Upala (a bus from here takes 45 minutes). Visiting with a tour company is the best way to see the park. ⚍ *$7* ⊘ *Daily 7–4.*

> ### WORD OF MOUTH
>
> "[Caño Negro Wildlife Refuge] is where we saw the most diversity in wildlife. We saw Jesus Christ lizards, caimans, iguanas, a sloth taking a bath right at the river edge, white-faced monkeys right next to the boat, [and] howler and spider monkeys in the trees in the distance."   –cachas

Outdoor Activities

Several La Fortuna–area tour companies have trips to Caño Negro: **Sunset Tours** (☎ 479–9800 ⊕ www.sunsettourscr.com) runs top-notch, informative daylong or half-day tours, among the best in the country, to Caño Negro for $48. Bring your jungle juice: the mosquitoes are voracious. **Jacamar Naturalist Tours** (☎ 479–9767 ⊕ www.arenaltours.com) is a well-established tour operator with three-hour boat trips ($50) on the Río Frío in the Caño Negro Nature Preserve.

Where to Stay

$$ 🏨 **Caño Negro Natural Lodge.** That such an upscale property exists in this remote place might amaze you, but this Italian-designed, family-operated resort on the east side of the reserve is never pretentious. Rooms have high ceilings, colorful drapes and bedspreads, and huge showers; some rooms have bunk beds. There are two- and three-day packages available for anglers and nonanglers alike. The lodge has a variety of meal options; most guests opt for taking all meals here, since there are few other restaurants in town. Horseback riding can be arranged and miniature golf, croquet, and badminton are a few of the on-site diversions. ⊠ *Caño Negro village* ☎ *471–1428, 265–2560 in San José* 🖷 *265–4561* ⊕ *www.canonegrolodge.com* ⤳ *22 rooms* ⚘ *Restau-*

CLOSE UP

A Biological Superpower

COSTA RICA'S FORESTS HOLD AN array of flora and fauna so vast and diverse that scientists haven't even named thousands of the species found here. The country covers less than 0.03% of the Earth's surface, yet it contains nearly 5% of the planet's plant and animal species. Costa Rica has at least 9,000 plant species, including more than 1,200 types of orchids, some 2,000 kinds of butterflies, and 876 bird species.

Costa Rica's biological diversity is the result of its tropical location, its varied topography, and the many microclimates resulting from the combination of mountains, valleys, and lowlands. It can also be attributed to Costa Rica's geological youth. Five million years ago this patch of land didn't even exist—in its place was a huge canal separating North and South America, where the Pacific and Atlantic oceans flowed together. About three million years ago the movement of tectonic plates created the land bridge that is now Costa Rica and Panama, which became a pathway for flora and fauna that had never coexisted.

Costa Rica's enormous natural diversity is in many ways the result of

the intercontinental exchange, but the country's flora and fauna actually add up to more than what has passed between the continents. Although it is a biological corridor, the isthmus also acts as a filter, a hospitable haven to many species that couldn't complete the journey from one hemisphere to the other. The rain forests of Costa Rica's Caribbean and southwestern lowlands, for example, are the most northerly home of such southern species as the crab-eating raccoon and the dreaded jungle pit viper known as the bushmaster. The tropical dry forests of the northern Pacific slope are the southern limit for such North American species as the white-throated magpie-jay and the Virginia opossum. And then there are the tourists—migrants, that is—such as the dozens of northern bird species that spend their winter holidays in Costa Rica, among them the Tennessee warbler, western tanager, and yellow-bellied sapsucker. Costa Rica's many physical barriers and microclimates have also fostered the development of indigenous plants and animals, such as the mangrove hummingbird and mountain salamander.

3

---

rant, pool, whirlpool tub, fishing, bar, laundry service, meeting room, tours; no room phones, in-room safes, no room TVs ⊟ *AE, MC, V* ⏍ *CP.*

$ ⌨ **Fishing Club Caño Negro.** Despite the name, all are welcome here, though the lodge is best known for its fishing tours, equipment and boat rental, and nearby lake filled with tarpon and bass. Four white bungalows of high-quality wood each contain two bright, sparkling rooms with terracotta tile floors, and are arranged around the wooded property. The produce from the lodge's citrus orchard ends up on your breakfast plate. ✉ *Caño Negro village* ☎ *471–1012* 🖷 *656–0260* ⊕ *www.canonegro. com* ⇱ *8 rooms* ⚒ *Restaurant, fans, fishing, horseback riding, bar, tours; no a/c, no room phones, no room TVs* ⊟ *AE, MC, V* ⏍ *BP.*

To & from Caño Negro
91 km/57 mi (1½ hrs) northwest of La Fortuna.

The highway from La Fortuna to Los Chiles is one the best maintained in the northern lowlands. You can catch public buses in San José at Terminal Atlántico Norte twice a day, a trip of about five hours. Public buses also operate between La Fortuna and Los Chiles. If they have room, many tour companies (Sunset Tours included) will allow you to ride along with them on their shuttles, for a cost of around $10.

THE PUERTO VIEJO LOOP

The Sarapiquí River gave its name to this region at the foot of the Cordillera Central mountain range. To the west is the rain forest of Braulio Carrillo National Park, and to the east are Tortuguero National Park and Barra del Colorado National Wildlife Refuge. These splendid national parks share the region with thousands of acres of farmland, including palm, banana, and pineapple plantations, as well as cattle ranching. Cheap land and rich soil brought a wave of Ticos to this area a half-century ago. Until the construction of Highway 126 in 1957, which connects the area to San José, this was one of the most isolated parts of Costa Rica, with little or no tourism. Government homesteading projects brought many residents, who cleared massive swathes of the rain forest for cattle grazing and agriculture. Now, ironically, old-growth lowland rain forest, montane cloud forest, and wetlands exist only within the borders of the national parks.

Poás Volcano

⑬ Towering to the north of Alajuela, the verdant mass of Volcán Poás is covered with a quilt of farms and topped by a dark green shawl of cloud forest. Arenal may be Costa Rica's most famous volcano, but you walk right up to the crater here at Poás. (Authorities are closely monitoring the volcano's activity following several eruptions in March 2006, the first significant activity since 1994. Access is open at this writing.) A paved road leads all the way from Alajuela to its 8,800-foot summit, winding past coffee fields, patches of forest, pastures, fern farms, and increasingly spectacular views of the Central Valley. Most of the volcano's southern slope is covered with coffee, but the higher altitudes, which are too cold for that crop, hold screened-in fern and flower farms, neat rows of strawberries, and the light green pastures of dairy farms. Only the volcano's upper slopes and summit are still covered with cloud forest, which stretches northward toward Cerro Congo and east toward Volcán Barva. The road divides at Poasito, not far from the summit, where the route to the left leads to the national park, and the one to the right heads toward the intersection of Vara Blanca. At Vara Blanca, you can turn left for the Waterfall Gardens and Northern Zone, or continue straight to wind your way down the slopes of Volcán Barva to Heredia.

Exploring

Fodor'sChoice The 57-square-km (22-square-mi) **Poás Volcano National Park** (Parque
★ Nacional Volcán Poás) protects epiphyte-laden cloud and elfin (small-

tree) forest near the summit as well as a blue-green crater lake and the volcano's massive active crater. The main crater, nearly 1½ km (1 mi) across and 1,000 feet deep, is one of the largest active craters in the world. The sight of this vast, multicolored pit with smoking fumaroles and a gurgling, gray-turquoise sulfurous lake is captivating. All sense of scale is absent here, as the crater is devoid of vegetation. No one is allowed to venture into the crater, or walk along its edge.

The peak is frequently shrouded in mist, and many who come here see little beyond the lip of the crater. Be patient and wait awhile, especially if some wind is blowing—the clouds can disappear quickly. ■ TIP→ **The earlier in the day you go, the better your chance of a clear view. Aim to get there before 10 AM.** If you're lucky, you'll see the famous geyser in action, spewing a column of gray mud high into the air. Poás last had a major eruption in 1953 and is thought to be approaching another active phase; at any sign of danger the park is closed to visitors. It can be very cold and wet up top, so dress accordingly. If you come ill equipped, you can duck under a *sombrilla de pobre* (poor man's umbrella) plant, the leaves of which grow to diameters of 4 to 5 feet.

The park has a paved road that leads from the visitor center to the edge of the active crater, from which two trails head into the forest. The second trail, on the right just before the crater, winds through a thick mesh of shrubs and dwarf trees to the eerie but beautiful **Laguna Botos** (Botos Lake), which occupies an extinct crater. It takes 30 minutes to walk there and back. ⊠ *From Alajuela, drive north through town, and follow signs.* ☎ *482–2424, 192 in Costa Rica* ⌑ *$7* ☉ *Daily 8:30–3:30.*

★ Five magnificent waterfalls are the main attractions at **La Paz Waterfall Gardens,** on the eastern edge of Volcán Poás National Park, but they are complemented by the beauty of the surrounding cloud forest, an abundance of hummingbirds and other avian species, and the country's biggest butterfly garden. A concrete trail leads down from the visitor center to the multilevel, screened butterfly observatory and continues to gardens where hummingbird feeders attract swarms of those multicolored creatures. The trail then enters the cloud forest, where it leads to a series of metal stairways that let you descend into a steep gorge to viewing platforms near each of the waterfalls. A free shuttle will transport you from the trail exit back to the main building, if you prefer to avoid the hike uphill. Several alternative paths lead from the main trail through the cloud forest and along the river's quieter upper stretch, providing options for hours of exploration—it takes about 1½ hours to hike down the waterfall trail. (Enter by 3:45 to give yourself adequate time.) The visitor center has a gift shop and open-air cafeteria with a great view. The gardens are 20 km (12 mi) northeast of Alajuela, and are a stop on many day-long tours from San José that take in the Poás volcano or are coffee tours. ⊠ *6 km/3 mi north of Vara Blanca* ☎ *482–2720, 225–0643 in San José* ⊕ *www.waterfallgardens.com* ⌑ *$25; $15 children under 12; $37 with lunch; $21 children under 12* ☉ *Daily 8:30–5:30.*

Outdoor Activities

HORSEBACK RIDING Guided horseback tours with **Poás Volcano Lodge** (⊠ 500 m west of gas station ☎ 482–2194) take place in the cloud forest of Finca Legua, a private reserve 5 km (3 mi) north of the lodge. Daily tours ($65), which include lunch, run from 9 AM to 2 PM. Make reservations.

Where to Stay & Eat

$–$$
Fodor'sChoice ★ ✕ **Chubascos.** Amid tall pines and colorful flowers on the upper slopes of Poás Volcano, this popular restaurant has a small menu of traditional Tico dishes and delicious daily specials. Choose from the full selection of casados and platters of *gallos* (homemade tortillas with meat, cheese, or potato fillings). The *refrescos* (fresh fruit drinks) are top-drawer, especially the ones made from locally grown *fresas* (strawberries) and *moras* (blackberries) blended with milk. ⊠ *1 km/½ mi north of Fraijanes* ☎ *482–2280* ▭ *AE, MC, V.*

$ ✕ **Jaulares.** Named after the *jaul,* a tree common in the nearby cloud forest, this spacious restaurant specializes in grilled meat, though there are also several fish dishes and *chicharrones* (deep-fried meaty pork rinds). All the cooking is done with wood, which adds to the rustic ambience of terra-cotta floors, bare wooden beams, and sylvan surroundings. The house specialty, *lomito Jaulares* (Jaulares tenderloin), is a strip of grilled meat served with *gallo pinto* (rice and beans) and a mild *salsa criollo* (creole sauce). Though primarily a lunch spot, Jaulares stays open until midnight on weekends for concerts—Latin music on Friday nights and rock on Saturday nights. Four basic cabinas in back are an inexpensive overnight option, though you'll need to reserve them early for concert nights. ⊠ *2 km/1 mi north of Fraijanes* ☎ *482–2155* ▭ *AE, DC, MC, V.*

★ **$$$–$$$$** ▤ **Peace Lodge.** These rooms overlooking the misty forest of La Paz Waterfall Gardens seem like something out of the *Lord of the Rings,* with their curved, clay-stucco walls, hardwood floors (note that all but the top floors can be noisy due to creaky footsteps), stone fireplaces (gas), and four-poster beds made of varnished logs, complete with mosquito-net canopy. They are proper abodes for elfin kings, especially the spacious, grottolike bathrooms with two showers, a whirlpool tub, tropical gardens, and private waterfall. Most hotels settle for a room with a bath. Peace Lodge gives you a bath with a room. And as if that weren't enough, you can soak in your second whirlpool tub on a porch with a cloud-forest view. Being able to explore the waterfall gardens before they open is another perk. The cuisine here is a couple of notches below the accommodations. ⊠ *3 km/2 mi north of Vara*

Blanca ☎ *482–2720, 225–0643 in San José* 📠 *482–2722, 225–1082 in San José* ⊕ *www.waterfallgardens.com* ⇋ *17 rooms, 1 villa* ⚲ *Restaurant, fans, in-room hot tubs, minibars, cable TV, massage, gift shop; no a/c, no room phones* ▱ *AE, DC, MC, V* ⎮○⎮ *BP.*

$–$$ ⊡ **Poás Volcano Lodge.** The rustic architecture of this former dairy farmhouse, with rough stone walls and pitched beam roof, fits perfectly into the rolling pastures and forests that surround it. The interior mixes Persian rugs with textiles from Latin America, and Guaitil Indian pottery with North American pieces. The oversize sunken fireplace may be the lodge's most alluring feature. All rooms are different, so if possible, look at a few before you decide: one has an exquisite stone bathtub. The less expensive rooms, while not as opulent, have a more dependable supply of hot water. A small dairy farm and garden supply the kitchen with ingredients for the hearty breakfasts. ⊠ *6 km/4 mi east of Chubascos restaurant, on road to Vara Blanca* ⛫ *Apdo. 5723–1000, San José* ☎ *482–2194* 📠 *482–2513* ⊕ *www.poasvolcanolodge.com* ⇋ *11 rooms, 9 with bath* ⚲ *Restaurant, billiards, horseback riding, Ping-Pong, laundry service, Internet, airport shuttle; no a/c, no room phones, no room TVs* ▱ *AE, DC, MC, V* ⎮○⎮ *BP.*

$ ⊡ **Siempreverde B&B.** A night at this isolated B&B in the heart of a coffee plantation might be as close as you'll ever come to being a coffee farmer. The attractive wooden house has four nicely decorated rooms upstairs, with hardwood floors and small windows; the room downstairs is a bit dark. There are also a living room, kitchen, lounge, and terrace in back where breakfast is served. Photos of the coffee harvest decorate the walls, and just beyond the yard and manicured gardens that surround the house, neat rows of coffee plants stretch off into the distance. ⊠ *12 km/5 mi northwest of Tribunales de Justicia de Alajuela, turn left at colegio (high school)* ☎ *449–5562* 📠 *239–0450* ⊕ *www.siempreverdebandb.com* ⇋ *7 rooms with bath* ⚲ *Restaurant; no a/c, no room phones, no room TVs* ▱ *AE, DC, MC, V* ⎮○⎮ *BP.*

To & from Poás Volcano

37 km/23 mi (45 mins) north of Alajuela, 57 km/35 mi (1 hr) north of San José.

■ TIP→ **Avoid taking a public bus to the park, as it can take up to five hours.** Taxis from San José are around $80 (and around $40 from Alajuela). From the Pan-American Highway north of Alajuela, follow the signs for Poás. The road is in relatively good condition.

Braulio Carrillo National Park

⓮ In a country where deforestation is still rife, hiking through Parque Nacional Braulio Carrillo is a rare opportunity to witness dense, primary tropical cloud forest. The park owes its foundation to the public outcry provoked by the construction of the highway of the same name through this region in the late 1970s—the government bowed to pressure from environmentalists, and somewhat ironically, the park is the most accessible one from the capital thanks to the highway. Covering 443 square km (171 square mi), Braulio Carrillo's extremely diverse terrain ranges from 108 feet to about 9,500 feet above sea level and extends from the central volcanic range down the Caribbean slope to La Selva research station near Puerto Viejo de Sarapiquí. The park protects a series of ecosystems ranging from the cloud forests on the upper slopes to the tropical wet forest of the Magsasay sector; it is home to 6,000 tree species, 500 bird species, and 135 mammal species.

For all its immense size and proximity to the capital, visitor facilities in the park are limited. Your exposure will most likely take place when you pass through on the way to the Caribbean, or when you stay at any of the lodgings that fringe Braulio Carrillo. Penetrating the park's depths is a project for the truly intrepid.

The **Zurquí ranger station** is to the right of the highway, ½ km (¼ mi) before the Zurquí Tunnel. Here a short trail loops through the cloud forest. Hikes are steep; wear hiking boots to protect yourself from mud, slippage, and snakes. The main trail through primary forest, 1½ km (1 mi) long, culminates in a *mirador* (lookout point), but alas, the highway mars the view. Monkeys, tapirs, jaguars, kinkajous, sloths, raccoons, margays, and porcupines all live in this forest, and resident birds include the quetzal and the eagle. Orchids, bromeliads, heliconias, fungi, and mushrooms live closer to the floor. Another trail leads into the forest to the right, beginning about 17 km (11 mi) after the tunnel, where it follows the Quebrada González, a stream with a cascade and swimming hole. There are no campsites in this part of the park. The **Carrillo ranger station,** 22 km (14 mi) northeast along the highway from Zurquí, marks the beginning of trails that are less steep. Farther north on this highway, near the park entrance/exit toward Guápiles is the **Quebrada Gonzalez** ranger station. To the east of Heredia, a road climbs **Barva Volcano** (⇨ *below*) from San Rafael. ☎ *283–8004 Sistemas de Areas de Conservación, 192 (national parks hotline)* 🖅 *$7* ⊘ *Daily 7–4.*

The 9,500-foot summit of **Barva Volcano** is the highest point in Braulio Carrillo National Park. Dormant for 300 years now, Barva is massive: its lower slopes are almost completely planted with coffee fields and hold more than a dozen small towns, nearly all of which are named after saints. On the upper slopes are pastures lined with exotic pines and the occasional native oak or cedar, giving way to the botanical diversity of the cloud forest near the top. The air is usually cool near the summit, which combines with the pines and pastures to evoke the European or North American countryside.

Barva's misty, luxuriant summit is the only part of Braulio Carrillo where camping is allowed, and it's a good place to see the rare resplendent quetzal early in the morning. Because it's somewhat hard to reach, Barva receives a mere fraction of the crowds that flock to the summits of Poás and Irazú. A two- to four-hour hike in from the Barva ranger station takes you to the main crater, which is about 540 feet in diameter. Its almost vertical sides are covered in *sombrillas de pobre* (poor man's umbrellas), a plant that thrives in the highlands, and oak trees laden with epiphytes (nonparasitic plants that grow on other plants). The crater is filled with an otherworldly, black lake. Farther down the track into the forest lies a smaller crater lake. ■ TIP→ **Bring rain gear, boots, and a warm shirt. Stay on the trail when hiking anywhere in Braulio; even experienced hikers who know the area have lost their way up here, and the rugged terrain makes wandering through the woods very dangerous. In addition, muggings of hikers have been reported in the park. Go with a ranger if possible.**

For access to the volcano, start from Sacramento, north of Heredia. North of Barva de Heredia the road grows narrow and steep. At Sacramento the paved road turns to dirt, growing worse as it nears the Barva ranger station. We recommend a 4WD vehicle, especially during the rainy season. From the ranger station you can take a 4WD vehicle over the extremely rocky road to the park entrance (dry season only), or hike up on foot. The walk through the cloud forest to the crater's two lakes takes two to four hours, but your efforts should be rewarded by great views (as long as you start before 8 AM, to avoid the mist). ⊠ *Access via the park's Barva ranger station* ☎ *283–5906, 192 in Costa Rica* ⤇ *$7 (in addition to $6 Braulio Carrillo Park entrance)* ⊘ *Tues.–Sun. 7–4.*

San Rafael de Heredia, 2 km (1 mi) northeast of Heredia, is a quiet, mildly affluent coffee town with a large church notable for its stained-glass windows and bright interior. The road north from the church winds its way up Barva Volcano to the hotels Chalet Tirol and La Condesa, ending atop the Monte de la Cruz lookout point.

Outdoor Activities

HIKING The upper slopes of **Barva Volcano** have excellent hiking conditions: cool air, vistas, and plentiful birds. The crater lakes topping the volcano can be reached only on foot, and if you haven't got a 4WD vehicle, you'll also have to trek from Sacramento up to the entrance of Braulio Carrillo National Park. The trails are frequently muddy; ask about their condition at the ranger station. The **Sendero Botello** trail, on the east side of the park (entrance near the Quebrada Gonzáles ranger station off the Guápiles Highway), is a better choice for casual hikers.

HORSEBACK Horseback-riding tours along the
RIDING upper slopes of Volcán Barva combine views of the Central Valley with close exposure to the cloud forest and resident bird life. **Canopy Adventure** (⊠ Passo Llano, 7 km/4 mi north of Barva de Heredia ☎ 266–0782) runs horseback tours suitable for all levels of riders in its private cloud-forest reserve above San José de la Montaña. Rides can be combined with a canopy tour and lunch ($75); reserve in advance.

> ### PURA VIDA, A WAY OF LIFE
>
> *Pura vida* means, literally, "pure life," and is used by Costa Ricans to express agreement, greeting, leave-taking, and basically anything positive. If someone asks "¿Pura vida?" (basically, "How's it going?") the response could also be "¡Pura vida!" ("Excellent!") It might also be used to wish someone luck or to say "Have fun!" Once you set foot in this ecological wonderland, you realize that pura vida is also a philosophy of life, and undoubtedly one reason why nearly 2 million visitors come here each year.

Where to Stay

$$ 🏨 **Hotel & Casino La Condesa.** The stone fireplace surrounded by armchairs and a small bar in the La Condesa lobby is one of the many facets of the hotel that suggest a lodge you'd expect to find in a more northern latitude. In the central courtyard, topped by a giant skylight, is one of the hotel's three restaurants. A tropical garden is similarly enclosed in the pool area. Guest rooms are carpeted and tastefully furnished, and each has a picture window. Suites have bedroom lofts, sitting areas, and the hotel's best views. ⊠ *Next to Castillo Country Club, 10 km/6 mi north of San Rafael de Heredia* ☎ *267–6000* 🖨 *267–6200* ⊕ *www. hotellacondesa.com* ⤶ *60 rooms, 36 suites* ⚲ *3 restaurants, in-room safes, some kitchens, minibars, cable TV, indoor pool, whirlpool tub, horseback riding, 2 bars, casino, laundry service, meeting room, car rental, tours; no a/c* ⊟ *AE, DC, MC, V* ¶◯¶ *BP.*

$ 🏨 **Las Ardillas.** Surrounded by old pines on a country road, these unpretentious log cabins are inviting retreats for those looking to lock themselves up in front of a fireplace and tune out the world. The small on-site spa is a good reason to venture from the comfortable, romantic rooms. The restaurant specializes in meats roasted over a wood fire and has a nice selection of Spanish wines. All rooms have modest wood furniture and queen-size beds. ⊠ *Main road, Guacalillo de San José de la Montaña* ⌂ *Apdo. 44–309, Barva* ☎ *260–2172* 🖨 *266–0211* ⤶ *18 cabins* ⚲ *Restaurant, kitchenettes, cable TV, whirlpool tub, massage, sauna, spa, bar; no a/c, no room phones* ⊟ *AE, MC, V* ¶◯¶ *BP.*

To & from Braulio Carrillo National Park
30 km/19 mi (45 mins) north of San José.

From San José, travel northeast on Calle 3, which becomes the Guápiles Highway (Hwy. 32), toward Limón. This highway winds through the park, entering at the main ranger station, Zurquí, and exiting at the Quebrada Gonzalez ranger station. The Barva station is on the west side of the park, north of Zurquí, and is the easiest to access. From Heredia, drive north to Sacramento on Highway 114. The station is 4 km (2½ mi) northeast of Sacramento on a trail that's accessible on foot or by 4WD (except during heavy rains).

Any bus going to Guapiles, Síquirres, and Puerto Viejo de Sarapiquí can drop you off at the Zurquí ranger station. Buses ($2) depart from San José Monday through Saturday from the TUASA bus station and Sundays from the central market and return from the park at 2:30 PM. A cab from San José costs $40–$50. A number of tour companies offer one-day tours from San José.

Puerto Viejo de Sarapiquí

⑮ In the 19th century, Puerto Viejo de Sarapiquí was a thriving river port and the only link with the coastal lands straight east, now Barra del Colorado National Wildlife Refuge and Tortuguero National Park. Fortunes nose-dived with the construction of the coastal canal from the town of Moín, and today Puerto Viejo has a slightly run-down air. The activities of the Nicaraguan Contras made this a danger zone in the 1980s, but now that the political situation has improved, boats once again ply the old route up the Río Sarapiquí to the Río San Juan on the Nicaraguan frontier, from where you can travel downstream to Barra del Colorado or Tortuguero. A few tour companies have Sarapiquí River tours with up to Class III rapids in the section between Chilamate and La Virgen with plenty of wildlife to see. If you prefer to leave the driving to them, many of the lodges operate boat tours on the tamer sections of the river.

> **CAUTION**
>
> Don't confuse Puerto Viejo de Sarapiquí with Puerto Viejo de Talamanca on the south Caribbean coast (Puerto Viejo de Talamanca, *in* Chapter 7). Locals refer to each as simply "Puerto Viejo." Buses for both towns depart from San José's Gran Terminal del Caribe with nothing more than a PUERTO VIEJO sign in the station to designate either.

Exploring

Bats are not blind, contrary to popular belief, and most have no interest in sucking your blood. Just a couple of things you learn on the **Bat Tour** at the nonprofit **Tirimbina Rainforest Center.** The center encompasses 750 acres of primary forest and 8 km (5 mi) of trails, some of them traversing hanging bridges at canopy level. Reservations are required for all tours. ⊠ *La Virgen de Sarapiquí, 17 km/11 mi southwest of Puerto Viejo* ☎ *761–1579* ⊕ *www.tirimbina.org* ⊠ *$10, $15 guided tour, $15 bat tour* ☉ *Daily 7–5, bat tour daily 7:30 PM, guided tours 8 AM and 2 PM.*

Costa Rica's indigenous peoples don't get the visibility of those in Guatemala or Mexico, probably because they number only 40,000 out of a population of 4 million. The **Museo de Culturas Indígenas Doctora María Eugenia Bozzoli** (Dr. María Eugenia Bozzoli Museum of Indigenous Cultures), part of the Centro Neotrópico Sarapiquís, provides a well-rounded all-under-one-roof introduction to the subject. Nearly 400 artifacts of the Boruca, Bribri, Cabécar, Guaymí, and Maleku peoples are displayed, including masks, musical instruments, and shamanic healing sticks. Start by watching a 17-minute video introduction, *Man and Nature in Pre-Columbian Costa Rica.* A botanical garden next door cultivates medicinal plants still used by many traditional groups. In 1999 researchers discovered an archaeological site on the grounds that contains pre-Columbian tombs and petroglyphs dating from the 15th century. The site is still under study. ⊠ *La Virgen de Sarapiquí, 17 km/11 mi southwest of Puerto Viejo* ☎ *761–1418* ⊕ *www.sarapiquis.org* ⊠ *$12 (includes guide)* ☉ *Daily 9–5.*

A working dairy farm and horse ranch, the **Hacienda Pozo Azul** runs guided tours of the ecologically sound 360-cattle dairy operation. It also has many adventure tours (⇨ Outdoor Activities, *below*). ⊠ *La Virgen de Sarapiquí, 17 km/11 mi southwest of Puerto Viejo* ☎ *761–1360, 877/810–6903 in North America* ⊕ *www.haciendapozoazul.com* ⊠ *$10* ☉ *By reservation.*

Heliconias abound at the aptly named **Heliconia Island** in the Sarapiquí River. Some 70 species of the flowering plant, a relative of the banana, are among the collections that populate five acres of botanical gardens here. Expect to see ample bird and butterfly life, too. ⊠ *La Chaves, 8*

km/5 mi south of Puerto Viejo de Sarapiquí ☎ *397–3948* 🖷 *766–6247*
⊕ *www.heliconiaisland.com* ✉ *$7.50* ⊙ *Daily 9–5.*

Outdoor Activities

Hacienda Pozo Azul (✉ La Virgen de Sarapiquí, 17 km/11 mi southwest
of Puerto Viejo ☎ 761–1360, 877/810–6903 in North America ⊕ www.
haciendapozoazul.com) is a dairy farm and ranch with biking, horseback riding, rafting, canopy tours, float tours, and rappelling excursions
that allow you to combine several activities in a day. **Hotel Gavilán Río
Sarapiquí** (☎ 766–6743 ⊕ www.gavilanlodge.com) runs wildlife- and
bird-watching tours from its site near Puerto Viejo de Sarapiquí up to
the San Juan River. Passports are required for the trip, since the San Juan
lies entirely within Nicaragua.

CANOPY TOUR   The canopy tour ($45) at **Hacienda Pozo Azul** (⇨ *above*) has 13 zip lines,
one topping 300 feet.

HORSEBACK   Dairy farm **Hacienda Pozo Azul** (⇨ *above*) is also a horse ranch and has
RIDING   riding excursions for all experience levels through the region around La
Virgen. A two-hour tour is $30; a half-day is $45.

MOUNTAIN   **Aventuras de Sarapiquí** (☎ 766–6768 ⊕ www.sarapiqui.com/biking.
BIKING   html) has half-day and multiday biking trips for casual and serious riders. **Costa Rica Biking Adventure** (☎ 225–6591 ⊕ www.bikingincostarica.
com) runs one-day mountain-biking tours of the area. **Hacienda Pozo Azul**
(⇨ *above*) has half-day, full-day, and two-day rough-and-tumble back-
roads bike tours ($30–$50).

RAFTING   The Virgen del Socorro area is one of the most popular "put-in points"
for white-water rafters, and offers both Class II and III rapids. Trips leaving from the Chilamate put-in are more tranquil, with mostly Class I
rapids. The put-in point depends on the weather and season.

Several operators lead tours on the Sarapiquí River. Old standby **Costa
Rica Expeditions** (☎ 222–0333 🖷 257–1665 ⊕ www.costaricaexpeditions.
com) offers full-day trips on the Sarapiquí from San José. La Fortuna-based
Desafío (☎ 479–9464 ⊕ www.desafiocostarica.com) brings you in from
the west to the Sarapiquí River, but the distance is no longer than making the trip from San José. **Ríos Tropicales** (☎ 233–6455 ⊕ www.
riostropicales.com) takes in the Sarapiquí on day excursions from San José.

RAPPELLING   **Hacienda Pozo Azul** (⇨ *above*) guides you on a 90-foot river canyon descent ($20).

Where to Stay

★ **$$–$$$**   🏨 **Selva Verde Lodge.** Built on stilts over the Río Sarapiquí, this expan-
sive complex stands on the edge of a 2-square-km (1-square-mi) private
reserve of tropical rain forest and caters primarily to natural-history tours.
The buildings have wide verandas strung with hammocks, and the
rooms come with polished wood paneling and mosquito blinds. Activities include guided walks, boat trips, canoeing, rafting, and mountain
biking. Room prices include a bird-watching tour. Reserve a few weeks
ahead, especially in high season; the place is very popular with tour groups.
✉ *7 km/4 mi west of Puerto Viejo de Sarapiquí* ⊙ *Apdo. 55, Chilamate* ☎ *766–6800, 800/451–7111 in North America* 🖷 *766–6011*

⊕ *www.selvaverde.com* 🛏 *40 rooms, 5 bungalows* ⌂ *Restaurant, fans, pool, boating, horseback riding, bar, library, laundry service, meeting room; no a/c in some rooms, no room phones, no room TVs* 🖬 *AE, MC, V* ⦿ *EP, FAP.*

🦋 **$$** 🏨 **Centro Neotrópico Sarapiquís.** Overlooking the Rio Sarapiquí, the CNS is an environmental educational center, museum, gardens, and hotel all rolled into one. Three indigenous-inspired circular palenque buildings with palm-thatched roofs house the ample-size rooms. All come with a tile floor, pre-Columbian-style decor, and a private terrace. There's an extra cost to visit the center's numerous attractions. ⊠ *La Virgen de Sarapiquí, 17 km/11 mi southwest of Puerto Viejo* ☎ *761–1004* 🖷 *761–1415* ⊕ *www.sarapiquis.org* 🛏 *44 rooms* ⌂ *Restaurant, coffee shop, fans, bar, library, gift shop, laundry service, meeting room; no a/c, no phones in some rooms, no room TVs* 🖬 *AE, DC, MC, V* ⦿ *EP.*

$ 🏨 **Hotel Gavilán Río Sarapiquí.** Beautiful gardens run down to the river, and colorful tanagers and three types of toucan feast in the citrus trees. The two-story lodge has comfortable rooms with white walls, terra-cotta floors, and decorative crafts. The food, Costa Rican *comida típica* (typical fare), has earned its good reputation. Prime activities are horseback jungle treks and boat trips up the Río Sarapiquí. ⊠ *700 m north of Comando Atlántico (naval command)* ⊕ *www.gavilanlodge. com* 🗁 *Apdo. 445–2010, San José* ☎ *766–6743, 234–9507 in San José* 🖷 *253–6556* 🛏 *11 rooms* ⌂ *Restaurant, fans, whirlpool tub, fishing, horseback riding; no a/c, no room phones, no room TVs* 🖬 *AE, DC, MC, V* ⦿ *BP.*

¢ 🏨 **Posada Andrea Cristina.** Alexander Martinez and his wife Florabel own and operate this friendly and comfortable bed-and-breakfast. High-ceilinged rooms have private bathrooms and hot water. Two A-frame bungalows share a (cold-water-only) bathroom. All bungalows and rooms have private gardens with hammocks. ⊠ *½ km/¼ mi west of town, La Guaíra* ☎🖷 *766–6265* ⊕ *www.andreacristina.com* 🛏 *5 rooms, 2 bungalows with shared bath* ⌂ *Restaurant, tours; no a/c* 🖬 *No credit cards* ⦿ *BP.*

To & from Puerto Viejo de Sarapiquí
6½ km/4 mi north of La Selva.

The Carretera Braulio Carrillo (Braulio Carrillo Highway) runs from C. 3 in San José and passes the Zurquí and Quebrada González sectors of Braulio Carrillo National Park. It branches at Santa Clara, north of the park, with the paved Highway 4 continuing north to Puerto Viejo de Sarapiquí. Alternatively, an older winding road connects San José with Puerto Viejo de Sarapiquí, passing through Heredia and Vara Blanca. The former route is easier, with less traffic; the latter route is more scenic but heavily trafficked. (If you are at all prone to motion sickness, take the newer road.) The roads are mostly paved, with the usual rained-out dirt and rock sections; road quality depends on the time of year, the length of time since the last visit by a road crew, and/or the amount of rain dumped by the latest tropical storm. Heavy rains sometimes cause landslides that block the highway near the Zurquí Tunnel. Check conditions before you set out. ■ TIP→ **There are gas stations on the Braulio**

Carrillo Highway at the turnoff to Puerto Viejo de Sarapiquí, as well as just outside of town. Fill the tank when you get the chance.

Puerto Viejo de Sarapiquí Essentials

Bank/ATM **Banco Nacional** ⊠ 100 m east of soccer field ☎ 766-6263. **Banco Popular** ⊠ West corner of soccer field.

Medical Clinic **Red Cross** ⊠ West end of town ☎ 710-6901.

La Selva Biological Station

☼ ⑯ At the confluence of the Puerto Viejo and Sarapiquí rivers, La Selva packs about 420 bird species, 460 tree species, and 500 butterfly species into just 15 square km (6 square mi). Spottings might include the spider monkey, poison dart frog, agouti, collared peccary, and dozens of other rare creatures. ■ TIP➔ **If you want to see wildlife without having to rough it, skip Rara Avis and come here.** Extensive, well-marked trails and swing bridges connect habitats as varied as tropical wet forest, swamps, creeks, rivers, secondary regenerating forest, and pasture. The site is a project of the Organization for Tropical Studies, a research consortium of 63 U.S., Australian, and Latin American universities, and is one of three biological stations OTS operates in Costa Rica. To see the place, take an informative 3½-hour morning or afternoon nature walk with one of La Selva's bilingual guides, who are some of the country's best. Walks start every day at 8 AM and 1:30 PM. You can add a noontime lunch to your walk for $10; schedule it in advance. For a completely different view of the forest, set off on a guided dawn walk at 5:30 AM, or the night tour at 7 PM. Or get a group of at least five together and enroll in the Saturday-morning Bird-watching 101 course or one of the nature photo workshops, which can be arranged anytime—either is $40 per person. Young children won't feel left out either with a very basic nature-identification course geared to them. Advance reservations are required for the dawn and night walks as well as for the birdwatching, photography, or kids' courses. ☎ 766-6565 or 524-0628 📠 766-6535 or 524-0629 ⊕ www. ots.ac.cr ✑ OTS, Apdo. 676-2050, San Pedro ⊠ Nature walk $34, morning and afternoon walks $40, dawn or night walk $40 ⊙ Walks daily at 8 AM and 1:30 PM.

Where to Stay

$$ ▦ **La Selva.** Other lodges provide more comfort for the money, but none can match La Selva's tropical nature experience. The dorm-style rooms have large bunk beds, tile floors, and lots of screened windows. The restaurant, something like a school cafeteria, serves decent food but has a very limited schedule (reserve ahead). It's a good idea to pay the full-board fee, which includes a guided nature walk and three meals a day with your room rate, since there's nowhere else to eat. Priority is given to researchers, so advance reservations are essential. ⊠ 6 km/3½ mi south of Puerto Viejo de Sarapiquí ☎ 766-6565, 524-0628 in San José ✑ OTS, Apdo. 676-2050, San Pedro 📠 524-0629 ➔ 60 bunk beds share 12 baths, 18 cabins � Dining room, fans, laundry facilities, gift shop; no a/c, no room phones, no room TVs � Reservations required ▭ AE, MC, V ▯ FAP.

To & from La Selva

6 km/3½ mi south of Puerto Viejo de Sarapiquí, 79 km/49 mi (2–4 hrs) northeast of San José.

To get here, drive south from Puerto Viejo and look for signs on the west side of the road. For those without wheels, La Selva is a $4 taxi ride from Puerto Viejo de Sarapiquí.

Rara Avis

⑰ Toucans, sloths, great green macaws, howler and spider monkeys, vested anteaters, and tapirs may be on hand to greet you when you arrive at Rara Avis, one of Costa Rica's most popular private reserves and open only to overnight guests. Ecologist Amos Bien founded Rara Avis with the intent of combining research, tourism, and the sustainable extraction of forest products. Bilingual guides take you along the muddy trails—boots are provided—and canopy observation platforms and help point out wildlife. Or go on your own to the orchid house and butterfly garden. Bring a camera: the reserve's lacy double waterfall is one of Costa Rica's most photogenic sights.

The town of **Las Horquetas** is the jumping-off point for the 13-square-km (8-square-mi) private reserve. The 16-km (10-mi) trip from Las Horquetas to the reserve can be accomplished in three hours on horseback, two to three hours by tractor (leaves daily at 8:30 AM), or one hour by 4WD vehicle, plus a rough 3-km (2-mi) hike up to the lodge proper. The trails are steep and rugged, but the flora and fauna en route are remarkable. ⚠ **There have been some complaints that, although the reserve itself is lovely, the guides and services are considerably less impressive.**

Where to Stay

$$–$$$ 🏨 **Rara Avis.** There are three lodging options here. The Waterfall Lodge, near a 197-foot waterfall, has hardwood-paneled rooms with chairs, firm beds, balconies, and hammocks. Despite the prices, accommodation is rustic, with minimal amenities and no electricity. More basic, Las Casitas are three two-room cabins with shared bath. On the high end, ideal for a rustic honeymoon, is the River Edge Cabin, a 10-minute walk through the forest (it's dark at night, but you're given a flashlight), with private bath and balcony and solar panel–generated electricity. Rates include guides and transport from Las Horquetas. It's time-consuming to get here—your journey from Las Horquetas is on a tractor-pulled cart—so the recommended stay is two nights. ✉ *Las Horquetas* ☎ *764–1111* 🖷 *764–1114* ⊕ *www.rara-avis.com* ⇨ *16 rooms, 10 with bath* ☖ *Restaurant; no a/c, no room phones, no room TVs* ▤ *AE, MC, V* ❢ *AI.*

$$ 🏨 **Sueño Azul Resort.** This nature lodge and wellness retreat is the most luxurious property in the area, and a favorite for honeymooners and those attracted by the wide variety of yoga and other "wellness" disciplines. Spacious rooms have high ceilings, two double beds, large bathrooms, and a private porch overlooking either one of the rivers or a small lake. One large junior suite has its own outdoor whirlpool tub. Meals are served in an open-air dining room with a view. A wide range of tours and activities is offered, including rain-forest hikes, horseback riding, mountain biking, and fly-fishing, as well as trips to major attractions.

The spa and yoga facility is impressive for area in which these ameni-ties are unheard of. ✉ *Just west of Horquetas, off Hwy 4* ☎ *764–1000* 🖷 *764–1049* ⊕ *www.suenoazulresort.com* ✈ *55 rooms* 🛆 *Restau-rant, fans, pool, whirlpool tub, spa, horseback riding, laundry service, gift shop, bar, meeting rooms; no a/c in some rooms* ▭ *MC, V* ⦿ *EP.*

To & from Rara Avis
17 km/11 mi (20 mins) south of Las Horquetas, 100 km/62 mi (2 hrs) north of San José.

From Braulio Carrillo, turn left at signs for Puerto Viejo de Sarapiquí and continue on to Las Horquetas.

THE NORTHERN PLAINS ESSENTIALS

Transportation

BY AIR
ARRIVING & DEPARTING NatureAir has daily flights from San José to La Fortuna (FTN). For more information, *see* Air Travel *in* Smart Travel Tips A to Z.

BY BUS
ARRIVING & DEPARTING For more information about bus travel between the Northern Plains and San José, *see* Bus Travel *in* Smart Travel Tips A to Z.

GETTING AROUND Buses in this region are typically large, clean, and fairly comfortable but often crowded Friday through Sunday. Don't expect air-conditioning. Service tends toward the agonizingly slow: even supposedly express buses marked *directo* (direct) often make numerous stops.

BY CAR
ARRIVING & DEPARTING Road access to the northwest is by way of the paved two-lane Pan-Amer-ican Highway (Carretera Interamericana, or CA1), which starts from the west end of Paseo Colón in San José and runs northwest through Cañas and Liberia and to Peñas Blancas at the Nicaraguan border.

GETTING AROUND This region manages to mix some of the country's smoothest highways with some of its most horrendous roads. (The road to Monteverde is legendary in the latter regard, but the final destination makes it worth the trip.) Four-wheel-drive vehicles are best on the frequently potholed roads. If you don't want to pay for 4WD, at least rent a car with high clearance. (Many rental agencies insist you take a 4WD vehicle if you mention Monteverde as part of your itinerary.) You'll encounter frequent one-lane bridges; if the triangular CEDA EL PASO faces you, yield to oncoming traffic.

La Fortuna is the only place in the region to rent a vehicle. Otherwise, rent in San José or Liberia.

🚗 Major Rental Agencies **Alamo** ✉ 100 m west of church, La Fortuna ☎ 479-9090 ⊕ www.alamocostarica.com.

🚗 Local Rental Agencies **Poás Rentacar** ✉ 50 m south of church, La Fortuna ☎ 479-8418.

BY SHUTTLE VAN

ARRIVING &
DEPARTING

If you prefer a speedier, more private form of travel, consider taking a shuttle. Gray Line has daily service between San José, La Fortuna and Arenal ($27), and Monteverde ($38). Comfortable air-conditioned vans leave various San José hotels early in the morning and return midafternoon. Purchase tickets at least a day in advance. Service is also provided from Arenal and Monteverde to several Pacific-coast beaches. Interbus also connects San José with La Fortuna and Monteverde (both $29) daily, with connections from there to a few of the North Pacific beaches. Apart from schedule, there's little difference between Gray Line and Interbus.

🛈 Shuttle Van Services **Gray Line Tourist Bus** ☎ 232-3681 or 220-2126 ⊕ www.graylinecostarica.com. **Interbus** ☎ 283-5573 ⊕ www.interbusonline.com.

Contacts & Resources

Banks and emergency contacts follow each town listed in the chapter.

BANKS & EXCHANGE SERVICES

Most larger hotels, tour companies, and retailers accept credit and debit cards. Visa and MasterCard predominate; a few retailers accept American Express. Changing U.S. dollars or traveler's checks is possible at Banco Nacional branches scattered throughout the region, but lines are long. Most hotels and larger businesses are prepared to accept U.S. dollars; smaller businesses usually will not.

You'll find a small but growing number of *cajeros automáticos* (ATMs) out here; Banco Nacional offices in La Fortuna and Santa Elena, as well as Banex in Ciudad Quesada and CooTilarán in Tilarán, are affiliated with the ATH (A Toda Hora) network, and accept Cirrus- and Plus-linked cards.

North Pacific

Conchal Beach

WORD OF MOUTH

"In the rainy season, go to Guanacaste, the driest region of Costa Rica. There are great beaches on the Nicoya Peninsula. At this time the nature is green, the beaches are not crowded, prices are lower, and it rains normally one hour a day in the late afternoon or in the night."

—costaklaus

WELCOME TO THE NORTH PACIFIC

TOP 5
Reasons to Go

1. **Beaches:** White sand, black sand, palm-fringed strands, beaches for swimming, partying, surfing, and sunbathing—you can't beat Guanacaste's beaches for sheer variety.

2. **Rincón de la Vieja National Park:** Mud pools bubble and fumaroles steam on the forested slopes of this active volcano. Turn up the heat with a soak in a hot sulphur spring.

3. **Surfing Witch's Rock and Ollie's Point:** The waves off the coast of Santa Rosa National Park are legendary.

4. **Turtle tours:** From October through April at Playa Grande and Playa Ostional, witness the life-and-death drama of thousands of sea-turtle hatchlings scurrying to the sea past a daunting array of predators.

5. **Scuba diving:** Forget the pretty tropical fish. Sharks, rays, sea turtles, and moray eels are the large-scale attractions for divers on the Guanacaste coast.

Dry, hot **Far Northern Guanacaste** is traditionally ranching country. But Rincón de la Vieja National Park, with wildlife and one of Costa Rica's five active volcanoes, is here; as is Bahía Salinas, second to Lake Arenal for wind- and kitesurfing.

Ostional Wildlife Refuge

Getting Oriented

This vast, inland chunk of land in northwestern Costa Rica—which comprises Guanacaste Province—is bordered by the Pacific Ocean to the west and the looming Cordillera de Guanacaste volcanic mountain range to the east. To the south is the Nicoya Peninsula, with almost continuous beaches along more than 60 miles of Pacific coastline, as the crow flies. Roads are mostly unpaved, so absent your own boat, the best way to get around is in a four-wheel-drive vehicle. Take a plane, bus, or shuttle van to Liberia and pick up your rental car there.

Church of San Blas, Nicoya

Playa Hermosa

National parks Palo Verde and Barra Honda are the main attractions in The Tempisque River Basin. The former is a prime bird- and wild-life-watching park; the latter has caves ripe for exploration.

The number and variety of beaches along The Nicoya Coast make it a top tourist destina-tion. Each beach has its specialty, be it surfing, fishing, diving, or just plain relaxing. Top hotels and restaurants are in generous supply.

Tamarindo Beach

NORTH PACIFIC PLANNER

When to Go

Guanacaste is the driest region of the country, with only 65 inches of average annual rainfall, and the hottest, with average temperatures around 30–35°C (86–95°F). The best time to visit is the shoulder season (mid-November–January), when the landscape is green, the evening air is cool, and hotels and restaurants energetically gear up for the tourist influx. Rainy-season travel (May–December) means lower prices and fewer crowds, but some restaurants and hotels are closed, and nearly every afternoon brings downpours. Avoid the January–March high season; skies are clear, but the heat is intense (apart from evening breezes near the beach), the landscape is brown and parched, and beaches and trails are packed. Mid-December to February, when school is out in Costa Rica, is especially busy.

■ TIP➜➜ Always apply bug repellent if you're going to be on the beach around sunset, when no-see-ums feast on unprotected ankles

Getting There

The Pan-American Highway heads northwest from San José to Liberia, then due north to the Nicaraguan border. But it's poorly maintained, potholed and hilly, and heavily trafficked by trucks and buses. The airport outside Liberia is the best way to access the region. Fly directly here from the U.S. or Canada or hop on a domestic flight from San José and save yourself four to five hours of difficult driving.

Ground Transportation from Liberia

At Daniel Oduber Airport in Liberia, official red taxis and hotel vans wait to meet each flight. When making a hotel reservation for the first night, ask if the hotel provides a cab or shuttle. If not, ask how much you should expect to pay for ground transportation from the airport. Fares vary widely, depending on how far away the hotel is and how many people are traveling together. In Guanacaste, it's usually safe to take *pirata* (pirate, or unofficial) taxis, but always negotiate the price before getting into the cab.

What to Do

ACTIVITY	WHERE TO DO IT
Fishing	Playa Flamingo, Tamarindo, Puerto Carrillo, Playas del Coco
Diving	Playa Hermosa, Playa Panama (Papagayo Peninsula area), Playa Potrero, Playas del Coco
Surfing	Tamarindo, Playa Grande, Playa Avellanas, Playa Negra, Santa Rosa National Park
Volcanoes	Rincón de la Vieja National Park
Turtle-watching	Playa Grande, Playa Ostional
Wildlife-watching	Palo Verde National Park, Rincón de la Vieja National Park, Santa Rosa National Park

How Much Time?

Ten days is what we recommend to get a taste of the North Pacific. Ideally, schedule at least a week to get into the rhythm of beach life. Logistically, you also need time for slow travel over bumpy roads. (By boat is faster and easier; tour operators will collect you from almost any beach.) A beach with lots of restaurants and nightlife can keep you entertained for a week or more, whereas a more solitary beach might merit only a couple of days. Outdoorsy types should consider spending a few days around Rincón de la Vieja National Park, hiking, bird-watching, horseback riding, and doing canopy tours.

Great Combinations

You can easily stop at Monteverde (⇨ chapter 3) en route to the coast from San José. From there, shuttle van connections to the beach are excellent. Macaw Air flies directly from Tamarindo or Liberia to Puerto Jiménez, where you can spend a few days in a jungle lodge off the grid in the Osa Peninsula, a contrast to developed Nicoya beaches.

Recommended Tour Operators

■ **Swiss Travel Service** (☎ 282-4898 ⊕ www.swisstravelcr.com) specializes in Guanacaste. Despite the name, it's operated by Costa Ricans with lots of local experience. Custom-design a guided private or small-group tour.

■ The excellent **Horizontes** (☎ 222-2022 ⊕ www.horizontes.com) has independent, private tours with your own guide/driver and small group tours.

■ **Lazy Lizard Catamaran Sailing Adventures** (☎ 654-4192 ⊕ www.sailingcostarica.com) four-hour sailing trips include guided snorkeling, kayaking, food, and drinks.

Choosing a Place to Stay

Balancing out super-expensive resorts like the Four Seasons are budget options like the $15/night grass shacks on the beach at Sámara. As in all of Costa Rica, the places we most recommend are the small owner-operated hotels and B&Bs that blend in with unspoiled nature and have one-on-one attention from the staff and owners. If your budget is tight, consider condo or apartment properties with kitchens (and no meals provided). That's how most Ticos travel. These places may not be fancy, but they put you where you want to be. Winter (January–March) tends to be the most stifling time of year, and a room with a/c is advisable.

4

Prices

WHAT IT COSTS in Dollars

	$$$$	$$$	$$	$	¢
Restaurants	over $25	$15–$25	$10–$15	$5–$10	under $5
Hotels	over $250	$150–$250	$75–$150	$50–$75	under $50

Restaurant prices are for a main course excluding tax and tip. Hotel prices are for two people in a standard double room in high season, excluding service and tax (16.4%).

FAR NORTHERN GUANACASTE

Dorothy
MacKinnon

The mountains, plains, and Pacific coastline north of Liberia up to the border of Nicaragua are encompassed in Far Northern Guanacaste. Liberia is the capital of Guanacaste province and is the closest town to Costa Rica's second-largest airport. You'll most likely pass through it on your way to the beaches west of the city or up north to the national parks of Guanacaste, Santa Rosa, or Rincón de la Vieja. Volcán Rincón de la Vieja, an active volcano that last erupted in 1991, is pocked with eerie sites such as boiling creeks, bubbling mud pools, and vapor-emitting streams—look, but don't touch!

Northwest of Rincón de la Vieja, on the coast, Santa Rosa National Park is a former cattle ranch where Costa Ricans defeated the invading mercenary army of American William Walker in 1856. Santa Rosa also protects some of the last remnants of the region's original dry tropical forest, as well as olive ridley sea turtles that come to lay their eggs on its beaches between August and November. Closer still to the Nicaraguan border are the remote beaches of Guanacaste National Park and the town of La Cruz, overlooking the lovely Golfo de Santa Elena and some windswept hotels on Bahía Salinas.

Rincón de la Vieja National Park

★ ❶ Parque Nacional Rincón de la Vieja is Costa Rica's mini-Yellowstone, with volcanic hot springs and boiling, bubbling mud ponds. The park protects more than 177 square km (54 square mi) of the volcano's upper slopes, much of which are covered by dry forest. The wildlife here is diverse: more than 250 species of birds, including long-tailed manakins and blue-crowned motmots; plus mammals such as brocket deer, monkeys, and armadillos. There may still be a jaguar or two left, but these large cats are elusive and rarely seen.

The Las Pailas park entrance is the most common place to enter the park because it has the most accessible trails and there are more hotels along the road leading up to it. ⚠ **If you want to explore the slopes of the volcano, go with a guide—the abundant hot springs and geysers have given unsuspecting visitors some very nasty burns.** In addition, the upper slopes often receive fierce and potentially dangerous winds—before ascending, check at either ranger station for conditions. The park does not have guides; we recommend the guides at Hacienda Guachipelín (⇨ *below*). You must sign a personal injury waiver before being admitted into the park. ☎ *661–8139 (after 1 PM only)* ✉ *$6* ۩ *Tues.–Sun. 7–5, last entry at 3 PM.*

Outdoor Activities

Buena Vista Lodge & Adventure Center (✉ Western slope of the volcano, 10 km/6 mi north of Cañas Dulces ☎ 661–8158 ⊕ www.buenavistacr. com) has horseback riding, waterfall hikes, a canopy tour, rappelling, tractor tours, and a 1,600-foot (long, not steep) waterslide through the forest. Tours are $15 to $30 per person; a combo ticket is $65. **Hacienda Guachipelín Adventure Center** (✉ Road to Rincón de la Vieja park

☎ 442–2818 ⊕ www.guachipelin.
com) has horseback riding, river
tubing, hot springs and mud baths,
and guided waterfall and volcano
hikes. The popular canyon tour in-
cudes rock climbing, rappelling, zip
lines, suspension bridges, and a
Tarzan swing. A one-day, all-you-
can-do adventure pass is $75. Tours
are designed for ages 8 to 80. Playa
Hermosa–based Maynor Lara Bustos of **Tours Your Way** (☎ 697–0210)
guides tours to Rincón de la Vieja National Park.

CANOPY TOURS   The zip-line canopy tour ($35) with **Buena Vista Lodge & Adventure Cen-
ter** (⇨ *above*) has cables that are up to 90 feet off the ground and up
to 450 feet long. **Top Tree Trails** (✉ Rincón de la Vieja Volcano Mountain Lodge ☎ 200–0238) runs four-hour horseback and canopy tours
($55), which include a 16-platform zip line, a ride to the Los Azufrales
sulfur springs, or a forest hike to a waterfall with a box lunch.

HIKING   Nearly all of the outfitters in the area have guided hikes through the
park to volcano craters, hot springs, or waterfalls.

If you're doing a self-guided hike, stop for trail maps and hiking information at the park stations at both entrance gates. The 8-km (5-mi) **trail
to the summit** heads up into the forest from the Las Pailas park entrance,
then emerges onto a windy, exposed shale slope that's slippery and
hard going, and has poor visibility owing to clouds and mist. It's a trip
for serious hikers, best done in dry season with preparation for cold
weather at the top. A less strenuous option is the fascinating 3-km (2-
mi) **loop through the park,** which takes about two hours to complete, starting at the Las Pailas entrance. Along the well-marked trail you'll see
fumaroles exuding steam, a *volcáncito* (baby volcano), and Las Pailas,
the boiling mud fields named after pots used for boiling down sugarcane. If you tread softly, you can spot many animals, including howler,
white-faced capuchin, and spider monkeys and raccoonlike coatis, looking for handouts. ■ TIP→ Remember the cardinal rule of wildlife encounters: Don't feed the animals. Another popular hike is a four-hour, 10-km
(6-mi) **La Cangreja Waterfall loop.** The *catarata* (waterfall) has a cool swimming hole below; the surrounding rocks have pockets of hot springs.

HORSEBACK   **Buena Vista Mountain Lodge & Adventure Center** (⇨ *above*) has horseback
RIDING   trips to hot springs ($15) and to Borinquen Waterfall ($25). If not
everyone in your party is a horse-lover, tractor transport ($25) is avail-
able to the hot springs as well. **Rincón de la Vieja Volcano Mountain Lodge**
(☎ 200–0238) has guides for hiking or horseback riding near the park.
Hacienda Guachipélin (⇨ *above*).

Where to Stay

$$$$ 🏨 **Borinquen Mountain Resort Thermae & Spa.** The luxury villas on this
12,000-acre ranch are shaded by old-growth trees on the volcano's windy
west slope. The spa has volcanic mud (*lodo*) baths, a wooden sauna

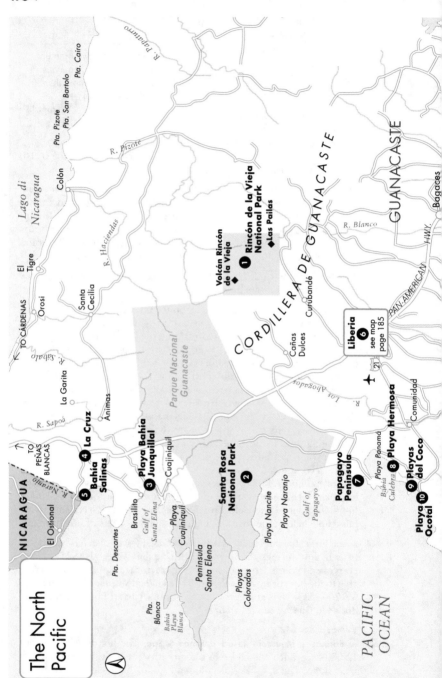

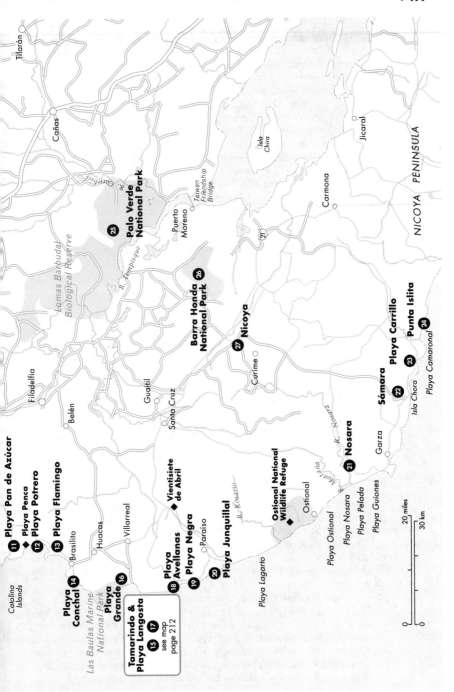

Tilarán

Cañas

Jicaral

Isla
Chira

R. Cañas

Palo Verde
National Park **25**

Taiwan
Friendship
Bridge

Lomas Barbudal
Biological Reserve

R. Tempisque

Puerto
Moreno

Carmona

21

NICOYA PENINSULA

Barra Honda
National Park **26**

Filadelfia

Playa Carrillo

Punta Islita **24**

Nicoya **27**

Playa Pan de Azúcar **11**

Playa Penca **12**
Playa Potrero

Cúrime

Sámara **22** **23**

Belén

Playa Flamingo **13**

Guaitil

Santa Cruz

Isla Chora

Playa Camaronal

Catalina
Islands

Villarreal

R. Nosara

Nosara **21**

Garza

Vientisiete
de Abril

Playa
Conchal **14**

Huacas

Brasilito

Playa
Grande **16**

Playa
Avellanas **18**

Playa Negra **19**

Paraíso

R. Rosario

Playa Junquillal **20**

Ostional National
Wildlife Refuge

Playa Ostional

Playa Nosara

Ostional

Las Baulas Marine
National Park

Tamarindo &
Playa Langosta **15** **17**

see map
page 212

R. Montaña

Playa Pelada

Playa Guiones

Playa Lagarto

20 miles

30 km

heated by steam from a fumarole, and naturally heated mineral pools—all included in room rates. The sulfur smell takes a little getting used to. Activities include hiking, horseback riding, ATV trips, a canopy tour, and a farm tour (with cow-milking). Getting to the restaurant and spa requires steep climbs, but the staff can transport you in a golf cart. The modern, two-room, hacienda-style villas have large private verandas; single villas are more private. The food is not on par with the rest of the hotel. ⊠ *13 km/8 mi northwest of Liberia on the Pan-American Hwy., then 29 km/18 mi north on the dirt road toward Cañas Dulces* ☎690–1900 🖷690–1903 ⊕ *www.borinquenresort.com* ⌨ *33 villas* ☖ *Restaurant, room service, refrigerators, satellite TV, pool, whirlpool tubs, spa, horseback riding, tours, bar, laundry service, Internet station* ⊟ *AE, DC, MC, V* †◎† *CP.*

$$ 🖼 **Posada El Encuentro B&B.** Cinematic views of valley, volcano, and the Gulf of Nicoya can be had from the main house and two-bedroom *casitas* (small houses) at this unexpectedly upscale B&B. The suites in the modern, hacienda-style house have queen-size four-poster beds, wicker sofas, and private baths. The casitas are similarly furnished, but a little more private; you can stay in one-half of the casita or rent both sides for a family. A big breakfast is served in a bright atrium room and there's a small dinner menu. After hiking in the nearby national park, you can watch the sun set while lounging on the large pool terrace. ⊠ *9 km/5 mi off the Pan-American Hwy., on road to Las Pailas park entrance* ☎848–0616, 389–1456 ⌨ *3 suites, 2 casitas* ☖ *Dining room, fans, pool, bar; no a/c, no room phones, no room TVs* ⊟ *AE, MC, V* †◎† *BP.*

★ $ 🖼 **Hacienda Guachipelín.** Day-trippers come here for hair-raising adventure tours (⇨ Outdoor Activities, *above*), but this 3,706-acre working ranch is also famous for its horses—all 120 of them—and its nature trails leading to waterfalls, hot springs, and mud baths. Rugged ranch hands swaggering around give the place a real cowboy flavor. This lodge is the best value in the Rincón area. Rooms are large and pleasantly furnished, with windows front and back to let in cool mountain air. The newest rooms, Nos. 40 and up, are the most elegant and quiet, though a bit of a walk from the restaurant. Avoid Rooms 24–31, right beside the corral, unless you enjoy the aroma of horses. Excellent buffet meals are served in the open-air restaurant, which has valley views. Dairy and beef products come fresh from the hacienda's own herd; vegetarians may have trouble finding meat-free dishes here. Large groups often stay here, but you can always find a quiet trail on the vast, partially forested property. ⊠ *17 km/10 mi north of the Pan-American Hwy., on road to Las Pailas park entrance* ☎666–8075 🖷442–1910 ⊕ *www.guachipelin. com* ⌨ *50 rooms* ☖ *Restaurant, fans, pool, horseback riding, tours, bar, playground, laundry service, Internet station; no a/c, no room phones, no room TVs* ⊟ *AE, DC, MC, V* †◎† *BP.*

¢ 🖼 **Rancho Curubandé Lodge.** Convenient to Rincón de la Vieja and Santa Rosa, these equipped bungalows and modern rooms are part of a working farm owned by a Costa Rican family. The tidy, two-bedroom bungalows ($40) have modern comforts, including hot water, and the seven spacious new motel-style rooms ($30–$35) have air-conditioning plus a view of the volcano from a deck under a giant Guanacaste tree. There is also a renovated wooden ranch home that used to host large family gatherings, with four rooms ($20 per double room) sharing two cold-

More Texan than Tropical

GUANACASTE, COSTA RICA'S "Wild West," looks different from the rest of Costa Rica. It was originally covered in vast, dry tropical forests, but beginning in early colonial times, and then picking up speed in the 1950s when cattle ranching became big business, the dry forest was cleared to create vast cattle ranges. (The harder-to-access forests covering the volcanic slopes survived.) The resulting flat, sun-baked landscape makes the inland parts of the province look a little like the American Southwest. Cowboy culture still takes center stage during seasonal fiestas and a few rodeos. But these days more and more *sabaneros* (cowboys) are turning in their horses for Toyota HiLux trucks.

water bathrooms and a kitchen. ⊠ *Just off Pan-American Hwy. on road to Las Pailas* ☎ *665–0374 or 369–8563* ✆ *ranchocurubande@gmail. com* ✇ *7 rooms, 2 villas* ⚭ *Dining room, fans, horseback riding; no a/c in some rooms, no room phones, no room TVs* ▭ *MC, V* ⵀ *EP.*

To & from Rincón de la Vieja National Park
25 km/15 mi (1 hr) northeast of Liberia.

There are two park entrances: the less traveled one at Hacienda Santa María on the road leading northeast from Liberia; and at Las Pailas, past Curubandé off the Pan-American Highway. To get to the Las Pailas entrance from Liberia, take the first entrance road 5 km (3 mi) northwest of Liberia off the Pan-American Highway. The turnoff is easy to miss—follow signs for Hacienda Guachipelín or the town of Curubandé. It's a rough 17-km (11-mi) dirt road, and you have to pay a small toll. The Santa María entrance is 25 km (15 mi) northeast of Liberia along the Colonia Blanca route, which follows the course of the Río Liberia. The turnoff from the Pan-American Highway to the hotels on the western slope of the volcano is 12 km (7 mi) northwest of Liberia, turning right at the road signed for Cañas Dulces. A 4WD vehicle is recommended, though not essential, for all of these slow and bone-rattling rides.

Santa Rosa National Park

Intrepid bird-watchers, naturalists, backpackers, and campers who like to rough it are the sort that visits this national park. Renowned for its wildlife, which is easy to spot due to less luxuriant, low-density foliage, Santa Rosa is the largest swath of tropical dry forest in Central America. Treetop inhabitants include spider, white-faced capuchin, and howler monkeys. If you station yourself next to water holes during the dry season, you may also spot deer, coyotes, coatis, or ocelots by day and armadillos and tapirs by night. Typical dry-forest vegetation includes oak, wild cherry, mahogany, calabash, bullhorn acacia, and gumbo-limbo.

Santa Rosa's wealth of flora and fauna is due in part to its remoteness, which also makes it very difficult to access. To get anywhere in the park, you must first hike the 7-km (4½-mi) paved road to park headquarters from the entrance gate. About halfway along this road is a wooden sign signaling that you are entering the old-growth area, with trees as old as 500 years. Within this dense, shady forest, temperatures drop by as much as 5°C.

⚠ **Visit areas beyond La Casona and accessible trails near the park headquarters only if you are a hardy hiker and backpacker.** In rainy season the park's rough trails cannot be accessed by even 4WD vehicles and require hours of trekking on foot. From the park's entrance it's 8 km (5 mi) to the park headquarters, another 13 km (8 mi) to **Playa Naranjo**—where famed Witch's Rock surf break is located (most surfers get there by boat)—and **Playa Nancite**—the world's only totally protected olive ridley turtle *arribada,* or mass nesting (accessible primarily to biologists and students; permit required)—is an additional 5 km (3 mi) beyond that. Only the first 20 km (12 mi) of trail is accessible by 4WD in the dry season.

✉ *Km 269, Pan-American Hwy., 35 km/22 mi north of Liberia* ☎ *666–5051* 💲 *$6* 🕙 *Daily 8–4.*

	WALKER'S LAST STAND

Santa Rosa Park was the site of the 1856 triumph over American invader William Walker in the famous Battle of Santa Rosa—one of the few military historic sites in this army-less country. The rambling colonial-style **Hacienda La Casona** farmstead was the last stand of a ragged force of ill-equipped Costa Ricans who routed the superior mercenary army of the notorious Walker. Disgruntled poachers burned La Casona to the ground in 2001, but it has since been rebuilt.

Outdoor Activities

HIKING The short (about 800 m) **La Casona nature-trail loop** from the park headquarters is worth taking to get a brief sampling of the woods. Look for the INDIO DESNUDO, or "Naked Indian," path, named after the local name for gumbo-limbo trees. ■ TIP➜ **Carry your own water; water holes are none too safe.**

The grueling **trails to the beaches** in Santa Rosa all start at the park headquarters, which is itself a 7-km (4-mi) hike along a hot, sunny road. The hike to Playa Naranjo is another 13 km (8 mi) and Playa Nancite is 5 km (3 mi) beyond that. You can get a map of the trails at the park entrance.

SURFING **Witch's Rock,** one of the oldest rock formations in the country, creates a
★ near-perfect beach break off Playa Naranjo in Santa Rosa Park. If you are interested in surfing Witch's Rock, take a boat tour from Playas del Coco, Playa Hermosa, or Playa Tamarindo, to the south.

Where to Stay

There are campsites within Santa Rosa Park, but they are very basic, some are quite remote, and there is limited availability. Call the park headquarters (☎ 666–5051) for information.

★ ☾ $ 🖻 **Los Inocentes Lodge.** So you want to be a cowboy? You can start by staying at this ranch in a private reserve bordering Guanacaste National Park. The ranch has horses, cattle, a herd of farm-raised peacocks (which account for the shrill shrieks you hear), and two pet scarlet macaws. The exquisitely maintained 115-year-old hardwood hacienda still has the original big rooms, which have high ceilings, huge closets, carved headboards, and only transom windows for ventilation. They're a little like elegant stables for people. Hot showers are across the corridors. Bungalows, about 200 meters from the hacienda, have private, solar-heated baths. The restaurant, which serves good traditional meals, and the second-floor veranda have views of verdant Orosi Volcano. Experienced guides, well-trained horses, and miles of trails get you into the forests. ⊠ *15 km/9 mi west of La Cruz* ☎ *679–9190* 🖷 *679–9224 or 265–1385* ⊕ *www.losinocentesranch.com* ✏ *Apdo. 228–3000, Heredia* ⌂ *11 rooms with shared bath, 12 bungalows* 🍴 *Dining room, fans, pool, whirlpool tub, horseback riding, bar; no a/c, no room phones, no room TVs* 🖃 *AE, MC, V* 🍽 *CP.*

To & from Santa Rosa National Park
35 km/22 mi (30 mins) northwest of Liberia.

The turnoff for Santa Rosa National Park from the CA1 (Pan-American Hwy.) is well marked. From Liberia you can hop on a bus heading north to La Cruz and get off at the park entrance.

Playa Bahía Junquillal

❸ This 2½-km (1½-mi), tree-fringed, Blue Flag beach is as close as you can get to a soft white-sand beach in this part of Guanacaste. The warm, calm water makes it one of the best swimming beaches on the Gulf of Santa Elena. Not to be confused with the Playa Junquillal on the western coast of the Nicoya Peninsula farther south, this beach is part of the Guanacaste National Wildlife Refuge to the north of Santa Rosa. Stay for the day or camp out in the shaded camping area close to the beach. You can snorkel if you've got your own gear. 🖾 *$4* ☎ *679–9692* 🕓 *7 AM–7 PM.*

To & from Playa Bahía Junquillal
22 km/14 mi north of Santa Rosa National Park. (30 mins from the Pan-American turnoff; 60 mins from Bahía Salinas).

From the Pan-American Highway, take the road signed for Cuajiniquil, 43 km (26 mi) northwest of Liberia and 8 km (5 mi) north of Santa Rosa Park. Follow the paved road 10 km (6 mi) to the beach turnoff, along a dirt road for another 4 km (2½ mi). From the Bahía Salinas area, take the scenic dirt road (4WD recommended); then follow the road near Puerto Soley (signed for Cuajiniquil) 7 km (4 mi) to the beach entrance. You can also take a public bus from Liberia to Cuanijiquil and walk 7 km (4 mi) to the beach.

La Cruz

❹ North of Guanacaste National Park on the west side of the highway is the turnoff to La Cruz, a scruffy, bustling little town. For travelers, it's noteworthy only for the stunning views of Bahía Salinas from its bluff and its proximity to the windswept beaches on the south shore of Bahía Salinas, the hamlet of Jobo, and the gentler beaches of the Golfo de Santa

Guanacaste National Park

THE 325-SQUARE-KM (125-square-mi) Parque Nacional Guanacaste, bordering the east side of the Pan-American Highway 30 km (18 mi) north of Liberia, was created in 1989 to preserve rain forests around Cacao Volcano (5,437 feet) and Orosi Volcano (4,847 feet), which are seasonally inhabited by migrant wildlife from Santa Rosa. The park isn't quite ready for tourism yet. There are no facilities (not even a toilet) and no well-marked trails. In rainy season, roads are impassable; a 4WD vehicle is required year-round. The park is a mosaic of interdependent protected areas, parks, and refuges; the goal is to eventually create a single Guanacaste megapark to accommodate the migratory patterns of animals, from jaguars to tapirs. Much of the park's territory is cattle pasture, which, it is hoped, will regenerate into forest. Today the park has more than 300 different birds and more than 5,000 species of butterflies.

To really explore the park, you must stay in the heart of it, at one of three biological stations. They are mostly reserved for students and researchers, but you can request accommodations from the **park headquarters** (☎ 666–5051).

Elena. The Nicaraguan border lies just north of La Cruz at Peñas Blancas. ⚠ **All travelers are stopped at two preborder checkpoints south of La Cruz for passport and cursory vehicle inspection. Police vigilance is heightened in the region.**

Where to Stay

¢ 🖼 **Amalia's Inn.** This breezy, bright, white inn on the cliff overlooking Bahía Salinas has big rooms furnished with a hodgepodge of mismatched furniture. Large-scale, dark, modern paintings and prints haunt the otherwise cheerful place. The view of the bay, from the garden or swimming pool, is the main selling point. A *soda* (informal restaurant) serving a *típico* breakfast is a block away. ⊠ *East of Central Park, on left of road heading into town* ☎☎ *679–9181* 🍽 *7 rooms* ⚑ *Pool, laundry service; no a/c, no room phones, no room TVs* ⊟ *No credit cards* 🍴 *EP.*

To & from La Cruz

65 km/40 mi (1 hr) northwest of Liberia.

La Cruz is a straight shot north of Liberia on the Pan-American Highway. Buses leave Liberia for La Cruz or you can flag down a bus, which says LA CRUZ on its windshield, anywhere along the highway north of Liberia.

La Cruz Essentials

🏧 Banks **Banco de Costa Rica** ⊠ 200 m north of Plaza Lopez ☎ 680–3252. **Banco Popular** ⊠ South of Central Park.

🏥 Hospital **Hospital Area de Salud La Cruz** ⊠ Main highway at entrance to town ☎ 679–9311.

💊 Pharmacies **Farmacia San Angel** ⊠ 2 blocks north of Central Park ☎ 679–8048.

Crossing into Nicaragua at Peñas Blancas

Costa Rica and Nicaragua share a busy border crossing at Peñas Blancas, 12 km (7 mi) north of La Cruz along a paved highway. ⚠ **Rental vehicles may not leave Costa Rica.** Tica Bus and Transnica bus companies (⇨ Bus Travel *in* Smart Travel Tips A to Z) cross into Nicaragua. The fee to cross the border is $7 (paid on the Nicaraguan side), plus a $2 surcharge if you cross from noon to 2 PM or on weekends. You can negotiate the border crossing on foot; taxis on the Nicaraguan side will take you to Rivas, the first city of any size, about 30 km (18 mi) from the border. Returning to Costa Rica is basically the same process in reverse; you are charged a $1 municipal tax and $2 exit tax to leave Nicaragua by land. The crossing is open daily 6 AM–8 PM; get there with time to spare or you *will* be stranded. Banks on both sides of the border change their own currency and U.S. dollars. Colones are not accepted or exchanged in Nicaragua; likewise for córdobas in Costa Rica. Overland border crossing procedures can be confusing if you don't speak Spanish.

Bahía Salinas

❺ The large windswept bay at the very top of Costa Rica's Pacific coast is the second windiest area in Costa Rica, after Lake Arenal, making it ideal for windsurfing and kitesurfing. The wind usually blows strong November through August (September and October are the height of the rainy season). Winds are generally not as powerful as those at Lake Arenal, but they're strong enough to make this a viable alternative. The south (bay) side has the strongest winds, and choppy, cold water. But on the sheltered Golfo Santa Elena to the west are two beaches that rank among the most beautiful in all of Costa Rica: Playas Rajada and Jobo.

Exploring

Playa Copal (✉ About 2 km/1 mi east of the branch road that leads to Ecoplaya) is one of the main venues for kitesurfing. It also has villas and rooms for rent. A couple of kilometers to the east, Playa Papaturro also has kitesurfing and new cabins.

Gorgeous, horseshoe-shape **Playa Rajada** (✉ 5 km/3 mi west of Ecoplaya Beach Resort or 3 km/2 mi north of the town of Jobo) is a wide sweep of almost-white, fine-grain sand. Shallow, warm waters make it perfect for swimming, and an interesting rock formation at the north end invites snorkelers. It's also a favorite beach for watching sunsets.

★ **Playa Jobo** (✉ 3 km/2 mi walk or drive, west from Ecoplaya Beach Resort) is a gem with fine sand, calm water, and rocky claws at each end of its horseshoe. It's fringed with acacia trees that have sharp thorns, so keep your distance. There's a shady parking area about 150 m off the beach where you have to leave your car.

Outdoor Activities

Ecoplaya Beach Resort (☎ 676–1010 ⊕ www.ecoplaya.com) organizes local adventure tours like kayaking, fishing, horseback riding, and diving, as well as farther-afield adventure tours to Isla Bolaños (a tiny bird-preserve island), Los Inocentes, and Hacienda Guachipelín, and overnight tours to Granada in Nicaragua.

At this writing, the **Kite Surfing Centre and School** (☎ 826–5221 ⊕ www. suntoursandfun.com/kitesurfing.htm) on Copal Beach is moving to Playa Papaturro (9 km/5½ mi west of La Cruz, turn right at sign for Papaturro). Nicola, a multilingual instructor with lots of experience, gives 10 hours of kitesurfing lessons for $250, including equipment use. The school has 10 new cabins with a restaurant, scheduled to open in 2006. **Eco-Wind** (☎ 676–1010 ⊕ www.ecoplaya.com) at Ecoplaya Beach Resort will fix you up for all your windsurfing needs. Equipment rental runs around $60 a day.

Where to Stay

$$ ⊡ **Ecoplaya Beach Resort.** How windy is it? Even with glass buffers and windbreak trees and shrubs, the large swimming pool usually has waves. This sprawling collection of villas and poolside rooms with bathtubs and king-size beds is bordered by a nearly 1-km-long (½-mi-long) beach with coarse brown sand flecked with sharp broken shells. Bird- and wildlife-filled estuaries hem in the beach. Jobo and Rajada beaches are just a short drive or hike away. The hotel organizes activities and tours, but many entail a jolting ride back to La Cruz and beyond. The restaurant serves good food. ⊠ *La Coyotera Beach, 15 km/10 mi west of La Cruz on a rough dirt rd.* ☎ *676–1010, 228–7146 in San José* ⓓ *Plaza Colonial, Escazú, No. 4, San José* 🏠 *289–4536 in San José* ⊕ *www.ecoplaya.com* 🛏 *16 villas, 20 rooms* ⚭ *Restaurant, in-room safes, some kitchens, pool, satellite TV, beach, windsurfing, diving, horseback riding, tour operator, bar, children's programs (high season only), playground, recreation room, laundry service* ▤ *AE, MC, V* ⦿*I FAP (including national-brand drinks).*

¢–$ ⊡ **Pura Vida Residence.** An affordable, unusually upscale base for exploring the area, this Italian-built and -managed hilltop residence overlooks Playa Copal, the premier beach for windsurfing and kitesurfing. Studio rooms are in a modern residence. Fully equipped villas are perfect for sharing. High ceilings, lots of cool stone, tile, and huge windows to catch the winds off the bay help you keep your cool despite the lack of air-conditioning. ⊠ *Playa Copal, 13 km/8 mi west of La Cruz* ☎ *389–6794* 🏠 *676–1055* ⊕ *www.progettopuravida.com* 🛏 *8 rooms, 7 villas* ⚭ *Restaurant (high season only), fans, some kitchens, some kitchenettes, pool, beach; no a/c, no room phones, no room TVs* ▤ *No credit cards* ⦿*I EP.*

To & from Bahía Salinas

15 km/9 mi (45 mins) west of La Cruz.

From a high point in La Cruz, the road to Salinas descends both in altitude and condition. It's only 15 km (9 mi) southwest to Hotel Ecoplaya, but they are the most jolting miles of broken road you can imagine. The road is actually signed for Puerto Soley and Jobo, an end-of-the-road hamlet, about 2 km (1 mi) past the turnoff for Ecoplaya. Playa Copal is about 13 km (8 mi) along the same road from La Cruz.

Liberia

❻ Liberia is the gateway to the national parks to the north and to the Nicoya Peninsula beaches to the south. The drive from San José takes between

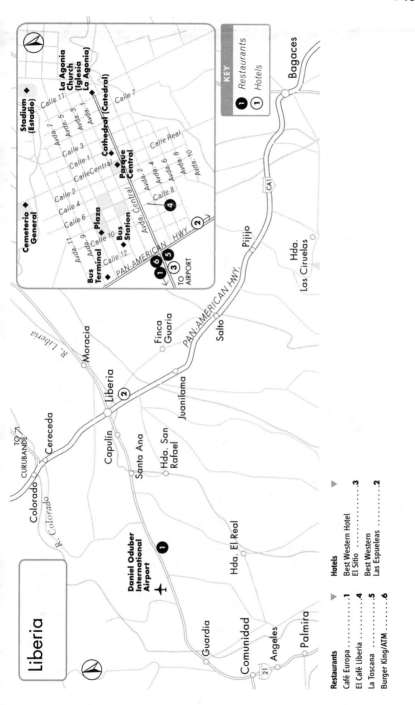

Liberia

KEY

1 Restaurants
① Hotels

Restaurants
Café Europa **1**
El Café Liberia **4**
La Toscana **5**
Burger King/ATM **6**

Hotels
Best Western Hotel
El Sitio **3**
Best Western
Las Espueleas **2**

four and seven hours, so it makes sense to fly directly into Liberia if you're going to the North Pacific. It's easy to rent a car near the airport, which you should do as soon as you arrive: the attractions of the city don't compare to the wonders of the nearby parks and beaches. Liberia is essentially a good place to have a meal and make a bank stop.

NAVIGATING
LIBERIA The *avenidas* (avenues) officially run east–west, while the *calles* (streets) run north–south. Liberia is not too big to walk easily, but there are always taxis lined up around the central park.

Exploring

For a true-grit taste of the sabanero life that is fast disappearing from Liberia, mosey on over to **Rancho Santa Alicia** (✉ Pan-American Hwy., 12 km/7 mi south of Liberia ☎ 671–2513) south of the city for a scenic trail ride by day or a romantic moonlight ride. The highlight is the Saturday-night **rodeo** when cowboys from all over Guanacaste come to compete in bull riding, bronco busting, and precision riding in a covered rodeo stadium. Barbecued beef, ribs, and some lighter choices are served ($6–$10). Additional entertainment includes *ranchero* music, mariachis, and a late-night disco.

Where to Stay & Eat

$ ✕ **La Toscana.** Billing itself as "spaghetteria, pizzeria, grigliata, and cafe," this restaurant is worth a trip to Liberia. Real Italian ingredients, such as properly aged Parmigiano cheese and prosciutto from Parma, give authenticity to its pastas and 40 types of wood-oven pizzas. Tender tuna or salmon carpaccios are tasty starters. Risottos are the chef's specialty; a nutty, brown, three-mushroom version is cooked perfectly *al dente* and flavored with truffle oil, rare in these parts. At this writing, the restaurant is leaving its historical, downtown mansion for a new pseudo–Spanish Colonial shopping center under construction. ✉ *In Centro Comercial Santa Rosa, across from Burger King, on road to airport* ☎ *665–0653* ▤ *AE, DC, MC, V.*

¢–$ ✕ **Café Europa/The German Bakery.** The aroma of baking bread is irresistible as you pass this bakery just south of the Liberia airport, whose baked goods are delivered all over the peninsula. Stop in for strudels, bundt cakes, and flaky fruit pastries. Lunch choices include (non-German) pizza and bratwurst with sauerkraut. It's open from 6 AM to 6 PM. ✉ *2 km/1 mi south of Liberia airport* ☎ *668–1081* ▤ *AE, MC, V.*

¢–$ ✕ **El Café Liberia.** The smell of roasting coffee is the best advertisement for this sophisticated café in the center of Liberia, where cheerful owner/chef Céline Goyette whips up cool, refreshing soups—the mint pea is a winner—and homemade desserts. Along with quiche, cakes, and hot sandwiches, Céline dishes out local information and helpful advice. A good selection of imported wines accompany the light meals. The café runs an English/French-language used-book exchange. ✉ *From Liberia's main street, 75 m south of Banco de Credito Agricola* ☎ *665–1660* ▤ *No credit cards* ⊘ *Closed weekends.*

$ ▦ **Best Western Las Espuelas.** Smaller and with more personal attention than the Best Western El Sitio on the other side of town, this motel-style hotel has some character thanks to local paintings and indigenous stone stat-

FODOR'S FIRST PERSON

Dorothy MacKinnon
Writer

We were rolling along the nearly deserted highway near Liberia when an aluminum ladder came loose from an open-bed truck and cartwheeled across the highway, heading straight for our windshield. My colleague swerved, catching the concrete abutment, flipping our rented KIA Sportage. We landed right side up, inches from a large tree.

Seconds later the highway was alive with people rushing to our aid. Two men, including the flying-ladder truck's driver, pried open our crumpled doors and pulled us out. Amazingly we had only minor cuts,

but the car was totaled and my driver was passing out from shock. An ambulance arrived in under five minutes. A passerby reported the accident to the traffic police and called my rental company. An elderly woman ran home to fetch salve for my injuries. A neighbor offered a glass of cold water and stayed with me for two hours.

Everyone, officials or not, was efficient. But more importantly, they were warm, treating two *extranjeras* (foreigners) like family. Within five hours of a potentially fatal accident our new KIA was loaded up and we were on our way with a better appreciation for Tico culture.

ues. Rooms are a little institutional, but there's great water pressure in the showers (hard to find in Costa Rica) and the air-conditioning is quiet. The suites, by the pool, have private whirlpool tubs. Rooms facing the highway can be a little noisy; Nos. 17 and up are quieter. The restaurant serves excellent coffee and a good buffet breakfast, but it's dark and gloomy. ⊠ *2 km/1 mi south of Liberia* ☎ *666–0144* 🖷 *666–2441* ✉ *es-puelas@racsa.co.cr* 🛏 *44 rooms, 2 suites* ⚓ *Restaurant, cable TV, pool, outdoor whirlpool tub, bar, meeting rooms* ⊟ *AE, D, MC, V* ⊙⊟ *BP.*

$ 🄷 **Best Western Hotel El Sitio.** Lacking warmth but with plenty of conveniences, this hotel has airy and spacious rooms with lots of storage space and some king-size beds. Elevated wooden walkways framed with greenery lead to rooms. Ask for an even-numbered room with a view of the pools shaded by an ancient Guanacaste tree in the hotel's garden court (an odd-numbered room is likely to face a wall). The restaurant is Italian. ⊠ *South of Burger King, on road heading west toward airport and beaches* ☎ *666–1211* 🖷 *666–2059* 🌐 *www.bestwestern.com* 🄿 *Apdo. 134–5000, Liberia* 🛏 *52 rooms* ⚓ *Restaurant, in-room safes, cable TV, 2 pools, spa, bar, casino, laundry service, Internet, meeting room* ⊟ *AE, MC, V* ⊙⊟ *BP.*

To & from Liberia
234 km/145 mi (4 hrs) northwest of San José.

From San José, follow the Pan-American Highway west past the Puntarenas exit, then north past Cañas to Liberia. The road is paved but is in various states of disrepair. It's a heavily traveled truck and bus route and there are miles and miles where it is impossible to pass, but many drivers try, making this a dangerous road. Frequent direct buses leave San José for Liberia each day, so it might be worth busing up to Liberia and renting a car from there.

Liberia Essentials

🏦 Banks **Banco de Costa Rica** ✉ Diagonal to the Central Park ☎ 666–9002.

🏦 ATMs **Bancredito** ✉ Avda. 0, 2 blocks north of Hwy. **Burger King ATH** ✉ Pan-American Hwy., at entrance to town.

🏥 Hospital **Liberia Hospital** ✉ North end of town ☎ 666–4250.

💊 Pharmacies **Farmacia Lux** ✉ C. 4 and Avda. 0 ☎ 665–0182 ⏱ Weekdays 8–6, Sat. 8–noon.

THE NICOYA COAST

Strung along the coast of the Nicoya Peninsula are sparkling sand beaches lined with laid-back fishing communities and hotels and resorts in every price category. As recently as the 1970s, fishing and cattle ranching were the area's mainstays. Development is barreling ahead full speed, though, bringing with it sophisticated restaurants, hotels, and shops, along with congestion, construction chaos, and higher costs. Roads are only starting to catch up, so you'll find the interesting anomaly of a fabulous restaurant or hotel plunked at the end of a tortuous dirt road.

Papagayo Peninsula

❼ If you are looking for resort or all-inclusive hotels in which to isolate yourself, Papagayo Peninsula, a crooked finger of land cradling the west side of Bahía Culebra (Snake Bay), is the place to do it. As of mid-2005, five large hotels and resorts were situated around the Papagayo Bay; upwards of 15 additional hotels have contracts to build in the near future. Though the hotels are modeled on Caribbean-Island resorts, beaches are distinctly Costa Rican, with brown sand and cloudy, rough water not recommended for swimming. Isolation is the name of the game, which means that getting out of man-made "paradise" to explore wilderness or anything off-property often entails hours in a van on a pricey tour.

> **ECO-OK?**
>
> The Papagayo Peninsula has been the center of controversy for a decade, pitting development companies against local environmentalists concerned about shrinking habitat and low water levels in this already parched area.

High season here coincides with dry season, so there's guaranteed sun January to April, but there's also intense heat and the landscape is brown and brittle. The sparkling water and spectacular sunsets are beautiful year-round. In the rainy season (August–December), the landscape is greener and lusher, and you can be outdoors more comfortably.

Continued on page 193

CHOOSING A BEACH

Tamarindo Beach, Guanacaste, Costa Rica

 Each beach along Nicoya's coast, most lined with palms and tamarind trees, has its distinct merits. Sand varies from pulverized black volcanic rock (Playa Negra) to crushed white shells (Playa Conchal) to picture-perfect, soft white sand (Playa Carrillo), with every shade of brown in between. Atmospherically, beaches vary from tranquil, secluded, Robinson Crusoe–like strands (Playa Rajada) to civilized beaches with restaurants so close to the ocean the surf spray salts your food (Playa Brasilito) to family-friendly spots with calm, swimmable waters and shade (Playas Hermosa and Sámara) to beaches with buff and beautiful, tattooed surfers (Playas Tamarindo and Negra) to those made for contemplative walks or dramatic sunsets (Playas Langosta and Pelada).

Playa Hermosa

BEACHES

 Diving
Snorkeling
Fishing
Surfing
Kayaking
Sailing
Swimming
Blue Flag Ecological Award

The main attraction on the **Papagayo Peninsula** beaches is the all-inclusive resorts that inhabit them.

Gulf of Papagayo

Puerto Culebra

Bahía Culebra

Playa Hermosa is one of the few Costa Rican beaches with calm, crystal-clear waters.

Aeropuerto Internacional Daniel Oduber

21

Guardia

Comunidad

Palmira

21

Playa Panamá

Panama

Playa Hermosa

Playas del Coco

Sardinal

Surfing, diving, and fishing are the name of the game at **Playas del Coco** and its scruffy beach town.

El Coco

Playa Ocotal

Playa Ocotal is a quiet beach with great views and good snorkeling.

Nuevo Colon

Playa Pan de Azúcar is difficult to access, but practically deserted once you get there.

Coyo

Playa Pan de Azúcar

Potrero

Tempate

Playa Potrero is the jumping-off point for diving trips to the Catalina Islands.

Playa Potrero

Isla Sta. Catalina

Playa Flamingo

Brasilito

155

Portegolpe

Llano

Huacas

Playa Conchal

Shells sprinkle the sand at chilled-out **Playa Conchal**, near a small fishing village.

Brasilito

Busy white-sand **Playa Flamingo** is ideal for swimming and sunning.

Playa Real

Matapalo

Salinas

Playa Grande

Las Baulas Marine National Park

Villarreal

155

Tamarindo

Tamarindo

Tamarindo is a hyped-up surfing and water-sports beach with wild nightlife.

Playa Langosta

Lively **Tamarindo** is a hyped-up surfing and water-sports beach with wild nightlife.

0   8 miles

0   12 km

Playa Langosta

Nosara

Playa Carrillo

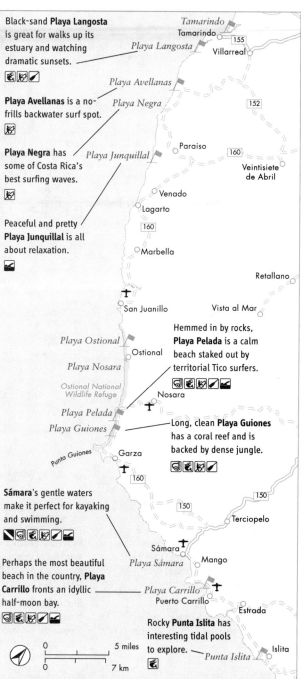

Black-sand **Playa Langosta** is great for walks up its estuary and watching dramatic sunsets.

Playa Avellanas is a no-frills backwater surf spot.

Playa Negra has some of Costa Rica's best surfing waves.

Peaceful and pretty **Playa Junquillal** is all about relaxation.

Hemmed in by rocks, **Playa Pelada** is a calm beach staked out by territorial Tico surfers.

Long, clean **Playa Guiones** has a coral reef and is backed by dense jungle.

Sámara's gentle waters make it perfect for kayaking and swimming.

Perhaps the most beautiful beach in the country, **Playa Carrillo** fronts an idyllic half-moon bay.

Rocky **Punta Islita** has interesting tidal pools to explore.

Tamarindo
Tamarindo
155
Playa Langosta
Villarreal

Playa Avellanas
152
Playa Negra

Paraiso
160
Playa Junquillal
Veintisiete de Abril

Venado
Lagarto
160
Marbella

Retallano

San Juanillo
Vista al Mar

Playa Ostional
Ostional
Playa Nosara
Ostional National Wildlife Refuge
Nosara
Playa Pelada
Playa Guiones
Punta Guiones
Garza

160
150
150
Terciopelo

Sámara
Playa Sámara
Mango

Playa Carrillo
Puerto Carrillo
Estrada

Punta Islita
Islita

0   5 miles
0   7 km

CHOOSING A BEACH

4

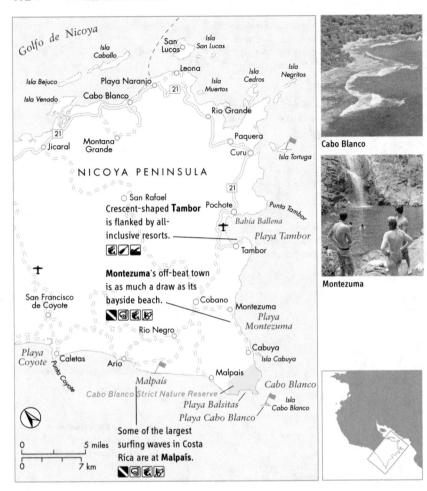

Cabo Blanco

Crescent-shaped **Tambor** is flanked by all-inclusive resorts. ⎯⎯

Montezuma's off-beat town is as much a draw as its bayside beach. ⎯⎯

Montezuma

Some of the largest surfing waves in Costa Rica are at **Malpaís**.

0   5 miles
0   7 km

MAKING THE MOST OF YOUR BEACH VACATION

■ Tamarindo, Nosara, and Sámara are good for beginning surfers. Playas Grande, Avellanas, and Negra are best left to those with experience; other surfing waters are somewhere in between.

■ Tamarindo, Nosara, Sámara, and Tambor are beaches with air service to San José.

■ The beach road connecting most Nicoya Peninsula beaches is hard to stomach any time of year, and virtually impassable during the August through December rains. Take easier inland routes instead.

■ Riptides are seriously dangerous and hardly any Costa Rican beaches have lifeguards; get information from your hotel about where to swim.

Outdoor Activities

CANOPY TOUR Taking advantage of one of the few remaining patches of dry tropical forest on the Papagayo Peninsula, **Witch's Rock Canopy Tour** (☎ 666–7546) gives you your money's worth: 23 platforms, with a thrilling 450-meter cable zip between two of them; four hanging bridges; a waterfall in rainy season; and hiking trails. The 1½-hour tour is $55 per person.

Where to Stay

$$$$ ▦ **Four Seasons Resort Costa Rica.** By far the most luxurious hotel in Costa Rica, the Four Seasons is extremely secluded (it's nearly 30 minutes from the main road). From the time you arrive to the time you sip your last umbrella drink, you won't have to lift a finger. Service, provided by a cream-of-the-crop, bilingual Tico staff, is faultless. The decor is anonymously tasteful and arty. Huge rooms have king-size beds, marble baths, and screened-in living-room terraces. The breezy 18-hole Arnold Palmer signature golf course has breathtaking views—and prices ($180 per round). The state-of-the-art spa is impressive but a little sterile. Dishes created at the dinner-only Di Mare restaurant are worth their wildly expensive price tags, but the rest of the hotel's food is disappointing. ✉ *25 km/15 mi west of Guardia; follow signs to Papagayo Allegro Resort, and continue to the end of the rd.* ☎ *696–0000* 🖷 *696–0010* ⊕ *www.fourseasons. com* 🛏 *123 rooms, 36 suites, 21 villas* ☖ *3 restaurants, room service, fans, in-room safes, refrigerators, satellite TV, 18-hole golf course, 4 pools, gym, spa, beach, tours, 2 bars, babysitting, children's programs, laundry facilities and service, concierge, in-room broadband, business center, meeting rooms, airport shuttle, car service* ▭ *AE, DC, MC, V* ⑩ *EP.*

☾ **$$$$** ▦ **Premier Fiesta Resort & Spa Papagayo.** This is the coziest of the large hotels around the bay; it also has the best beach. Pretty bungalows, half with king-size beds, are spread out on the hills overlooking the bay; however, the 21 new bungalows under construction may change the landscape. The pool and beach are the noisy hubs for most of the organized activities. But an adults-only, resistance lap pool is near the spa and fitness center. Ask for a bungalow near the spa if you seek quiet. Avoid the concrete high-rise block of less private rooms at the top of the hill. Book early in the morning for à la carte meals. ✉ *Playa Arenilla, just north of Playa Panama* ☎ *672–0000* 🖷 *672–0181* ⊕ *www.fiestapremier. com* 🛏 *142 rooms in 71 bungalows, 60 high-rise rooms* ☖ *3 restaurants, fans, in-room safes, refrigerator, cable TV, 2 pools, gym, spa, beach, dive shop, tours, bicycles, kayaking, 3 bars, casino, nightclub, babysit-*

The Ecological Blue Flag

THE WORLD GIVES HIGH MARKS to Costa Rica for its environmental awareness, but a visit here shows that the accolades don't always match the reality. Deforestation occurs at an alarming rate and the country has major trash-disposal issues. Recognizing that three-quarters of visitors to Costa Rica make a beach excursion, the national water utility, Aqueductos y Alcantarillados, in conjunction with the Instituto Costarricense de Turismo, began evaluating and ranking water and environmental quality in coastal communities in 1996. Those that achieved a 90 percent score were awarded a Bandera Azul Ecológica (ecological blue flag) to fly as a symbol of excellence.

The program, modeled on one begun in Spain in 1986 and now used in the European Union, awards flags as prizes for communities, rather than to individual hotels. Participating areas are required to form a Blue Flag committee, a move that brings together diverse sectors of an area's population, many of which otherwise fiercely compete for tourist dollars. In true developing-country fashion, Costa Rica's wealth concentrates in the capital and the Central Valley. But the Blue Flag program has prompted less affluent lowland and coastal communities to put resources into improving environmental quality of life for themselves and for their guests.

Only 10 beaches earned a Blue Flag that first year, a fact that Costa Rica sheepishly decided not to publicize, not wanting to call attention to the high number of communities that *didn't* make the cut. When 19 succeeded the following year, the results went public. Officials inspect heavily visited beaches once a month. More isolated communities get bimonthly assessments. They evaluate water quality—both ocean and drinking water—trash cleanup, waste management, security, signage, and environmental education. In 2002, the competition was opened to inland communities.

Blue flags fly proudly in the following communities covered in this book:

Central Valley: Carrizal (Alajuela).

Northern Plains: La Fortuna, Las Horquetas de Sarapiquí, San Rafael de Heredia, Vara Blanca.

North Pacific: Bahía Junquillal, Nosara (Playa Guiones, Playa Pelada), Ostional, Playa Avellanas, Playa Carrillo, Playa Conchal, Playa Grande, Playa Hermosa, Playa Junquillal, Playa Langosta, Playa Ocotal, Playa Pan de Azúcar, Playa Panamá, Punta Islita, Tamarindo.

Central Pacific: Barú, Isla Tortuga, Malpaís, Manuel Antonio (Playa Manuel Antonio, Playa Espadilla Sur, Puerto Escondido, Playa Gemelas), Puntarenas, Punta Leona (Playa Blanca, Playa Limoncito, Playa Mantas).

South Pacific: Ballena National Marine Park (Playa La Colonia, Playa Piñuela, Playa Ballena, Punta Uvita), Dominical, San Gerardo de Rivas, San Marcos de Tarrazú.

Caribbean Coast: Cahuita (Puerto Vargas, Playa Blanca, Playa Negra), EARTH, Puerto Viejo de Talamanca (Playa Negra, Playa Chiquita, Playa Cocles, Punta Uva), Gandoca-Manzanillo National Wildlife Refuge.

ting, children's programs, laundry facilities, concierge, Internet ☐ AE, DC, MC, V ⊙ AI.

To & from Papagayo Peninsula

All hotels here have airport pickup. To get to the Four Seasons from the Liberia airport (the hotel refuses to put up directional signs in order to "protect its privacy"), drive 10 km (6 mi) south of Guardia, over the Río Tempisque Bridge, then take the turn on the right signed for Papagayo Allegro Resort. Follow this road about 20 km (12 mi) to its end at the entrance to the resort. For Fiesta Premier, the best route is via Comunidad, then 20 km (12 mi) north to Playa Panamá, all on paved roads. The Grand Papagayo is 30 km (19 mi) north of Guardia toward Nacascolo, then follow signs.

Playa Hermosa

❽ Beautiful Playa Hermosa is one of the last laid-back beach towns on this part of the coast. It's the kind of place where the beach is still the town's main throroughfare, filled with joggers, people walking their dogs, and families out for a stroll. Not to be confused with the mainland surfers' beach of the same name south of Jacó, this Playa Hermosa is experiencing heavy development pressures, with new crops of sunny villas springing up each year and filling up with American and Canadian expatriates. Clusters of condominiums climb up the surrounding hillsides. Luckily, though, the full length of the beach has long been occupied by small hotels, restaurants, and homes, so the newer hotel behemoths and other developments are forced to set up shop off the beach or on other beaches in the area. There is a positive side to all this growth: new restaurants and a wider choice of accommodations.

Hermosa's mile-long crescent of dark gray volcanic sand attracts heat, so the best time to be out on the beach is early morning or late afternoon, in time for the spectacular sunsets. The beach fronts a line of trees, so there's a welcome respite from the heat of the sun. The crystal-clear water—it's a Blue Flag beach—is usually calm, with no strong currents and with comfortable temperatures of 74°F–80°F. Sea views are as picturesque as they get, with bobbing fishing boats, jagged profiles of coastline, rocky outcroppings, and at night the twinkling lights of the Four Seasons Resort across the bay. At the beach's north end, low tide creates wide, rock-lined tidal pools.

Outdoor Activities

Aqua Sport (✉ Beach road; heading south, take second entrance to Playa Hermosa and follow signs ☎ 672–0050 ⊕ www.costa-rica-beach-hotel.com) organizes fishing, surfing, and snorkeling trips and rents every kind of boat and board. **Charlie's Adventure** (✉ Hotel Condovac, north end of beach ☎ 672–0275) organizes ATV tours, horseback riding, fishing trips, snorkeling, diving, and sunset sails, as well as boat tours of a mangrove and Hermosa Bay. At the north end of the beach, below Hotel Condovac La Costa, an independent **kiosk** rents Boogie boards, plastic kayaks, Jet Skis, and other water toys.

BOATING **The Giuseppina** (☎ 305–1584), a 48-foot replica of a Grand Banks trawler, can be chartered by the hour (three-hour minimum) or overnight, from $200/hour to $245 per person overnight (four-person minimum). **Hotel el Velero** (⊠ 100 m north of Aqua Sport ☎ 672–0036 ⊕ www. costaricahotel.net) will take you out for a five-hour sunset cruise on their 38-foot sailing yacht ($45 per person). Tours include snorkeling, cave exploring, and sunbathing.

DIVING & Average temperatures of 75°F to 80°F, 20 to 60 feet of visibility, and
SNORKELING frequent sightings of sea turtles, sharks, manta rays, mora eels, and very big fish make Hermosa a great place to dive.

Charlie's Adventure (⇨ *above*) organizes snorkeling and diving trips. **Diving Safaris** (⊠ Second entrance road to Playa Hermosa, across from Villa Huetares Hotel ☎ 672–0012, 877/853–0538 in U.S. ⊕ www. costaricadiving.net) has a range of scuba activities, from beginner training to open-water PADI certification courses. Multitank dives are organized at more than 30 sites. Guides and trainers are very good, and their safety standards have the DAN (Divers Alert Network) seal of approval. This dive shop has also earned the coveted five-star, gold-palm status from PADI. Prices range from $75 for two-tank morning dives, to $375 and up for PADI open-water and Dive Master certification courses.

There are no reefs for snorkeling here, but there are coral formations and rocky outcroppings to explore. You need a boat and a guide to find the best spots. **Aqua Sport** (⇨ *above*) sends snorkelers out with a knowledgeable local guide who's excellent at finding marine life. A three-hour tour with guide, boat, and equipment is $20 per person (minimum of 3 people).

FISHING The fishing at Playa Hermosa is mostly close to the shores, and yields edible fish like dorado (mahimahi), amberjack, and yellowfin tuna. Local restaurants are happy to cook your catch for you. You can rent a boat with **Aqua Sport** (⇨ *above*). **Charlie's Adventure** (⇨ *above*) runs fishing trips.

Where to Stay & Eat

★ ¢–$ ✕ **Ginger Restaurant Bar.** This all-appetizer restaurant, in a modernistic glass-and-steel treehouse cantilevered on the side of a hill, is a big hit. The Cordon-Bleu–trained chef has created a half-Asiatic, half-Mediterranean menu with fun offerings like seasoned shoestring fries dipped in roasted garlic mayonnaise and a taco basket filled with seared pepper-crusted tuna and pickled ginger slaw. Portions look small, but layerings of condiments and garnishes make them satisfying. Save room for the elaborate desserts. ⊠ *Main highway, just south of Hotel Condovac entrance* ☎ *672–0041* ▤ *MC, V* ⚐ *Reservations essential Jan.–Mar.* ☺ *Closed Mon. No lunch.*

★ $$ ▥ **Hotel El Velero.** This hotel is always hopping, with local expats and visitors exchanging fishing, boating, and real-estate stories. The Canadian general manager is an ebullient host, full of local lore and advice. Spacious, attractive rooms at this two-story, white beachfront hotel have arched doorways, terra-cotta tiles, bamboo furniture, and large windows. The hotel runs daily snorkeling and sunset cruises on its own handsome 38-foot sailboat. In the restaurant, jumbo shrimp and always-fresh mahimahi are fixtures. Come on Wednesday or Saturday for beach barbecue nights, when there's live music. Drinks are two-for-one every day during Happy Hour, 4 to 6 PM. ⊠ *Second entrance to Playa Hermosa, then north 100 m along beach rd.* ☎ 672–0036 📠 672–0016 ⊕ *www. costaricahotel.net* 🖙 *22 rooms* ⏥ *Restaurant, in-room safes, cable TV, pool, snorkeling, boating, Jet Skiing, bar, laundry service, gated parking* ▭ *AE, MC, V* ¶◎¶ *EP.*

$ 🔲 **Hotel Playa Hermosa Bosque del Mar.** Shaded by massive, hundred-year-old trees, this low-lying hotel is pleasantly laid back. The most popular activity here is lounging in hammocks strung around the garden. But floating in the new, lushly landscaped pool is a close second. Flashes of sunlit ocean, just a few barefoot steps away, periodically penetrate the cool greenery. The rooms, lined up in one-story brick blocks, are being revamped at this writing, with new mattresses, sunny color-washed walls, ceramic bathrooms with hot water, cable TV, and quiet, remote-controlled air conditioners. Beachfront rooms are the smallest but you can open the screened windows at night and catch the breeze and the sound of the ocean. The restaurant serves truly fresh fish and beef tenderloin raised on the owner's ranch. ⊠ *End of the first entrance to Playa Hermosa* ☎ 672–0046 📠 672–0019 ⊕ *www.hotelplayahermosa.com* 🖙 *20 rooms* ⏥ *Restaurant, fans, beach, bar* ▭ *AE, DC, MC, V* ¶◎¶ *EP.*

$ 🔲 **Villas Huetares.** The best bargain in town, this long-established family hotel with two-bedroom garden villas also has a pleasant, two-story annex with 16 spacious rooms. In a quiet corner of the large garden, behind the pool, the newer rooms have two double beds, small refrigerators, cable TV, and air-conditioning. Two ground-floor rooms are wheelchair accessible. Oddly, a few of the rooms have only cold water, or as the Ticos like to say, *agua corriente* (room-temperature water). If you're willing to cook for yourself, the bungalows are a bargain, especially for families or groups. Be prepared for the sound of kids playing in the pool and garden. The walk to the beach is about 10 minutes. ⊠ *Second entrance road to Playa Hermosa, 100 m (1 block) in from the main hwy* ☎ 672–0052 📠 672–0051 🖙 *16 rooms, 15 villas* ⏥ *Snack bar, fans, some kitchens, some refrigerators, cable TV, 2 pools; no a/c in villas, no room phones* ▭ *AE, DC, MC, V* ¶◎¶ *EP.*

Nightlife

Hotel El Velero (⊠ Second entrance to Playa Hermosa, then 100 m north of Aqua Sport on beach rd.) hosts beach barbecues with live music on Wednesday and Saturday nights in high season. The crowd is 30-ish and up. Weekend nights in high season there's live mellow jazz, as well as some classic rock at **Villa del Sueño** (⊠ First entrance to Playa Hermosa, 350 m west of main hwy.). The band takes its cues from what the audience wants to hear.

Shopping

You can shop for a beach picnic at the **Aqua Sport** (⊠ Second entrance to Playa Hermosa; follow signs heading south on beach rd.) minimarket and liquor store and buy souvenirs in the gift shop. The **Villa del Sueño gift shop** (⊠ First entrance to Playa Hermosa, 350 m west of main hwy.) has original oil paintings, exotic crafts from around the world,

Making a Difference

YOUR NATIONAL-PARK or -reserve entrance fee helps support the preservation of Costa Rica's wildlife and places. You can also make your visit beneficial to the people living nearby by hiring local guides, horses, or boats; eating in local restaurants; and buying things (excluding wild-animal products) in local shops. You can go a few steps farther by making donations to local conservation groups or to such international organizations as Conservation International, the Rainforest Alliance, and the Worldwide Fund for Nature, all of which support important conservation efforts in Costa Rica. It's also helpful to explore private preserves off the beaten path, and stay at lodges that contribute to environmental efforts and to nearby communities. By planning your visit with an eye toward grassroots conservation efforts, you join the global effort to save Costa Rica's tropical ecosystems and help ensure that the treasures you traveled so far to see remain intact for future generations.

locally made mother-of-pearl jewelry, and unique ivory bracelets made of local brahma cow bones. **Kaltak Art and Craft Market** (⊠ South of airport on road to Santa Cruz) has five rooms of high-quality crafts and gifts, including organic-cotton blouses and dresses and traditional leather-and-wood rocking chairs, which they will ship for you.

To & from Playa Hermosa
27 km/17 mi (30 mins) southwest of Liberia airport.

From the Comunidad turnoff of Highway 21, heading from Liberia, Playa Hermosa is about 15 km (9 mi) northwest. The paved road forks after the small town of Sardinal, with the right fork heading into Hermosa and the left leading to Playas del Coco. Local directions usually refer to the first and second entrance roads to the beach, with the first entrance being the southern one. There is no through beachfront road, so you have to approach the beach from either of these two roads. Empresa Esquivel buses leave from Liberia for Playa Hermosa daily at 4:45, 7:30, and 11:30 AM and 1, 3:30, and 5:30 PM.

Playa Hermosa Essentials
Playa Hermosa has few resources. Get what you need in Liberia or Playas del Coco, to the south.

🖥 Internet **Villa Acacia** ⊠ Second entrance to Playa Hermosa; south on beach rd. ☎ 672-1000.

Playas del Coco

🟢 Messy, noisy, colorful, and interesting, Playas del Coco is first and fore-most a fishing port, with a Port Captain's office, a fish market, and an ice factory for keeping fish fresh—not for cooling margaritas, although many are drunk here. The town (called "El Coco" by locals) is not particularly scenic. The dark-sand beach is mostly a workplace, and it hasn't yet met the Blue Flag standards of cleanliness. The main street becomes a sea of mud when it rains and a dustbowl when it doesn't. So why do visitors flock here? They come to eat at the many excellent seafood restaurants and to shop at the big supermarket and myriad souvenir shops. But primarily they come to dive, surf, and fish. If you like your resorts to have some local color, Coco's slightly down-at-the-heels appearance can be appealing. It's also one of the most accessible beaches from San José in Guanacaste. The north part of the beach has a couple of lovely restaurants and hotels, although condominium developers have moved in and the sounds of construction will be ringing out for a few years to come.

Outdoor Activities

BOATING
You can sail off into the sunset for $55, including open bar and appetizers, on **Drums of Bora Bora** (☎ 670–1033), a 50-foot teak yacht.

DIVING & SNORKELING
Half a dozen dive shops crowd into this small town. This coast doesn't have the coral reefs or the clear visibility of the Caribbean coast, but it does have a lot of plankton (hence the lower visibility) that feeds legions of fish, some of them really, really big. Manta rays and sharks (white-tipped, nurse, and bull varieties) are among the stars of the undersea show. It takes about 20 to 45 minutes to reach the local sites.

Most of the dive shops have instruction, including **Summer-Salt Dive Center** (✉ Main St. ☎ 670–0308 ⊕ www.summer-salt.com). **Deep Blue Diving Adventures** (✉ Main street, in Hotel Coco Verde parking lot ☎ 670–1004 ⊕ www.scuba-diving-in-costa-rica.com) has the cheapest dives (from $50). **Drums of Bora Bora** (⇨ Boating, *above*) runs daytime snorkeling trips ($65). **Rich Coast Diving** (✉ Main street, across the street and one block north of Hotel Coco Verde ☎ 670–0176 ⊕ www.richcoastdiving.com) has enthusiastic guides and instructors and limits tours to 5 divers per Dive Master and 10 divers per boat.

FISHING
Fishing charter boats go out 15 to 40 mi seeking yellowfin tuna, mahimahi, grouper, and red snapper close-in, and sailfish, marlin, and roosterfish offshore (beyond 40 mi). Boats, moored here and in nearby Ocotal, can pick you up from a beach near your hotel. **TranquilaMar** (✉ Behind Louisiana Bar & Grill, off main st. ⊕ www.tranquilamar.com ☎ 670–0833) has three 28-foot Cummins diesel-powered boats moored in nearby Ocotal and can pick you up at any local beach. Just bring sunscreen and your hat, says the owner. Trips are $400 for a half-day and $600 for a full day. **Blue Marlin Service** (✉ Main St. ☎ 670–0707, 353–5011) goes out in either a 25-foot boat for close-in fishing ($285/half-day) or in a luxury, 52-footer for a full day offshore ($1,600).

SURFING
★
Legendary **Witch's Rock and Ollie's Point** surfing spots are a one-hour boat ride away from Playas del Coco off the coast of Santa Rosa National Park. Overcrowding led the park authorities to limit the number of daily surfers to 25 in 2004, but that stricture has gone by the boards. Now you can surf as long as you pay the $6 park entrance fee.

You can sign up for a surfing trip with any beach-town tour operator, but local authorities only allow excursions to Witch's Rock and Ollie's Point to originate from the main dock at Playas del Coco, in boats owned by local boat owners, in order to curb overcrowding and undue environmental stress. **Roca Bruja Surf Operation** (✉ Main street, about 3 blocks from beach ☎ 670–1020 ⊕ www.costaricasurftrips.com) is the operator that officially represents the local association of boat operators. The trip is around $50 per person (five surfers per boat at $250 for the boat), plus the park entrance fee.

Where to Stay & Eat

$$–$$$ ✕ **Vida Bar y Peruvian Cuisine.** The newest place in town is also the most expensive and the most sophisticated. Celebrating ceviche, which was invented in Peru by early 19th-century Japanese immigrants, this place is the quintessence of cool. There's live jazz weekends on a stage where the backdrop features huge photos of guitar greats. You can sip Pisco Sours—a Peruvian specialty made with grappa and egg whites—on a breezy veranda lounge. Avoid the overpriced local beers. The vast menu is authentically and deliciously Peruvian, from starters to desserts. If you can't make a choice, try the excellent sampler plates. ✉ *Main street, across from Coco Verde Hotel* ☎ 670–0605 ▭ *MC, V* ☉ *Open 11:30 AM to 2 AM in high season, to 10 PM in low season.*

$–$$ ✕ **Restaurante Papagayo Pura Vida.** The best way to enjoy the beach and the bay is to sit yourself down at an outdoor table at this beachfront Tico restaurant. The food is straightforward, reliably fresh, and flavorful. Sip a fruit smoothie, sample a ceviche of fish and shrimp, or slurp up a seafood soup generously packed with shrimp, calamari, fish, and crab. The lobster here is the best buy in town. There's also a lobster kabob for those who don't like the work of cracking shells. ✉ *Main street, right at the beach* ☎ 670–0272 ▭ *AE, DC, MC, V.*

★ $ ✕ **El Sol y La Luna.** Finding haute-Italian cuisine in a romantic alfresco restaurant in Playas del Coco is a pleasant surprise. Host Alessandro Tolo brought his design ideas and superb jazz CD collection from Rome, and his wife, Silvia Casu, brought her culinary skills from her native Sardinia. Diners are often repeat visitors, returning for homemade pasta and homegrown basil, along with other distinctively Italian tastes, including a wide selection of Italian wines, sparkling San Pellegrino mineral water, and aromatic sambuca liqueur. For dessert, try the Arenal, a moist, chocolate cake floating in a lake of chocolate sauce. If you're staying nearby, there's also pizza to go. ✉ *La Puerta del Sol hotel, 180 m to right, off main road to Playas del Coco* ☎ 670–0195 ▭ *MC, V.*

$$ ✕⌂ **La Puerta del Sol.** The most luxurious hotel in the area is a tranquil enclosure of stylish suites facing a formal garden with sculpted shrubs and a lovely pool. The modern, airy Mediterranean-style guest rooms are shot through with hot, tropical colors: fuchsia, orange, and aqua. King-size beds roost atop adobe platforms, and gleaming white, tiled bathrooms have high ceilings. Pasha, the resident Newfoundland dog, can usually be found lolling around the reception area and there are various pet cats prowling in the garden. The restaurant, El Sol y La Luna (⇨ *above*), is excellent. ✉ *180 m to right (north) off main road to town* ☎ 670–0195 ⎙ 670–0650 ⊕ *hotelsol@racsa.co.cr* ⤳ *10 suites* ⚐ *Restaurant, in-room safes, refrigerators, cable TV, pool, gym* ▭ *MC, V* ⦿ *BP.*

$$ ⌂ **Rancho Armadillo.** The eye-popping avenue of pink bougainvillea lining the long drive to this B&B is just a hint of the riotous garden beyond that attracts hummingbirds, butterflies, birds, and small beasts.

At the foot of a forested mountain, the hotel has views of greenery as far as the eye can see, and azure sea in the distance. There's nothing fussy here: this is a place to relax, with decks, terraces, and an elevated hammock house. The handsome rooms are large, with queen- and king-size beds with carved-wood headboards. Big bathrooms have rain forest shower heads. You are welcome to cook in the commercially equipped kitchen, but owner and former culinary arts teacher Rick Vogel will cook dinner for you on request. He also gives cooking lessons ($20 plus cost of the ingredients, which you get to eat). ⊠ *First left turn, just before divided boulevard, at entrance to Playas del Coco* ☎ *670–0108* 🖷 *670–0441* ⊕ *www.ranchoarmadillo.com* ⋽ *6 rooms, two of which are 2-bedroom suites* ♨ *Shared kitchen, fans, cable TV, pool, Internet; no room phones* ☰ *AE, MC, V* ⌶⊙⌶ *BP.*

$–$$ 🖾 **Villa Flores.** Extremely popular, this comfortable B&B with floral motifs inside and out books up quickly all year round. Comments in the guest book uniformly praise the homey feeling and the personalized attention by the American owners. The high-ceilinged upstairs suites are spacious, while the downstairs rooms are fairly small but cozy, with smallish bathrooms. The gardens are awash in flowering shrubs and the pool is inviting, as are the hammocks slung between an avenue of tall palm trees. A hearty breakfast is served in a tiled terrace restaurant and dinner, too, by reservation. Restaurant Sol y Luna is just around the corner. ⊠ *180 m east of main st.* ☎ *670–0269* 🖷 *670–0787* ✆ *Apdo. 2, Playas del Coco* ⊕ *www.hotel-villa-flores.com* ⋽ *7 rooms, 2 deluxe rooms* ♨ *Restaurant, fans, pool, whirlpool tub, laundry service; no room phones, no TV in some rooms* ☰ *V* ⌶⊙⌶ *BP.*

Nightlife

At the **Lizard Lounge** (⊠ Next to Hotel Coco Verde) there's dancing every night on a big thatched-roof dance floor. The reggae and rap beats appeal to a very young surfing crowd. There's a happy hour and gambling every night at the **Hotel Coco Verde** (⊠ Main street through town). Occasionally, there are dances down by the dock at the **Coco Mar** (⊠ On beach, turn left from plaza) when a live band comes to town and the locals come from miles around. Dancing doesn't get under way until after 10 PM.

Shopping

If you can't find it at **Galería & Souvenirs Susy** (⊠ Main street, next to Coco Verde Hotel), chances are they don't make it in Costa Rica. Along with a huge selection of interesting notebooks and albums made of botanical materials, they also sell locally made shell belts ($11). Open-air souvenir stands pop up along Main Street and there's a classier Artisans' Market in a garden next door to Senor Pizza.

To & from Playas del Coco
25 km/16 mi (30 mins) southwest of Liberia airport.

It's an easy drive from the Liberia airport to Playas del Coco. This is the first major town, with lots of services, south of Liberia. The paved highway turns into a grand, divided boulevard as you enter town and then dissolves into the dusty main street that leads directly to the beach.

If you don't have a car, the best way to get here from Playa Hermosa is in a taxi, for about $7.50 each way.

Playas del Coco Essentials

🏧 Bank/ATM **Banco Nacional** ⊠ Main street, at entrance to town.

🏧 Hospital **Public Health Clinic** ⊠ Next to Hotel Coco Verde ☎ 670–0987.

🏧 Pharmacies **Farmacia Cocos** ⊠ 100 m east of Banco Nacional ☎ 670–1186 🕐 Mon.–Sat. 8:30–8, Sun. 10–6 ☞ Resident doctor.

Playa Ocotal

❿ One of the most dramatic beaches in the country, this serene crescent is ringed by rocky cliffs. The sparkling, clean turquoise water contrasts with the black sand. It's only ⅓-mi long but the vistas are endless, with offshore islands and the jagged profile of the Santa Elena Peninsula 21 mi away. Right at the entrance to the Gulf of Papagayo, it's a good place for sportfishing enthusiasts to hole up between excursions. There's good diving at Las Corridas, just 1 km (½ mi) away, and excellent snorkeling in nearby coves and islands, as well as right off the beach around the rocks at the east end of the beach.

Outdoor Activities

DIVING & SNORKELING
The **dive shop** at **El Ocotal Beach Resort** (⊠ 3 km/2 mi south of Playas del Coco ⊕ www.ocotaldiving.com) is the only PADI Gold Palm Resort in Costa Rica, so it's pretty much a sure thing that they have excellent equipment, safety standards, and instruction. It rents snorkeling equipment for $10 per day. The rocky outcrop at the north end of the beach near Los Almendros is good for snorkeling.

FISHING
El Ocotal Beach Resort (⊠ 3 km/2 mi south of Playas del Coco ⊕ www.ocotalfishing.com) has a sportfishing operation with three 32-foot Morgan hulls powered by twin 260HP Cummins engines ($499/half-day; $800 full day for up to five fishers). Marlins are catch-and-release but you can keep—and eat—the mahimahi, yellowfin tuna, and Amber Jack you catch.

HIKING
Take an exhilarating and engrossing morning walk ($15) in the hills of Ocotal with retired vet and very active naturalist **Dr. Will Abrams** (☎ 670–0553). The energetic, knowledgeable Kentucky native entertains and educates with stories about the secret lives of trees, plants, and animals spotted along the way.

Where to Stay & Eat

♨ **$$** ✕ **Picante.** It's hot and it's tropical and, as the name warns (*picante* means "spicy"), everything here makes your tastebuds tingle. The menu spices up (literally) local fish and tropical fruits in dishes like fresh-tuna *salade niçoise* and grilled mahimahi with spicy mango sauce. (There's also a milder kids' menu.) The large terrace restaurant is poolside, facing the gorgeous beach backed by a cookie-cutter condominium development at Bahía Pez Vela. The cheap dinette furniture is out of sync with the innovative food, but you'll forgive the furniture faux pas when you taste the tart Margarita Pie or Mango Cobbler. ⊠ *At the beach, Bahía Pez Vela, 1½ km/1 mi south of Ocotal* ☎ 670–0901 ▭ AE, DC, MC, V.

$$ ⊞ **Los Almendros.** If you don't mind cooking for yourself, consider settling into this residential/hotel complex on a steep hill rising right up from the beach. Its pleasant, two-bedroom, two-bath apartments are in a great location with mature gardens and good snorkeling right at their doorstep. Kitchens are modern and well equipped. The best apartments are No. 7 or 9, with a trail right down to a tidal-pool natural bathtub. There are also four-bedroom, cottage-style houses for rent but these are a little scruffy and poorly furnished. ⊠ *East end of Playa Ocotal* ☎ *670–0582* 📠 *670–0526* ⊕ *www.losalmendros.com* ⤵ *20 apartments* ♨ *Fans, kitchens, cable TV, 3 pools, beach* ▤ *AE, DC, MC, V* ⑩ *EP.*

★ **$$** ⊞ **Hotel Villa Casa Blanca.** For romance, you can't beat this Victorian-style, all-suites B&B in a hillside building buried in a bower of tropical plantings. Four-poster beds, plush furniture, and Victorian detailing set the mood. The Honeymoon Suites have deep soaking tubs built for two. The pool is small but pretty. There's no room service but the obliging staff can arrange for local restaurants to deliver dinners *á deux,* to be enjoyed by candlelight at the pool or on the terrace. Waffles, pancakes, muffins, and savory dishes provide fuel in the morning, and breakfast entertainment is provided by two pet parrots who are vociferous as well as notorious moochers. Judging by the guest comments, people love them. ⊠ *Just inside gated entrance to El Ocotal Beach Resort* 📞📞 *670–0448* ⊕ *www.hotelvillacasablanca.com* 🗋 *Apdo. 176–5019, Playas del Coco* ⤵ *12 suites* ♨ *Pool, fans, outdoor whirlpool tub; no room phones, no room TVs, no smoking* ▤ *AE, MC, V* ⑩ *BP.*

Nightlife

Enjoy a quiet margarita with an ocean view at **Father Rooster Sports Bar & Grill** (⊠ El Ocotal Beach Resort, 3 km/2 mi south of Playas del Coco) on the beach. The action heats up later in the evening with big-screen TV, music, pool, beach volleyball, and Tex-Mex bar food. During peak holiday weeks, huge crowds of partiers descend on the bar to dance by torchlight.

To & from Playa Ocotal

3 km/2 mi (10 mins) of Playas del Coco.

The drive from Playas del Coco is on a paved road to the gated entrance of Playa Ocotal. The road winds through a heavily populated Tico residential area, so be on the lookout, especially at night, for bicyclists without lights, children, dogs, cows, and horses on the road. There are no buses from Playas del Coco to Ocotal, but it's $5 by taxi.

Playa Pan de Azúcar

⓫ Playa Pan de Azúcar (Sugar Bread Beach) has a quality that can be hard to come by in this area: privacy. With only one built-up property, the entire stretch of brown-sugar sand feels practically deserted. The north end of the beach has some good snorkeling and the swimming is good here—the ocean floor is soft and sandy. Playa Penca, a short walk south along the beach, has good swimming as well.

Outdoor Activities

Most of the operators who work out of Flamingo (⇨ *below*) cover this whole area, which is very close as the boat speeds, although more spread out via road.

Where to Stay

$$–$$$ ☒ **Hotel Sugar Beach.** Picture a thin, curving beach and a secluded hotel and shimmering pool shaded by tropical trees. The years-long construction is finally finished and the hotel now boasts some huge new suites. They're ultrasophisticated, with elegant wicker furniture, high ceilings, and private terraces with idyllic sea views. A nice touch is a coffeemaker and milk in the minifridge to go with it. If you like serenity and want to spend a little less on lodging, opt for one of the original rooms in the cool, maturely landscaped garden. Each room has a wooden door with a hand-carved local bird or animal, and a veranda with a garden or ocean view. The open-air rotunda restaurant serves good seafood dishes ($$–$$$, excluding the pricey lobster) and there's a kids' menu. ☒ *8 km/5 mi north of Playa Flamingo* ☎ *654-4242* 🖷 *654-4239* ⊕ *www.sugar-beach.com* 🛏 *18 rooms, 5 suites, 2 houses* ⚘ *Restaurant, in-room safes, some kitchens, refrigerators, cable TV, pool, snorkeling, boating, diving, horseback riding, bar, laundry service, airport shuttle (from Liberia), Internet, gift shop* ☰ *AE, D, MC, V* ⋈ *BP.*

To & from Playa Pan de Azúcar

8 km/5 mi (20 mins) north of Flamingo Beach.

Getting to this beach is an adventure in itself. It's still a very bumpy road from Flamingo Beach. If you have four-wheel drive and an excellent sense of direction, you can attempt to drive (dry season only) the 16-km (11-mi) Monkey Trail, which cuts through the mountains from Coco to Flamingo. But even some Ticos get lost on this route, so keep asking directions along the way. There are no buses to Playa Pan de Azúcar; a taxi from Playa Flamingo costs about $15.

Playa Potrero

❿ The small town of Potrero is a classic Tico community, with a church, school, and supermarket arranged around a soccer field. But Potrero Beach stretches for 4 km (2½ mi) all the way south from the village to the skyline of Flamingo. Development is picking up speed, with large houses and condominium developments springing up on any hill with a view. There's a large Italian contingent here, adding some style and flavor to area hotels. There are also some affordable, self-catering resorts, where you can set yourself up comfortably for a week or more. The brown-sand beach is safe for swimming and the quietest stretch is midway between Flamingo and Potrero town. The best beach view and best breeze are from a bar stool at Bar Las Brisas. About 10 km (6 mi) offshore lie the Catalina Islands, a barrier-island mecca for divers and snorkelers.

Outdoor Activities

DIVING   Marked as Santa Catarina on maps, the **Catalina Islands,** as they are known locally, are a major destination for dive operations based all along the coast. These barrier islands are remarkable for their versatility, and appeal to different levels of divers. On one side, the islands have 20- to 30-foot drops, great for beginner divers. The other side has deeper drops of 60 to 80 feet, better suited to more experienced divers. The two premier diving sites around the Catalina Islands are **The Point** and **The Wall.** From January to May, when the water is colder, you are almost guaranteed manta-ray sightings at these spots. Cow-nosed and devil rays are also spotted here in large schools. Dive operators from Playa Hermosa south to Tamarindo offer trips to these islands. Reserve through your hotel.

Costa Rica Diving (⊠ 1 km/½ mi south of Flamingo on the main Hwy. ☎ 654–4148 ⊕ www.costarica-diving.com) has been specializing in Catalina Islands dives for 16 years, with two-tank, two-location trips limited to five divers. The German owners also offer courses and are noted for their precision and high standards.

Where to Stay & Eat

$ ✕ **Ristorante Marco Polo.** They came, they saw, they built a whole Tuscan-style village and imported a chef from Italy to cater to a demanding Italian clientele. Marco Polo, the main restaurant at the Villagio Flor de Pacífico mega-development of red-roofed villas east of Potrero, serves properly *al dente* pasta with homemade sauces and excellent wood-oven pizza. Tablecloths and elegant table settings add a Continental touch. It's open for meals or pizza from noon to 10 PM. ⊠ *1 km/½ mi east of Potrero* ☎ *654–4664* ▭ *AE, DC, MC, V.*

¢–$ ✕ **Bar Las Brisas.** The perfect beach bar, Las Brisas is a shack with a view, and what a view: the entire sweep of Playa Potrero. The kitchen serves up excellent Mexican-inspired food and seafood. The fish tacos are outstanding—breaded strips of fish smothered in lettuce, tomato, and refried beans and encased in both a crisp taco and a soft tortilla shell. Monday night is reggae night and Wednesday is ladies' night (9:30 to 11 PM) and karaoke, when the joint really jumps. The place is decorated with old surfboards, rusty U.S. license plates, and wall murals. ⊠ *Beside the supermarket* ☎ *654–4047* ▭ *No credit cards.*

¢–$ ✕ **El Castillo Gourmet Eatery.** You won't find a better peanut-butter cookie in the country. This bakery/restaurant, formerly known as Harden's Garden, is also famous for its gooey cinnamon buns and pizza by the slice or pie. You can call in your order and pick up your pizza to eat on the beach or in your hotel. A mix of Latin and American food—from breakfast eggs Benedict through lunchtime taco salads and fish-and-chips—is served at casual terrace tables shaded by an ancient fig tree. The restaurant serves meals from 7 AM to 2:30 PM and the bakery café stays open until 5 PM ⊠ *Across from Club Bahía Potrero* ☎ *654–4271* ▭ *No credit cards* ☉ *Wed.*

$ ▤ **Bahía Esmeralda Hotel & Restaurant.** Although it's not on the beach, this Italian-run hotel has lots of style at an affordable price. It's a great place for families or groups. Ochre-colored villas are spread out around a pretty pool in a sunny, mature garden. Large, glass doors bring in lots of light and clay-tile roofs keep the villas cool. The equipped apartments ($$–$$$) are for four, six, or eight people. All rooms and apartments have handsome, modern fabrics and elegantly Italian bathrooms tiled in cool green. An alfresco restaurant serves breakfast and light Italian dishes. The friendly, owner/manager is always on site. It's a five-minute walk through the village to the beach. ⊠ *1 block east of Potrero village* ☎ *354–6322* 🖷 *654–4480* ⊕ *www.hotelbahiaesmeralda.com* 🛏 *4 rooms, 14 apartments* ㋡ *Restaurant, fans, some kitchens, cable TV, pool, bicycles, laundry service; no room phones* ⊟ *MC, V* ⦿ *EP apartments, BP rooms.*

To & from Playa Potrero
4 km/2½ mi (15 mins) north of Flamingo.

Just before crossing the bridge at the entrance to Flamingo, take the right fork signed for Potrero. The road, which is alternately muddy or dusty, is rough and follows the shoreline. You don't need four-wheel drive as long as you take it nice and slow. If you've come via the four-wheel-drive-only Monkey Trail from Coco, you'll reenter civilization at Potrero. Local buses run from Flamingo to Potrero, but it's so close that you're better off taking a taxi.

Playa Flamingo

⓭ Flamingo was the first of the northern Nicoya beaches to experience the wonders of overscale resort development, a fact immortalized in the concrete towers that straggle up the hill overlooking Flamingo Bay. The place is still a bevy of real estate activity, only now the realtors are selling condominiums and house lots all around the bay. Any ledge of land with a view is now a building site. The beach, hidden away to the south of the town, is one of the few truly white-sand beaches in Costa Rica. This beach is great for swimming, with a fine-sand bottom and no strong currents. There's a bit of surf, so keep your eye on little paddlers. Except for a few spindly trees, there is no shade along the beach's kilometer-long stretch and no services. To find the beach, as you enter town, instead of going up the hill, turn left past Marie's Restaurant and follow the road past the entrance to the Flamingo Beach Resort to the end, where it becomes a dirt beach road.

Outdoor Activities

Aquacenter Diving (⊠ Flamingo Marina Resort, hill above Flamingo Bay ☎ 352–4031 ⊕ www.aquacenterdiving.com) has diving trips, kayaking, snorkeling, cruises, kids' activities, and more.

BOATING   With **Lazy Lizard Catamaran Sailing Adventures** (☎ 654–4192 ⊕ www.sailingcostarica.com), sail off for an afternoon of snorkeling and sunbathing on a 38-foot Australian-built catamaran. The catamaran's two hulls make for smoother sailing, minimizing seasickness. A four-hour sail leaving at 2 PM is $75, including guided snorkeling, kayaking, beer, wine, rum, and lots of food. Sunsets appear as you sail into port. If you're up for a more energetic sea expedition, paddle with **Costa Rica Outriggers** (☎ 383–3013 ⊕ www.guanacasteoutriggers.com) to hard-to-reach beaches for snorkeling, swimming, beachcombing, and kayaking ($45, including fruit buffet). Canoes seat seven, plus two guides.

Sail off for an afternoon of snorkeling, snacking, and sunset drinks on **Samonique III** (☎ 654–5280 ⊕ www.costarica-sailing.com), a *trés jolie* 52-foot French ketch ($75). The ship sails daily at 2 and returns at 6:30 PM.

> ### THE GUANACASTE TREE
>
> Massive and wide-spreading, with ear-like seed pods, the Guanacaste is Costa Rica's national tree.

FISHING Although the marina is still closed down while officials consider proposals (and incentives) for reopening it, there are plenty of sportfishing boats bobbing in Flamingo Bay. In December the wind picks up and many of the smaller, 31-foot-and-under boats head to calmer water farther south. But marlin (blue, black, and striped) love colder, choppier water, so January to April is prime catch-and-release marlin season. Sailfish abound, too, and there are tournaments galore. Closer in, the edible catch usually includes dorado, yellowfin tuna, wahoo, grouper, and red snapper. One of the established fishing operations that sticks around all year is **Billfish Safaris** (⊠ Lower level, Mariner Inn, at entrance to town ☎ 828–2173 or 654–4272 ⊕ www.billfishsafaris.com). Its 42-foot boat with twin 350-horsepower diesel engines can go anywhere in any kind of sea. Trips on smaller boats are also available. Half-day close-in trips are $550 for up to five fishers; or $800 for a day. Offshore trips are $650 (for up to seven people) for a half-day; $900 for the whole day. You can also go out night-fishing for snapper and grouper ($100 per person)

Where to Stay & Eat

★ $-$$ ╳ **Marie's Restaurant.** A Flamingo institution, this veranda restaurant serves reliably fresh and delicious seafood in large portions at reasonable prices. Settle in at one of the sliced-tree-trunk tables painted with sea creatures for delightful ceviche and a delicious *plato de mariscos* (shrimp, lobster, and fish fillets served with garlic butter, potatoes, and salad). Save room for the dark and delicious banana-chocolate bread pudding. At breakfast, try unusual papaya pancakes and French toast made with cream cheese and jam. ⊠ *Main road, near north end of beach* ☎ 654–4136 ▭ V.

☾ $$ ▦ **Flamingo Beach Resort.** After years of lying dormant, this modest, concrete hotel, the only hotel actually fronting Flamingo Beach, has risen again under new management that has its act together. The family-friendly hotel has been smartened up and now has the comfortable but slightly anonymous look of an international hotel. You can't beat its beach-accessible location, though, or the huge, centerpiece swimming pool, with Olympic-length laps along one side. The kids' pool has a sunburn-preventive cover. There's a dive shop on site and water equipment, plus game rooms and lots of kids' activities. The beach is just across the beach-access road. Rooms are huge, each with a private balcony. The restaurants are not exciting, so if you're looking for spectacular cuisine, don't take the all-inclusive option. A few good restaurants are within walking distance, including Marie's, and some beachfront seafood places at the entrance to Flamingo. ⊠ *Hotel entrance just past Marie's Restaurant, on left side of rd.* ☎ *654–4444, 283–8063 in San José* 🖷 *654–4060, 253–1593 in San José* ⊕ *www.resortflamingobeach.com* ⇗ *63 rooms, 20 junior suites, 8 2-bedroom suites* ⌂ *Restaurant, fans, in-room safes, refrigerators, some kitchens, cable TV, fitness room, 2 pools, beach, dive shop, 2 bars, casino, disco, babysitting, children's programs, laundry service, Internet, meeting rooms* ▭ *AE, MC, V* ⑩ *EP or AI.*

$ 🏠 **Hotel Guanacaste Lodge.** On the outskirts of Flamingo, this Tico-run lodge is good value for this pricey area. Ten large rooms in five houses have high beamed ceilings, and are comfortably furnished with wood furniture and walk-in closets. Bathrooms are tiled and spacious. Each room has a picture window looking out onto the pool and a cascading fountain. At this writing, two new rooms are under construction. The attached Rancho Grande Restaurant/Bar serves Tico, Mexican, and Spanish dishes in a huge, open rancho with handmade wooden furniture. There's a big-screen TV for karaoke and occasional live music, so there could be some noisy times here and service is leisurely, to put it mildly. ⊠ *200 m south of the Potrero-Flamingo crossroads* ☎ *654–4494* 🖷 *654–4495* ✉ *portolsa@racsa.co.cr* ⇗ *12 rooms* ⌂ *Restaurant, fans, in-room safes, cable TV, pool, bar, laundry service* ▭ *MC, V* ⑩ *BP.*

Nightlife

The **Mariner Inn Bar** (⊠ Bottom of the hill, entering Flamingo) is always boisterous and thick with testosterone, as fishermen trade fishtales. If you're interested in fishing of a different sort, or just like to watch, restaurant, disco, and casino **Amberes** (⊠ Halfway up hill in Flamingo) has recently been given a face-lift and is the late-night meeting place.

To & from Playa Flamingo

80 km/50 mi (3 hrs) southwest of Liberia.

To get to Playa Flamingo from Liberia, drive 45 km (28 mi) south to Belén on a good, paved road and then 35 km (22 mi) west on an abysmally bad, potholed road to Flamingo. (Pre-potholes, the trip from Liberia took only 1½ hours.) If you're coming from the Playas del Coco and Ocotal area, you can take a 16-km (10-mi) shortcut, called the Monkey Trail, starting near Sardinal and emerging at Potrero. It's then 4 km (2½ mi) south to Flamingo. Only attempt this in dry season and in a four-wheel-drive. You can also take a bus from Liberia (⇨ Bus Travel *in* Smart Travel Tips A to Z).

Playa Flamingo Essentials

🏧 Bank/ATM **Banco de Costa Rica** ⊠ Main street, halfway up hill, in Condominio Marina Real ☎ 654–4984.

🏥 Hospital **Pacific Emergencies** ⊠ Crossroads at Huacas ☎ 653–8787 or 378–8265 ⊙ Daily 8–8.

💊 Pharmacy **Santa Fe Medical Center & Pharmacy** ⊠ Halfway up hill ☎ 654–9000 ⊙ Daily 8–8.

Playa Conchal

❶❹ Lovely, secluded Playa Conchal is aptly named—it's sprinkled with shells atop a base of fine white sand. Although you can access the beach from the water and by walking south from Brasilito at low tide, you can't get to it from the road without passing through the rigid security of the sprawling Paradisus Playa Conchal resort. The road north of the resort is also sprinkled—but with a cluster of restaurants and shops.

Exploring

A small, scruffy fishing village just 1 km (½ mi) north of Conchal, **Brasilito** has ramshackle houses huddled around its main square, which doubles as the soccer field. It's cluttered, noisy, and totally Tico, a lively contrast to the controlled sophistication of Playa Conchal. Fishing boats moor just off a wide beach, about 3 km (2 mi) long, with golden sand flecked with pebbles and a few rocks. The surf is a little stronger here than at Flamingo Beach but the shallow, sandy bottom keeps it swimmable. The beach fronting the town of Brasilito is lined with casual, Tico *marisquerias* (seafood snack bars) and a couple of notable restaurants.

Outdoor Activities

GOLF   One of the best golf courses in the country, the Paradisus Playa Conchal megaresort's **Garra de Léon Golf Course** (⊠ Paradisus Playa Conchal, entrance less than 1 km/½ mi south of Brasilito ☎ 654–4123) is a par-72 course designed by Robert Trent Jones Jr. Hotel guests and nonguests who reserve at least one day in advance can try out their swing on 18 holes for $150 or go 9 holes for $85, cart included.

Where to Stay & Eat

★ $$–$$$ ✕ **Gecko's Restaurant/Bar.** This wildly popular Tamarindo dining fixture has moved to the Hotel Brasilito, trading road dust for fresh sea breezes and adding a lighter lunch menu to its tried-and-true dinner dishes. For the first time, it's also accepting reservations. Chef John Szilasi is in a new, improved kitchen, turning out his signature Gecko's Pasta, a mountain of garlicky linguine studded with jumbo shrimp, set on fire with jalapeño peppers and served on a bed of bitter arugula. Along with local shrimp, tuna, and calamari, there's also local pork tenderloin to sink your teeth into. The divine chocolate cake is worth driving the potholed road to Brasilito. At lunch, there are ceviches, a salade niçoise with fresh tuna and Po'Boy shrimp or fish sandwiches. The open-air dining room is straightforward and simple, surrounded by potted plants, backed by a sea view. With more dining space, there's now a kids' corner with tiny tables. ⊠ *In the Hotel Brasilito, on the beach* ☎ *654–4596* ▭ *AE, MC, V* ☉ *Sat.*

$–$$ ✕ **El Camarón Dorado.** Much of the appeal of this bougainvillea-drenched bar-restaurant is its shaded location on Brasilito's beautiful beach. Some tables are practically on the beach, with the surf lapping just yards away, perfect for sunset drinks. The white-plastic tables and chairs are not up to the standards of the food and service, though. A small-vessel fishing fleet anchored offshore assures you of the freshness of the bountiful portions of seafood on the menu. If you have a reservation, a van can pick you up from Flamingo or Tamarindo hotels. ⊠ *200 m north of Brasilito Plaza, Brasilito* ☎ *654–4028* ▭ *AE, DC, MC, V.*

¢–$$ ✕ **Il Forno Restaurant.** For a break from seafood, try lunch or dinner at this romantic Italian garden restaurant. There are 17 versions of thin-crust pizzas, plus fine, homemade pastas and risotto, and veal marsala. Vegetarians have lots of choices (if you can get past the thought that veal is on the menu), including an eggplant lasagna and interesting salads. At dinner, fairy lights and candles glimmer all through the garden, and some private tables are set apart under thatched roofs. Spanish and Italian wines are available by the glass or bottle. ⊠ *Main road, 200 m south of the bridge in Brasilito* ☎ *654–4125* ▭ *No credit cards* ⊙ *Closed Mon, Tues.*

$$$$ ⊡ **Paradisus Playa Conchal Beach & Golf Resort.** So vast that guests ride around in trucks covered with striped awnings and staff get around on bicycles, this all-inclusive resort, the top of the line of the Spanish Meliá hotel chain, is luxurious, if lacking a bit in personality. The grounds encompass almost 4 square km (1½ square mi) that include a distant, picture-perfect beach. But in the labyrinthine guest village, the ocean disappears and the only views are of gardens and other villas exactly like yours. The split-level Spanish Colonial–style villas have huge marble bathrooms and elegant sitting rooms. There are two kids' clubs for different ages, and grown-ups amuse themselves with nightly live shows, a casino, a gorgeous 18-hole golf course, and the largest—and perhaps warmest—pool in Central America. ⊠ *Entrance less than 1 km/½ mi south of Brasilito* ☎ *654–4123* 🖶 *654–4181* ⊕ *www. paradisusplayaconchal.com* ⟳ *292 villas* ⌥ *7 restaurants, fans, in-room safes, minibars, cable TV, 18-hole golf course, pro shop, 4 tennis courts, pool, gym, beach, jet skiing, bicycles, casino, nightclub, babysitting, children's programs, laundry service, Internet, meeting room* ▭ *AE, DC, MC, V* ⟦◎⟧ *AI.*

¢–$ ⊡ **Hotel Brasilito.** For adventurers only, this vintage, all-wood hotel is definitely sans decorating frills, but it does have hot water now and its seafront location makes it the best—and only—choice if you want to stay right at Playa Brasilito. Be prepared for some noise: kids playing, dogs barking, and motors revving. The sparely furnished rooms occupy both floors of an old but well-maintained two-story wooden building behind the restaurant. Ask for one of the two larger rooms above the restaurant; they share a veranda with unobstructed sea views. You can't beat the price for seaside rooms. And now Gecko's Restaurant (*see above*) occupies the open-air lobby. ⊠ *Next to the square and soccer field, Brasilito* ☎ *654–4237* 🖶 *654–4247* ⊕ *www.brasilito.com* ⟳ *15 rooms* ⌥ *Restaurant, fans, beach, laundry service, horseback riding; no a/c in some rooms, no room phones, no room TVs* ▭ *MC, V* ⟦◎⟧ *EP.*

Nightlife

Live music, both acoustic guitar and rowdier dance bands, keeps the **The Happy Snapper** (⊠ Brasilito, on the main street across from the beach in Brasilito) hopping on Friday and Saturday nights. Owner Mike Osborne often mans the bar and spikes the drinks with his own brand of wry humor.

To & from Playa Conchal

8 km/5 mi (10 mins) south of Flamingo.

The drive south from Flamingo is on a paved highway. Both town and beach are just 1 km (½ mi) north of the entrance to Paradisus Playa Conchal. Buses run from Flamingo to Conchal three times daily, at 7:30 and 11:30 AM and 2:30 PM. A taxi from Flamingo is about $6.

Playa Conchal Essentials

The closest bank and ATM are in Flamingo.

🏨 Hospital **Pacific Emergencies** ⊠ Crossroads at Huacas ☎ 653-8787 or 378-8265 ⊗ Daily 8-8.

💊 Pharmacies **Farmacia El Cruce** ⊠ Crossroads at Huacas ☎ 653-8787 ⊗ Daily 8-10.

EN ROUTE Gas stations are few and far between in these hinterlands. If you're heading down to Tamarindo from the Flamingo/Conchal area, fill up first. There's a station near Brasilito, but it's unreliable and often closed. Your best bet is the 24-hour Oasis Exxon, 3 km (2 mi) east of Huacas.

> **HELP ON THE ROAD**
>
> The more remote the area, the more likely that someone will stop to help you change a tire or tow you out of a river. Usually, good samaritans won't accept any payment and are more trustworthy than those who offer to "help" in the States. Near Ostional, there's a farmer named Valentin who regularly pulls cars out of the flooded river with his tractor. So he is known as Valentin *con chapulin* (with a tractor).

4

Tamarindo

⓯ Once a funky beach town full of spacey surfers and local fishermen, Tamarindo has become a pricey, hyped-up hive of commercial development and U.S. fast-food franchises, with the still-unpaved roads kicking up dust and mud alternately, depending on the season. At this writing, the whole community is virtually one noisy construction site. On the plus side, there's a dizzying variety of shops, bars, hotels, and probably the best selection of restaurants anywhere in Costa Rica. Strip malls and high-rise condominiums have obscured views of the still-magnificent beach, and some low-life elements are making security an issue. But once you're on the beach, almost all the negatives disappear. Wide and flat, the sand is packed hard enough for easy walking and jogging. After losing its Blue Flag clean-beach status, thanks to overdevelopment and the total absence of water treatment, concerned residents worked hard and managed to win it back in 2006. ⚠ **Strong currents at both ends of the beach get a lot of swimmers into trouble, especially when they try to cross the estuaries during tidal changes.**

Outdoor Activities

BOATING Rocky Isla El Capitán, just offshore, is a close-in **kayaking** destination, full of sand-dollar shells. Exploring the tidal estuaries north and south of town is best done in a kayak at high tide, when you can travel farther up the temporary rivers. Arrange kayaking trips through your hotel. **Iguana Surf** (⊠ Road to Playa Langosta ☎ 653–0148 ⊕ www.iguanasurf.net) has an office with information on guided kayaking tours of the San Francisco Estuary and a full roster of local tours, including snorkeling. Experienced sailors can rent a four-passenger Hobie Cat (on the beach, south of Nogui's) ☎ 653–0073, 302–3549 for $25 an hour, plus a $20 setup charge. Sail off into the sunset aboard a 50-foot traditional schooner with cruise company **Mandingo** (☎ 653–0623). Soft drinks, beer and wine, and bocas are included on the three-hour cruise.

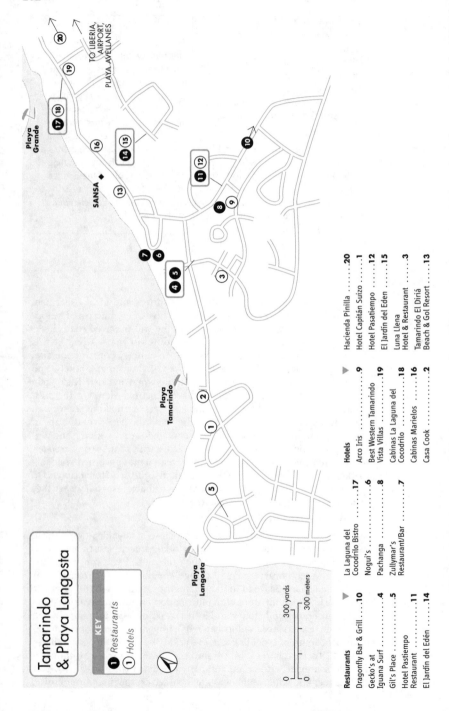

Tamarindo & Playa Langosta

KEY

1 *Restaurants*

1 *Hotels*

0   300 yards
0   300 meters

Playa Grande

SANSA ◆

Playa Tamarindo

Playa Langosta

TO LIBERIA, AIRPORT, PLAYA AVELLANES

Restaurants ▶

Dragonfly Bar & Grill **10**
Gecko's at
Iguana Surf **4**
Gil's Place **5**
Hotel Pastiempo
Restaurant **11**
El Jardín del Edén **14**
La Laguna del
Cocodrilo Bistro **17**
Nogui's **6**
Pachanga **8**
Zullymar's
Restaurant/Bar **7**

Hotels ▶

Arco Iris **9**
Best Western Tamarindo
Vista Villas **19**
Cabinas La Laguna del
Cocodrilo **18**
Cabinas Marielos **16**
Casa Cook **2**
Hacienda Pinilla **20**
Hotel Capitán Suizo **1**
Hotel Pasatiempo **12**
El Jardín del Edén **15**
Luna Llena
Hotel & Restaurant **3**
Tamarindo El Diriá
Beach & Gol Resort **13**

The boat leaves at 3 PM from in front of El Pescador restaurant on the beach ($50 per person).

FISHING A number of fishing charters in Tamarindo cater to saltwater anglers. The best among them is probably **Tamarindo Sportfishing** (☎ 653–0090 🖷 653–0161 ⊕ www.tamarindosportfishing.com), run by Randy Wilson, who has led the way in developing catch-and-release techniques that are easy on the fish. Wilson has roamed and fished the Guanacaste waters since the 1970s, and he knows where the big ones lurk. His boat, the *Talking Fish,* is equipped with a marlin chair and a cabin with a shower. Soaring fuel costs have upped the price for up to six fishers, to $1,200, half-days $675. A full-day fishing trip on the smaller, 27-foot *Salsa* costs $725; $450 a half-day.

GOLFING Mike Young, who has designed some of the best golf courses in the southern United States, designed the par-72 championship course at **Hacienda Pinilla** (✉ 10 km [6 mi] south of Tamarindo via Villa Real ☎ 680–7062 ⊕ www.haciendapinilla.com). It has ocean views and breezes, and plenty of birds populate the surrounding trees. J.W. Marriott has announced it is building a huge new hotel in Hacienda Pinilla, and it is rumored that the golf course may soon close to the public.

SURFING **Iguana Surf** (✉ At beach near Frutas Tropicales ☎☎ 653–0148). **Iguana Surf 2** rents surfboards, Boogie boards, and offers lessons (for ages 3 to 88). **Maresias Surf Shop** (✉ Next to Banco Nacional ☎ 653–0224) has equipment, lessons, and lots of local knowledge. Check out the **Robert August Surf Shop** (✉ Tamarindo Vista Villas ☎ 653–0114) for boards to buy or rent, wax, surfing gear, swimsuits, and sunblock. It also operates a kids' surfing school as well as adult lessons. **High Tide Surf Shop** (✉ Road to Langosta, about 200 m west of Hotel Pasatiempo ☎ 653–0108) has high-end surfing equipment and clothing and a large selection of beachwear in a second-story shop; Tamarindo Adventures downstairs in the same building organizes kayaking, ATV tours, and surf lessons, as well as snorkeling tours.

TURTLE TOURS Numerous tour operators organize turtle tours in season for $35–$45 per person. **Papagayo Excursions** (✉ Next to Banco Nacional, main st. ☎ 653–0254) is the oldest turtle-tour operator in Tamarindo. Tours ($45) include hotel pickup, boat transport to Playa Grande, park entrance fee, and an expert guide. Pickup is usually around 7:30 PM and the tour lasts until you see a turtle.

Where to Stay & Eat

★ $$–$$$ ✕ **Laguna del Cocodrilo Bistro.** It's not often you get to experience haute cuisine at the beach, but Argentine chef Leonardo Elbiza, taking over from the restaurant's original French chef, dresses up perfectly cooked fish and seafood with designer sauces of balsamic vinegar reductions, drizzles of flavored oils, and dollops of spicy fruit marmalades. Portions are generous and the wind-and-surf combination plate is a tour de force: a tower of pink South Pacific salmon with a shrimp sauce, a crusty crostini topped with spicy mussels, and a duck leg confit. Wines by the glass are served out of a temperature-controlled dispenser, and the list is long and carefully conceived with unusual, high-end Argentine wines. The garden setting, under palm trees lit by fairy lights, is casual, but the food and service are anything but. The bar opens at 4 PM. ☒ *Hotel Laguna del Cocodrilo, north end of Tamarindo* ☎ 653–0255 ☰ *AE, MC, V* ⊘ *Closed Sun. No lunch.*

★ **$–$$** **Dragonfly Bar & Grill.** A huge tent with tree-trunk poles, simple but sculptural Ikea lamps, and a cool soundtrack are the components of this immensely popular, ultracool restaurant. A new chef has introduced a limited but enticing, lighter menu. It's attracting standing-room-only crowds, eager to tingle their tastebuds with shiitake-crusted filet mignon paired with an ethereally light goat-cheese pudding or Thai-style crispy fish cake with curried sweet corn. There are interesting vegetarian options, too, daily fish specials, and a new sushi bar to complement the Asian accent of many of the creative dishes here. ☒ *100 m east of Hotel Pasatiempo* ☎ 653–1506 ⊕ *www.dragonflybarandgrill.com* ☰ *No credit cards* ⌖ *Reservations essential* ⊘ *Closed Sun., end of Sept. and Oct. No lunch.*

$–$$ ✕ **Nogui's.** Considered by a loyal legion of local fans as the most affordable seafood restaurant in town, Nogui's, practically on the beach, has been dishing out huge salads and seafood at lunch and a full seafood menu at dinner since 1974. The homemade pies are legendary, notably the coconut cream. The newest addition to the menu is a meal-sized, garlicky steak sandwich, loaded with cheese, mushrooms, and onions on freshly baked bread. Instead of the ubiquitous rice and beans on the side, Nogui's has a purée of *tiquisque*, a local, potato-like vegetable. They also serve a signature Tamarindo Margarita, made with tamarind fruit. Nogui's location is practically on the beach. ☒ *South side of Tamarindo Circle, on the beach* ☎ 653–0029 ☰ *AE, DC, MC, V* ⊘ *Closed Wed. and 2 wks in Oct.*

★ **$–$$** ✕ **Pachanga.** In a casual but chic setting, Shlomi Koren, a Cordon Bleu–trained Israeli chef, transforms fresh local ingredients into elegant Mediterranean dishes you would pay a fortune for on the Riviera. Ours was red snapper fillet in a sauce of white wine, thyme, and sundried tomatoes, followed by a sublime chocolate soufflé. With tangerine walls and a sunburst mural, the small terrace restaurant shimmers in a golden light. Tables in the recently expanded garden make for even more romantic, starlit dining. ☒ *Across from Hotel Pasatiempo* ☎ 368–6983 ☰ *No credit cards* ⊘ *No lunch. Closed Sun. and two weeks in May.*

¢–$ ✕ **Gil's Place.** You gotta love a guy who has the chutzpah to print this slogan on his menu: "No shoes, no shirt—we don't care; Come on in and grab a chair." Poetry it isn't, but the breakfast burritos are worthy of a laureate's praises. The hand-rolled, paper-thin tortillas are good enough to eat all on their own, but instead they are wrapped around generous combinations of scrambled eggs, cheese, sautéed vegetables, and breakfast meats, served with a flavorful but mild salsa. (Hot sauce is kept under the counter.) Go. Eat. You won't be disappointed. ☒ *Next to Iguana Surf shop on road to Playa Langosta* ☎ 836–3345 ☰ *No credit cards* ⊘ *Closed Sun.*

$$$ ✕▦ **El Jardín del Edén.** There is trouble in this "Garden of Eden," formerly a two-tier, Mediterranean-style, pink hotel residing amid lush hillside gardens. At this writing, 14 new rooms were under construction in a three-story annex, almost doubling the hotel's capacity and infringing on the garden and the former tranquility. Most of the original rooms were redecorated by French owners with a penchant for crisp blue-and-white Moroccan and hot Polynesian decor. The lowest-priced double rooms are very tiny indeed, fine for one person but a little tight for two. Most rooms have ocean views, and two tiny but lovely pools provide the missing water element. The recently expanded thatch-roof restaurant ($$) has lost its intimacy but still serves excellent Mediterranean-style fresh seafood, pastas, and steaks. ⊠ *From Hotel El Milagro on main road, go up hill 180 m, then right for 180 m* ☎ *653–0137* 🖷 *653–0111* ⊕ *www.jardindeleden.com* ⬦ *35 rooms, 2 apartments* ⟁ *Restaurant, fans, in-room safes, mini fridges, some kitchens, cable TV, 2 pools, whirlpool tub, bar, laundry service, Internet* ⊟ *AE, MC, V* ⌾ *BP.*

$$ ✕⌤ **Hotel Pasatiempo.** Come for Sunday football projected on a large screen, open mike on Tuesday nights, or great eggs Benedict any morning. One way or another, you are bound to pass some time at this friendly, laid-back place where there's always something happening. Energetic owners Ron and Janet Stewart throw legendary parties and raise money for community projects. This is one of the last relatively tranquil and resort-like hotels in the sea of Tamarindo construction. Comfortable bungalow rooms are scattered around lushly landscaped grounds and a beautiful pool. Each unit, named after a Guanacaste beach, has a patio with a hammock or swinging chair and a unique hand-painted mural. Suites have one bedroom and daybeds in the living room. The restaurant ($–$$) serves a mix of above-average bar food and pizza, along with more sophisticated fare, like seared tuna with wasabi, or chicken in a Stroganoff sauce. There's also a pizzeria, to eat in, take out or have delivered. Early-morning coffee and breakfast cake are complimentary. ⊠ *Off dirt road to Playa Langosta, 180 m from beach behind Tamarindo Circle* ☎ *653–0096* 🖷 *653–0275* ⊕ *www.hotelpasatiempo.com* ⬦ *15 bungalows, 2 suites* ⟁ *Restaurant, fans, pool, bar, laundry service; no room TVs, no room phones* ⊟ *AE, MC, V* ⌾ *EP.*

$$$ ⌤ **Hotel Capitán Suizo.** For folks who like luxury, small scale, and a beautiful beach setting, this is the best choice in town. On a relatively quiet stretch of Tamarindo's gorgeous beach, elegant balconied rooms and luxurious bungalows surround a large, shaded pool set in a mature garden. The stunning, two-story rooms have high, angled ceilings, recently updated bathrooms, and a collection of vintage sepia photos of 19th-century Costa Rican life decorating the walls. The two-level bungalows have Swiss-made, adjustable, king-size beds and sensuous bathrooms with sunken tubs, beautiful tile work, and outdoor garden showers with hot water. The four-bedroom apartment has a kitchen and whirlpool tub. A beautifully decorated restaurant serves contemporary cuisine and hosts lively beach barbecues. Service is friendly and polished. ⊠ *Right side of road toward Playa Langosta* ☎ *653–0075 or 653–0353* 🖷 *653–0292* ⊕ *www.hotelcapitansuizo.com* ⬦ *22 rooms, 8 bungalows, 1 apartment* ⟁ *Restaurant, in-room safes, refrigerators, pool, kayaking, fishing, bicycles, horseback riding, tours, shop, laundry service; no a/c in some rooms, no room TVs* ⊟ *AE, MC, V* ⌾ *BP.*

FodorśChoice
★

$$ ☒ **Luna Llena Hotel & Residence.** This place looks a little like a Fellini film set of a fantasy tropical village. Bright-yellow conical thatched-roof huts on different levels circle a central pool. Interiors are colorful and whimsical, with unusual fabrics, furniture, and walls painted by co-owner Simona Daniela, who, along with husband Pino Trimarchi, adds Italian panache to the place. Downstairs, the bungalows have a kitchen, a king-size bed, and a bathroom. Up a steep, curving ladder stair, there's a loft right under the thatched roof, with its own air conditioner. Four double rooms in a two-story building are spacious and just as creatively decorated. One room sleeps four. The hotel is far from the beach in a quiet, woodsy area. There's a new Internet café and gift shop. ⊠ *From road to Playa Langosta, first left (uphill); one block past Iguana Surf* ☎ *653–0082* 🖶 *653–0120* ⊕ *www.hotellunallena.com* ⇆ *7 bungalows, 6 rooms* ⚭ *Dining room, fans, in-room safes, some kitchens, cable TV, pool* ▤ *AE, MC, V* ⦿| *CP.*

$ ☒ **Cabinas Marielos.** In high season Tamarindo has few decent bargain rooms; judging by the happy comments in the guest book, these cabinas are among the best. Decorated with painted floral motifs in the style of the artisans of Sarchí, the rooms (not literally cabinas) are in two wings, flanking a colorful flower garden well back from the road. Guests sometimes share their meals in the well-equipped common kitchen. The atmosphere is surprisingly serene and the staff friendly and helpful. There is no hot water except in the three newest air-conditioned rooms. ⊠ *Across main dirt road from beach, north of town center (follow signs)* ☎🖶 *653–0141* ✑ *cabinasmarielos@hotmail.com* ⇆ *20 rooms* ⚭ *Fans, some refrigerators; no a/c in some rooms, no room phones, no room TVs* ▤ *AE, MC, V* ⦿| *EP.*

¢–$ ☒ **Arco Iris.** This arty hotel, on the hill above the road to Playa Langosta, is like a trip around the world. The four funky cabinas are painted in primary colors and decorated with distinct ethnic themes by the creative Italian sisters who own the hotel. Aerobics, stretching, kickboxing, dance, art, and yoga sessions are taught on-site, and a massage therapist is on hand in case it all gets too strenuous. There's a new vegetarian dinner restaurant ($), featuring African, European, Indian, and Indonesian dishes. One new cabin has a huge bathroom, and there's a new new spa with a therapy pool. The sisters donate $1 of the room rate to a fund to keep the beach clean. ⊠ *Follow signs past Hotel Pasatiempo and go up hill to right* ☎ *653–0330* ⇆ *5 cabinas* ⚭ *Restaurant, fans, refrigerators, fitness classes, spa; no a/c, no room phones, no room TVs* ▤ *No credit cards* ⦿| *BP.*

Nightlife

Tamarindo is one of the few places outside of San José along with Jacó, in the Central Pacific, where the nightlife really jumps. In fact, it has the dubious distinction of being featured on Entertainment Television's explicit *Wild On* series, which spotlights the rowdiest party scenes around the world.

While party-hearty hot spots come and go with the tides, Tamarindo does have some perennial, low-key options. For a relatively sedate Saturday evening, try barbecue on the beach at the **Capitán Suizo Hotel**

(✉ Right side of road toward Playa Langosta; veer left before circle), starting at 6:30 with a cocktail, then on to a lavish barbecue buffet and live folk music and dancing ($35, reserve in advance). During the week, **Hotel Pasatiempo** (✉ Off dirt road to Playa Langosta) has wildly popular Tuesday open-mike sessions, with a $5 cover or two-drink minimum charge. Friday nights at **The Monkey Bar** (✉ Tamarindo Vista Villas, main road entering Tamarindo) is Ladies Night and usually a big party. The live Latin dance music (no cover) attracts a locals who really know how to dance. **Restobar La Caracola** (✉ Tamarindo Circle, beside Nogui's) often has live Latin music and dancing on weekends, and tango, salsa, and merengue dance lessons on request. Shared bocas and tropical cocktails, backed by a pulsing soundtrack, make for instant parties at the Lazy Wave, just a block past Etcetera Restaurant.

Shopping

Most stores in the strip malls lining the main road sell the same souvenirs and beachwear. It's hard to leave town without at least one sarong in your suitcase. But at Calypso (in the new Shops of Diria attached to the Tamarindo el Diria Hotel ☎ 653–1436), Parisian Anne Loriot has raised the bar on beach fashion with fabulous Indonesian and Mexican-style cover-ups and elegant, cool dresses, available in real women's sizes. In the same complex, Amo La Vida (☎ 653–1507) offers high-end home accessories, with half the store devoted to Moroccan imports, such as stained-glass sconces and leather hassocks, and the other half to Costa Rican–made lamps, picture frames, and natural-material novelties. You'll also find original clothing and jewelry at **Azul Profundo** (✉ Main street, Plaza Tamarindo ☎ 653–0395), designed by a talented young Argentine woman. All her jewelry is made with real and semiprecious stones. For a good selection of swimsuits and a wide range of kiddie beach wear, check out **Tienda Bambora** (✉ On beach, south side of Tamarindo Circle; attached to Nogui's restaurant).

To & from Tamarindo

82 km/51 mi (1hr 15 mins) southwest of Liberia.

Both NatureAir and SANSA fly to Tamarindo from San José. Macaw Air flies between Liberia and Tamarindo and to other Nicoya Peninsula towns. By car from Liberia, travel south on the highway to the turnoff for Belén, then head west and turn left at the Huacas crossroads to Tamarindo. Stretches of the paved road from Belén are in deplorable states of disrepair. There are no direct bus connections between Playa Grande or Playa Avellanas and Tamarindo. Taxi is the way to go from nearby towns if you don't have wheels. The **Tamarindo Shuttle** (☎ 653–1326 ⊕ www.tamarindoshuttle.com) ferries passengers among the various beaches in a comfortable van.

Tamarindo Essentials

🏧 Bank/ATM **Banco Nacional** ⊠ Across from Hotel Diría ☎ 653-0366.

🏥 Hospital **Pacific Emergencies Clínic** ⊠ Next to Farmacia Tamarindo ☎ 653-1226.
Emergencias 2000 ⊠ 4 km/2½ mi east of Tamarindo at Villa Real crossrd. ☎ 380-4125.

💊 Pharmacies **Farmacia Tamarindo** ⊠ Main road into town ☎ 653-1239.

🚕 Taxi Service **Olman Taxi** ☎ 653-1143, 356-6364 (cell); the SANSA shuttle van from the airport into town ☎ 653-0244 charges $3 per person.

Playa Grande

16 A very bumpy 21 mi from Tamarindo by road, but only 5 minutes by boat across a tidal estuary, lies Playa Grande. The beach had largely escaped overdevelopment, thanks in part to a surfer who came ashore more than 30 years ago and traded in his surfboard for a conservationist's agenda. Louis Wilson, owner of Las Tortugas Hotel, spearheaded the campaign to create a wildlife refuge—now Las Baulas Marine National Park—to protect nesting *baulas* (leatherback turtles). The brown-sand, Blue Flag beach, edged by creeping sea-grape, is still a paradise for surfers and sunbathers by day and a haven for nesting turtles by night. The whole beach and miles of water offshore are, in fact, part of the national park.

Exploring

Both **Las Baulas Marine National Park** (Parque Nacional Marino Las Baulas), which protects the long Playa Grande, and the **Tamarindo Wildlife Refuge,** a mangrove estuary with some excellent bird-watching, have been under some developmental pressure of late. Playa Grande hosts the world's largest visitation of nesting giant leatherback turtles. From October 1 to February 15, during the peak nesting season, the beach is strictly off limits from 6 PM to 5 AM. You can only visit as part of a guided tour, waiting your turn at the park entrance, beside Hotel Las Tortugas, until spotters find a nesting turtle. Then you silently sprint down the beach in darkness to witness the remarkable sight of a 500-pound creature digging a hole in the sand large enough to deposit up to 100 golfball-size eggs. Just as impressive is the sight of hundreds of hatchlings scrambling toward open water in the early morning about sixty days after. The best way to go is with a turtle-watching tour run by one of numerous Playa Grande or Tamarindo hotels and tour operators. Environmental activist Louis Wilson, also the owner of the Hotel Las Tortugas, struggled for a decade to protect this area. An evening spent discussing ecotourism and ecopolitics with him is a real education. ⊠ *North of Tamarindo, across an estuary* ☎ *653–0470* 💲 *Free, Oct. 1–Feb. 15, $16 after 6 PM includes guided tour (Spanish only)* ☉ *Oct. 1–Mar. 15 by reservation only after 6 PM.*

El Mundo de la Tortuga (Turtle World) is a French-run museum with creative displays about the life cycle of the giant leatherback and the threats it faces. Audio tours (available in English) through the interactive exhibits last 20 minutes. The museum runs nighttime turtle tours (⇨ *below*). ⊠ *Road to Hotel Las Tortugas* ☎ *653–0471* 💲 *$5* ☉ *4 PM until tours return. Closed May–Oct.*

Outdoor Activities

⚠ **Unless you are a strong swimmer attached to a surfboard, don't swim here.** There is some calmer water for snorkeling about a 20-minute walk north of Las Tortugas, at Playa Carbón.

Hotel Las Tortugas (✉ Las Baulas Marine National Park ☎ 653–0423 ⊕ www.cool.co.cr/usr/turtles) has a full menu of nature tours, including guided walks to pristine, remote areas; snorkeling at Playa Carbón; and canoeing and nature photography tours ($20–$30).

SURFING Playa Grande is renowned for having the most consistent surf breaks in the country and impressive barrels. Only experienced surfers should attempt them. The waves are best at high tide and it's customary to share waves. **Hotel Las Tortugas** (⇨ *above*) rents boards for $20 a day. **Hotel Bula Bula** (✉ Palm Beach Estates, 2 km/1 mi east of Playa Grande ☎ 653–0975, 877/658–2880 in U.S. ⊕ www.hotelbulabula.com) rents both long and short boards for $25/day.

TURTLE TOURS Lots of tour operators in Tamarindo organize turtle tours in season for about $35 to $45 per person, including guide, snacks, and transportation. **El Mundo de la Tortuga** (✉ Road to Hotel Las Tortugas ☎ 653–0471) conducts excellent turtle tours almost every night from October 20 to February 15, depending on high tide, and returning not earlier than 11 PM (and sometimes as late as 3 AM).

Where to Stay & Eat

★ **$$** ✕⛶ **Hotel Bula Bula.** At the far east end of Palm Beach Estates, Bula Bula (happy, happy) has its own dock and boat for ferrying guests and restaurant customers the short distance to and from Tamarindo for free. Rooms march in two straight lines, forming a 45-degree angle to the curvy pool bordered by an impressive cactus garden (be careful where you walk in the dark!). Some people may find the rooms too close together, but others may like the four adjoining rooms, perfect for families. Walls painted in brilliant jewel colors, king-size beds, and generous bathrooms make for a very comfortable stay. Complimentary sarongs, bottled water, coffeemakers, and fluffy pool towels are unexpected touches of luxury in this boutique-style hotel. The beach is about 300 m away. The menu at the excellent, alfresco Great Waltini Restaurant & Bar ($–$$) reads like a U.S.-style eatery: peel'n'eat shrimp, lobster tails, filet mignon, and New York strip steak. ✉ *Palm Beach Estates, 3 km/2 mi east of Playa Grande* ☎ *653–0975, 877/658–2880 in U.S.* ⊕ *www.hotelbulabula.com* ⇌ *10 rooms* ⚖ *Restaurant, fans, refrigerators, cable TV, pool, beach, bar, laundry service, boat service, Internet, Wi-Fi; no room phones* ▤ *AE, MC, V* ❢◎❢ *BP.*

$$ ✕⛶ **Hotel La Cantarana.** This hotel is essentially a restaurant with hotel rooms. Chef Manfred Margraf brings to the table 30 years of cooking experience in Switzerland, Germany, and the Caribbean. The menu changes depending on availability of local ingredients—think lots of seafood—and on the chef's inspired whims, but is always classically continental, with elegant presentation. Clean lines, modern ceramic bathrooms, and twin beds make rooms, in a two-story terra-cotta building facing a beautifully landscaped pool, a comfortable if not exciting place to spend the night after an evening of feasting. The beach is a short walk away. ☒ *Palm Beach Estates, 2 km/1 mi east of Playa Grande, across from Hotelito Sí Sí Sí* ☎ *653–0486* 🖷 *653–0491* ⊕ *www.hotelcantarana. com* ⤵ *5 rooms* ⌂ *Restaurant, fans, in-room safes, cable TV, pool* ▭ *AE, MC, V* 🍽 *BP.*

¢–$ 🏠 **Hotel El Manglar.** If you like cooking for yourself, consider the apartments at this French-run hotel. Painted in hot tropical colors, they also have a Provençal touch, with French doors and lace curtains. King-size beds, sitting rooms, kitchens, and terraces give you lots of room to relax. No. 3, with its own BBQ grill on the terrace, is the favorite. The upstairs guest rooms are more basic, with modernly minimalist decor and un-air-conditioned loft bedrooms. But they're very cheap. The hotel has a very pretty garden and a pool inlaid with bright mosaic tile. It's a short walk to the beach. ☒ *Palm Beach Estates, 2 km/1 mi south of Playa Grande, beside Hotel La Cantarana* ☎🖷 *653–0952* ⊕ *www.hotel-manglar.com* ⤵ *6 rooms, 4 apartments* ⌂ *Fans, some kitchens, pool; no a/c in some rooms, no room phones, no room TVs* ▭ *No credit cards* 🍽 *EP.*

To & from Playa Grande
21 km/13 mi (40 mins) north of Tamarindo.

Ten kilometers (6 mi) of the road from Tamarindo is paved, as far as Huacas, and then 11 km (7 mi) is a rough dirt road. Palm Beach Estates is about 3 km (2 mi) of bumpy but nicely shaded road east of the Playa Grande entrance of Las Baulas Marine National Park. Alternatively, you can take a small boat across the Tamarindo Estuary for about 50¢ per person and walk 40 minutes along the beach to Playa Grande; boats are at the guide kiosk at the north end of Tamarindo. Or you can take a ferry with Las Palmas Tours (☎ 653–1502) from the Tamarindo side and return with the Hotel Bula Bula ferry (☎ 658–2880) from the Playa Grande side. Ferries runs 6 AM–11 PM during high season, for about $2 per person each way.

Playa Langosta

⑰ Every foot of beachfront property in beautiful Playa Langosta has been built up, but now the contractors' hammers are ringing out in every building space inland. This formerly quiet, leatherback turtle nesting beach is now an upscale, gentrified extension of Tamarindo, connected by a heavily traveled dirt road. The beach is separated from Tamarindo Beach by a rocky headland at high tide. Luckily, most of the development is tucked behind mangrove trees, so you can enjoy an unsullied dramatic beachscape, with surf crashing against rocky outcroppings. The sand here is coarse, black pulverized rock and shell, though there's a wider, whiter, softer stretch in front of the Barceló Resort. At low tide you can walk across the San Francisco estuary and walk a ways up the tidal river in search of wading birds: showy snowy egrets; hunting little blue herons; tail-bobbing spotted sandpipers; and if your eyes are sharp, tiny white-lored gnatcatchers, endemic to these parts.

Outdoor Activities
Tour operators in Tamarindo, just a few miles north, offer activities in the Playa Langosta area.

Where to Stay & Eat

★ **$–$$** ✕ **Maria Bonita Restaurant.** This popular, intimate, Latin-Caribbean restaurant is owned by a couple with years of hotel and restaurant experience in Cuba and throughout the Caribbean. Cheerful Adela serves (and makes delicious desserts) while Tom slaves away in the kitchen, turning out mouth-watering, perfectly spiced dishes such as smoked pork chops smothered in a tart tamarind sauce. The wine list focuses on South American vintages. There are just six tables in the pretty patio garden and four tables inside the restaurant—and they fill up fast. ⊠ *Beside the Playa Langosta supermarket* ☎ *653–0933* ▤ *MC, V* ⚓ *Reservations essential in high season* ⊗ *Closed Sun. and Oct. No lunch.*

$$$ ⌂ **Sueño del Mar.** A garden gate opens into a dreamy world of intimate gardens and patios with frescoes, antique tiles, and a jungle of exotic *objets d'art.* This nearly flawless B&B occupies an adobe-style house. A stepped passageway is lined with double rooms with queen-size beds, and Balinese showers open to the sky. Casitas have large kitchens, sitting rooms, and a loft bedroom. The downstairs rooms are a little dark and closed-in but full of interesting and often amusing pieces of folk art, such as a tissue dispenser in the shape of an Easter Island statue. If privacy is paramount, opt for the breezy honeymoon suite, recently transformed into a sensuous, sultan's lair with rich, red fabrics, rugs, and hanging glass lamps bought on the owners' recent trip to Turkey. A lavish breakfast is served on the patio looking onto a tiny garden pool. Or you can take your morning coffee on the beach, sitting on driftwood furniture, desert-island style. ⊠ *130 m south of Capitán Suizo, turn right for 45 m, then right again for about 90 m to entrance gate, across from back of Cala Luna Hotel* ☎ *653–0284* ▤ *653–0558* ⊕ *www.sueno-del-mar.com* ⇨ *3 rooms, 1 suite, 2 casitas* ⚐ *Dining room, fans, some kitchens, pool, beach, snorkeling, bicycles, horseback riding, laundry service, Internet; no room phones, no room TVs* ▤ *MC, V* ⊚ *BP.*

FodorśChoice
★

★ **$$$** ⌂ **Villa Alegre.** A visit here is like coming to stay with friends who just happen to have a really terrific house on a fantastic beach. Owned by congenial and helpful Californians Barry and Suzye Lawson, this homey but sophisticated Spanish-style B&B is close to a stand of trees and a somewhat rocky but swimmable beach, which is visible from the pool. Rooms and casitas are furnished with souvenirs from the Lawsons' international travels, including Japan, Russia, and Guatemala. The new Mexican honeymoon suite has a Frida Kahlo–esque canopy bed and a huge outdoor bathroom/lounge area. Breakfast is lavish served on a terrace overlooking the infinity pool with a small waterfall. The hotel often plans and hosts weddings; ceremonies take place at a huge boulder on the beach dubbed Marriage Rock. ⊠ *Playa Langosta, 300 m south of Hotel Capitán Suizo* ☎ *653–0270* ▤ *653–0287* ⊕ *www.villaalegrecostarica.com* ⇨ *4 rooms, 2 villas, 1 casita* ⚐ *Fans, pool, beach, no-smoking rooms; no room phones, no room TVs* ▤ *AE, MC, V* ⊚ *BP.*

To & from Playa Langosta

2 km/1 mi (5 mins) south of Tamarindo.

The dirt road from Tamarindo is alternately dusty or muddy, but reliably rough. Or you can walk along the beach, at low tide, all the way from Tamarindo Beach. Most car-free visitors get picked up from Tamarindo by their hotels. Or you can take a taxi.

Playa Avellanas

⑱ Geographically and atmospherically separate from Tamarindo, this relatively undeveloped beach's main claim to fame is surfing. As you bump along the very rough beach road, most of the cars you pass have surfboards tied on top. But Tamarindo escapees are slowly encroaching, building private houses and a smattering of new hotels. The beach is a beautiful 1-km (½-mi) stretch of pale-gold sand with rocky outcroppings, a river mouth, a mangrove swamp, and a very big pig named Lola, who likes to cool off in the surf. Unfortunately, security here has become an issue, with posted signs warning visitors not to leave anything of value in parked cars or unattended on the beach.

Outdoor Activities

SURFING Apart from taking photos of Lola the pig with waves washing over her, the main action here is surfing. Locals claim there are eight surf spots when the swell is strong. There are no tour operators based in Playa Avellanas. Tamarindo-based surf shops bring surfers down here whenever the surf is up. You can rent boards and find kindred surfing spirits at **Cabinas Las Olas** (⊠ Road to Avellanas; follow signs ☎ 658–8315), $2.50/hour, $22 per day.

Where to Stay & Eat

$-$$ ✕ **Lola's.** In deference to Lola, the owners' pet pig who freely roams the beach, the menu at this hip beach café is heavily vegetarian. Seating, or more precisely, lolling is all on the sand. The low driftwood tables, reclining wood chairs, and colorful throws and cushions slung around the beach recall a Roman-style beach banquet. Along with the fresh-fruit smoothies and vegetarian pizzas of past seasons, the menu includes organic chicken, mushroom crepes, and "responsible fish" (fish caught in nets that don't mistakenly trap turtles). Seared ahi tuna with sundried tomato and olive tapenade served on ciabatta bread is a winner, as are the delectable fries served Dutch-style with garlic mayonnaise. You can arrange in advance for private beach dinners by candlelight (pig not invited). ⊠ At main entrance to Playa Avellanas ☎ 658–8097 ▤ No credit cards ☯ Closed Mon. and mid-Sept.–mid-Nov.

¢-$ ▥ **Cabinas El Léon.** Accommodations here are basic but surfers don't seem to mind, as long as they are near the beach. Comforts in these four simple, concrete-block rooms extend as far as fans and hot water. The Italian owners cook Italian-style, family dinners for their guests. Rooms aren't pretty, but are cleaner than most of the shabby surfers' camps along the beaches here. The beach is a two-minute walk away. ⊠ Beach road, just south of Cabinas Las Olas ☎ 658–8318 ⊕ www.cabinaselleon.com ➷4 rooms ⚹ Fans, beach, laundry service. ▤ No credit cards ❢❂ EP.

You have to drive inland from Tamarindo to VillaReal and then 13 km (8 mi) down a very bumpy road to reach Playa Avellanas. There are many rivers to cross in rainy season and huge potholes to avoid in dry season. If you're sans car, have your hotel pick you up in Tamarindo.

To & from Playa Avellanas
17 km/11 mi (30 mins) south of Tamarindo.

You have to drive inland from Tamarindo to Villa Real and then 13 km (8 mi) down a very bumpy road to reach Playa Avellanas. There are many rivers to cross in rainy season and huge potholes to avoid in dry season. If you're sans car, have your hotel pick you up in Tamarindo or take the **Tamarindo Shuttle** (☎ 653–1326 ⊕ www.tamarindoshuttle.com) van, $25 one way for one to four people, $40 return.

Playa Negra

⑲ Surfer culture is apparent here in the wave of beach-shack surfer camps along the beach road. But there's also a big residential development here called Rancho Playa Negra, with more upscale development on the drawing boards. The beach is rocky and, true to its name, has very dark, hard-packed sand. Spindly mangrove trees edge the beach and there are views north of the wavy coastline.

> **A SURF CLASSIC**
>
> Americans—surfer Americans at least—got their first look at Playa Negra in 1994's *The Endless Summer II,* a film by legendary surf documentarian Bruce Brown.

Outdoor Activities

SURFING Surfing cognoscenti dig the waves here, which are almost all rights, with beautifully shaped barrels. The beach also has a spectacular rock-reef point break. Ask at Hotel Playa Negra, where some of the best breaks are, or just scan the ocean to see where everybody else is. **Hotel Playa Negra** (⊠ 4 km/2½ mi northwest of Paraíso on dirt road [watch for signs for Playa Negra], then follow signs carefully at forks in rd. ☎ 658–8034 ⊕ www.playanegra.com) has a surfing school that specializes in beginners and Boogie board lessons, and rents boards. Trips to Ollie's Point and Witch's Rock can be arranged.

Where to Stay & Eat

¢–$ ✕ **Café Playa Negra Bistro.** The stylish creation of Peruvian glass artist Andrea Raffo, this huge, modern, hacienda-like hall showcases her art, with squares of stained glass built into the walls. There's also a separate art gallery and an Internet café. Andrea matches her passion for art with a talent for food, featuring such Peruvian specialties as ceviche and *causa,* cold mashed potatoes studded with shrimp and tuna chunks. Desserts are homemade and delicious. The only drawback is very slow service. There are also six, simple un-air-conditioned B&B rooms ($20 per person) upstairs with colorful Peruvian fabrics, fans, private baths, and a shared terrace. ⊠ *Main Street, Playa Negra* ☎☎ 658–8351 ▤ *No credit cards.*

★ $ ▥ **Hotel Playa Negra.** This ocean-front place is gorgeous: a little village of brilliantly colored thatch-roof cabinas sprinkled across sunny lawns strewn with tropical plantings. The cabinas are perfectly round, and the two swimming pools are elliptical. Each hut has built-in sofas that can double as extra beds, and beautiful, curvaceous tile bathrooms. There's no air-conditioning but the high, conical thatch roofs keep the cabinas cool. The ocean has tidal pools, swimming holes, and rock reefs providing some shelter. This is paradise found for surfers, with a good swell running right in front of the hotel. The round, rancho restaurant serves typical food with a few Continental touches left over from a now-departed French chef. There's a new air-conditioned Internet café and beach boutique. ⊠ 4 km/2½ mi northwest of Paraíso on dirt road (watch signs for Playa Negra), then follow signs carefully at forks in rd. ☎ 658–8034 🗐 658–8035 ⊕ www.playanegra.com ➷ 10 cabinas ♨ Restaurant, fans, in-room safes, pool, beach, horseback riding, bar, laundry service; no a/c, no room phones, no room TVs ▤ AE, DC, MC, V ⭦ EP ☉ Restaurant closed Sept. 15–Nov. 1.

> **THE YOUNGEST PROVINCE**
>
> Guanacaste was a political monkey-in-the-middle for centuries, bouncing between Spain, Nicaragua, and independence. In 1858 Guanacastecans finally voted to annex themselves to Costa Rica, an event celebrated every July 25 with a national holiday.

To & from Playa Negra

3 km/2 mi (10 mins) south of Playa Avellanas.

From Playa Avellanas, continue south on the rough beach road to Playa Negra, or if you don't have 4WD or it's rainy season, approach along a more civilized route from Santa Cruz. Drive 27 km (16½ mi) west, via Vientisiete de Abril, to Paraíso, then follow signs for Playa Negra for 4 km (2½ mi). Taxi is the easiest way to get around if you don't have a car.

Playa Junquillal

❷⓿ Seekers of tranquility need look no farther than Junquillal (pronounced hoon-key-*yall*). To the south of Playa Negra, this long swath of picturesque beach stretches about 3 km (2 mi), with only one old, wooden hotel/bar on the entire beach. A surprisingly cosmopolitan *mélange* of restaurants—Peruvian, German, Italian, Swiss—is adding an international flavor, and away from the beach, Junquillal is definitely getting livelier. There's finally a small supermarket in the village with a public Internet connection. Although it qualifies as a Blue Flag beach, the surf here is a little strong, so watch children carefully. There's a kids' playground right at the beach. If you're child-free, it's also a perfect beach for taking long, romantic strolls.

Outdoor Activities

HORSEBACK RIDING   At German-run **Paradise Riding** (☎ 658–8162 ⊕ www.paradiseriding. com) the 14 horses are in tip-top shape, as is the impressive tack room, with top-quality saddles lined up in a neat row. There are two-hour trail rides ($29), sunset rides, or you can set off for a whole day of riding. The maximum number of riders they can handle is 10. You saddle up at the friendly owner's house, across from the entrance to Guacamaya Lodge.

Where to Stay & Eat

★ **$$$** ✕ **La Puesta del Sol.** Italian food aficionado Alessandro Zangari and his wife, Silvana, have created what he modestly calls "a little restaurant in my home." But regulars drive all the way from San José to sit at one of the four tables and enjoy the dinner-only, haute-Italian menu. Alessandro spares no expense or effort to secure the best ingredients, and each fall he travels to Italy to buy white and black truffles in season. The softly lit patio restaurant, tinted in tangerine and deep blue, evokes a Moroccan courtyard. All the pasta is made from scratch; the fettucine *boscaiolo* contains a woodsy trio of cremini, porcini, and Portobello mushrooms and the *tagliolini al limón* is tartly sublime. ⊠ *Just north of Playa Junquillal* ☎ *658–8442* ⌲ *Reservations essential* ▤ *No credit cards* ⊘ *Only open for dinner in high, daily in high season Nov. 15 to Easter week.*

★ ☾ **$–$$** ▥ **Guacamaya Lodge.** Secluded Guacamaya, on a breezy hill, has expansive views of surrounding rolling countryside and a generous-sized pool set amid lush landscaping. The three-meal restaurant serves excellent, reasonably priced food, including such Swiss specialties as *rösti* potatoes, as well as calorie-conscious "fitness plates" and delicious, dense homemade bread. The spacious cabinas have lovely curtains and bedspreads and modern bathrooms. At night, you don't even need the new quiet air conditioners; screened windows let in the cooling evening breezes. The modern house has a full kitchen and a large covered veranda; the equipped suites are the newest addition to the property, perfect for families. There's also a kids' pool, a playground, and a resident little girl happy to have playmates. The place fills up fast, so book early or come off-season. ⊠ *275 m off Playa Junquillal* ☎ *658–8431* 🖷 *658–8164* ⊕ *www.guacamayalodge.com* 🖃 *Apdo. 6, Santa Cruz* ⇆ *6 cabinas, 4 suites, 1 house* ⌂ *Restaurant, fans, some kitchens, pool, volleyball, bar, shop, playground, laundry service, Internet; no room phones, no room TVs* ▤ *AE, MC, V* ⅋ *EP.*

$–$$ ▥ **Hotel Iguanazul.** On a bluff overlooking black tidal pools, this hotel is a 10-minute walk from surfing waves to the north and a 30-minute walk from Playa Junquillal to the south. The joint is jumping for surfervideo nights, happy hours, and Monday-night football on a large screen. There's a great pool, beautifully maintained gardens, and pleasant, recently spiffed-up, high-ceilinged bungalows. Some rooms have no airconditioning, but do have screened windows to let in ocean breezes. No. 6 has ocean views and the most privacy (but no air-conditioning). Food is adequate in the spacious alfresco restaurant with, sadly, dismal plastic furniture. Service is friendly but slow. A row of slightly obtrusive, cookie-cutter condominiums baking in a pasture behind the hotel are also for rent. ⊠ *North end of Playa Junquillal* ☎ *658–8124* 🖷 *658–8123* ⊕ *www.hoteliguanazul.com* ⇆ *24 rooms* ⌂ *Restaurant, fans, in-room safes, pool, beach, bar, laundry service; no a/c in some rooms, no room TVs* ▤ *AE, MC, V* ⅋ *CP.*

$ ▥ **Hotel Tatanka.** This Italian hotel has great style and great food. Ten big rooms are lined up under a tile-roofed veranda facing a kidney-shaped pool. They have firm mattresses, big windows, and Mayan-motif wall paintings, arty bamboo closets, and scarlet fixtures in the tiled bathrooms. Wood-oven pizzas and homemade pastas—the *spaghetti a la carbonara* is *delicioso*—are served in a huge alfresco restaurant with elegant furniture. The beach is a three-minute walk away. ☒ *Main Junquillal road, south of Guacamaya Lodge, 300 m from the beach* ☎ *658–8426* 🖷 *658–8312* ⊕ *www.crica.com/tatanka.com* ⬩ *10 rooms* ⌂ *Restaurant, fans, pool; no a/c in some rooms, no room phones, no room TVs* ▤ *MC, V* ☽ *Closed Sept.–Oct.; restaurant closed Mon.* ⑩ *BP.*

Shopping
The **Hotel Iguanazul gift shop** (☒ North end of Playa Junquillal) has interesting glass jewelry made by a Peruvian artist who lives in Playa Negra. There is also truly different and fabulous shell jewelry, including cuff bracelets, made by a local company called Organic Jewelry.

To & from Playa Junquillal
4 km/2 ½ mi (30 mins) south of Paraíso. 34 km/22 mi (1 hr) south of Santa Cruz.

In rainy season, the 4-km-long (2½-mi-long) beach road from Playa Negra to Playa Junquillal is often not passable, and even in dry season and with a 4WD vehicle, it's challenging. Your safest bet is driving down from Santa Cruz on a road that's paved part of the way. Or take a bus. The Castillos company (☎ No phone) runs a bus to Junquillal from the central market in Santa Cruz three times a day (at 10:30 AM, and 2 and 5:30 PM); the trip takes about an hour. If you don't have a car, Junquillal is a bit difficult to access. A taxi from Santa Cruz costs about $20; from Tamarindo, $30.

Playa Junquillal Essentials
The closest town for most services is Santa Cruz, 33 km/21 mi east.

🏥 Hospital **Clínica** ☒ Vientesiete de Abril, 16 km/10 mi northeast of Playa Junquillal.
🌐 Internet **Supermercado Junquillal** ☒ Near beach entrance.

Nosara

㉑ One of the last beach communities for people who want to get away from it all, Nosara's attractions are the wild stretches of side-by-side Playas Pelada and Guiones, with surfing waves and miles of beach to comb. The town itself is inland and not very interesting. The Nosara Yoga Institute is increasingly a draw for health-conscious, new-age visitors. Regulations here limit development to low-rise buildings 200 meters from the beach, where they are thankfully screened by trees. Americans and Europeans, with a large Swiss contingent, are building at a fairly rapid pace, but there appears to be an aesthetic sense here that is totally lacking in Tamarindo.

The access roads to Nosara are abysmal, and the labyrinth of woodsy roads around the beaches

> **CAUTION**
>
> To approach Nosara along the coast from Junquillal to the north, you have to ford many rivers, including the Río Ostional, impossible during most of the wet season. This beach road is in really bad shape and is extraordinarily slow going even in dry season; 23 km (14 mi) can take two hours to drive. You are better off driving via Nicoya on the paved road.

and hard-to-read signs make it easy to get lost. ■ TIP→ **It's a good idea to scout out your dinner spot earlier in the day.** For local news and happenings, check out *The Voice of Nosara* (⊕ www.voiceofnosara.com).

Exploring

With some of the best surf breaks around, **Playa Guiones** attracts a lot of surfboard-toting visitors. But the breezy beach, with tendrils of sea grape curling almost down to the high-tide mark, is also a haven for shell seekers and sun lovers. The only building in sight is the bizarre, surreal Hotel Nosara, chronically under construction. Otherwise, this glorious beach has 7 km (4 mi) of hard-packed sand, great for jogging and riding bikes. Since there's a 3-meter tide, it's safer to go swimming at either high or low tide, and avoid the strong currents when the tide is turning. Most hotels post tide charts. Guiones is at the south end of the Nosara agglomeration, with three public accesses. The easiest one to find is just past the Hotel Harmony, formerly the Hotel Villa Taype.

Ostional National Wildlife Refuge (Refugio Nacional de Fauna Silvestre Ostional) protects one of Costa Rica's major breeding grounds for olive ridley turtles. Locals have formed an association to run the reserve on a cooperative basis, and during the first 36 hours of the *arribadas* (mass nesting) they are allowed to harvest the eggs, on the premise that eggs laid during this time would likely be destroyed by subsequent waves of mother turtles, or stolen by poachers. There are two nesting seasons. The largest arribadas, with thousands of turtle, occur from June to December during Costa Rica's "winter"; smaller, less frequent arribadas occur from January to May. Guided tours of the nesting and hatching areas cost for $7 per person, plus the entrance fee of $7. Stop at the kiosk at the entrance road to the beach to ask for a tour. Before you go to the refuge, try to get a sense from the locals of when, if ever (some years they come in very small numbers), the turtles will arrive. ⊠ *7 km/4½ mi north of Nosara; during the rainy season a 4WD vehicle is needed to cross the river* ☎ *682–0428* ☜ *$7* ☉ *Oct.–Apr., by tour only.*

★ At the north end of Nosara, the **Reserva Biológica Nosara** is a natural treasure. The 125-acre private reserve includes trails through a huge mangrove wetland and old-growth forest along the Nosara River. A concrete walkway passes over an eerily beautiful mangrove swamp, with fantastical roots and snap-crackling sound effects from respiring mollusks. More than 250 bird species have been spotted here and there's an observation platform for observing wading birds. There are always crabs, lizards, snakes, and other creatures rustling in the grass or monkeys, iguanas, and boa constrictors hanging from the trees. Pick up a self-guided trail map from the Lagarta Lodge (near the trailhead); call ahead to the lodge if you want to hire a guide ($6 entrance fee). There's also a guided Botany tour for an extra $3. ⊠ *Trailhead 168 steps down from Lagarta Lodge, top of hill at the north end of Nosara* ☎ *682–0035.*

MASSAGE & YOGA **The Nosara Yoga Institute** (⊠ Southeast end of town, on main road to Sámara ☎ 682–0071, 866/439–4704 in U.S. ⊕ www.nosarayoga.com) focuses on teacher certification, but also offers daily yoga classes to the public, weeklong workshops, and retreats. Relaxing massages in a jungle setting ($45/hour) are available by appointment at **Tica Massage**

(⊠ Across from the Hotel Harmony [formerly the Hotel Villa Taype] ☎ 682–0096), plus spa services such as facials and salt glows.

Outdoor Activities

Iguana Expeditions (⊠ Gilded Iguana, Playa Guiones ☎ 682–4089 ⊕ www.iguanaexpeditions.com) organizes canopy tours, kayaking, horseback riding, fishing, and nature tours. The **Harbor Reef Lodge** (⊠ Follow signs from Café de Paris turnoff, Playa Guiones ☎ 682–0059 ⊕ www.harborreef.com) has an excellent tour desk that can arrange fishing, surfing, snorkeling, and nature tours.

BIRD-WATCHING On river trips with **Toni's Birdwatching** (⊠ Boat moored at bottom of hill leading to Lagarta Lodge, follow the yellow-fish signs to mouth of Nosara River ☎ 822–1806 or 682–0610), you glide up the Nosara and Montaña rivers in a flat-bottomed catamaran with an almost noiseless electric motor. Wading herons, egrets, roseate spoonbills, ospreys, and kingfishers are common sights. The German-born naturalist guide also knows where river otters play and crocodiles hunker down in mud caves along the riverbank. Trips are $60 for 1 person; $30 per person for two or more.

HORSEBACK RIDING German equestrienne Beate Klossek and husband Hans-Werner take small groups of two to four people on 2½-hour horseback nature tours through the jungle and along the beach ($30 to $50 per person, depending on size of group) with **Boca Nosara Tours** (⊠ 150 m below Lagarta Lodge, at the mouth of the Nosara River ☎ 682–0280). Horses are well mannered and well treated. Up to eight people can go on day-long rides into the mountains, stopping at a comfortable hotel for lunch and a swim ($90).

SURFING If you ever wanted to learn to surf, Nosara is the place. Guiones is the perfect beginners' beach, with no strong undercurrents and no reef to worry about. Local surf instructors say that the waves here are so consistent that there's no week throughout the year when you won't be able to surf. In February there's a local tournament organized by Safari Surf School, with guest celebrity surfers. In March, the Costa Rican National Surf Circuit comes here for surf trials. Especially recommended for beginners, **Safari Surf School** (⊠ Road to Playa Guiones; ask for directions at Nosara Surf Shop ☎ 682–0573 ⊕ www.safarisurfschool.com) is run by two surfing brothers from Hawaii, one of whom lives here year-round. It's closed in October. **Corky Carroll's Surf School** (⊠ Near Casa Romántica, on the Playa Guiones Rd. ☎ 682–0385 ⊕ www.surfschool.net) has its own hotel for surfing students. **Coconut Harry's Surf Shop** (⊠ Main road, across from Café de Paris ☎ 682–0574) has gear, boards, wax, and lessons. **Nosara Surf Shop** (⊠ Café de Paris road to Playa Guiones ☎ 682–0186) rents boards by the day ($15 to $25) or week and has lots of gear, too.

Where to Stay & Eat

$-$$ ✕ **Marlin Bill's.** Sink your teeth into classic American-style rib-eye steak, pork chops, and lobster in large American portions at this established, open-air restaurant with a distant ocean view. Lighter choices include eggplant Parmesan and delicious "dorado fingers"—battered fish fillet strips served with tartar sauce. The decor is decidedly fishy, with a mounted marlin, fish murals, and a photo wall of happy fishers and their prize catches. Fishing and real estate talk over beer and chicken wings keeps the U-shaped bar abuzz. ✉ *Hilltop above main road, near Coconut Harry's Surf Shop* ☏ 682–0458 ▭ *MC, V* ☾ *Closed Sun.*

★ **$** ✗ **Giardino Tropical Restaurant Pizzería.** Famous for its crispy-crusted, wood-oven pizzas loaded with toppings and homemade chili-pepper sauce, this thatch-roof, two-story restaurant casts a wider net to include excellent fresh seafood and fish—the carpaccio of sea bass is a sure bet. Service is always fast and friendly. ✉ *Giardino Tropical Hotel, main street, past entrance to Playa Guiones* ☏ 682–0258 ▭ *AE, DC, MC, V.*

$–$$ ✗ 🏠 **Casa Romántica Hotel.** The name (Romantic House) says it all: the Spanish Colonial–style house has a balustraded veranda upstairs and a graceful arcade below. New Swiss owners have renovated the original rooms and built two new rooms. They are bright, with big bathrooms and views of the glorious garden and extra-large pool covered by a thatched cabana. The short path to the beach is lined with aloe, cactus, and costus (similar to flowering ginger) and populated with birds. There is a small patio restaurant where breakfast is served; at night it becomes a candlelit, romantic restaurant with a sophisticated international menu, featuring excellent seafood. ✉ *Turn down road at Il Giardino Tropicale, Playa Guiones* ☏☏ 682–0272 ⊕ *www.casa–romantica.net* ⤳ *10 rooms* ♿ *Restaurant, refrigerators, fans, pool, massage, beach, Internet; no a/c in some rooms, no room phones, no room TVs* ▭ *MC, V* ⏐⊙⏐ *BP.*

$$$ 🏠 **Condo Canadiense del Sol Villas.** Steps from Playa Guiones, these clean and comfortable white villas face the garden's riot of color surrounding a sparkling blue pool. They have great kitchens, all-wood furniture, and queen beds in the high-ceilinged bedrooms. Living areas have both a double and a single futon, and large terraces have dining tables. New air-conditioning units are quiet, as are the ceiling fans. ✉ *Across from Casita Romántica, Playa Guiones* ☏ 682–0350, 403/938–1112 in Canada 🖷 403/938–3051 in Canada ⊕ *www.condocanadiense.com* ⤳ *4 villas* ♿ *Fans, kitchens, pool* ▭ *MC, V for online reservations; cash only in Costa Rica* ⏐⊙⏐ *EP.*

$$–$$$ 🏠 **Harmony Hotel.** Surf's up . . . scale, that is. Hotel Villa Taype, a frayed old surfer's haunt, has been reborn as an ultracool, ultrasophisticated retreat. The new American owners are surfers, too, but of an age where comfort and quiet are more appealing than partying. The huge garden and gorgeous pool are oases of soft sage-and-cream-colored tranquility. Every spacious room, villa, and bungalow has a king-size bed dressed in all-white linen. Quiet, new air-conditioning and ceiling fans, updated bathrooms, outdoor decks with hot showers, a juice bar, and a retro '60s lounge bar with basket chairs all add to the harmonious vibe here. The lobby restaurant, not yet opened at this writing, will serve a simple, healthy menu. The best surf breaks are just 200 meters down a shaded path to the beach. ✉ *From Café de Paris, take road almost all the way to Playa Guiones* ☎ *682–0571* 🖷 *682–0187* ⊕ *www.harmonynosara.com* 🛏 *24 rooms; 9 standard rooms, 7 1-bedroom bungalows, 4 2-room bungalows, 3 with connecting doors* ⚘ *Restaurant, fans, in-room safes, refrigerators, coffeemakers, bar, pool, beach, surfing, Ping-Pong, Wi-Fi, Internet* ▭ *AE, MC, V* ⊙ *EP.*

★ **$$** ⊞ **Luna Azul.** The most luxurious, tasteful hotel in the Nosara area, Luna Azul is full of clever designs and healthful attributes—supplied by the zoologist and homeopathist Swiss owners. Birds and wildlife are abundant thanks to the surrounding private nature reserve. Rooms are spacious, and the bathrooms are elegant, with hot-water showers open to nature. Three separate rooms have very private decks, cooled by overhead fans; four others share two buildings but each has a private garden. A new room in the main building has all the same amenities but no terrace. Acupuncture and homeopathic treatments and massages are available. The chic seafood restaurant overlooking the gorgeous infinity pool is drawing customers from Nosara (even when the river is flooded) with perfectly prepared seafood, Swiss fondues, and culinary theme nights. Breakfasts are hearty and delicious. The only drawback to this picture-perfect place is that it's hard to get to when the Ostional River overflows in rainy season, but you can always reach it via the slow but sure road from Veintisiete de Abril. ✉ *1 km/½ mi north of Ostional, 5 km/3 mi north of Nosara* ☎ *821–0075* ⊕ *www.hotellunaazul.com* 🛏 *3 bungalows, 4 rooms in two buildings, 1 room in main building* ⚘ *Restaurant, fans, refrigerators, in-room safes, pool, whirlpool tub, bar* ▭ *AE, DC, MC, V* ⊙ *BP.*

$–$$ ⊞ **Casita Romántica.** This small terra-cotta hotel used to be the annex to Casa Romántica next door. Now run as a separate hotel, the five modern, comfortable suites all have kitchenettes and share a pool, a garden, and a pathway to the beach. Each suite has a wonderful wall mural, loads of light, and stylish furnishings. One large suite has a full kitchen and room for four. The management is Swiss. ✉ *Beside Casa Romántica* ☎ *682–0019* ⊕ *www.hotelcasaromantica.com* 🛏 *5 suites* ⚘ *Fans, kitchenettes, pool, beach; no a/c in some rooms, no room phones, no room TVs* ▭ *MC, V* ⊙ *EP.*

$–$$ ⊞ **The Gilded Iguana.** This lively hotel/bar/restaurant has been a Nosara fixture for more than 15 years. Televised sports, live music, and lots of friendly regulars keep this popular place casual. The on-site tour desk can arrange almost any outing you can think of. Six large, newer, air-conditioned rooms are lined up behind a beautiful pool, complete with a refreshing waterfall. For traditionalists, the original rooms have more character, in a shaded wooden building, with louvered, screened windows letting in fresh breezes. Spacious, woodsy No. 4 is the favorite. ✉ *Playa Guiones, Nosara* ☎ *682–0259* ⊕ *www.gildediguana.com* 🛏 *9 rooms, 3 suites* ⚘ *Restaurant, fans, refrigerators, pool, kayaking, tours, bar, laundry service; no a/c in some rooms, no room phones, no room TVs* ▭ *MC, V* ⊙ *EP.*

★ **$** ⊞ **Lagarta Lodge.** A birders' and nature-lovers' mecca, this magnificent property on a promontory has the best views of Ostional National Wildlife Refuge. The private Nosara Biological Reserve is directly below the lodge. A 10-minute steep walk down takes you through a monkey-filled forest to beautiful Playa Guiones and surfing waves. Swiss managers Regina and Amadeo Amacker have renovated and brightened up formerly dark rooms. The eagle's-nest lobby-restaurant, with great views, has family-style seating and a Swiss-inspired menu. The breakfast buffet is delicious, with fresh breads and homemade jams. ⊠ *Top of hill at the north end of Nosara* ☎ *682–0035* 🖷 *682–0135* ⊕ *www. lagarta.com* ⌁ *6 rooms* ⌂ *Restaurant, fans, pool, beach, laundry service, Internet; no a/c, no room phones, no room TVs.*

Nightlife
There's always plenty of surfing talk at **Blew Dog's Surf Club** (⊠ Playa Guiones 682–0080). Friday nights, **Café de Paris** (⊠ Entrance to Playa Guiones) shows DVD movies on a big outdoor screen. **The Gilded Iguana** (⊠ Playa Guiones), a popular sports bar, has live acoustic music on Tuesday nights that draws a big crowd. Sip a margarita or one of a myriad other cocktails and watch the sun set at tony **La Luna Bar&Grill** (⊠ Playa Pelada, 200 m north of Olga's). Sunset is the main evening event on the Nosara beaches, and people gather on Playa Pelada to down a local beer at **Olga's Bar** (⊠ Playa Pelada), a ramshackle beach bar. Saturday nights, the dance action is at the popular Tropicana Disco/Bar in downtown Nosara, beside the soccer field.

Shopping
Arte Guay (⊠ Commercial center, just past Café de Paris on road to Playa Guiones ☎ 682–0943) has local crafts. Along with surfing wear and gear, **Coconut Harry's Surf Shop** (⊠ Main road, across from Café de Paris) has an interesting selection of jewelry and bottled hot sauces made by Harry himself. (The Iguana Atomic Hot Sauce will rip your tongue out!) At the **Nosara Boutique** (⊠ Commercial center, just past Café de Paris on road to Playa Guiones), the Nosara Yoga Institute sells yoga books, new-age CDs, and yoga wear. **Nosara Surf Shop** (⊠ Café de Paris road to Playa Guiones) has a great selection of straw hats to keep the sun from frying your hair and face.

To & from Nosara
28 km/17 mi (1 hr) southwest of Nicoya.

From Nicoya, drive south, almost to Sámara, but take the very first road signed for Nosara, 1 km (½ mi) south of the big gas station before Sámara. This higher road is rough, too, for about 8 km (5 mi) but there are bridges over all the river crossings. When you join up with the beach road near Garza, you still have a very bumpy 10 km (6 mi) to go. Whichever way you go, the roads into Nosara are in really bad shape, and a 4WD vehicle is definitely recommended. Even the high-speed highway buses for Nosara transfer passengers to crummy old buses to negotiate the last 20 km (12 mi). You can also fly directly to Nosara on daily scheduled SANSA and Nature Air flights or take an air-conditioned shuttle van from San José.

Nosara Essentials
🏦 Bank/ATM **Banco Popular** ⊠ Beside Café de Paris, at entrance to Playa Guiones ☎ 682–0267 ⊙ Bank open Mon. and Fri. only; ATM available some days.

🏥 Hospital **Clínica Pública** ⊠ In front ot Super Nosara ☎ 682-0166.

💊 Pharmacies **Farmacia** ⊠ Next to soccer field ☎ 682-0282 ⊘ Mon.-Sat. 8-noon and 2-4.

🚕 Taxi Independent drivers provide taxi service. **Abel's Taxi** ☎ 812-8470 is reliable.

Sámara

㉒ The drive to Sámara from Nicoya may be one of the most scenic in Costa Rica, past rolling hills and green vistas. Long a favorite with well-off Ticos, many of whom built summer houses on the beach, Sámara is flourishing and attracting a lot of Europeans. The town even has a sidewalk.

A branch of the Heredia-based language school **Intercultura** (☎ 656-0127) attracts students of all ages. But despite a distinctively Italian flavor, Tico culture—school, soccer field, and church—still rules, along with a certain amount of characteristically Tico clutter.

Outdoor Activities

Sámara is known more for gentle watersports such as snorkeling and kayaking than for surfing or diving, although there are a couple of surfing and dive shops. There are also two high-flying adventures here: zipline tours and ultralight flights and flying lessons. ATV tours, tearing along dirt roads, are also becoming popular. For information on area activities, visit the town's official Web site at ⊕ www.samarabeach.com.

Tío Tigre Tours (☎ 656-0098 ⊠ 50 m east of the school and 100 m north) has a full line of guided outdoor tours, including snorkeling, kayaking, in-shore fishing, horseback riding, and dolphin- and whale-watching tours. **Carrillo Tours** (⊠ Main street, across from Las Brasas restaurant ☎ 656-0935 in Sámara, 656-0543 in Carrillo ⊕ www.carrillotours.com) is another reputable general tour operator, with a small office in Sámara and the main office in nearby Carrillo.

CANOPY TOURS **Wing Nuts Canopy Tour** (⊠ In the hills above Sámara ☎ 656-0153) is a three-hour, 12-platform zip-line tour through dry tropical forest, with ocean views from some of the platforms ($50; $30 for 17 years and under).

DIVING & SNORKELING The reef just offshore is the best place to snorkel. Kayakers also paddle out to Isla Chora to snorkel around the island. The lone dive shop here, French-run **Pura Vida Dive** (⊠ Downtown Sámara, around corner from Villas Kalimba ☎ 843-2075) takes divers (five maximum) about 5 mi out for guided dives around rock formations off Playa Buena Vista and Playa Carrillo. Turtles, white-tipped sharks, and lots of big fish are the star sightings. They also rent scuba equipment and make snorkeling trips.

KAYAKING **Tio Tigre** (⇨ *above*) is the main kayaking outfitter in Sámara. **PoPo's Adventures** (⇨ Playa Carrillo, *below*) also runs kayaking trips in the area.

SURFING The surf is relatively gentle around Sámara, so it's a good place for beginners. The challenging waves for more experienced surfers are farther south, past Puerto Carrillo at Playa Camaronal, which has both left and right breaks. **Jesse's Original Sámara Beach Surf School** (⊠ Northwest end of the beach ☎ 656-0055) specializes in teaching beginners and also rents boards. **C&C Surf Shop** (⊠ Across from Hotel Belvedere in town

☎ 656–0628) has a beach-front surf school ($30 per lesson) and gives one free surf lesson with weekly board rental ($80).

ULTRALIGHT FLIGHTS   **Flying Crocodile Lodge** (⊠ Playa Buena Vista, 6 km/4 mi northwest of Sámara ☎ 656–8048 ⊕ www.flying-crocodile.com) gives ultralight flights and flying lessons ($60 for 20-min tour; $110 for instruction plus cost of flights).

Where to Stay & Eat

$–$$ ✕ **Restaurante Las Brasas.** Seafood and meat grilled over hot *brasas* (coals) are the specialties at this Spanish restaurant, along with paella, gazpacho, and a variety of Spanish *tortillas* (hearty omelets). Avocado stuffed with shrimp salad makes an excellent shared starter or a light lunch. An upstairs balcony is perfect for sipping Spanish wines. Downstairs, enormous green elephant-ear leaves frame the rustic wooden-railed restaurant, decorated with oxen horns and yokes. ⊠ *Main road to beach, beside soccer field* ☎ 656–0546 ▭ MC, V.

$ ✕ **Restaurant El Dorado.** After one visit to Costa Rica, Andrea Dolcetti and his wife, Luigina Sivieri, sold their restaurant in Ferrara, Italy, and opened one here. We're glad they did. Their open-air *palenque* (wood-and-thatch building) specializes in seafood, pasta, and at dinner, wood oven–baked pizzas. Andrea brings home the fish and Luigina works magic in the kitchen. Pasta is made from scratch, and real Parmesan cheese and salami are imported from Italy. Luigina's lasagna is the lightest imaginable and the spaghetti *al mare* is an inspired marriage of local shellfish and Italian cooking. For dessert, there are fruit *crostatas* (tarts) and chocolate "salami." ⊠ *West off main road, just past church in Sámara* ☎ 656–0145 ▭ AE, DC, MC, V ☻ *Closed Thurs. No lunch May–early Dec.*

★ **¢–$** ✕ **Pizza & Pasta a Go-Go.** Exceptionally fine Italian food, including 25 fabulous pizzas, 26 pasta choices, generous salads, and a lengthy Italian wine list are just a few reasons to drop in at this sidewalk trattoria with glass tabletops showcasing shells. Save room for a tiramisu that transcends the tropics and delivers your taste buds to Italy. ⊠ *Hotel Giada lobby, main strip, 150 m from beach* ☎ 656–0132 ▭ MC, V.

$$$ ▦ **Villas Playa Sámara.** Families come back year after year for good reasons: there's lots to do; the villas are spacious; and the setting is fabulous. The long stretch of picture-perfect beach has clean, clear water that's shallow and safe enough for swimming. The pretty one-, two-, and three-bedroom, white-stucco villas are sprinkled throughout the property's mature trees and gardens. New, quiet air conditioners keep the villas cool. Villa 11B, near the beach with a shaded terrace, has one of the most idyllic beach views. The restaurant food is not terrific; it's best to cook for yourself or dine in Sámara, which you can walk to in 20 minutes along the beach (it's perfectly safe at night). ⊠ *Off main road, 2 km/1¼ mi south of Playa Sámara* ☎▦ 656–0372; 256–8228 in San José ✆ htlvilla@racsa.co.cr ⇄ 58 villas ⚗ Restaurant, fans, some cable TV, kitchens, pool, beach, boating, fishing, horseback riding, bar; no room phones, no TVs in some rooms ▭ AE, MC, V ⍾ EP.

$–$$ ▦ **Las Brisas del Pacífico.** One of the few beachfront hotels in Sámara, Las Brisas has two rows of white, Spanish-style bungalows hugging the bottom of a steep, landscaped hill. The well-maintained bungalows face a gorgeous pool and thatch-roof restaurant. "Sky rooms," in the two-story building at the top of the hill, have ocean-view balconies and a pool topside, as well as a separate parking lot, so you don't have to climb up and down the hill except for meals and beach walks. The hotel's tour desk can arrange diving trips and other outings. The only downside is the rather surly German owner. ⊠ *South end of beach* ☎ *656–0250* 🖶 *656–0076* ⊕ *www.brisas.net* 🛏 *22 bungalows, 16 rooms* ⚐ *Restaurant, fans, in-room safes, some cable TV, 2 pools, 2 outdoor whirlpool tubs, beach, snorkeling, bar; no a/c in some rooms, no room phones, no TV in some rooms* ⊟ *AE, D, MC, V* ❑ *BP.*

$ ▦ **Casa del Mar.** Less than a block from the beach, you can't beat this pleasant, well-tended hotel for value. The bright, tidy rooms have dark-wood furniture, white walls, and ceramic floors. Eleven of the rooms have private bath, TVs, and a/c and some have queen-size beds. Six of the rooms have fans only and shared baths. The hotel has a giant cold-water whirlpool in a small garden and a big cage with pet parrots. Evening beach breezes help to cool down the rooms without air-conditioning. ⊠ *Main strip, 45 m east of school* ☎ *656–0264* 🖶 *656–0129* ⊕ *www. casadelmarsamara.com* 🛏 *17 rooms, 11 with bath* ⚐ *Dining room, fans, in-room safes, some refrigerators, bar; no a/c in some rooms, no room phones, no TV in some rooms* ⊟ *AE, MC, V* ❑ *BP.*

$ ▦ **Hotel Belvedere.** After a day on the beach, it's refreshing to retreat to this small hotel buried in a dense, cool garden. There's a shaded swimming pool with a trickling waterfall, and a cool whirlpool. Friendly German owners Manfred and Michaela run a tight ship, keeping the garden moisture out of the large, bright rooms housed in a two-story, white-stucco building. Breakfast comes with ocean views and the total bill is a hard-to-beat bargain. The beach is a 10-minute walk through town. ⊠ *Entering Sámara, go 100 m left at the first cross st.* ☎ *656–0213* 🖶 *656–0215* ⊕ *www.belveresamara.net* 🛏 *20 rooms* ⚐ *Dining room, fans, cable TV, in-room safes, some kitchenettes, refrigerators, pool, whirlpool tub; no room phones* ⊟ *MC, V* ❑ *BP.*

★ $ ▦ **Hotel Giada.** The gem of Sámara's small hotels, Giada, which means "jade," is the polished creation of artistic Italian owners. Watermelon, terra-cotta, and yellow washes give the walls an antique Mediterranean look. In contrast, thatch roofs overhang private terraces, which overlook a tropical garden and curvaceous blue pool. The large rooms have elegant bamboo furniture, and whimsical sea creatures are hand-painted on the bathroom tiles. Pizza & Pasta a Go-Go (⇨ *above*) is an excellent Italian restaurant. The hotel's only drawback is that the upstairs roadside rooms can be noisy; ask for a room overlooking the pool or one of the newer rooms in the back garden. ⊠ *Main strip, 150 m from beach* ☎ *656–0132* 🖶 *656–0131* ⊕ *www.hotelgiada.net* 🛏 *24 rooms* ⚐ *Restaurant, fans, some refrigerators, safety boxes, cable TV, 2 pools, whirlpool tub, tours, car rental, laundry service* ⊟ *MC, V* ❑ *BP.*

Nightlife

The liveliest, noisiest beach bar is at **Las Olas** (⊠ Northwest end of the beach). Three pool tables, bright lights, and a pulsing Latin soundtrack attract locals and young backpackers staying in cold-water, thatch huts next to the bar. **Sol y Mar** (⊠ Northwest end of the beach) has popular karaoke nights; just ask in town for the schedule. **Shake Joe's** (⊠ On beach,

center of town) is the place for music, juices, drinks, and an international
★ menu. Ultracool **La Vela Latina** (⊠ Across from Villas Kalimba, on the beach) is the place for grown-up soft music and cocktails on the beach.

Shopping

Souvenir stands set up along the main street and at the entrance to the beach. Most shops here have pretty much the same beachwear and souvenirs for sale. **Tienda Licia** (⊠ main St.) has a wall hung with pretty glass fish and butterfly ornaments made by a San José artist. Arts and crafts gallery **Dragonfly Galería** (⊠ Across the street from Licia) sells local paintings and carvings, and shell, feather, and bead jewelry. It also paints temporary henna tattoos.

To & from Sámara

36 km/23 mi (1 hr) southwest of Nicoya. 26 km/16 mi (2 ½ hrs) south of Nosara.

The road from Nicoya is paved all the way for the scenic 36 km (23 mi) to Sámara. ⚠ **Potholes are spreading, so keep your eyes on the road instead of the beautiful views.** A rough beach road from Nosara is passable in dry season (it's more direct, but takes just as long); do not attempt this road when it rains. To get from Nosara to Sámara via the paved road, drive south, 5 km (3 mi) past Garza. At a T intersection, ignore the road toward Sámara (the beach road) and take the road to the left, toward Nicoya. This will take you uphill to merge with the main Nicoya-Sámara highway. No matter which way you go, the drive to Sámara is long and bumpy. Buses leave Nicoya for Sámara, from a stop 300 m east of the central park, almost every hour on the hour from 5 AM to noon and on the half-hour, from 1:30 to 6:30 Monday to Friday; last bus is at 9:45.

Sámara Essentials

🔋 Bank/ATM **Mobile Banco Nacional** ⊠ Beach entrance, in front of police station ⊙ ATM available when satellite communication working.

🔋 Hospital **Medical Care Beach Services** ☎ 304-2121 ⊙ 24-hour emergency hotline.

🔋 Pharmacies **Farmacia Sámara** ⊠ North end of soccer field ☎ 656-0123.

🔋 Taxi Independent taxi drivers include Felo 356-4288 and Osvaldo 390-3271.

Playa Carrillo

❷❸ With its long, reef-protected beach backed by an elegant line of swaying palms and sheltering cliffs, Playa Carrillo (interchangeably called FodorśChoice Puerto Carrillo) is a candidate for the most picturesque beach in Costa ★ Rica. Totally unmarred by even a single building, it's ideal for swimming, snorkeling, walking, and lounging—just remember not to sit under a loaded coconut palm. There are some round, concrete tables and benches but they get snapped up quickly. The main landmark here is the Hotel Guanamar, high above the beach. Unfortunately the former private fishing club and previously grand hotel has been bought and sold so often that its charm has faded. But its bar still has the best view.

Exploring

☺ Most nature lovers are no fans of zoos, but **La Selva Zoo & Bromeliad Garden,** a small zoo with mostly rescued, small animals is a great chance to see them up close, in low, chest-high corrals under the shade of trees.

The zoo's focus is on hard-to-see nocturnal animals, so the best time to visit is at sunset when the armadillo and big-eyed kinkajou are starting to stir. There are also a skunk, spotted pacas, raccoons, and scarier species like bats, boas, poison-dart frogs, caimans, and crocodiles (the latter two, very small babies). A bromeliad and orchid collection is artistically arranged around the zoo. If you come early in the day, your ticket is also good for a return evening visit. ⊠ *Road behind Hotel Esperanza* ☎ *305–1610* ✉ *$5* ☺ *Daily 10–9.*

Outdoor Activities

ATV TOURS   **Hotel El Sueño Tropical** (⊠ 2 km/1 mi south of Puerto Carrillo, along a dirt rd. ☎ 656–0151 ⊕ www.elsuenotropical.com) guides ATV tours along beach trails south of Puerto Carrillo.

KAYAKING   Energetic, friendly Tad Cantrell at **PoPo's Adventures** (⊠ Off main Carrillo road, just south of Hotel Esperanza ☎ 656–0086) knows his birds and trees and he'll point them out as you float down the Río Ora in brand-new sit-on-top kayaks, the cadillac of kayaks, says Tad. He also has skirted, cockpit kayaks for more experienced paddlers. The four-to-five-hour trip is designed for anyone aged 2 to 102, he says, and includes a picnic lunch. Cantrell also runs a sea kayaking school; organizes longer, more challenging kayaking trips; and has surfing and snorkeling trips as well.

FISHING   From January to April, sportfishing boats moored off the beach take anglers on fishing expeditions. Experienced local Capt. Rob Gordon lives right in Puerto Carrillo and runs fishing trips on **Kitty Kat** (☎ 656–0170 or 359–9039 ⊕ www.sportfishcarrillo.com), a 28-foot aluminum boat with twin diesels ($800 full-day offshore fishing for up to five people; $500 half-day including lunch). He'll find catch-and-release marlin and sailfish out in the ocean as well as good-eating dorado, yellowfin tuna, and wahoo for you. There are also dolphins and whales to watch if the fishing is slow.

Where to Stay

$$ ⊞ **Puerto Carrillo Sunset Luxury B&B.** High on a hill, these rooms are a little pricey, but can't be beat for spectacular views of distant Sámara Bay and nearby Carrillo Beach. Rooms are spacious and sunny, with carvings of fish adorning the wooden headboards. Huge blue-tiled bathrooms have solar-heated hot water. Breakfast is served poolside in an open rancho facing the view. Surrounded by secondary forest, the garden has flowers that lure hummingbirds and butterflies. The road to the hotel is incredibly steep and often heavily rutted after rain, but you can usually get up it in dry season without four-wheel drive. ⊠ *500 m up steep road to left of public parking area in Playa Carrillo* ☎ *656–0011* 🖨 *656–0009* ⊕ *www.carrillosunset.com* 🛏 *6 rooms* ⚭ *Fans, pool; no room phones, no room TVs* ⊟ *No credit cards* ⑩ *BP.*

$ ✕⊞ **Hotel Esperanza.** The best thing about this modest but comfortable B&B is the garden, an oasis with hammocks, lounge chairs, an old-fashioned swing seat, and a pretty dining terrace. Beds are comfy, there's lots of hot water, and the rooms, which sleep two to seven, are always fresh and well maintained. At night, in high season, the breakfast terrace becomes El Ginger Restaurant (¢–$), specializing in grilled jumbo shrimp, fish and beef tenderloin, and a bananas flambé ending. The hotel organizes a waterfall hiking tour and fishing excursions. ✉ *90 m west of Hotel Guanamar* 🕾🕾 *656–0564* ⊕ *www.hotelesperanza.com* 🔦 *7 rooms* ⚒ *Restaurant, fans; no a/c, no room phones, no room TVs* 🖃 *MC, V* ⑩ *BP.*

To & from Playa Carrillo
7 km/4 mi (15 mins) southeast of Sámara.

You can fly into Playa Carrillo on SANSA or Nature Air and land at the airstrip, or head south on the smooth, paved road from Sámara. If you're not staying at a hotel in Carrillo, you'll have to park your car either in a sun-baked concrete lot halfway along the beach or on the grassy road median at the south end of the beach. You can also leave the driving to Interbus (⇨ The North Pacific Essentials, end of chapter) and get here via air-conditioned van.

Playa Carrillo Essentials
Sámara is the closest town for banks and other services.

Punta Islita

㉔ Punta Islita is named for a tiny tuft of land that becomes an island at high tide but the name is synonymous in Costa Rica with Hotel Punta Islita, one of the country's most luxurious and gorgeous resorts. The curved beach is rather rocky but good for walking, especially at low tide when tidal pools form in the volcanic rock. Another interesting stroll is through the small village, which has become a work of art in progress, thanks to a community art project, led by renowned Costa Rican artists recruited by Hotel Punta Islita, who use town buildings as their canvas. Everything—from outdoor activities to food—revolves around and is available through the resort.

Where to Stay

$$$$ 🖾 **Hotel Punta Islita.** Overlooking the Pacific from a forested ridge, this
FodorśChoice exquisite, secluded hotel is luxury incarnate. Hidden around the hill-
★ side are villas, casitas, suites, and spacious rooms, each with a private porch and a hammock. Beds have rough-hewn wooden bedposts, and bathrooms are tiled, with deep tubs. Casitas have their own private plunge pools or outdoor whirlpools and private gardens, one of the main attractions for the many honeymooners. A massive thatched dome covers the restaurant and opens onto an infinity-edge pool with a sea view and a swim-up bar. If you overdo with activities here—which include golfing, zip-line canopy tours (shorter and lower to the ground than most canopy tours), and mountain biking—stop by the spa for unique massage treatments using local herbs. ✉ *South of Playa Carrillo* 🕾 *661–4044, 231–6122 in San José* 🖷 *661–4043, 231–0715 in San José* ⊕ *www.hotelpuntaislita.com* 🖘 *Apdo. 242–1225, Plaza Mayor, San José* 🔦 *15 bungalows, 13 casitas, 6 suites, 5 villas* ⚒ *2 restaurants, minibars, cable TV (some with VCR or DVD), driving range, 2 tennis courts, 2 pools, gym, spa, beach, boating, fishing, hiking, horseback riding, tours, 2 bars, laundry service, Internet, airstrip, helipad* 🖃 *AE, DC, MC, V* ⑩ *CP.*

To & from Punta Islita
8 km/5 mi (15 mins) south of Playa Carrillo in dry season; 50 km/31 mi (1½ hrs) south of Carrillo by alternate route in rainy season.

In rainy season, it's often impossible to cross the Río Ora, south of Carrillo, so you have to make a much longer detour along dirt roads with spectacular mountain views but lots of potholes. Most guests fly into the hotel's private airstrip.

THE TEMPISQUE RIVER BASIN

The parks in and around the Río Tempisque are prime places to hike, explore caves, and watch birds and other wildlife. The town of Nicoya is the commercial and political hub of the northern Nicoya Peninsula. By road, Nicoya provides the best access to Sámara, Nosara, and points south and north and is linked by a smooth, well-paved road to the artisan community of Guaitil and the northern Nicoya beach towns.

Palo Verde National Park

25 One of the best wildlife and bird-watching parks in Costa Rica, Palo Verde is bordered on the west by the Río Tempisque. Extending over 198 square km (76 square mi), the park protects a significant amount of deciduous dry forest. The forest is less dense than rain forest, which makes it easier to spot birds and animals. The terrain is fairly flat—the maximum elevation in the park is 268 meters (879 feet)—and the main attraction is bird-watching. Its swampland and the nearby river are temporary homes for thousands of migratory birds toward the end of the rainy season, as well as crocodiles year-round. From September through March you can see dozens of species of aquatic birds, including herons, wood storks, jabirus, and elegant, flamingo-like roseate spoonbills. ■ TIP→ A raised platform near the ranger station, about 8 km (5 mi) past the park entrance, gives you a vantage point over a marsh filled with ducks and jacanas. But be prepared to climb a narrow metal ladder. Camping in rustic dormitory facilities ($13) and meals ($5 breakfast; $7 for lunch or dinner) can be arranged through the park headquarters. ☎ 200–0125 ⤴ $6 ⊗ *Daily 8–4; entrance gate closed noon to 1 PM.*

Just 3 km (2 mi) north of the Palo Verde road at Bagaces, take the dirt road signed for **Llanos de Cortés,** to get to this hidden waterfall less than 2 km (1 mi) off the highway. About half a kilometer along the dirt road you'll see on your right a large rock with CATARATAS scrawled on it. Follow this bumpy road about 1.3 km to its end and then clamber down a steep path to the pool at the bottom of a spectacular, wide, 50-foot waterfall. This is a great place for a picnic. ■ TIP→ Don't leave anything of value in your car.

Sad but sobering, one of the few places left in the country where you are guaranteed to see large wild cats, including a jaguar, is **Las Pumas rescue shelter** (⌂ 4½ km/3 mi north of Cañas on main Hwy. ☎ 669–6044 ⊕ www.laspumas.com). The small enclosures also hold jaguarundis, pumas, margays, ocelots, and oncillas. Some small animals and birds are rehabilitated and released into the wild. But the larger cats are probably here for life; it's too dangerous (for them) to be released. The refuge relies on contributions. It's open daily, 8 AM to 4 PM.

Outdoor Activities

The **Organization for Tropical Studies** (☎ 524–0628 ⊕ www.ots.ac.cr) runs half-day hiking, mountain biking, and boat tours in Palo Verde Park, and has some nighttime tours. Packages combine a guided walk with three meals and lodging in small, bunk-bedded double rooms with private bath ($50 per person).

BIRD-WATCHING   A boat excursion to Isla Pájaros along the Río Tempisque is a must for birders. Toward the end of rainy season, this tiny 6-acre island, across from Puerto Moreno, is an exciting place to see hundreds of nesting wood storks, cormorants, and anhingas. You can get close enough to see chicks being fed in nests. ■ TIP➔ **The best time to go is very early in the morning, to avoid heat and to guarantee the most bird sightings. Aventuras Arenal** (☎ 479–9133 ⊕ www.arenaladventures.com) guides have good eyes and usually know the English names for birds. The company specializes in ecological tours and runs bird-watching boat tours ($35 per person) to Isla Pájaros, leaving from docks along the Río Tempisque, including the dock at Palo Verde. It will pick up passengers from as far south as Tamarindo and Sámara. **CATA Tours** (☎ 674–0180, 296–2133 in San José ⊕ www.catatours.com) runs wildlife and bird-watching boating adventures ($45 person; $75 with hotel pickup) down the Río Bebedero into Palo Verde. Arrange hotel pickup from Nicoya beaches and Papagayo Peninsula with your reservation.

RIVER RAFTING   **Ríos Tropicales** (☎ 669–6262 ⊕ www.riostropicales.com) has relatively easy Class I and II rafting trips down the Río Corobicí. The one-, two-, or three-hour trips ($20–$45) start from the Restaurante Rincón Corobicí, on the main highway 5 km (3 mi) north of Cañas. It's a good way to get an introduction to rafting without being scared to death by fast rapids.

WILDLIFE   On a calm adventure trip with **Safaris Corobicí** (✉ Follow signs from high-
WATCHING   way to Km 193 ☎ 669–6191 ⌨ 669—6091 ⊕ www.safariscorobici.
   com), guides do the rowing on large inflatable rafts while you look at the passing scene and wildlife. The three-hour float trips ($45, including snack) cover wildlife-rich territory not far from Palo Verde. Trips require two or more passengers. They have a kiosk in front of the Restaurante Corobicí, too. Another recommended operator is **CATA Tours** (⇨ Bird-Watching, *above*).

Where to Stay near Palo Verde

$ ⊡ **La Ensenada Lodge.** This is the most comfortable base for bird-watching and nature appreciation near the Río Tempisque. Part of a national wildlife refuge, the property is also a 1,000-acre cattle-fattening ranch and salt producer. The salt flats and nearby shallow waters attract wading birds, and crocodiles that snack on them. The good-sized pool has a gulf vista, and there's a motor boat for wildlife touring. The Isla Pájaros Biological Reserve, the country's largest breeding grounds for black-crowned night herons, is a short boat ride away. The wood cabins are small but comfortable, with verandas and views and big screened windows for breezes. The rancho restaurant serves Italian/Costa Rican meals, buffet-style, including beef raised on the ranch. ✉ *13 km/8 mi along a dirt road from the Pan-American Hwy., 27 km/17 mi south of Cañas* ☎ *289–6655* 🖷 *289–5281* ⊕ *www.laensenada.net* ⮡ *22 cabin rooms* ⌂ *Restaurant, fans, pool, horseback riding, bar, laundry service* ▭ *No credit cards* ⍾ *FAP.*

To & from Palo Verde
52 km/32 mi (3 hrs) south of Liberia.

To get to Palo Verde from Liberia, drive south along the Pan-American Highway to Bagaces, then turn right at the small, easy-to-miss sign for Palo Verde, along a rough dirt road for 28 km (17 mi). Count on an hour to drive the distance from the main highway to the park entrance; it's a very bumpy road. (You'll have to pay the $6 park entrance fee to get to the OTS station.) The OTS station is about 7 km (5 mi) beyond the park entrance; the park headquarters is just another kilometer farther. The gatekeeper takes lunch from noon to 1 PM, so don't arrive during that time. Day visitors must be out of the park by 6 PM.

EN
ROUTE

The approach to the town of Santa Cruz from the east is like a giant pit stop, with one car-parts shop after another. One of the few reasons to visit is to eat at **Coope-Tortillas** (✉ Drive through business district, 200 m past church turn right and look for peaked-roof metal structure, Santa Cruz ☎ 680–0688), where you can watch hand-rolled corn tortillas being cooked the old-fashioned way over an open fire. Friendly women in blue uniforms, members of a local women's cooperative, heap your plate with your choice of traditional *Guanacasteco* foods and bring it to one of the picnic tables in a high-ceilinged, corrugated-metal building. Try the delicious *arroz de maíz,* a corn stew. The restaurant is open 4 AM to 6 PM. Tortillas sometimes run out before 4 PM.

Barra Honda National Park

� ㉖ Once thought to be a volcano, 1,184-foot **Barra Honda peak** actually contains an intricate network of caves, a result of erosion after the ridge emerged from the sea. Some caves on the almost 23-square-km (14-square-mi) park remain unexplored, and they're home to abundant animal life, including bats, birds, blindfish, salamanders, and snails.

Every day from 7 AM to 1 PM local guides take groups 58 feet down to the **Terciopelo Cave,** which shelters unusual formations shaped like fried eggs, popcorn, and shark's teeth. You must wear a harness with a rope attached for safety. The tour costs $12 total for equipment rental for 1 to 8 people, plus $16 for a guide for one to four people, in addition to park admission. Kids under 12 are not allowed to visit this cave but they can visit the kid-size La Cuevita cavern that also has interesting stalagmites. Both cave visits include interpretive nature hikes.

If caving leaves you feeling claustrophobic, you can climb the 3-km (2-mi) Los Laureles trail (the same trail that leads to the Terciopelo cave) to Barra Honda's summit. From here you have fantastic views sweeping across the islet-filled Gulf of Nicoya. Wildlife includes howler monkeys, skunks, coatis, deer, parakeets, and iguanas. It's a good idea for hikers, as well as cavers, to hire a local guide from the **Asociación de**

Guias Ecologistas (☎ 659–1551). An off-site **park office** (✉ Across from colonial church, Nicoya ☎ 686–6760) provides information and maps of the park. It's open weekdays 7–4. The park has camping facilities; and a community tourism association provides guides and runs a simple, inexpensive restaurant and lodge ($4.50 per person) by the park entrance. Make reservations for weekend food or lodging in the park. ☎ 659–1551 ☜ $6 ☉ Daily 7–4.

To & from Barra Honda
100 km/62 mi (2 hrs) South of Liberia. 13 km/8 mi west of Río Tempisque Bridge.

From the Río Tempisque Bridge, drive west along a paved highway. Then follow a dirt road (signed off the highway) for 10 km (6 mi) to the park entrance. There are buses from the town of Nicoya but they don't leave until 12:30 and 4 PM, which is a little late to start a hike. You can also take a taxi from Nicoya to the park entrance or go with one of many tour companies in beach towns on the Nicoya Peninsula.

Nicoya

㉗ Once a quaint, provincial town, known as Guanacaste's colonial capital, Nicoya is now a boomtown, thanks to increased traffic from the Río Tempisque Bridge. The town has spruced up old buildings and added modern new ones, and has Internet cafés and ATMs that takes international cards.

Exploring
Nicoya's only colonial landmark, is whitewashed, mission-style **Church of San Blas.** Originally built in 1644, the current church was reconstructed after an 1831 earthquake. The spare interior is made grand by seven pairs of soaring, carved-wood columns. Inside are folk-art wood carvings of the stations of the cross arrayed around the stark white walls, a small collection of huge, 18th-century bronze mission bells, and some antique wooden statues of saints. Arched doorways frame verdant views of park greenery and distant mountains. ✉ *North side of central park* ☎ *No phone* ☜ *By donation* ☉ *Erratic hours.*

Outdoor Activities
Hiking in Barra Honda is the main outdoor adventure here. If that's too strenuous for you, **Tempisque Eco Adventures** (✉ 4 km/2½ mi west of Río Tempisque Bridge ☎ 687–1110 or 687–1212) can show you flora and fauna similar to Barra Honda's on their seven-cable canopy tour ($35). For a fun day, you can combine the

> ### CHOROTEGAN POTTERY
>
> In the country village of Guaitil 24 km/15 mi north of Nicoya, artists—most of them women—have revived a vanishing tradition by producing clay pottery handmade in the manner of pre-Columbian Chorotegans. The town square is a soccer field, and almost every house facing it has a pottery shop out front and a round, wood-fired kiln in back. Pottery designs range from imitation Mexican to inspired Cubist abstractions. Prices range from $12 to $300, depending on size; most are around $30. Pieces do crack easily, so pack them carefully.

4

canopy tour with a Palo Verde Boat Tour for wildlife watching and lunch in their charming, open-air restaurant accompanied by traditional marimba music ($60).

Where to Stay & Eat

¢–$ ✕ **Restaurante Nicoya.** There are many Chinese restaurants from which to choose in Nicoya. This one is the most elegant, with hanging lanterns, a colorful collection of international flags, and an enormous menu with 85 Asian dishes, such as stir-fried beef with vegetables, along with some familiar favorites, such as fried chicken. The fresh sea bass sautéed with fresh pineapple, chayote, and red peppers is excellent. ⊠ *Main road, 70 m south of Coopmani Bldg.* ☎ *685–5113* ⊟ *No credit cards* ☉ *Closed 3–5.*

¢ ✕ **Soda Colonial.** One of the last vestiges of local color in town is this vintage all-day restaurant with white-adobe walls. Facing the shady central park, it's a great place to watch small-town life go by. Sit at a wooden bench in the wainscotted interior and sip a tamarindo refresco or order hearty portions of typical Tico food, heavy on the beans and rice. ⊠ *Southeast corner of central park* ⊟ *No credit cards.*

$ ▦ **Hotel de Lujo Río Tempisque.** There aren't many reasons to stay overnight in Nicoya, unless you're on a shopping spree. But if you're staying, the rooms here, with high wooden ceilings and big picture windows, are comfortable by any standards, and on the road to Santa Cruz they are a marvel. The owner is in the hardware business, and the hotel has high-quality materials inside and out, including palatial iron gates at the entrance. Huge, white-tile bathrooms have mirrored closets and showers big enough for two. The gardens and pool area are beautifully landscaped. There is no restaurant, but room refrigerators are stocked with juice and soft drinks. ⊠ *Highway north to Santa Cruz, just outside Nicoya* ☎ *686–6650* ⇄ *30 rooms* ⚘ *Restaurant, fans, refrigerators, cable TV, pool; no room phones* ⊟ *AE, MC, V* ⦿ *EP.*

To & from Nicoya

27 km/15 mi (40 mins) west of the Río Tempisque Bridge.

The town of Nicoya is west of the Río Tempisque Bridge on a newly paved road. If you're running out of gas, oil, or tire pressure, the Servicentro Nicoyano on the north side of Nicoya, on the main road, is open 24 hours.

Nicoya Essentials

▣ Banks **Banco de Costa Rica** ⊠ West side of central park ☎ 685–5110.

▣ ATMs **Coopmani ATH** ⊠ Main street, beside Fuji Film store.

▣ Hospital **Hospital de L'Anexion** ⊠ Main road into town from hwy ☎ 685–5066.

▣ Pharmacies **Farmacia Clinica Medica Nicoyana** ⊠ Main street, near Restaurante Nicoya ☎ 685–5238 ☉ Weekdays 8–7:30, Sat. 8–6.

▣ Taxi **Taxi Service** Call 686–2466.

THE FIRST GUANACASTECOS

The Chorotega tribe first settled the Guanacaste area and grew corn and fished. Chief Nicoya was the Chorotegan leader who greeted the conquistadors in 1523 and bequeathed his name to the town and peninsula.

Understanding Costa Rica's Climate

ALTHOUGH YOU MAY associate the tropics with rain, precipitation in Costa Rica varies considerably, depending on where you are and when you're there. This is a result of the mountainous terrain and regional weather patterns. A phenomenon called rain shadow—when one side of a mountain range receives much more than the other—plays an important ecological role in Costa Rica. Four mountain ranges combine to create an intercontinental divide that separates the country into Atlantic and Pacific slopes; thanks to the trade winds, the Atlantic slope receives much more rain than the Pacific. The trade winds steadily pump moisture-laden clouds southwest over the isthmus, where they encounter warm air or mountains, which make them rise. As the clouds rise, they cool, lose their ability to hold moisture, and eventually dump most of their liquid luggage on the Caribbean side.

During the rainy season—mid-May to December—the role of the trade winds is diminished, as regular storms roll off the Pacific Ocean and soak the western side of the isthmus. Though it rains all over Costa Rica during these months, it often rains more on the Pacific side of the mountains than on the Atlantic. Come December, the trade winds take over again, and while the Caribbean prepares for its wettest time of the year, hardly a drop falls on the western side until May.

Climate variation within the country results in a mosaic of forests. The combination of humidity and temperature helps determine what grows where; but whereas some species have very restricted ranges, others seem to thrive just about anywhere. Plants such as strangler figs and bromeliads grow all over Costa Rica, and animals such as the collared peccary and coati—a long-nosed cousin of the raccoon—can pretty much live wherever human beings let them. Other species have extremely limited ranges, such as the mangrove hummingbird, restricted to the mangrove forests of the Pacific coast, and the volcano junco, a gray sparrow that lives only around the highest peaks of the Cordillera de Talamanca.

4

NORTH PACIFIC ESSENTIALS

Transportation

BY AIR

ARRIVING & DEPARTING

International Aeropuerto Internacional Daniel Oduber (LIR) in Liberia is a good gateway to the coast. Tamarindo, Playa Nosara, Playa Sámara, Playa Carrillo, Punta Islita, and Tambor also have airstrips. Flying in from San José to these airports is the best way to get here if you are already in the country. If your primary destination lies in Guanacaste or Nicoya, make sure you or your travel agent investigates the possibility of flying directly into Liberia instead of San José, which saves some serious hours on the road. For more information, *see* Air Travel *in* Smart Travel Tips A to Z.

GETTING
AROUND Macaw Air, based in Tamarindo, flies five-passenger Cessna 206 planes between Liberia, Tamarindo, Nosara, and Tambor on the Nicoya Peninsula, and over to Quepos on the mainland and as far south as Puerto Jiménez in the South Pacific. They also have a daily scheduled shuttle flight between Tamarindo and Liberia at 10 AM ($45). SANSA and Nature Air have scheduled flights between San José and Guanacaste beach destinations, as well as connecting flights within Guanacaste.

BY BUS

ARRIVING &
DEPARTING For information about bus travel to and from the North Pacific, *see* Bus Travel *in* Smart Travel Tips A to Z.

GETTING
AROUND Bus service connects the larger cities to each other and to the more popular beaches, but forget about catching a bus from beach to beach; you'll generally have to backtrack to the inland hubs of Nicoya and Liberia unless you take a minibus, which may take just as long as a bus, although they're usually more comfortable. Your hotel front desk should be able to confirm which station specific buses and lines depart from. Buses don't serve Rincón de la Vieja National Park.

BY CAR

ARRIVING &
DEPARTING The northwest is accessed via the paved two-lane Pan-American Highway (CA1), which begins at the top of Paseo Colón in San José. Take the bridge across the Río Tempisque to get to the Pacific beaches south of Liberia. Paved roads run down the spine of the Nicoya Peninsula all the way to Playa Naranjo, with many unpaved and potholed stretches. Once you get off the main highway, the pavement holds out only so far, and then dirt, dust, mud, potholes, and other factors come into play. The roads to Playa Sámara, Playas del Coco, and Ocotal are paved all the way; every other destination requires some dirt-road maneuvering. If you're headed down to the coast via unpaved roads, be sure to get advance information on road conditions.

GETTING
AROUND If you want to drive around the Nicoya Peninsula, be prepared to spend some serious time in the car. The road to Nicoya's southern tip is partly paved and partly just gravel, and it winds up and down and around various bays. Some roads leading from Liberia to the coast are intermittently paved. As you work your way toward the coast, pay close attention to the assorted hotel signs at intersections—they may be the only indicators of which roads to take to your lodging.

Stick with the main rental offices in San José and their branches in Liberia—they have more cars available and you're more likely to reach an English-speaking agent on the phone; some have local satellite offices. Alamo has pickup and car delivery in Liberia. Budget has branches in San José and also 6 km (4 mi) west of Liberia's airport. Economy, Alamo, and Elegante rent cars in Tamarindo; Economy has a good supply of automatic four-wheel-drive vehicles.

▨ TIP➜ Four-wheel-drive vehicles are recommended, but not essential, at least not in the dry season, for most roads. If you don't rent a four-wheel-drive vehicle, at least rent a car with high clearance—you'll be glad you did.

🛪 Major Rental Agencies **Alamo** ✉ 2 km/1 mi north of Liberia airport, Liberia 🕾 668-1111, 800/462-5266 in U.S. ✉ Hotel Diría, main road, Tamarindo 🕾 653-0727. **Budget** ✉ 6 km/4 mi southwest of Liberia airport, Liberia 🕾 668-1118 ✉ Hotel Zullymar, main road just past Hotel Diría, Tamarindo 🕾 653-0756. **Economy** ✉ 3½ km/2 mi southwest of Liberia airport, Liberia 🕾 666-2816 or 666-7560 ✉ Main road entering Tamarindo, next to Restaurant Coconut, Tamarindo 🕾 653-0728.

🛪 Local Rental Agencies **Elegante** ✉ 5 km/3 mi southwest of Liberia airport, Liberia 🕾 667-0511. **Sol Rentacar** ✉ In front of Hotel El Bramadero, across from Burger King at intersection of Pan-American Hwy. and entrance to town, Liberia 🕾 666-2222 ✉ Hotel Giardini de Papagayo, Playa Panamá 🕾 885-4086.

BY SHUTTLE VAN

ARRIVING & DEPARTING You can ride in a comfortable, air-conditioned minibus with Gray Line Tourist Bus, connecting San José, Liberia, Playa Flamingo, Playa Hermosa, Tamarindo, and other destinations in Guanacaste. Fares range from $27 to $38, depending on destination. The Gray Line Tourist Bus from San José to Tamarindo and Liberia begins picking up passengers from hotels daily around 6 AM. The return bus leaves Tamarindo around 2 PM and passes through Liberia around 3:30 PM; there's also an early bus leaving Tamarindo at 7 AM. Interbus has door-to-door minivan shuttle service from San José hotels to all the major beach destinations (Papagayo, Panama, Hermosa, Flamingo, Tamarindo, Cocos, Ocotal, Nosara, and Sámara in Nicoya), for $29 to $39 per person. Reserve at least one day in advance.

🛪 Shuttle Van Services **Gray Line Tourist Bus** 🕾 232-3681 or 220-2126 ⊕ www. graylinecostarica.com. **Interbus** 🕾 283-5573 ⊕ www.interbusonline.com.

Contacts & Resources

Banks and emergency contacts follow each town listed in the chapter.

MAIL & SHIPPING

Finding a post office in beach towns is almost impossible since most beach areas are not incorporated towns. Liberia, La Cruz, Nicoya, Nosara, Playas del Coco, Sámara, and Santa Cruz all have post offices.

Central Pacific

Scarlet Macaw

WORD OF MOUTH

"Manuel Antonio National park is my favorite. There is so much to do there . . . comb the mountain's many trails, zip through the trees like Tarzan, or go horseback riding."

—hopabout

"Montezuma is a place that I am glad I visited . . . I most definitely saw more hippies than I have seen since the '60s. But . . . we enjoyed ourselves."

—dfarmer

WELCOME TO THE CENTRAL PACIFIC

Surfing at Playa Jacó

TOP 5
Reasons to Go

1 **Nature and wildlife:** Explore seaside flora and fauna at Manuel Antonio National Park, Curú National Wildlife Refuge, and Cabo Blanco Nature Reserve.

2 **Fishing:** Deep-sea fishing at Quepos almost guarantees your snapshot alongside a swordfish, marlin, or yellowfin tuna.

3 **Waterfalls:** In Montezuma, hike to a waterfall with two swimming holes or ride horseback to a cascade falling into the sea. Near Tárcoles, get refreshed in a majestic 656-foot waterfall.

4 **Surfing:** This is Costa Rica's surf central. Jacó, Malpaís and Playa Hermosa swarm with surfers, from beginners to pros.

5 **Adventure sports:** Snorkel among colorful fish, get muddy on ATV mountain rides, and zip through treetops near Jacó, Manuel Antonio, or Montezuma.

On the Southern Nicoya Tip, across the gulf from the "mainland," towns are more tranquil and more spread out. Beaches and surfing dominate. Montezuma is a popular hub.

Kayaking, Quepos

Getting Oriented

Most of the Central Pacific is mountainous, and beach towns are backed by forested peaks. Humid evergreen forests, coffee fields, and cattle pastures blanket the land. The coastal highway connects all towns from Tárcoles to the southern Pacific. The hub town of Jacó makes a good base for visiting surrounding beaches and wildlife areas. Farther south are Quepos and its neighbor, Manuel Antonio, followed by smaller towns barely touched by tourism. Across the Gulf of Nicoya, the more tranquil southern tip of the Nicoya Peninsula is also surrounded by impressive mountains, but with dry tropical forests that change radically from the rainy to the dry season. Distances are longer between towns here. Many folks like to use Montezuma as a regional hub.

Carara National Park

Humid evergreen forests, coffee fields, and cattle pastures blanket the Inland portions of the Central Pacific. Lagoon-ridden Carara Biological Reserve is here.

Boy jumping through waterfalls, Montezuma

Carara Biological Reserve

Tárcoles

34

Jacó

Pavona

PUNTARENAS

Parrita

Esterillos Este

Quepos

Manuel Antonio

34

Pacific Ocean

Manuel Antonio National Park

Rey

From Tárcoles, the highway along the Coast connects lively tourist hubs Jacó, Quepos, and Manuel Antonio, and on down to the South Pacific. This is the place to surf, do a multitude of active tours, laze on the beach, and explore Manuel Antonio National Park.

Manuel Antonio National Park

CENTRAL PACIFIC PLANNER

When to Go

Masses arrive during the dry season (late December–May), driving hotel prices up; in Manuel Antonio high-season prices kick in even earlier. Holy Week and the last week of December are the hardest times to find a room. Consider May to August, when the weather tends to sunny days and occasional light rain. Avoid the tip of Nicoya in September and October—heavy rains make road crossing difficult, and many businesses close.

Crowd Control

Most tourist towns in Costa Rica spring into action after Christmas, but Manuel Antonio's high season activates at the start of December, with rising hotel prices, long park entrance lines, and overcrowded beaches. To avoid the crunch, go June–November. To beat the crowds at the park, get there early—around 7 AM.

Great Combinations

South of Quepos along the coastal highway lie tranquil beaches, where time seems to stand still, a real contrast with the busy Manuel Antonio area. Dominical makes a great surf spot after Jacó, and Punta Uvita has calm waters and more wildlife than people. From the southern tip of Nicoya, head up the west coast to hop along the endless stretch of beaches. Or ferry back to the mainland to explore Monteverde's cloud forest.

Getting There

If you're not pressed for time, rent a car or travel by bus, shuttle, or private driver instead of flying from San José to experience beautiful landscapes and typical rural towns. Distances from San José are not overwhelming, and the ferry ride across the Gulf of Nicoya has great views of the mountainous coast and its islands. Buses are timely and economical, but if you prefer an air-conditioned ride, shuttles leave from San José and can drop you off at your hotel's doorstep. Most travelers heading to the southern tip of the Nicoya Peninsula arrive by car from points north or take the ferry from Puntarenas to Paquera. You can also fly into Tambor's airstrip.

What to Do

ACTIVITY	WHERE TO DO IT
Fishing	Quepos, Playa Herradura, Tambor, Malpaís
Snorkeling	Isla Tortuga, Manuel Antonio, Cabo Blanco Nature Reserve
Surfing	Jacó, Playa Hermosa, Malpaís
Wildlife-viewing	Manuel Antonio National Park, Tárcoles River, Cabo Blanco Nature Reserve, Curú National Wildlife Refuge, Carara National Park
Yoga	Montezuma, Malpaís, Jacó, Manuel Antonio
Zip-line tours	Malpaís, Montezuma, Jacó, Playa Herradura, Playa Hermosa, Manuel Antonio, Quepos

Choosing a Place to Stay

The southern Nicoya Peninsula has a good mix of high-quality hotels, nature lodges, and *cabinas* (low-cost Tico-run hotels, often laid out like motels). The Central Pacific "mainland" has some of the country's priciest lodgings, but as a rule, prices drop 20 to 30 percent during the rainy season. Reserve as far in advance as possible during the busy dry season. Near Manuel Antonio National Park, Manuel Antonio is the more activity-rich, attractive, and expensive place to stay (though we've culled the best budget options). Quepos has a wider range of economy hotels and is not as popular, making it ideal for last-minute reservations.

Recommended Tour Operators

■ **Costa Rica's Temptations** (CRT; ☎ 777-0607 ⊕ www.costarica4u.com) has a variety of Central Pacific tours, plus car rentals, private drivers, shuttle vans, and a 4WD off-the-beaten-path "adventure" transfer between San José and Manuel Antonio.

■ **Cruise West** (☎ 800/397-3348) runs four 11- to 15-day cruises originating in Miami that visit Panama and Costa Rica.

■ **King Tours** (☎ 637-7343, 643-2441 ⊕ www.kingtours.com) arranges trips to the top Central Pacific attractions, including Manuel Antonio National Park and Carara Biological Reserve.

■ **Ríos Tropicales** (☎ 233-6455, 888/722-8273 ⊕ www.riostropicales.com), a high-quality adventure tour company, runs a four-day, three-night sea-kayaking trip ($600) that leaves from Curú National Wildlife Refuge and meanders among the islands of the Gulf of Nicoya. Transport is provided from San José or from Paquera. One-day whitewater trips begin at $75.

Spring Break All Year

Nightlifers of all ages, including Ticos and tourists, flock to Jacó to party till sunrise, making it the country's liveliest beach town. Jacó draws everyone from partying college kids to groups of men seeking to savor the local beer and ladies, some too young to be legal. (That's a *warning*, not a tip.)

5

How Much Time?

A week gives you enough time to visit several beaches on the central coast or get a good grasp of the tip of Nicoya. Don't try to hit every beach in the Central Pacific or you'll defeat the purpose of your vacation: to relax. The larger towns of Manuel Antonio, Jacó, and Montezuma take more time to explore.

Prices

	$$$$	$$$	$$	$	¢
Restaurants	over $25	$15–$25	$10–$15	$5–$10	under $5
Hotels	over $250	$150–$250	$75–$150	$50–$75	under $50

Restaurant prices are per-person for a main course at dinner. Hotel prices are for two people in a standard double room in high season, excluding service and tax (16.4%).

THE SOUTHERN NICOYA TIP

Updated by
Brian Kleupfel

Catch a breathtaking ferry ride that lasts about an hour from Puntarenas to the southern tip of the Nicoya Peninsula, and you'll be just a bumpy bus hop away from gorgeous beaches with waterfalls and tidal pools. Within the region are quiet, well-preserved parks where you can explore caves and pristine forests or travel by boat or sea kayak to remote islands and wildlife preserves for bird-watching, snorkeling, diving, and even camping. Not too remote, and thus at times overcrowded with tours, Isla Tortuga is ringed by some of Costa Rica's most beautiful beaches. If you like to mix nightlife with your outdoor adventures, the towns of Montezuma and Malpaís are often jammed with an international cast of surfers, ecotourists, and eccentrics of all sorts, from practitioners of alternative lifestyles to expatriate American massage therapists living out their dreams. For those who prefer the convenience of luxury resorts, Tambor's got several to choose from.

Puntarenas

❶ A stroll around Puntarenas's once glorious neighborhoods quickly reveals that the city's golden age has long since passed. Today, it's a docking point for international cruise ships and the launching pad for ferries heading to the southeast coast of the Nicoya Peninsula. Unless you're waiting to catch the ferry, there's really no other reason to stay in Puntarenas. Parts of its urban beach look almost like a dumpster, especially toward its tip. How it got the blue flag for beach cleanliness is a mystery (some suspect political bribery). Nonetheless, it's a city with personality due to its past as an affluent port town and principle vacation spot for San José's wealthy, who arrived by train in the last century. Once the port closed and roads opened to other beaches, Puntarenas's economy crashed. Recent attempts by politicians and hotel owners to create tourism-boosting diversions have been unsuccessful thus far. But if you have some down time here, walk along the Paseo de los Turistas, a beachfront promenade lined with sidewalk lamps and concrete benches along which locals pass on bicycles. From this narrow spit of sand—*punta de arenas* (literally, "point of sand")—which protrudes into the Gulf of Nicoya, you get impressive sunsets and vistas toward the peninsula. On days when cruise ships arrive, the town really livens up and local artisans sell their wares at a market near the dock.

Where to Eat

$$–$$$ ✕ **Restaurante La Yunta.** This steakhouse is one of Puntarenas's best restaurants. In a 1928 wooden building that originally served as a vacation house for San José's upper class, the old-fashioned restaurant is presided over by mounted ox heads (*la yunta* means a yoked pair of oxen), and has a veranda with a view of the ocean and of passersby strolling down the Paseo. Its specialty is *churrasco* (tenderloin), though its diverse menu includes seafood dishes like sea bass cooked 10 different ways, and lobster. The liquor list is impressively long. ✉ *West end of Paseo de los Turistas, 100 m east of Hotel Tioga* ☎ *661–3216* ▭ *AE, DC, MC, V.*

$–$$ ✕ **Gugas.** Simple but elegant, Gugas receives high praises from locals for its fine dining alfresco. "Chicken of the Sea" (fish stuffed with shrimp and spices), pasta dishes, vegetarian options, seafood, and meat plates are all on the menu of this German-owned restaurant. ⊠ *100 m north of the cruise-ship port or 100 m from the bus terminal, across from the fishing pier* ☎ *661–4231* ⊟ *AE, DC, MC, V.*

To & from Puntarenas
110 km/68 mi (3 hrs) west of San José.

Buses to Puntarenas leave every hour from San José. From Puntarenas, jump on the ferry to Paquera to explore the southern tip of the Nicoya Peninsula. Located near Puntarena's tip, the ferry dock is about a 20- to 25- minute walk from the bus station; taxis frequently drive by and can get you there in minutes. Ferries cross with passengers and cars (and livestock). If you don't have a car and you're heading on to a beach town, grab a bus or taxi from the Paquera ferry dock.

Passenger and car ferries run by **Naviera Tambor** (☎ 661–2084) and the **Asociación de Desarrollo Integral Paquera** (☎ 641–0118) connect Puntarenas with Paquera. The trip takes on average 1½ hours, and ferries leave nine times daily at 4:30, 6:30, 8:30, and 10:30 AM, and 12:30, 2:30, 6:30, 8:30, and 10 PM, with an equal number of return trips at 4:30, 6, 8:30, and 10 AM, and noon, 5:30, 6, and 9:30 PM. Expect long waits on all car ferries in high season and on weekends. Avoid Sunday afternoon crossings from Paquera at any time of the year.

Puntarenas Essentials
🏧 Bank/ATM **Banco de Costa Rica (BCR)** ⊠ 100 m north of the municipal market. **Mutual Alajuela ATH** ⊠ Across from Ferretería Tung Sing, near central market ⌕ ATM only.
🏧 Tourist Information **La Camera de Turismo** ⊠ Plaza de las Artesanias, in front of Muelle de Cruceros ☎ 661-2980 ⊙ Open weekdays 8–12:30 and 1:30–5:30; weekends when cruise ships are in port. **La Oficina de Información Turistica** ⊠ Near car ferry terminal ☎ 661-9011 ⊙ Open daily 8-5.

EN ROUTE If you take the ferry from Puntarenas to the southern tip of the Nicoya Peninsula, you'll arrive at a ferry dock 5 km (3 mi) north of the small community of **Paquera**. The only reason to spend time here is to pick up supplies or fill up your tank on the way to the beach.

Curú National Wildlife Refuge

🐾 ❷ Established by former farmer and logger turned conservationist Federico Schutt in 1933, Refugio Nacional de Vida Silvestre Curú was named after the indigenous word for the pochote trees that flourish here. Trails lead through the forest and high-salinity mangroves where you see hordes of phantom crabs on the beach, howler and white-faced capuchin monkeys in the trees, and plenty of hummingbirds, kingfishers, woodpeckers, trogons, and manakins (including the coveted long-tailed manakin). The refuge is working to reintroduce spider monkeys and scarlet macaws into the wild. Some very basic accommodations, originally designed for students and researchers, are available by the beach ($6 per

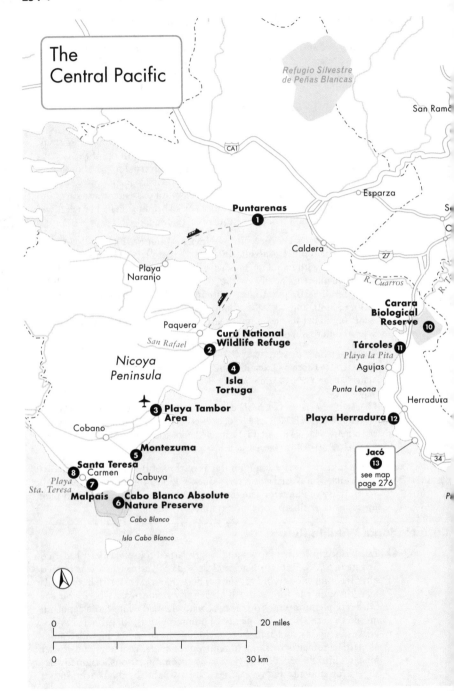

The Central Pacific

Refugio Silvestre de Peñas Blancas

San Ramó

CA1

Esparza

S

Puntarenas
1

Caldera

27

C

R. Cuarros

Playa Naranjo

Carara Biological Reserve **10**

Paquera

San Rafael

Curú National Wildlife Refuge
2

Tárcoles **11**
Playa la Pita
Agujas

Nicoya Peninsula

4
Isla Tortuga

Punta Leona

Herradura

3 **Playa Tambor Area**

Playa Herradura **12**

Cobano

5 **Montezuma**

Santa Teresa
8 Carmen
Playa Sta. Teresa **7** Cabuya

Jacó
13
see map page 276

34

Malpaís **6** **Cabo Blanco Absolute Nature Preserve**

Cabo Blanco

P

Isla Cabo Blanco

0   20 miles
0   30 km

Grecia

Alajuela

Atenas
❾

PAN AMERICAN HWY.
CA2

San Joaquin

Escazú

Heredia

San José

n Mateo

otina

Cartago

CA2

SAN JOSÉ

San Pablo de
León Cortés

San Marcos

Santa
María

R. Tulin

R. Palma

Fila Chonta

R. Parrita

R. Cañas

R. Naranjo

**Playa
Hermosa**

Parrita

LA COSTANERA

Judas

Esterillos
Oeste

Esterillos
Este

Playa
Palo
Seco

see map
page 287

Quepos ⓯

Manuel Antonio ⓰

Manuel
Antonio
National
Park

34

Playa Espadilla

Isla Mogote

Punta Catedral

Playa Escondido

Playa Manuel
Antonio

PACIFIC OCEAN

see map page 287

KEY
🚢 Ferry lines

person); call ahead to arrange for lodging, guides, and early-morning bird-watching walks. ☎ 641–0100 ⊕ *www.curuwilderefuge.com* ✉ *$8* ☉ *Daily 7–4.*

Outdoor Activities

Luis Schutt Tours (✉ Main road, across from Esso station, Paquera ☎ 641–0004, 834–7343 (cell) ⊕ www.curutourism.com) gives horseback tours of the refuge and also has a ride to a sparkling white beach.

To & from Curú National Wildlife Refuge

7 km/4½ mi south of Paquera; 1½ to 2 hrs southwest of Puntarenas by ferry.

From the town of Paquera you can drive or catch a bus toward Cóbano and get dropped off before Tambor. The dirt road leading to the refuge's gate isn't marked. Visits should be arranged in advance, so call for specific directions or to get a taxi.

EN ROUTE Paquera is the closest city to Tambor, but if you're headed to Montezuma or Malpaís, you'll pass through **Cóbano**, 12 km (7½ mi) west of Tambor, a bustling crossroads with supermarkets, a bank, restaurants, shops, and a gas station.

Playa Tambor Area

❸ Known for luxe hotels and high-end housing developments, wide, treeless Playa Tambor runs along the large half-moon Bahía Ballena, whose waters are much more placid than other beaches in Nicoya's southern tip. Its cleanliness, however, remains dubious after environmental infractions pinned on the mammoth Barceló resort, owner of most of the land in Tambor.

Outdoor Activities

Unlike other beach towns, in Tambor you won't find tour operators on every corner or rentals of any kind, not even for a basic bike. The Barceló has a tour desk, and all other hotel receptions have information on organized tours. Eduardo at Cabinas Cristina, across from the church, gives tourist information and the inside scoop on the area's hidden treasures.

HIKING One of the few things that you can do on your own in Tambor is hike. From the town's beach access, swing a right and walk along a shady trail, over rocks and sand around the Piedra Amarilla point to Tango Mar Resort—about 8 km (5 mi). The trees along the way resound with the throaty utterings of male howler monkeys.

> **¿HABLA INGLES?**
>
> Although some Central Pacific areas like Jacó and Manuel Antonio are very touristy, don't assume everyone speaks English. For example, oftentimes taxi and bus drivers won't understand your directions in English. To make traveling smoother, write down the Spanish name of the place your headed to or ask your hotel's reception desk attendee to write out directions in Spanish, which you can pass on with a smile to your driver.

A Darker Side of Tourism

DESPITE COSTA RICA'S RELATIVE affluence in Central America–in large part due to its thriving tourism industry–the fact remains that 10% of the country's population still lives in poverty. And while burgeoning tourism has benefitted portions of the population, it has manifested itself in less fortunate ways in more impoverished sectors of society by giving rise to a sex-for-sale trade that some experts say rivals that in Thailand.

The case is bleak for impoverished Costa Ricans, but is worst for women and young girls. Forty percent of girls do not attend school and 41% of births in Costa Rica are to unwed mothers. Prostitution is legal for those over 18 in Costa Rica, but pimping is not, and prostitution of minors certainly is not. There are no statistics on the number of minors involved in prostitution, but it's clear from the many Web sites promoting travel to Costa Rica as a sex-tourism paradise

with plenty of young girls available, that the problem is ongoing. In 1996 the National Institute for Children (PANI) targeted Limón, San José, and Puntarenas as the places where poor children are most susceptible to entering into prostitution; Jacó is another problem area.

In 2004 the U.S. Human Trafficking Report listed Costa Rica as one of the world's worst offenders in the trafficking of women and children into prostitution. To its credit, the administration of President Abel Pacheco has taken steps to combat the problem of the underage sex trade, a refreshing change from his predecessor, Miguel Angel Rodríguez, who famously denied in an interview on the ABC News program *20/20* in 2001 that such a problem existed. Steps taken thus far have included crackdowns on brothels, closer surveillance, harsher penalties for offenders, and a Web site that lists photos of missing children.

SPORTFISHING   Sailfish, marlin, dorado, tuna, and wahoo are in abundance from December to February, when deep-sea fishing is best. Peak coastal fishing season is November and December, but local fisherman and their small boats are your best guides to finding fish almost year-round. Prices range from $250 half-day trips to $400 for a full-day excursion. Tambor's best catch and release, deep-sea fishing boat is the 29-foot *Phoenix* owned by **End of the Line Sportfishing.** Robert, the owner, captains the boat for nine-hour full-day excursions ($900/group) or half-day trips that last around five hours ($400/group). The boat can carry six people. Lunch, drinks, and fishing gear are included. ⊠ *Road from Paquera, just before Tambor's entrance* ☎ *683–0453.*

Where to Stay & Eat

$–$$ ✕ **Perla Tambor.** Between the row of private residences built along the right-hand side of Playa Tambor is this Swiss-owned restaurant that serves a dozen different pasta dishes, cheese fondue, and chicken *cordon bleu,* among other international plates. Surrounded by thick foliage, tables are arranged on an open-air terrace area beneath a white stucco building. The restaurant is a couple of minutes from town on foot along the beach. ✉ *In Tambor, across from the ocean on the main st.* ☎ *683–0152* ▭ *MC, V* ☺ *Breakfast served.*

¢–$$ ✕ **Bahía Ballena Yacht Club.** Get fishing tips and the day's catch in butter and garlic or grilled at this old dockside fisherman's haunt. Don't bother asking for a menu—this laid-back joint doesn't have one. Friday is rotisserie chicken day, and Saturday serves up thick-crust pizza. Burgers and other basics can be cooked to order. A large central bar, TVs, a pool table, and dart board provide entertainment. ✉ *Road from Paquera, after the entrance to Tambor, left before hill; at the dock* ☎ *683–0213* ▭ *No credit cards.*

★ $$$–$$$$ ▦ **Tambor Tropical.** In the town of Tambor, a stone's throw from the beach, this small hotel offers many of the fine touches of bigger hotels, but in a more intimate setting. The floors, ceilings, walls, and even toilet seats of its cabins are made from strips of more than 14 tropical Costa Rican woods. (The fact that many of these trees are rare should raise the eyebrows of any nature lover.) That said, the cabins are beautifully constructed and maintained, with every inch perfectly varnished. The large windows running across the front keep them full of light. Beds are on a platform so you can view the sunrise; second-floor cabins have the best views. The sea breeze and ceiling fans cool the rooms better than air-conditioning, and the TV-less living room area inspires reading and resting. ✉ *Main street of Tambor toward beach, left* ☎ *683–0011* 🖷 *683–0013* ⊕ *www. tambortropical.com* ↩ *12 suites* ♿ *Restaurant, room service, fans, kitchens, golf privileges, pool, whirlpool tub, massage, beach, horseback riding, bar, laundry services, airport shuttle; no a/c, no room phones, no room TVs, no kids under 16* ▭ *AE, MC, V* ❍| *BP.*

To & from Tambor

27 km/17 mi south of Paquera.

You can fly directly to Tambor from San José on SANSA and NatureAir (⇨ Air Travel *in* Smart Travel Tips A to Z for schedules). Otherwise, when you arrive by ferry from Puntarena, hop on the bus to Montezuma and ask to get dropped off at Tambor's entrance. Buses depart daily at 6:15, 7:30, and 10 AM and 12:30, 4:30, and 6:15. Drivers, head down the road toward Cóbano.

Tambor Essentials

🖪 Internet **Compu-Office del Pacífico** ✉ In small strip mall on left after Costa Coral Hotel, coming from Paquera ☎ 683–0582 ☺ 9–7.

Isla Tortuga

☾ ❹ Soft white sand and casually leaning palms fringe this island of tropical dry forest off the southern coast of the Nicoya Peninsula. Sounds heavenly? It would be if there weren't so many people. Tours from Jacó, Herradura, San José, Puntarenas, and Montezuma take boatfuls of visitors to drink from coconuts and snorkel around a large rock. You'll see a good number of colorful fish, though in the company of many tourists. But it does make for an easy day trip out to sea. On the boat ride from Montezuma you might spot passing dolphins. A 40-minute hiking trail wanders past monkey ladders, strangler figs, bromeliads, orchids, and the fruit-bearing *guanabana* (soursop) and *marañón* (cashew) trees up to a lookout point with amazing vistas. Though state-owned, the island is leased and inhabited by a Costa Rican family who funded efforts to reintroduce such species as deer and wild pig to the island some years ago.

Outdoor Activities

KAYAKING **Luis Schutt Tours** (✉ Main road, across from Esso station, Paquera ☎ 641–0004 ⊕ www.curutourism.com), run by the son of the owner, arranges year-round kayak excursions to Isla Tortuga for $25; snorkeling equipment is extra. **Calypso Tours** (☎ 256–2727 ⎙ 256–6767 ⊕ www.calypsocruises.com) takes you to Isla Tortuga from San Jose, with bus and boat transportation included.

To & from Isla Tortuga
90 mins by boat from Puntarenas.

Every tour operator in Montezuma (⇨ below) offers trips to Isla Tortuga, one of the area's biggest activities, or take a kayak trip from the nearby Curú National Wildlife Refuge. Admission to the island is $7 (included in tour prices).

5

Montezuma

❺ Beautifully positioned on a sandy bay, Montezuma is hemmed in by a precipitous wooded shoreline. Its small, funky town center is a pastel cluster of New Age health-food cafés, trendy beachwear shops, and jaunty tour kiosks mixed with older Tico *sodas* (casual eateries) and noisy open-air bars. Most hotels are clustered in or around the town's center, making it very pedestrian friendly. Montezuma has been on the international vagabond circuit for years, attracting backpackers and alternative-lifestyle types. It has an infamous drug reputation, but the community has been changing over the past years, with Internet cafés and more sophisticated hotels and restaurants. Thankfully, its development remains manageable, compared to other beach towns that have been invaded by large franchise hotels and strip-mall developers. Despite its growth, Montezuma retains its very green atmosphere and holistic personality.

The **Karen Mogensen Fischer Museum** (✉ Internet Café, El Sano Banano Restaurant) details conservation contributions to the area's forests made by Nicolas and Karen Wessberg, who founded the Cabo Blanco Absolute Nature Preserve (⇨ *below*). It includes photos of the Wessbergs living in the virgin jungle.

Outdoor Activities

Almost every second storefront is occupied by a tour operator in central Montezuma. They seem to work together more than against each other, and have standarized costs for the most popular activities, saving you the hassle of comparing prices. **Aventuras en Montezuma** (⇨ ATV Tours, *below*) can give you information about the area's activities, like boat and fishing trips. The oldest and most experienced tour group in Montezuma, **Cocozuma Traveller** (✉ Main road, next to El Sano Banano Internet Montezuma ☎ 642–0911 ⊕ www.cocozuma.com) offers just about every activity that's popular in the area, including horseback riding tours to the beachfront waterfall, full-day snorkeling trips to Isla Tortuga, fishing trips, canopy rides, and excursions to the nearby Curú reserve.

ATV TOURS **Aventuras en Montezuma** (✉ Main rd. ☎ 642–0050 ⊕ www.zumatours. com) is your only connection to ATV tours, which visit the other side of the peninsula.

HORSEBACK A Montezuma favorite is the horse ride along the beach to the "Chorro"
RIDING oceanfront waterfall, which used to be more impressive and swimmable prior to a landslide. Guides usually will take you afterward for a refreshing dip in a nearby river. Hop on an organized tour with any operator in town, including Cocozuma Traveller (⇨ *above*). Trips around sunset are highly recommended.

HIKING Hiking is one of the best ways to explore Montezuma's natural treasures, including beaches, jungles, and waterfalls. There are plenty of options around town or in nearby parks and reserves. Just over a bridge, 10 minutes south of town, a slippery path patrolled by howler monkeys leads upstream to two waterfalls, the second one an impressive 108 feet,
★ with a fun **swimming hole.** If you value your life, don't jump or dive from the waterfalls. Guides from any tour operator in town can escort you, but save your money. This one you can do on your own. To reach the famous **El Chorro waterfall** on the beach, head left from the main beach access. The beautiful cascade lost some height and magnitude after a rough rainy season instigated a landslide that left it smaller and unswimmable, but still impressive. The roughly 2½-hour walk along the sand takes you across seven adjacent beaches. Bring water and good sunblock.

Where to Stay & Eat

$$–$$$ ✗ **Playa de los Artistas.** This open-air Italian restaurant with driftwood
Fodor'sChoice tables scattered along the beach specializes in modern Mediterranean-
★ style seafood. Flickering lanterns combine with crashing surf to create a romantic and relaxed dinner experience. Portions are plentiful and dramatically presented on huge platters. Eighty percent of the eclectic menu changes daily, and an outdoor, coffee-wood oven gives a tropical aroma to pizza, fish, and pork. Try the tuna carpaccio, a raw tuna appetizer seasoned with oregano and garlic, and soak up the marinade with freshly baked, savory focaccia. ✉ *275 m south of town, just past Los Mangos Hotel* ☎ *642–0920* ▤ *No credit cards* ⊘ *Closed Sun. and Sept. 20 through the first week of Nov.*

$–$$ ✗ **El Sano Banano Restaurant.** Seafood, hormone-free chicken, and a half-dozen pasta dishes are included on the mostly vegetarian menu at Montezuma's first natural-food restaurant, named after the dried bananas the owners originally sold. A terrace café provides excellent people-watching, as well as tall glasses of sinfully delicious Mocha Chiller, made with frozen yogurt, and a wide variety of coffee drinks and desserts. A battalion of ceiling fans keeps the air moving in the spacious, adobe-style restaurant with green plastic chairs. It's open for breakfast from 7 AM; a free movie is shown nightly at 7:30 PM in the dining room. ✉ *Main rd.* ☎ *642–0638* ▤ *AE, MC, V.*

$ ✗▥ **El Sano Banano Hotel Village.** Smack in the middle of Montezuma, above the restaurant of the same name, guests of this hotel can walk to Ylang-Ylang to swim in the pool and use its other facilities. Rooms have huge showers. Aside from faint traces of music, the place is amazingly quiet for its location near the town's nightlife. Cooking smells sometimes drift into the hallway from the kitchen below. Ask for a room with a window to the garden or street, or you'll be staring at the wall of an adjacent building. ✉ *Main rd.* ☎ *642–0638* 🖶 *642–0631* 🌐 *www.elbanano.com* ⤶ *14 rooms* ⚬ *Restaurant, cable TV, bar, laundry service, Internet café, no-smoking rooms; no room phones* ▤ *AE, MC, V* ⦿| *BP.*

$$–$$$ ⛉ **Ylang-Ylang Beach Resort.** Secluded and quiet, this tropical resort
FodorsChoice (formerly the El Sano Banano Beach Hotel) with a holistic slant is a
★ 10-minute beach walk from town. Nestled between the sea and a lush forest, the geodesic-dome bungalows are snug but charming, with outdoor showers and terraces. Some have direct sea views and cozy loft sleeping areas for two. Facing the beach, a two-story building has three comfortable suites with balconies and three double rooms below. Adding to the romance is a garden-fringed pool with a waterfall. An array of yoga classes and spa services are offered, and a restaurant with tables under the stars serves some of the tastiest fusion dishes in Montezuma. The reception desk is at the El Sano Banano Restaurant in town. ✉ *700 m north of school in Montezuma, on the beach* ☎ *642–0636* 🖶 *642–0068* 🌐 *www.elbanano.com* ⤶ *3 rooms, 3 suites, 8 bungalows* ⚬ *Restaurant, fans, in-room safes, refrigerators, pool, massage, beach, bar, shop, laundry service; no a/c, no room phones, no room TVs* ▤ *AE, MC, V* ⦿| *BP.*

★ **$–$$** ⛉ **Nature Lodge Finca los Caballos.** A long dirt road leads to this cozy equestrian paradise high on a hill, with 10 horses grazing around its vast 14 acres, just a short ride from Montezuma center. Five different horse tours are offered to nearby waterfalls, mountains, or the Curú Reserve. Bird-watching is also a popular activity here. The open-air restaurant, reading chairs, and pool have bird's-eye views of the ocean and valley below. Designed with a southwestern U.S. motif, the small, simple rooms have pastel walls decorated with stencils of lizards and frogs; all have hammocks in front, but only four have forest views. The others have views of the property. The restaurant serves dinner to nonguests by reservation. ✉ *3 km (2 mi) north of Montezuma on main rd.* ☎🖶 *642–0124* 🌐 *www.naturelodge.net* ⤶ *12 rooms* ⚬ *Restaurant, fans, pool, massage, horseback riding, bar, laundry service, airport shuttle, no-smoking rooms; no a/c, no room phones, no room TVs* ▤ *MC, V* ⦿| *EP* ⊗ *Closed Sept. and Oct.*

$ ⛉ **Hotel Amor de Mar.** Take the time to walk the ¼ mi south of town to find this ruggedly handsome, two-story wooden hotel across from the waterfall's entrance. A grassy lawn stretches to the rocky seashore, where you can cool off in a natural tidal pool or in a palm-shaded hammock. It has a peaceful and intimate atmosphere, coupled with great homemade breakfasts. The wood-paneled rooms are rustic but comfortable; second-floor rooms have more windows. Two of the rooms share a bathroom and are a few bucks cheaper. A two-story, equipped oceanfront house has four bedrooms. ✉ *300 m south of town, just past bridge, left-hand side* ☎🖶 *642–0262* 🌐 *www.amordemar.com* ⤶ *11 rooms, 9 with private bath; 2 houses for up to 6 guests* ⚬ *Restaurant, fans, some refrigerators, laundry service; no a/c, no room phones, no room TVs* ▤ *MC, V* ⦿| *EP.*

5

$ 🏨 **Hotel El Tajalín.** A short walk from the beach and in a quiet part of town, this hotel has spacious rooms but a somewhat sterile atmosphere. Rooms are spread out across the concrete building's three floors, and only one has a private balcony. Skip the dull first-floor rooms; those on the second level are much roomier, and have refrigerators and wood floors. On the top floor an open-air lounge has hammocks, tables, and books. ✉ *Behind the soccer field* ☎ *642–0061* 📠 *642–0527* ⊕ *www.tajalin. com* 🛏 *12 rooms* ♨ *Some fans, some refrigerators; no room phones, no room TVs* ▤ *MC, V* ❋⦿❋ *BP.*

¢ 🏨 **Hotel Lucy.** Montezuma's first hotel is still run by the same hospitable family and retains some of the lowest prices in town. The two-story renovated structure stands directly facing the sea, and though not every room enjoys the view, a communal veranda facing the ocean is open to all. Most of the spartan rooms share a cold-water shower. Private (cold-water) baths cost extra. Rooms on the second floor heat up during the day. There's no formal reception, so you may have to walk to the side of the building, where family members are usually sitting in the shade. Lucy, the owner's daughter, runs a seaside restaurant next door that serves good and inexpensive breakfasts, lunches, and dinners. ✉ *200 m south of town, in front of Hotel Los Mangos* ☎ *642–0273* 🛏 *19 rooms, 7 with bath* ♨ *Fans, laundry service; no a/c, no room phones, no room TVs* ▤ *No credit cards* ❋⦿❋ *EP.*

Nightlife

Though options are extremely limited, Montezuma's nightlife scene is growing. Locals and foreigners mix at pool tables or late-night clubs, refreshing after larger beach towns where the clientele tends to be more segregated. Streetside artisans selling their creations oftentimes animate the area with drumming and dancing that draws passersby to stop and shake their hips, too.

Chico's Bar (✉ Center of town, next to Hotel Moctezuma), blasts music from its dark, uninviting entrance, but farther back is a brighter, spacious deck with pool tables and dancing. Directly behind Chico's Bar is **Chico's Playa,** an open-air bar that has softer music, tables in the sand, and a more laid-back atmosphere. The bar at the entrance of open-air seafood eatery **Restaurante Montezuma** (✉ Center of town, next to Hotel Moctezuma ☎ 643–0657) is a favorite with locals and serves the cheapest beers in Montezuma. At night, tables in the sand are lit by candles and moonlight.

To & from Montezuma

7 km/4½ mi southeast of Cóbano, 45 km/28 mi (15 mins) south of Paquera, 18 km/11 mi (1½–2 hrs) south of Tambor.

There are two routes into town, both bumpy and unpaved. Buses to Montezuma stop in Cóbano. They depart from Paquera daily at 6:15, 7:30, and 10 AM and 12:30, 4:30, and 6:15. Buses drop you off in the center of town. To continue to Malpaís, you have to switch buses in Cóbano. For Tambor, take a Paquera bus and ask the driver to stop at the town's entrance. Air-conditioned bus transfers can be arranged with any tour operator.

Montezuma Essentials

🏧 ATM **Yacamares** ✉ In front of Super Mamatea.

Cabo Blanco Absolute Nature Preserve

❻ Conquistadores named this area Cabo Blanco on account of its white earth and cliffs, but it was a more benevolent pair of foreigners—Nicolas Wessberg and his wife, Karen, arriving here from Sweden in 1950—who made it a preserve (Reserva Natural Absoluta Cabo Blanco, in Spanish). Appalled by the first clear-cut in the Cabo Blanco area in 1960, the couple launched a pioneering and international appeal to save the forest. In time their efforts led not only to the creation of the 12-square-km (4½-square-mi) reserve but also to the founding of Costa Rica's national park service, the National Conservation Areas System (SINAC). Wessberg was murdered on the Osa Peninsula in 1975 while researching the area's potential as a national park. A reserve just outside Montezuma was named in his honor. A reserve has also been created to honor his wife, who dedicated her life to conservation after her husband's death.

Informative natural-history captions dot the trails in the moist evergreen forest of Cabo Blanco. Look for the sapodilla trees, which produce a white latex used to make gum; you can often see V-shape scars where the trees have been cut to allow the latex to run into containers placed at the base. Wessberg cataloged a full array of animals here: porcupine, hog-nosed skunk, spotted skunk, gray fox, anteater, cougar, and jaguar. Resident birds include brown pelicans, white-throated magpies, toucans, cattle egrets, green herons, parrots, and turquoise-browed motmots. A fairly strenuous 4-km (2½-mi) hike, which takes about two hours in each direction, follows a trail from the reserve entrance to **Playa Cabo Blanco.** The beach is magnificent, with hundreds of pelicans flying in formation and paddling in the calm waters offshore—you can wade right in and join them. Off the tip of the cape is the 7,511-square-foot **Isla Cabo Blanco,** with pelicans, frigate birds, brown boobies, and an abandoned lighthouse. As a strict reserve, Cabo Blanco has restrooms and a visitor center but no other tourist facilities. Rangers and volunteers act as guides. ☎ 642–0093 ✎ $8 ☉ *Wed.–Sun. 8–4.*

To & from Cabo Blanco Preserve

10 km/6 mi southwest of Montezuma, about 11 km/7 mi south of Malpaís.

Roads to the reserve are usually passable only in the dry season, unless you have a 4WD. From Montezuma or Malpaís, take the road to Cabuya. Taxis can take you to or from Montezuma, but buses toward the park also leave from Montezuma daily at 8 AM and 10 AM.

Malpaís & Santa Teresa

❼ ❽ This remote fishing village was once frequented only by die-hard surfers in search of some of the country's largest waves and by naturalists en route to the nearby Cabo Blanco Nature Preserve. The town and its miles of beach are accessible only down a steep gravel road. But now hotels, restaurants, and shopping centers are springing up at an alarming rate—especially toward the Santa Teresa side—despite the bad roads.

Coming from Montezuma, the road ends at a T intersection, with the beach (the west coast of the peninsula) ahead of you. To the left is Malpaís, a tranquil fishing village with a handful of hotels and restaurants along its gravel road, but primarily residential homes. (Rumor has it that a large chain hotel is on its way, though.) Playa Malpaís is rockier than Playas Santa Teresa and Carmen, but has tidal pools and is ripe for beachcombing. To the right at the intersection is the Santa Teresa area, which is more commercial, with more hotels, restau-

rants, markets, and a strip mall. Santa Teresa is parallel to Playa Carmen, the area's best place for surfing and swimming. Malpaís and Santa Teresa are so close that locals disagree on where one begins and the other ends. You could travel up the road parallel to the ocean that connects them and not realize you've moved from one town to the other.

Outdoor Activities

Your hotel's reception is probably the best resource for area activities. Otherwise, the Internet café next to Frank's Place offers tourist information. If you speak some Spanish, you can ask locals in Malpaís's fishing village to take you out to sea or horseback riding along the beach or into nearby mountains.

CANOPY TOUR **Canopy del Pacífico** (⊠ In front of fisherman's village, Malpaís ☎ 640–0360, 817–1679 ⊕ www.canopy.malpais.net) is the only canopy tour in the area ($35 for two-hour, nine-platform tour). You can walk, glide, or rappel through 64 acres of forest.

SURFING **Playa Carmen** is the area's most consistent surf spot for all levels. In rocky Malpaís, across from **Mar Azul**, more advanced surfers like to catch stronger waves that result from swells. The handful of surf shops in Santa Teresa can connect you with experienced surfing teachers and board rentals and repairs.

Where to Stay & Eat

$$–$$$ ✕ **Nectar.** Resort Florblanca's alfresco restaurant is laid out by the pool with some tables enjoying calming sea views. Aside from a vegetarian and pasta menu, expect to find grilled filet mignon and fresh seafood that changes according to the day's catch. Green salads are organic, and the restaurant's international chef stresses a French-Asian influence in his dishes. There is a "sunset sushi" special buffet on Tuesday and Saturday. ⊠ Resort Florblanca, 2 km/1 mi north of soccer field, Santa Teresa ☎ 640–0232 ▭ AE, DC, MC, V ☺ Breakfast served.

★ $$ ✕ **Soma.** This small restaurant within the Milarepa hotel serves up delicious and creative Latin-inspired plates. Specials change each night, and can include garlic papaya soup, seared tuna with plantains, or pork chops with mashed sweet potatoes. A vegetarian special is also always offered in this tranquil restaurant, whose name comes from the Huxley classic *Brave New World*. Tables are arranged under an open-air poolside deck. ✉ *Milarepa hotel, toward the end of town, beside Resort Florblanca, Santa Teresa* 🕾 *640–0023* 🚫 *No credit cards* ☾ *May close for dinner Sept.–Nov. Breakfast served.*

¢–$ ✕ **Piedra Mar.** With all the new restaurants popping up along the beach road, the favorite standby is still this old shack down on the beach. Tables and plastic chairs are set up under a corrugated tin roof, and the only decor is the rocky seascape, 10 feet away. Your shrimp or lobster (for less than $10) comes flavored with garlic and—on windy days—the sea spray crashing against the rocks. Sunset is popular with locals in the know, so come early. Or come for breakfast at 7 and watch the early morning sun lighting up the ocean. ✉ *275 m south of Blue Jay Lodge, Malpaís* 🕾 *640–0069* 🚫 *No credit cards* ☾ *Breakfast served.*

$$$$ ✕▨ **Resort Florblanca.** Named for the white flowers of the frangipani
FodorsChoice trees that shade the beachfront property, this collection of simply lux-
★ urious villas ministers to body and soul with a heavy Eastern-influenced decor. Secluded at the northern end of Santa Teresa, the handsome and spacious villas have outdoor Balinese-inspired bathrooms and sunken tubs. Most villas have one air-conditioned bedroom with a king-size bed; two-bedroom villas have a second room with twin beds. Three villas have sea views. A dojo for yoga classes faces the ocean, and a massage therapist is on staff to work out your kinks. The only TV is in a comfortable lounge. Two pools flow into each other in front of Nectar (⇨ *above*), the hotel's restaurant. ✉ *2 km (1 mi) north of soccer field, Santa Teresa* 🕾 *640–0232* 🖷 *640–0226* ⊕ *www.florblanca.com* ⤵ *10 villas* ⚘ *Restaurant, room service, fans, in-room safes, refrigerators, 2 pools, fitness room, massage, spa, beach, snorkeling, mountain bikes, hiking, horseback riding, bar, shop, Internet; no room TVs, no kids under 8* 🚫 *AE, DC, MC, V* ⦿❘ *BP.*

☾ $$ ▨ **Blue Jay Lodge.** This enchanting nature lodge evokes the old Disney flick
FodorsChoice *Swiss Family Robinson.* Tucked in a forested mountainside, the wooden
★ cabins feel like treehouses. Raised walkways lead to the rustic aeries built on stilts, with only screens for walls on three side. Hot-water showers and balconies with hammocks add to the simple comforts. Ceiling fans keep the air moving, but warm blankets are on hand for cool, breezy nights. Breakfast is in the wooden-terrace restaurant at ground level. The beach is 200 meters away, or you can climb the mountain trail to look for birds and howler monkeys. Apart from campsites, it's rare to find a place where you're so entrenched in the forest. ✉ *From the crossroads, 800 m south toward Malpaís* 🕾 *640–0089 or 640–0342* 🖷 *640–0141* ⊕ *www. bluejaylodgecostarica.com* ⤵ *10 cabins* ⚘ *Restaurant, fans, pool, massage, bicycles, horseback riding, snorkeling, laundry service; no a/c, no room phones, no room TVs* 🚫 *AE, D, MC, V* ⦿❘ *BP.*

☾ ¢ ▨ **Frank's Place.** This is the first hotel you'll see when you arrive in the area, and it was the second hotel built in Malpaís. Owned by a former fisherman, it has grown significantly and is oftentimes full, owing to its location and low prices. Some rooms share a bathroom, others have their own (cold-water) shower, and the most expensive ones have air-conditioning, cable TVs, and hot water, and include breakfast. Rooms lie around the pool and gardens. The friendly staff is helpful in giving tourist information and rents ATVs. Skip the restaurant; local food can be found at better prices elsewhere. An Internet café is just next door. ⊠ *At the crossroads, on main road into Malpaís* 🖼🖼 *640–0096* ✉ *frank5@racsa.co.cr* 🛏 *21 rooms, 6 with shared bath* ⚒ *Restaurant, room service, Jacuzzi, some fans, some kitchens, some cable TV, pool, massage, bicycles, ATVs, bar; no a/c in some rooms, no room phones* ➦ *AE, D, MC, V* 🍴 *CP.*

¢ 🖼 **Los Tres Pinedas.** Behind Soda la Sirenita, a low-cost local eatery in front of Playa Carmen, this small, family-run motel has some of the cheapest rooms in the area. Two rows of rooms face each other, separated by a large green lawn with mountains in the background. The sky-blue rooms have either two twin beds or one double. Those with their own bathroom also have a refrigerator; bathrooms do not have hot water. A front porch has chairs for reading and relaxing. ⊠ *50 m north of Frank's Place, Malpaís* 🖼🖼 *640–0172* 🛏 *8 rooms with shared bath* ⚒ *Restaurant, fans, some refrigerators; no a/c, no room phones, no room TVs* ➦ *No credit cards* 🍴 *EP.*

To & from Malpaís & Santa Teresa

12 km/7½ mi southwest of Cóbano, 52 km/33 mi south of Paquera.

From Paquera, take the road to Cóbano and then on to Malpaís passing by San Isidro. The dirt road to Malpaís can become quite muddy in the rainy season. There are no direct buses from Paquera to Malpaís; you have to change buses in Cóbano. Paquera–Cóbano buses depart at 6:15, 7:30, and 10 AM and 12:30, 4:30, and 6:15 daily. Cóbano–Malpaís buses depart at 10:30 AM and 2:30 PM. To head to Montezuma or back to Paquera, catch corresponding buses from Cóbano. **Extreme Boat** (🖼 640–0600 ⊕ www.extboat.com) shuttles surfers between Malpaís and Jacó, Monday and Friday.

Malpais & Santa Teresa Essentials

🏧 Bank/ATM ⊠ Tourist information office next to Frank's Pl.

INLAND

Beaches may be this region's biggest draw, but the countryside holds some splendid scenery, from the steep coffee farms around Atenas to the tropical forests of the lowlands. In the wilderness of Carara Biological Reserve and surroundings, you might encounter white-faced capuchin monkeys in the trees or crocodiles lounging on a riverbank. The region is extremely diverse biologically, making it a boon for bird-watchers and other wildlife enthusiasts.

Atenas

9 Known for its excellent cool-evening climate, Atenas is a pleasant, friendly town surrounded by a hilly countryside of coffee and cane fields, cattle ranches, and patches of forest. The small city has some charming mountaintop bed-and-breakfasts with breathtaking views that make for a relaxing stay on your way to or from the Central Pacific beaches. Plus, the fact that it's not on the tourist circuit means that here, unlike other highly popular destinations, you'll walk alongside more Costa Ricans than foreigners and get a more authentic idea of the country. Gazing at the tree-covered peaks and exploring the forest by horseback or mountain motorcycle are the main activities in this traditional town. Atenas's center has a concrete church, some well-kept wooden and adobe houses, and a central park dominated by royal palms.

Outdoor Activities

Local hotels can recommend guides for horseback trips. **Villas de la Colina** (✉ 4 km/2 mi west and 2 km/1 mi north of Coopeatenas ☎ 446–5015 📠 446–8545) rents motorcycles and leads motorcycle tours through the nearby mountains.

Where to Stay & Eat

¢–$ ✕ **Mirador del Cafetal.** An obligatory stop even if it's just for a cup of coffee, this open-air restaurant next to the road between Atenas and Jacó is a great spot to enjoy the view of steep hillsides covered with coffee trees. The best view is from the long countertops with stools that line the edge of the building, but the wooden tables and chairs might be more comfortable. A mix of Costa Rican and Mexican cuisine is served, including side orders like miniature tamales, black-bean purée, and *patacones* (fried, squashed plantain slices). If you're hungry for more, try chicken in a tomato-and-onion sauce or *sopa azteca* (a tomato-based soup). The restaurant's own brand of coffee is sold by the pound. ✉ *Road to Jacó, 6 km (3 mi) west of Atenas* ☎ *446–7361.*

¢ ✕ **C@fé K–puchinos.** A good place to get a bite and check your e-mail (via a high-speed connection), this corner café in a papaya-colored 1900s house stands across from the town's palm-shaded central park. The Spanish owners serve a good selection of breakfast items, coffee drinks, pizzas, pastas, sandwiches, and salads, as well as meals such as sautéed shrimp and salmon in a wine sauce. Spanish culture influences menu items such as sangria and the *tortilla española* (Spanish omelet, with potatoes and onions). This is the only place we found in town with tourist information. ✉ *Across from northwestern corner of central park* ☎ *446–8771* 🚫 *No credit cards* ☾ *Closes at 8 PM Apr.–Dec (and at 10 PM Jan.–Nov.).*

SIDESTEP SAN JOSÉ

Some visitors to Costa Rica prefer using Atenas as their first- and last-night base camp instead of San José, since Atenas is smaller, friendlier, more tranquil, and safer. The international airport is geographically closer to Atenas, but the hilly roads make the ride slightly longer than on San José's express highway.

$$–$$$ El Cafetal Inn. This extremely charming B&B feels and looks more
FodorśChoice like a friend's house than a hotel. The living room area has wedding pic-
★ tures of the friendly Salvadorean-Colombian owners, who go out of their
way to make you feel at ease and help with your travel plans. On a hilltop coffee farm, the two-story concrete lodge has comfortable accommodations with fabulous vistas. The second-floor corner rooms are
larger and have curved windows for panoramic views. Breakfast, which
includes home-grown and -roasted coffee, is served on the back garden
patio. ⊠ *8 km (5 mi) north of Atenas; heading west from San José on
highway to Puntarenas, turn left (south) just before bridge 5 km (3 mi)
west of Grecia, then follow signs, Santa Eulalia de Atenas* ☎ *446–5785*
🖷 *446–7028* ⊕ *www.cafetal.com* ↪ *12 rooms* ⚹ *Restaurant, fans, pool,
bar, laundry service, no-smoking rooms; no a/c, no room phones, no
room TVs* ▤ *AE, MC, V* ⍥ *BP.*

$ Villas de la Colina. A Costa Rican family owns and operates this hill-
top retreat in the countryside north of town with rustic wooden cabinas and sweeping views of the surrounding countryside. A green lawn
with an archway of flowers covers the footpaths to most rooms. Hummingbirds add to the natural beauty. The upper rooms cost a bit more
but are brighter and have private balconies with hammocks. You can
also rent motorcycles here for exploring the area's forested mountains.
⊠ *4 km (2 mi) west and 2 km (1 mi) north of Coopeatenas*
🖷☎ *446–5015* ↪ *7 cabinas* ⚹ *Fans, kitchenettes, pool, horseback riding, laundry service; no a/c, no room phones, no room TVs* ▤ *No credit
cards* ⍥ *BP.*

To & from Atenas
42 km/26 mi (1 hr) west of San José.

Buses to Atenas leave frequently from the Coca-Cola station in San José
and arrive near the center of town. You can also catch a bus to Jacó and
request to be dropped off at the entrance to Atenas. If you're driving
from San José, hop on the Pan-American Highway west toward Alajuela past the airport, and turn right on overpass after the giant RECOPE
storage tanks (on left). Turn left from the exit, stay on the main road
and follow the signs.

Atenas Essentials
🏧 Bank/ATM **Banco de Costa Rica (BCR)** ⊠ 200 m west of Catholic church. **Banco
Nacional** ⊠ Northern corner of central park.
🏥 Hospital **Clínica Pública** ⊠ 150 m south of the fire station ☎ 446–5522.
💊 Pharmacy **Farmacia Don Juan** ⊠ West side corner of Catholic church ☎ 446–5055.
ℹ️ Tourist Information **C@fé K-puchinos** ⊠ Northwest corner of Parque Central
☎ 289–0082.

Carara Biological Reserve
❿ On the east side of the road between Puntarenas and Playa Jacó, Parque Nacional Carara protects one of the last remnants of an ecological
transition zone between Costa Rica's drier northwest and the more
humid southwest. It consequently holds a tremendous collection of
plants and animals. Much of the 47-square-km (18-square-mi) park is

covered with primary forest on steep slopes, where the massive trees are laden with vines and epiphytes. The sparse undergrowth makes wildlife easier to see here than in many other parks, but nothing is guaranteed. If you're lucky, you may glimpse armadillos, basilisk lizards, blue-crowned motmots, chestnut-mandibled toucans, trogons, coatis, and any of several monkey species.

The first trail on the left shortly after the bridge that spans the Río Tár-coles (a good place to spot crocodiles) leads to a horseshoe-shape *laguna meandrica* (oxbow lake). The small lagoon covered with water hyacinths is home to turtles, crocodiles, and waterfowl such as the northern jacana, roseate spoonbill, and boat-billed heron. It is a two-to four-hour hike from the trailhead to the lagoon. ⚠ **Cars parked at the trailhead have been broken into, so ask at the main ranger station (several miles south of the trailhead) whether there is a ranger on duty at the *sendero laguna meandrica* lagoon. If there isn't, you may be able to leave your belongings at the main ranger station, where you can also buy drinks and souvenirs and use the restroom.**

Two trails lead into the forest from the parking lot. One short stretch is wheelchair-accessible. A longer trail connects with the Quebrada Bonita loop, which takes two to three hours to hike. The latter can be quite muddy during the rainy months, when you may want rubber boots. Carara's proximity to San José and Jacó means that tour buses arrive regularly in high season, scaring some animals deeper into the forest. Come very early or late in the day to avoid crowds. Bird-watchers can call the day before to arrange admission before the park opens. Camping is not permitted.

Local travel agencies and tour operators arrange transport to and guides through the park (⇨ Park Tours, *below*). The park itself has guides, but you have to arrange in advance. ☎ *200–5023, 383–9953* ✉ *$8* ☉ *Daily 7–4.*

Park Tours

Costa Rica Expeditions (☎ 222–0333 🖨 257–1665 ⊕ www.costaricaexpeditions.com) and **Horizontes** (☎ 222–2022 🖨 255–4513 ⊕ www.horizontes.com), the country's two premier nature-tour operators, have expert guides and can arrange tours that visit Carara, Manuel Antonio, or both. Tour operators in Jacó and Herradura (⇨ *below*) have trips to Carara. The Jungle Crocodile Safari (⇨ Tárcoles, *below*) has a day tour from San José that combines Carara Reserve with the Tárcoles riverboat tour.

To & from Carara Biological Reserve

43 km/25 mi southwest of Atenas, 85 km/51 mi (2½ hrs) southwest of San José.

From Atenas, pass through Orotina and follow the signs to Tárcoles and Jacó. The reserve is on left after you cross Río Tárcoles. From San José, hop on a bus to Jacó, Quepos, or Manuel Antonio and ask to be dropped off near the entrance of the park.

THE COAST

Along a short stretch of Costa Rica's Pacific Coast from Tárcoles to Manuel Antonio are patches of undeveloped jungle, the popular Manuel Antonio National Park, and some of the country's most accessible beaches. The proximity of these strands to San José leads Costa Ricans and foreigners alike to pop down for quick beach vacations. Surfers have good reason to head for the consistent waves of Playas Jacó and Hermosa, and anglers and golfers should consider Playa Herradura for its links and ocean access. You might find most of these beaches overrated and overdeveloped. Manuel Antonio could be accused of the latter, but nobody can deny its spectacular natural beauty.

Tárcoles

⓫ Crocodile boat tours on the Río Tárcoles are this small town's claim to fame and the only reason to stop here. In fact, you don't actually have to drive to Tárcoles to do the tour, since operators can pick you up in San José or Jacó. The muddy river has gained the reputation as the country's dirtiest thanks to San Jośe's inadequate sewage system, but it amazingly remains an impressive refuge for wildlife. An inordinate diversity of birds results from a combination of transitional forest and the river, which houses crocodiles, herons, storks, spoonbills, and other waterbirds. Spot them on a boat tour along the river or hiking in the private reserves nearby, one of which houses a spectacular waterfall.

You can hike, ride by horseback, or drive to the beautiful 656-foot **Manantial de Agua Viva Waterfall** deep in a lush forest. Its 10 natural pools are great for a refreshing dip after your ride or hike. The waterfall is within the private Complejo Ecológico la Catarata (Waterfall Ecological Reserve), which has guides who lead tours to the waterfall. The horseback ride is four hours. A tough 2½-km (1½-mi) trail makes a loop through the woods, passing the waterfall and pools; it takes between 40 minutes and two hours to hike, depending on how much bird-watching you do. Good physical condition and hiking shoes are necessary. Parrots, monkeys, scarlet macaws, and most of the other animals found in the nearby Carara Biological Reserve live in the forest here. ⊠ *From the coastal highway south to Jacó, turn left onto dirt road at Hotel Villa Lapas sign. The reserve is about 9 km/5½ mi past Villa Lapas* ☎ *661–8263* 💰 *$10 on foot, $15 in car, $40 guided horseback ride (includes entrance fee). Entry on foot not highly recommended* ☉ *Daily 8–4, horseback tours at 8:30 am and 2:00 pm.*

Outdoor Activities

BOAT TOURS   On the two-hour **river-boat** tours through mangrove forest you might see massive crocodiles, Jesus lizards, iguanas, and some of roughly 50 colorful bird species, including the turquoise browed motmot and boatbilled heron. Tours reach the river's mouth, providing nice sea views, especially at sunset. ■ TIP→ **Around noon is the best time to spot crocs sunbathing; bird enthusiasts prefer afternoon rides to catch scarlet macaws. During the rainy season (May–November), the river may grow too rough for boats.**

Diving the Deep at Coco Island

RATED ONE OF THE TOP DIVING DESTINATIONS in the world, Isla del Coco is uninhabited and remote, and its waters are teeming with marine life. It is no place for beginners, but serious divers enjoy 100-foot visibility and the underwater equivalent of a big-game park: scalloped hammerheads, white-tipped reef sharks, Galápagos sharks, bottlenose dolphins, billfish, and manta rays mix with huge schools of brilliantly colored fish.

Encompassing about 22½ square km, or 14 square mi, Isla del Coco is the largest uninhabited island on earth. Its isolation has led to the evolution of dozens of endemic plant and animal species. The rocky topography is draped in rain forest and cloud forest and includes more than 200 waterfalls. Because of Isla del Coco's distance from shore (484 km/300 mi) and its craggy topography, few visitors to Costa Rica—and even fewer Costa Ricans—have set foot on the island.

Costa Rica annexed Coco in 1869, and it became a national park in 1978. Today only extremely high-priced specialty-cruise ships, park rangers and volunteers, and scientists visit the place Jacques Cousteau called "the most beautiful island in the world." The dry season (November–May) brings calmer seas and is the best time to see silky sharks. During the rainy season, large schools of hammerheads can be seen, but the ocean is rougher.

Most dive cruises to Isla del Coco are about 10 days, and include three days of travel time on the open ocean. The **Okeanos Aggressor** (☎ 289–2261, 800/348-2628 in U.S. ⊕ www. aggressor.com) and the **Undersea Hunter** (☎ 228–6613, 800/203–2120 in U.S. ⊕ www.underseahunter.com) run trips year-round at a cost of roughly $3,500.

Two brothers run **Crocodile Man Tour** (✉ Main road into Tárcoles ☎ 637–0426 or 637–0771 [cell 822–9042] ⊕ www.crocodilemantour. com), started by a pioneer in the area's crocodile encounters, for $25 per person. Small scars on their hands prove they continue the tour's original (and optional) attraction: feeding fish to the crocs. The boats are small enough to slide up alongside the mangroves for a closer look. Transportation is provided from nearby beaches, but not from San José.

CANOPY TOUR **Hotel Villa Lapas** (✉ Off Costanera, 3 km/2½ mi after bridge over Tárcoles River, turn left on dirt road, up 600 m ☎ 637–0232 ☎ 637–0227 ⊕ www.villalapas.com) manages a suspension-bridge nature walk and a zip-line tour. **Sky Way** consists of five suspension bridges spread out over a 2½-km (1½-mi) old-growth-forest nature trail. You can do the trail with a guide ($20) or without a guide ($15). A shuttle picks you up at the Hotel Villa Lapas. **Villa Lapas Canopy** has zip lines through primary forest. The tour is $35 per person.

HIKING Trails in this area—in Manantial de Agua, the Complejo Ecológico, and at Hotel Villa Lapas's Sky Way—can keep you afoot for a couple of days, crossing suspension bridges in old growth forests or trekking up to one of the country's highest waterfalls, which you can also reach on horseback.

Where to Stay & Eat

¢–$ × **Soda las Veraneras.** This small and simple tiled-floor eatery serves standard homemade *soda* food, like filling *casados* (plates of rice, beans, salad, and fish, chicken, or meat). ⊠ *Near entrance to Tárcoles* ☎ 637–0418 ▱ *No credit cards.*

★ ☾ $$ ▦ **Hotel Villa Lapas.** Within a tranquil rain-forest preserve, far from other hotels (and the beach), Villa Lapas is a great escape for nature lovers, but also has on-site entertainment to keep you busy, such as a large-screen television, a pool table, and foosball. Cross a suspension bridge to a small replica of a Costa Rican colonial village with a restaurant, cantina, church, and gift shops. Follow the river flowing through the protected forest for a pleasant hike. For the adventurous, there is a canopy tour on the property. The austere rooms are nothing special, but have terra-cotta floors, hardwood ceilings, and large baths. An all-inclusive meal plan is available. ⊠ *Off Costanera, 3 km (2 mi) after bridge over Tárcoles River, turn left on dirt road, up 600 m* ☎ 637–0232 ➧ 637–0227 ⊕ *www. villalapas.com* ➪ *55 rooms* ☾ *2 restaurants, fans, in-room safes, pool, 3 bars, recreation room, 3 shops, laundry service, meeting room; no room TVs* ▱ *AE, DC, MC, V* ⦿ *AI.*

To & from Tárcoles

90 km/54 mi (1½ hrs) southwest of San José.

Any bus traveling to Jacó can drop you off at the entrance to Tárcoles; just let the driver know in advance. By car, follow the signs on the Costanera to Orotina and continue toward Jacó. The entrance to the town of Tárcoles is on the west side of the road; across the highway is a dirt road that leads to the Hotel Villa Lapas and the waterfall reserve.

⌐
EN
ROUTE   Even if you choose to bypass Tárcoles and its crocodile tours, you can still get a peek of the huge reptiles as they lounge on the riverbanks: on the Costanera, pull over just after crossing the Río Tárcoles bridge and walk back onto it. Bring binoculars if you have them. As always, lock your car—vehicles have been broken into here.

Between Tárcoles and Playa Herradura

Past Tárcoles, the first sizable beachtown of the Central Pacific coast is Playa Herradura. In between, you'll pass two of the area's most exclusive hotels, hidden from roadside view at the end of long winding roads. About a kilometer (½ mi) south after the entrance to Tárcoles, the Costanera passes a small beach called **Playa La Pita,** which provides your first glimpse of the Pacific if you're coming down from the Central Valley. The beach is rocky, and its proximity to the Tárcoles River makes the water murky and unfit for swimming, but it's a nice spot to stop and admire the ocean. La Pita lies within a calm-water cove, where fishermen anchor their boats off its southern end. Watch pelicans diving into the water, and in the distance, you might see the mountains of the southern tip of the Nicoya Peninsula. Farther down, you'll come across the entrances of elegant lodgings Villas Caletas and Hotel Punta Leona, which have access to other small beaches along the coast.

Where to Stay & Eat

$$–$$$ ✕ **El Mirador Restaurant.** White tablecloths, glass walls, and yellow-and-blue-checkered curtains contribute to the sophisticated but not overly stuffy atmosphere of this restaurant at the Villa Caletas hotel. A reasonable prix fixe includes your choice of appetizer, main dish, and dessert. Add a little more for nightly specials or choose à la carte. Mango snook, cognac chicken supreme, and beef tenderloin béarnaise are a few of the delectable entrées. A covered terrace is popular for sunset viewing over a cocktail. ⊠ *Villa Caletas hotel, off coastal highway, 3 km (1½ mi) south of Punta Leona, on the right* ☎ *637–0505* ▤ *AE, DC, MC, V* ✆ *No lunch.*

¢–$$ ✕ **Steve n' Lisa's.** A convenient location, an ocean view, and good food make this roadside restaurant overlooking Playa La Pita a popular pit stop for those traveling between San José and the Central Pacific beaches. Sit on the covered porch or at one of the concrete tables on the adjacent patio, and enjoy the view of the Gulf of Nicoya through the palm fronds. The menu includes breakfast options and a wide selection of lunch and dinner entrées that ranges from tacos and hot dogs to a pricy surf and turf. There's a salad bar, and an eclectic mix of appetizers includes a chicken quesadilla, two types of *ceviche,* onion rings, and deep-fried cauliflower. ⊠ *On the Costanera, 1 km (½ mi) south of Tárcoles turnoff, on the right* ☎ *637–0594* ▤ *AE, MC, V* ✆ *Breakfast served.*

★ **$$–$$$$** ✕🏠 **Hotel Punta Leona.** This 740-acre private reserve and resort community is an odd and overwhelming mix of nature, residential development, and vacation spot. Punta Leona's attractions include three beaches, a tropical forest, a butterfly farm, and guided bird-watching hikes. Punta Leona (Lion's Point) made headlines as the main site of the Ridley Scott film *1492: Conquest of Paradise* and more recently for controversially blocking the public's access to its beaches, which is illegal in Costa Rica. The little "city" contains everything from multiple restaurants and pools to a grocery store and church, plus plenty of amusements, including a zip-line tour, tennis court, and mini–golf course. Frequent shuttles travel between the rooms, restaurants, and beaches. Hotel guests, homeowners, and time-share members contribute to crowded beaches on weekends, especially in the dry season. Nonguests who choose to dine or use any facility at Punta Leona must pay a $20 surcharge. ⊠ *Off the Costanera, on road to Jacó* ☎ *231–3131 or 625–8825* 🖷 *282–9701* ⊕ *www.hotelpuntaleona.com* ✄ *108 rooms,*

THE CART WITHOUT OXEN

If you're out late one night and hear a slow scraping of wheels against the road, it just might be the *carreta sin bueyes* (cart without oxen) of ghostly legend. Its owner reputedly stole building materials from a church, and was condemned to perpetually traverse the country's highways and byways in the cart he used to transport his stolen goods. (The oxen were blameless for their role and escaped the curse.) Hurry back to your hotel.

---

13 suites, 92 apartments △ 3 restaurants, 2 snack bars, in-room safes, refrigerators, cable TV, 3 pools, beach, snorkeling, hiking, 3 bars, shops, laundry service, Internet ⊟ AE, DC, MC, V ⍾⊙⍾ EP.

Playa Herradura

⑫ If sportsfishing and golf are your priorities, this is a good option. If you're looking for nature, seclusion, a beautiful beach, or a bargain, keep driving. Rocky Playa Herradura, a poor representative of Costa Rica's breathtaking beaches, gets its name from the Spanish word for "horseshoe," referring to the shape of the deep bay in which it lies. Its tranquil waters make it considerably safer for swimming than most central and southern Pacific beaches, and that, coupled with its proximity to San José, has turned it into a popular weekend getaway for Josefinos, who compete for shade beneath the sparse palms and Indian almond trees.

Outdoor Activities

A few activities are available directly in Playa Herradura, but that doesn't mean you have to settle for less. Most of the area's diverse outfitters can pick you up at your hotel for activities near Jacó and Playa Hermosa. Your hotel's reception desk is often a good source of information.

King Tours (⊠ Main road into Playa Herradura, in front of Los Sueños resort ☎637–7343, 643–2441, 800/213–7091 [toll free in U.S.] ⊕www.kingtours.com) arranges trips to renowned attractions like Manuel Antonio National Park and Carara Biological Reserve, as well as crocodile boat tours, deep-sea and coastal fishing trips, horseback riding, and canopy tours. It also books tours elsewhere in the country, to destinations such as Poás and Arenal volcanoes, Monteverde Cloud Forest, and Isla Tortuga. **Marlin del Rey** (⊠ On the main road into Playa Herradura, shortly after the entrance to Los Sueños resort, on the left ☎ 637–7249 or 386–6786) specializes in fishing tours, snorkel trips to Isla Tortuga, and sunset catamaran rides.

Where to Stay & Eat

$$$$ ✕⍾ **Marriott Los Sueños Ocean and Golf Resort.** This mammoth multi-million-dollar resort contains condos and a hotel. The palatial terra-cotta, colonial-style buildings, reminiscent of a theme park, combine modern amenities with traditional Central American decorative motifs, like Nicaraguan barrel-tile roofing and hand-painted Costa Rican tiles. Its rooms, though attractive and some of the country's most expensive, are nothing special compared with those at other hotels in this price range. They have marble baths, wooden furniture, and tiny balconies. Be sure to get a room with an ocean view, or you'll be contemplating condominiums. An enormous pool with islands and swim-up bars, a Ted Robinson golf course, a modern marina, and various diversions are designed to keep you on-site and entertained. ⊠ *On road to Jacó from San José, follow signs on right at entrance of road to Playa Herradura; hotel's entrance on right, shortly before end of road, clearly marked* ☎630–9000, 800/228–9290 in U.S. ⍾ 630–9090 ⊕*www.marriott.com* ⍽ *191 rooms, 10 suites △ 5 restaurants, 2 bars, in-room safes, minibars, cable TV, 18-hole golf course, canopy tours, 2 tennis courts, pool, gym, massage, beach, casino, shops, children's programs (ages 5–15),* *laundry service, business services, meeting rooms, no-smoking rooms, Internet, airport shuttle* ⊟ *AE, DC, MC, V* ⧀ *EP.*

To & from Playa Herradura
12 km/7 mi (20 mins) south of Punta Leona.

By bus, hop on one heading to Jacó. By car, head straight down the Central Pacific highway. The town's entrance is on right-hand side. A long paved road leads to the beach: follow the signs to the Marriott.

Jacó

⓭ Its proximity to San José has made Jacó the most developed beach town in Costa Rica. Nature lovers and solitude-seekers should skip this place, which is known for its nightlife, surf scene, and blatant prostitution. More than 50 hotels and cabinas back its long, gray-sand beach, and the mix of restaurants, shops, and bars lining Avenida Pastor Diaz (the town's main drag), gives it a cluttered appearance devoid of any greenery. Any real Costa Rican–ness evaporated years ago; U.S. chain hotels and restaurants have invaded, and you can pretty much find anything you need, from law offices and dental clinics to DVD rental shops and appliance stores. In terms of tours and outdoor activities, it's also got a bit of everything and makes a hub for exploring neighboring beaches and attractions.

Long, palm-lined **Playa Jacó,** just east of town, is a pleasant enough spot in the morning, but can burn the soles of your feet on a sunny afternoon. Though the gray sand and beachside construction make it less attractive than most other Costa Rican beaches, it's a good place to enjoy a sunset. Playa Jacó is popular with surfers for the consistency of its waves, making it less than ideal for swimmers.

Outdoor Activities
You don't have to physically step into any tour office, since everyone from a reception desk attendant to a boutique salesperson can book you a local adventure. Almost every tour can pick you up at your hotel's doorstep. ■ TIP→ Keep in mind that part of your price tag includes the salesperson's commission, so if you hear higher or lower prices from two different people, it's likely a reflection of a shift in the commission. You can try negotiating a better deal directly from the outfitter.

Costa Tropical Expeditions (☎ 393–6622) is a small Jacó tour operator that specializes in trips to Carara Biological Reserve, but can arrange all kinds of personalized excursions. **Fantasy Tours** (⊠ Best Western Jacó Beach Resort ☎ 643–2231, 220–2126 [main office in San José]) is the biggest operator in Jacó and deals primarily with large groups, arranging day trips from Jacó to Arenal and Poás volcanoes, Manuel Antonio National Park, Sarchí, Tortuga Island, and rafting on the Savegre River, plus local tours like zip-line adventures and kayak and snorkeling trips, among many others. **Pacific Travel and Tours** (⊠ Centro comercial La Casona [La Casona shopping center] ☎ 643–2520, 643–2449 ⊕ www.pacifictravelcr. com) organizes tours for numerous activities in and around Jacó.

ATV TOURS Since ATV tours are fairly new here, the vehicles are in good condition. But they're not exactly the most eco-friendly way to see the area's rain

5

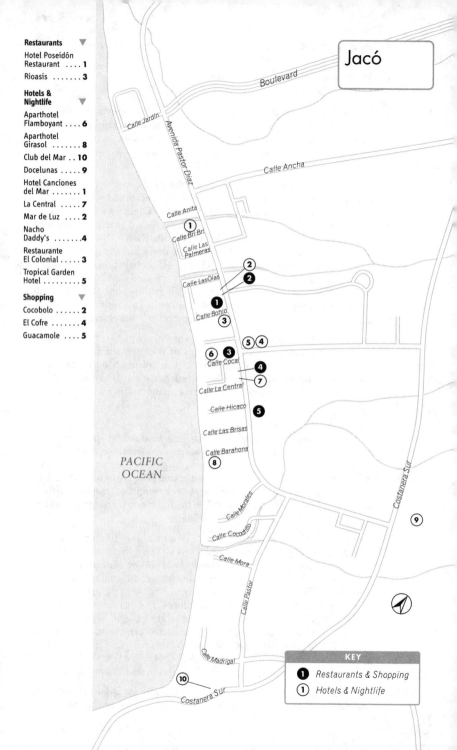

Jacó

Restaurants ▼
Hotel Poseidón
Restaurant 1
Rioasis 3

Hotels & Nightlife ▼
Aparthotel
Flamboyant 6
Aparthotel
Girasol 8
Club del Mar .. 10
Docelunas 9
Hotel Canciones
del Mar 1
La Central 7
Mar de Luz 2
Nacho
Daddy's 4
Restaurante
El Colonial 3
Tropical Garden
Hotel 5

Shopping ▼
Cocobolo 2
El Cofre 4
Guacamole 5

Boulevard

Calle Jardín

Avenida Pastor Díaz

Calle Ancha

Calle Anita

Calle Bri Bri

Calle Las Palmeras

Calle Las Olas

Calle Bohío

Calle Cocal

Calle La Central

Calle Hicaco

Calle Las Brisas

Calle Barahona

Calle Morales

Calle Cocodrillo

Calle Mora

Calle Pastor

Calle Madrigal

Costanera Sur

Costanera Sur

PACIFIC
OCEAN

KEY
1 Restaurants & Shopping
1 Hotels & Nightlife

forest and wildlife. Some operators will ask you to put up a credit card voucher of roughly $500. **ATV Tours** (☎ 778–8172, 812–1789) runs two- or three-hour tours ($65–$85) through rain forests, rivers, and waterfalls that lie about 15 minutes south of Jacó. **Paraíso Adventures** (☎ 225–0858, 814–5018 ⊕ www.paraisocostarica.com) has shorter tours with longer breaks than most companies, which means you spend less time riding the quad. Trips are $65 for two hours, $85 for three hours, and $95 for four hours. **Ricaventura** (✉ In the center of Playa Jacó, behind Subway ☎ 818–6973 or 643–3395) is considered by locals to be the best ATV tour with the longest routes. Ricaventura offers three options: a two-hour sunset tour ($65), a four-hour Carara Park and nearby river tour ($90), and a six-hour Pacayal Waterfall trip ($150).

CANOPY TOURS
In the hills across the highway from Jacó Beach, **Canopy Adventure Jacó** (☎ 643–3271 ⊕ www.adventurecanopy.com) takes you sliding through the forest along cables strung between 13 treetop platforms ($55), some of which have views of the coast. **Waterfalls Canopy Tour** (☎ 643–3322 ⊕ www.waterfallscanopy.com), in a private reserve 4 km/2½ mi from Jacó, is a zip-line tour ($55) through trees, with a view of rain forest and waterfalls. You can combine the tour with a visit to a butterfly and frog garden.

HANG GLIDING &
ULTRALIGHT
FLIGHTS
A truly unique experience for the adventurous, hang gliding gives you the chance to see not just Jacó, but a huge expanse of Pacific coastline from above. With **Hang Glide Costa Rica** (☎ 353–5514 ⊕ www.hangglidecostarica.com), you can take a tandem hang-gliding flight or fly in a three-seat, open cockpit ultralight plane. You are picked up in Jacó and taken to the airstrip 6 km/4 mi south of Playa Hermosa. Prices start at around $70 per person.

HORSEBACK
RIDING
Horse Tours at Hacienda Agujas (☎ 643–2218, 838–7940) are serene enough for all ages and skill levels. Late-afternoon tours are on a cattle ranch about 25 minutes north of Jacó, include a trail ride through the rain forest and down a beach, and end with a colorful sunset bang. For much less, you can take a tour with one of the locals who are usually walking their horses along the beach, but don't expect insurance coverage in the price.

KAYAKING AND
CANOEING
Kayak Jacó Costa Rica Outriggers (☎ 643–1233 ⊕ www.kayakjaco.com) takes you to less restless waters than those at Jacó Beach with sea-kayaking tours for novices and seasoned adventurers and Hawaiian-style outrigger canoe trips. Both include snorkel excursions (conditions permitting) at secluded beaches. For a bit more activity, you can take a white-water kayaking or rafting trip.

SURFING
Jacó has several beach breaks, all of which are best around high tide, specifically three hours before and three hours after (local maps and promotional magazines carry tide charts). Surfboard-toting tourists abound in Jacó, but you don't need to be an expert to enjoy the waves—the swell is often small enough for beginners. Surf shops, which have popped up on almost every corner, rent boards and give surf lessons, although pretty much any local can teach you how to stand on a board. (Jacó has

Catch the Wave

COSTA RICA GETS HIGH MARKS among surfers for its warm, clean ocean water, beautiful tropical scenery, consistent waves, and not-too-crowded conditions. (The place hasn't yet turned into California or Hawaii.)

Tamarindo anchors a popular surfing region on the North Pacific coast. Its protected bay offers smaller waves that translate into great conditions for beginners. The exception is December and January, when the bay is exposed to southern swells that create bigger waves. North of town to Playa Grande and south to Playas Avellanas and Negra always get exposed to those swells and are experts-only destinations year-round.

Farther down the coast, **Sámara** is little mentioned in surfing circles, but is a good beginner's beach for its small waves.

Some of the country's finest surfing is at **Malpaís,** at the tip of the Nicoya Peninsula. The town is gradually becoming more popular, despite its remoteness.

The Central Pacific town of **Jacó** gets mixed reviews. As the closest surfing destination to San José, it draws the crowds. Surfers say its waves close out early (good for beginners) but tend toward quick shore breaks (conditions best negotiated by experts).

Playa Hermosa, just south, has 8- to 10-foot waves. The beach is

enormously popular, but the waves are long enough that crowding is rarely a problem.

The South Pacific's **Dominical** is a nice alternative to Jacó. It's a bit farther from San José and therefore less crowded, and its wide beach break and cool beach-town atmosphere make it worth the trip.

Staring at each other from across the entrance to the Golfo Dulce are the point breaks and resulting big waves at **Matapalo** and **Pavones.** The latter in particular is famed in surfing circles for being one of the world's longest left-breaking waves.

While the Pacific has consistent year-round conditions, the Caribbean coast has a narrower January–April window of top-notch surfing. In theory, the north coast has the waves, but it's tough enough to get yourself here, let alone a board, and shark-infested waters make it a no-go. Heading south, the reef breaks at **Limón** draw a few surfers. (It's just not a popular tourist destination.) Cahuita's **Playa Negra** is fairly consistent for a beach break.

Just beyond Puerto Viejo de Talamanca is the consistent beach break at **Playa Cocles.** The famed—and revered—**Salsa Brava,** an experts-only reef break, is visible from the town of Puerto Viejo.

no surf schools.) Prices range from $25 to $45 an hour and usually include a board and transportation. If you plan to spend more than a week surfing, it might be cheaper to buy a used board and sell it before you leave (⇨ Shopping, *below*). If you don't have much experience, don't go out when the waves are really big—Jacó sometimes gets very powerful swells, which result in dangerous rip currents. During the rainy season, waves are more consistent than in the dry months, which can bring flatter waves.

SWIMMING The big waves and dangerous rip currents that make surfing so popular here make swimming dangerous. Lifeguards are on duty only sporadically, so plan on being on your own. If the ocean is really rough, stay on the beach—dozens of swimmers have drowned over the years. When the waves are small, this can be a good place for strong swimmers to body surf. In general, if you're swimming and a wave is about to break on top of you, dive deep underneath it.

> **CAUTION**
>
> Riptides (or rip currents), common in Jacó and Manuel Antonio's Playa Espadilla, are dangerous and have led to deaths in the area. If you get caught in one, don't panic and don't try to swim against it. Let the current take you out just past the breakers, where its power dissipates, then swim parallel to shore. Once the current is behind you, swim back to the beach. The best policy is not to go in deeper than your waist when the waves loom large.

When the ocean is calm, you can swim just about anywhere along Jacó Beach. But always avoid the northern and southern extremes, and the areas around any of several small rivers that flow into the ocean, where the beach and ocean bottom are littered with rocks. The most frequently voiced advice is to not go deeper than your waist and to make sure you're always touching the ground.

Where to Stay & Eat

★ $$–$$$$ ✕ **Hotel Poseidon Restaurant.** One of Jacó's best restaurants, this spot has patio seating, friendly service, an intimate atmosphere, good music, and an open grill at the entrance. Its small selection of inventive dishes always includes seafood, meat, chicken, and vegetarian options whose preparation changes every few days. Cooking flavors you might come across are Caribbean jerk-style, oyster peppercorn sauce, toasted pecans, and balsamic demi-glace. ⊠ *C. Bohío, 25 m west of main road. Across from the Parqueo El Paso* ☎ 643–1642 ⊟ AE, D, DC, MC, V.

☾ ¢–$ ✕ **Rioasis.** With an eclectic menu of Tex-Mex dishes, pastas, and salads, this large, colorful place on the main drag is popular with families and surfers, who head here for cheap eats. Pizza is the best bet: 34 varieties are baked in an outdoor wood-burning oven. You can eat on the front patio or under a high roof hung with ceiling fans. There's a long bar in back, a pool table, and foosball for after-dinner entertainment. ⊠ *Avda. Pastor Diaz, north of Banco Nacional* ☎ 643–3354 ⊟ MC, V ☉ *Closed Tues. May–Nov.*

$$$–$$$$ ✕🏨 **Club del Mar.** Secluded on the beach's southern extreme, far from Fodor'sChoice Jacó's din and masses, Club del Mar is the area's priciest option. In the ★ main building, above the restaurant, bar, and reception, standard green-and-cream-hued rooms have private teak balconies with screen doors that keep the sea breeze circulating. For the price, you can find better options elsewhere. Instead, go for the comfortable condos, clustered in a dozen two-story buildings amid massive trees and verdant lawns. The one- and two-bedroom apartments have modern kitchens, pleasant

decor, abundant windows, and washing machines. Some apartments stand in front of the sea (Nos. 13–16); those farthest back lie close to the highway. Restaurant Las Sandalias ($–$$) serves some of the area's finest dinners, from chateaubriand to grilled lobster. It also serves breakfast. The split-level, open-air space has a bar on top and tables below, all facing the pool and ocean. The penthouse has two bedrooms, one with a king-size bed and the other with two twins. ⊠ *Costanera, 275 m south of gas station* ⌖ *Apdo. 107–4023* 🕾🖷 *643–3194, 1–866/978–5669 toll free in US* ⊕ *www.clubdelmarcostarica.com* 🖘 *8 rooms, 22 condos, 2 suites* ⌂ *Restaurant, fans, in-room safes, kitchens, cable TV, pool, massage, bar, shop, beach, laundry service, laundry facilities, kayaking, in-room data ports, Internet* ☰ *AE, MC, V, DC* ⏀ *BP.*

$$–$$$
Fodor'sChoice
★
✕🖾 **Docelunas.** Most of Jacó's hotels and visitors huddle around the beach and bars, but "Twelve Moons" has a radically different holistic atmosphere across the highway. With a mountainous green backdrop, this choice hotel spreads out across 5 acres. Paintings (for sale) decorate the spacious teak furniture–filled rooms, and large bathrooms have showers, bathtubs, and double sinks. Yoga classes are given daily in a hilltop, hardwood-floor room with windows for walls. The full-service spa uses the hotel's own homemade beauty products and the open-air restaurant ($$–$$$) serves up creative seafood, meat, vegetarian, and vegan dishes that change weekly. A lovely sun mosaic decorates the large pool with a waterfall flowing into it. Each Sunday local residents arrive for movie night. ⊠ *On coastal highway, coming from San José, pass the first entrances to Jacó; take dirt road on left with signs for Docelunas to the end (if you reach the gas station on the right, next to the last entrance to Jaco, you passed it)* 🕾 *643–2211* ⊕ *www.docelunas.com* 🖘 *20 rooms* ⌂ *Restaurant, room service, bar, fans, in-room safes, refrigerators, cable TV, pool, spa, shop, laundry service, in-room data ports, business center, meeting room, no-smoking rooms* ☰ *MC, V* ⏀ *BP.*

$$–$$$
Fodor'sChoice
★
🖾 **Hotel Canciones del Mar.** The poetically named "Songs of the Sea" is a tranquil, intimate, and charming hotel with rooms that are among the closest to the ocean of those in any area hotel. Except for one bamboo-lined room, spacious suites are the only option. Tastefully and individually decorated, the one- and two-bedroom suites are in a two-story cream-colored building, with well-equipped kitchens. Each has a porch overlooking lush gardens and a blue-tile pool, except for the honeymoon suite, which faces the beach. Breakfast and drinks can be enjoyed under a thatch roof next to the beach or in the shade of palms on the beach itself. A communal treehouse-like space behind the pool makes a pleasant reading or relaxing spot. ⊠ *End of C. Bri Bri* 🕾 *643–3273* 🖷 *643–3296* ⊕ *www.cancionesdelmar.com* 🖘 *1 room, 9 condos, 1 honeymoon suite, 1 2-bedroom suite* ⌂ *Fans, in-room safes, kitchens, refrigerators, cable TV, pool, laundry service, Internet, no-smoking rooms; no room phones* ☰ *AE, MC, V* ⏀ *BP.*

🕙 **$$**
🖾 **Aparthotel Girasol.** A great option for families or groups looking for comfort and quiet, Girasol is a small beachfront hotel with a neighborly feel. The cozy apartments face the small pool and grill area and include a living and dining room, a complete kitchen, lots of windows, and a terrace with chairs. A winding pathway crosses the well-maintained front lawn, with an impressive tree in the middle, and leads to a small gate

that opens directly onto the beach, where you should take at least one evening to enjoy a spectacular sunset. ⊠ *End of C. Los Almendros; 300 m south and 75 m west of Más X Menos supermarket* ☎ *643–1591* ⊕ *www.girasol.com* ⋈ *16 apartments* ⚷ *Fans, kitchens, cable TV, pool, laundry service; no phones in some rooms* ▭ *MC, V* ⦿ *EP.*

★ **$–$$** ▦ **Tropical Garden Hotel.** As its name suggests, this hotel's special charm comes from the impressive lush gardens that fill almost every inch of its property, making it one of the most verdant places in Jacó. Meters from the beach and from the main strip, rooms lack decor but have convenient kitchenettes and comfortable front porches for iguana- and bird-spotting. Though one of Jacó's earliest hotels (formerly known as Villas Miramar), it has modern perks like wireless Internet. Poolside breakfast is served for an extra $5 and the deluxe suite's two rooms sleep up to six people. ⊠ *In front of Il Galeone mall, toward the beach* ☎ *643–3003* ⊟ *643–3617* ⊕ *www.tropicalgardenhotel.com* ⋈ *11 rooms, 1 suite* ⚷ *Fans, in-room safes, kitchenettes, cable TV, pool, massage, in-room data ports, Wi-Fi; no a/c in some rooms* ▭ *AE, MC, V* ⦿ *EP.*

$ ▦ **Aparthotel Flamboyant.** Though nothing special, this small tranquil hotel is a good deal, especially if you take advantage of the cooking facilities. Half the rooms have small kitchenettes; the others have air-conditioning instead. Larger apartments can fit five to six people. Terraces with chairs overlook a garden and pool area, where there's a grill for your use. Second-floor rooms have balconies with sea views. It's all just a few steps from the beach, and a block east of Jacó's busy main strip. ⊠ *100 m east of Centro Comercial Il Galeone* ☎ *643–3146* ⊟ *643–1068* ✍ *flamboya@racsa.co.cr* ⋈ *20 rooms, 3 apartments* ⚷ *Fans, in-room safes, some kitchenettes, pool; no a/c in some rooms, no TV in some rooms* ▭ *AE, DC, MC, V* ⦿ *EP.*

☿ **$** ▦ **Mar de Luz.** It may be a few blocks from the beach, and it doesn't look like much from the street, but Mar de Luz is a surprisingly pleasant, quiet place full of flowering plants and shady, bird-attracting trees. The Dutch owner is dedicated to cleanliness and providing extra amenities, such as poolside grills, a kids' gameroom, microwaves and refrigerators in each room, plentiful common areas—like the large open-air reading lounge with comfortable couches—and inexpensive tours. Rooms vary in feel and decor: the bright, pastel-hue rooms have two queen-size beds and kitchenettes; top-floor rooms have a small living room with checkered sofas and a double bed; the cozy split-level rooms with kitchenettes and stone walls are reminiscent of European B&Bs. Few places can match Mar de Luz's helpful and accommodating staff. Breakfast is served at an additional cost. ⊠ *Just east of Avda. Pastor Diaz, behind Onyx bar* ☎ *643–3259, 1–877/623–3198 toll-free in US* ⊕ *www.mardeluz.com* ⋈ *27 rooms, 2 suites,* ⚷ *In-room safes, some kitchenettes, refrigerators, microwaves, cable TV, 2 pools, massage, laundry service, Internet; no room phones* ▭ *V* ⦿ *EP.*

Nightlife & the Arts

While other beach towns may have a bar or two, Jacó has an avenue full of them, with enough variety for many different tastes. After-dinner spots range from restaurants perfect for a quiet drink to loud bars with pool tables to dance clubs or casinos.

BARS For a laid-back cocktail, people-watching, and a tropical feel, head to **Restaurante El Colonial** (✉ Avda. Pastor Diaz, across from Il Galeone mall ☎ 643–3326), on the main drag, which has a large circular bar in the center and lots of wicker chairs and tables in the front. Sometimes it has live music. A mix of bar and disco, **Nacho Daddy's** (✉ Avda. Pastor Diaz, first floor of Il Galeone mall ☎ 643–2270) draws crowds of all ages and nationalities. Its carpeted floors and air-conditioning make it Jacó's cushiest nightspot.

DANCE CLUBS **La Central** (✉ On the beach, end of the street across from Más x Menos ☎ 643–3076) is a club that plays a mix of popular dance music in different genres, has air-conditioning, and attracts a wide variety of late-night partygoers. No one arrives before 11 PM, and it stays open until 5 AM.

Shopping

The two neighboring shops at **Cocobolo** (✉ Avda. Pastor Diaz, next to Banana Café ☎ 643–3486) are jam-packed with merchandise hanging from the ceiling, walls, and shelves. It's much of what you find in other stores, but with more international and tasteful items and richer variety. **El Cofre** (✉ Avda. Pastor Diaz, across from Banco Nacional ☎ 643–1912) claims to sell only handmade goods and specializes in mostly wooden furniture, including heavy Guatemalan pieces and Indonesian teak, but sells masks, drums, Morroccan lamps, and even carved doors. Curious religious statues of saints and angels from Central America are big sellers.

Guacamole (✉ Il Galeone mall ☎ 643–3297 ✉ Centro Comercial Costa Brava ☎ 643–1120) sells beautiful and comfortable batik clothing produced locally, along with Brazilian bathing suits, Costa Rican leather sandals and purses, and different styles of jewelry.

SURFBOARDS & GEAR **Carton** (✉ Calle Madrigal ☎ 643–3762) sells new and used boards and has a selection in surfwear, sunglasses, and accessories. **El Pana Bikinis and Surf** (✉ Avda. Pastor Diaz, next to Cocobolo souvenir shop ☎ 812–2803) has less variety than the other three shops in town, but more affordable prices. It rents and sells new and used surfboards and Boogie boards, and fixes small dings. **Jass** (✉ Centro comercial Ureña ☎ 643–3549) has a good variety of surf gear at decent prices. It sells new and used boards.

■ TIP→ **Most shops that sell boards also buy used boards.**

To & from Jacó
2 km/1 mi south of Playa Herradura, 114 km/70 mi (2½ hrs) southwest of San José.

Buses leave from San José's Coca-Cola station five times daily. From here it's easy to catch a bus to the surrounding beaches or back to the capital, and many private shuttles offer transfers to other parts of the country. If you're driving, head down the Costanera, past Playa Herradura; get off before Playa Hermosa. **Extreme Boat** (☎ 640–0600 ⊕ www.extboat.com) shuttles surfers between Malpaís and Jacó, Monday and Friday.

Jacó Essentials
🏦 Bank/ATM **BAC San José** ✉ Il Galeone mall. **Banco Nacional** ✉ Avda. Pastor Diaz.
🏥 Hospital **Ambulance** ☎ 643–1690 **Clínica Pública** ✉ In front of the Plaza de Deportes ☎ 643–1767)

🏠 Pharmacy **Farmacia Jacó** ✉ Diagonal from Mas X Menos supermarket ☎ 643–3205.

🏠 Taxis **Taxi services** ☎ 643-2020, 643-2121, or 643-3030

🏠 Tourist Information **Pacific Travel and Tours** ✉ Centro comercial La Casona (La Casona shopping center) ☎ 643-2520 or 643-2449 ⊕ www.pacifictravelcr.com.

Playa Hermosa

⑭ Just over the rocky ridge that forms the southern edge of Jacó is Playa Hermosa, a swath of gray sand and driftwood stretching southeast as far as the eye can see. Despite its name, there's nothing really pretty about it. The wide beach lacks palm trees or other shade-providing greenery; its sand is scorchingly hot in the afternoon and frequent rip currents make it unsafe to swim when the waves are big. But board-toters find beauty in its jaw-dropping surf breaks. The beach's northern end is popular for its angle, which often has waves when Jacó and other spots are flat. For nonsurfers, outdoor options include horseback and canopy tours in the nearby forested hills or ultralight and hang-gliding flights along the coast. But all of these can be done from other beaches. As for the town itself, there's really not much. Most of the restaurants, bars, and hotels have cropped up one after the other on a thin stretch separating the highway and the beach. From August to December, olive ridley turtles nest on the beach, on nights when there's not much moonlight.

Outdoor Activities

You can arrange activities throughout the Central Pacific from Playa Hermosa. Most tour operators and outfitters include transportation in their prices. For more options than we list here, *see* Outdoor Activities *in* Jacó, *above,* or consult your hotel's reception.

CANOPY TOUR **Chiclets Tree Tour** (✉ West of Costanera, ½ km/¼ mi north of Hermosa ☎ 643–1880 ⊕ www.jacowave.com) has four guided tours daily that take you through the rain-forest canopy. Cables strung between platforms perched high in a dozen trees have views of tropical foliage, wildlife, and the nearby coast.

HORSEBACK RIDING Tours with **Discovery Horseback** (☎ 643–7151, 838–7550 ⊕ www.discoveryhorsetours.com) lead you through the nearby mountains and along the beach, and also offers riding lessons.

SURFING Most people who bed down at Playa Hermosa are here for the same reason—the waves that break just a shell's toss away. One of the country's most consistent surf spots, Hermosa often has waves when other beaches are flat. There are a half-dozen beach breaks scattered along the beach, but the surf is always best around low and high tide. Because it is a beach break,

> **WORD OF MOUTH**
>
> "We left Quepos around 9:30 AM for our long ride to Arenal. Stopped at Playa Hermosa to see the surfing beach. While walking back to our car, saw a huge cloud of dust from the dirt road. When the dust cleared, what emerged was a Tican cowboy herding about two dozen cattle! What a great sight. Kodak picture moment! We would have missed opportunities like these without our rental car."
> —Kwoo

5

though, the waves here often close out, especially when the surf is big. If you don't have much experience, don't go out when the waves are really big—Hermosa sometimes gets very powerful swells, which result in dangerous rip currents. In fact, if you're a beginner, don't go out at all. Surf instructors in Hermosa take their students to Jacó, an easier place to stand on a board for the first time.

Reggae-themed **Restaurante Jammin'** (✉ In front of Cabinas Las Arenas 🖼 643–1853) also has surf trips and lessons (2-hr lesson is $45; package is $100/day) and buys, rents, and sells boards as they're available. Andrea, a professional, Quiksilver surfer with **Waves Costa Rica** (✉ Next to the Backyard 🖼 829–4610 ⊕ www.wavescr.com), takes surf students to calmer Playa Jacó for two-hour lessons ($45; $100 for day-long package). She also has surf camp packages for women, which include room and board, yoga sessions, and surf lessons.

Where to Stay & Eat

¢–$ ✕ **Jungle Surf Cafe.** This colorful, open-air eatery next to the Costanera serves some of Hermosa's best food. Seating is on a patio shaded by tropical trees, with a view of the road and soccer field. Breakfasts are hearty, and the eclectic lunch selection ranges from shish kebabs to fish sandwiches. The dinner menu changes nightly, but usually includes fresh tuna and mahimahi, and pork chops or chicken (preparation varies). ✉ *Costanera, north of soccer field* 🖼 *643–1495* ▭ *No credit cards* 🍴 *BYOB* ⊙ *Closed Wed.*

¢ ✕ **The Backyard.** The only bar in Playa Hermosa, the Backyard has a North American atmosphere and several seating areas, each with its own bar. Inside, TVs on the wraparound bar show sports matches and surf videos. A wooden deck with plastic tables closer to the beach gets great sea breezes. The usual bar food, like pizza, burgers, and sandwiches, accompanies local seafood starters, including ceviche and peel-and-eat shrimp. It's a popular nightspot, especially on Wednesday and Friday's Ladies Night. ✉ *Next to the hotel by the same name* 🖼 *643–3936* ▭ *AE, DC, MC, V.*

$$–$$$ 🏨 **The Backyard.** Surfers—not the budget backpacking kind—are the main clientele at this small two-story, cream-colored hotel on the beach. Rooms have high ceilings, clay-tile floors, and sliding-glass doors that open onto semiprivate balconies and terraces, most of which have good views of Playa Hermosa. Second-floor rooms have better views, as do the two spacious corner suites with separate bedrooms and large balconies—they're a good deal for small groups. ✉ *Costanera, southern end of town, 4 km south of Jacó* 🖼 *643–1311* ⊕ *www.backyardhotel. com* 🛏 *6 rooms, 2 suites* ⌂ *Bar, fans, in-room safes, minibars, cable TV, pool, massage, bar, laundry service, Internet; no room phones* ▭ *AE, DC, MC, V.*

$$ 🏨 **Hotel Terraza del Pacífico.** Playa Hermosa's largest hotel is self-sufficient and secluded, about 500 meters from the other hotels and businesses. Loud lime-colored, two-story buildings with white verandas surround the large pool with a swim-up bar and a green lawn and beach chairs. Near the beach are a sand volleyball court, a raised tikihut bar, and an open-air restaurant with tables that are probably the closest to the ocean in Hermosa. Rooms have clay-tile floors, balconies,

simple wooden furniture, and original oil paintings from a resident artist who sometimes displays his work by the restaurant. The more spacious superior rooms on the second floor are better kept than the regular standards, with surfboard racks. Suites, which are mostly occupied by time shares, have kitchens and DVD players, a rare luxury. ⊠ *Costanera, at the start of Playa Hermosa, first hotel on right* ☎ 643–3222, 440–6862 for reservations 🖷 643–3424 ⊕ www.terrazadelpacifico. com ↩ 40 rooms, 2 suites ⚷ Restaurant, room service, in-room safes, minibars in some rooms, cable TV, pool, 3 bars, laundry service, some rooms with kitchen, beach, car service, airport shuttle ☰ AE, MC, V.

$ 🏨 **Casa Pura Vida.** Hidden from public view behind tall walls and a large fortress-style wooden door, Casa Pura Vida seems as secretive as Oz. Inside, the extremely intimate and tiny hotel is elegant and secluded enough to please a recluse millionaire—at a working man's rates. The two-story, Spanish-style building has just three apartments, each with two bedrooms and a kitchenette. The second-floor apartment has an ocean view and private balcony; the two downstairs open onto a gravel patio with a small green-tile pool and a kiosk with tables and rocking chairs. The beach is just across a bare lawn with a playground. Perks such as filtered water, a fully equipped communal kitchen by the pool, and attentive owners who live on-site make this a homey place to stay. ⊠ *Costanera, 100 m south of soccer field* ☎☎ 643–2039 ⊕ www.casapuravida.com ↩ 3 apartments ⚷ Fans, in-room safes, kitchenettes, cable TV, pool, massage, playground, laundry service ☰ AE, MC, V ⦿⧵ EP.

♻ ¢–$ 🏨 **Vista Hermosa.** Older and more rustic than other Hermosa hotels, this place facing the beach has rooms that sleep two to eight people. It's behind a shady palm-tree grove on the beach, hard to find in bare Playa Hermosa. Two small budget cabins in a separate building from the rooms share a bathroom. Only some rooms have hot water. The rooms and restaurant surround two pools shaded by large tropical trees. Common areas have hammocks and diversions like foosball and Ping-Pong. ⊠ *Costanera, 150 m south of soccer field* ☎☎ 643–3422 ⊕ www. vistahermosa.20m.com ↩ 12 rooms, 2 cabins with shared bath ⚷ Restaurant, fans, some kitchenettes, cable TV, 2 pools, laundry service; no a/c in some rooms, no room phones ☰ No credit cards ⦿⧵ BP.

To & from Playa Hermosa

5 km/3 mi south of Jacó, 113 km/70 mi southwest of San José.

From Jacó take a taxi or local bus toward Quepos. Some hotels can pick you up from Jacó. On coastal highway, drive 5 km/3 mi past Jacó. You'll see the cluster of businesses on the right.

Playa Hermosa Essentials

🛈 Tourist Information **Restaurante Jammin'** ⊠ In front of Cabinas Las Arenas ☎ 643–1853.

Quepos

⑮ This tourist-rich party town draws visitors with its world-famous sportfishing, laid-back pace, and 24-hour bars. The somewhat seedy gateway to Manuel Antonio is also the area's hub for banks, supermarkets, and other services. Quepos's name stems from the indigenous tribe that inhabited the area until the violence, slavery, and disease that accompanied the Spanish conquest wiped them out. For centuries the town of Quepos barely existed, until the 1930s, when the United Fruit Company built a banana port and populated the area with workers from other parts of Central America. The town thrived for nearly two decades, until Panama disease decimated the banana plantations in the late 1940s. The fruit company then switched to less lucrative African oil palms, and the area declined. Only since the 1980s have tourism revenues lifted the town out of its slump, a renaissance owed to the beauty of the nearby beaches, to Manuel Antonio National Park, whose forests begin just south of town, and to the massive Talamanca Mountain Range, some 10 km (6 mi) to the east, which holds one of the largest expanses of wilderness in Central America. Forests immediately to the north and east of Quepos were destroyed half a century ago, and that landscape is now dominated by oil-palm plantations.

Spread over Fila Chota, a lower ridge of the Talamanca Range 22 km (13 mi) northeast of Quepos, **Rainmaker** is a private nature reserve which protects more than 1,500 acres of lush and precipitous forest. The lower part of the reserve can be visited on guided tours from Manuel Antonio, or as a stop on your way to or from Quepos. Tours ($45; entrance free included) begin at 8:30 and 12:30, and can include lunch. There are two tours available: a walk up the valley of the Río Seco, which includes a dip in a pool at the foot of a waterfall; or a hike into the hills above the waterfall and over a series of suspension bridges strung between giant tropical trees. The better value is a half-day package ($75; entrance fee included) that includes transport from Manuel Antonio or Quepos, a guided tour, a river swim, and breakfast and lunch. The reserve is home to most of the species found in Costa Rica, and you may spot birds here that you won't find in Manuel Antonio. It isn't as good a place to see animals as the national park, but Rainmaker's forest is different from the park's—lusher and more precipitous—and the view from its bridges is impressive. It's best to visit Rainmaker in the morning, since—true to its name—it often rains in the afternoon. ⊠ *15 km/9 mi north and 7 km/4 mi east of Quepos* ☎ *777–3565* ✇ *$65* ⊙ *Mon.–Sat., 8–4.*

Outdoor Activities

Your hotel's reception desk, a tour operator, or travel agency can arrange most activities, but some outfitters give discounts if you book directly through them. **Costa Rica's Temptations** (CRT; ⊠ Downtown, next to Adobe car rental ☎ 777–0607 ⊕ www.costarica4u.com) has various area tours.

For more options in the area, *see* Outdoor Activities *in* Manuel Antonio, *below.*

KAYAKING & RAFTING   **Iguana Tours** (⊠ Downtown Quepos, across from the soccer field ☎ 777–1262 ⊕ www.iguanatours.com) specializes in exploring the area's natural beauty through river-rafting excursions on the Naranjo and Savegre rivers and kayak adventures by sea or in a mangrove estuary.

Quepos & Manuel Antonio

Restaurants ▼

Billy's Beach
Karolas **3**

Café Milagro . . . **4**

El Gran
Escape **1**

Hotel Vela Bar
Reataurant **5**

Mar y Sombra . . **6**

Sunspot
Bar and Grill . . . **2**

Hotels ▼

Cabinas
Arenas **18**

Cabinas
Piscis **10**

Cabinas
Ramase **2**

Cabinas
Ramirez **11**

Costa Verde **8**

Hotel Los
Almendros . . . **15**

Hotel Casitas
Eclipse **7**

Hotel Ceciliano . . **3**

Hotel Inn
on the Park . . **16**

Hotel Malinche . . **1**

Hotel Manuel
Antonio **19**

Hotel Playa
Espadilla **13**

Hotel Sí
Como No **6**

Hotel
Vela Bar **12**

Hotel
Villabosque . . . **14**

El Mango
Moon **5**

La Mariposa . . . **4**

La Posada **17**

Villas
de La Selva **9**

TO SAN JOSÉ ↑   TO AIRPORT ↗

Quepos

SEE INSET

KEY

❶ *Restaurants*

① *Hotels*

Manuel Antonio

Fincas Naturales

Doctor's
Beach

Biesanz
Playa

Punta
Quepos

PACIFIC OCEAN

Playa
Escondida

Playa
Espadilla

Islas Gemelas

Isla
Largo

Playa
Manuel
Antonio

Manuel Antonio National Park

↑
TO ARCO
IRIS

Pali
Supermarket   ②

Bus
Station   Control
Market

El Banco
Bar   Super Mas
Market

Post
Office

Dos Locos
Restaurante   Soccer
Field   Nature
Air Office

③ SANSA
Office

Quepos

CANOPY TOUR The dry season is the best time to glide through the area's rain forests. If you're here during the rains, do a tour first thing in the morning. There are many zip-line tours in the area, but **Canopy Safari** (⊠ Downtown, next to the Poder Judicial ☎ 777–0100 or 777–3079 ⊕ www. canopysafari.com) has a earned a reputation for long and fast-paced rides. Its privately owned forest is about a 45-minute car ride from Quepos, and the tour ($65) includes a meal and swim in a river pool.

HIKING Manuel Antonio National Park is the most popular place to hike, but Rainmaker (⇨ *above*) is more tranquil and lush.

SPORTSFISHING Quepos is one of the best points of departure for deep-sea fishing in southwestern Costa Rica. **Bluefin Tours** (⊠ Downtown, across from the soccer field ☎ 777–2222 or 777–1676 ⊕ www.bluefinsportfishing.com) has catch-and-release sportfishing, conventional, and fly-fishing on half- and full-day charters ($380–$800) aboard 25-, 28-, or 31-foot boats. **Costa Mar Dream Catcher** (⊠ Entrance to Quepos, next to Café Milagro ☎777–0593, 877/435–8068 toll-free in U.S. ⊕www.costamarsportfishing. com) has half- and full-day charters ($450–$1,000) on the largest variety of boats in Quepos; 11 boats range from 25 to 42 feet. Half-, three-quarter-, and full-day catch-and-release fly and conventional trips ($625–$900) with **Luna Tours Sportfishing** (⊠ Downtown, next to Casino Kamuk ☎ 777–0725 ⊕ www.lunatours.net) are available on 27-, 32-, or 33-foot boats.

MOUNTAIN BIKING The area's green mountains are great for biking, but in the dry season, it's hot—very hot. The rainy season is cooler, but be prepared to get muddy. **Cycling Estrella** (⊠Downtown, across the street from Restaurante El Pueblo ☎ 777–1286, 843–6612 ⊕ www.puertoquepos.com/ecotourism/ mountain-biking.html) has bike tours for intermediate and expert riders. One- to five-day trips range from $140 to $520 and include equipment, meals, lodging in mountain cabins, and in the dry season, nighttime rides. Single-day tours ($95) and 2-hour tours ($45) are also available.

Where to Stay & Eat

★ **$–$$** ✕ **El Gran Escape.** A favorite with sportfishermen ("You hook 'em, we cook 'em"), the Great Escape is the best place for seafood in this area. The menu is dominated by marine entrées, from shrimp scampi to the highly recommended fresh tuna with mushrooms, but you can also get hearty burgers and a handful of Mexican dishes. You won't find any cooked billfish, like marlin or swordfish, owing to its conservation policy, but the back wall is covered with pictures of them (and their proud reelers). Weathered fishing caps hang from the bar's ceiling. ⊠ *150 m north of Hotel Kamuk* ☎ *777–0395* ▭ *AE, DC, MC, V* ☻ *Closed Tues.*

$ ▦ **Cabinas Ramase.** Within walking distance of the heart of Quepos, this budget hotel has rooms with fans or air-conditioners. A large Indian almond tree in the center and a talkative caged parrot provide a bit of greenery. Aside from the bars around some of the television sets, the no-frills tile-floor rooms are pleasant enough. ⊠ *Eastern corner of the Palí supermarket* ☎▦ *777–0590* ⇗ *6 rooms* ⚴ *Fans in some rooms, refrigerators, cable TV; no a/c in some rooms, no room phones* ▭ *No credit cards* ❏ *EP.*

¢–$ ⊞ **Hotel Malinche.** The older rooms in the main building of this centrally located hotel are cooled by ceiling fans and have private baths without hot water. For double the price, the concrete annex holds larger, newer rooms with carpeted floors, air-conditioning, cable TV, hot water, and small balconies. ⊠ *½ block west of Quepos bus station* 🕾🕾 *777–0093* ✍ *hotelmalinche@racsa.co.cr* ➷ *24 rooms* ⚭ *Fans, refrigerators in some rooms, laundry service; no a/c in some rooms, no TV in some rooms, no room phones* ⊟ No credit cards ⦶ *EP.*

¢   ⊞ **Hotel Ceciliano.** If you arrive in town late or just want to sleep and go, consider this budget hotel with bare, basic rooms. The more expensive, but still economical, rooms include private bath, hot water, and cable TV. Half-price rooms share cold-water showers. It's a tranquil, simple hotel, with a green courtyard in the middle. ⊠ *Downtown, road to Manuel Antonio, in front of the Escuela Republica de Korea* 🕾 *777–0192* ➷ *24 rooms* ⚭ *Fans in some rooms, cable TV in some rooms; no a/c in some rooms, no room phones* ⊟ No credit cards ⦶ *EP.*

Nightlife

Large, air-conditioned **El Arco Iris** (⊠ Over the last bridge into Quepos 🕾 777–0449) is the only dance club in the area. Quepos locals and Manuel Antonio tourists of all ages pack in after midnight, after warming up in other bars. A DJ spins a mix of salsa, merengue, reggae, and pop. It's open every day, but there's not much activity apart from weekends and holidays.

El Banco Bar (⊠ Downtown Quepos 🕾 777–0478) is a laid-back bar with a pool table frequented by younger North American tourists. Happy hour is every day from 4 to 6 PM. Speakers blare pop/rock from the States. It's closed Wednesday. Older American expats often congregate at Tex-Mex **Dos Locos Restaurante** (⊠ Avda. Central at C. Central, diagonal from the bus station 🕾 777–1526) day and night to people-watch or, on Wednesday and Friday nights, to listen to live music.

To & from Quepos

23 km/14 mi south of Parrita, 174 km/108 mi (3 hrs) southwest of San José.

Buses from San José to Manuel Antonio can drop you off in Quepos. Direct buses leave three times daily; other buses leave six times daily. Buses make the short trip from Quepos to Manuel Antonio every half hour daily from 7 to 7, then hourly until 10 PM. Buses leave Quepos for Dominical (2½-hour trip) fairly frequently. By car from Playa Hermosa, continue south on the coastal highway to Quepos and from there head to Manuel Antonio.

Quepos Essentials

🔳 Bank/ATM **BAC San José** ⊠ Avda. Central. **Banco Nacional** ⊠ 50 m west and 100 m north of bus station.

🔳 Hospital **Ambulance** 🕾 380–4125. **Quepos hospital** ⊠ 4 km on road to Dominical 🕾 777–0922.

🔳 Pharmacy **Farmacia Fischel** ⊠ Near bus station, in front of municipal market 🕾 777–0816.

🔳 Taxis **Taxi services.** 🕾 777–0425, 777–0734, or 777–1068

Manuel Antonio

⑯ You need merely reach the top of the forested ridge on which many of Manuel Antonio's hotels are perched to understand why it is one of Costa Rica's most popular destinations. That sweeping view of beaches, jungle, and shimmering Pacific dotted with rocky islets confirms its reputation. And unlike the tropical forests in other parts of the country, Manuel Antonio's humid tropical forest remains green year-round. The town itself is spread out across a hilly and curving 5-km (3-mi) road that originates in Quepos and dead-ends at the entrance to Manuel Antonio National Park. Along this main road, near the top of the hill or on its southern slope, are the area's most luxurious hotels and fine-dining restaurants, with amazing views of the rain forest, beaches, and offshore islands. The only problem with staying in one of those hotels is that you'll need to drive or take public transportation to and from the main beach and national park, about 10 to 15 minutes away. More hotel and restaurant options are available at the bottom of the hill, within the touristy center, which is lined with Internet cafés, tour operators, and souvenir shops. Nearly the entire ridge is covered with thick foliage.

Manuel Antonio is a very gay-friendly town. Many hotels and bars cater exclusively to foreign gay travelers and Costa Ricans who come on holiday from San José. The area doesn't cater to budget travelers, so backpackers may want to steer clear. While there are inexpensive accommodations, cheap eats are harder to find. Former *sodas* (low-cost Costa Rican eateries) have been turned into full-scale restaurants, and the overpriced central market lacks fresh fruits and vegetables. Hardly any locals live in touristy Manuel Antonio, and those that do work in hotels and restaurants and bus in from Quepos.

As the road approaches the national park, it skirts the lovely, forest-lined beach of **Playa Espadilla,** which stretches for more than a mile north from the rocky crag that marks the park's border to the base of the ridge. One of the most popular beaches in Costa Rica, Playa Espadilla fills up with sunbathers, surfers, volleyball players, strand strollers, and sand-castle architects on dry-season weekends and holidays, but for most of the year it is surprisingly quiet. Even on the busiest days it is long enough so that you can escape the crowd, which tends to gather around the restaurants and lounge chairs near its southern end. Though it is often safe for swimming, beware of rough seas, which create deadly rip currents.

☾ **Fincas Naturales,** a former plantation, has been reforested to allow native trees to spring back and introduced not-so-native trees like teak. A footpath winds through part of the 30-acre tropical forest, and naturalist guides do a good job of ecological instruction and identifying birds. The reserve is home to three kinds of monkeys, as well as iguanas, motmots, toucans, tanagers, and large rodents called agoutis. Guided walks are given throughout the day: the first starts at 6:30 AM for bird-watching, and the last is a nighttime jungle trek that departs at 5:30 PM. Unfortunately, you can't explore the reserve at your own pace; only the Butterfly Botanical Garden can be seen without a guide. ✉ *Entrance across street from Sí Como No Hotel* ☎ *777–0850* ⊕ *www.*

Continued on page 296

MANUEL ANTONIO NATIONAL PARK

Fodor's Choice ★ **GOOD THINGS COME IN SMALL PACKAGES.** Case in point, Costa Rica's smallest park packs in an impressive collection of natural attractions: lots of wildlife, rain forest, white-sand beaches, coral reefs, and rocky coves with abundant marine life. Trails are short, well maintained, and easy to walk. The forest is dominated by massive ficus and gumbo-limbo trees, and is home to two- and three-toed sloths, green and black iguanas, agoutis, four species of monkeys, and nearly 200 species of birds.

FAST FACTS

Size: 7 square km (3 square mi)

Established: 1972

Dry season: December–April

Wettest months: September–October

What to do: Nature hikes, bird-watching, wildlife-watching, kayaking, snorkeling, swimming

Geography: 5 km (3 mi) of coastline; 700 hectares (1,730 acres) of primary, secondary, and mangrove forest; 12 islands

Number of species catalogued: 184 birds, 109 mammals, 60 fish, 4 turtles

- One of two places in Costa Rica to see squirrel monkeys.
- One of two places in Costa Rica to see all four of Costa Rica's monkey species.
- One of the best places in Costa Rica to see three-toed sloths.
- Despite being Costa Rica's smallest national park, this is its second most-visited, after Poás Volcano.

Make no mistake about it: Manuel Antonio is no undiscovered wilderness. It's one of Costa Rica's most-visited attractions, so if you're looking for an undisturbed natural oasis, this is not it. But what Manuel Antonio *does* have is great diversity of wildlife, all easily spotted from the well-marked trails. And because animals are so used to humans, this is one of the best places to see them up close.

ATTRACTIONS

From the ranger station a trail leads through the rain forest behind **Playa Espadilla Sur,** the park's longest beach. It's also the least crowded because the water can be rough. ⚠ Riptides are brutal at Playa Espadilla when the surf is up; more than a few unsuspecting tourists have been swept away. Snorkeling, however, is good in the tidal pools. The coral reefs and submerged volcanic rocks of white-sand **Playa Manuel Antonio** also make for good snorkeling. The 1/2-mile-long beach, tucked into a deep cove, is safe for swimming. At low tide you can see the remains of a Quepos Indian turtle trap on the right—the Quepos stuck poles in the semicircular rock formation, which trapped turtles as the tide receded. Olive ridley and green turtles come ashore on this beach May through November. Espadilla and Manuel Antonio beaches lie on opposite sides of a tombolo, or a sandy strip that connects the mainland to **Punta Catedral** (Cathedral Point), which used to be an island. The steep path that leads up Punta Catedral's rocky hill draped with thick jungle, passes a lookout point from which you can gaze over the Pacific at the park's islands. ⚠ Theft is a problem on the beaches; don't leave your belongings unattended while you swim and don't leave anything of value in your car.

Farther east, **Playa Escondido** (Hidden Beach) is rocky and secluded, but it's also more difficult to access. Before you head out to Escondido, find out when the tides come in so you're not stranded. **Playa Playita**, south of Escondido, is Costa Rica's only nude beach, though unofficially so. It also tends to be a favorite of gay sun-seekers. It's quiet and secluded. Kayaking trips might take you down to **Punta Serrucho** near the southern border of the park, whose jagged peaks explain its name. (*Serrucho* means "saw.")

Trails from the entrance to Punta Catedral and Playa Manuel Antonio are in good shape. Trails farther east to Escondido and Playita are progressively rougher going.

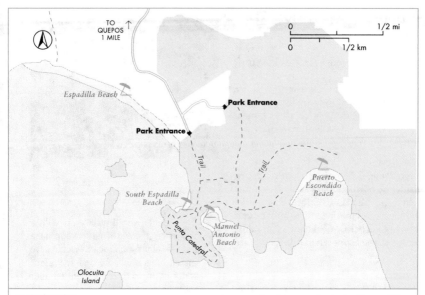

TO QUEPOS 1 MILE

Espadilla Beach

Park Entrance

Park Entrance

Trail

Trail

South Espadilla Beach

Punta Catedral

Manuel Antonio Beach

Puerto Escondido Beach

Olocuita Island

0   1/2 mi
0   1/2 km

Squirrel Monkey

MONKEY BUSINESS

Monkeys are undoubtedly the superstars of Manuel Antonio wildlife. It's nearly impossible to tour the park without seeing at least one species. ⚠ Never feed or touch the monkeys: they have been known to bite overly friendly visitors and they can get sick, or even die from eating improper foods. Some monkeys are kleptomaniacs, so keep your backpack tightly zipped.

The **squirrel monkey** (*mono tití* in Spanish), the world's smallest monkey, is critically endangered, with only 1,200 to 1,500 remaining. Manuel Antonio

is one of only two places in Costa Rica (the Osa Peninsula being the other) and three places in the world inhabited by squirrel monkeys.

Monkeys can't thrive only within the small park's border. To allow them to access areas outside the park, forested corridors have been built connecting the habitats. Suspended bridges allow monkeys to travel above roads around the park. Still, growing infrastructure around the park threatens the monkey population.

A SHAKY START

Before 1972 the land that now constitutes the park had a succession of foreign private owners intent on making a profit from tourism. These owners alienated the local community by cutting off their access to the park and, in the case of the final owner, razing tracts of forest and allegedly dumping pesticides to throw a wrench in the government's plan to create a protected area. The government seized the land shortly thereafter.

ACTIVITIES

KAYAKING

Iguana Tours (☎ 777–1262 ⊕ www.iguanatours.com) runs sea-kayaking trips ($65) to the park's islands—which require some experience when the seas are high—and a mellower paddle through the mangrove estuary of Isla Damas, where you see monkeys, crocodiles and birds.

SNORKELING

Playa Manuel Antonio, the third beach inside the national park, is a good snorkeling spot thanks to calm, clear waters and the varied marine life on and around submerged rocks. Snorkeling is best during the dry season, when tidal pools are clear.

SWIMMING

Manuel Antonio's safest swimming area is sheltered **Playa Manuel Antonio,** whose white sand makes it attractive for lounging while keeping an eye on pint-sized swimmers.

TOP WILDLIFE

Top on our list of animals to see here are:

- howler monkeys
- white-faced capuchin monkeys
- squirrel monkeys
- two- and three-toed sloths
- agoutis
- coatis
- magnificent frigate birds
- olive ridley turtles (May–November)
- green turtles (July–September)

For information on these and other species, *see* the Wildlife & Plant Glossary *in* Understanding Costa Rica, at the back of the book.

Sloth

TIPS

- Hire a guide—you'll walk away with a basic understanding of the flora and fauna and see things you probably would have missed otherwise. Hire one at the entrance of the park or through any tour operator in town.

- Beware of *manzanillo* trees (indicated by warning signs)—their leaves, bark, and applelike fruit secrete a gooey substance that irritates the skin.

- Get here as early as possible—between 7 and 8 AM is ideal. Rangers permit only 600 to 800 people inside at a time, and during peak season visitors line up to enter. Early morning is also the best time to see animals. Avoid weekends and major holidays, particularly around Christmas and the week before Easter, when the park is packed.

- Camping is not allowed in the park, and there are no lodges or food.

- Park beaches do not have lifeguards, but that doesn't mean that swimming is always safe. Riptides are dangerous everywhere except at Manuel Antonio Beach.

- If you want to snorkel, come during the December–April dry season; at other times of the year, heavy rains cloud the water.

A FRAGILE BEAUTY

Deforestation, development, cattle ranching, pollution, and tourism place environmental stress on the park. Tourism brings in enough revenue for the federal government to sustain the park, but the majority of the money goes to fund social programs. The major problems facing Manuel Antonio today are:

- Hotel and resort development that encroaches on natural wildlife corridors and traps animals within the park, diminishing their gene pool and threatening biodiversity

- Endangered squirrel-monkey population

- Solid-waste pollution

- Overwhelming growth that outruns development of infrastructure to handle it

- Lax regulations, corruption of park management, and poor relationship between the park and the municipality

PARK INFO

Hours of Operation: Tuesday–Sunday 7–4. Closed Monday.

Contacts: 777–0654

Admission: $7

Getting There: From San José, 3½ hours by car, 4 hours by bus, or a 30-minute flight to Quepos, then 15 minutes by car. Entrance at the end of the main road from Quepos. Parking is less than $2. ■ TIP→→ The park entrance is across a shallow estuary that is so deep when the tide changes in the early morning and late afternoon that you have to pay a boatman (less than $1) to ferry you across it.

HOW MUCH TIME? A few hours is sufficient to tour the short trails and see some wild animals, but we recommend an entire day that includes lounging on the beaches, and/or hiking the challenging trails toward Puerto Escondido.

butterflygardens.co.cr ✉ *$15–$35, depending on the tour* ☉ *Daily 7 AM–6 PM.*

Outdoor Activities

Manuel Antonio's list of outdoor activities is almost endless. But all this excitement doesn't come cheap, and most tours range between $40 to $60 per person. Arrange tours through your hotel's reception desk or any of the tour operators in town, or contact outfitters directly. During the rainy season some outdoor options might lose their appeal; but clouds usually let loose in the afternoon, so take advantage of the sunny mornings. (⇨ For more activities, *see* Outdoor Activities *in* Quepos, *above.*)

> **IN THE THICK OF IT**
>
> There's more rain forest on private land than in Manuel Antonio National Park, which means it's not unusual to see many of the animals the park is famous for from the balcony of your hotel room or from your breakfast table. It also means that local landowners play an important role in conserving the area's flora and fauna.

TOUR OPERATORS A small company run by friendly young locals with a good grasp of the area's activities, **Espadilla Tours** (☎ 777–5334) can arrange basically any kind of activity in the Quepos/Manuel Antonio area, from surf lessons to sunset sails. The Internet café next to the Marlin Restaurant has information.

CANOPY TOUR **Titi Canopy Tours** (☎ 777–1020 or 777–1646 [reservations] ⊕ www.
★ titicanopytours.com) has a slower-paced zip-line tour ($55) than the one at Canopy Safari (⇨ Quepos, *above*), which gives you a better chance to spot animals and take in the scenery. It's also closer to Manuel Antonio. Guides go above and beyond to make you feel comfortable and safe.

HIKING Highly visited Manuel Antonio National Park is the obvious place to go, but in private reserves like Fincas Naturales (⇨ *above*) and Rainmaker (⇨ Quepos, *above*) you can do more solitary hikes, gaining a richer appreciation of the local forests' greenery and wildlife. ■ TIP→ **Bring binoculars!**

HORSEBACK **Brisas del Nara** (☎ 779–1235 ⊕ www.horsebacktour.com) takes riders
RIDING of all ages and levels through the protected Cerro Nara mountain zone, 10 mi from Manuel Antonio, and ends at a 350-foot waterfall within its property. Full-day tours include three hours on horseback, although the half-day tour lasts two hours on easier terrain. All tours include a meal. **Finca Valmy Tours** (☎ 779–1118 ⊕ www.valmytours.com) is known for its attentive service and expert guides. Its half-day (six-hour) horseback tours take you through the forested mountains above Villa Nueva, east of Manuel Antonio. Lunch and swimming in a pool below a waterfall are included.

Beach riding is the specialty of **Rancho Savegre** (☎ 779–4430 or 834–8687). Run by two cowboy hat–wearing brothers, trips set out from a cattle ranch about 15 minutes south of Manuel Antonio and include a stop at a waterfall for swimming or trail walking. Of the two half-day tours, only the morning tour includes a meal.

KAYAKING **Iguana Tours** (☎ 777–1262 ⊕ www.iguanatours.com) runs sea-kayaking trips ($65) to the islands of Manuel Antonio National Park—which require some experience when the seas are high—and a mellower paddle through the mangrove estuary of Isla Damas, where you might see monkeys, crocodiles, and various birds.

SNORKELING Multiple tour operators in town can put you on an organized snorkel excursion. Or for a more personalized and inexpensive experience, hire one of the locals waiting to take visitors on a short boat ride to the best snorkel spots. They're usually hanging out along Playas Espadilla and Biesanz. **Playa Biesanz,** near the Hotel Parador and ½ km (¼ mi) south of Makanda by the Sea, is in a protected cove full of rocks that provide habitat for marine life and calm swimming. **Playa Manuel Antonio,** the third beach inside the national park, is a good snorkeling spot thanks to calm, clear waters and the varied marine life on and around submerged rocks.

SWIMMING When the surf is up, riptides are a dangerous problem on long Playa Espadilla (⇨ *above*), Manuel Antonio's main beach, which runs parallel to the road to the park's entrance. For a less turbulent swim and smaller crowds, head to **Playa Biesanz** (⊠ Near Hotel Parador), which lies within a sheltered cove and also makes for great snorkeling. Manuel Antonio's safest swimming area is sheltered **Playa Manuel Antonio,** which lies within the national park. Its white sand makes it attractive for lounging around, and it's also good place for snorkeling. ⚠ **Never leave your valuables unattended while you're swimming.**

ULTRALIGHT **Sky Riders** (☎ 777–4101) has open-cockpit, slow-flying ultralights that
FLIGHTS & glide between sea level and 1,000 feet. One tour is a one-passenger, 24-
PARASAILING minute ride over Manuel Antonio and several surrounding beaches ($72). The other is a two-person 35-minute flight over Damas Island's canals and mangroves ($105).

WHITE-WATER The three white-water rivers in this area have limited seasons. The rains
RAFTING from August to October raise the rivers to their perfect peak. **Río Savegre,** which flows past patches of rain forest, has two navigable stretches: the lower section (Class II–III), which is a mellow trip perfect for neophytes, and the more rambunctious upper section (Class III–IV). It is usually navigable from June to March. **Río Naranjo** (Class III–IV) has a short but exciting run that requires some experience and can be done only from June to December. **Río Parrita** (Class II–III) is a relatively mellow white-water route, and in the dry season it can be navigated only in two-person, inflatable duckies.

Manuel Antonio's original rafting outfitter, **Amigos del Río** (☎ 777–1084 ⊕ www.adventuremanuelantonio.com), leads trips down the Savegre and Naranjo on two-day, full-day, and half-day tours. Naranjo River tours can be combined with kayaking in the nearby estuary. **Rios Tropicales** (☎ 777–4092 ⊕ www.aventurash2o.com), the biggest rafting outfitter in the country, runs kayaking excursions and rafting trips on the Savegre and Naranjo.

Getting Married in Costa Rica

COUPLES LONG AGO DISCOVERED that Costa Rica's rain forests, volcanoes, beaches, and sunsets make the country a prime honeymoon destination. A growing number are deciding to start that honeymoon early and tie the knot here as well.

First the marriage legalities:

• Any two people of the opposite sex at least 18 years old may marry in Costa Rica.

• Your passport must have at least six months' remaining validity.

• Your witnesses, who may not be your relatives, must meet the same requirements.

• You need to demonstrate that any former marriage is no longer in effect by providing a copy of a divorce decree or death certificate of a prior spouse; a Costa Rican consulate in the country where those documents were issued must translate them into Spanish and notarize them.

• A woman must wait at least 10 months after the end of a previous marriage or provide a medical statement attesting to not being pregnant (presumably with her ex-husband's child); a man has no waiting period.

Judges, attorneys, and Catholic priests have legal authority to certify a marriage in Costa Rica. While the law provides for complete freedom of religion, it grants the Catholic Church special "state church" status, meaning that if you have an official other than a Catholic priest preside over your service, a lawyer or judge will have to make it legal, either at the ceremony or at his or her office later. The priest (in a Catholic ceremony), a lawyer, or a judge will register the marriage with the Civil Registry and your own embassy. The license takes three months to issue and is sent to your home address. Virtually all Western countries recognize the legality of a Costa Rican marriage.

While the country offers no shortage of impressive backdrops for a ceremony, the Central Pacific coast sees the most tourist weddings, hands down. (May and June are the most popular months.) Manuel Antonio's Makanda by the Sea, La Mariposa, and Sí Como No and Punta Leona's Villa Caletas are among the many lodgings here with events staffs well versed in planning ceremonies and tending to the legalities. You need only say, "I do." Private wedding planner **Tropical Occasions** (☎ 249-0773 ⊕ www.tropicaloccasions.com) comes highly recommended and has over 450 weddings under its belt. It also has arranged a few same-sex commitment ceremonies, although Costa Rican law does not recognize these as legally binding.

Where to Stay & Eat

★ $$ ✕ **Billy's Beach Karolas.** Off the main road and tucked in the forest just below Barba Roja, plastic chairs and tables with candles are arranged under several covered and uncovered patio areas. The food is tasty, but some argue that it's overpriced. The tranquil setting makes up for the lack of ocean view. The most popular dishes are fresh tuna, shrimp, or the "Plato Gordo," a mix of local seafood for two. Tenderloin, ribs, and Caribbean chicken are also top-notch, as are the desserts—leave room for a slice of macadamia pie. ✉ *Down steep driveway south of Barba Roja* ☎ *777–5067* ▭ *AE, MC, V.*

★ **$–$$** ✕ **Hotel Vela Bar Restaurant.** This small open-air, roadside restaurant retains an intimate atmosphere behind a minijungle of tropical foliage. Beneath a conical thatched roof it serves a variety of dishes in generous proportions, including shrimp in ginger, pork chops in pineapple sauce, vegetarian options, and nightly specials. Service can be slow when the place fills up. ✉ *Up road from Marlin Restaurant, on left* ☎ *777–0413* ▭ *AE, DC, MC, V* ☺ *Breakfast served.*

$–$$ ✕ **Sunspot Bar and Grill.** The open-air, poolside restaurant of the exclusive Makanda by the Sea hotel has tables beneath purple cloth tents, which overlook the sea and surrounding trees. Its kitchen is cleverly hidden beneath and serves up such succulent treats as jumbo shrimp in a ginger sauce and grilled beef tenderloin with different sauces. The menu also includes poultry and pasta dishes, along with nightly specials that sometimes list tender New Zealand lamb. ✉ *Makanda by the Sea hotel, 1 km/½ mi west of La Mariposa* ☎ *777–0442* ▭ *V* ⚲ *Reservations essential.*

¢–$$ ✕ **Mar y Sombra.** You haven't been to Manuel Antonio unless you've contemplated the sea from one of the circular concrete tables in the sand at Mar y Sombra, one of the area's first enterprises popular with nationals and internationals alike. The food may not win any awards, but it's hard to top the view of Playa Espadilla and the island-studded sea and the decor, a roof of Indian almond trees and thick lianas draped with moss, ferns, and orchids. Try a typical *gallo pinto* at breakfast or *casado* for lunch, but the best bet is the fresh dorado and other seafood. Even if you don't eat, have a drink here, preferably at sunset. ✉ *Across from Cabinas Ramirez, on Playa Espadilla* ☎ *777–0003* ▭ *AE, MC, V* ☺ *Breakfast served.*

¢ ✕ **Café Milagro.** The only place in town that serves its own fresh-roasted coffee, Café Milagro is a colorful, cozy place for breakfast food any time of the day, or to satisfy a chocolate-chip-cookie craving. The North American menu includes bagels, breakfast burritos, baked goods like brownies and muffins, an inventive selection of sandwiches, and a fruit plate with granola. Tables on the front porch overlook the road, but there's also seating in the back garden. **El Patio,** an affiliated gourmet Latin bistro in Quepos, is worth the drive for dinner (Monday–Saturday only). ✉ *Main road to the park, across from Karolas, on the left* ☎ *777–0794* ▭ *AE, DC, MC, V* ☺ *Breakfast served.*

★ **¢–$$** ✕▭ **Hotel Vela Bar.** Abutting the jungle a mere 100 meters up a dirt road from Playa Espadilla, this low-key eclectic hotel has rooms of varying size and amenities at competitive rates. Though small, each room has its own rustic charm, with simple wooden furniture, terracotta tile or wooden floors, and minimal decor. For two, white-walled Room 7 is particularly charming, with large windows and a bathtub. Balconies and terraces with rocking chairs and hammocks overlook the tall, lush gardens. The casita, with a private patio, air-conditioning, and TV, sleeps four. The restaurant (⇨ *above*) is excellent. ✉ *Up road from Marlin Restaurant, on left* ☎ *777–0413* 🖷 *777–1071* ⊕ *www.velabar.com* 🛏 *10 rooms, 1 casita* ♿ *Restaurant, fans, some in-room safes, some kitchenettes, some refrigerators, cable TV in some* *rooms, bar, laundry service, Internet; no a/c in some rooms, no room phones* ▭ *AE, DC, MC, V.*

★
☾ $$$–$$$$ ▣ **Hotel Sí Como No.** As is evident from the partial solar power, energy-efficient air-conditioning, and plantation wood, Sí Como No makes an effort to be eco-friendly and is a level-four member of the Certificate of Sustainable Tourism. (Level five is the highest.) Family-friendly is a another adjective that could be used to describe this place. Rooms of varying sizes (and prices) are in two-story concrete buildings. Request a room away from the road, and spring for a deluxe room for a sea view. Two pools—one for adults only—have cascades, swim-up bars, and adjacent restaurants. A free shuttle heads frequently to the beach, about 2 mi away, and movies are shown nightly. Concrete painted to resemble bamboo and palm trees evokes Disneyland, but the forest and ocean views are 100 percent Costa Rica. ✉ *Road to park, just after of Villas Nicolás, right-hand side* ☎ *777–0777* 🖷 *777–1093* ⊕ *www.sicomono.com* 🗪 *60 rooms, 4 honeymoon suites* ♨ *2 restaurants, fans, in-room safes, some kitchenettes, minibars, 2 pools, 2 whirlpool tubs, spa, 2 bars, shop, laundry service, Internet; no room TVs* ▭ *AE, MC, V* ⦿ *BP.*

$$$–$$$$
Fodor's Choice
★ ▣ **La Mariposa.** The best view in town—a sweeping panorama of verdant hills, the aquamarine Pacific, and offshore islands—is Mariposa's claim to fame. Accommodations range from standard rooms overlooking the rain forest to bright suites with ocean-view balconies to a comfortable master suite to a penthouse. All are spacious, with hand-carved furniture and large baths, and are located in a series of buildings between the jungle and gardens ablaze with colorful flowers. The white four-story main building with external spiraling stairways on both sides holds the lobby, restaurant, pools, and suites, which have semiprivate balconies. Transportation is provided to the beach, about 2½ mi away. ✉ *Road to park, 100 m past Café Milagro, on the right* ⊕ *www. hotelmariposa.com* ☎ *777–0355, 800/572–6440 in U.S.* 🖷 *777–0050* 🗪 *60 rooms* ♨ *Restaurant, room service, in-room safes, some kitchenettes, 3 pools, 2 bars, shop, laundry service, concierge, Internet, in-room broadband; no room TVs* ▭ *AE, DC, MC, V* ⦿ *EP.*

★ $$–$$$ ▣ **Costa Verde.** You're likely to see monkeys, iguanas, and all kinds of birds on the forest trails surrounding this extensive hotel's buildings, which are scattered on both sides of the main road, about 800 meters from the beach. Adult-only studios are spacious, with large balconies and screened walls that let the breeze through. Those in the other buildings are smaller, but can be closed and air-conditioned. Splurge for a Studio-Plus, which means it has an ocean view. Three fully equipped bungalows are also available for groups of six or less. The cheaper, standard rooms are a mixed lot—only those in Building D, in the jungle overlooking the sea, are recommended. Transportation vestiges, like a plane from 1954, stand curiously next to two of the hotel's restaurants, and its reception and Internet café are inside antique train wagons. ✉ *Road to park, at Km 6* ☎ *777–0584, 777–0187, 1–866/854–7958* 🖷 *777–0560* ⊕ *www. costaverde.com* 🗪 *3 rooms, 36 studios, 3 bungalows* ♨ *3 restaurants, fans, kitchenettes, cable TV, 3 pools, 4 bars, laundry service, Internet; no a/c in some rooms, no room phones* ▭ *AE, MC, V* ⦿ *EP.*

★ $$–$$$ ▣ **Hotel Casitas Eclipse.** Perched on a hilltop about half a mile from the beach, this hotel with its Mediterranean-style architecture gives you the impression you're in the Greek Isles, until you spot the exuberant tropical forest below. The spacious two-story, white casitas with clay-tile roofs can be rented out entirely to include two separate bedroom areas and a kitchen, or by floors. Though the dull interior decor falls far behind the exterior, the casitas are comfortable, luminous, and ideal for groups. The balconies of the bottom casitas are closest to the jungle. The charmless standard rooms in the hotel section are worth skipping. ⊠ *Road to park, at Km 5, in front of El Avión restaurant* ☎ *770–0408* 🖷 *777–1738* ⊕ *www.casitaseclipse.com* ➘ *10 casitas, 13 rooms* ⌂ *Restaurant, fans, in-room safes, kitchenettes, refrigerators, cable TV, 3 pools, fitness room, massage, 2 bars, laundry service, no-smoking rooms* ▭ *AE, MC, V* ⏎❘ *BP.*

★ **\$\$–\$\$\$** ▥ **El Mango Moon.** This B&B's intimate atmosphere and hospitable owners make you feel like you're with a friend rather than at a hotel. The comfy, open living-room area extends to a balcony lined with a wooden counter and stools with views to the mango-shaped pool below and a tranquil cove dotted with boats. The cream-color rooms vary in size and amenities; some have private or semiprivate balconies. Rooms on the top floor can connect for families and functions. Monkey-attracting mango trees surround the building, and a 15-minute trail leads to a secluded beach. Plush bathrobes and fine chocolates are among the hotel's personal touches. ⊠ *Between La Mariposa and Hotel El Parador, on the right if coming from La Mariposa* ☎ *777–5323* 🖷 *777–5128* ⊕ *www.mangomoon.net* ➘ *7 rooms, 5 suites* ⌂ *Fans, some kitchens, some refrigerators, cable TV, pool, massage, Internet, no-smoking rooms; no room phones, no kids under 12* ▭ *V* ⏎❘ *BP.*

★ **\$\$–\$\$\$** ▥ **Villas de la Selva.** Hidden from the main road behind a mural of monkeys, almost as if to keep this place a secret, lies this unique, tiny hillside hotel with comfortable accommodations and great views of the Pacific. Straight down the long stairway, and perched on a cliff facing the ocean, stand three charming and airy rooms, each with its own colorful decor, kitchenette, and ample terrace. There's also a casita that fits several people. Up the side of the hill, two much smaller rooms have reduced balconies with great views and local artisanal decor, but small bathrooms. A 300-meter trail leads to the beach. ⊠ *Road to park, on right (coming from Quepos) after Costa Verde and La Arboleda hotels* ☎ *777–1137* 🖷 *777–0434* ⊕ *www.villasdelaselva.com* ➘ *7 rooms, 1 casita* ⌂ *Some fans, cable TV, Internet, some in-room safes, some kitchenettes, pool, laundry service; no a/c in some rooms, no room phones* ▭ *MC, V* ⏎❘ *EP.*

★ ♺ **\$\$** ▥ **Hotel Inn on the Park.** This family-friendly inn has a quiet central location, personalized service, and spacious rooms. From the outside it looks like an apartment building, and has three floors with two rooms each. Half are larger master suites, which have a separate bedroom and sizable kitchen. Upper rooms in the papaya-colored building share balconies. A small pool area with a wooden deck has a grill, and the gregarious English owner, who lives next door, is very attentive. The hotel has Boogie-board and surfboard rentals. ⊠ *Up the road to the right of the Marlin Restaurant, turn right at Hotel Villabosque, on the left* ☎ *777–5115 or 777–5232* 🖷 *777–3468* ⊕ *www.innontheparkhotel. com* ➘ *6 rooms* ⌂ *Fans, in-room safes, some kitchens, cable TV, pool, laundry service, no-smoking rooms* ❘ *BP.*

⏱ **$$** ▦ **Hotel Playa Espadilla.** Close to the beach and park, this friendly hotel spreads back across rectangular grounds, bordered on two sides by the tall trees of its private reserve, with a trail. The simple but spacious mint-green rooms with big windows are housed in two-story concrete buildings surrounded by green lawns; for a bit more, some rooms have good-sized kitchens with modern appliances. A small blue-tile pool and patio area have a pleasant adjacent bar area with a billiard table. Directly behind is a large, open-air restaurant with elegant table settings, followed by a tennis court. ⊠ *End of dirt road, to the right of Marlin Restaurant* 📠 *777–2135* ⊕*www.espadilla.com* ⇲ *16 rooms* ↺ *Restaurant, snack bar, room service, some fans, in-room safes, some kitchenettes, cable TV, tennis court, pool, bar, laundry service, in-room data ports* ▭ *AE, DC, MC, V* ⍟ *BP.*

★ **$$** ▦ **Hotel Villabosque.** In "downtown" Manuel Antonio, this cramped, overbuilt hotel has pleasant rooms with wooden furniture, soft-colored walls, and one small painting each. Most are in a two-story motel-style building facing the gravel parking lot out front; others open onto a communal TV area and have less natural light. Rooms above the restaurant are smaller, but have private balconies with a table and chairs. (Room 11 has the best forest view.) A peaceful river runs behind the hotel amid tall trees and intertwined lianas (corner Room 18 is the closest), but unfortunately it's mostly hidden behind the construction. The shadeless pool is raised above the reception area. ⊠ *From the Marlin Restaurant, 200 m east, end of the rd.* 📞 *777–0463* 📠 *777–0401* ✉ *hotelvilla-bosque@racsa.co.cr* ⇲ *17 rooms* ↺ *Restaurant, in-room safes, cable TV, pool, massage, bar, laundry service; no room phones* ▭ *AE, DC, MC, V* ⍟ *CP.*

$$ ▦ **La Posada.** Nestled on the edge of the national park, this small group
Fodor'sChoice of bungalows is a rare gem within Manuel Antonio, and only a short
★ walk from the beach. Each bungalow has its own theme—Fisherman, Birds of Paradise, and Jungle are a few—and is decorated accordingly. The palm-thatched covered terraces face the small pool and lush greenery of the rain forest next door. As the charming North American owner who lives on-site says, it's as close as you'll get to sleeping in the park. ⊠ *Next to the park's exit* 📠 *777–1446* ⊕ *www.laposadajungle.com* ⇲ *4 bungalows, 2 apartments* ↺ *Fans, microwaves, refrigerators, pool, lunch (pizza), whirlpool tub, laundry service, no-smoking rooms; no room phones* ▭ *MC, V* ⍟ *BP.*

★ **¢–$** ▦ **Cabinas Arenas.** On a quiet street next to the park's exit, this tiny hotel rents three basic but comfortable rooms only a few minutes from the beach. Two have a double bed and one single; the third contains two doubles. Directly next to it stands an Italian eatery and souvenir shop with park-themed items. ⊠ *Next to the park's exit* 📞 *777–5113* ⇲ *3 rooms* ↺ *Fans, microwaves, refrigerators; no room phones* ▭ *No credit cards* ⍟ *EP.*

¢–$ ▦ **Cabinas Piscis.** Shaded by tall trees a short walk through the woods from the beach, this older, tranquil hotel is one of the area's best deals. Most rooms are in a concrete building with a wide porch; they are simple but spacious, with small bathrooms and lots of windows. The tiny, lower-price rooms that share a separate, cold-water bathhouse are geared toward backpackers. Also available is a separate cabin with a refrigerator and an open-room, fully equipped *casita* for four. A small restaurant serves breakfast and light lunches. Bathrooms do not have hot water. ⊠ *Road to park, right after Hotel Karahe, on right* 📠 777–0046 or 777–5320 ✐ *vivipisc@racsa.co.cr* 🖙 *15 rooms, 9 with bath; 1 casita; 1 cabin* ৬ *Restaurant, fans, laundry service; no a/c, no room phones, no room TVs* ⊟ *MC, V* ⦿Ⅰ *EP.*

★ ¢–$ 🏨 **Hotel Los Almendros.** On a large, palm-filled lot, these budget rooms are within walking distance of Manuel Antonio's main attractions, are well kept, and are a good deal for the price. But light sleepers keep away; the on-site Argentinian grill has live music every night until about 11 PM. Choose from air-conditioned or economical fan-ventilated rooms. Bathrooms are small, and front porches with plastic chairs face the large tiled pool. The restaurant serves all three meals. ⊠ *From the Marlin Restaurant, 300 m west* 📠 777–0225 🖙 *21 rooms* ৬ *Some fans, pool, bar, Internet; no a/c in some rooms, no room phones, no room TVs* ⊟ *No credit cards* ⦿Ⅰ *EP.*

★ ¢–$ 🏨 **Hotel Manuel Antonio.** One of Manuel Antonio's original hotels, this economical place has the closest beds you'll find to the park's entrance and is across the street from the beach. Choose from rustic rooms above an open-air restaurant, which are a good option for budget travelers, or larger, newer rooms in a two-story yellow concrete building next door, with cable TVs and air-conditioning. The new rooms have simple pastel drapes and bedspreads and large balconies; be sure to get one with an ocean view, preferably on the second floor. ⊠ *End of the road to the park, across from beach* ☎ 777–1237 or 777–1351 📠 777–5172 ✐ *hotelmanuelantonio@racsa.co.cr* 🖙 *29 rooms* ৬ *Restaurant, room service, fans in some rooms, in-room safes, some cable TV, massage, bar, laundry service, Internet, no-smoking floors; no a/c in some rooms* ⊟ *AE, MC, V* ⦿Ⅰ *EP.*

★ ¢ 🏨 **Cabinas Ramirez.** Manuel Antonio's first cabinas, owned by the same family as owns Mar y Sombra, Ramirez retains its cheap and simple accommodations that sleep up to 12 people, only 50 meters from the beach. Some have kitchenettes, but a communal kitchen is also available. Not all private baths have hot water. Rooms and their front terraces face the parking lot or garden areas. Campers can pitch their tents in a palm-shaded area. ⊠ *Road to the park, to the right of the entrance to "downtown" Manuel Antonio* ☎ 777–5044 🖙 *22 rooms* ৬ *Fans, some kitchenettes, laundry service; no a/c, no room phones, no room TVs* ⊟ *No credit cards* ⦿Ⅰ *EP.*

Nightlife

BARS **Barba Roja** (⊠ Road to park, in front of Hotel Divisamar ☎ 777–0331)
★ has a popular sunset happy hour. It's primarily a restaurant, but the bar sometimes stays busy until 10 or 11. Try its famous nachos. The **Billfish Bar** (⊠ Byblos Hotel, across from Barba Roja ☎ 777–0411) fills up on game nights for its large-screen TVs and pool tables. The casino next door is the only one in Manuel Antonio. **Bambu Jam** (⊠ Road to park, ½ mi from Quepos ☎ 777–3369), an open-air French-and-tropical-fusion restaurant, has live music on Fridays in a variety of styles.

DANCE CLUB **Cockatoo** (⊠ 200 m north of Barba Roja, above La Hacienda Restaurant ☎ No phone) plays danceable music in a Spanish-style building. It has a gay bar on the second floor. **Mar y Sombra** (⊠ Next to Cabinas Ramirez ☎ 777–0003), the most popular restaurant on the beach, becomes an open-air dance party Thursday through Saturday after 10:30. Saturday is the busiest night, when the locals come in from Quepos.

Shopping

There's no shortage of shopping in this town. Near the entrance to the park vendors in kiosks sell T-shirts and Indonesian fabrics. More authentic handicrafts, like seed jewelry, are sold at night by artisans positioned along the sidewalk in central Manuel Antonio. Plenty of souvenir shops across the main road sell typical Costa Rican crafts, similar to those you'd find anywhere else in the country. Quepos (⇨ *above*) has a handful of tasteful gift shops worth exploring.

(⇨ *above*)

HIGH-WIRE ACTS

Though the construction of hotels and other buildings has altered the natural landscape, the surrounding forest has largely been left intact. The greatest danger most animals face is the traffic that flows between Quepos and Manuel Antonio, which is why local conservationists have strung ropes over the road between large trees, so that monkeys can cross the street without risking their simian necks. Conservation group **ASCOMOTI** (⊕ www.ascomoti.org) is working with local landowners to preserve forest corridors for the monkeys between remaining islands of wilderness.

La Buena Nota (⊠ Road to park, on right after Hotel Karahe ☎ 777–1002) has an extensive selection of beachwear, souvenirs, sunscreen, hats, postcards, international newspapers, Costa Rican CDs, and magazines. The second floor has English-language used books and a café. The friendly owner, one of the first North Americans to settle in Manuel Antonio, relates historical anecdotes about the area. **Regalame** (⊠ Next to Sí Como No Hotel ☎ 777–0777) is primarily an art gallery, with paintings, drawings, pottery, and jewelry by dozens of artists, but it also sells wood handicrafts and other souvenirs.

To & from Manuel Antonio

3 km/2 mi south of Quepos, 179 km/111 mi (3½ hrs) southwest of San José.

Buses from San José leave for Manuel Antonio (via Quepos) nine times daily; three buses are direct. When leaving Manuel Antonio, head to the bus terminal in Quepos, which has service to San José. Buses make the short trip from Quepos to Manuel Antonio every half hour daily from 7 to 7, then hourly until 10 PM. Buses leave Quepos for Dominical (2½-hour trip) fairly frequently. By car, once you cross the Quepos Bridge, the road swings inland several kilometers through forested hills until you reach downtown Manuel Antonio. To get to Dominical, return to the coastal highway and head straight south.

Manuel Antonio Essentials

🏦 Bank/ATM **Banca Proamerica** ⊠ Next to Economy Rent A Car.
💊 Pharmacy **Farmacia Manuel Antonio** ⊠ Across from Marlin Restaurant ☎ 777–5370.
🚕 Taxis **Taxi services** ☎ 777–0425, 777–0734, or 777–1068.

CENTRAL PACIFIC ESSENTIALS

Transportation

BY AIR

ARRIVING & DEPARTING The 30-minute flight between San José and Quepos can save you the 3½-hour drive or bus trip, which involves a steep mountain road. Flights from San José get you to Tambor in a fraction of the time it takes to drive to Puntarenas and ferry over. For more information about bus travel between the Central Pacific and San José, *see* Air Travel *in* Smart Travel Tips A to Z.

BY BUS

ARRIVING & DEPARTING Buses are very inexpensive and easy to use. From San José to Puntarenas you'll pay about $2. Buses to Manuel Antonio vary; the faster and slightly fancier direct ones cost about $4; a "collective" that makes several stops costs about $3. All buses heading toward San José that pass through Alajuela can drop you off at the airport, but you need to ask the driver when you board, and then remind him again as you draw near the stop. For more information about bus travel between the Central Pacific and San José, *see* Bus Travel *in* Smart Travel Tips A to Z.

GETTING AROUND The buses are run-down and the ride might wrack your nerves, especially as they slowly rattle up the hills (sometimes reversing to gain more momentum), but don't sweat it. You'll make it. Not every town has direct buses, so you may have to hop on a connecting bus to get to some destinations. Ask any local or your hotel's reception where the oftentimes unmarked bus stop is located and for departure times. Before handing a bill over to the bus driver, ask how much the fare costs to ensure you get the proper change.

BY CAR

ARRIVING & DEPARTING The quickest way to get to this region from San José is to take the Pan-American Highway (CA1) west to the exit for Atenas, where you turn left (south). Once you leave the highway, the road is one lane in each direction for the rest of the route, and between Atenas and Orotina it is steep and full of curves. If you don't have experience in mountain driving, you're better off taking a bus, shuttle van, or flight to the coast. The coastal highway, or Costanera, heads southeast from Orotina to Tárcoles, Jacó, Hermosa, and Quepos. It is well marked and, except for a few stretches near bridges, well paved. An asphalt road winds its way over the hill between Quepos and Manuel Antonio National Park.

From San José the best way to get to the southern tip of Nicoya is to drive to Puntarenas, and from there board your car on the ferry bound for Paquera. Take the road to Cóbano, which passes Tambor. From Cóbano the road south to Cabuya branches out to Montezuma and Malpaís.

GETTING AROUND It's best to stick with the main rental offices in San José, because they have more cars available and you're more likely to reach an English-speaking agent on the phone; some have local satellite offices. Montezuma

Expeditions coordinates the delivery of rental cars from major agencies in Liberia.

⚑ Major Rental Agencies **Alamo** ⊠ Downtown, 50 m south of Korean school, Quepos ☎ 777-3344, 800/462-5266 in U.S. ⊕ www.alamo.com. **Budget** ⊠ Avda. Pastor Diaz, Jacó ☎ 643-2665 ⊕ www.budget.com. **Economy** ⊠ Avda. Pastor Diaz, Jacó ☎ 643-1098 ⊠ Next to Banca Proamerica, Manuel Antonio ☎ 777-5353 ⊕ www.economycarrental.com. **National** ⊠ Avda. Pastor Diaz, Jacó ☎ 643-1752 ⊕ www.nationalcar.com.

⚑ Local Rental Resources **Elegante/Payless** ⊠ Avda. Pastor Diaz, Jacó ☎ 643-3224 Jacó, 777-0115 Quepos ⊠ 75 m east of Catholic church, Quepos ☎ 777-0115. **Montezuma Expeditions** ⊠ Main road, near El Sano Banano restaurant, Montezuma ☎ 440-8078 ⊕ www.montezumaexpeditions.com.

BY SHUTTLE VAN

ARRIVING & DEPARTING A more comfortable, air-conditioned, and quicker alternative to regular bus service to Montezuma, Tambor, Paquera, Puntarenas, Punta Leona, Playa Herradura, Jacó, Manuel Antonio, and some destinations in between is the hotel-to-hotel shuttle service offered by Interbus. Another luxury bus service, Gray Line Tourist Bus, has service to Jacó and Manuel Antonio. Prices on Interbus range from $17 to $38, depending on the distance from San José. Gray Line is $21 to Jacó and $25 to Manuel Antonio. You can request that vans to Jacó drop you off at Carara Biological Reserve. Vans to Manuel Antonio can drop you off in front of Playa Hermosa's hotels.

⚑ Shuttle Van Services **Gray Line Tourist Bus** ☎ 232-3681 or 220-2126 ⊕ www.graylinecostarica.com. **Interbus** ☎ 283-5573 ⊕ www.interbusonline.com.

Contacts & Resources

Banks and emergency contacts are listed at the end of each town entry.

BANKS & EXCHANGING SERVICES

There are various ATMs in Jacó, Puntarenas, Atenas, and Quepos that accept either Visa or MasterCard, or both. Ask the receptionist at your hotel where the nearest one is. In the unlikely event that you come upon an ATM that's out of order, you should be able to find another one nearby. Malpaís and Montezuma also have ATMs. Banks in Jacó, Puntarenas, Herradura, Cóbano, Atenas, Manuel Antonio, and Quepos exchange U.S. dollars, though it's quicker to get Costa Rican currency from an ATM, when available. Most hotels, restaurants, tour operators, taxi drivers, gift shops, and supermarkets will accept or change U.S. dollars, though at slightly less than the bank rate. Canadian, Australian, and New Zealand dollars and English pounds must be exchanged in banks.

South Pacific

Matapalo Beach

WORD OF MOUTH

"Everything that everyone talks about being great and wonderful about Costa Rica is in the Osa! . . . It is hot and humid but you can't beat the beaches or the rain forest."

—coryandcarissa

"There are some great things to be said about the [Golfo Dulce] area. Hardly any tourism, which means long stretches of beach with no tourists. Great fishing, horseback riding, swimming, and surfing."

—Ally

www.fodors.com/forums

WELCOME TO THE SOUTH PACIFIC

Howler monkeys, Corcovado National Park

TOP 5
Reasons to Go

1. **Enormous Corcovado National Park** is the last refuge of endangered species like jaguars and squirrel monkeys.

2. **Mountain hikes** range from easy daytime treks from luxurious lodges to Costa Rica's toughest: 12,500-foot Cerro Chirripó.

3. **Kayaking** the Golfo Dulce or along the Sierpe or Colorado rivers' jungly channels.

4. **Bird-watching** yields beauties like scarlet macaws and the resplendent quetzal.

5. **Wild places to stay** include top ecolodges, platform tents on the beach, and mountain retreats.

The main road climbs more than 7,000 feet over mountains and above the clouds of the Central Highlands before descending into the huge Valle de El General agricultural region. Highlights are fabulous mountain lodges and Chirripó National Park.

The Coast consists of miles of beaches and small beach communities, including unassuming surfer town Dominical.

Cerro de la Muerte

Cerro Chirripó/Chirripó National Park

San Isidro

SAN JOSÉ

C2

Juntas

Dominical

VALLE DE EL GE

244

Ballena National Park

34

Palmar Norte

Rincón

San Pedrillo

Corcovado National Park

Sirena

Pacific

The wild Osa Peninsul consists almost enirel of Corcovado Nationa Park, 445 square mile of primary and secon ary rain forest straigh out of a Tarzan film.

Iguana-crossing road sign, Dominical   Cerro de la Muerte Mountain

**CUIDADO !
BE CAREFUL !**

Yo también uso el camino
I use the road too

Getting Oriented

The most remote part of Costa Rica, the South Pacific encompasses the southern half of Puntarenas Province and La Amistad National Park. The region descends from mountainous forests just a couple of hours south of San José to the humid Golfo Dulce and the richly forested Osa Peninsula, 8 to 10 hours from the capital by car.

Matapalito Beach

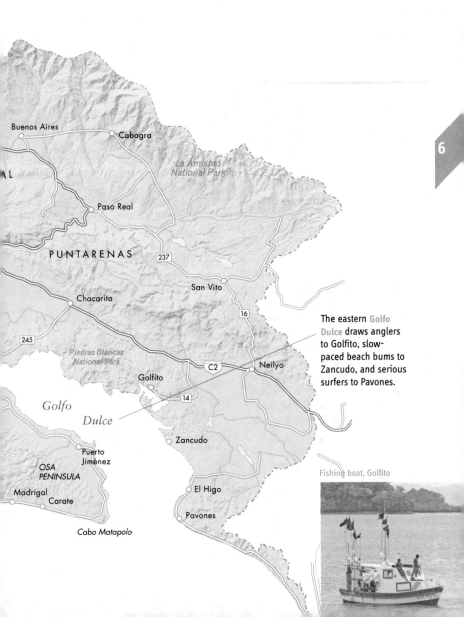

6

The eastern Golfo Dulce draws anglers to Golfito, slow-paced beach bums to Zancudo, and serious surfers to Pavones.

Fishing boat, Golfito

SOUTH PACIFIC PLANNER

When to Go

The May to December rainy season is the worst in the Osa Peninsula, where rains usually last through January, and roads flood and lodges might close in the rainiest months (Oct.–Nov.). Elsewhere, mornings tend to be brilliant and sunny, with rain starting in mid-afternoon. Climate swings wildly in the south, from frigid mountain air to steamy coastal humidity. In the mountains it's normally around 24°C (75°F) during the day and 10°C (50°F) at night, though nighttime temperatures on the upper slopes of Cerro de la Muerte can be close to freezing. Temperatures in coastal areas are usually 24–32°C (76–90°F), but it's the humidity that does you in.

Getting There

For points between San José and San Vito, driving is a viable option, as long as you have lots of time. Direct buses to San Isidro, Golfito, and Puerto Jiménez are cheap and reliable and most are quite comfortable. But the best and fastest way to get to the far south is to fly directly to Golfito, Puerto Jiménez, Drake, Palmar Sur, or Carate. Many lodges arrange flights, taxi, and boat transfers all the way from San José.

DRIVING ALERT: The Cerro de la Muerte is often covered with fog in the afternoon. If you're driving, plan to cross the mountains in the morning.

■ TIP→→ Don't try to cover too much ground. You can't easily hop from one destination in the south to the other. It is impossible to estimate how long it takes to drive the roads or make transportation connections in this part of the country.

What's Your Beach Style?

Family	Playa Platanares
Relaxation	Playa Zancudo
Safe Swim	Playa Platanares, Playa Uvita
Water Sports	Ballena Marine Park, Playa Dominical, Playa Pavones

What to Do

ACTIVITY	WHERE TO DO IT
Bird-watching	San Gerardo de Dota, San Gerardo de Rivas, Ballena Marine Park, San Vito, Corcovado Park
Fishing	Dominical, Ballena Marine Park, Golfito, Playa Zancudo, Puerto Jiménez, Cabo Matapalo
Diving	Ballena Marine Park, Caño Island
Hiking	San Gerardo de Dota, Chirripó Park
Snorkeling	Ballena Marine Park, Caño Island
Surfing	Dominical, Playa Pavones, Cabo Matapalo
Whale-watching	Ballena Marine Park, Puerto Jiménez, Drake Bay
Wildlife-viewing	La Amistad Park, Corcovado Park

Choosing a Place to Stay

Expect reasonable comfort in unbelievably wild settings. Small hotels and lodges are run by hands-on owners, many of them foreigners who fell in love with the place on a visit and stayed. Generally speaking, the farther south and more remote the lodge, the more expensive it is. Bad roads (causing supply problems) and lack of electricity and communications make hotel-keeping costly, especially in the Osa Peninsula and Golfo Dulce. But most of these places include meals, transport, and guides in the price.

How Much Time?

You need at least a week to truly experience any part of the Osa Peninsula. Even if you fly, transfers to lodges are slow, so plan two days for travel. Choose one home base and take day trips. In three weeks you can experience the entire Southern Zone: mountains, beaches, and the Osa Peninsula. If you only have a few days you could make a quick mountain sortie from San José to tour the Route of the Saints and go hiking in the Cerro de la Muerte.

Recommended Tour Operators

■ **Horizontes Nature Tours** (☎ 222-2022 ⊕ www.horizontes. com) is an expert generalist.

■ **Costa Rica Expeditions** (☎ 257-0766 ⊕ www. costaricaexpeditions. com) organizes trips with overnights at the Corcovado Lodge Tent Camp.

Living off the Grid

Many hotels in the South Pacific generate their own electricity, so don't count on air-conditioning, using a hair dryer, or paying with a credit card (unless it's arranged in advance). Pharmacies are few, and often low on supplies. Pack with Mother Nature in mind. Bring:

■ Flashlight with extra batteries

■ Insect repellent (lots of it)

■ Sunscreen (ditto)

■ All toiletries or medicine that you might conceivably need

■ Sturdy, breathable hiking shoes and lots of socks (your feet *will get wet*)

■ Waterproof walking sandals

■ Binoculars

■ Sun hat

■ Water bottle

Prices

WHAT IT COSTS in Dollars

	$$$$	$$$	$$	$	¢
Restaurants	over $25	$15–$25	$10–$15	$5–$10	under $5
Hotels	over $250	$150–$250	$75–$150	$50–$75	under $50

Restaurant prices are per-person for a main course at dinner. Hotel prices are for two people in a standard double room in high season, excluding service and tax (16.4%).

THE CENTRAL HIGHLANDS

By Dorothy MacKinnon

Less than an hour south of San José the Pan-American Highway climbs up into the scenic Central Highlands of Cerro de la Muerte, famous for mountain vistas, high-altitude coffee farms, cloud-forest eco-lodges, and challenging mountain hikes.

Zona de Los Santos

Empalme, at Km 51 of the Pan-American Highway, marks the turnoff for Santa María de Dota, the first of the blessed coffee-growing towns named after saints that dot this mountainous area known as the Zona de Los Santos (Zone of the Saints). The scenic road that winds through the high-altitude valley from Empalme to San Pablo de León is appro-

★ priately called **La Ruta de Los Santos** (Route of the Saints). It's well paved to facilitate shipping the coffee produced in the region, which is central to Costa Rica's economy. On the 30-minute (24-km [15-mi]) drive from Santa María de Dota to San Pablo de León Cortés, you see misty valleys ringed by precipitous mountain slopes terraced with lush, green coffee plants. The route also captures the essence of a traditional Tico way of life built around coffee growing. Stately churches anchor bustling towns full of prosperous, neat houses with pretty gardens and 1970s Toyota Landcruisers in a rainbow of colors parked in front.

NAVIGATING THE ROUTE OF THE SAINTS

Santa María de Dota is 65 km/40 mi (1½ hrs) south of San José. The Route of the Saints is 24 km/15 mi long.

From San José, drive southeast on the paved Pan-American Highway, heading toward Cartago, then follow the signs south for San Isidro de El General. The two-lane road climbs steeply and there are almost no safe places to pass heavy trucks and slow vehicles. Make an early start, because the road is often enveloped in mist and rain in the afternoon. At Km 51 turn right at Empalme to reach Santa María de Dota, 14 km (8½ mi) along a wide, curving, paved road.

Where to Stay & Eat

¢ ✕ **Café de Los Santos.** This pretty café serves more than 30 different kinds of local coffees. The most typical of the region, billed on the menu as "a celestial drink of the land of the saints," is high-altitude *arabica* Tarrazú, for which this area is famous. The café also has homemade sweet and savory pastries. It's open weekdays 9–6:30, Saturday 2–5:30, and Sunday noon–5:30. There's also a conveniently located outpost on the highway at Empalme, called La Ruta del Café (open daily 10:30–6). ⊠ *50 m east of church, 6 km west of Santa María de Dota, San Marcos de Tarrazú; look for the sign with a chubby monk with a halo, pouring a cup of coffee* ☎ *546–7881* ▭ *No credit cards* ⊠ *Pan-American Hwy., at entrance to Ruta de Los Santos, Empalme* ☎ *571–1118* ▭ *No credit cards.*

$ ▦ **El Toucanet Lodge.** For serenity and mountain greenery, you can't beat this family-run lodge with a 270-degree panorama of pastoral scenery from its dining room. Each of the six large rooms in three wooden cabins above the main lodge has its own private veranda and skylit tile bathroom. No. 5 is the newest and most private room. One rustic three-bedroom cabin has a kitchen and fireplace. Owners Gary and Edna Roberts are excellent cooks, well known for hearty breakfasts, baked trout dinners, and creative vegetarian dishes. Gary leads guests on bird-watching excursions,

> **THE FINAL FRONTIER**
>
> The Southern Zone was the very last part of Costa Rica to be settled. The first road, from San José to San Isidro, was built in the 1950s.

including a free quetzal hunt every day at 7 AM. He also arranges horseback rides, mountain hikes, and tours of neighboring coffee *fincas* (farms). With at least six hours' notice, Gary can fire up the natural-stone hot tub for an end-of-day soak under the stars. ⊠ *7 km/4 mi east of Santa María de Dota (along steep, winding paved road), Copey; or from Km 58 of the Pan-American Hwy., turn right at sign for Copey and follow dirt road 7 km/4 mi* ☎☎ *541–3045* ☎ *541–3131* ⊕ *www. eltoucanet.com* ⟳ *6 rooms, 1 cabin* ⅄ *Dining room, hot tub, horseback riding; no a/c, no room phones, no TV* ⊟ *AE, MC, V* ⊘ *Sept.* ⏣ *BP.*

Shopping

The best—and cheapest—place to buy local coffee is where the farmers themselves bring their raw coffee beans to be roasted and packed into jute bags, the **Coopedota Santa María** (⊠ Main road, just after the bridge, as you enter Santa María de Dota ☎ 541–2828). You can buy export-quality coffee here for less than $5 per kilo (2.2 pounds) *en grano* (whole bean) or *molido* (ground), and choose between light or dark roast. It's open Monday through Friday, 6–5 PM and Saturday 6–11 AM. You can also arrange for a free tour of the coffee co-op by calling ahead.

San Gerardo de Dota

❶ Cloud forests, cool mountain air, pastoral scenery, and excellent bird-watching make San Gerardo de Dota one of Costa Rica's premier nature destinations. The village is in the narrow Savegre River valley, 9 km (5½ mi) down a twisting, partially asphalted track that descends abruptly to the west from the Pan-American Highway. The peaceful surroundings look more like the Rocky Mountains than typical Central America, but hike down the waterfall trail and the vegetation quickly turns tropical again. Beyond hiking, activities include horseback riding and trout fishing.

Outdoor Activities

BIRD-WATCHING This area is a must for bird-watchers, who flock here with small package tours (⇨ Tours & Packages *in* Smart Travel Tips A to Z). Individual birders can choose from a roster of expert local guides; check with ★ your hotel for recommendations. **Savegre Hotel de Montaña** (☎ 740–1028 ⊕ www.savegre.co.cr) has the best bird guides in the area ($55 for a half-day) and organizes hiking tours in the surrounding mountains.

Although you can see many birds from your cabin porch, most bird-watching requires hiking, some of it along steep paths made extra challenging by the high altitude (from 7,000 to 10,000 feet above sea level).

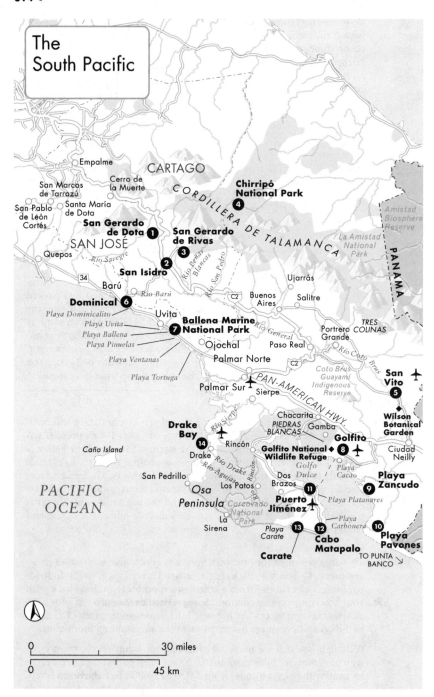

The South Pacific

PACIFIC OCEAN

Empalme

CARTAGO

San Marcos de Tarrazú

Cerro de la Muerte

Santa María de Dota

Chirripó National Park **④**

San Pablo de Léon Cortés

San Gerardo de Dota ①

CORDILLERA DE TALAMANCA

SAN JOSÉ

Quepos

Río Savegre

San Gerardo de Rivas ③

②

Amistad Biosphere Reserve

La Amistad National Park

PANAMA

San Isidro

Barú

34

Río Barú

Río Peñas Blancas

Río San Pedro

Ujarrás

Dominical ⑥

Playa Dominicalito

Uvita

C2

Buenos Aires

Salitre

TRES COLINAS

Playa Uvita

Ballena Marine National Park ⑦

Río General

Portrero Grande

Playa Ballena

Playa Pinuelas

Ojochal

Paso Real

Río Coto Brus

San Vito ⑤ ✈

Playa Ventanas

Palmar Norte

C2

Playa Tortuga

Palmar Sur

PAN-AMERICAN HWY.

Sierpe

Coto Brus Guaymí Indigenous Reserve

Wilson Botanical Garden ◆

Río Sierpe

Chacarita

PIEDRAS BLANCAS

Gamba

Drake Bay ⑭ ✈

Rincón

Golfito National Wildlife Refuge ◆

Golfito ⑧ ✈

Ciudad Neilly

Caño Island

Drake

Río Drake

Golfo Dulce

Playa Cacao

San Pedrillo

Río Agujas

Dos Brazos

Playa Platanares

Playa Zancudo ⑨

PACIFIC OCEAN

Osa Peninsula

Los Patos

Río Rincón

Puerto Jiménez ⑪ ✈

Corcovado National Park

La Sirena

Playa Carate

⑬

Playa Carbonera

⑫

Cabo Matapalo

⑩

Playa Pavones

Carate

TO PUNTA BANCO ↘

0   30 miles

0   45 km

Come fit and armed with binoculars and layers of warm clothing. The early mornings are brisk up here, but you'll warm up quickly with the sun and the exertion of walking.

HIKING Some of the best hiking in the country is in this valley. Expert birder Marino Chacón of Hotel de Savegre (⇨ *above*) leads a daylong natural-history hike ($90 for 1 to 10 people) that starts with a drive up to the *páramo* (high-altitude, shrubby ecosystem) of **Cerro de la Muerte**. The trail begins near the cluster of communication towers, near Km 89, and descends through the forest into the valley. Miles of prime bird-watching/hiking trails wind through the forest reserve belonging to the Chacóns.

⚠ **Night temperatures on the slopes of Cerro de la Muerte can approach freezing—it's called the Mountain of Death for the very simple reason that long-ago travelers attempting to cross it on foot often froze to death during the night. Pack accordingly.**

★ The most challenging trail in the area is the one that begins at the Hotel Savegre and follows the **Río Savegre** down to a spectacular waterfall. To get to the trailhead, follow the main road past Savegre Hotel to a fork, where you veer left, cross a bridge, and head over the hill to a pasture that narrows to a footpath. Although it is only 2 km (1¼ mi) each way, the hike is steep and slippery, especially near the bottom, and takes about three hours.

Where to Stay & Eat

¢–$ ×☐ **Las Cataratas.** One of the best deals—and meals—in the valley is at this restaurant and cabins run by a lovely Tico family, who all join in (kids, too) to help serve meals. Three simple, wooden cabins have wood-burning fireplaces. The red-velvet decor borders on bordello, but the cabins are cheap and comfortable enough. There are also some short, steep forest trails to explore. At the restaurant you can dine on fresh trout—pulled directly out of the adjoining pond when you place your order—with salad, vegetables, dessert, and juice for under $5. If you haven't got the time or the courage to face the steep road all the way down to San Gerardo, this is a good compromise, only 3 km (2 mi) in from the highway. ✉ *3 km/2 mi down steep road to San Gerardo de Dota* ☎ *393–9278, beeper 257–8585* ⊕ *www.cataratas. guiapz.com* ⇝ *3 cabins* ⚐ *Restaurant, fishing, hiking; no a/c, no room phones, no room TVs* ⊟ *No credit cards.*

★ $–$$ ☐ **Savegre Hotel de Montaña.** Famous for quetzals and miles of bird-

---

THE RESPLENDENT QUETZAL

The damp, epiphyte-laden oak-tree forest around San Gerardo de Dota is renowned for resplendent quetzals, considered by many to be the most beautiful bird in the Western world. Male quetzals in full breeding plumage are more spectacular than females, with metallic green feathers, crimson stomachs, helmetlike crests, and long tails—especially dramatic in flight. Quetzals commonly feed on *aguacatillos* (avocado-like fruits) in the valley's trees. Ask guides or hotel staff about common quetzal hangouts; early morning during the March–May nesting season is the best time to spot them.

watching trails, this formerly rustic hotel has been upgraded to luxury, with handsome furniture, tile baths, space heaters, and hair dryers—unthinkable luxuries back in the 1950s when Don Efrain Chacón first bushwhacked his way through the mountains to homestead here. Nine cabin-suites even have fireplaces and deep bathtubs. The most secluded cabin is No. 105, across a bridge over a small stream. Still run by Efrain's affable sons, the main lodge has a big fireplace, a cozy bar, and a veranda with hummingbird feeders. Breakfast and lunch can be served on a sunny terrace. Homegrown trout is the restaurant's specialty. You can avoid the twisting drive here by taking a bus to Km 80 on the Pan-American

WORD OF MOUTH

"As we were approaching [Savegre Hotel de Montaña] my husband caught a glimpse of a quetzal on the post on the side of the road. We were beside ourselves! We had seen one from a great distance in Monteverde a few years earlier. This one (a female) was within 10 feet of us. We got great pictures. Another female (immature male?) flew in. And then the MALE. He was farther away but within very clear sight and we got great pictures of him as well! So we said, Well, okay, we can go home now, ha ha."   –glover

Highway and arranging to get a lift to the hotel ($10). ✉ *Turn right at sign to San Gerardo de Dota on Pan-American Hwy., about 80 km/50 mi southeast of San José, and travel 9 km/5½ mi down very steep, gravel road with some paving* ☎ *740–1028* 🖨 *740–1027* ✉ *Apdo. 482, Cartago* ⊕ *www.savegre.co.cr* 🛏 *22 cabinas, 9 cabin-suites* ⚒ *Restaurant, fishing, bird-watching, hiking, horseback riding, bar, Internet; no a/c, no room TVs* ▭ *AE, MC, V* ⦿ *FAP.*

$ ⌂ **Albergue Mirador de Quetzales.** The main attraction at this 8,530-foot-high perch is the resplendent quetzal, which swoops its famous tail feathers around the 106-acre cloud-forest reserve, also known as Finca Eddie Serrano (Eddie Serrano's Farm). The price of a room in a rustic A-frame cabin overlooking a misty valley includes a hearty breakfast, lunch, dinner, and a guided tour. Electric space heaters and hot-water bottles at the foot of your bed take the chill off at night, when the temperature can drop close to freezing. The reserve's 4-km (2½-mi) El Robledal trail wends past gnarly 1,500-year-old cypress trees and 14-million-year-old marine fossils. Day visitors can pay $6 to walk the trail. You can also take a horseback ride past a sobering, old plane wreck to a waterfall. ✉ *Km 70 off Pan-American Hwy.* ☎ *381–8456* ⊕ *www. exploringcostarica.com/mirador/quetzales.html* 🛏 *11 cabins* ⚒ *Restaurant, hiking, horseback riding; no a/c, no room phones, no room TVs* ▭ *No credit cards* ⦿ *MAP.*

To & from San Gerardo de Dota

89 km/55 mi (3 hrs) southeast of San José. 52 km/32 mi (1 hr) south of Santa María de Dota.

At Km 80 on the Pan-American Highway, turn down the dirt road signed SAN GERARDO DE DOTA. It's a harrowing, twisting road for most of the 9 km (5½ mi), with signs warning drivers to gear down and go slow. Some newly paved sections help to ease the worst curves. Tourist vans often stop along the road when the guides spot birds; grab your binoculars and join them!

VALLE DE EL GENERAL REGION

The Valle de El General (The General's Valley) is bounded to the north and west by the central highlands of the massive Cordillera de Talamanca and to the south by La Amistad International Park, above San Vito. The valley is named for the Río de El General, one of the many rivers that rise in the Talamancas and run down through the valley, making it ideal for farming. This area includes vast expanses of highland wilderness, on the upper slopes of the Cordillera de Talamanca and the high-altitude *páramo* (shrubby ecosystem) of Chirripó National Park, as well as prosperous agricultural communities amid vast, sun-baked fields of pineapple and sugarcane.

San Isidro

2 Although San Isidro has no major attractions, the bustling market town is a good place to have lunch, get cash at one of the many ATMs (the majority accept only Visa/Plus cards), or fill your tank: the main highway into town is lined with service stations, some operating 24 hours.

Exploring

The **National Parks Service** (✉ Across from Cámara de Cañeros ☎ 771–3155) has information on Chirripó and is the central reservation agent for lodging in the park's hostel. Before you head up to the park entrance in San Gerardo de Rivas, you need to stop in here and pay up front for your park lodging.

In a lush valley 7 km (4½ mi) northeast of San Isidro, the community-managed **Las Quebradas Biological Center** is a *centro biológico* (nature reserve) that protects 1,853 acres of dense forest in which elegant tree ferns grow in the shadows of massive trees and colorful tanagers and euphonias flit about the foliage. A 3-km (2-mi) trail winds through the forest and along the Río Quebradas, which supplies water to San Isidro and surrounding communities. Overnights in a rustic lodge (⇨ Where to Stay & Eat, *below*) are available. ✉ *At bottom of mountain as you approach San Isidro, take sharp left off Pan-American Hwy. at sign for Las Quebradas, go 7 km/4½ mi northeast; center is 2 km/1 mi north of town, along unpaved rd.* ☎ *771–4131* 🎟 *$5* ⊙ *Daily 8–3.*

Los Cusingos Neotropical Bird Sanctuary is the home of the late Dr. Alexander Skutch, Central America's preeminent ornithologist/naturalist and a co-author of *A Guide to the Birds of Costa Rica*, the birders' bible. His 190-acre estate, an island of forest amid new farms and housing developments, is now run by the Tropical Science Center, which, at this writing, is improving the trails and restoring the simple house where Dr. Skutch lived—without electricity—from 1941 until his death in 2004, just a week shy of his 100th birthday. Bird species you might see include fiery-billed aracaris, colorful, small members of the toucan family, and mixed tanager flocks. The plan is to open the trails and museum by May 2006. ✉ *12 km (7½ mi) southeast of San Isidro,* *near Santa Elena; phone for precise directions, Quizarrá ☎ 253–3267 ⊕ www.cct.or.cr ⊠ $8 ⊗ By appointment, daily 7 AM–3:30.*

Outdoor Activities

Selva Mar (⊠ Half a block south of the cathedral ☎ 771–4582 ⊕ www.exploringcostarica.com) is the most experienced Southern Zone tour operator.

HIKING The major tourist draw is climbing Mount Chirripó (the highest peak is 3,820 meters or about 12,530 feet high) in Chirripó National Park. **Costa Rica Trekking Adventures** (☎ 771–4582 ⊕ www.chirripo.com), run by Selva Mar, can arrange everything you need to climb the mountain, including transportation, guide, porters to carry your gear, meals, snacks, and beverages. But you still have to make the tough climb yourself, about eight hours uphill to the park lodge, and five hours to come down. The three-night, four-day packages are around $400 per person. The company also arranges multiday hikes across the Talamanca Mountains.

BIRD-WATCHING **Birding Escapes** (☎ 771–4582 ⊕ www.birdwatchingcostarica.com), run by Selva Mar, has multiday bird-watching packages and arranges customized tours. At the **Los Cusingos Neotropical Bird Sanctuary** (⇨ Exploring, *above*), the home of the late Dr. Alexander Skutch, a co-author of *A Guide to the Birds of Costa Rica,* you might spot scarlet-rumped tanagers, blue-crowned motmots, green honeycreepers, and turquoise cotingas.

Where to Stay & Eat

☺ ¢–$ ✕ **El Trapiche de Nayo.** This rustic open-air restaurant with a panoramic valley view serves the kind of food Ticos eat at *turnos* (village fund-raising festivals), including hard-to-find *sopa de mondongo* (tripe soup). Easier to stomach are the *gallos* (do-it-yourself filled tortillas), which you can stuff with heart of palm, other root vegetables, and wood-fire-cooked chicken. On Saturdays, raw sugarcane is pressed in an antique mill and boiled in huge iron cauldrons to make smooth *sobado,* a molasses-flavored fudge. The restrooms—with seatless toilets—leave much to be desired. ⊠ *Pan-American Hwy., 6 km/4 mi north of San Isidro* ☎ *771–7267* ⊟ *AE, MC, V.*

¢ ▦ **Hotel Zima.** One of the newest accommodations in town, modern Hotel Zima is close to the bus station. The pleasant rooms are in a nicely landscaped row, reminiscent of a 1950s motel. Some rooms have queen-size beds and air-conditioning; others have double or single beds. Have breakfast at the small terrace restaurant or cross the highway and for-

---

HITTING THE TRAILS

The hiking in the south is simply splendid, so don't leave home without your boots. The most challenging hike in the country is Chirripó Mountain, a 6- to 10-hour haul up to the national-park hostel, a base camp for exploring surrounding peaks. Dramatic but less challenging hikes include the well-maintained, wide trails in the cool high-altitude forests of the Savegre Valley; the narrow Coastal Path south of Drake; and forest trails to waterfalls and swimming holes in the Golfo Dulce, Osa Peninsula, and around Dominical.

A Mosaic of Forests

THOUGH THE RAIN FOREST IS the most famous region in Costa Rica, there are other types of forests here equally rich in life and well worth exploring. The **tropical dry forests** of the northwestern lowlands are similar to rain forests during the rainy season, but once the weather turns dry, most trees lose their leaves, and some burst simultaneously into full flower, notably the yellow-blossom buttercup tree and the pink tabebuia. Cacti, coyotes, and diamondback rattlesnakes can be found, in addition to typical rain-forest flora and fauna.

The **cloud forests** on the upper reaches of many Costa Rican mountains and volcanoes are so deeply lush that it can be hard to find the bark on a tree for all the growth on its trunk and branches. Vines, orchids, ferns, aroids, and bromeliads are everywhere. More light reaching the ground means plenty of

undergrowth, too. Cloud forests are home to a multitude of animals, ranging from delicate glass frogs, whose undersides are so transparent that you can see many of their internal organs, to the legendary resplendent quetzal. The foliage and mist can make it hard to see wildlife.

Along both coasts are extensive **mangrove forests,** extremely productive ecosystems that play an important role as estuaries. Mangroves attract animals that feed on marine life, especially fish-eating birds such as cormorants, herons, pelicans, and ospreys. The forests that line Costa Rica's northeastern coast are dominated by the water-resistant *jolillo* palm or *palma real*. Mangroves are home to many of the same animals found in the rain forest—monkeys, parrots, iguanas—as well as river dwellers such as turtles and crocodiles.

6

age among the inexpensive sodas in town. ⊠ *Half a block east of main highway into San Isidro, across from MUSOC bus terminal* ☎ *770–1114* 🖨 *770–9394* 🖅 *19 rooms* ⚭ *Dining room, fans, cable TV, laundry service, Internet; no a/c in some rooms; no room phones* ▤ *AE, MC, V* ⍾ *EP.*

To & from San Isidro
54 km/34 mi (1½ hrs) south of San Gerardo de Dota.

The Pan-American Highway takes you straight into San Isidro. It's 129 km (80 mi) south of San José and about 50 km (31 mi) south of the San Gerardo de Dota highway exit. Truck traffic can be heavy. Buses to Dominical leave San Isidro from a stop 100 meters south and 200 meters east of the cathedral, near the main highway. Buses to San Gerardo de Rivas, the starting point of the trail into Chirripó National Park, depart from San Isidro at 5 AM from the central park and at 2 PM from a stop at the central market.

San Isidro Essentials
🏧 Bank/ATM **Banco de Costa Rica** ⊠ Northeast corner of park ☎ 229–2231. **ATH Coopealianza** ⊠ South side of central park, beside Hotel Chirripó ☞ (ATM only).
🏥 Hospital **Hospital Escalante Pradilla** ⊠ North end of town ☎ 661–3122.

📕 Pharmacy **Farmacia Santa Marta** ⊠ Across from the cultural center ☎ 771-4506.
📕 Visitor Information **Ciprotur** ⊠ Behind the MUSOC bus station, where the San José buses arrive ☎ 771-6096. **Selva Mar** ⊠ 45 m south of central park ☎ 771-4582 ⊕ www.exploringcostarica.com.

San Gerardo de Rivas

❸ Chirripó National Park is the main reason to venture to San Gerardo de Rivas, but if you aren't up for this physically challenging adventure there are less difficult hikes, and the town is still a great place to spend a day or two. Spread over steep terrain at the end of the narrow valley of the boulder-strewn Río Chirripó, San Gerardo de Rivas has a cool climate, good bird-watching, spectacular views reminiscent of Nepal, and an outdoor menu that includes waterfall hikes.

Exploring

🕘 The **Aguas Termales** (Hot Springs), on a farm above the road to Herradura, are a favorite tourist stop. To get here, you must cross a river on a rickety footbridge, then it's a steep climb on foot to a combination of natural rock and concrete pools in a forested area. It can be crowded with locals on weekends. ⊠ *Above road to Herradura, about 1½ km/1 mi past the ranger station, north of town* ☎ *$3* ⊘ *Daily 7–6.*

🕘 **Cloudbridge Reserve,** a private nature reserve, has an easy trail to a waterfall, plus almost 20 km (12 mi of river and ridge trails bordering Chirripó National Park. It's a pleasant alternative for hikers who aren't up to the challenge of Chirripó. ⊠ *2 km/1 mi northeast of San Gerardo de Rivas* ☎ *By donation* ⊕ *www.cloudbridge.org* ⊘ *Daily, sunrise to sunset.*

Outdoor Activities

Selva Mar (⇨ San Isidro, *above*) runs tours around San Gerardo de Rivas.

HIKING   If Chirripó isn't on your hiking list, you can still get some good walks in the area around San Gerardo de Rivas. Guide **Eric Kang** (⊕ www.climbcostarica.com) at the Cloud Bridge Reserve arranges longer hiking trips and naturalist tours, starting at $15 for a half-day up to $345 for a four-day trek.

Where to Stay

$ 🏨 **Río Chirripó Retreat.** A popular place for yoga retreats, this lodge with its clear mountain air, rushing river, and huge conical-roofed adobe temple hung with a monastery bell and Tibetan prayer flags makes you feel as though you have arrived in the Himalayas. The bougainvillea-bedecked B&B is also great place for acclimatizing before climbing Chirripó, for bird-watching, and for clambering along the river rocks, strewn with Druidic-looking stone seats and altars. A new hot tub overlooks the river. Two-story wood cabins are cantilevered over a steep ravine, with twig-railing porches. The comfortable rooms have large bathrooms and walls stenciled with runic symbols. ⊠ *Down a steep drive, just past cemetery* ☎ *364–9527, 707/937–3775 in U.S., Apr. 1–Dec. 1* ⊕ *www.riochirripo. com* ⇥ *8 rooms, 1 cabin* ⚶ *Dining room, pool, hiking; no a/c, no room phones, no room TVs* ▤ *No credit cards* ⊙⚏ *BP.*

¢ ▦ **Albergue de Montaña El Pelícano.** On a ridge south of town, this wooden lodge is named for a chunk of wood that resembles a pelican—and that's not its only oddity. The property also has a museum to house the dozens of idiosyncratic wooden sculptures carved out of tree roots by owner Rafael Elizondo. Above the restaurant, which has a gorgeous view of the valley below San Gerardo, are economical small rooms with shared bath. There are also two private wooden cabins with kitchenettes, near the pool. The owners can arrange everything for a climb up Chirripó, including a free lift to the park entrance. The climb to the hotel itself is quite steep and requires 4WD. ⊠ *260 m south of national park office* ☎ *390–4194* 🖷 *770–3526* 🖃 *Apdo. 942–8000, San Gerardo de Rivas* ⊕ *www.hotelelpelicano.net* ↩ *10 rooms with shared bath, 2 cabins* ᕫ *Restaurant, tennis court, pool, horseback riding; no a/c, no room phones, no room TVs* ▭ *AE, MC, V,* ⦿⦿ *EP.*

To & from San Gerardo de Rivas

20 km/12½ mi (1 hr) northeast of San Isidro.

More than half the distance from San Isidro is on a very rocky, very hilly, dirt road; 4WD is strongly recommended. There is a bus from San Isidro and it is a slow, dusty ride up the mountain.

Chirripó National Park

❹ The ascent to Mount Chirripó, the highest mountain in Costa Rica, is the most popular and challenging hike in the country. Unfortunately, it is also the most exclusive. A recent environmental-impact study led officials to limit the number of hikers in the park on any one day to 40. Thirty reservations are prebooked, usually months ahead, leaving only 10 spaces for hikers who show up at the park. The park service office in San Isidro takes phone reservations every two months, starting in January. This means they take reservations in January, for February and March; then in March for April and May, and so forth. To access the challenging trail, you must first hike about 6 km (4 mi) uphill from San Gerardo de Rivas to the park's official boundary. From there it's a tough climb to the base camp—6 to 10 hours from the official park entrance, depending on your physical condition—so most hikers head out of San Gerardo at the first light of day. There is a modern but unheated (and chilly) **hostel** near the top ($10/night). This will be your base for a night or two if you want to continue your hike up to the peaks. The hostel has small rooms with four bunks each, cold-water bathrooms, and a cooking area. In 2004, bathrooms were newly tiled and the septic system was improved. You can rent camp stoves, blankets, and sleeping bags here, but you should bring a better-quality sleeping bag, and you must bring food and water. ■ TIP→ **Pack plenty of warm clothes.** Trails from the hostel lead to the top of Chirripó—the highest point in Costa Rica—and the nearby peak of Terbi, as well as to glacier lakes and the *páramo*—a highland ecosystem common to the Andes, with shrubs and herbaceous plants.

You are required to report to the **San Gerardo de Rivas National Parks Service** (⊠ *Main St.* ☎ *200–5348*) before you start, either the day before—or the morning of—your climb. The office is open 6:30–4 and has trail maps. Don't try to sneak in: a park ranger will stop you at a checkpoint on the trail and ask to see your reservation voucher. To reserve or pay for lodging in the park, you must visit the **San Isidro National Parks Service office** (⇨ *above*).

🖃 *$10* ⊙ *Last two weeks in May; all of Oct.*

Outdoor Activities
Hikes and other activities in the park are arranged by **Selva Mar** (⇨ San Isidro, *above*).

To & from Chirripó National Park
The park entrance is a 5-km (3-mi) hike uphill from San Gerardo de Rivas.

San Vito

5 Except for the tropical greenery, the rolling hills around the bustling hilltop town of San Vito could be mistaken for a Tuscan landscape. The town actually owes its 1952 founding to 200 Italian families who converted forest into coffee, fruit, and cattle farms. The Italian flavor lingers in outdoor cafés serving ice cream and pastries and an abundance of shoe stores. A statue dedicated to the *pioneros* stands proudly in the middle of town. San Vito is also the center of the Coto Brus coffee region. Many of the coffee pickers are from the Guaymí tribe, who live in a large reserve nearby and just over the border in Panamá. They're easy to recognize by the women's colorful cotton dresses.

Exploring
Fodor'sChoice The compelling tourist draw here is the world-renowned **Wilson Botan-**
★ **ical Garden,** a must-see for gardeners and bird-watchers and enchanting even for those who are neither. Paths through the extensive grounds are lined with exotic plants and shaded by avenues of palm trees and 50-foot-high bamboo stalks. In 1961, U.S. landscapers Robert and Catherine Wilson bought 30 acres of coffee plantation and started planting tropical species, including palms, orchids, bromeliads, and heliconias. Today the property extends over 635 acres, and the gardens hold around 2,000 native and more than 3,000 exotic species. The palm collection—more than 700 species—is the second-largest in the world. Fantastically shaped and colored bromeliads, which usually live in the tops of trees, have been brought down to ground in impressive mass plantings, providing one of many photo opportunities. The property was transferred to the Organization for Tropical Studies (OTS) in 1973, and in 1983 it became part of Amistad Biosphere Reserve. Under the name **Las Cruces Biological Station,** Wilson functions as a research and educational center, so there is a constant supply of expert botanists and biologists to take visitors on natural history tours in the garden and the adjoining forest trails. If you spend a night at the garden lodge, you have the garden all to yourself in the late afternoon and early morning, when wildlife is most active. ⊠ *6 km/4 mi south of San Vito on road to Ciudad Neily* ⌂ *Apdo. 73–8257, San Vito* ☎ *773–4004* 🖷 *773–4109* ⊕ *www.esintro.co.cr* 🖃 *$6* ⊙ *Daily 8–4.*

Outdoor Activities

BIRD-WATCHING   In addition to its plants, **Wilson Botanical Garden** (⇨ Exploring, *above*) is renowned for its birds. More than 320 species have been recorded here, along with more than 800 butterflies. Naturalist guides lead visitors on birding and natural history tours through the garden ($15 per person). The Río Java trail, open only to overnight guests of Wilson, is a great place to see birds.

WILDLIFE-   If you are an overnight guest at **Wilson Botanical Garden** (⇨ Exploring,
WATCHING   *above*), you can walk the Río Java trail, through a forest thick with wildlife.

Where to Stay & Eat

★ $ ✕ **Pizzeria Liliana.** Treat yourself to real Italian pizza at the classiest restaurant in town. The large, friendly, family-run restaurant has an elegant indoor dining room and an attractive garden terrace out back. Pizzas have crispy olive-oil crusts and are generously sized. Or dig into the macaroni *sanviteña*-style, with white sauce, ham, and mushrooms. The classics are here as well, and they're all homemade—lasagna, canneloni, and ravioli. The authentically Italian vinaigrette salad dressing is a welcome change from more acidic Tico dressings. ⊠ *150 m west of central Sq.* ☎ *773–3080* ⊟ *V.*

¢   ✕ **Panaderia y Reposteria Flor.** In a town famous for coffee, ice cream, and pastry shops, this emporium stands out. You can't miss the hot-pink sign on the main street. Stop in and grab a pair of tongs and a tray and help yourself to sweet and savory buns, breads, and an array of doughnuts, cakes, cookies, and puddings. The *pièces de résistance* are the elegant pastry swans filled with pastry cream. Enjoy your treats at the sidewalk tables or bag them and eat them en route to your next destination. ⊠ *Main street, halfway down the hill.*

$$ ▥ **Wilson Botanical Garden.** A highlight of any Costa Rican visit for gardeners and bird lovers, this magical botanical garden has comfortable rooms in two modern buildings built of glass, steel, and wood that blend into a forested hillside. Private balconies cantilevered over a ravine make bird-watching a snap even from your room. Each room is named after the exotic plant growing at the doorway. Room rates include three excellent home-style meals, a guided tour, and 24-hour access to the garden. Staying overnight is the only way to see the garden at dusk and dawn, and it's also the only way to walk the Sendero Río Java, a trail that follows a stream through a forest teeming with birds and monkeys. The staff here are cheerful and professional, and the youthful enthusiasm of visiting research students is contagious. ⊠ *6 km/4 mi south of San Vito on road to Ciudad Neily* ♺ *OTS, Apdo. 676–2050, San Pedro* ☎ *524–0628* 🖶 *524–0629* ⊕ *www.esintro.com* ⇆ *12 rooms* ♨ *Dining room, fans, hiking, tours, Internet; no a/c, no room TVs* ⊟ *AE, MC, V* ⍩⃝ *FAP.*

Fodor'sChoice
★

¢   ▥ **Hotel El Ceibo.** The best deal in town, El Ceibo is a well-maintained two-story hotel tucked in a quiet cul-de-sac behind the main street. The architecture is reminiscent of Italy, with graceful arcades and decorative balustrades. Rooms are compact but tidy, bright, and comfortable; Rooms 1–10 and 21–32 have small balconies that open onto a wooded ravine alive with birds. The restaurant, illuminated by a skylight, serves homestyle Italian and Tico food at reasonable prices. ✉ *140 m east of San Vito's central park, behind Municipalidad* ☎ *773–3025* 🖶 *773–5025* 🛏 *40 rooms* ⚒ *Restaurant, fans, cable TV, bar; no a/c, no room phones* ▭ *V* ⑩ *EP.*

Shopping

In an old farmhouse on the east side of the road between San Vito and the botanical garden, **Finca Cántaros** (✉ Road to Ciudad Neily, 3 km/2 mi south of San Vito ☎ 773–3760) sells crafts by indigenous artisans from near and far, including Guaitil ceramic figures and *molas* (colorful appliqué work) made by Kuna women from the San Blas Islands in Panama. You can also find a great selection of colorful, high-glaze ceramics from San José artists. Profits help support the adjacent children's library.

To & from San Vito

110 km/68 mi southeast of San Isidro, 61 km/38 mi northeast of Golfito.

If you are driving south from San Isidro, your best route is along the wide, smooth Pan-American Highway via Buenos Aires to Paso Real, about 70 km (43 mi). Then take the scenic high road to San Vito, 40 km (25 mi) farther along. This road has its share of potholes but it is the most direct route and the prettiest. Another route, which many buses take, is via Ciudad Neilly, about 35 km (22 mi) northeast of Golfito, and then 24 km (15 mi) of winding steep road up to San Vito, at almost 1,000 meters (3,280 feet) above sea level. There are direct buses from San José three times a day; and buses from San Isidro six times a day. You can also fly to Coto 47 and take a taxi to San Vito.

San Vito Essentials

Most of the banks in town have cash machines that accept foreign cards.
🏧 Bank/ATM **Banco Nacional** ✉ Across from central park ☎ 773-3601. **ATH Coopealianza** ✉ Center of town, north of hospital ⚲ ATM only.
🏥 Hospital **Hospital San Vito** ✉ South end of town on road to Wilson Botanical Garden ☎ 773-3103.
💊 Pharmacy **Farmacia Coto Brus** ✉ Center of town across from La Flor pastry shop ☎ 773-3939.
🚕 Taxis **Taxi service** ✉ Taxi stand beside park at center of town ☎ 773-3939.

EN ROUTE The 33-km (21-mi) road from **San Vito to Ciudad Neily** is twisting and spectacular, with views over the Coto Colorado plain to the Golfo Dulce and Osa Peninsula beyond. Much of this steep terrain is covered with tropical forest, making it an ideal route for bird-watching and picture-taking. The road from **San Vito to Paso Real** is equally scenic, traveling along a high ridge with sweeping valley views on either side. As you descend, the wide valley of the El General River opens up before you, planted with miles of spiky pineapples and tall sugarcane. Sadly, the formerly perfectly paved road is now pitted with potholes. But if you pick your way carefully, the scenery is still worth the drive.

La Amistad National Park

BY FAR THE LARGEST PARK IN Costa Rica, at more than 1,980 square km (765 square mi), La Amistad it's a mere portion of the vast La Amistad Biosphere Reserve that stretches into western Panama. Altitudes range from 1,000 meters (3,280 feet) to 3,500 meters (11,480 feet). There are miles of rugged, densely forested trails and plenty of wildlife (two-thirds of the country's vertebrate species live here), but because access is extremely difficult, it's not worth visiting the park unless you plan to spend several days, making this a trip only for experienced hikers. Tour operators don't do trips (yet), but you can—and

should. Unless you're comfortable being lost in the wilderness, hire a park guide. The three-day guided trips have overnights at a ranger station with potable water and restrooms. The alternative is rustic camp sites (bring your own tent) for $5 per person. Reserve space about a week in advance. To get to the park (4WD essential), drive 31 km (20 mi) west from San Vito along the road to Paso Real. Turn right at the park sign at Guacimo, near two small roadside restaurants. Then drive about 20 km (13 mi) uphill on a rough road. There is no public transport. ☎ 730-0846 🎟 *$6 per day* ⊙ *Daily 8-4.*

THE COAST

On the other side of a mountain ridge, just a scenic 50-minute drive southwest of San Isidro, you reach the southern Pacific coast with its miles of beaches for sunning, surfing, kayaking, and snorkeling. Ballena National Marine Park alone encompasses almost 10 km (6 mi) of protected beaches. Scattered along the coast are small communities with increasing numbers of international residents and interesting restaurants and lodging options.

Dominical

❻ Sleepy fishing village turned scruffy surfer town, Dominical is changing again, as luxury villas pop up all over the hillsides above the beaches, bringing new wealth that is fueling the local economy. For now, it's still a major surfing destination, with a lively surfer-fueled restaurant and nightlife scene. Bars and restaurants come and go with the waves of itinerant young people, so don't hesitate to try something new. Dominical's real magic, though, lies beyond the town, in the surrounding terrestrial and marine wonders: the rain forest grows right up to the beach in some places, and the ocean offers world-class surfing.

Exploring

★ ☼ The **Hacienda Barú** nature reserve is a leader in both ecotourism and conservation, with a turtle protection project and nature education program in the local school. The bird-watching is spectacular, with excellent guides. You can stay at the cabins or just come for the day to walk the forest and mangrove trails, zip through the canopy on cables, or climb a tree or stake out birds on an observation platform. ✉ *3 km/2 mi north of bridge into Dominical* ☎ *787–0003* ⊕ *www.haciendabaru.com* 🖼 *$6, tours $20–$60/person* ⊘ *Daily dawn–dusk.*

☾ Five years in the making, **Parque Reptilandia** is an impressive reptile house, with more than 150 species of snakes, lizards, frogs, turtles, and other reptilian creatures in terrariums and large enclosures. There's also a maternity ward showcasing newborn snakes. The snakes live under a retractable roof that lets in sun and rain. They become much more active when it rains, so this is a great rainy-day-at-the-beach alternative activity. Night tours ($10) can also be arranged to watch nocturnal animals at work. ✉ *13 km/8 mi east of Dominical on road to San Isidro* ☎ *787–8007* 🖼 *$10* ⊘ *Daily 9:30 AM–4 PM.*

☾ **Cataratas de Nauyaca** (Nauyaca Waterfalls), a massive double cascade tumbling down 45 meters (150 feet) and 20 meters (65 feet), is one of the most spectacular sights in Costa Rica. The waterfalls—also known as Barú River Falls—are on private property, so the only way to reach them is to take a hiking or horseback tour (⇨ Outdoor Activities, *below*).

Playa Dominical is long and flat, rarely crowded, and good for beachcombing among all the flotsam and jetsam that the surf washes up onto the brown sand. Swimmers should beware of fatally dangerous rip currents. In high season, flags mark off a relatively safe area for swimming, under the watchful gaze of a professional lifeguard.

Playa Dominicalito, just 1 km (½ mi) south of Playa Dominical, is usually calmer and more suited to Boogie boarding.

☾ A considerably smaller waterfall than Cataratas de Nauyaca, **Pozo Azul** is in the jungle about 5 km (3 mi) south of town. Off the main highway, head up the road toward Bella Vista lodge and take the first road to the right, past the new school and through a stream; follow the road straight uphill for about 300 meters to where the road widens. You can park here and climb down the steep trail to the river on the right, where there is a lovely swimming hole and waterfall, often populated by local kids when school is out. Be sure not to leave anything of value in your parked car; there have been reports of theft here.

Outdoor Activities

Southern Expeditions (✉ At entrance to town on right ☎ 787–0100 ✉ With a tour desk in Villas Río Mar hotel, 1 km/½ mi west of Dominical ☎ 787–0052 ⊕ www.southernexpeditionscr.com) is the major tour operator in the area, and can arrange kayaking, white-water rafting, scuba diving, fishing, and nature tours in and around Ballena Marine National Park, Caños Island, and all the way down to Corcovado National Park.

Much of the lush forest that covers the steep hillsides above the beaches is protected within private nature reserves. By leading hikes and horseback tours, several of these reserves, such as Hacienda Barú and La Merced (⇨ Ballena Marine National Park), are trying to finance preservation of the rain forest.

FISHING Angling options range from expensive sportfishing charters to a trip in a small boat to catch red snapper and snook for supper. The five most common fish species here are yellowfin tuna, wahoo, dorado, marlin, and sailfish. **Mark Hendry** (☎ 787–8224 ⊕ www.dominical. biz/mako1) runs trips 28 nautical miles out to the Furuno Bank, which he claims is the most reliable area for finding the big ones, including sailfish and marlin. Trips ($600/ day) are in a 21-foot Mako boat and include food, drinks, and gear. Hendry has been fishing here since

PACK YOUR BOARD

The surfing is great in Dominical, thanks to the runoff from the Barú River mouth, which constantly changes the ocean bottom and creates well-shaped waves big enough to keep intermediate and advanced surfers challenged. The best surfing is near the river mouth, and the best time is two hours before or after high tide, to avoid the notorious riptides.

1992. **Steve Sandusky** (☎ 787–0230) has a high-powered boat that can go long distances fast to find sailfish and marlin ($650/day, including food, drinks, gear).

HORSEBACK RIDING **Don Lulo's tour** (☎ 787–8137 or 787–8013) to Nauyaca Falls departs daily at 8 AM from the road to San Isidro, 10 km (6 mi) northeast of Dominical. The tour is $45 and includes breakfast and lunch at Don Lulo's family homestead near the falls. You can swim in the cool pool beneath the falls, so bring a bathing suit. The ride is easy; horses proceed at a walk.

Friendly, well-trained horses at **Bella Vista Lodge** (✉ 5 km/3 mi south of Dominical ☎ 787–8069 or 388–0155) also take riders to the Nauyaca (or Barú River Falls as they are also known), following a shorter route, with lunch and a ride in an aerial tram included for $45. Or you can go for a gallop on the beach, morning or afternoon, depending on tides. These tours include breakfast before morning tours or sunset beers and bocas after the afternoon ride ($45). The three- to four-hour tours start at the lodge, then head down the steep Escaleras road, 2 km (1 mi) past Pozo Azul.

SURFING **Green Iguana Surf Camp** (☎ 787–0157 ⊕ www.greeniguanasurfcamp. com) gives two-hour individual lessons ($50) and has week-long packages that include lodging, board rental, lessons, and transport to whichever nearby beach has the best waves each day (from $240).

Where to Stay & Eat

Lodgings in the lowlands of Dominical and the area a little to the north tend to be hot and muggy and not as comfortable (excluding Río Mar) as the more luxurious, private, and breezy places up in the hills above Dominicalito, to the south.

DOMINICAL AND THE LOWLANDS $–$$ ✕ **Coconut Spice.** If you like rice with spice, you came to the right place. This sophisticated restaurant has authentic Southeast Asian flavor in both the food and furnishings. Try the hot-and-sour Tom Yan Goong soup, tart with lemongrass and limes and heated up with chilies. The jumbo shrimp vary in price and can get quite expensive, but they're worth it:

buttery and sweet, and cooked in spicy coconut sauce. There are also satays, curries, and other Indian dishes. The best tables at this second-floor restaurant are out on the star-lit veranda, where it's cooler. ⊠ *Second floor, Plaza Pacífica, on the highway just above Dominical* ☎ *829–8397* ▤ *MC, V* ☺ *Closed Mon.*

¢–$ ✕ **Restaurant Su Raza.** Among the handful of sodas in town serving typical Costa Rican food, this one is notable for its whole fish and hearty portions of seafood served on a wooden veranda that's a great bird-watching spot. Bring your binoculars, especially if you come just before sunset or for breakfast. Stick to the *desayuno típico* for breakfast, with traditional rice and beans and eggs. The omelettes are great but they come with limp frozen french fries, the bane of Tico restaurants today. ⊠ *Across from San Clemente Grill, main st.* ☎ *787–0105* ▤ *No credit cards.*

¢–$ ✕ **San Clemente Bar & Grill.** Signs you're in the local surfer hangout: dozens of broken surfboards affixed to the ceiling, photos of the sport's early years adorning the walls, and a big sound system and dance floor. Fresh seafood, sandwiches, and Tex-Mex standards like burritos and nachos make up the menu. The bargain "starving surfer's breakfast"—two eggs with gallo pinto or pancakes, plus coffee—is very popular. Owner Mike McGinnis is famous for making great hot sauces and for being a super source of information about the area. ⊠ *Main St.* ☎ *787–0055* ▤ *AE, MC, V.*

¢–$ ✕ **Tortilla Flats.** A popular surfer hangout along the lines of the San Clemente Grill, this place has the advantage of being right across from the beach. Fresh-baked baguette sandwiches are stuffed with interesting combinations; the California grilled chicken, avocado, tomato, and mozzarella is the most popular. Light eaters can buy half a sandwich. Fresh fish specials and typical Mexican fare round out the casual menu. The margaritas are excellent and ladies drink free anise-and-*guaro* (sugarcane liquor) shots on Thursday nights. Upstairs there's a new air-conditioned pool room with a beach view. ⊠ *On the beach, Dominical* ☎ *787–0168* ▤ *AE, MC, V.*

$$ ▦ **Plaza Suites Luxury Rentals.** Seemingly straight from the pages of a home-decorating magazine, these tastefully furnished apartments come equipped with a multitude of appliances and comforts, picture-perfect kitchens, and enormous stone-lined showers. Each unit has its own design theme, reflected in fabrics and accessories. The 1,000-square-foot units share a small pool and barbecue area and a glorious garden that backs onto a river and forested hill with a trail to a waterfall. Dominical Beach is within a 10-minute walk. The only drawback here is the road noise from the nearby highway, which can be drowned out by the remote-controlled air-conditioning. ⊠ *Main highway above Dominical, 100 m south of Plaza Pacífica* ☎ *787–0012* 🖷 *787–0049* 📭 *4 suites* ⊕ *www.caracolicostarica.com* ♻ *Pool, cable TV, kitchens* ▤ *AE, MC, V* ⦿ *EP.*

♻ $ ▦ **Hacienda Barú National Wildlife Refuge and Ecolodge.** Base yourself in these spacious but simple cabinas to explore the surrounding forests, mangroves, and Blue Flag beach. Four of the six cabins were freshened up in 2004, so be sure to ask for one of them when you reserve. Cabins, with tile floors and sitting rooms with bamboo furniture, sleep three or four people. Linger for an hour or two atop a lofty bird obser-vation platform in the hotel's rain-forest canopy, zip along the canopy tour, climb a 114-foot-high tree with ropes, or stay overnight at a shel-ter in the heart of the forest. Excellent local guides interpret the miles of trails, or you can follow the self-guided trail with the help of a hand-book. There's a great gift shop here with lots of local crafts. ⊠ *3 km/2 mi north of bridge into Dominical* ✉ *Apdo. 215–8000, Pérez Zeledón* ☎ *787–0003* 🖷 *787–0057* ⊕ *www.haciendabaru.com* ➟ *6 cabinas* ⚲ *Restaurant, fans, kitchens, hiking, beach; no a/c, no room phones, no room TVs* 🖃 *AE, MC, V* ¶⊙¶ *CP.*

$ 🏨 **Río Lindo Resort.** This modest, two-story, concrete hotel has an old-fashioned resort-like feel, with a round pool ringed by gardens, and an idyllic view of the wide Barú River as it meets the ocean. Hunkered under the highway bridge that crosses the same river, there's some road noise but the pool fountain helps to mask it. Simple rooms are five up, five down, with the top rooms open to breezes (and road noise) and the bot-tom ones air-conditioned. Breakfast is served on a veranda with a river view. At night there's occasional live music at the funky Rum Bar, dec-orated with fantastical wall murals; there's always great bar food, in-cluding spicy chicken wings and stand-out *stromboli* (pizza rolls), as well as the best pizza in town. A guard watches the parking lot all night. ⊠ *En-trance to Dominical, beside the river* ☎ *787–0028* 🖷 *787–0078* ⊕ *www. riolindo.com* ➟ *10 rooms* ⚲ *Restaurant, pool, fans, 2 bars; no a/c in some rooms, no room phones, no room TVs* 🖃 *AE, MC, V* ¶⊙¶ *CP.*

★ $ 🏨 **Villas Río Mar.** The fanciest hotel in town is upriver from the beach on exquisitely landscaped grounds adrift in clouds of terrestrial orchids and aflame with bright bougainvillea and hibiscus. Rooms are in adobe-style, round cabinas with thatched roofs and cane ceilings, and have clean white bathrooms. The newer junior suites have cable TV, king-size beds, and a/c—which is necessary, since they are on a hill, baking in the sun. Every room has a private porch screened with mosquito netting and fur-nished with bamboo chairs and hammocks. Plants and elegant table set-tings fill the thatch-roof restaurant where the breakfast buffet ($6) is a good deal. A luxurious, large pool has a swim-up bar and handsome teak pool furniture. The spa can arrange yoga sessions. ⊠ *1 km/½ mi west of Dominical; turn right off highway into town and then right again under bridge and follow bumpy river rd.* ☎ *787–0052* 🖷 *787–0054* ⊕ *www.villasriomar.com* ✉ *Apdo. 1645–2050, San José* ➟ *40 rooms, 12 junior suites* ⚲ *Restaurant, refrigerators, tennis court, pool, whirlpool tub, massage, spa, beach, bicycles, bar, convention center, tours, Inter-net; no a/c in some rooms, no TV in some rooms* 🖃 *AE, MC, V* ¶⊙¶ *EP.*

THE HIGHLANDS SOUTH OF DOMINICAL

$$$ 🏨 **Casí el Cielo.** The name, which means "almost heaven," is accurate at this unequaled, luxury B&B with a twist: a full staff at your service all day. The views from the villa's lofty perch alone are worth the price tag: the Pacific coast stretching south to the Osa Peninsula and north to Manuel Antonio. The four rooms, all with queen beds topped by pil-low-soft mattresses, have themes of shells, birds, jungle, or fish. Exquis-ite details echo the room motif, down to the towel racks in the bathrooms. A coffee tray appears at 6:30 AM on your private terrace with a view. Enticing you to leave your room are the pretty pool; a resident natural-

ist ready to lead tours; and the friendly Tico staff, who prepare creative breakfasts and elegant dinners on a breezy terrace. ⊠ *Top of Bella Vista road at Km 147 of the Costanera, then 4 km/2 mi up* ☎ *813–5614* ⊕ *www.casielcielo.com* ↪ *4 rooms* ⌂ *Dining room, safety box, hairdryer, pool, car service, Internet; no room phones, no room TVs* ▭ *MC, V* ⭕ *MAP.*

★ **$–$$** ⌧ **The Necochea Inn.** Though the forest setting feels primeval, the decor at this handsome B&B mountain retreat is a sophisticated mix of plush, contemporary furniture, at home in the huge rooms. Downstairs living and dining rooms face a wall of sliding glass doors looking onto a stone-decked pool with jungle and a slice of ocean for a view. For TV and video-game fans, there's an air-conditioned media room. Two streams run through the forested property, supplying a natural sound track. A curved stone stairway leads up to two luxurious, large rooms that share a spacious bath; and two suites, each with private porch, decadent bathrooms with deep tubs or whirlpool tubs for two, antique armoires, and gleaming hardwood floors. Hosts Yvonne and Carlos, transplants from Los Angeles, are full of energy and make every guest feel at home. ⊠ *2 km/1 mi up Bella Vista road just south of Km 147, past the Pozo Azul, Dominicalito* ☎ *787–8072 or 395–2984* ⊕ *www. thenecocheainn.com* ↪ *2 rooms with shared bath, 2 suites* ⌂ *Dining room, some in-room whirlpool tubs, pool; no a/c, no room phones, no room TVs* ▭ *MC, V* ⭕ *BP.*

★ **$–$$** ⌧ **Pacific Edge.** Unbeatable views and stylishly rustic cabins at affordable prices set this place apart. The forest grows right up to the edge of the property, high on a mountain ridge south of town. Private, spacious wood cabinas—one sleeps six; others sleep two to four—have newly tiled bathrooms, hammocks strung on wide porches, and comfortable orthopedic mattresses covered with colorful Guatemalan bedspreads. Host Susie Anderson serves great breakfasts in the lodge's bamboo-roofed, pagoda-style dining room. Dinner—spicy Thai shrimp, perhaps—is cooked on request. Two lookout towers at each end of the tiny pool catch the spectacular sunsets and passing whale pods. The road up to this lofty perch requires a 4WD ve-

> **WORD OF MOUTH**
>
> "[Pacific Edge has a] fabulous setting on a ridge with what must be a 270-degree clear view of the coast. We saw whales from there."
> –glover

hicle, but a hotel shuttle can pick you up in town with advance notice. Be prepared for a barky welcome; Susie and her husband, George, love big (but gentle) dogs. The reception desk closes at 6 PM. ⊠ *Turn inland 4 km/2½ mi south of Dominical at Km 148, up a rough road 1.2 km/1 mi* ☎ *787–8010* ⊕ *www.pacificedge.info* ↪ *4 cabinas* ⌂ *Dining room, refrigerators, pool, bar; no a/c, no room phones, no room TVs* ▭ *AE, MC, V.*

Nightlife

During the high season, Dominical hops at night, and when the surfers have fled to find bigger waves, there are enough locals around to keep some fun events afloat. Wednesday night there's live music at **Jazzy's River-**

house (⊠ Behind the Pueblo El Rio complex ☎ 787-0310), when a mix of professional and local musicians jam after a fixed-menu vegetarian dinner. At Friday night's **Movies in the Jungle** (⊠ High up on Marina Drive in a private house with no sign; call for directions ☎ 787–8065), a pot luck dinner is at 5 and the movies start at 6. Movie buff Harley "Toby" Toberman presents self-proclaimed weird shorts from his huge collection plus a full-length feature on a huge screen, with state-of-the-art equipment. Admission is by $4 donation to the projection bulb fund. Saturday nights the dance action is at the **Roca Verde** (⊠ 1 km/½ mi south of Dominical), with a mixed crowd that doesn't usually get warmed up until 11 PM. Friday night there's live music at **San Clemente Bar** (⊠ On main st.) and noisy, rowdy dancing at **Thruster's** (⊠ Near the beach at south end of town), which attracts a fairly young, boisterous crowd.

To & from Dominical

34 km/21 mi (50 mins) southwest of San Isidro, 40 km/25 mi (1½ hrs) south of Quepos.

The paved road west over the mountains and down to Dominical is scenic at its best and fog-enshrouded at its worst. There are lots of curves, and potholes pop up unexpectedly, so take your time and enjoy the scenery along the route from San Isidro. From Quepos, the road south is the only section of the Costanera still not paved, and it's a bumpy, dusty ride past palm-oil plantations. Buses from San Isidro and Quepos leave twice a day.

Dominical Essentials

🔲 Bank/ATM **Banco de Costa Rica** ⊠ Plaza Pacífica.

🔲 Hospital **Clínica González Arellano** ⊠ Next to pharmacy ☎ 787-0129.

🔲 Pharmacy **Farmacia Dominical** ⊠ Pueblo del Río Center, at entrance to town ☎ 787-0197.

🔲 Visitor Information **Southern Expeditions** ⊠ Entrance to town ☎ 787-0100.

🔲 Taxis ⊠ Taxi stand on main street, at bus stop in front of San Clemente Bar & Grill.

Ballena Marine National Park

❼ There's great snorkeling and whale-watching at Parque Nacional Marino Ballena (Whale Marine National Park), which protects several beaches stretching for about 10 km (6 mi), a mangrove estuary, a recovering coral reef, and a vast swath of ocean with rocky isles and islets. Along with the tropical fish you'll see while snorkeling, there are also humpback whales. They can be seen with their young from December to April and again in late July through late October. Dolphins are also common sights. Above the water there are frigate birds and brown boobies, a tropical seabird, nesting on the park's rocky islands. ☎ 743–8236 ☒ $6 (*$1 if you enter at Playa Uvita*) ☉ *Daily 6–6.*

At the park's northern end, palm-fringed, Blue Flag **Playa Uvita** stretches out into Punta Uvita, a long swath of sand, or *tombolo,* connecting a former island to the coast. At low tide the brown sand bar resembles a whale's tail fanning out on either side of the point, hence the name of the bay: Bahía Ballena, or Whale Bay. This is the best place to enter the park, since it only costs $1 and there are restrooms and lots of restaurants nearby. The other entrance at Playa Ballena, staffed by park rangers, costs $6.

Playa Ballena, 6 km (4 mi) to the south of Playa Uvita in the park, is a lovely strand backed by lush vegetation. The price to enter the park here is $6.

Tiny **Playa Piñuela,** 3 km (2 mi) south of Playa Ballena and outside the park boundaries, is in a deep cove that serves as the local port.

Playa Ventanas, just 1½ km (1 mi) south of Ballena Marine Park, is a beautiful beach that's popular for sea-kayaking, with some interesting tidal caves. The mountains that rise up behind these beaches hold rain forests, waterfalls, and wildlife.

⟲ At **La Merced National Wildlife Refuge,** owned by Selva Mar, you can ride the range on horseback, explore the forest on a nature hike, or go bird-watching with an excellent guide. Tours include transportation from your hotel and a guide; the full-day tour includes lunch. ⊠ *Road between Dominical and Playa Uvita* ☎ *771–4582* ⊕ *www.wildlifecostarica. com* ⊠ *$25 half-day tour; $65 full-day tour* ☉ *By tour only.*

Outdoor Activities

Outfitters in Dominical (⇨ *above*) run tours to the park and surrounding beaches. **La Merced National Wildlife Refuge** (⇨ *above*) has birding, forest hikes, and horseback riding.

DIVING & SNORKELING **Mystic Dive Center** (☎ 788–8636 ⊕ www.mysticdivecenter.com) specializes in dive and snorkel trips to Caño Island, about 50 km (31 mi), or an hour and 15 minutes, from Playa Uvita. ($85 full-day snorkeling; $145 full-day diving including equipment)

The best spot for snorkeling in the park is at the north end of Playa Ballena, near the whale's tail. **Ballena Tour** (☎ 831–1617) has a combination tour ($65) that includes snorkeling in the park, swimming in the ocean to hear the whales sing, or swimming with sociable bottlenosed dolphins when they're around, plus exploring the caves at Ventana Beach. The tours are led by Chumi, a local who has fished and guided all his life here. His boat's four-stroke engine is extra quiet and environment-friendly. **Delfin Tours** (☎ 743–8169), with an office very close to the beach, rents snorkeling gear and organizes snorkeling and fishing trips.

FISHING **Ballena Tour** (⇨ Diving & Snorkeling, *above*) organizes fishing trips for mahimahi, tuna, and mackerel, as well as catch-and-release sailfish and marlin. A half-day costs $250; a whole day $400, including drinks, snacks, and all equipment.

KAYAKING **Club Fred** (⊠ On the Costanera, 200 m south of bridge to Ojochal ⟲ ☎ 363–9042 ⊕ www.clubfredcr.com)leads adventurous kayaking trips from mid-November to May in and around the caves at Playa Ventana ($40). They also offer river kayaking and ocean snorkeling trips to Isla Ballena ($40). Kayaks are comfortable sit-on-tops with back rests.

ULTRALIGHT FLIGHTS For a bird's-eye view of Bahía Ballena and the park, take off in an ultralight flying machine with aeronautical engineer Georg Kiechle and ☼ **Skyline Nature Ultralight Flying Tours** (✉ Road into Uvita ☎ 743–8037 ⊕ www.fly-ultralight.com). Tours cost $65–$150 for 20 minutes to an hour.

WHALE & DOLPHIN TOURS When you head out to snorkel, chances are you'll be on the lookout for whales and dolphins, too. **Ballena Tour** (☎ 831–1617) has a popular combo ☼ tour (⇨ Diving & Snorkeling, *above*).

Where to Stay & Eat

$–$$ ✕ **Citrús Floating Restaurant.** Breezy and pretty, this restaurant is on the beautifully restored riverboat *Manglar Sur*—floating in a blue lagoon with a green mountain backdrop. Run by a Belgian/French chef, Citrús is as refreshing as its name, with *haute cuisine*—for example, duck breast with cranberry sauce and baked goat cheese and smoked salmon— served Jungle Queen–style. You can dine dockside or charter the boat for an elegant lunch or sunset dinner cruise through the mangroves. It's open for lunch and dinner. ✉ *At Km 178 on the Costanera, at the dock, just south of Ojochal* ☎ 786–5175 ▬ *No credit cards* ☾ *Closed Mon. Dec.–Apr.; Closed Mon.–Wed. May–Dec.*

★ $ ✕ **Pizzeria El Jardin Tortuga.** Ordering a pizza doesn't get any simpler than this: vegetarian or meat. The German pizza baker can make only six individual pizzas at a time in his wood-fired clay oven, but it's worth the wait for thin-crust pies heaped with toppings. The only other menu items are lasagna and salad. ✉ *Ojochal, past supermarket, left on bridge and first right* ☎ 786–5059 ▬ *No credit cards* ☾ *Closed Tues.*

★ $$–$$$ ▥ **Cristal Ballena Hotel Resort.** High on a hillside with spectacular ocean views, this Austrian-owned hotel is now the most luxurious base for exploring the Uvita/Dominical area. The jewel in this blue-and-white, Mediterranean-style hotel is a sparkling, 400-square-meter swimming pool that commands both mountain and sea views. Spacious, elegant rooms and suites set in carefully landscaped grounds have canopy beds, large tile bathrooms with sinks for two and sliding-glass doors leading out to private terraces, each with an ocean view. If you tire of the view (not likely), there are large TVs set on swivel bases. Four rustic Adventure Lodges are set close together in a lush garden, but they get quite hot and don't have an ocean view. Breakfasts are hearty and the Pura Vida poolside restaurant serves excellent fish, along with some tasty Austrian specialties. Service is on the slow side, but with an ocean vistas and refreshing breezes, who really cares? ✉ *7 km/4 mi south of Uvita on the Costanera* ☎ 365–6258 🖷 212/901–6980 ⊕ *www.cristal-ballena. com* ➲ *19 suites, 4 cabins* ⟋ *Restaurant, bar, fan, pool, satellite TV, safety boxes, coffeemakers, minibars, wireless Internet; no a/c, no TV, no minibar in 4 cabins* ▬ *AE, MC, V.*

$ ▥ **Diquis del Sur Resort.** An ideal—and affordable—tropical retreat for the winter-weary, this formerly rundown hotel in the hills above Ojochal has been given new life by a French-Canadian couple who abandoned the Great White North almost the moment they saw this property. The views look to mountains and ocean and a garden full of mature fruit trees and flowering shrubs. Four freshly painted white bungalows with

6

two rooms each are spread around the pretty grounds. Some have a kitchen and air-conditioning; some have only a fan. But the shade trees keep the cabins cool. The full breakfast has a French accent—crepes, French toast, omeletes—and is served in a thatched-roof dining room overlooking an inviting pool with a waterfall. Owners Renée and Pierre Beaupré are just as delighted as their guests to be in this "earthly paradise." There is a two-day minimum stay. ⊠ *1 km/½ mi up dirt road signed* Calle Papagayo, *off Ojochal main Rd.* ☎ *786–5013* ⊕ *www. diquiscostarica.com* ⇄ *8 rooms* ⚲ *Dining room, pool, fans, some kitchens, bar; no a/c in some rooms, no room TVs, no room phones* ⊟ *No credit cards* ⏏ *BP.*

☾ $ 🏠 **Rancho La Merced.** Be a cowboy for a day, herding and riding the range, at this 1,235-acre hillside cattle ranch. Or hike mountain trails in search of wildlife and birds. The rambling, 60-year-old farmhouse where you bed down is made of wood that was shipped in from Puntarenas and then carried uphill on men's backs, before there were roads or cars in this area. The avocado-green hacienda has four simple but comfortable rooms that can accommodate up to 10 people; they share a modern bathroom with two solar-powered showers and toilets. A homey eat-in kitchen is equipped with a microwave, coffeemaker, stove, and fridge. A separate cabin sleeps three. Resident guides can take you on foot or horseback into the forest. ⊠ *1.5 km/1 mi north of Uvita, then 700 m up steep mountain road, Uvita* ☎ *771–4582* 📠 *771–8841* ⊕ *www.wildlifecostarica.com* ⇄ *4 rooms, 1 cabin* ⚲ *Fans, hiking, horseback riding; no a/c, no room phones, no room TVs* ⊟ *AE, MC, V* ⏏ *FAP.*

Shopping

Next door to Mystic Dive Center is **Green Leaf Arts & Artesania** (⊠ Centro Comercial Ventanas, near Km 174, north of Ojochal ☎ 788–8636), with a great selection of quality local art and indigenous crafts. You can also find huge bowls and vases made of recycled ojoche wood, which used to cover all of Ojochal.

To & from Bahía Ballena

20 km/12 mi (30 mins) southeast of Dominical.

The park area encompasses the communities of Uvita, Bahía Ballena, and Ojochal, all easily accessed off the Costanera. The park officially begins 20 km (12 mi) south of Dominical along a wide, newly paved highway. As soon as you get off the highway, however, the roads are bumpy and dusty. While Uvita and Bahía have phones, the phone lines have just reached Ojochal, and many hotels and restaurants still have no service. The communications hub is an Internet café in the center of the village. Alternatively, take a taxi or bus from Dominical. Buses leave Dominical at 4:30 and 10:30 AM daily and there are longer-haul buses that pass along the Costanera and can drop you off in Uvita.

THE GOLFO DULCE

One of only three tropical fjords in the world, the Golfo Dulce has 600-foot-deep waters in the center of the gulf that attract humpback

Going Fishing?

COSTA RICA TEEMS WITH a constant supply of *pescado* (fish), some of which might seem unique to North Americans. Below are some local catches and where you'll find them.

Gaspar (alligator gar), found in Barra del Colorado River and Lake Arenal, looks like a holdover from prehistoric times and has a long narrow snout full of sharp teeth; they make great sport on light tackle. Gar meat is firm and sweet (some say shrimplike), but the eggs are toxic to humans.

Guapote (rainbow bass) make their home in Lake Arenal. It's a hard-hitting catch: 5- to 6-pounders are common. Taxonomically, guapote are not related to bass, but are caught similarly, by casting or flipping plugs or spinner bait. Streams near the Cerro de la Muerte, off the Pan-American Highway leading south from San José, are stocked with guapote. The fish tend to be small, but the scenery makes a day here worthwhile.

Marlin and sailfish migrate northward through the year, beginning about November when they are plentiful in the Golfito region. From December into April they spread north to Quepos, which has some of the country's best deep-sea fishing, and are present in large numbers along the Nicoya Peninsula at Carrillo and Sámara from February to April, and near Tamarindo and Flamingo from May to September. Pacific sailfish average over 45 kilos (100 pounds), and are usually fought on a 15-pound line or less. Costa Rican laws require that all sails, except record catches, be released.

Tarpon and snook fishing is big on the Caribbean coast, centered at the mouth of the Barra del Colorado River. The acrobatic tarpon, which averages about 85 pounds here, is able to swim freely between saltwater and freshwater and is considered by many to be the most exciting catch on earth. Tarpon sometimes strike like a rocket, hurtling 5 meters (16 feet) into the air, flipping, and twisting left and right. Anglers say the success rate of experts is to land about one out of every 10 tarpon hooked. In the Colorado, schools of up to 100 tarpon following and feeding on schools of *titi* (small, sardinelike fish) travel for more than 160 km (100 mi) to Lake Nicaragua. Snook also make this long swim. The long-standing International Game Fishing Association all-tackle record was taken in this area.

6

whales. At Chacarita, 33 km (20 mi) South of Palmar Sur, the southern coast assumes a multiple personality. Heading west, you reach the Osa Peninsula and, eventually, the Pacific Ocean and the wildest region of Costa Rica. Continuing due south is the Golfo Dulce, which means Sweet Gulf and suggests tranquil waters. This gulf creates two shorelines: an eastern shore that is accessible only by boat above Golfito, and a western shore, which is the eastern side of the Osa Peninsula. South of Golfito the coast fronts the Pacific Ocean once again (rather than the tranquil gulf), with beaches that beckon surfers and nature lovers.

Golfito

❽ Overlooking a small gulf (hence its name) and hemmed in by a steep bank of forest, Golfito has a great location and little else—that is, unless you're an angler. Sport- and fly-fishing have taken off in this area, and many lodges here run world-class fishing trips. The gulf water is warm, salty, and crystal clear in the early mornings. The sun sets behind the rolling silhouette of the Osa Peninsula and some nights you can spot phosphorescent fish jumping. Golfito was a thriving banana port for several decades—United Fruit arrived in 1938—with elegant housing for its plantation managers. After United Fruit pulled out in 1985, Golfito slipped into a state of poverty and neglect. The town itself consists of a pleasant older section and a long, ugly strip of newer buildings, dilapidated former workers' quarters, and abundant seedy bars. Visiting U.S. Navy ships dock here, and small cruise ships moor in the harbor. The Costa Rica Coast Guard Academy is also here.

NAVIGATING GOLFITO Taxis and boats take you wherever you need to go in and around Golfito. You can hire taxi boats at the city dock in Golfito (about $50 to go to area lodges or across to Puerto Jiménez). The only way to reach the remote Golfo Dulce lodges above Golfito is by boat. Early morning is the best time, when the water in the gulf is at its calmest. Most lodges include the boat transport in their rates.

Exploring

The northwestern end of town is the so-called **American Zone,** full of wooden houses on stilts, where the expatriate managers of United Fruit lived amid flowering trees imported from all over the world. These houses were purchased by Costa Ricans when the company departed, and a few are now very basic B&Bs.

Golfito doesn't have a beach of its own, but **Playa Cacao** is a mere five-minute boat ride across the bay from town. Hire a boat at the city dock or from a mooring opposite the larger cruise-ship dock, north of Golfito's center. Playa Cacao has two casual restaurants and one collection of basic cabinas, but it makes a cooler, quieter option when the heat and noise in Golfito get unbearable.

Piedras Blancas National Park, adjacent to the Golfito National Wildlife Refuge, has some great birding. The park is covered in verdant forest and is home to many species of endemic plants and animals. It's an important wildlife corridor because it connects to Corcovado National Park, and it's one of the few places in Costa Rica where jaguars still live. Follow the main road northwest through the old American Zone, past the airstrip and a housing project: the place where a dirt road heads into the rain forest is ground zero for bird-watchers. ✉ *Adjacent to Golfito National Wildlife Refuge* ☎ *No phone* 💲 *Free* ☉ *Daily dawn–dusk.*

★ A Garden of Eden with mass plantings of ornamental palms, bromeliads, heliconias, cycads, orchids, and flowering gingers, **Casa Orquideas** is accessible only by boat. It has been tended with care for more than 25 years by American owners Ron and Trudy MacAllister. The three-hour tour includes touching, tasting, and smelling, plus spotting toucans and hummingbirds. Tours are $5 per person for four or more. The guided tour costs a minimum of $20. The water taxi from Golfito to the garden (about $60 for up to four people, including the return trip) is a tour in itself. ⊠ *North of Golfito on the Golfo Dulce* ☎ *775–1614* 🎟 *$5* ☺ *Tours Sat.–Thurs. at 8:30* AM.

Outdoor Activities

FISHING The open ocean holds plenty of sailfish, marlin, and roosterfish during the dry months, as well as mahimahi, tuna, and wahoo during the rainy season; there's excellent bottom fishing any time of year. Captains are in constant radio contact with one another and tend to share fish finds.

Banana Bay Marina (☎ 775–0838 ⊕ www.bananabaymarina.com) has one of the biggest charter fleets in town, with a dozen boats and world-record-holding captains. **C-Tales** (⊠ Las Gaviotas Hotel ☎ 775–0062 ⊕ www.c-tales.com) operates fishing boats with English-speaking captains. **Golfito Sailfish Rancho** (☎ 380–4262, 800/450–9908 in U.S.) has a big fishing charter operation with 11 boats. **King & Bartlett Sportfishing International Marina** (☎ 775–1624 ⊕ www.kingandbartlett.com) ★ arranges sportfishing charters. **Roy Ventura** (⇨ Playa Zancudo, *below*) has some of the area's best charter trips. **Land Sea** (⊠ Waterfront next to Banana Bay Marina ☎☎ 775–1614 ⊕ www.marinaservices-yachtdelivery.com) arranges day trips with independent captains in the area.

Where to Stay & Eat

The atmosphere of the in-town Golfito hotels (Hotel Samoa del Sur and Hotel Las Gaviotas) differs dramatically from the lodges in the delight-fully remote east coast of the Golfo Dulce above Golfito. The latter is a world of jungle and blue water, birds and fish, and desert-island beaches, with lodges accessible only by boat, from either Golfito or Puerto Jiménez.

GOLFITO ✕**Banana Bay.** For consistently good American-style food, you can't beat $–$$ this breezy marina restaurant with a view of very expensive yachts and fishing boats. Locals complain that the prices are high, but portions are hefty, and include generous salads, excellent chicken fajitas wrapped in homemade tortillas, interesting pastas, and a delicious grilled dorado fish sandwich with a mountain of fries—a deal at $7. Jumbo shrimp, for which Golfito's commercial fleet is famous, are expensive at $14 but worth it. While you're waiting for your order, check your e-mail at their high-speed Internet café. ⊠ *Golfito main street, south of town dock* ☎ *775–0838* ▭ *MC, V* ☺ *Breakfast served.*

$ ✕**Restaurante Mar y Luna.** Strings of buoys, nets, and fishing rods give a nautical air to this casual terrace restaurant that juts out into Golfito Harbor. Even after the hottest day, there are cool evening breezes here and the restaurant's twinkling fairy lights frame a pleasant harbor view. The seafood-heavy menu includes shrimp and grilled whole fish. Chicken fillets smothered in a mushroom sauce and vegetarian dishes are non-fish choices. The quality varies, depending on who's in the kitchen, but during a recent visit, the kitchen was in top form. ⊠ *South end of Golfito main street, just north of Hotel Las Gaviotas* ☎ *775–0192* ▭ *AE, MC, V* ☺ *Closed Mon.*

☾ $ ✕🏠 **Hotel Samoa del Sur.** Nautical kitsch at its best, this dockside hotel has a ship-shaped bar/restaurant ($–$$), complete with a sail and a mermaid figurehead. This is definitely fishermen territory, with a pool table, loud music, and big TVs. Unexpectedly, the breakfast omeletes may be the best in Costa Rica. The seaside theme carries through to spacious rooms, from shell-patterned bedspreads to shell-shaped hand soap. Rooms have two double beds, quiet, remote-controlled air-conditioning, and tile bathrooms with hot water (a rarity). Mattresses are a little soft, and you are at the mercy of adjoining neighbors and the bass from the bar, but things usually quiet down by 11 PM. The eccentric French owner/architect designed a swimming pool in the shape of two butterfly wings, plus a kids' pool and play area. After midnight you are warned not to leave your room to avoid a nasty encounter with the guard dogs. ⊠ *Main street, 1 block north of town dock* ☎ *775–0233* 🖷 *775–0573* ⊕ *SamoaSur@racsa.co.cr* ↩ *14 rooms* ♻ *Restaurant, fans, cable TV, pool, bicycles, kayaks, bar, laundry service; no room phones* ☰ *AE, MC, V* ⊚| *EP.*

THE GOLFO DULCE 🏠 **Golfito Sailfish Rancho.** Embraced by gulf and jungle, this comfy
$$$$ white-stucco lodge attracts serious fishermen and celebrity sports figures who come to fish, fish, fish! All-inclusive, first-rate fishing packages range from $1,900 for three days to $3,900 for seven days and include San José transfers and hotel; flight, taxi, and boat transportation to the lodge; plus all meals, snacks, beer and wine, and fishing gear. Two wings of comfortable rooms with tile verandas look onto a narrow strip of beach. The convivial restaurant serves buffet meals. Spacious rooms have racks for storing fishing rods. The Rancho's fleet includes 10 up-to-date fishing boats, where you spend the majority of your days. ⊠ *15-min boat ride north of Golfito* ☎ *775–2157, 877/726–2468 in U.S.* 🖶 *427 58th St., West Palm Beach, FL 33407* 🖷 *561/848–8988 in U.S.* ⊕ *www.golfitosailfish.com* ↩ *10 rooms* ♻ *Restaurant, fans, beach, fishing, bar; no a/c, no room phones, no room TVs, no kids under 12* ☰ *AE, MC, V* ⊚| *AI.*

★ $$$$ 🏠 **Playa Nicuesa Rainforest Lodge.** Hands down, this is the best lodge on the gulf, with friendly but professional service and an emphasis on adventure. Out the front door of the lodge are beach, bay, and mangroves, with kayaks, snorkeling, fishing, sailing, and swimming; out the back door is a forested mountain with hiking trails, a waterfall, and plenty of wildlife and a resident naturalist to interpret the trails. The two-story main lodge is a palatial treehouse, crafted from 15 kinds of wood. Luxurious, hexagonal wooden cabins with open-air showers are scattered around a lush garden that ensures privacy. A stucco guesthouse with four large, comfortable rooms is shaded by mango trees. Solar power ensures a steady supply of electricity and there's always lots of hot water. Imaginative meals are served in the second-story dining room–cum–lounge with an unbeatable tropical-garden view. ⊠ *Golfo Dulce, north of Golfito; accessible only by boat from Golfito or Puerto Jiménez* ☎ *735–5237 voice mail* ⊕ *www.nicuesalodge.com* ↩ *5 cabins, 4 rooms* ♻ *Restaurant, beach, snorkeling, boating, fishing, hiking, bar; no a/c, no room phones, no room TVs, no kids under 6* ☰ *MC, V* ☺ *Closed Oct.–Nov. 15* ⊚| *AI.*

$$$ 🏠 **Esquinas Rainforest Lodge.** This well-managed eco-lodge is run by an Austrian nonprofit group who have tried to instill a sense of Teutonic order. But the tidy gravel paths winding past wooden cabins in manicured gardens are being encroached upon by wild forest, with the garden looking wilder every year. Rooms have tile floors, good reading lamps, and airy bathrooms with plenty of hot water. A spring-fed pool is delightful, and the candlelit dining room serves excellent food. Fragrant white ginger and ylang-ylang encircle a pond with resident caimans. Wild and thrilling trails head to the waterfalls and primary forest of Piedras Blancas Park. Local guides lead river walks and bird-watching tours. More than 80 percent of the guests here are from Germany and Austria. If you have 4WD, you can get here by following the dirt road through the heart of Piedras Blancas National Park. In the dry season when it's passable, this back route can cut miles off a trip from the north, and it passes through some gorgeous wilderness. ⊠ *Near La Gamba, 5 km/3 mi west of Villa Briceño turnoff* 🖀🖨 *775–0901 lodge, 775–0140 Golfito office* ⊕ *www.esquinaslodge. com* ⮫ *14 rooms* ♦ *Dining room, fans, pool, hiking, horseback riding, bar; no a/c, no room phones, no room TVs* 🖃 *AE, MC, V* ⦿ *FAP.*

> ## TO FLUSH OR NOT TO FLUSH?
>
> Costa Rican toilets *do* flush, but in most of Costa Rica septic systems weren't designed to accommodate toilet tissue (the pipes are too narrow). If you don't want to be the *gringo* who clogs up the works, watch for signs asking you not to put anything in the toilet—that includes toilet paper. A wastebasket (*basurero*) is almost always provided to hold used tissue. Even upscale resorts and other places with modern septic systems have the basket, since the habit has been ingrained in locals.

Shopping

★ In a class all its own, the **Mercado Artesania** (⊠ Hotel Samoa Sur, main street, 1 block north of town dock) is the biggest emporium in the Southern Zone, filled with every imaginable—and unimaginable—souvenir. Large paintings by local artists, huge painted fans from Thailand, hammocks, beach clothes, and life-size snake carvings are just a few of the offerings here. Even if you don't buy a thing, it's fun to look. Ask the hotel manager to unlock the door and visit the Shell Museum, the hotel owner's personal, life-long collection of shells.

Nightlife

The bar at **Banana Bay Marina** (⊠ Main street, south of town dock) is usually full of English-speaking fishermen in the evening. Every night, **Bar Los Comales** (⊠ Near the large dry dock at the north end of town) has late-night dancing and karaoke until 2 AM in a rougher section of town, near the large dry-dock. Be a little careful here; go with a group and leave in a taxi.

Samoa del Sur bar (⊠ Hotel Samoa del Sur, main street, 1 block north of town dock) has a mix of Ticos and foreigners, mostly of the male persuasion, and loud music until 11 PM.

To & from Golfito

339 km/212 mi (8 hrs by car; 1 hr by plane) southeast of San José.

From San José the trip is a long and often grueling drive along paved roads but over often-foggy mountains. Your best bet, especially if you are visiting one of the lodges on the gulf, is to fly to Golfito. Direct buses from San José leave twice daily.

Golfito Essentials

🏧 Bank/ATM **ATH Coopealianza** ✉ Across from hospital, north end of town. **Banco Nacional** ✉ South of hospital ☎ 775-1101.

🏥 Hospital **Regional Hospital** ✉ American Zone, near Deposito ☎ 775-1001.

💊 Pharmacy **Farmacia Golfito** ✉ Main street, across from city park ☎ 775-2442.

🚕 Taxis **Taxi service** ☎ 775-2020.

ℹ Visitor Information **Land Sea Services** ✉ Next to Banana Bay Marina on left as you enter town ☎ 775-1614. Also sells SANSA tickets.

Playa Zancudo

❾ For laid-back beaching involving hammocks strung between palms and nothing more demanding than watching the sun set, you can't beat breezy Playa Zancudo, with its miles of wide, flat beach and views of the Osa Peninsula. It isn't particularly beautiful: the 10 km (6 mi) of dark brown sand is often strewn with flotsam and jetsam. But there's a constant breeze and a thick cushion of palm and almond trees between the beach and the parallel dirt road through town. The standout feature is the magnificent view across the gulf to the tip of the Osa Peninsula. The beach runs almost due north–south, so you have center-stage seats for sunsets, too. Away from the beach breezes, be prepared for biting *zancudos* (no-see-ums).

NAVIGATING PLAYA ZANCUDO — Getting around Playa Zancudo doesn't take much, as it's so small. Rent an electric golf cart ($100, three-day minimum; $225 per week) at Brad's Shop (☎ 776-0161) across from the Supermercado Buen Precio. Or rent a bike at Cabinas Sol y Mar or Tres Amigos Supermercado, both on the main road in Zancudo, for about $10 per day.

Outdoor Activities

FISHING — If you've got your own gear, you can do some good shore fishing from the beach or the mouth of the mangrove estuary, or hire a local boat to take you out into the gulf. The main edible catches are yellowfin tuna, snapper, and snook; catch-and-release sportfish include marlin, roosterfish, and swordfish.

Roy Ventura (✉ Roy's Zancudo Lodge, north end of town on main rd. ☎ 776-0008) runs the biggest charter operation in the area, with 12 boats ranging in length from 25 feet to 28 feet. Packages include room, food, and drink, and you can arrange to be picked up in Golfito, Puerto Jiménez, or San José. Captain John Olson at **Sportfishing Unlimited** (☎ 776-0036) fishes from 28-foot, center-console boats with both fly and conventional tackle. The rate is $550 per day for two fishers, which includes lunch, drinks, and gear. Born and raised in Golfito, **Captain Ronny** (☎ 776-0048) has worked at all the area fishing lodges. He uses a VHF

Radio fish finder on his 26-foot boat with 240 HP diesel engines. The daily rate is an all-inclusive $650.

HORSEBACK RIDING ☪ Early-morning rides over hills, through jungle, and along the beach ($50) set off at 7 AM from a farm 4 mi inland and finish at **Oasis on the Beach** (☎ 776–0087) for a full breakfast. A shorter ride, from 4 to 6 PM ($30), takes you to a hilltop for a sunset view over the gulf.

KAYAKING The kayaking is great at the beach and along the nearby Río Colorado, lined with mangroves. **Cabinas Los Cocos** (⊠ Beach Rd. ☎ 776–0012) has a popular tour ($40) that takes you for a 1½-hour motorboat ride up the river, then a two-hour kayak tour along a jungly mangrove channel, before motoring back to Zancudo. The company also rents user-friendly, sit-on-top kayaks with back rests for $5 per hour.

Where to Stay & Eat

¢–$ ✕ **Macondo.** There's absolutely nothing fancy about this tiny restaurant, but it serves the best homemade pasta in the Southern Zone. Chef Daniel Borello comes from the Piemonte region in northern Italy and his pasta is light, almost tissue-paper thin, and perfectly sauced. There's no written menu, just a recitation of pasta shapes available with your choice of sauce. There are also meat or spinach-and-cheese ravioli and, sometimes, lasagna, as well as jumbo shrimp and tenderloin. But stick to the pasta—it's a sure bet. The only disappointment is that none of the wine choices is worthy of the food. End your meal with an authentic espresso or cappuccino. ⊠ *Across from the Ferreteria, on beach road, center of town* ☎ 776-0157 ▤ *No credit cards* ⊘ *Closed Sept.–Nov.*

$ ✕▥ **Oasis on the Beach.** This is the ideal, laid-back beachfront hotel. The three wooden cabins are reminiscent of old Nantucket cottages. The cabins have two bedrooms each, bright ceramic bathrooms, and porches to sit on to catch the constant breeze and admire the view of coconut palms, hammocks, blue sea and sky, and white surf. Mini-fridges are stocked with juice and milk. The newest additions are the two air-conditioned rooms in a two-story villa. The contemporary restaurant/bar (⇨ *above*) is the coolest place in Zancudo. ⊠ *Main beach road, as you enter town* ☎ 776–0087 ⊕ *www.oasisonthebeach.com* ⇴ *3 cabins, 2 rooms* ⚏ *Restaurant, refrigerators, beach, horseback riding, bar; no a/c in some rooms, no room phones, no room TVs* ▤ V ⭕ *EP.*

¢–$ ✕▥ **Cabinas Sol y Mar.** As its name implies, Cabinas Sol y Mar has sun and sea, plus a beach fringed by coconut palms. Peach-colored cabinas with porches and high ceilings look onto the gulf and have views of the Osa Peninsula. Each roomy cabina has a sunny bathroom with a pebble-paneled shower and sleeps

6

¿HABLA INGLES?

Although some Central Pacific areas like Jacó and Manuel Antonio are very touristy, don't assume everyone speaks English. For example, oftentimes taxi and bus drivers won't understand your directions in English. To make traveling smoother, write down the original Spanish name of the place you're headed to or ask your hotel's reception desk attendee to write out directions in Spanish, which you can pass on with a smile to your driver.

four. The alfresco restaurant (⇨ *above*) consistently serves the best food in town. The popular U-shaped bar is an easy place to meet new friends, including the friendly Canadian-American owners. A shop sells colorful sarongs and clothing from Thailand. ⊠ *Main road, south of Cabinas Los Cocos, Playa Zancudo* 🕾 *776–0014* ⊕ *www.zancudo.com* 🛏 *5 cabinas, 1 house* ⚖ *Restaurant, fans, beach, bar, gift shop; no a/c, no room phones, no room TVs* 🗖 *No credit cards* 🍴 *EP.*

$$$$ 🏨 **Roy's Zancudo Lodge.** Most people who stay here are anglers on all-inclusive sportfishing packages, taking advantage of Roy's 12 fishing boats. But the comfortable, modern hotel is a good choice even if you've never caught anything but a cold. It's right on the beach—the ample, verdant grounds surround an inviting pool, and an open-air restaurant serves buffet meals. The nonfishing rate includes all meals and "national-brand" drinks (locally made brands of alcohol). Women are more than welcome, but just remember this place is usually full of sometimes rowdy fishermen. The sea foam–green two-story hotel has huge rooms with hardwood floors, two firm double beds, and ocean views. Four suites are in cozy private cabinas, and there are two smaller, cheaper rooms. ⊠ *Main road, north end of town, 200 m past police post, Playa Zancudo* 🕾 *Apdo. 41, Golfito* 🕾 *776–0008* 🖷 *776–0011* ⊕ *www.royszancudolodge.com* 🛏 *14 rooms, 4 cabinas* ⚖ *Restaurant, fans, refrigerators, TV, pool, whirlpool tub, beach, fishing, bar* 🗖 *AE, MC, V* 🍴 *FAP.*

$ 🏨 **Cabinas Los Cocos.** This little beachfront colony of four self-catering cabins is designed for people who want to kick back and enjoy the beach. Artist Susan England and her husband, Andrew Robertson, are Zancudo fixtures and can organize any activity, including river safaris, kayaking tours, and visits to nature preserves. Two idyllic tropical cabins have thatched roofs and hammocks. The other two cabins are renovated 40-year-old banana-company houses moved here from Palmar Norte. These charming white-and-green wooden cottages give you the rare chance to live a little bit of Costa Rican history. ⊠ *Beach road, about 300 m north of Sol y Mar* 🕾 *776–0012* ⊕ *www.loscocos.com* 🛏 *4 cabins* ⚖ *Kitchens, beach; no a/c, no room phones, no room TVs* 🗖 *No credit cards* 🍴 *EP.*

Nightlife

Hanging out at the bar at **Sol y Mar** (⊠ Main road, south of Cabinas Los Cocos) and Oasis on the Beach constitutes nightlife here, although there is sometimes karaoke or a disco in town. An itinerant mariachi band shows up at restaurants and bars all over town.

To & from Playa Zancudo
51 km/32 mi (2½ hrs) south of Golfito.

The road from Golfito is paved for the first 11 km (7 mi), but after the turnoff at El Rodeo the trip entails almost two hours of bone shaking and a short ride on—but sometimes long wait for—a cable river ferry. You are much better off without a car here. You can hire a boat at the municipal dock in Golfito for the 25-minute ride ($30 for two) or take a *collectivo* boat that leaves Zancudo daily at 7 AM except on Sundays and docks at Hotel Samoa del Sur in Golfito; the return boat leaves Samoa del Sur at noon ($5 each way). **Cabinas Los Cocos** (⊠ Beach Rd. ☏ 776–0012) has water-taxi service to Golfito ($15 per person; minimum 2 people) and service to Puerto Jiménez ($15 per person; minimum 4 people).

Playa Pavones

❿ One of the most scenic beaches to drive past is remote Playa Pavones, on the southern edge of the mouth of Golfo Dulce. Through a fringe of palms you catch glimpses of brilliant blue, white surf crashing against black rocks, and the soft silhouette of the Osa Peninsula across the gulf. The area attracts serious surfer purists, but also has pristine black-sand beaches and virgin rain forest. The beach is very rocky, so it's important to ask around for the best swimming areas. One of the best places to swim is in the Río Claro, under the bridge or at the river mouth (dry season only). The town of Pavones itself is an unprepossessing collection of *pensiones* and sodas clustered around a soccer field.

Outdoor Activities

SURFING Pavones is famous for one of the longest waves in the world, thanks to the mouth of the Río Claro, which creates ideal sand banks and well-shaped waves. The ocean bottom is cobblestoned where the surfing waves break. The most consistent waves are from April to September, and that's when the surfing crowd heads down here from the Central Pacific Coast beaches. But even at the crest of its surfing season, Pavones is tranquility central compared to the surfing hotspots farther north.

6

Most surfers here are serious about their sport and bring their own boards, but you can rent surfboards—$25 long, $20 short—and Boogie boards at **Sea Kings Surf Shop** (⊠ In town, by the soccer field ☏ 393–6982 or 829–2409 ⊕ www.surfpavones.com). Surf lessons are $35, including board rental. **Cabinas La Ponderosa** (⇨ Where to Stay & Eat, *below*) rents surfboards and Boogie boards, as well as bicycles.

Where to Stay & Eat

¢–$ ✕ **Cafe de la Suerte.** Lucky for food-lovers, the "Good Luck Café" serves truly astonishing vegetarian food that even a carnivore could love, along with intriguing exotic juice combinations and thick fruit smoothies. The homemade yogurt is a revelation: light, almost fluffy, and full of flavor. The Israeli owners serve it over a cornucopia of exotic fruits, sprinkled with their own granola, and mix it into refreshing fruit-flavored *lassis* (yogurt-based drinks from India). Healthy sandwiches are heavy on excellent hummus, and hot vegetarian daily specials might include curried hearts of palm. Don't leave

> **CAUTION**
>
> In the unlikely event that you are bitten by a snake, stay calm, move slowly, and try to remember what the snake looked like, to tell the clinic staff. Only allow antivenin to be administered by a trained person, in case of side effects. Five hours is the window before any tissue loss. To avoid snakebites, stay on trails and wear long pants; in some areas high rubber boots are recommended. *Never* reach out to touch a snake or poke it with a stick, à la Jeff Corwin.

without buying a fudgy brownie or a brown-sugar oatmeal square for the road. ⊠ *Next to soccer field* ☎ *No phone* ⊟ *No credit cards.*

$$$
Fodor'sChoice
★

⊡ **Tiskita Jungle Lodge.** One of the premier attractions in the Southern Zone for nature lovers, Tiskita was begun in 1977 by Peter Aspinall, a passionate farmer and conservationist, and his wife, Lisbeth. The property includes a vast fruit orchard, with more than 100 varieties of trees that attract monkeys, coatis, birds, and other wildlife. Surrounding the orchard are 800 acres of primary and secondary forest, a habitat for the more than 275 species of birds and a 90-strong troop of squirrel monkeys. Peter leads tours of the orchard, and expert naturalist guide Luis Vargas leads bird-watching and nature tours. Comfortable, screened wooden cabins on stilts are surrounded by lush vegetation and have rustic furniture and modern, open-air bathrooms. Trails invite you to explore the jungle on your own and a cascading waterfall with freshwater pools. Very simple, rather meager buffet meals are served in an open-air dining room; but throughout the day you can help yourself to freshly squeezed tropical juices in the fridge, and the cookie jar is always full. Cabins are spread out, with lots of steps to climb. No. 6 has the most privacy, and a beautiful ocean view. The beach, with swimmable waters, is a steep 15-minute downhill walk. Most guests arrive by air taxi at the hotel's private airstrip. ⊠ *6 km/4 mi south of Playa Pavones* ✉ *Apdo. 13411–1000, San José* ☎ *296–8125* 🖷 *296–8133* ⊕ *www.tiskita-lodge.co.cr* ➷ *16 rooms in 3 single cabins, 3 doubles, and 1 triple* ⌂ *Dining room, fans, pool, beach, bicycles, hiking, horseback riding, bar, airstrip; no a/c, no room phones, no room TVs* ⊟ *AE, MC, V* ⊘ *Closed Sept. 15–Oct. 15* ⦿ *AI.*

☾ $
⊡ **Casa Siempre Domingo.** High on a breezy hill, this B&B has the best view in town of the Golfo Dulce meeting the Pacific Ocean. Two of the four enormous rooms have 20-foot ceilings and two double beds set high to catch the view out the large windows. The other two rooms have pretty garden views. Even the big outdoor stone shower has narrow slits to capture the view. The owners have a young son and welcome playmates. Substantial breakfasts are served at a large communal table in a screened-in great room with wicker furniture, and there's a communal fridge to store food and drinks. The only drawback here is the very steep driveway up to this lofty perch. You'll need 4WD and nerves of steel or else you can build up a set of steely muscles climbing up. ⊠ *2 km/1mi south of town; follow signs after Río Claro Bridge* ☎ *820–4709* ⊕ *www.casadomingo.com* ➷ *4 rooms* ⌂ *Fans, surfing; no room phones, no room TVs* ⊟ *No credit cards* ⦿ *BP.*

$
⊡ **Riviera.** Brand new at this writing, each of these spacious, one-bedroom villas next to the Río Claro has a large modern kitchen, two double beds, and a futon. Huge tile patios look out onto a garden and there's a trail to the river, great for a cool swim. You're close enough to the beach to hear the surf, just a two-minute walk away. ⊠ *300 m southwest of Supermercado Siete Mares* ☎ *823–5874* ➷ *3 villas* ⌂ *Kitchen, beach; no phone, no TV* ⊟ *No credit cards* ⦿ *EP.*

Shopping

At **Arte Nativo** (⊠ Beside soccer field ☎ 821–6563) the best buys are charming watercolors painted by owner/artist Candyce Speck and beautifully matted with decorated banana paper ($15–$50). They're a much more evocative souvenir of the beach than the usual T-shirt. There's also a selection of high-quality indigenous crafts and funky jewelry and mobiles made from natural materials.

Nightlife

La Manta (✉ 1 km/½ mi north of town, on beach rd.) is the main event here, an open-air surfer bar where surfer videos shot by the owner are played every evening, DVD movies are shown on a big screen, and Tex-Mex is the cuisine of choice.

To & from Playa Pavones

53 km/33 mi (2½ hrs) south of Golfito.

There's no avoiding the bumpy road from Golfito to Conte, where the road forks north to Zancudo and south to Pavones. But the dirt road to Pavones is usually well graded. A public bus leaves from Golfito very early in the morning. A taxi from the airstrip in Golfito costs more than $60.

THE OSA PENINSULA

Costa Rica's most breathtaking scenery and most abundant wildlife thrive on the Osa Peninsula, one-third of which is covered by Corcovado National Park. You can hike into the park on any of three routes or fly in on a charter plane. Corcovado also works for day trips from nearby luxury nature lodges, most of which lie within private preserves that are home for much of the same wildlife you might see in the park. And complementing the peninsula's lush forests and pristine beaches is the surrounding sea, with great sportfishing.

There are two sides to the Osa: the gentle Golfo Dulce side, much of it accessible by car, albeit along rocky roads; and the much wilder and dramatic Pacific side, which is only accessible by boat or charter plane, or by hiking a sublimely beautiful coastal trail.

Puerto Jiménez

⓫ When you see Puerto Jiménez, you'll be surprised that this dusty, one-iguana town is the largest on the Osa Peninsula. Main-street traffic consists mostly of bicycles and ancient pickup trucks. But the place has a certain frontier charm, and new restaurants, hotels, Internet cafés, and "green" newcomers are lending an interesting, funky edge. It's also the last civilized outpost on the peninsula. Heading south, you fall off the grid. That means there is no public electricity or phone service. So make your phone calls, send e-mails, get cash, and stock up on supplies here. Be prepared for the humidity and mosquitoes—Jiménez has plenty of both.

The reason to come to Puerto Jiménez is to spend a night before or after visiting Corcovado National Park, since the town has the best access to the park's two main trailheads and an airport with flights from San José. It's also the base for the *collectivo* (public transport via pickup truck) to Carate.

FODOR'S FIRST PERSON

Dorothy MacKinnon
Writer

In search of wild nightlife, I set out with entomologist Tracie Stice one moonless night on the Osa Peninsula. Equipped with headlamps and night-vision optics, we carefully moved along the jungle trail. After studying, then steering clear of a venomous fer-de-lance snake, we came across a whip scorpion and a dozen huge,

industrious spiders. At a rickety suspension bridge, Stice felt a vibration. She signaled for silence while she scanned the bridge with her infra-red flashlight for an animal large enough to make the bridge move. In a flash we recognized the creature. Eyes wide with terror, we silently beat a hasty retreat, narrowly escaping an encounter with the most dreaded animal in the forest: the skunk.

The **National Parks Service Headquarters** (✉ Next to airport ☎ 735–5036 🖷 735–5276) has information about hiking trails in Corcovado National Park. The office is open weekdays 8 AM to 4 PM.

NAVIGATING
PUERTO JIMÉNEZ
Once you get to the main street in town, you can get around by foot. If you don't have a car and are staying at one of the Playa Platanares hotels or at Bosque del Río Tigre or Villa Corcovado—all outside of town—you are at the mercy of taxis to get anywhere. Water taxis, hired at the city dock, can take you to waterfront lodges, nearby beaches, or Golfito. There's also a passenger launch every morning at 6:30 to Golfito.

Outdoor Activities

Escondido Trex (✉ Restaurante Carolina, center of town, 200 m south of soccer field ☎ 735–5210 🖷 735–5196 ⊕ www.escondidotrex.com) arranges kayaking ($35 for a mangrove tour), charter-fishing, and small-boat outings for watching wildlife, in addition to a number of land-based outings. Isabel Esquivel, at **Osa Tropical** (✉ Across from Banco Nacional on main st. ☎ 735–5062 🖷 735–5043 ⊕ www.osatropical. com), runs the best generalist tour operation on the peninsula. Whatever travel question you ask the locals, they will usually say: "Ask Isabel." Along with arranging flights, ground transport, hotel bookings, tours, and car rentals, Osa Tropical is the radio communications center for all the Osa lodges and tour operators.

BIRD-WATCHING
The birding around the Osa Peninsula is world renowned, with more than 400 species. Endemic species include Baird's trogon, yellow-billed cotinga, whistling wren, black-cheeked ant tanager, and the glorious turquoise cotinga. There have even been sightings of the very rare harpy eagle in the last couple of years. One of the best spots on the peninsula to find a yellow-billed cotinga or a white-crested coquette is the bridge over the river at **Rincón** (✉ 40 km/25 mi north of Puerto Jiménez), if you get there before 7 AM.

★ The best English-speaking birding guides are Liz Jones and Abraham Gallo, who run **Bosque del Río Tigre Lodge** (✉ Dos Brazos del Tigre, 12 km/7½ mi northwest of Puerto Jiménez ☎ 735–5725 ⊕ www.osaadventures.com). They lead birding trips all around the peninsula, including in Corcovado National Park.

FISHING Along with Golfito across the water, Puerto Jiménez is a major fishing destination, with plenty of billfish and tuna, snapper and snook, almost all year, with the exception of June and July, when things slow down.

Escondido Trex (⇨ *above*) has charter-fishing trips and unique fishing-by-kayak trips. **Osa Sportfishing** (⊠ Next to Restaurant Carolina ☎ 735–5675 ⊕ www.fishosa.com) runs offshore fishing trips on a 30-foot Stamas boat, $900 for up to six fishers; inshore fishing trips are $550 for up to three. Sunset party cruises ($55) are aboard *The Delfin Blanco,* a 50-foot custom tour boat, with the chance to see dolphins and bioluminescent microbes during a scenic 3½-hour cruise around the gulf.

Parrot Bay Village (☎ 735–5180 🖷 735–5568 ⊕ www.parrotbayvillage.com) is one of the biggest operations around. Its state-of-the-art boats have quiet four-stroke engines and customs rods and lures. Guides recommend arriving 10 days before or after the new moon to ensure lots of fish. Most fishers come on a fishing package tour, but a full-day offshore fishing in a boat for two costs $850. The largest charter company in the area is **Roy Ventura** (⇨ Playa Zancudo, *above*).

HIKING If you have 4WD, it's just a 30-minute ride west to the village of Dos Brazos and the **Tigre Sector** of the park. Few hikers come here because it's difficult to access, which means it's more pristine and you'll likely have it to yourself. You can take a taxi to Dos Brazos and hike from here or use rustic but comfortable Bosque del Río Tigre Lodge as a base.

★ **Osa Aventura** (☎🖷 735–5758 ☎ 836–4114 ⊕ www.osaaventura.com) specializes in multiday Corcovado hiking adventures, led by Mike Boston, an ebullient tropical biologist who sounds like Sean Connery and looks like Crocodile Dundee. Mike has also hired three young bilingual biologists to lead hikes and conduct scientific research projects, in which visitors can sometimes participate.

HORSEBACK RIDING The most popular horse trails in the area are at remote **Río Nuevo Lodge** (⊠ Office next to La Carolina Restaurant, main st. ☎ 735–5411), about 12 bumpy km (7½ mi) west of town. Rides along the river and up onto scenic forested ridges last from three to seven hours and include transportation there and back and a home-cooked hot meal for $50–$65 per person.

KAYAKING Puerto Jiménez is a good base for sea-kayaking trips on the calm Golfo Dulce and for exploring the nearby mangrove rivers and estuaries. Alberto Robleto, an enterprising local, has amassed an impressive fleet of kayaks with excellent safety equipment at **Aventuras Tropicales Golfo Dulce** (⊠ South of airport on road to Playa Platanares ☎ 735–5195 🖷 735–5692 ⊕ www.aventurastropicales.com). Tours include snorkeling, dolphin-watching, and bird-watching. The most popular is the

Where Have All the Forests Gone?

THE WORLD GIVES HIGH MARKS to Costa Rica for its environmental awareness, but accolades don't always match reality. In the last half century more than two-thirds of Costa Rica's original forests have been destroyed. Forests have traditionally been considered unproductive land, and their destruction was for a long time synonymous with development. In the 1970s and 1980s, international and domestic development policies fueled the destruction of large tracts of wilderness. Fortunately, in the 1970s alarmed Costa Rican conservationists began creating what is now the best national park system in Central America. The government has since made progress in curbing deforestation outside the national parks, too.

As you travel through Costa Rica, you see that its predominant landscapes are not cloud and rain forests but the coffee and banana plantations and cattle ranches that have replaced them. Deforestation not only spells disaster for endangered animals like the jaguar and the harpy eagle, but can have grave consequences for human beings. Forests absorb rain and release water slowly, playing an important role in regulating the flow of rivers—which is why severely deforested regions often suffer twin plagues of floods during the rainy season and drought during the dry months. Tree covers also prevent topsoil erosion, thus keeping the land fertile and productive; in many parts of the country erosion has left once-productive farmland almost worthless.

---

three-hour mangrove tour ($25). A three- to nine-day kayaking tour ($80 per day, with four participants) teaches survival skills in the tropical forest. **Escondido Trex** (⇨ *above*) has sea-kayaking trips and rents sit-on-top kayaks by the hour for $5.

Where to Stay & Eat

Playa Platanares is only about 7 km (4 mi) outside of Puerto Jiménez, but lodgings there have a very different feeling from those in town, as they are on a lovely and quiet beach. Bosque del Río Tigre, Villa Corcovado, and Río Nuevo Lodge are also outside of town, but in forested areas.

★ $$ ✕ **El Restaurante Jade Luna.** Haute cuisine is not what you'd expect in Puerto Jiménez, but New York chef Barbara Burckhardt has set a whole new standard at her elegantly arcaded terrace restaurant. Already famous for her ice creams and sorbets, Barbara has scoured the country to find goat cheese, the best smoked trout, and the freshest herbs, and solicited local fishermen to deliver fresh seafood, to create outstanding dinners as well. The menu changes daily, but you can count on such creative dishes as grilled red snapper in a coconut curry broth, grilled loin pork chop with a coriander, cumin, orange, and black-peppercorn rub, and succulent coconut and macadamia-fried shrimp. Italian and French wines are reasonably priced ($16–$30). The chef spares no expense in her ingredients, her raw materials, and her attention to presentation and service. For dessert, the coconut and dulce de leche macadamia-nut pie with chocolate sauce is a hit. ✉ *500 m east of airport on road to Playa*

Platanares ☎ 735–5739 🖃 *No credit cards* ☾ *No lunch. Closed Sun; closed Sept. 15 to Thanksgiving.*

¢–$ ✕ **Juanita's Mexican Bar & Grill.** Swing open the saloon doors of this cantina and you might think you're in another south-of-the-border frontier town. The popular bamboo bar dispenses signature margaritas to go along with the Tex-Mex menu of fajitas, burritos, and taco salads. The food is only so-so, but the brightly colored tablecloths and art enliven the eating experience. It's open for breakfast, too, with the only breakfast buffet in town. ⊠ *Beside CaféNet El Sol, center of town* ☎ 735–5056 🖃 *No credit cards.*

¢–$ ✕ **Restaurante Carolina.** This simple alfresco restaurant in the heart of Puerto Jiménez serves decent *comida típica* (typical food) and reliably fresh seafood. It's also the central meeting place for every tourist and foreigner in town, ergo a good place to pick up information. Don't count on using a credit card, as phone lines are dodgy. ⊠ *Main street, center of town* ☎ 735–5185 🖃 *MC, V.*

★ $$$$ 🏨 **Iguana Lodge.** If a long stretch of deserted beach is your idea of heaven, this luxury lodge with breezy, screened-in cabins among mature trees is for you. The gentle Golfo Dulce waters are perfect for swimming, sea-kayaking, and Boogie boarding. Cabins are furnished elegantly in bamboo, with thoughtful touches, including Egyptian cotton sheets and a raft of candles for romantic evenings. The upper-level cabins have the best views and catch the best breezes. The pebble-lined showers have plenty of solar-heated hot water and excellent water pressure. Buffet-style dinners, with exotic foods reflecting the owners' worldwide travels, are served in a thatched-roof dining room with a huge table that can accommodate up to 32. The lavish breakfasts are worth getting up for. There are also a communal kitchen, a yoga platform, and a Japanese soaking tub. Birds are plentiful in the Playa Preciosa Platanares Mixed Refuge, which borders the lodge. ⊠ *Playa Platanares, 5 km/3 mi south of Puerto Jiménez airport* ☎ 848–0752 🖷 735–5436 ⊕ *www. iguanalodge.com* ⤳ *4 rooms (in 2 bungalows), 2 (2-bedroom) family cabins, 1 (3-story, 3-room) house* ⚭ *Dining room, fans, beach, tours, snorkeling, kayaking, Boogie boards; no a/c, no room phones, no room TVs* 🖃 *MC, V* ⦿| *AI.*

$$$$ 🏨 **Villas Corcovado.** Extravagant ecotourism is the theme here. Argentine owners have built the sumptuous villas, each a symphony of rare hardwoods, with handmade four-poster beds, high-quality cotton sheets, outdoor garden showers as well as nice indoor bathrooms, and private verandas with Golfo Dulce views. The pool is the largest in the South Pacific, meant for serious swimmers (the owner's daughter swims competitively for Argentina). Bright-blue wicker beach chairs add a touch of whimsy to the elegant grounds. Service is top-notch in the gulf-view alfresco restaurant, and the food has Italian and Argentine accents plus sushi and a vegetarian menu. A resident naturalist guide organizes kayaking, dolphin- and whale-watching, fishing, and organic-farm tours. You can also hike steep forest trails within the property and help monitor the local poison-dart frog population. The road down to the waterfront resort is so steep that you need 4WD and nerves of steel to drive it. Most guests arrive by boat from Puerto Jiménez. This place is

not recommended (by the owners' admission) for kids under 6. ✉ *30 km/19 mi north of Puerto Jiménez, at the top of the Golfo Dulce* ☎ *817–6969* 🖷 *770–8061* ⊕ *www.villascorcovado.com* ⇌ *8 villas* ⚬ *Dining room, fans, refrigerators, pool, massage, beach, kayaking, tour operator, bar, laundry service, airport shuttle; no a/c, no room phones, no room TVs* ⊟ *MC, V* ⅃◯⅃ *FAP.*

⟳ **$$** ▦ **Río Nuevo Lodge.** You have to cross five rivers to get to this Tico-run tent camp on the western edge of Corcovado National Park. But it's worth the trip, and the bumpy truck ride from Puerto Jiménez is included in the affordable rate, along with three meals. This is camping even ardent anticampers can enjoy. The mold-free, green plastic tents sit atop wooden platforms with private porches. Inside, mattresses and bed linens are fresh and clean; eight tents sleep two and two new tents sleep three. The views from the tents are of misty mountains, Río Nuevo, and a gorgeous tropical garden. Family-style meals usually consist of hearty Costa Rican stews and lots of vegetables, cooked on a wood-fire stove. The shared bathhouse is clean and lit by solar-powered lightbulbs (bring a flashlight). The main event is horseback riding, and many day visitors come out just for a three-hour ride and a hot lunch ($50). It's also a starting point for hiking into Corcovado National Park. ✉ *12 km/7 mi west of Puerto Jiménez; office in Puerto Jiménez, next to Carolina Restaurant* ☎ *735–5411* 🖷 *735–5407* ⊕ *www.rionuevolodge.com* ⇌ *10 tents with shared baths* ⚬ *Dining room, shared cold-water bath, horseback riding, hiking; no a/c, no room phones, no room TVs* ⊟ *MC, V* ⅃◯⅃ *FAP.*

$ ▦ **La Choza de Manglar.** Just steps from the airport, this hotel has comfort with pizzazz. Spectacular hand-painted murals in the huge restaurant area create an indoor rain forest, and the bathrooms are immersed in a sea of painted underwater life. An amazing amount of real wildlife makes appearances in the surrounding mangrove forest. Rooms are on the small side, with tile floors and colorful, hand-carved wooden furniture made in Nicaragua. The garden cabins are larger, with ceiling fans instead of air-conditioning, and hammocks on the porches. ✉ *100 m west of airport* ☎ *735–5002* 🖷 *735–5605* ⊕ *www.manglares.com* ⇌ *6 rooms, 4 cabins* ⚬ *Restaurant, fans, bar, wireless Internet; no a/c in some rooms, no room phones, no room TVs* ⊟ *AE, MC, V* ⅃◯⅃ *BP.*

¢–**$** ▦ **Cabinas Marcelina.** Two elderly Italian sisters run the best bargain hotel in town. The lavish Continental breakfast, served in the garden ($4), is optional. Fresh, bright, spotlessly clean rooms look out onto the pleasant garden and have homey, old-fashioned touches like lace shower curtains. All have private bath and hot water and half the rooms are air-conditioned. If you're traveling solo or need a break from your traveling companion, two single rooms are $16 each. ✉ *Main street, north side of the Catholic church* ☎🖷 *735–5268* ⊕ *cabmarce@hotmail.com* ⇌ *8 rooms* ⚬ *Fans, garden; no a/c in some rooms, no room phones, no room TVs* ⊟ *No credit cards* ⅃◯⅃ *EP.*

Nightlife

The sidewalks are usually rolled up by 9 PM in Puerto Jiménez, but there are a few evening options. **La Taberna** (✉ 1½ blocks east of main street, at Oro de Verde hotel turnoff) is a mellow lounge with intimate seating arrangements, a jungle garden, and large-screen TVs that show

Wildlife-Watching Tips

IF YOU'RE ACCUSTOMED TO nature programs on TV, with visions of wildebeest and zebra swarming across African savannah, your first visit to a tropical forest can be a bewildering experience. If these forests are so diverse, where are all the animals? Web sites, brochures, and books are plastered with lovely descriptions and close-up images of wildlife that give travelers high hopes. Reality is much different but no less profound. Below are some tips to make your experience more enjoyable.

• Don't expect to see rarely sighted animals. It might happen; it might not. Cats, especially jaguars, harpy eagles, and tapirs are a few rare sightings.

• Monkeys can be the easiest animals to spot, but while they are as reliable as the tides in some locations, in others they are rare indeed.

• Remember that nearly all animals spend most of their time avoiding detection.

• Be quiet! Nothing is more unsettling to a wary animal than 20 *Homo sapiens* conversing as they hike. It's best to treat the forest like a house of worship—quiet reverence is in order.

• Listen closely. Many visitors are surprised when a flock of parrots overhead is pointed out to them,

despite the incredible volume of noise they produce. That low-pitched growl you hear is a howler monkey call, which is obvious if nearby, but easily missed over the din of conversation. Try stopping for a moment and closing your eyes.

• Slowly observe different levels of the forest. An enormous caterpillar or an exquisitely camouflaged moth may be only a few inches from your face, and the silhouettes in the tree 100 meters away may be howler monkeys. Scan trunks and branches where a sleeping sloth or anteater might curl up. A quick glance farther down the trail may reveal an agouti or peccary crossing your path.

• In any open area such as a clearing or river, use your binoculars and scan in the distance; scarlet macaws and toucans may be cruising above the treetops.

• Cultivate some level of interest in the less charismatic denizens of the forest—the plants, insects, and spiders. On a good day in the forest you may see a resplendent quetzal or spider monkey, but should they fail to appear, focus on an intricate spiderweb, a column of marching army ants, mammal footprints in the mud, or colorful seeds and flowers fallen from high in the canopy.

music videos. It's a great place to hang out with the locals. **Pearl of the Osa** (⇨ Where to Stay & Eat, *above*) attracts a big crowd Friday nights with live salsa music and a special pasta menu. The crowd is a mix of ages, and of tourists and locals. The music is loud and a lot of fun. Some Saturday nights there's live music—usually salsa or rock—at **La Choza de Manglar** (✉ Beside airport). At **Juanita's** (✉ Next to CaféNet El Sol in the middle of town) there's occasional karaoke and live music. A weekend **discothèque** (✉ North end of town) is mostly frequented by teens.

Shopping

★ Jewelry maker **Karen Herrera** (⊠ Beside airport) has collected the finest arts and crafts in the area and displayed them in an impressive shop. **Jagua Arts & Crafts** (⊠ Beside airport) has some rare items, including colorful cotton dresses and original, woven Panamá hats made by the Guaymí people. Other interesting items are bird carvings made by a family in Rincón, stained-glass mosaic boxes, mirrors and trivets made by a San José artist, local paintings, and serious art ceramics. There's also a selection of natural-history field guides and books.

To & from Puerto Jiménez

130 km/86 mi (3 hrs by car; 90 mins by boat) west of Golfito, 364 km/226 mi (8 hrs by car; 1 hr by plane) from San José.

Most visitors fly to Puerto Jiménez from San José, since the bus ride or drive is grueling and long. The drive from Golfito is not recommended either—the road from Chacarita to Rincón is notoriously potholed and the road from Rincón to Jiménez is dust-filled dirt all the way. A better option is the 90-minute water-taxi ride from Golfito. You can hire taxi boats at the city dock. Prices are $50–$75 between Golfito and Puerto Jiménez. Water taxis can also take you to beachfront lodges. A ricketylooking launch ($2.50 each way) leaves from Golfito's *muellecito* (small municipal dock) at 11:30 AM every day. It returns the next morning from the concrete pier at Puerto Jiménez at 6 AM.

A *collectivo*, an open-air communal truck ($8), leaves Puerto Jiménez twice daily for Cabo Matapalo and Carate. It's the cheapest way to travel but the trip is along a very bumpy road—not recommended in rainy season (May–December). The collectivo leaves from Autotransportes Blanco, 200 m west of the Super 96, at 6 AM and 1:30 PM.

Puerto Jiménez Essentials

🏦 Bank/ATM **Banco Nacional** ⊠ 500 m south of Super 96, directly across from the church ☎ 735-5020.

🏥 Hospital **Public Clinic and First Aid Station** ⊠ 25 m west of post office ☎ 735-5063.

ℹ️ Visitor Information **Osa Tropical** ☎ Across from Banco Nacional on main street ☎ 735-5062 🖷 735-5043 ⊕ www.osatropical.com.

Cabo Matapalo

⑫ The southern tip of the Osa Peninsula, where virgin rain forest meets the sea at a rocky point, retains the kind of natural beauty that people travel halfway across the world to experience. From its ridges you can look out on the blue Golfo Dulce and Pacific Ocean, sometimes spotting whales in the distance. The forest is tall and dense, with the highest and most diverse tree species in the country, usually draped with thick lianas. The name "Cabo Matapalo" means "cape strangler fig," a reference to the fig trees that germinate in the branches of other trees and extend their roots downward, eventually smothering the supporting tree by blocking the life-giving light with their roots and branches. Flocks of brilliant scarlet macaws are another draw here.

Outdoor Activities

Outfitters in Puerto Jiménez run tours in this area. Each of the lodges listed here has resident naturalist guides to take guests on nature hikes.

For extreme forest sports, **Everyday Adventures** (☎ 353–8619 ⊕ www.psychotours.com) takes you on not-so-everyday adventures: rappelling down waterfalls ($75), climbing up a 140-foot strangler fig tree ($55), ocean kayaking (with an optional 30-foot dive), and rain-forest hiking.

SURFING   On the eastern side of Cabo Matapalo, waves break over a platform that creates a perfect right, drawing surfers from far and wide, especially beginners. Mike Hennessey of **Captain Mike's Surf School** (☎ 382–7796) gives surfing lessons ($50) on long boards in the relatively safe waves at Playa Pan Dulce, in front of Lapa Ríos, where he lives. Mike guarantees you'll stand up on the board the first wave you try. He's taught everyone from kids to 70-year-olds.

FISHING   **Cabo Matapalo Sportfishing** (☎ 735–5531 ᕊ 735—5351 ⊕ www.cabomatapalo.com) has excellent, experienced fishing captains and top-of-the-line, well-equipped boats ($925 full day; $700 half-day). Captain Mike Hennessey is always in demand as one of the most entertaining and fun guys to go fishing with in the Gulf.

Where to Stay

★ $$$$ **Bosque del Cabo.** On a cliff at the tip of Cabo Matapalo, this lodge has unparalleled views of blue gulf waters meeting blue ocean. The property, with hundreds of acres of animal-rich primary forest, also has the most beautiful landscaping on the peninsula. Deluxe cabins have king-size beds, and all the luxurious thatch-roof cabins have private, outdoor (hot-water!) garden showers. For the ultimate in romantic seclusion, ask for the Mariposa cabin, which has the most private porch. A suspension bridge through the forest links the main lodge with three more rustic cabins. Appetizing meals are served in a rancho restaurant overlooking a garden alive by day with hummingbirds. Lantern-lighted dinners are accompanied by a chorus of frogs. Solar/hydro power provides enough light to read by, and ocean breezes make air-conditioning superfluous. Resident guides are on hand to lead you along dense forest trails—on foot or along a canopy zip line—and down to the beach with its natural warm tidal whirlpools and river waterfalls. ⊠ *22 km/14 mi south of Puerto Jiménez on road to Carate* ☎☎ *735–5206* ⊕ *www.bosquedelcabo.com* ⌦ *6 deluxe cabins, 4 standard cabins, 3 garden cabins, 2 houses* ₰ *Dining room, some kitchens, pool, beach, kayaking, fishing, horseback riding, bar, Internet; no a/c, no room phones, no room TVs* ⊟ *MC, V* ⊺⊙⊺ *FAP.*

$$$$ **Lapa Ríos.** This is the most spectacular eco-resort in Costa Rica, winning awards worldwide for its mix of conservation and comfort. It's one of only two hotels in the country to have (deservedly) garnered five leaves, the tourism ministry's top ecotourism designation. After catching your breath when you see the view from the high, breezy jungle ridge rife with wildlife, your next sharp intake may be when you see the bill. But in this case the price is not inflated. Spacious, airy cabins, built of gleaming hardwood with high, thatched roofs, have four-poster queen beds,

Fodor's Choice ★

up-to-date luxury bathrooms, and showers with one screened wall open to nature. Private teak-decked garden terraces allow you to view passing monkeys and toucans from a lounge chair. There's an infinity pool, a spa, and a new yoga deck. Inspired meals, served in a newly refreshed rancho with a soaring thatch roof, include lots of seafood, exotic local fruits and vegetables, and mouthwatering desserts. You can eat whenever—and as much as—you want. Resident naturalist guides lead tours through pristine wilderness and to nearby beaches on foot or on horseback. There's also a new Sustainability Tour highlighting the efforts made to limit the lodge's impact on its environs. Along with the high cost of transporting and providing all these luxuries in a remote location, it's the exceptional service that justifies the high price tag, which includes transfers from Puerto Jiménez in new 4X4s, unlimited food, and nonalcoholic drinks. Lapa Ríos also has more of a luxury hotel feel than the other equally beautiful but more casual lodges nearby. ■ TIP➡ **If you don't like to climb stairs, request a cabin close to the main lodge.** ✉ *20 km/12 mi south of Puerto Jiménez* ✆ *Apdo. 100, Puerto Jiménez, or Box 025216, SJO 706, Miami, FL 33102-5216* ☎ *735–5130* 🖷 *735–5179* ⊕ *www.laparios.com* 🛏 *16 cabinas* ⚒ *Restaurant, pool, spa, beach, fishing, hiking, horseback riding, bar, laundry service; no a/c, no room phones, no room TVs* 🖃 *AE, MC, V* ⦿ *FAP.*

To & from Matapalo
21 km/14 mi (1 hr) south of Puerto Jiménez.

If you drive south from Puerto Jiménez, be prepared for a bumpy ride and a lot of river crossings. In rainy season cars are sometimes washed out along rivers to the ocean. Most hotels arrange transportation in 4WD taxis or their own trucks. The cheapest—and the roughest—way to travel is by *collectivo,* an open-air communal truck ($8) that leaves Puerto Jiménez twice a day (at 6 AM and 1:30 PM). Buses do not serve Cabo Matapalo.

Carate

⓭ Carate is literally the end of the road. The black volcanic-sand beach stretches for over 3 km (2 mi), with surf that's perfect for Boogie boarding and body surfing but not for serious board surfing or swimming. The main entertainment at the beach is watching the noisy but magnificent scarlet macaws feasting on almonds in the beach almond trees that edge the shore. Carate has no phones; a few lodges have cell phones but radio is the main line of communication.

Outdoor Activities
Activities here revolve around Corcovado National Park and its surrounds. Hikes, canopy tours, and other adventures must be organized through your hotel.

Where to Stay
$$–$$$ ▦ **Luna Lodge.** Luna's charm lies in its almost ethereal remoteness and tranquillity. On a mountain overlooking the Pacific and the rain forest, it's a true retreat, with a huge hardwood pavilion for practicing yoga or contemplating magnificent sunsets. Just below, there's an ele-

gant new massage hut with views and professional therapists. Round bungalows, spaced apart for privacy around the garden, have thatched roofs, garden showers, and decks for bird-watching or relaxing in wood-and-leather rocking chairs. Three new deluxe rooms with private baths share a spacious deck. Or you can semirough it in a well-ventilated, comfortable tent. Guided hikes to nearby waterfalls and swimming holes are precipitous and thrilling, and a large new swimming pool is cool and shaded. Healthful meals have an imaginative vegetarian flair, tempered with servings of fish and chicken spiced with herbs from a hilltop organic garden. When there's a large group, dinners are buffet-style and they are true feasts. Host Lana Wedmore is a model of amiable helpfulness. Prices include a waterfall tour ⊠ *2 km/1 mi up a steep, partially paved road from Carate* ☎ *380–5036, 358–5848, 888/ 409–8448 in U.S.* ⊕ *www.lunalodge.com* ⟿ *Box 025216–5216, Miami, FL 33102* ⟿ *8 bungalows, 3 rooms, 7 tents* ⚮ *Restaurant, massage, kayaks, horseback riding, bar, spa; no a/c, no room phones, no room TVs* ▭ *MC, V* ⭑❙ *FAP.*

★ ⚬ **$$** ▤ **Corcovado Lodge Tent Camp.** Fall asleep to the sound of surf pounding the beach in a tent on a wooden platform. Ecotourist pioneer Costa Rica Expeditions owns this rustic lodge and its 400 acres of forest reserve adjoining Corcovado National Park. Side by side facing the ocean, the white tents have two single beds, no electricity, and share eight showers and toilets. Unsightly plastic lounge chairs are messily scattered around, but the excellent naturalist guides still make this a prime destination for nature lovers. Family-style meals are served in an open-air thatched restaurant with communal tables overlooking the ocean. Skip the "canopy tour" that hoists you up into a 90-foot tree: you don't see much wildlife, so it's not worth the $69 price tag. Bring a flashlight (there's no electricity after 9 PM), insect repellent, and sandals for river hikes. The package with all meals is a great deal, especially since there's nowhere to buy food nearby. Packages usually include a charter flight to Carate. The walk from Carate is 2 km (1 mi; 30–45 minutes) along a hot beach, so bring a sun hat. A horse and cart can pick up your luggage from the store with advance notice. ⊠ *On beach 2 km/1 mi north of Carate; 30–45 min by foot* ☎ *222–0333 or 257–0766* ☎ *257–1665, 800/886–2609 from U.S.* ⊕ *www. costaricaexpeditions.com* ⟿ *Apartado 6941–1000 San José* ⟿ *20 tents with shared bath* ⚮ *Dining room, beach, horseback riding, hiking, bar, laundry service; no a/c, no room phones, no room TVs* ▭ *AE, MC, V.*

To & from Carate
60 km/37 mi (2 hrs) west of Puerto Jiménez.

The road from Matapalo to Carate covers 40 suspension-testing km (25 mi) and it is never easy; you're better off taking the *collectivo* from Puerto Jiménez (⇨ To & from Puerto Jiménez, *above*). Or give yourself a break and fly via charter plane to Carate's small airstrip, arranged through your lodge. From here it's just a 3-km (2-mi), or roughly 40-minute, walk, along the beach to the La Leona ranger station entrance to Corcovado National Park. In rainy season (May–December) it is sometimes impossible to cross the raging Río Carate that separates the landing strip from the beach path to the park, and you may end up stranded on either side. Parking at the store in Carate is $5 per day.

Drake Bay

⑭ This is castaway country, a real tropical adventure, with plenty of hiking and some rough but thrilling boat rides. The rugged coast that stretches south from the mouth of the Río Sierpe to Corcovado probably doesn't look much different from what it did in Sir Francis Drake's day (1540–96), when the British explorer anchored here. Small, picture-perfect beaches with surf crashing against dark, volcanic rocks are backed by steaming, thick jungle. Nature lodges scattered along the coast are hemmed in by the rain forest, which is home to troops of monkeys, sloths, scarlet macaws, and hundreds of other bird species.

The cheapest accommodations in the area can be found in the town of **Drake,** which is spread out along the bay. A trio of nature lodges—Drake Bay Wilderness Resort, Aguila de Osa Inn, and La Paloma Lodge—are also clumped near the Río Agujitas on the bay's southern end. They all offer comprehensive packages, including trips to Corcovado and Caño Island. Lodges farther south, such as Punta Marenco Lodge and Casa Corcovado, run excursions from even wilder settings. During the dry season you can reach the town of Drake via a graded dirt road from Rincón.

Outdoor Activities

Jinetes de Osa (✉ Drake village, west side of bay ☎ 236–5637 ⊕ www.costaricadiving.com) has diving and snorkeling ($65) and dolphin-watching tours ($95), as well as a canopy tour ($55) with some interesting bridge, ladder, and rope transitions between platforms.

Where to Stay

$$$$ ▣ **Aguila de Osa Inn.** The spacious rooms here have gorgeous hardwood interiors, huge bamboo beds, and luxurious tile bathrooms. Stained-glass and Tiffany-style lamps with tropical themes and hand-carved doors add artistic flair. Be prepared for a steep climb up a concrete path to your room with a view of Drake Bay. Morning coffee arrives outside your room before 6 AM, and the food is sophisticated and plentiful. The inn has two boats for sportfishing, its specialty. Scuba diving, snorkeling, and other excursions are easily arranged. ✉ *South end of Drake, at mouth of Río Agujitas* ☎ *296–2190 in San José* 🖶 *232–7722* ⊕ *www.aguiladeosa. com* ✉ *898 Box 025635, Miami, FL 33102* ✑ *11 rooms, 2 suites* ⚭ *Restaurant, fans, refrigerators, massage, snorkeling, boating, fishing, horseback riding, bar, laundry service, Internet; no a/c, no room phones, no room TVs* ▤ *AE, MC, V* ⦿ *FAP.*

★ **$$$$**   ▣ **Casa Corcovado.** This hilltop jungle lodge has it all: a prime location on the edge of Corcovado National Park, resident naturalist guides, luxury accommodations, and first-class

> ### WORD OF MOUTH
>
> "[S]wimming in the ocean near Drake Bay on the Osa was heavenly! Warm water, tropical birds flying overhead, even able to do a bit of snorkling (fun, but not great). No crocs, but my husband did 'get' to share his swimming space with a poisonous water snake!"   –Molly2

Continued on page 362

CORCOVADO NATIONAL PARK

FOR THOSE WHO CRAVE UNTAMED WILDER-NESS, Corcovado is the experience of a lifetime. Covering one-third of the Osa Peninsula, the park is blanketed primarily by virgin rain forest and holds Central America's largest remaining tract of lowland Pacific rain forest. The remoteness of Corcovado and the difficult access to its interior results in its being one of the most pristine parks in the country—barely disturbed by human presence—where massive *espavel* and *nazareno* trees tower over the trails, thick lianas hang from the branches, and toucans, spider monkeys, scarlet macaws, and poison dart frogs abound.

FAST FACTS

Size: 445 square km (172 square mi)

Established: 1975

Dry season: January-April

Wettest months: October–November

What to do: Nature hikes, bird-watching, wildlife-watching, river walks, sea kayaking, camping, deep-sea fishing

Geography: 37 km (23 mi) of beach; 44,500 hectares (109,961 acres) of tropical wet forest

Number of species catalogued: 10,000 insects, 700 trees, 367 birds, 140 mammals, 123 butterflies, 117 amphibians and reptiles

- 15 of Costa Rica's 30 endangered animal species live here
- Corcovado has the largest population of scarlet macaws in Costa Rica
- Nearly 200 inches of rain falls here every year
- The hike between any two ranger stations takes at least a day
- The harpy eagle, thought to have been extinct, has been sighted here since 2003

6

CORCOVADO NATIONAL PARK

Your chances of spotting endangered species, such as boa constrictors, squirrel monkeys, and five wild cats, are better here than anywhere else in the country. The rarest and most sought-after are the jaguar and Baird's tapir. In and around the park are some of Costa Rica's most luxurious jungle lodges and retreats, all of which are contributing to the effort to save Corcovado's wildlife.

For day trips into the park, the most convenient place to base yourself is either in Drake Bay or at the Corcovado Lodge Tent Camp near Carate. There are three entrances: **La Leona** (to the south), **San Pedrillo** (to the north), and **Los Patos** (to the east). The park has no roads, however, and the roads that approach it are dirt tracks that require 4WD most of the year.

ROUGHING IT

If you have a backpack, strong legs, and a reservation for a tent site or a ranger-station bunk, you can spend days deep in the wilds. Bunks at the Sirena ranger station (which is in a deplorable state of disrepair at the moment) are very limited. Bring your own sheets, a pillow, and a good mosquito net. Basic meals can be arranged at Sirena if you reserve in advance with the National Parks Service office in Puerto Jiménez.

During the dry season the park takes reservations for bunks and camping on the first day of each month for the following month. You may be asked to deposit money into the Environment Ministry's account in the Banco Nacional to reserve space. Reconfirm your reservation a few days before you enter the park. Camping is allowed at the Sirena,

ENDANGERED ANIMALS

Corcovado has significant populations of species that are in danger of extinction, including:

- Baird's tapir
- boa constrictor
- American crocodile
- harpy eagle
- howler monkey
- jaguar
- jaguarundi
- little spotted cat (*caucel*)
- margay
- ocelot
- puma
- scarlet macaw
- Southern River otter
- spider monkey
- squirrel monkey

BIRD CHECKLIST

Check the following off your "life list":

- Baird's trogon
- black-bellied wren
- black-hooded antshrike
- black-cheeked ant-tanager
- black-headed brush finch
- brown pelican
- fiery-billed aracari
- golden-naped woodpecker
- harpy eagle
- laughing gull
- mangrove hummingbird
- orange-collared manakin
- riverside wren
- scarlet macaw
- spotted-crowned euphonia
- turquoise cotinga
- whistling wren
- white-crested coquette
- yellow-billed cotinga

American crocodile

scarlet macaw

squirrel monkey

jaguar

purple gallinule

roseate spoonbill

hummingbird

brown pelican

laughing gull

howler monkey

three-toed sloth

Baird's tapir

6

CORCOVADO NATIONAL PARK

SAVING THE CATS

The park has been under heavy pressure from poachers who have been killing the peccaries and pacas (small mammals) that the jaguars, ocelots, margays, and other cats feed on. Local and international groups are raising money to fund new park rangers to stop illegal hunting. In 2004 one non-profit conservation fund in the U.S. earmarked $8 million to protect and preserve the park. Much of the money has gone to hiring more park rangers.

ocelot

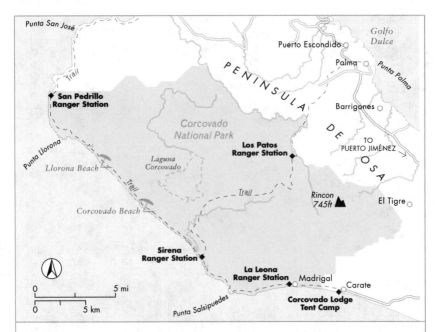

La Leona, Los Patos, and San Pedrillo stations, but only 35 people are allowed to camp at any given station, so reservations with the National Parks Service in Puerto Jiménez are essential in high season.

⚠ Swimming on the beach near Sirena is not advised due to rip currents and bull sharks. Also steer clear of the brackish Río Sirena, home to crocs, bull sharks, and snakes. The only advisable swimming area is the Río Claro.

HOW MUCH TIME?
Most first-time visitors to Corcovado come on a day-long boat tour or hike. But to get to the most pristine, primary growth areas, you need to walk, and that means a minimum of three days: one day to walk in; one day to walk out out; and one day inside.

HIRING A GUIDE
If your reason for coming to the Osa is Corcovado, choose a lodge that has resident naturalist guides. On the Drake Bay and gulf sides of the park, all the lodges arrange guided trips into Corcovado, most with their own guides, but some with freelance guides. Corcovado Lodge Tent Camp, on the southern edge of the park, has its own guides. Outdoors outfitters in Puerto Jiménez and Drake Bay also run guided trips in the park.

HIKING
There are three main hiking routes to Corcovado. One begins near Puerto Jiménez, at the **Los Patos** entrance. There are also two beach trails to the park: one begins in Drake Bay and follows the coast down to the **San Pedrillo** entrance to the park; the other is an easy 40-minute beach walk from Carate to the **La Leona** entrance. Hiking is always tough in the tropical heat, but the forest route (Los Patos) is cooler than the two beach hikes (La Leona and San Pedrillo), and the latter are accessible only at low tide.

The hike between any two stations takes all day or more, and the longest hike is

San Pedrillo to Sirena; it's 21 km (13 mi) along the beach, then 7 km (4 mi) on the forest trail. ■ TIP →→This trail is passable only in the dry season, as the rivers get too high to cross in the rainy months and the river mouths are home to snakes, bull sharks, and crocodiles! But for hardy hikers who attempt it, the reward is walking through majestic forest as you approach Sirena.

The hike from **La Leona to Sirena** is about 16 km (10 mi) and requires crossing one big river mouth and a stretch of beach that can only be crossed at low tide. It takes planning ahead, and some guides do it at night, by the light of the moon and stars, to avoid the blistering heat along the beach.

The 17.4-km (10.8-mi) trail from **Los Patos to Sirena** is lovely and forested. But to get to the Los Patos station you first walk 8 km (5 mi) along the verdant Río Rincón valley. The **Sirena ranger station** has great trails around it that can easily fill a couple of days. Osa Aventura (⇨ Outdoor Activities *in* Puerto Jiménez, *above*) specializes in wildlife tours.

ESSENTIALS

Hours of Operation: Ranger stations are officially open from 8 AM to 4 PM daily, but you can walk in almost any time as long as you pay in advance.

Contacts: 735–5036 (National Parks Service in Puerto Jiménez)

Admission: $8 per day; $17 per person for stays of 4–5 days

Getting There: The easiest way to visit remote Corcovado is on a day trip via boat from a Drake Bay lodge or on foot from the Corcovado Lodge Tent Camp. The 20-minute boat trip from Drake Bay gets you to the San Pedrillo entrance in the dry season (January–April). The boat trip from Drake to Sirena takes 45 min. to 1 hour. The Corcovado Lodge

HIKING TIPS

- Stay on the trails, for your safety and for the well-being of animals and plants

- Animals here are less used to humans than those in more touristed parks; be quiet and keep your eyes and ears open

- Apply mosquito repellent only as needed. Repellent reduces your ability to sweat

- Take plenty of water with you, even on short hikes. Don't ever drink water from streams. Every ranger station has potable water.

- Bring a flashlight. Darkness falls quickly in the forest.

- Plan your hikes around high tides, which can block park entrances

- Bring a sun hat and sunblock, and wear comfortable shoes.

Tent Camp is a 10-minute walk from the La Leona entrance.

For getting to Corcovado from elsewhere, the most expensive option—but also the easiest way to get right to the heart of the park—is flying in on a small charter plane ($275) to the tiny La Sirena airstrip in the park. Contact **Alfa Romeo Aero Taxi** (⊠ Puerto Jiménez airport ☎ 735–5178).

Less expensive is hiring a taxi in Puerto Jiménez ($45) to the Los Patos trailhead, or at least to the first crossing of the Río Rincón (from which you hike a few miles upriver to the trailhead).

The cheapest, and least convenient, option is to take a morning bus for less than $1 from Puerto Jiménez at 8 AM to La Palma and then hike or take a taxi to the Los Patos entrance.

6

CORCOVADO NATIONAL PARK

service and food. A trail leads right into the park from here, so you can explore its forests hours before anyone else arrives. Spanish colonial–style cabinas are spread around a garden for maximum privacy. The guest rooms have elegant furniture, four-poster beds, and huge tile bathrooms with separate vanity, shower, and toilet areas. Alas, there are no clotheslines in some cabins, but there is laundry service for an extra charge. There's a sunset margarita bar at the top of the very steep hill that climbs up from the beach where you make a thrilling, very wet landing: a tractor-towed cart transports guests and luggage. Guests arrive by boats outfitted with fresh-smelling life jackets and plenty of towels (a wave may smack you). The restaurant serves upscale dinners and packs gourmet picnic lunches. Rooms have their own pure-water dispenser and each guest receives a personal nalgene bottle to refill. The minimum stay is two nights, but the best deal is a three-night package that includes transportation from San José by plane, taxi, and boat, all meals, and a trip to Caño Island and Corcovado National Park. ⊠ *Northern border of Corcovado* ☝ *Apdo. 1482–1250, Escazú* ☎ *256–3181, 888/896–6097 in U.S.* 📠 *256–7409* ⊕ *www.casacorcovado.com* 💭 *14 rooms* ♨ *Dining room, fans, 2 pools, beach, snorkeling, boating, hiking, horseback riding, 2 bars; no a/c, no room phones, no room TVs* ☱ *AE, MC, V* ☯ *Closed Sept.–mid-Nov.* ⎩*AI.*

★ **$$$$** ☷ **La Paloma Lodge.** Sweeping ocean views and sophisticated furnishings make these secluded cabinas the area's most romantic. Planted in a jungle garden on a ridge jutting out into Drake Bay, the elegant wooden villas have bedroom lofts and large porches with pretty green wicker furniture, huge wooden armoires, hammocks, and elegant bathrooms. All the cabins have been renovated, but Nos. 1 and 2 have the best views. The four rooms in a low-lying building have porches but are less private. A small tiled pool overlooks forest and ocean, or you can head down the hill to Playa Cocolito, the hotel's gem of a beach at the edge of the coastal path that eventually leads to Corcovado The hotel runs a diving school and offers river kayaking, along with trips to Corcovado and Caño Island. The flower-filled restaurant serves delicious, fresh tropical fare and there's always afternoon tea and banana bread. Longtime manager Nichole Dupont maintains a very high standard of personal service. There's a three-night minimum stay; packages are the best bet and include transportation from San José, all meals, and some tours. ⊠ *Drake Bay, 300 m past Drake Bay Wilderness Resort* ☝ *Apdo. 97–4005, Heredia* ☎ *293–7502* 📠 *239–0954* ⊕ *www.lapalomalodge.com* 💭 *4 rooms, 7 cabinas* ♨ *Dining room, pool, beach, snorkeling, fishing, diving, horseback riding; no a/c, no room phones, no room TVs* ☱ *AE, MC, V* ☯ *Closed Oct.* ⎩ *FAP.*

☭ **$$$–$$$$** ☷ **Drake Bay Wilderness Resort.** Spread over a grassy point between the Río Agujitas and the ocean, this resort has the best wide-open views of Drake Bay. It's also kid-friendly with a pool, lots of open ground to play on and tidal pools to explore. Keep an eye out for the small troop of precocious squirrel monkeys. The wooden cabins are camp-style with three to a building. But with hot water, new tile bathrooms, wall murals, and carved animal bedposts supporting firm queen-size beds, this is very comfortable camping. Kayaks are at your disposal for paddles along the river. Most guests come here to see the rain forest, but you can also opt for mangrove, scuba diving, sportfishing, and dolphin- and whale-watching tours. The minimum stay is three nights. ⊠ *On peninsula at mouth*

Snorkelers' Paradise

MOST OF UNINHABITED 2½-square-km (1-square-mi) **Caño Island Biological Reserve** is covered in evergreen forest that includes fig, locust, and rubber trees. Coastal Indians used it as a burial ground, and the numerous bits and pieces unearthed here have prompted archaeologists to speculate about pre-Columbian long-distance maritime trade. Occasionally, mysterious stones that have been carved into perfect spheres of varying sizes are still found on the island. The uninhabited island's main attraction now is the ocean around it, superb for scuba diving and snorkeling. The snorkeling is best around the rocky points flanking the island's main beach; if you're a certified diver you'll probably want to explore Bajo del Diablo and Paraíso, where you're guaranteed to encounter thousands of good-size fish.

of Río Agujitas, on southern end of bay 🚣🚣 770–8012 ☎ 384–4107 ⊕ www.drakebay.com ✉ Apdo. 1370010–1000, San José ☎ 561/371–3437 in U.S. ⋈ 20 rooms ⏶ Two dining rooms, fans, saltwater pool, boating, fishing, horseback riding, bar, laundry facilities, Internet; no a/c, no room phones, no room TVs ▤ AE, MC, V ⏹ FAP.

$$–$$$ 🏨 **Jinetes de Osa.** The most comfortable and reasonably priced place to stay right in the village of Drake, this bay-side hotel and open-air restaurant has simple rooms, some larger and more expensive than others, all with tile floors and hot-water showers. The on-site tour and diving operations are well run and the lodge is often filled with groups of divers. A nice touch is the coffee delivered outside your room early in the morning. ✉ Drake village, west side of bay ☎ 826–9757 🖷 241–2906 in San José ⊕ www.costaricadiving.com ⋈ 9 rooms ⏶ Restaurant, fans, beach; no a/c, no room phones, no room TVs ▤ MC, V ⏹ FAP.

$$ 🏨 **Delfin Amor Eco Lodge.** Dolphin fans will do back flips over this lodge devoted to marine mammals. Six private wooden cabins buried in a hilly garden are just steps from the ocean and dolphin motifs grace every imaginable nook. Meals are tasty vegetarian, with some fish but absolutely no shrimp served. (Shrimp boats dragging the ocean floors with long-line nets are the bane of marine environmentalists.) The often-buggy, open-air dining room is in the process of being rebuilt. The highlight of a visit here is a six-hour, naturalist-guided boat tour in search of whales and the many species of dolphin that frequent these waters. The lodge stays open during the rainy season, the best time to catch close-ups of migrating humpback whales. Boat tours are pricey at almost $100 per person, but some of the fee goes to a dolphin research and conservation foundation. On land, there's hiking and birding along the sublimely beautiful Coastal Path that passes in front of the hotel. Kids under 12 are half-price for both lodging and dolphin tour. ✉ About 45-min walk south of La Paloma, 5 mins by boat from Drake village ☎ 847–3131 ⊕ www.divinedolphin.com ⋈ 6 cabins ⏶ Dining room, fans, beach, hiking, yoga, snorkeling, tours, kayaks, Internet; no a/c, no room phones, no room TVs ▤ AE, MC, V ⏹ FAP.

6

Nightlife

When you're on the Osa Peninsula, the wildest nightlife is outdoors. Join
★ ☾ entomologist Tracie Stice, also known as the Bug Lady, on the **Night Tour**
(☎ 382–1619 ⊕ www.thenighttour.com) of insects, bats, reptiles, and
anything else moving around at night. Tracie is a wealth of bug lore,
with riveting stories from around the world. Special night-vision optics
and infrared flashlights help you see in the dark. Tours are $35 per person; Tracie will meet you at your hotel.

To & from Drake Bay

*18 km/11 mi north of Corcovado, 40 km/25 mi southwest of Palmar
Sur, 310 km/193 mi (7 hrs by car; 50 mins by plane) south of San José.*

The fastest way to get to Drake Bay is to fly directly to the airstrip. You
can also fly to Palmar Sur and take a taxi to Sierpe and then a boat to Drake
Bay. From the airport, it's a 25-minute taxi ride to Sierpe; small, open boats
leave at low tide, usually 11–11:30 AM for the one-hour trip to Drake. Often,
the captains will stop along the way to view wildlife in the river mangroves.
Many lodges arrange boat transportation from Drake Bay or Sierpe. From
Rincón you can drive to Drake on a 20-km (12-mi) graded dirt road. The
drive from San José to Drake is scenic, but exhausting.

Exceptionally fit backpackers can hike to the northern entrance of Corcovado along a 18-km (11-mi) coastal path that follows the shoreline,
cutting through shady forest when the coast gets too rocky. But it is impossible to walk during rainy season (September–December), when
rivers flood and tides are too high.

Drake Bay Essentials

Drake just got electricity in 2004, so there are still very few services.
🖪 Visitor Information **Corcovado Expeditions** ☎ 818–9962, beside the high school
in Drake village.

THE SOUTH PACIFIC ESSENTIALS

Transportation

BY AIR

SANSA and NatureAir have direct flights to Golfito, Drake Bay, Palmar Sur, Coto 47 (for San Vito), and Puerto Jiménez. For more information about air travel to the South Pacific from San José, *see* Air
Travel *in* Smart Travel Tips A to Z.

Alfa Romeo Aero Taxi, at the Puerto Jiménez "airport" (really more of
an airstrip), flies small charter planes to Carate and Corcovado National
Park's airstrip at La Sirena.
🖪 **Alfa Romeo Aero Taxi** ☎ 735-5178.

BY BUS

ARRIVING & Bus fares from San José to destinations in the South Pacific range from
DEPARTING about $2 to $7, depending on distance and number of stops. For more
information about bus travel between the South Pacific and San José,
see Bus Travel *in* Smart Travel Tips A to Z.

GETTING AROUND | The best way to get around the region's roads is by bus—let someone else do the driving. Bus fares are cheap and you'll meet the locals. But the going is generally slow, buses often leave very early in the morning, and schedules change frequently, so check the day before you want to travel.

BY SHUTTLE VAN

ARRIVING & DEPARTING | Interbus has van service from Quepos to Sierpe ($30); a minimum of four passengers is required.

🚐 Shuttle Van Services **Interbus** ☎ 283-5573 ⊕ www.interbusonline.com.

BY CAR

ARRIVING & DEPARTING | Owing to the dismal state of the roads and hazardous driving conditions—flooded rivers and potholes—we don't recommend driving to the South Pacific, especially in rainy season. If you decide to drive, make sure your vehicle has 4WD and a spare tire. Give yourself lots of time to get to where you are going.

GETTING AROUND | Driving is fairly straightforward, if slow, around Cerro de la Muerte, San Isidro, Dominical, and Uvita. But as soon as you get off the main paved highways, the roads are rough and slow-going and require 4WD. On the Osa Peninsula and around the Golfo Dulce, the last thing you want is a car. Boat taxis and land taxis will save you time, if not money, and save your energy for activities that are more fun than navigating really rough roads.

Solid Car Rental now has an office in Puerto Jiménez with four-wheel-drive vehicles (including some with automatic transmission); they also have cars available in Golfito and Palmar Norte; the other agencies' closest outposts are in Quepos. Selva Mar can arrange for a rental car to be picked up in San Isidro, and you can drop off the car anywhere down south and avoid the drive back. Alamo, in Dominical, also allows drop-off at various points south. But you'll incur steep drop-off fees, which range from $50 to $125.

🚗 Major Rental Agencies **Solid Car Rental** ⊠ Main street, near Catholic church, Puerto Jiménez ☎ 735-5777 ⊕ www.solidcarrental/com.

🚗 **Selva Mar** ☎ 771-4582 ⊕ www.exploringcostarica.com.

Contacts & Resources

Banks and emergency contacts are listed at the end of each town entry.

BANKS & EXCHANGING SERVICES

In the major centers—San Isidro, Golfito, and San Vito—banks and ATMS are plentiful. But in Puerto Jiménez there is only one bank with one ATM, which may or may not be working. Many other places have no banking facilities at all. Don't count on being able to use a credit card, since phone lines—where they exist—are often out of order. Arrange in advance to pay lodges.

Caribbean

La Selva Biological Station

WORD OF MOUTH

"Don't miss out on Tortuguero! We loved it. Take the boat in—it is definitely part of the experience. The wildlife viewing is incredible there. We saw everything, and plenty of it."

—tanya0070

"I'm a big fan of the Caribbean side of CR. It's less crowded, less touristy, and generally cheaper than the usual destinations. The beaches all down the coast are beautiful and practically deserted."

—rbrazill

WELCOME TO THE CARIBBEAN

Braulio Carrillo Park

TOP 5
Reasons to Go

1. **Turtles:** People from around the world flock to the northern Caribbean for the annual nesting of four species.

2. **Food and flavors:** Leave gallo pinto behind in favor of mouthwatering *rondón* (meat or fish stew), or *caribeño* (Caribbean) rice and beans, stewed in coconut milk.

3. **Dolphin-watching:** Bottlenose, tucuxi, and Atlantic-spotted dolphins ply the southern Caribbean coast.

4. **Music:** Mix reggae and calypso with your salsa. Rhythms waft in from the far-off Caribbean Islands; and home-grown musicians are making names for themselves, too.

5. **Sportfishing:** World-class tarpon and snook attract serious anglers to the shores off Barra del Colorado and Tortuguero national parks.

NICARAGUA

Barra del Colorado

Barra del Colorado Wildlife Refuge

Tortu...

Canta Gallo

Tortugue... National P...

Campo Cinco

Cariari

LIMÓN

247

Rio Jimenez

248

32 Flores

Guapiles

The Northern Lowlands have little to offer tourists in their own right, but are close to Braulio Carrillo Park and rafting-trip put-in points.

0   10 mi
0   10 km

Pichara Lodge

Getting Oriented

This flat, expansive region just a few meters above sea level stretches from the eastern slope of the Cordillera Central, east through banana-growing country, and down to pristine beaches. North to the Nicaragua border, it encompasses the coastal jungles and canals of Tortuguero National Park and Barra del Colorado Wildlife Refuge. In the central and southern Caribbean, nearly everything of tourist interest lies along the main artery to Limón (the Guápiles Highway) and the coastal highway south.

Limón, Central Caribbean

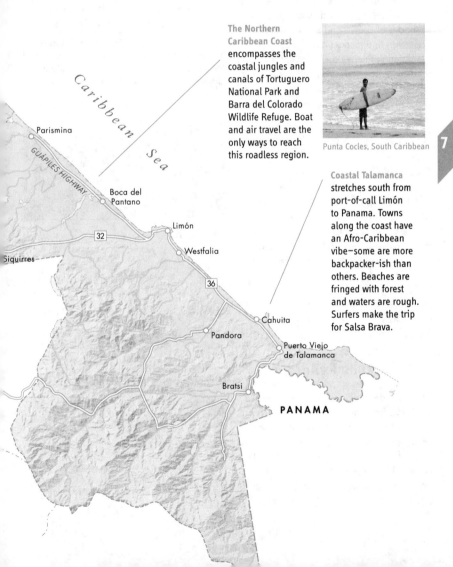

The Northern Caribbean Coast encompasses the coastal jungles and canals of Tortuguero National Park and Barra del Colorado Wildlife Refuge. Boat and air travel are the only ways to reach this roadless region.

Punta Cocles, South Caribbean

7

Coastal Talamanca stretches south from port-of-call Limón to Panama. Towns along the coast have an Afro-Caribbean vibe—some are more backpacker-ish than others. Beaches are fringed with forest and waters are rough. Surfers make the trip for Salsa Brava.

Caribbean Sea

Parismina

GUÁPILES HIGHWAY

Boca del Pantano

Limón

32

Westfalia

Siquirres

36

Cahuita

Pandora

Puerto Viejo de Talamanca

Bratsi

PANAMA

CARIBBEAN PLANNER

Not *that* Caribbean

Costa Rica's Caribbean coast is sometimes called its Atlantic coast, so as not to confuse tourists looking for the white sand and clear-blue waters of the Caribbean Islands. This Caribbean is very different, with sands in shades of brown and black, waters that are rough and murky (ideal for surfing), dense jungle, heavy and frequent rain, and a less sophisticated, laid-back approach to tourism. It is beautiful and fascinating in its own way, but it's definitely not St. Barths.

When to Go

The Caribbean lacks a true dry season, though February–April and September–October could be called *drier* seasons with many sunny days and intermittent showers. The heaviest rains (and periodic road closures) come in December and January, prime tourist months elsewhere. During the rainiest months prices are lower and tourists fewer. Temperatures remain constant year-round, with daily highs of 29–31˚C (84–88˚F) and lows of 21–23˚ C (69–73˚F).

Don't Get the Runaround

Check road conditions before you set out for the Caribbean from points west. Most of the time it is one of the country's most easily reached regions, but occasional closures of the route through Braulio Carrillo National Park north of San José necessitate passing through Turrialba, which can add a couple of hours to your journey.

Getting There

This historically isolated sector of Costa Rica is today one of the most accessible. The southern coast is a 3- to 4-hour drive from San José, over decent roads (by Costa Rican standards), and public transportation is frequent. The northern Caribbean coast is another story: the total absence of roads means you have to arrive by plane or boat. Most travelers go with a tour or book at one of the large hotels that include transport to and from San José.

DRIVING ALERT: When visiting the Caribbean coast by car, remember that fog often covers the Braulio Carrillo mountains after noon, making driving hazardous. Cross this area in the morning.

What to Do

ACTIVITY	WHERE TO DO IT
Fishing	Barra del Colorado, San Juan River, Tortuguero
Diving	Gandoca-Manzanillo Wildlife Refuge
Snorkeling	Gandoca-Manzanillo Wildlife Refuge
Surfing	Cahuita, Puerto Viejo de Talamanca
Turtle-watching	Gandoca-Manzanillo Wildlife Refuge, Tortuguero
White-water rafting	Siquirres
Wildlife-viewing	Barra del Colorado, Gandoca-Manzanillo Wildlife Refuge, Tortuguero

Choosing a Place to Stay

The glitzy resorts of the Pacific coast are nowhere to be found in the Caribbean, where the norm is small, independent lodgings, usually family owned and operated. Fewer tourists in this region means plenty of decent lodging at affordable prices. And unless you travel during Christmas or Easter weeks you can usually find a place to stay without much advance planning. But tourism *is* growing, so it's risky to show up without reservations. Surprisingly few places here have air-conditioning; but sea breezes and ceiling fans usually provide sufficient ventilation. Smaller places don't take credit cards; those that do may give discounts if you pay with cash.

How Much Time?

Attractions near Guápiles and Siquirres lend themselves to long day trips from San José. Tour operators also have whirlwind day-long Tortuguero trips from San José. Avoid these—the area really deserves two or three days, which is the length of the classic Tortuguero package that includes transportation, lodging, food, and tours. Choose a single Caribbean destination and stay put if you have just a few days. If you have a week, you can tackle the north and south coasts.

Package Tours

■ **Horizontes**
(☎ 222-2022
⊕ www.horizontes.
com) tours include naturalist guides and transport by 4WD vehicle.

■ **Río Indio Adventure Lodge**
(☎ 296-0095
⊕ www.rioindiolodge.
com) has all-inclusive guided trips from San José to a luxury eco-hotel just over the border in Nicaragua.

■ **Talamanca Adventures**
(☎ 224-3570
⊕ www.talamanca-adventures.com) leads off-the-beaten-path tours familiarizing you with everything from Caribbean cooking to rain-forest conservation.

Prices

	$$$$	$$$	$$	$	¢
Restaurants	over $25	$15–$25	$10–$15	$5–$10	under $5
Hotels	over $250	$150–$250	$75–$150	$50–$75	under $50

WHAT IT COSTS in Dollars

Restaurant prices are per-person for a main course at dinner. Hotel prices are for two people in a standard double room in high season, excluding service and tax (16.4%).

Rain Check

Packing for wet weather is a necessity. Be sure to bring:

■ a collapsible umbrella

■ a poncho

■ Zip-lock bags for cameras and other things you'll take on hikes and tours

■ waterproof sandals

■ quick-drying clothing

THE COMPLETE PACKAGE

If you don't want to be bothered arranging the logistics of transportation to remote Tortuguero, consider booking a package tour. Many lodges listed in the chapter have similar packages, varying in length from one night to two weeks, that include transport from San José, overnights, meals, and guided tours.

7

THE NORTHERN LOWLANDS

By Jeffrey
Van Fleet

That proverbial fork in the road presents you with a choice just beyond the immense Braulio Carrillo National Park north of San José. The highway branches at Santa Clara, having completed its descent onto the Caribbean plain. A left turn takes you north to Puerto Viejo de Sarapiquí and the forest-clad hills of the eastern slope of the Cordillera Central. If you stay on the well-maintained main Guápiles Highway, head southeast toward Limón and the Caribbean coast. The highway passes through sultry agricultural lowlands, home to large banana and cacao plantations, but bypasses the region's three main communities, burgeoning Guápiles and the smaller towns of Guácimo and Siquirres. You may not see any reason to stop when driving through the region—the Caribbean coast beckons, after all—but a couple of decent lodgings and lesser-known sights might be incentive to take a break.

Guápiles

❶ Guápiles is fast becoming the hub of northeastern Costa Rica, and with all the facilities in town, residents of the region find little need to trek to San José anymore. The smaller town of Guácimo lies 12 km (7 mi) east on the Guápiles Highway.

Exploring

Curious how those tropical houseplants you have at home started out? Ornamental plant farm **Costa Flores** conducts one-and-a-half-hour English-language tours—advance reservations are required—through its gardens and facilities. (Riotously colored heliconias are a specialty here.) The tour ends at the packing house, where you see how plants are prepared for export. Then you get to create your own floral bouquet to take with you as a souvenir. ⊠ *3½ km/2 mi north of Guácimo on road to Río Jiménez* ☎ *716–6457* ☜ *$15* ☉ *Weekdays, 8–4; weekends by reservation.*

Where to Stay

¢ ▦ **Hotel Río Palmas.** Think of it as a hacienda motel. Proximate to EARTH (⇨ *below*), near the town of Guácimo, the Río Palmas has a red-tile-roof open-air restaurant that grabs your eye as you're speeding by on the highway. The restaurant is a popular stop for tour buses or individual travelers en route to and from the Caribbean. Behind an arched, whitewashed entry gate, one-story tile-roof cabinas wrap around a central courtyard with a fountain. Exotic plantings abound, and the staff can arrange hikes, farm and jungle tours, and horseback rides to private waterfalls. ⊠ *Pocora de Guácimo, 15 km/9 mi east of Guápiles on Guápiles Hwy.* ☎ *760–0330* 🖷 *760–0296* ⊕ *www.hotelriopalmas.com* ↩ *28 rooms* ⚇ *Restaurant, fans, cable TV, pool, horseback riding, laundry service; no a/c in some rooms, no room phones* ▭ *AE, DC, MC, V.*

To & from Guápiles

60 km/38 mi (1 hr) northeast of San José.

Guápiles lies just north of Braulio Carrillo National Park and straddles the highway to the Caribbean. It is easily accessible from San José just

60 km (38 mi) to the southwest or Limón 84 km (50 mi) to the east. Empresarios Guapileños buses connect San José's Gran Terminal del Caribe with Guápiles every hour from early morning until late evening.

Guápiles Essentials

🏦 Bank/ATM **Banco Nacional** ✉ 400 m east and 50 m north of hospital ☎ 713–2000. **BAC San José** ✉ Across from Instituto Nacional de Seguros ☎ 710–7434.
🏥 Hospital **Hospital de Guápiles** ✉ 90 m south of fire station ☎ 710–6801.
💊 Pharmacy **Farmacia San Martín** ✉ Across from Palí ☎ 710–1115. **Farmacia Santa Marta** ✉ Across from Banco Nacional ☎ 710–6253.

EARTH

❷ The nonprofit institution of higher education EARTH (Escuela de Agricultura de la Región Tropical Húmeda, or Agricultural School of the Humid Tropical Region) researches the production of less pesticide-dependent bananas and other forms of sustainable tropical agriculture, as well as medicinal plants. The university graduates some 100 students from Latin America and Africa each year. EARTH's elegant stationery, calendars, and other paper products made from banana stems, tobacco leaves, and coffee leaves and grounds, and are sold at the on-site Oropéndola store and in many tourist shops around the country. The property encompasses a banana plantation and a forest reserve with nature trails. Half-day tours are $10; full-day, $15–$20; and lunch is $4 for day visitors. Though priority is given to researchers and conference groups, you're welcome to stay in the school's 50-person lodging facility, with private bathrooms, hot water, and ceiling fans, for $55 a night, which includes the use of a swimming pool and exercise equipment. The site is a favorite of bird-watchers; some 250 species have been spotted here. Reservations are required. ✉ *Pocora de Guácimo, 15 km/9 mi east of Guápiles on Guápiles Hwy.* ✆ *Apdo. 4442–1000, San José* ☎ *713–0000* 🖷 *713–0001* 🌐 *www.earth.ac.cr.*

To & from EARTH

The entrance to EARTH lies just east of the town of Guácimo. Stop and check with the guard at the gate off the highway. If you're taking the bus, drivers should drop you off at the stop in front of the gate.

Siquirres

❸ Its name is a corruption of the words "*Si quieres*" (if you want), fittingly impassive for this lackluster town. It anchors a fertile banana- and pineapple-growing region, and marks the transition point between the agricultural lowlands and the tropical, palm-laden coast. Siquirres has the unfortunate historical distinction of at one time being the westernmost point to which Afro-Caribbeans could migrate. The law was implemented in the late 1880s—when large numbers of Afro-Caribbeans immigrated (mainly from Jamaica) to construct the Atlantic Railroad—but was abolished by the 1949 constitution.

Exploring

Pineapples don't get the same attention in world circles as Costa Rican coffee and bananas, but the **AgriTour Pineapple Tour** (✉ On the highway

NICARAGUA

San Juan
del Norte

Barra del
Colorado
5

San Juan

Colorado

BARRA DEL COLORADO
NATIONAL WILDLIFE
REFUGE

Tortuguero
4
see map
page 378

Puerto
Viejo de
Sarapiqui

Suerte   La Pavona

Tortuguero

TORTUGUERO
NATIONAL PARK

La Selva
Biological
Station

4

Cariari

Rara Avis

Perismina   Parismina

Guápiles   **2** EARTH

Aguas Zarcas

Santa   **32**   **1**
Braulio Carrillo   Clara   Costa   Guácimo   San Rafael
National Park   Flores

Guápiles Hwy.

Volcán
Barva   Rain Forest
               Arial Tram   Siquirres

Sacramento   **3** AgriTour/
                                              Pineapple
Cordillera Central   Tour   Matina
Zorqui

32   **32**   Stratford
                                              Bristol
Heredia   Reventazón   Liverpool
                                   10 Pacuare

San Jose   Volcán Irazú
                      National Park
                            GUAYABO
                            NATIONAL   Tres Equis
          Pacayas   MONUMENT

Cartago   Juan
                 Viñas

TAPANTÍ
NATIONAL WILDLIFE
REFUGE

San
Marcos

Santa   **CA**
Maria   **2**

0   20 miles

0   20 kilometers

The
Caribbean
Coast

Caribbean Sea

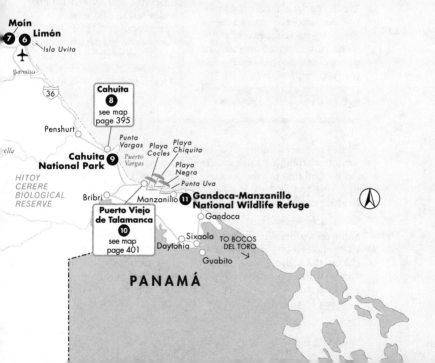

Moín

Limón

Isla Uvita

Banano

36

Penshurt

Cahuita
8
see map
page 395

Punta
Vargas

Playa
Cocles

Playa
Chiquita

Cahuita
National Park **9**

Puerto
Vargas

Playa
Negra

Punta Uva

HITOY
CERERE
BIOLOGICAL
RESERVE

Bribri

Manzanillo **11** **Gandoca-Manzanillo**
National Wildlife Refuge

Gandoca

Puerto Viejo
de Talamanca
10
see map
page 401

Sixaola

Daytonia

TO BOCOS
DEL TORO

Guabito

PANAMÁ

Rain Forest Aerial Tram

JUST 15 KM (9 MI) BEYOND the northeastern boundary of Braulio Carrillo, a 4-square-km (2½-square-mi) preserve houses a privately owned and operated engineering marvel: a series of gondolas strung together in a modified ski-lift pulley system. (To lessen the impact on the jungle, the support pylons were lowered into place by helicopter.) The tram gives you a way of seeing the rain-forest canopy and its spectacular array of epiphyte plant life and birds from just above, a feat you could otherwise accomplish only by climbing the trees yourself. The founder, Dr. Donald Perry, also developed a less elaborate system of canopy touring at nearby Rara Avis; of the two, this is more user-friendly. Though purists might complain that it treats the rain forest like an amusement park, it's an entertaining way to learn the value and beauty of rain-forest ecology.

The 21 gondolas at the original site hold five people each, plus a bilingual biologist-guide equipped with a walkie-talkie to request brief stops for gaping or snapping pictures. The ride covers 2½ km (1½ mi) in 1½ hours. The price includes a biologist-guided walk through the area for ground-level

orientation before or after the tram ride. You can arrange a personal pickup in San José for a fee; alternatively, there are public buses (on the Guápiles line) every half hour from the Gran Terminal del Caribe in San José. Drivers know the tram as the *teleférico.* Many San José tour operators make a daylong tour combining the tram with another half-day option; combos with the Britt Coffee Tour or INBioparque in Santo Domingo, both near Heredia, are especially popular. Ten rustic (no a/c or TV) but cozy cabinas are available on-site for $94 per person. The facility operates the lodging only if at least two cabins are being rented at the same time. (Reservations are required.) Electricity shuts off after 9 PM. Cabin rates include meals, tram tours, and guided walks. A café is open to all for breakfast and lunch. Reservations: Avda. 7 at C. 7, San José ☎ 257–5961, 866/759–8726 in North America 🖷 257–6053 ⊕ www.rainforestram.com ✉ $55; $74.50 includes round-trip transportation from San José hotels 🚍 AE, MC, V ⊙ Tours Mon. 9–4, Tues.–Sun. 6:30–4. Call for reservations 6 AM–9:30 PM.

7 km/4 mi east of Siquirres ☎ 768–8192, 282–1349 in San José ⊕ www.agritourscr.com), affiliated with Del Monte Foods, can acquaint you with the life and times of the country's lesser-known crop, from cultivation to drying and packing at a farm just east of town. The two-hour tour is $15, samples included. Call to make a reservation.

Outdoor Activities

RAFTING ★ Siquirres's proximity to the put-in sites of several classic rafting excursions makes it an ideal place to begin a trip. Old standby **Ríos Tropicales** (⊠ On the highway in Siquirres ☎ 233–6455 ⊕ www.riostropicales.com) has tours on a Class III–IV section of the Pacuare River between Siquirres and San Martín, as well as the section with the same difficulty between Tres Equis and Siquirres. Not quite so wild, but still with Class

FODOR'S FIRST PERSON

Suzanna Starcevic
Writer

The road ended southeast of Guápiles. We removed our shoes at the riverbank (a useless measure, since by day's end we would have sunk knee-deep in mud) and waded across to another world. The Costa Rican Humanitarian Foundation brought us to this Cabécar village to teach Spanish and help the women to develop crafts (most indigenous peoples in Costa Rica have lost ties to their traditions), but in the end, *we* may have learned the most. It was the kind of travel experience that can't fit within the confines of a postcard.

III rapids, is the nearby Florida section of the Reventazón. Day excursions normally begin in San José, but if you're out in this part of the country, you can kick off your excursion here at the company's operations center in Siquirres.

To & from Siquirres
28 km/17 mi, 30 mins east of Guápiles.

Siquirres lies just off the main highway and is easily accessible from the east, west, or south (if you're arriving from Turrialba). Autotransportes Caribeños buses connect San José's Gran Terminal del Caribe with Siquirres several times daily.

Siquirres Essentials
🏧 Bank/ATM **Banco Nacional** ✉ 50 m south of Servicentro ☎ 768-8024.
🏧 Clinic **Centro de Salud de Siquirres** ✉ East side of soccer field ☎ 768-6138.
🏧 Pharmacy **Farmacia Santa Lucía** ✉ 50 m west of fire station ☎ 768-9304.

THE NORTHERN CARIBBEAN COAST

Some compare this densely layered greenery highlighted by brilliantly colored flowers, whose impact is doubled by the jungle's reflection in the mirror-smooth canal surfaces, to the Amazon. That might be stretching it, but there's still an Indiana Jones mystique to the journey up here, especially when you get off the main canals and into the narrower lagoons. The region remains one of those Costa Rican anomalies: roadless and remote, it's nevertheless one of the country's most-visited places. The tourism seasons here are defined not by the rains or lack thereof (it's wet here most of the year) but by the months of prime turtle hatching in Toruguero, or by what's biting in sportfishing paradise Barra del Colorado.

In 1970 a system of canals running parallel to the shoreline was constructed to provide safer access to the region than the dangerous journey up the seacoast. You can continue up the canals, natural and man-made, that begin in Moín, near Limón, and run all the way to Tortuguero and beyond to the less visited Barra del Colorado Wildlife Refuge. Or you can embark at various points north of Guápiles and Siquir-

Casa
Marbella 6

Evergreen
Lodge 4

Laguna
Lodge 2

Mawamba
Lodge 3

Pachira
Lodge 5

Tortuga
Lodge 1

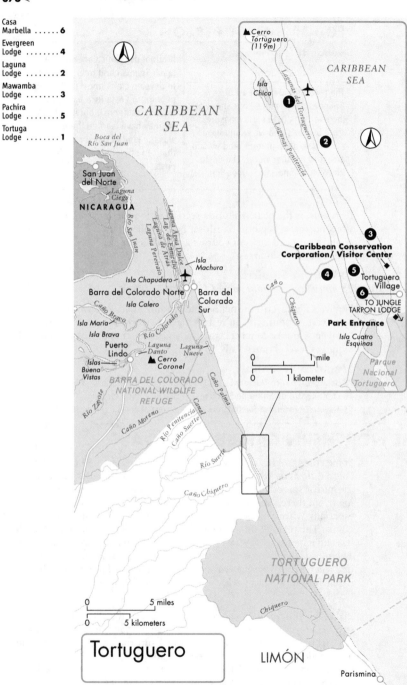

Tortuguero

res, as do public transportation and most of the package tours. (The lodges' minivans bring you from San José to the put-in point, where you continue your journey by boat.)

Tortuguero

④ North of the national park, the hamlet of Tortuguero is a pleasant little place with 600 inhabitants, two churches, three bars, a handful of souvenir shops, and a growing selection of inexpensive lodges. (And one more plus: there are no motor vehicles here, a refreshing change from the traffic woes that plague the rest of Costa Rica.) You can also take a stroll on the 32-km (20-mi) beach, but swimming is not recommended because of strong riptides and large numbers of bull sharks and barracuda.

The stretch of beach between the Colorado and Matina rivers was first mentioned as a nesting ground for sea turtles in a 1592 Dutch chronicle. Nearly a century earlier, Christopher Columbus compared traversing the north Caribbean coast and its swimming turtles to navigating through rocks. Because the area is so isolated—there's no road here to this day—the turtles nested undisturbed for centuries. By the mid-1900s, however, the harvesting of eggs and poaching of turtles had reached such a level that these creatures faced extinction. In 1963 an executive decree regulated the hunting of turtles and the gathering of eggs, and in 1970 the government established Tortuguero National Park, and modern Tortuguero bases its economy on tourism.

Exploring

The **Caribbean Conservation Corporation** (CCC) runs a visitor center and a museum with excellent animal photos, a video narrating local and natural history, and detailed discussions of the latest ecological goings-on and what you can do to help. There's a souvenir shop next door. For the committed ecotourist, the **John H. Phipps Biological Field Station**, affiliated with the CCC, has camping areas and dorm-style quarters with a communal kitchen. If you want to get involved in the life of the turtles, helping researchers to track turtle migration (current research, using satellite technology, has tracked turtles as far as the Florida Keys), or helping to catalog the population of neotropical migrant birds, arrange a stay in advance through the center. ⊠ *From beach, walk north along path and watch for sign* ☎ *709–8091, 297–5510 in San José, 352/373–6441 or 800/678–7853 in U.S.* ⊕ *www.cccturtle.org* ✉ *Apdo. 246–2050, San Pedro* ⊠ *$1* ☉ *Mon.–Sat. 10–noon and 2–5, Sun. 2–5:30.*

Outdoor Activities

Tortuguero is one of those "everybody's a guide" places. Quality varies, but most guides are quite knowledgeable. If you stay at one of the lodges, guided tours are *usually* included in your package price. (Check when you book.) If you hire a private guide, $5 per person per hour is the going rate, with most excursions lasting three hours.

WORD OF MOUTH
"My first comment is about Tortuguero. Go! The package deals are not so pricey when you consider that they are all-inclusive. You literally will spend hardly a dime more."   –Lair

Continued on page 383

TORTUGUERO NATIONAL PARK

TORTUGUERO MEANS "TURTLE REGION," which is apt, since turtles are the main attraction. Four species of turtles—green, hawksbill, loggerhead, and giant leatherback—lumber up the 35 km (22 mi) of beach at various times of the year and deposit their eggs for safekeeping. The park was, in fact, established to protect the sea turtles' nesting habitat and to protect the turtles themselves. From the time that Europeans set foot on Costa Rican shores in the mid-1500s up until the early 20th century, turtles were aggressively hunted, and their eggs and carapaces exported. Some people still believe the turtle eggs to be a delicacy and some bars (illegally) serve them as snacks.

FAST FACTS

Size: 189 square km (73 square mi)

Established: 1975

"Dry" Season: February–April and September–October (But it's never *completely* dry here.)

Wettest months: January, June, and July

What to do: Turtle tours, canal tours, fishing

Geography: Lowland rain forests, swamp forests, beaches, canals, and lagoons

Number of species catalogued: 309 birds, 85 freshwater fish, 60 mammals, 7 river turtles, 4 sea turtles

Turtles have the limelight at Tortuguero, but also keep your eyes peeled for **non-turtle species** such as tapirs (in Jolillo groves), jaguars, anteaters, ocelots, howler monkeys, white-faced capuchin monkeys, three-toed sloths, collared and white-lipped peccaries, raccoons, otters, skunks, coatis, and blue morpho butterflies.

The palm-lined **beaches** of Parque Nacional Tortuguero stretch off as far as the eye can see. You can wander the beach independently, but riptides make swimming dangerous, and shark rumors persist.

Tours
It's virtually impossible to get around Tortuguero on your own. A package tour is the best way to go. Most Tortuguero tours are packaged through local lodges, with one- or two-night stays, and include transportation, meals, and guided tours. ■ TIP→→ Opt for at least two nights. The one-night tours give you a scant 18 hours to spend in Tortuguero, with the rest of your time spent coming and going.

Turtle watching is the name of the game most of the year here, and various guides in and around the village of Tortuguero can take you on excursions. For information on package tours, *see* The Caribbean Planner, at the start of this chapter.

The Turtle-Nesting Ritual
Every two to four years, female turtles come ashore, nesting two to five times in a 12-day period. Each turtle digs a pit with her flippers and scoops out a chamber for depositing about 100 eggs. She fills and conceals the chamber before heading back out to sea. After a 60-day incubation period, the hatchlings emerge. In the ultimate in team effort, they scurry up the sides of the chamber, kicking sand down to the bottom, gradually raising the level of the base of the pit, allowing them to escape, and make a mad dash to the sea. Biologists believe that the nesting site's sand leaves an imprint on the hatchlings—though it's not known exactly how—that draws the females back as adults to the same stretch of beach, to continue the ritual that has taken place for thousands of years. Less than one percent of the hatchlings will make it to adulthood. Most fall victim to birds, dogs, sharks, and humans. That the turtle population survives at all is a remarkable feat of nature.

River and rain forest tour

Tortuguero National Park

The Endangered Manatee

It is estimated that only about 100 manatees (*vacas marinas,* or "sea cows" in Spanish) remain in Tortuguero even though they were common here prior to 1950. It is thought that numbers have dwindled due to pesticides used on banana plantations, which seep into the water, killing the manatees' food supply and changing the aquatic environment. Also, because the manatees move extremely slowly, they are easy prey and often hit by motorboats.

SEA-TURTLE SPECIES	NESTING SEASON
● Giant Leatherback	February–July
● Green	July–October
● Hawksbill	March–October
● Loggerhead	Infrequently year-round

The green turtle is the most numerous species, so its nesting season is the most impressive to see.

Ironically, efforts to save Tortuguero's turtles have pushed manatees to the margins: Increased boat traffic bringing tourists to help guide turtle hatchlings to sea means more opportunities for manatees to be hit by boats, and scares them deeper into obscure canals. In another bit of irony, manatees provide a service to the very boats that threaten them by eating water hyacinths, which can clog up waterways if they grow unchecked.

Manatees, which are generally 3–3½ meters (10–12 feet) long and weigh 450–800 kilos (1,000–1,800 pounds), are vegetarians, and eat up to 75 kilos (150 pounds) of fresh- and saltwater plants every day. They are the only exclusively herbivorous marine mammals. Their slow digestion makes for lots of gas, so a good way to spot a manatee is to stop and look around for bubbles in the water! Count yourself lucky if you see one of these rare and cute (in a bulldog sort of way) creatures.

Park Info

Hours of Operation: Daily 6–6

Contacts: 710–2929 or 710–2939

Admission: $7

Getting There: The north entrance to the park lies at the southern edge of Tortuguero village. If you come here on a package tour with one of the lodges, your boat trip to and from will take you through the park. Hiking in the park is best accomplished on a guided tour that provides transportation.

TOUR GUIDES AND OPERATORS   Call or stop by the visitor center at the **Caribbean Conservation Corporation** (☎ 709–8091, 297–5510 in San José ⊕ www.cccturtle.org) to get a recommendation for good local guides.

★ **Daryl Loth** (☎ 833–0827 or 709–8011) is a wealth of information about the area and conducts boat excursions on the canals and responsible turtle-watching tours in season with advance notice. **Victor Barrantes** (☎ 709–8055 or 838–6330) is the local SANSA agent who conducts hiking tours to Cerro Tortuguero and around the area when he's not meeting the early-morning flights.

FISHING   You have your choice of mackerel, tarpon, snook, and snapper if you fish in the ocean; snook and calba if you fish in the canals. If you opt for the latter, the National Parks Service levies a $30 license fee (you are fishing in the confines of Tortuguero National Park), good for one month. Operators add the fee to your price.

Longtime area fishing expert **Eddie Brown** (☎ 710–8016) is based out of Tortuga Lodge and has daylong fishing packages for $500. **Elvin Gutiérrez** (☎ 709–8071 or 709–8072), known as "Primo" to everyone in town, takes two passengers out for two hours or more, at $50 per hour, or for a full nine-hour day ($350). Prices include boat, motor, guide, and refreshments.

TURTLE WATCHING   If you want to watch the *deshove* (egg laying), contact your hotel or the parks office to hire a certified local guide, required on turtle-watching excursions. Note that you won't be allowed to use a camera—flash or nonflash—on the beach and only your guide is permitted to use a flashlight (and that must be covered with red plastic), because lights can deter the turtles from nesting. ⚠ **A few unscrupulous locals will offer to take you on a turtle-watching tour outside the allowed February-through-November season, disturbing sensitive nesting sites in the process. If it's not the season, don't go on a turtle excursion. As the signs around town admonish:** DON'T BECOME ANOTHER PREDATOR.

Where to Stay & Eat

The big lodges here offer one- or two-night excursion packages. Rates are expensive, but prices include everything from guides, tours, meals, and snacks to minivan and boat transport, and in some cases air transport to and from San José. If you stop and calculate what you get, the price may not be as bad as it first seemed.

$ ✕ **Budda Café.** "Hip" was never a word that went hand in hand with Tortuguero, but this place has changed the rules. Pizza, crepes, pastas, and fresh fish are on the menu at this small, canal-side café in the center of town. Lattice wood over the windows, a thatched roof, and of course, a Buddha statue make up the furnishings. Jazzy cha-cha or a Dean Martin ballad might be playing in the background. ⊠ *Next to police station, Tortuguero village* ☎ 709–8084 ▭ *No credit cards* ⊘ *Closed Wed.*

¢–$ ✕ **Miss Junie.** If Tortuguero had royalty, it would be Miss Junie, the village's best-known cook, who continues a tradition started by her mother more than a half century ago and serves cheap, filling, tasty food at an open-air restaurant adjoining her home. (Fidel Castro and Che Guevara

A Province Apart

THE CAPITAL'S HISTORIC neglect of this region has given rise to an "us vs. them" outlook among the people here. It extends to the tourism industry as well, with laments that the Instituto Costarricense de Turismo (Costa Rican Tourism Institute, or ICT) would rather promote the sunnier Pacific coast to international markets. Some here charge that subtle racism is at play. (Memories of early-20th-century government racial policies that segregated this region still remain.) The San José press doesn't help matters by splashing stories of crime in the Caribbean on front pages while giving little attention to comparable problems in Jacó, Tamarindo, or the capital. Any racial issues that *do* exist in Costa Rica—and that analysis goes way beyond the scope of this book—pale in comparison to those of many other countries. And the true cause for the Caribbean's lighter tourism may be as nonsociological as the weather: the fact remains that it's rainier here than elsewhere in the country; it's just not the typical fun-in-the-sun mass-tourist destination. And it's exactly that road-less-traveled aspect of the Caribbean and its unique ethnic makeup that make the region worth visiting.

---

were among the early diners here.) Selection is limited, and it's best to call ahead, but you can usually count on a chicken, beef, or fish platter with rice and beans simmered in coconut milk. Your meal includes a beverage and dessert. ⊠ *150 m north of Paraíso Tropical, Tortuguero village* ☎ *709–8102* ▤ *No credit cards.*

¢ ✕ **The Vine Bakery.** Pastas, pizzas, and sandwiches are on the menu, but this small bakery and coffee shop is also a great place to stop for breads made with banana, carrot, and *natilla* (cream), for example. ⊠ *25 m north of Catholic church, Tortuguero village* ☎ *709–8132* ▤ *No credit cards* ☽ *No dinner. Breakfast served.*

$$$$ ▥ **Evergreen Lodge.** Owned by the Pachira people, the Evergreen offers
Fodor'sChoice an entirely different (and intimate) concept in Tortuguero lodging: While
★ other lodges have cabins arranged around a clearing, at Evergreen they penetrate deep into the forest. A network of walking trails extends to Canal Chiquerito, the third waterway inland. Cabins are made from deep red almondwood or gypsum wood. All contain one double and one single, as well as venetian blinds for privacy. Honeymooners make up a substantial portion of the clientele here. Watch for the whimsical ANT CROSSING signs as you walk around the grounds. ⊠ *2 km/1½ mi from Tortuguero village on Canal Penitencia* ✉ *Apdo. 1818–1002, San José* ☎ *257–2242, 800/644–7438 in North America* ▤ *223–1119* ⊕ *www. pachiralodge.com* ⟿ *30 cabins* △ *Restaurant, kayaking, bar, meeting room; no a/c, no room phones, no room TVs* ▤ *AE, DC, MC, V* ⍵ *AI.*

$$$$ ▥ **Laguna Lodge.** Laguna is the largest of the Tortuguero lodges, and it hums with activity. Jam-packed package tours begin in San José and embark boats at Caño Blanco, north of Siquirres. A mix of concrete and wood buildings spread out over 12 acres of grounds on a thin sliver of land between the ocean and the first canal inland. Rooms have wood

paneling and floors, and tiled bathrooms. The property includes a butterfly garden and a small network of trails through secondary forest. Meals are served buffet style at the open-air restaurant that extends out over the canal. The snazzy combo reception–gift shop–meeting room building seems to have sprung straight from the mind of Gaudí. ☎ 225–3740 📠 283–8031 ⊕ *www.lagunatortuguero.com* ⇨ *80 rooms* 🕭 *2 restaurants, fans, pool, 2 bars, meeting room; no a/c, no room phones, no room TVs* 🖃 *AE, DC, MC, V* ¶◎¶ *AI.*

★ **$$$$** 🏨 **Mawamba Lodge.** Nestled between the river and the ocean, Mawamba is the perfect place to kick back and relax. It is also the only jungle lodge within walking distance (about 10 minutes) of town. Packages include transport from San José; when you arrive at the river town of Matina, you're whisked in a 2½-hour launch ride to a 15-acre site with comfortable (hot-water!) rustic cabinas with garden views. Meals are taken in the spacious dining room, and are included in the price, along with transfers and guided tours of the jungle and canals; trips to turtle-heavy beaches cost $10 extra. Packages begin at about $210 per person. ✉ *½ km/¼ mi north of Tortuguero on ocean side of canal* 🏠 *Apdo. 10980–1000, San José* ☎ 293–8181

⊕ *www.grupomawamba.com* 🏠 *Apdo. 10980–1000, San José* 📠 *239–7657* ⇨ *58 cabinas* 🕭 *Restaurant, dining room, fans, pool, whirlpool tub, beach, bar, shop, laundry service, meeting room; no a/c, no room phones, no room TVs* 🖃 *AE, DC, MC, V* ¶◎¶ *AI.*

$$$$ 🏨 **Pachira Lodge.** This is the prettiest and most luxurious of Tortuguero's
Fodor'sChoice lodges, but not the costliest. Each almond-wood cabina in the lush, well-
★ manicured gardens contains four guest rooms with high ceilings, king-size beds, and bamboo furniture. The stunning pool is shaped like a giant sea turtle: the head is a whirlpool tub, the left paw is a wading pool, and the right paw is equipped for swimmers with disabilities. There is no cross-river transportation into town. Package deals include transport from San José, a jungle tour, and all meals; rates begin at about $260 per person. Pachira is known for being the most competitive marketer of the lodges here, and the place is often full. ✉ *Across river from Mawamba Lodge* 🏠 *Apdo. 1818–1002, San José* ☎ 256–7080 or 257–2242, 800/644–7438 in North America* ⊕ *www.pachiralodge.com* 🏠 *Apdo. 1818–1002, San José* 📠 *223–1119* ⇨ *44 rooms* 🕭 *Dining room, fans, pool, bar, laundry service; no a/c, no room phones, no room TVs* 🖃 *AE, MC, V* ¶◎¶ *AI.*

★ **$$$$** 🏨 **Tortuga Lodge.** Lush lawns, orchids, and tropical trees surround this thatched riverside lodge owned by Costa Rica Expeditions and renowned for its nature packages and top-notch, personalized service. Tortuga sets itself apart with its smaller size and markets itself to a higher-budget clientele than do its major competitors here (Laguna, Mawamba, and Pachira). Guest rooms are comfortable, with much-appreciated mosquito blinds. The chefs do an excellent job of preparing hearty food, which is served family style rather than in a buffet line as at other lodges. Tortuguero National Park is 20 minutes south by boat. ⊠ *Across the river from the airstrip, 2 km/1 mi from Tortuguero* ☎ *710–8016, 257–0766, or 222–0333* 🖶 *257–1665* ⊕ *www.costaricaexpeditions.com* 🖶 *257–1665, 800/886–2609 from U.S.* ⇙ *26 rooms* ⌂ *Dining room, fans, pool, fishing, hiking, bar, laundry service; no a/c, no room phones, no room TVs* ☰ *AE, MC, V* |Ol *FAP.*

¢ 🖾 **Casa Marbella.** The best of the in-town hotels is a real find. Cana-
Fodor's Choice dian owner and naturalist Daryl Loth is a respected authority on all things
★ Tortuguero, and one of the community's biggest boosters. If he's unable to take you out in his boat himself, he'll find someone who can. Immaculate rooms have tile floors and varnished wood finishing with vaulted ceilings and skylights in the bathrooms. Ample breakfasts are served on the covered back patio facing the lodging's own private canal dock. The terrace is also a relaxing place for a coffee break on a rainy afternoon. There's a small kitchenette for your use. ⊠ *Across from Catholic church, Tortuguero village* ☎ *833–0827 or 709–8011* ⊕ *casamarbella.tripod.com* ⇙ *5 rooms* ⌂ *Fans, travel services; no a/c, no room phones, no room TVs* ☰ *No credit cards* |Ol *BP.*

Shopping

★ Octagonal **Jungle Shop** (⊠ 25 m north of Catholic church, Tortuguero village ☎ 709–8072) has the best selection of souvenirs in town. Tiles, feather paintings, and original-design T-shirts are the standouts, and they are things you won't find at every other store in Costa Rica. The town's largest souvenir emporium, **Paraíso Tropical** (⊠ West side of Tortuguero school, Tortuguero village ☎ 709–8095) has a huge selection of wood carvings and sandals in addition to the standard T-shirt and postcard fare. You can't miss it; it's right at the pier where the lodges' boats dock for their afternoon tours of the village. **Souvenirs Pura Vida** (⊠ Across from police station, Tortuguero village ☎ 709–8037) is small but has a nice variety of colorful T-shirts and wood carvings.

To & from Tortuguero

It's easier than you'd think to get to remote Tortuguero. Flying is the quickest (and most expensive) option. SANSA and NatureAir provide early-morning flights to and from San José. SANSA agent **Victor Barrantes** (☎ 709–8055 or 838–6330) meets both planes—they arrive and depart within 15 minutes of each other—and offers boat-taxi service to and from town for $3. Call and confirm with him the day before if you need a ride. If you're staying at one of the lodges, its boat will meet you at the airstrip.

The big lodges all have packages that include transportation to and from San José along with lodging, meals, and tours. Guide-staffed

> **CAUTION**
>
> The conditions that make the Caribbean so popular among surfers spell danger for swimmers. Drownings occur each year. Strong riptides can pull you out to sea, even in waist-deep water, before you realize what's happening. Never swim alone in these parts— good advice anywhere.

minivans pick you up at your San José hotel and drive you to the put-in site, usually somewhere north of Siquirres, where you board a covered boat for the final leg on the canals to Tortuguero. The trip up entails sightseeing and animal viewing. The trip back to San José stops only for a lunch break. This is the

> **CAUTION**
>
> Wear mosquito repellent in low-lying coastal areas, where a few cases of dengue have been reported.

classic "leave the driving to them" way to get to Tortuguero.

A boat from the port of Moín, near Limón, is the traditional budget method of getting to Tortuguero if you are already on the Caribbean coast. Arrive at the docks by 9 AM and you should be able to find someone to take you there. The going price is $30 one way; $50 round-trip; and travel time is about three hours. **Alexis Soto and Sebastián Torres** (☎ 900/296–2626 beeper) partner to provide a reliable boat service between Moín and Tortuguero for about $50 round-trip. Arrange in advance. If you arrive in Moín in your own vehicle, JAPDEVA, Costa Rica's Atlantic port authority, operates a secure, guarded parking facility for your car while you are in Tortuguero.

It's entirely possible to make the trip independently from San José, a good option if you are staying in the village rather than at a lodge. A direct bus departs from San José's Gran Terminal del Caribe to Cariari, north of Guápiles, at 9 AM. At Cariari, disembark and walk five blocks to the local terminal, where you can board a noon bus for the small town of La Pavona. From there, boats leave at 1:30 PM to take you to Tortuguero, arriving around 3 PM. The Cariari–La Pavona–Tortuguero bus–boat service is provided by **COOPETRACA** or **Viajes Clic-Clic** (☎ 709–8155, 844–0463, or 308–2006) for $10 one way. La Pavona has secure parking facilities. ⚠ **Avoid Rubén Bananero, a company that provides bus–boat transport from Cariari via an inconvenient route through the Geest banana plantation. They begin to hustle you the minute you get off the bus in Cariari, insisting the La Pavona route does not exist. They also require that you buy a round-trip ticket, limiting your return options, and do everything they can to steer you toward hotels that pay them a commission. Others will also try to take you to their own dedicated "information dock" in the village, steering you toward their own guides. If you've made advance reservations for guides or hotels, stand your ground and say "No, gracias."**

Water taxis provide transport from multiple points in the village to the lodges. Expect to pay about $2–$3 per trip.

Tortuguero Essentials

🌐 Internet **La Casona** ✉ North side of soccer field ☎ 709–8092.

🌐 Visitor Information **Kiosk** ☎ Town center ☞ Information on the town's history, the park, turtles, and other wildlife; no staff. **Tortuguero Information Center** ✉ Across from Catholic church ☎ 709–8011 or 833–0827

Barra del Colorado

⑤ Up the coast from Tortuguero is the ramshackle hamlet of Barra del Colorado, a popular sportfishing hub characterized by plain stilted wooden houses, dirt paths, and a complete absence of motorized land vehicles (though some locals have added motors to their hand-hewn canoes).

Exploring

Bordered to the north by the Río San Juan and the frontier with Nicaragua is the vast, 905-square-km (350-square-mi) **Barra del Colorado Wildlife Refuge** (Refugio Nacional de Vida Silvestre Barra del Colorado), really the only local attraction for nonanglers. Most people arrange trips here through their lodge. Transportation once you get here is almost exclusively waterborne, as there are virtually no paths in this swampy terrain. The list of species that you're likely to see from your boat is almost the same as that for Tortuguero; the main difference here is the feeling of being farther off the beaten track. You can realistically get as far as the 640,000-acre **Río Indio-Maíz Biological Reserve** when crossing the border here. The reserve is a continuation of the Barra del Colorado Wildlife Refuge, but in Nicaraguan territory. If you want to venture there, book a room at the Río Indio Adventure Lodge (⇨ *below*) in Nicaragua, which takes care of all border-crossing protocol. ☏ *No phone* ☒ *Free* ⊙ *24 hours.*

Outdoor Activities

FISHING Fishing is the name of the game here, and your lodge in Barra del Colorado will handle all the arrangements for you.

Where to Stay

$$$$ ⌂ **Río Colorado Lodge.** This long-established lodge caters almost exclusively to sportfishing folk and tours, complete with a modern fleet of 10- and 26-foot sportfishing vessels. (Tarpon and snook are the catch here.) Guest rooms have twin beds, paneled ceilings, white curtains, and basket lampshades. The all-inclusive packages include airport pickup, all meals, and fishing trips; rates begin at about $1,500 per person. Alternatively, there are some fly-in, boat-out nature-tour packages that include Tortuguero National Park and are considerably cheaper. Given the logistics of getting here, it doesn't pay to stay only one night. ✉ *35-min flight from San José* ☏ *710–6879, 232–4063 San José, 800/243–9777 in North America* 🖷 *231–5987, 813/909–4467 in U.S.* ⊕ *www.riocoloradolodge.com* ✍ *Apdo. 5094–1000, San José* ⇆ *24 rooms*

THE NICARAGUA CANAL

Spurred by the 1840s California Gold Rush, the San Juan River became an important crossroads allowing miners and gold to move between New York and San Francisco some 70 years before the Panama Canal opened. Cornelius Vanderbilt financed the dredging of the waterway to allow ships to pass up the river to Lake Nicaragua. From there a rail line connected to the Pacific Ocean. As the Panama Canal ages, there is again talk of resurrecting this "wet-dry" canal. So far, plans remain on the drawing board.

♺ *Restaurant, fans, fishing, bar, laundry service; no room phones, no room TVs* ▤ *AE, DC, MC, V* ▯❂▯ *AI.*

$$$$ **Río Indio Adventure Lodge.** Near the small village of San Juan del Norte, in the midst of the Río Indio-Maiz Biological Reserve (⇨ *above*), was Nicaragua's first true ecotourism lodge, and it still has a rustic luxury. Thatch-roof-covered walkways lead through the forest connecting the main building to your room, with hardwood floors and huge windows. All is well ventilated here despite the heat in this part of southern Nicaragua. Packages include van transport from San José to Puerto Viejo de Sarapiquí, with continuation by boat another three hours up the Sarapiquí and San Juan rivers to the lodge. Or you can opt for air transport to Barra del Colorado with another hour's boat journey up the Río Colorado to the site. So tied is San Juan del Norte to its southern neighbor that the lodge's information offices and telephone numbers are in Costa Rica rather than Nicaragua. ✉ *San Juan del Norte, Nicaragua* ☎ *296–0095, 866/593–3176 in North America* 🖷 *291–0835* ⊕ *www. rioindiolodge.com* ⟿ *34 rooms* ♺ *Restaurant, fans, in-room safes, pool, babysitting, laundry service, Internet, bar, travel services; no a/c, no room phones, no room TVs* ▤ *AE, DC, MC, V* ▯❂▯ *AI.*

To & from Barra del Colorado
25 km/16 mi northwest of Tortuguero.

SANSA and NatureAir have very early-morning flights from San José. You're likely staying at a fishing lodge if you come this far, and a representative will meet your flight and escort you to your lodge and back.

Crossing into Nicaragua via the San Juan River

Crossing into Nicaragua here is both difficult and easy. A stay at the Río Indio Lodge offers the easiest (and most expensive) option, with guided transportation included in your package price. The lodge will handle the $10 immigration fee levied by Nicaraguan authorities. (Depending on the state of relations between the countries, Nicaraguan authorities periodically levy a $20 charge. The border remains a thorny issue between Costa Rica and its northern neighbor, but other than this little annoyance, it need not concern you as a visitor.) Less formally, a 40-km (24-mile) boat trip from Puerto Viejo de Sarapiquí up the Río Sarapiquí takes you to the San Juan and lets you officially enter Nicaragua. Passports are required for the trip, but you won't acquire a Nicaraguan stamp as a souvenir if you remain on the river, as is the case for most excursions. Venturing any farther into Nicaragua on your own is impossible here; you run up against the largely forested eastern half of the country. It remains essentially roadless, much like Tortuguero and Barra del Colorado immediately to the south. The western immigration point at Peñas Blancas provides a much easier entry into Nicaragua (⇨ *Chapter 4*).

COASTAL TALAMANCA

The landscape along the Guápiles Highway changes from farmland to tropical as you approach the port city of Limón. Place names change, too. You'll see signs to towns called Bristol, Stratford, and Liverpool, reflecting the region's British Caribbean heritage.

Limón

❻ The colorful Afro-Caribbean flavor of Costa Rica's most important port (population 90,000) is the first sign of life for seafaring visitors to Costa Rica's east coast. Christopher Columbus was the first visitor: he dropped anchor here on his final voyage to the New World in 1502. Limón (sometimes called "Puerto Limón") is a lively, if shabby, town with a 24-hour street life. The wooden houses are brightly painted, but the grid-plan streets look rather worn, largely because of the damage caused by a 1991 earthquake. Street crime, including pickpocketing and nighttime mugging, is not uncommon here. Long charged with neglecting the city, the national government has now turned attention to Limón. New businesses are coming in, a positive sign of urban renewal, and the town has beefed up security with a more visible police presence.

Limón receives thousands of visitors every year, owing in large part to its newest incarnation as a port of call. Carnival, Celebrity, Cunard, Holland America, Norwegian, Princess, and Royal Caribbean cruise ships all dock at the Terminal de Cruceros, downtown, during the October–August season, with December–March seeing one or two boats each day, but many fewer outside those peak months. (At this writing, Cunard's new luxury liner, the *Queen Mary II,* is scheduled to make an occasional call here at Limón.) This is the place to find telephones, Internet cafés, manicurists—they do quite a brisk business—a tourist-information booth, and tour-operator stands, too. Downtown shopkeepers have all learned how to convert their colón prices to dollars, and post the day's exchange rate. St. Thomas or Puerto Vallarta it is not—perhaps someday, residents hope—but Limón has a tourist vibe these days that the city has never before experienced. The terminal contains souvenir stands staffed by low-key vendors who invite you to look, but don't pester you if your answer is "*No, gracias.*"

NAVIGATING
LIMÓN

Avenidas (avenues) run east and west, and *calles* (streets) north and south, but Limón's street-numbering system differs from that of other Costa Rican cities. "Number one" of each avenida and calle begins at the water and numbers increase sequentially as you move inland, unlike the evens-on-one-side, odds-on-the-other scheme used in San José. But the scarcity of street signs means everyone uses landmarks anyway. Official red taxis ply the streets, or wait at designated taxi stands near Parque Vargas, the Mercado Municipal, and the cruise-ship terminal.

CRUISING INTO LIMÓN

If you arrive in Limón on a cruise ship, a day in the Caribbean is yours for the taking. The Tortuguero canals, the beaches at Puerto Viejo de Talamanca, or the sloth rescue center at Aviarios del Caribe near Cahuita are three popular excursions. A few hardy souls venture as far away as the Rain Forest Aerial Tram or San José. But many remain in Limón to shop and explore. (The terminal is right downtown.) A legion of taxi drivers waits at the terminal exit.

Caribbean Carnaval

IF YOU'RE HERE IN EARLY OR mid-October, don't miss Limón's Carnaval, arguably Costa Rica's biggest blowout. The weeklong celebration is held around October 12 (Columbus Day in the U.S.), which is celebrated by the rest of Latin America as the Dí de la Raza (Day of the Race), with "race" referring to the mixed population resulting from the encounter of European and indigenous peoples, a day that tends to have decidedly leftist political overtones. But the holiday is the Día de las Culturas (Day of the Cultures) in Costa Rica, and is a joyous multicultural celebration of the encounter of New and Old Worlds in the country's most multicultural city. Historians here debate whether or not Carnaval was ever intended to coincide with the holiday. Most agree that it was simply a revitalization of the October Sin Kitt harvest celebrations once held on the Caribbean island of St. Kitts, the native home of 19th-century Afro-Caribbeans who immigrated to Costa Rica to work on the Atlantic Railroad. Expect a week's worth of colorful parades and vibrant reggae and calypso music. Book lodging weeks in advance if you plan to be in Limón during that time.

Exploring

The aquamarine wooden port building faces the cruise terminal, and just to the east lies the city's palm-lined central park, **Parque Vargas.** From the promenade facing the ocean you can see the raised dead coral left stranded by the 1991 earthquake. Nine or so Hoffman's two-toed sloths live in the trees of Parque Vargas; ask a passerby to point them out, as spotting them requires a trained eye.

A couple of blocks west of the north side of Parque Vargas is the lively enclosed **Mercado Municipal** (Municipal Market; ⊠ Pedestrian mall, Avda. 2, between Cs. 3 and 4), where you can buy fruit for the road ahead, and experience the sights, sounds, and smells of a Central American market.

On the left side of the highway as you enter Limón is a large **Chinese cemetery,** Chinese workers having made up a large part of the 1880s railroad-construction team that worked here. Thousands died of malaria and yellow fever. Look for the COLONIA CHINA and corresponding sign in Chinese on the hill in the cemetery.

Outdoor Activities

Limón's growing crop of tour operators serves cruise-ship passengers almost exclusively. **Laura Tropical Tours** (⊠ Terminal de Cruceros ☎ 758–1240) has excursions to banana plantations, Tortuguero, and Cahuita National Park. **Mambo Tours** (⊠ Terminal de Cruceros ☎ 798–1542) can take you on 3- to 8-hour excursions around the region, and even on an all-day trip to the Rain Forest Aerial Tram or San José.

Where to Stay & Eat

$–$$ ✕ **Brisas del Caribe.** Here's a case study in what happens when cruise ships come to town. This old downtown standby, once charmingly as off kilter as the crooked umbrellas on its front tables, got rid of its video poker machines (and the locals who always hoped to get lucky playing them) and tiled the floors and remodeled. The food is still good— seafood and surprisingly decent hamburgers, a real rarity in Costa Rica, are the fare here—but a bit of the local color has faded. ✉ *North side of Parque Vargas* ☎ *758–0138* 🖃 *AE, DC, MC, V* ☉ *Breakfast served.*

$ 🏨 **Hotel Maribú Caribe.** Perched on a cliff overlooking the Caribbean Sea between Limón and Portete, these white conical thatched huts have great views but you're a long way from the ocean itself. The lovely grounds have green lawns, shrubs, palm trees, and a large, kidney-shape pool. The poolside bar discourages exertion. The hotel is immensely popular on weekends, but during the week you'll likely have the place to yourself. ✉ *4 km/2½ mi north on road to Portete, Apdo. 623–7300* ☎ *795–2543* 🖴 *795–3541* ⊕ *www.vacationcity.com/costa-rica/hotel/ maribu-caribe* ⇨ *52 rooms* ♨ *Restaurant, cable TV, bar, laundry service* 🖃 *AE, DC, MC, V* ⫪ *EP.*

¢ 🏨 **Hotel Park.** The prices can't be beat here in this pastel-and-pink business-class hotel in central Limón. All rooms have modern furnishings and private balconies, so opt for one fronting the ocean. The air-conditioned dining room is a pleasant respite from the heat of the port city. ✉ *Avda. 3, between Cs. 2 and 3* ☎ *798–0555* 🖴 *758–4364* ✐ *irlyxie@racsa.co.cr* ⇨ *32 rooms* ♨ *Restaurant, cable TV, meeting room* 🖃 *AE, DC, MC, V.*

Shopping

The cruise-ship terminal contains an orderly maze of souvenir stands. Vendors are friendly; there's no pressure to buy. Many shops populate the restored port building across the street. Spelling is not its forte, but the **Caribean Banana** (✉ 50 m north Terminal de Cruceros, west side of Parque Vargas ☎758–3619) stands out from the other shops in the cruise-terminal area with a terrific selection of wood carvings.

To & from Limón

100 km/62 mi southeast of Guápiles, 160 km/100 mi (3½ hrs) east of San José.

If you're coming to the Caribbean coast, you'll pass through Limón. The Guápiles Highway that began in San José ends here at the ocean, but bypasses the heart of downtown by a couple of blocks. Just after the sign to Sixaola and the coastal highway south to Cahuita and Puerto Viejo de Talamanca is the city center. The main bus terminal lies at Avenida 2 and Calle 8, across from the soccer stadium and serves routes from San José, Guápiles, and Siquirres, with buses arriving several times daily from each. Opt for the *directo* (express) service from San José rather than the *corriente* buses, which make many stops along the route. Buses to Cahuita and Puerto Viejo de Talamanca and all points on the south coast arrive and depart from a stop across from Radio Casino on Avenida 4 between calles 3 and 4.

The Old Atlantic Railroad

CHRISTOPHER COLUMBUS became the Caribbean's (and the country's) first tourist when he landed at Uvita island near Limón during his fourth voyage to the New World in 1502. But the region was already home to thriving, if small, communities of Kekoldi, Bribrí, and Cabécar indigenous peoples. If Costa Rica was an isolated backwater, the Caribbean remained even more remote from colonial times through most of the 19th century.

New York industrialist Minor Keith changed all that in 1871 with his plan to launch the British-funded Atlantic Railroad, a mode of transportation that would permit easier export of coffee and bananas to Europe. Such a project required a massive labor force, and thousands of West Indians, Asians, and Italians were brought to Costa Rica to construct the 522 km (335 mi) railroad from Limón to San José. Thousands are reputed to have died of yellow fever, malaria, and snakebite during construction of the project. Those who survived were paid relatively well, however, and by the 1930s many Afro-Caribbean residents owned their own small plots of land. When the price of cacao rose in the 1950s, they emerged as comfortable landowners. Until the Civil War of

1948, black Costa Ricans were forbidden from crossing into the Central Valley lest they upset the country's racial balance, and they were thus prevented from following work when United Fruit abandoned many of its blight-ridden northern Caribbean plantations in the 1930s for green-field sites on the Pacific plain.

Costly upkeep of rail service, construction of the Braulio Carrillo Highway to the coast, declining banana production, and an earthquake that rocked the region in 1991 all sounded the death knell for the railroad. The earthquake was also a wake-up call for many here. The long lag time for aid to reach stricken areas symbolized the historic neglect for the region on the part of the central government. Development has been slower to reach this part of the country. (Telephones and electricity are still newfangled inventions in some smaller communities here.) As elsewhere in the country, communities now look to tourism to put colones in the coffers. San José has just begun to reinstate commuter-rail service; a few folks here hold out faint hopes of beginning Caribbean train service once again, but that's likely a long way off.

Limón Essentials

🏦 Bank/ATM **BAC San José** ⊠ Avda. 3, between Cs. 2 and 3 ☎ 798-0155. **Banco Nacional** ⊠ Avda. 2, between Cs. 3 and 4 ☎ 758-0094. **Scotiabank** ⊠ Avda. 3 and C. 2 ☎ 798-0009

🏥 Hospital **Hospital Dr. Tony Facio** ⊠ Highway to Portete ☎ 758-2222.

💊 Pharmacy **Farmacia Buenos Aires** ⊠ 25 m east of Mercado Municipal ☎ 798-4732. **Farmacia Limonense** ⊠ First floor, Radio Casino ☎ 758-0654.

ℹ️ Visitor Information **JAPDEVA** (Atlantic Port Authority) ⊠ Terminal de Cruceros ☞ Accessible to cruise-ship passengers only.

Moín

❼ The docks at Moín are a logical next stop after visiting neighboring Limón, especially if you want to take a boat north to explore the Caribbean coast. You'll probably be able to negotiate a waterway and national-park tour with a local guide, and if you call in advance, you can arrange a tour
★ with the man considered the best guide on the Caribbean coast: **Modesto Watson** (☏ 226–0986 ⊕ www.tortuguerocanals.com), a local Miskito Indian guide. He's legendary for his bird- and animal-spotting skills as well as his howler monkey imitations. The family's *Riverboat Francesca* can take you up the canals for two-day–one-night excursions to Tortuguero.

To & from Moín
5 km/3 mi north of Limón.

Moín is a quick taxi ride from the center of Limón.

Cahuita

❽ Dusty Cahuita, its main dirt street flanked by wooden-slat cabins, is a backpackers' vacation town—a hippie hangout with a dash of Afro-Caribbean spice tossed in. And after years of negative crime-related publicity, Cahuita has beefed up security—this is one of the few places in the country where you will be conscious of a visible and reassuring, though not oppressive, police presence—and is making a well-deserved comeback on the tourist circuit. Tucked in among the backpackers' digs are a few surprisingly nice get-away-from-it-all lodgings and restaurants with some tasty cuisine at decent prices. No question that nearby Puerto Viejo de Talamanca has overtaken Cahuita and has become the hottest spot on the southern Caribbean coast. But as Puerto Viejo grows exponentially, Cahuita's appeal is that it remains small and manageable.

NAVIGATING   Cahuita's tiny center is quite walkable, if dusty in the dry season and
CAHUITA   muddy in the wet season. It's about a 30-minute walk to the end of the Playa Negra road to Hotel La Diosa. Take a taxi if going to or from Playa Negra after dark. Cahuita has no formally licensed red taxis, with transportation provided informally instead by private individuals. To be on the safe side, have your hotel or restaurant call a driver for you.

Bicycles are a popular means of utilitarian transport in Cahuita. Seemingly everyone rents basic touring bikes for $4–$8 per day, but quality varies widely. **Cabinas Brigitte** (✉ Playa Negra road, 1½ km/1 mi from town ☏ 755–0053) rents good bikes for $8 per day. **Cahuita Tours** (⇨ *below*) also has bike rentals.

Exploring
A full-fledged nature center a few
Fodor'sChoice   miles north of Cahuita and well
★   worth a stop, **Aviarios del Caribe** has dense gardens that have at-

> **RECYCLE!**
>
> Unfortunately it's difficult to recycle most places in Costa Rica, but Cahuita and Puerto Viejo de Talamanca have made it a breeze. Deposit your aluminum cans and glass and plastic beverage bottles in the blue *Recicaribe* barrels found around either community.

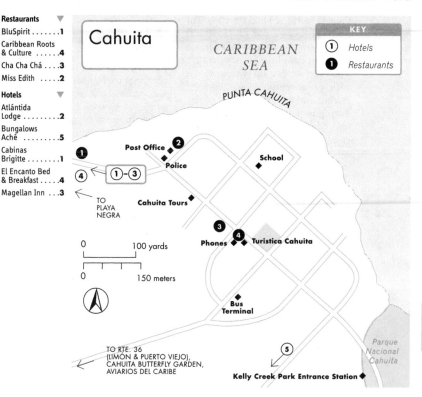

Restaurants ▼

BluSpirit **1**

Caribbean Roots
& Culture **4**

Cha Cha Chá **3**

Miss Edith **2**

Hotels ▼

Atlántida
Lodge **2**

Bungalows
Aché **5**

Cabinas
Brigitte **1**

El Encanto Bed
& Breakfast **4**

Magellan Inn . . .**3**

tracted over 300 bird species. Proceeds go to goodhearted owners Judy and Luis Arroyo's sloth rescue center on the premises. Buttercup, the very first of their charges, holds court in the nature-focused gift shop. ⊠ *9 km/5 mi north of Cahuita, follow signs on Río Estrella delta* ☎ *750–0775* ⊕ *www.slothrescue.org.*

At most butterfly gardens around Costa Rica you get wet during the rainy season. (The mesh enclosures don't offer much protection from the moisture.) But that's not the case at the **Cahuita Butterfly Garden,** where a bamboo roof covers the perimeter of the 1,100-square-meter facility. The friendly owners conduct tours in English, French, and Spanish. There's a souvenir shop and small café that serves refreshments, as well as a lounge area outfitted with whimsical wooden chairs. (The owner is a sculptor.) ⊠ *Coastal highway, 200 m before main entrance to Cahuita* ☎ *755–0361* ⊠ *$8* ⊙ *Daily 8:30–3:30.*

Outdoor Activities

Cahuita is small enough that its tour operators don't focus simply on the town and nearby national park but instead line up excursions around the region, even as far away as the Tortuguero canals to the north and Bocas del Toro, Panama, to the south.

Cahuita Tours (✉ Main street, 180 m north of Ricky's Bar ☎ 755–0000 or 755–0101) is the town's largest and most established tour operator. They can set you up with any of a variety of adventures, including river rafting and kayaking, tours of the Tortuguero canals and mountains, and of indigenous reserves (for a glimpse into traditional life). They can also reconfirm flights and make lodging reservations. We recommend them over their competitors.

CAUTION

That man on the street who asks you, "Do you want a smoke?" isn't offering you a Marlboro. A simple "*No, gracias,*" is all you need. The problem is no worse here than anywhere else in Costa Rica, but drugs get more publicity in the Caribbean.

Where to Stay & Eat

$–$$ ✕ **BluSpirit.** The Caribbean-Italian couple that owns this small beach restaurant on Playa Negra has "married" their respective native cuisines. The menu is small and handwritten, but you can opt for spaghetti *al pomodoro* (with tomato sauce), red snapper, or something in between. Try the *fruta del mar* pasta that mixes shrimp, lobster, and crab in a tangy barbecue sauce. There's live entertainment many evenings, and the manager makes amazing piña coladas. ✉ *200 m west of police station on Playa Negra Rd.* ☎ *755–0122* ▤ *No credit cards* ⚖ *Reservations required* ⊘ *Closed Wed. No lunch.*

$–$$ ✕ **Cha Cha Chá.** Québécois owner Bertrand Fleury's sign triumphantly
Fodor'sChoice announces CUISINE OF THE WORLD at the entrance to his restaurant on
★ Cahuita's main street. (He counts French, Italian, Brazilian, and Canadian heritage in his family tree.) Thai shrimp salad and Tex-Mex fajitas are two of the typically eclectic dishes. The menu is small, but what's done is done impeccably well. A delectable specialty is *langosta cha cha chá,* lobster in a white-wine garlic sauce with fresh basil. Paintings by local artists hang on the walls of the candlelit outdoor dining area, separated from the street by miniature palm trees. The place is (deservedly) popular and has a scant 11 tables. ✉ *Main street, 200 m north of Ricky's Bar* ☎ *394–4153* ▤ *MC, V* ⚖ *Reservations essential* ⊘ *Closed Mon. No lunch.*

$ ✕ **Caribbean Roots & Culture.** Miss Edith's daughter Elizabeth learned to cook at her mother's side, and the results show at her spun-off restaurant on Cahuita's main street. Jerk and rondón are on the menu here, but Elizabeth has spiced up her mother's recipes—the veggie curries pack a bit of a punch. The clientele is a bit spicier, too: the largely young backpacking crowd has turned this into a fun, lively place to hang out in the evening. ✉ *Main street, 100 m north of Ricky's Bar* ☎ *755–0248* ▤ *No credit cards* ⊘ *Closed one day each week. Varies. No lunch.*

$ ✕ **Miss Edith.** Miss Edith is revered for her flavorful Caribbean cooking, vegetarian meals, and herbal teas for whatever ails you. Back in the old days, she served on her own front porch; she's since moved to more ample surroundings on an easy-to-miss side street at the north end of town. A bit of the mystique disappeared with the move, but her made-to-order dishes—*rondón* (stew of vegetables and beef or fish) and spicy jerk chicken—are good no matter where they are served.

⊠ *East of police station* ☎ *755–0248* ▭ *No credit cards* ☾ *Breakfast served Mon.–Sat.*

★ **$–$$** ✕🔲 **Magellan Inn.** Arguably Cahuita's most elegant lodging, this group of bungalows is graced with tile-floor terraces facing a pool and gardens growing on an ancient coral reef. Carpeted rooms have original paintings and custom-made wooden furniture. Feast on intensely flavored French and creole seafood specialties at the Casa Creole ($–$$), open for dinner each evening on the hotel's patio; don't miss the house pâté or the homemade ice cream. The open-air bar rocks to great blues and jazz recordings in the evenings and mellows with classical music at breakfast. ⊠ *2 km/1 mi north of town at end of Playa Negra Rd.* ⌂ *Apdo. 1132–7300, Limón* 🔳🔳 *755–0035* ⊕ *www.magellaninn. com* ⇆ *6 rooms* ⌂ *Restaurant, fans, pool, bar; no a/c in some rooms, no room phones, no room TVs* ▭ *AE, MC, V* ⧉ *CP.*

$ 🔲 **Atlántida Lodge.** Attractively landscaped grounds, the beach across the road, and a large pool are Atlántida's main assets. You're welcomed to your room by a lovely assortment of fresh and dried flowers; the rooms themselves are a little on the rustic side, but have tile floors and pretty terraces. All the coffee and bananas you can drink and eat are yours as well. ⊠ *Next to soccer field at Playa Negra* ☎ *755–0115* 🔳 *755–0213* ⊕ *www.atlantida.co.cr* ⇆ *30 rooms* ⌂ *Restaurant, fans, pool, gym, whirlpool tub, massage, kayaking, bar, laundry service, meeting room; no a/c, no room phones, no room TVs* ▭ *AE, DC, MC, V.*

$ 🔲 **El Encanto Bed & Breakfast.** Zen Buddhist owners have cultivated a serene and beautiful environment here, ideal for physical and spiritual relaxation. Lodgings are in a garden with an extensive bromeliad collection and Buddha figures. Choose between comfortable rooms or bungalows, all decorated with art from around the globe; some rooms have a double vaulted ceiling with strategically placed screens that keep the place wonderfully ventilated. Amenities include queen-size beds, hot water, and secure parking. Breakfast comes complete with homemade breads and cakes. The beach is across the street, and massage and yoga classes are available on weekends. ⊠ *200 m west of police station on Playa Negra Rd.* ☎ *755–0113* 🔳 *755–0432* ⊕ *www.elencantobedandbreakfast.com* ⌂ *Apdo. 7–7302, Cahuita* ⇆ *3 rooms, 3 bungalows, 1 apartment* ⌂ *Fans, some kitchenettes, pool; no a/c in some rooms, no room phones, no TV in some rooms* ▭ *AE, MC, V* ⧉ *BP.*

FodorsChoice
★

¢ 🔲 **Bungalows Aché.** Like Alby Lodge next door, Aché scatters wooden bungalows—three octagonal structures in this case—around wooded grounds near the center of town, yet seemingly far away. You get newer buildings here with bed, rocking chair, and porch hammock. The largest bungalow sleeps four. The Swiss owner accepts euros, as well as dollars and colónes, for payment. ⊠ *180 m west of national park entrance* ⌂ *Box 740–7300, Limón* ☎ *755–0119* ⊕ *www.bungalowsache.com* ⇆ *3 bungalows* ⌂ *Fans, refrigerators; no a/c, no room phones, no room TVs* ▭ *No credit cards.*

Nightlife

Other than two local bars, Cahuita's nightlife centers on restaurants, all pleasant places to linger over dinner for the evening. Lively reggae,

7

soca, and samba blast weekend evenings from the turquoise **Coco's Bar** (⊠ Main rd.). The assemblage of dogs dozing on its veranda illustrates the rhythm of local life. **Ricky's Bar** (⊠ Opposite corner from Coco's) is more subdued, quiet, and touristed than Coco's.

To & from Cahuita

44 km/26 mi (45 mins) southeast of Limón.

Autotransportes MEPE buses travel from San José four times a day, and hourly throughout the day from Limón and Puerto Viejo de Talamanca. Car travel is straightforward: watch for signs in Limón and head south on the coastal highway. Road conditions wax and wane with the severity of the previous year's rains, and with the speed at which highway crews patch the potholes. Cahuita has three entrances from the highway: the first takes you to the far north end of the Playa Negra road, near the Magellan Inn; the second, to the middle section of Playa Negra, near the Atlántida; and the third, to the tiny downtown.

The proximity of the Panamanian border means added police vigilance on the coastal highway. No matter what your mode of transport, expect a passport inspection and cursory vehicle search at a police checkpoint just north of Cahuita.

Cahuita National Park

❾ The only Costa Rican park jointly administered by the National Parks Service and a community, Parque Nacional Cahuita starts at the southern edge of the town of Cahuita. The park's rain forest extends right to the edge of its curving, utterly undeveloped 3-km (2-mi) white-sand beach. Roughly parallel to the coastline, a 7-km (4-mi) trail passes through the forest to Cahuita Point, encircled by a 2½-square-km (1½-square-mi) coral reef. The hike takes only a few hours, but you have to ford several rivers on the way, so check conditions beforehand, as they can be prohibitive in the rainy season.

There's good snorkeling off Cahuita Point—watch for blue parrot fish and angelfish as they weave their way among equally colorful species of coral, sponges, and seaweeds. Sadly, the coral reef is slowly being killed by sediment, intensified by deforestation and the erosive effects of the 1991 earthquake. ■ TIP➔ **Use a local guide to find the best reefs (or to snorkel independently, swim out from the beach on the Puerto Vargas side), and don't snorkel for a few days after it rains, as the water is sure to be murky.** You can take a ride in a glass-bottom boat from Cahuita; visibility is best in September and October. The road to the park headquarters at Puerto Vargas is 5 km (3 mi) south of Cahuita on the left. Here you find the ranger station as well as campsites that have been carved out of the jungle, scattered along the beachfront. ☎ 755–0461 *Cahuita entrance,* 755–0302 *Puerto Vargas entrance* ✉ *By donation at Cahuita entrance; $7 at Puerto Vargas entrance* ☉ *Daily 6–5 Cahuita entrance; Daily 7–4 Puerto Vargas entrance.*

Reefs at Risk

ONE OF THE MOST COMPLEX organisms in the marine world, a coral reef is an extraordinary and extraordinarily delicate habitat. Coral reefs are the result of the symbiotic relationship between single-cell organisms called zooxanthellae and coral polyps. The zooxanthellae grow inside the cells of the polyps, producing oxygen and nutrients that are released into the coral tissues. Corals secrete calcium carbonate (limestone) that, over time, forms the vast coral reef "superstructure." Zooxanthellae require exposure to sunlight to thrive. The healthiest coral reefs are in clear, clean, tropical seawater at a temperature of 70°F to 80°F (20°C to 25°C). Healthy coral reefs are biologically rich gardens occupied by a diverse selection of life forms, from microscopic unicellular algae and phytoplankton to a wide range of fish.

Unfortunately, coral reefs in Costa Rica are in danger. Dirt and sediment from banana plantations and logging areas, as well as runoff from pesticide use, are killing them. The dirty runoff literally clogs the pores of the zooxanthellae and smothers them. In the Golfo Dulce, 98% of one of the oldest reefs in Costa Rica have been destroyed by this sedimentation. The once-enormous reefs of Cahuita are almost entirely gone.

Human visitors, including careless snorkelers, have also damaged reefs. Just touching a reef damages it. When exploring a coral reef, look but don't touch, and snorkel only on its outer side, preferably in calm weather. Can the reefs be saved? With commitment and time, yes. Coral is resilient, and will grow back—if the Costa Rican government makes it a priority.

7

Outdoor Adventures

Operators in Cahuita or Puerto Viejo de Talamanca can hook you up with excursions to and in the park, or you can go on your own, especially if you use the entrance at the south edge of the village.

BICYCLING You can bike through Cahuita National Park, but the trail gets pretty muddy at times, and you run into logs, river estuaries, and other obstacles. Nevertheless, mountain bikes are a good way to get around on the dirt roads and trails surrounding Cahuita and Puerto Viejo de Talamanca. (The southern entrance to the park is close enough to Puerto Viejo that you could bike there just as easily as from Cahuita.) Cycling is easiest in the dry season, though many hardy souls are out during the long rainy season. Rent bikes in Cahuita or Puerto Viejo.

HIKING A serious hiking trail extends as far as Puerto Vargas. If you're coming from Cahuita, you can take a bus or catch a ride into Puerto Vargas and hike back around the point in the course of a day. Be sure to bring plenty of water, food, and sunscreen. Along the trail you might spot howler and white-faced capuchin monkeys, coatis, armadillos, and raccoons.

SNORKELING Cahuita's reefs are just one of several high-quality snorkeling spots in the region. Rent snorkeling gear in Cahuita or Puerto Viejo de Talamanca or through your hotel; most hotels also organize trips. It's wise to work with a guide, as the number of good snorkeling spots is limited and they're not always easily accessible. Cahuita established a community lifeguard team in 2002, unusual in Costa Rica. ⚠ **As elsewhere up and down the Caribbean coast, the undertow poses risks for even experienced swimmers. Use extreme caution and never swim alone.**

To & from Cahuita National Park
Just south of Cahuita.

Choose from two park entrances: one is at the southern end of the village of Cahuita; the second is at Puerto Vargas, just off the main road, 5 km (3 mi) south of town. If you don't have a car, you can get there easily via bike or taxi.

Puerto Viejo de Talamanca

❿ This muddy, colorful little town has become one of the hottest spots on the international budget-travel circuit, and swarms with surfers, New Age hippies, beaded and spangled punks, would-be Rastafarians of all colors and descriptions, and wheelers and dealers—both pleasant and otherwise. Time was when most kids came here with only one thing on their mind: surfing. Today many seem to be looking for a party, with or without the surf.

But if alternative lifestyles aren't your bag, there are plenty of more "grown-up" offerings on the road heading southeast and northwest out of town. At last count, some 44 nationalities were represented in this tiny community, and most are united in concern for the environment and orderly development of tourism. (Few want to see the place become just another Costa Rican resort community.) Some locals bemoan the loss of their town's innocence, as drugs and other evils have surfaced, but only in small doses: this is still a fun town to visit, with a great variety of hotels, cabinas, and restaurants in every price range. Unlike other parts of Costa Rica, no one has been priced out of the market here.

Locals use "Puerto Viejo"—and they always drop the "de Talamanca" part—to refer to the village. You have access to the beach right in town, and the Salsa Brava, famed in surfers' circles for its pounding waves, is here off the coast, too. The best strands of Caribbean sand are outside the village: Playa Cocles, Playa Chiquita (technically a series of beaches), and Punta Uva, all dark sand, line the road heading southeast from town. Playa Negra—not the Playa Negra near Cahuita—is the black-sand beach northwest of town. Punta Uva, with fewer hotels and the farthest from the village, sees fewer crowds and more tranquillity. Playa Negra shares that distinction, too—for now—but developers have eyed the beach as the next area for expansion.

NAVIGATING PUERTO VIEJO DE TALAMANCA You can manage the town center quite easily on foot, though it is dusty in the dry season and muddy when it rains. Everyone gets around via bike here, and seemingly everyone has one for rent. Quality varies widely. Expect to pay a $4–$8 per day for a good bike. **Cabinas Grant** (⊠ 100 m south of bus stop ☎ 750–0292) has the best selection of quality bikes in town. Priority is given to guests at **Cabinas Casa Verde** (⊠ 200 m south and 200 m east of bus stop ☎ 750–0015), but there

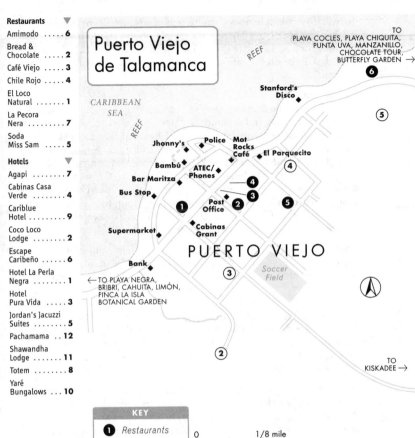

Restaurants ▼

Amimodo **6**

Bread &
Chocolate **2**

Café Viejo **3**

Chile Rojo **4**

El Loco
Natural **1**

La Pecora
Nera **7**

Soda
Miss Sam **5**

Hotels ▼

Agapi **7**

Cabinas Casa
Verde **4**

Cariblue
Hotel **9**

Coco Loco
Lodge **2**

Escape
Caribeño **6**

Hotel La Perla
Negra **1**

Hotel
Pura Vida **3**

Jordan's Jacuzzi
Suites **5**

Pachamama ..**12**

Shawandha
Lodge **11**

Totem **8**

Yaré
Bungalows ...**10**

**Puerto Viejo
de Talamanca**

CARIBBEAN
SEA

REEF

REEF

TO
PLAYA COCLES, PLAYA CHIQUITA,
PUNTA UVA, MANZANILLO,
CHOCOLATE TOUR,
BUTTERFLY GARDEN →

Stanford's
Disco

Jhonny's Police Mot
Rocks
Café El Parquecito

Bambú ATEC/
Phones

Bar Maritza

Bus Stop

Post
Office

Supermarket Cabinas
Grant

PUERTO VIEJO

Bank

← TO PLAYA NEGRA,
BRIBRI, CAHUITA, LIMÓN,
FINCA LA ISLA
BOTANICAL GARDEN

Soccer
Field

TO
KISKADEE →

KEY

● Restaurants
① Hotels

0 ————————— 1/8 mile

0 ————————— 1/8 kilometer

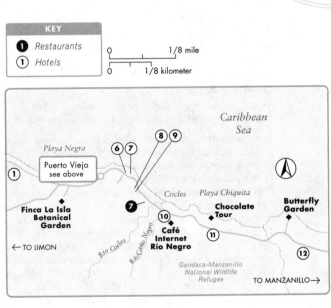

Caribbean
Sea

Playa Negra

Puerto Viejo
see above

Cocles Playa Chiquita

Finca La Isla
Botanical
Garden

← TO LIMON

Río Cocles

Río Cabo Negro

Café
Internet
Río Negro

Chocolate
Tour

Butterfly
Garden

Gandaca-Manzanillo
National Wildlife
Refuge

TO MANZANILLO →

are usually enough bikes for you to rent one for a half- or full day even if you don't stay here. There are a couple of official red licensed cabs, but most taxi service here is informal, with private individuals providing rides. To be on the safe side, have your hotel or restaurant call one for you.•

Exploring

At the **Finca La Isla Botanical Garden** you can wander around a working tropical fruit, spice, and ornamental plant farm. Sloths abound, and you could see a few poison dart frogs. A $10 guided tour includes admission and a glass of the farm's homemade fruit juice. You get the fruit juice if you wander around on your own, too, and can purchase a $1 self-guide tour book in English, Spanish, French, or German. Watch the demonstration showing how cacao bean are turned into chocolate, and sample some of the product at the end of the tour, too. ☒ *½ km/¼ mi west of town at Playa Negra* ☎ *750–0046* ⊕ *www.greencoast.com/garden.htm* ☜ *$5* ☾ *Fri.–Mon. 10–4.*

Cacao once ruled the Talamanca region, but few plantations are left these days. One friendly Swiss couple continues the tradition and gives you a **Chocolate Tour** of their working plantation. Follow the the little-known life cycle of this crop from cultivation to processing. There's sampling at the tour's conclusion. Call to reserve a tour (you need a minimum of four people) and to be picked up from the Playa Chiquita School. Since these folks are Swiss, they can tailor the commentary in German, French, or Italian, in addition to English or Spanish. ☒ *6 km/4 mi southeast of town at Playa Chiquita* ☎ *750–0075* ☜ *$15/person* ☾ *Open for tours only.*

☾ Unlike most such establishments in Costa Rica, which are for show only, the working **Butterfly Garden** cultivates 60 to 80 species of butterflies, three of which are unique to the area, for shipment to similar facilities around the world. The knowledgeable staff provides guided tours with bilingual commentary. ☒ *7 km/4½ mi southeast of town at Punta Uva* ☎ *750–0086* ☜ *$5; children under 12, free* ☾ *Daily 8–4.*

Outdoor Activities

As in Cahuita, tour operators and outfitters here can set up tours and activities anywhere on the south Caribbean coast.

Tours with **ATEC** (Association for Ecotourism and Conservation of Talamanca; ☒ Across from Restaurant Tamara ☎☎ 750–0191 ⊕ www.greencoast.com/atec.htm) have an environmental or cultural bent, such as Afro-Caribbean or indigenous-culture walks—tours to the nearby Kekoldi indigenous reserve are especially popular—rain-forest hikes, coral-reef snorkeling trips, fishing trips, bird-watching tours, night walks, and adventure treks. Local organizations and wildlife refuges receive 15%–20% of ATEC's proceeds. Well-established operator **Terraventuras** (☒ 100 m south of bus stop ☎ 750–0750 ⊕ www.terraventuras.com) can lead you around Puerto Viejo de Talamanca and Cahuita, or take you on excursions to Tortuguero, the Gandoca-Manzanillo Wildlife Refuge, and Bocas del Toro in Panama. It also rents good-quality surfboards, bicycles, boogie boards, and snorkeling gear.

CLOSE UP

Afro-Caribbean Heritage

COSTA RICA DOESN'T GET MORE ethnically diverse than its Caribbean region. Roughly a third of the people here are Afro-Caribbean, descendants of West Indians who arrived in the late 19th century to build the railroad and remained to work on banana and cacao plantations. Although Jamaicans brought some aspects of British colonial culture with them, such as cricket and the maypole dance, these habits have long since given way to reggae, salsa, and soccer, much to the chagrin of the older generation. The substantial East Asian population here also counts railroad workers as its ancestors, and small pockets of indigenous peoples have lived here since pre-Columbian times.

The Atlantic coast's long African-Caribbean heritage makes it the likeliest place in the country to find English-speakers, though residents will speak a Caribbean-accented English that may sound unfamiliar to you. "Okay" is a general all-purpose greeting heard on the coast, and is gradually replacing the older generation's traditional "Wha' happin!" (What's happening?) With Spanish now the language of instruction in all schools, young people here are less likely than their elders to speak English.

RAFTING Rafting excursions lie about two hours away, but one San José–based outfitter has an office here. New kid on the block in Costa Rican rafting circles, **Exploradores Outdoors** (✉ Across from ATEC ☎ 750–0641 or 222–6262 ⊕ www.exploradoresoutdoors.com) is already highly regarded. It has day excursions on the Pacuare and Reventazón rivers, with a pickup point here or in San José, and the option to start in one place and be dropped off at the other.

SURFING Surfing is the name of the game in Puerto Viejo, for everyone from newbies to Kelly Slaters. The best conditions are late December through March, but there's action all year. Longtime surfers compare the south Caribbean to conditions found in Hawaii, but without the "who-do-you-think-you-are?" attitude. There are a number of breaks here, most famously **Salsa Brava,** which breaks fairly far offshore and requires maneuvering past some tricky currents and a shallow reef. Hollow and primarily right-breaking, Salsa Brava is one gnarly wave when it gets big. If it gets *too* big, or not big enough, check out the breaks at Punta Uva, Punta Cocles, or Playa Chiquita. Boogie-boarders and bodysurfers can also dig the beach-break waves at various points along this tantalizingly beautiful coast.

If you're, say, over 30, but have always wanted to try surfing, consider the friendly, three-hour $35 surf school at **Aventuras Bravas** (✉ Across from Stanford's ☎ 849–7600). You start out with a small wave near the bus stop, and get a money-back guarantee that you'll be standing by the end of the lesson. You can also rent equipment here. A youthful surfing crowd staffs the small **Salsa Brava Surf Shop** (✉ Next to Hotel

Puerto Viejo ☎ 750–0668), which rents, sells, and repairs surfboards and boogie boards.

Where to Stay & Eat

★ **$–$$$** ✕ **Amimodo.** The name translates "my way," and the exuberant Italian owners really do it their way, combining the cuisine of northern Italy, from where they came, with Caribbean flavors. Your antipasto might be classic bruschetta or *jamón de tiburón* (shark ham with avocado dressing). Or your ravioli might be stuffed with tropical shrimp, pineapple, and curry, with avocado sauce on the side. The tropical veranda with gingerbread trim spills over onto the beach with abundant greenery, and the restaurant is a popular gathering place for Puerto Viejo's Italian community. ⊠ *200 m east of Stanford's* ☎ *750–0257* ⊟ *AE, DC, MC, V.*

$–$$ ✕ **Café Viejo.** This has fast become the hot place to see and be seen on Puerto Viejo's main drag. The owners, four brothers who learned to cook at the knee of their Italian grandmother back in Rimini, have concocted a menu, several pages long, of pizzas and handmade pastas. Recorded reggae and mambo music bops in the background. ⊠ *Across from ATEC* ☎ *750–0817* ⊟ *AE, DC, MC, V* ☽ *Closed Tues., no lunch.*

$–$$ ✕ **La Pecora Nera.** Though the name means "black sheep" in Italian, there's

FodorśChoice nothing shameful about this thatch-roof roadside restaurant. There's al-
★ ways a lot more to choose from than what appears on the sparse-looking menu. Wait for owner/chef Ilario Giannoni to come out of the kitchen and triumphantly announce—with flair worthy of an Italian opera—which additional light Tuscan entrées, appetizers, and desserts they've concocted that day. Be prepared for a long, leisurely dining experience with attentive service. It's worth the wait; this is one of the country's top Italian restaurants. ⊠ *3 km/2 mi southeast of town at Playa Cocles* ☎ *750–0490* ⊟ *No credit cards* ☽ *Closed Mon. Apr.–Nov.*

$ ✕ **Chile Rojo.** There's not a thing about the name or furnishings to reflect its Thai and Middle-Eastern offerings, and you might miss this hole-in-the-wall place driving by on Puerto Viejo's main street. Choose from Thai grilled tuna, falafel, hummus, and somosa. Sushi is available on Saturday. In deference to the town's European tourist trade, the restaurant accepts euros as payment, too. ⊠ *Across from ATEC* ☎ *750–0025* ⊟ *No credit cards.*

$ ✕ **El Loco Natural.** El Loco Natural epitomizes Puerto Viejo: lively, or-

FodorśChoice ganic, all the rage, but confident enough in itself to not have to be too
★ trendy. Ordering is by sauces: Thai peanut, Indonesian-Caribbean curry, Mexican chipotle, or Malaysian-guayaba curry. Then select vegetables, chicken, shrimp, or fish (marlin or tuna). Bar stools on the balcony face the street and let you survey the goings-on below. You'll be better able to converse with your fellow diners if you sit at the tables inside: live music gets going later on Thursday and Saturday evenings, and during the December–April high season, often on one other night of the week, too. It's easy to miss its second-floor location above the Color Caribe souvenir shop; look up as you walk by. ⊠ *100 m south of bus stop* ☎ *750–0263* ⊟ *No credit cards* ☽ *Closed Wed. Dec.–Apr. and June–Sept.; closed May and Oct.*

★ **¢** ✕ **Bread & Chocolate.** The take-away line for brownies forms at the gate before this place opens at 6:30 AM, but stick around and fortify yourself with a hearty breakfast of cinnamon-oatmeal pancakes, French toast, or creamy scrambled eggs, washed down with a cup of French-press coffee. Lunch gives way to jerk chicken, tomato hummus, and roasted red peppers. Everything is homemade, right down to the mayonnaise. This is one of several bakery-slash-breakfast-and-lunch cafés to open in town; the friendly, chatty owners who park their vegetable oil–powered vehicle out in front give this place the edge. ⊠ *50 m south of post office* ☎ *750–0051* ▭ *No credit cards* ⊘ *Closed Mon. and Tues. No dinner. Breakfast served.*

¢ ✕ **Soda Miss Sam.** The front-porch is always full of diners, and Miss Sam has been dishing up hearty Caribbean cuisine for years, though she prefers not to divulge how many. She usually has rice and beans going, or can fix a casado with chicken, beef, pork, or fish and freshly squeezed fruit juices as accompaniment. ⊠ *300 m south, 200 m east of bus stop* ☎ *750–0108* ▭ *No credit cards* ⊘ *Closed Tues. Breakfast served.*

$$ ▦ **Cariblue Hotel.** The youthful Italian owners who came here to surf

★ years ago stayed on and built a lodging that combines refinement with that hip Puerto Viejo vibe in exactly the right proportions. Cariblue's finely crafted all-wooden bungalows are spaciously arrayed on the edge of the jungle, across the road from the splendid white-sand beaches of Punta Cocles. Cabinas are linked to the main ranch-style building by paths that meander through a gently sloping lawn shaded with enormous trees. Expansive verandas and beautiful bathroom-tile mosaics add an air of refinement; hammocks add an air of relaxation. Breakfasts are huge. ⊠ *2 km/1 mi southeast of town at Playa Cocles* ⌂ *Apdo. 51-7304, Puerto Viejo de Talamanca* ☎ *750–0035 or 750–0518* ▦ *750–0057* ⊕ *www.cariblue.com* ⋗ *16 bungalows* ⌂ *Restaurant, fans, pool, whirlpool tub, massage, 2 bars, shop, laundry service; no room phones, no room TVs* ▭ *AE, MC, V* ⫶◉⫶ *BP.*

★ $$ ▦ **Shawandha Lodge.** The service is personalized and friendly at Shawandha, whose spacious, beautifully designed bungalows are well back from the road at Playa Chiquita. The thatch-roof bungalows have elegant hardwoods, four-poster beds, and verandas with hammocks. Each bathroom has a unique and beautiful tile mosaic. The hearty breakfast starts off with an impressive fruit plate. A white-sand beach lies 180 meters away, across the road. Even if you don't stay here, stop by and enjoy a distinctive French-Caribbean dinner in the open-air restaurant. ⊠ *6 km /4 mi southeast of town at Playa Chiquita* ☎ *750–0018* ▦ *750–0037* ⊕ *www.shawandhalodge.com* ⋗ *12 bungalows* ⌂ *Restaurant, fans, in-room safes, bar, laundry service; no a/c, no room phones, no room TVs* ▭ *AE, DC, MC, V* ⫶◉⫶ *BP.*

$–$$ ▦ **Jordan's Jacuzzi Suites.** As befits the name of the place, each of the three suites here—and more are being constructed at this writing—contains its own whirlpool tub. What's atypical of Puerto Viejo is the use of Japanese styling in each large unit, with statuary, fabric, and local woods used throughout, as well a four-poster king-size bed and air-conditioning. The suites bear names such as "Shogun," "Samurai," and "Geisha." ⊠ *200 m east of Stanford's* ☎ *750–0232* ⊕ *www.lotusgarden. net* ⋗ *7 suites* ⌂ *Restaurant, fans, kitchenettes, whirlpool tubs; no room phones, no room TVs* ▭ *AE, DC, MC, V.*

$ ⬚ **Escape Caribeño.** Wonderfully friendly Italian owners Gloria and Mauro Marchiori are what make this place: they treat you like family. A dozen immaculate hardwood bungalows line a pleasant garden area amply populated with hummingbirds, just outside of town. All cabins have hammocks, mosquito nets, double beds, and even a bunk bed or two for larger groups. Across the road lie two stucco cabins in a wooded area on the beach, both with kitchenette. Breakfast is served in a thatch-roof dining area in the center of the garden. You'll receive a small discount if you pay with cash. ✉ *400 m southeast of Stanford's* 🕾 *750–0103* ⊕ *www.escapecaribeno.com* ➷ *14 cabins* ♤ *Fans, in-room safes, some kitchenettes; no a/c in some rooms, no room phones, no room TVs* ▤ *AE, DC, MC, V.*

$ ⬚ **Hotel La Perla Negra.** The owners' previous experience as designers is evident in the fine construction of this handsome, two-story wooden structure across a tiny dirt road near the end of Playa Negra. All rooms have balconies, half with ocean views, half with jungle views. The three-meal restaurant features grilled meats and fish. Between the building and the beach is a spacious, inviting pool. ✉ *Playa Negra, 1 km/½ mi north of Puerto Viejo* 🕾 *750–0111* 🖷 *750–0114* ⊕ *www.perlanegra-beachresort.com* ➷ *25 rooms, 7 houses* ♤ *Restaurant, fans, pool, tennis, kayaking, bar, laundry service; no a/c in some rooms, no room phones, no room TVs* ▤ *AE, DC, MC, V* ¶◎¶ *CP.*

$ ⬚ **Totem.** Each of the tropical-blue units contains a living room and bedroom with bamboo furnishings, a queen bed, and bunks. We like the two rooms on the upper balcony with stupendous ocean views, and overlooking the gurgling, fountain-fed pool. The restaurant serves Italian food. ✉ *1½ km/1 mi southeast of town at Playa Cocles* 🕾 *750–0758* 🖷 *750–0825* ⊕ *www.totemsite.com* ➷ *6 cabinas* ♤ *Restaurant, fans, cable TV, pool, bar, Internet; no a/c in some rooms* ▤ *AE, DC, MC, V* ¶◎¶ *BP.*

$ ⬚ **Yaré Bungalows.** The sound of the jungle is overpowering, especially at night, as you relax in your brightly pastel-painted Yaré cabina. All rooms have hot water and verandas with hammocks. The restaurant is open for breakfast, lunch, and dinner. ✉ *3½ km/2 mi southeast of town at Playa Cocles* ⬚ *Apdo. 117–1007, San José* 🕾 *750–0106* 🖷 *750–0420* ⊕ *www.bungalowsyare.com* ➷ *22 rooms* ♤ *Restaurant, fans, some kitchenettes, refrigerators, bar, laundry service; no room phones, no room TVs* ▤ *AE, DC, MC, V* ¶◎¶ *CP.*

¢–$ ⬚ **Agapi.** Agapi means "love" in Greek, and Costa Rican–Greek owners Cecilia and Tasso lovingly watch over their guests with some of the most attentive service around. Seven furnished apartments overlook the beach and come complete with fully equipped kitchen, hot-water bath, hammock, mosquito nets over the beds, and private balcony. An additional six rooms have two full-size beds each, and all have an ocean view. A common area in the back contains a beachside barbecue. ✉ *1 km/½ mi southeast of Stanford's* 🕾 *750–0446* 🖷 *750–0418* ⊕ *www.agapisite.com* ➷ *5 rooms, 7 apartments* ♤ *Fans, some kitchens; no a/c, no room phones, no TV in some rooms* ▤ *AE, DC, MC, V* ¶◎¶ *EP.*

¢–$ ⬚ **Cabinas Casa Verde.** If you've graduated from your backpacker days and are a bit more flush with cash but still want to be near the action, this old standby on a quiet street a couple of blocks from the center of town is ideal. The comfortable cabinas are decorated with an interest-

FodorśChoice
★

ing variety of touches such as shell mobiles, watercolor frescoes, and indigenous tapestries. Overall, rooms have a neat-as-a-pin quality. Exotic birds flutter constantly through the lush plantings that screen the cabinas from the street. The place is immensely popular, since the price is low and it's clean and well run; reserve well in advance. ⊠ *200 m south and 200 m east of bus stop* ☎ *750–0015* ⊞ *750–0047* ⊕ *www. cabinascasaverde.com* ⊕ *Apdo. 37–7304, Puerto Viejo de Talamanca* ⊅ *15 rooms, 9 with bath* ⚫ *Cafeteria, fans, some refrigerators, massage, bicycles, laundry service; no room phones, no room TVs* ▭ *AE, DC, MC, V* ℣ *EP.*

¢ ▦ **Coco Loco Lodge.** The cool, forested grounds here lie close to the center of town but seem so far away. The Austrian owners lavish you with lots of personal attention. The bungalows on stilts are simply furnished but contain hot-water baths, mosquito nets over the beds (you'll need them), and hammocks on the porch. There's also one fully furnished house available for short- or long-term rental. Great coffee is included in the room rate; a huge buffet breakfast is extra. You'll receive a small discount if you pay with cash. ⊠ *180 m south of bridge at entrance to town* ☎☎ *750–0281* ⊕ *www.cocolocolodge.com* ⊅ *8 cabins, 1 house* ⚫ *Fans; no a/c, no room phones, no TV in some rooms* ▭ *MC, V.*

¢ ▦ **Hotel Pura Vida.** The friendly owners help make this the nicest of the lowest-end budget lodgings in the center of town. Rooms are basic, but clean, bright, and well ventilated and arranged around a center patio. Guests have use of the shared kitchen. ⊠ *270 m south of bus stop* ☎ *750–0002* ⊞ *750–0296* ⊅ *10 rooms, 5 with bath* ⚫ *Fans; no a/c, no room phones, no room TVs* ▭ *AE, MC, V.*

¢ ▦ **Pachamama.** So cool and shady is this place set within the confines of the Gandoca-Manzanillo Wildlife Refuge that the owners took out the ceiling fans. No one ever needed them. Though still within sight of the Puerto Viejo–Manzanillo road, Pachamama delivers a get-away-from-it-all nature experience at a fraction of the cost of other Costa Rican eco-lodges. Cozy wood cabins are simply furnished with two beds and mosquito netting and colorful spreads and drapes. A house can be rented by the week or month. Personal touches such as breakfast brought to the porch of your cabin are standard. ⊠ *9 km/5½ mi southeast of town at Punta Uva* ☎ *759–9196* ⊕ *www.greencoast.com/pachamama. htm* ⊅ *2 bungalows, 1 house* ⚫ *Bicycles, kayaking, laundry service; no a/c, no room phones, no room TVs* ▭ *No credit cards* ℣ *BP.*

Nightlife

The distinction between dining spot and nightspot blurs as the evening progresses, with many restaurants becoming pleasant places to linger over dinner. Bars each have their special nights for live music. The town's main drag between El Loco Natural and Salsa Brava is packed with pedestrians, bicycles, and a few cars most evenings, with the block between Café Viejo and El Parquecito getting the most action. Wander around; something is bound to entice you in. ■ TIP➜ **When out after dark, ask a staff member at the restaurant, bar, or club to call you a taxi at the end of the night.**

BARS Play billiards, and chow down on pizza or sandwiches at **El Dorado** (⊠ Across from ATEC), a much quieter alternative to the noisier bars.

Maritza Bar (✉ 50 m east of bus stop) is frequented by locals, and has live music on Sunday night. **Oasis Tropical** (✉ Across from Stanford's) is little more than a big green awning under which you'll find a *típico* restaurant with a karaoke machine. Tex-Mex appetizers and all types of cocktails are the draw at **Sunset Tapas Bar** (✉ On beach near bus stop), a block off the main drag. You can watch U.S. football on television during the season.

DANCE CLUBS Ticos come from miles around for the Friday and Monday reggae nights at **Bambú** (✉ Next to Jhonny's), but the place is closed most other evenings. **Jhonny's Place**

> **A BAD RAP**
>
> The Caribbean has a reputation among Costa Ricans for being crime-ridden, mainly because of a few high-profile cases here years ago, the nearness of the Panamanian border, and the fact that this is an impoverished region compared to other parts of the country. In actuality, the problem is no better or worse here than elsewhere. Just take the standard precautions you would when you travel anywhere and stick to well-traveled tourist paths.

(✉ 230 m east of bus stop) has nights variously devoted to reggae, jazz, R&B, and hip-hop. **Stanford's Disco** (✉ 100 m from the town center on the road to Manzanillo) is the place to merengue or salsa the weekend nights away.

LIVE MUSIC Caribbean and Italian restaurant **El Parquecito** (✉ 50 m east of ATEC) pulls live-music duty Tuesday, Friday, and Saturday evenings. You're bound to hear "No Woman No Cry" and all the other reggae anthems. Second-floor organic-food restaurant **El Loco Natural** (✉ 150 m west of ATEC ☎ 750–0263) has live music Thursday and Saturday evenings, and some Sundays.

Shopping

Vendors set up stands at night on the beach road near El Parquecito, with jewelry being the prime fare. But the town counts a few honest-to-goodness souvenir stores, too.

★ Puerto Viejo's best shop, **Luluberlu** (✉ 200 m south and 50 m east of bus stop), sells a wonderful selection of local indigenous carvings—balsa and *chonta* wood are especially popular—and jewelry, paintings, and ceramics by 30 artists from the region.

To & From Puerto Viejo de Talamanca
16 km/10 mi (15 mins) south of Cahuita.

The turnoff to Puerto Viejo de Talamanca is 10 km (6 mi) down the coastal highway south of Cahuita. (The highway itself continues south to Bribrí and Sixaola at the Panamanian border.) The village lies another 5 km (3 mi) beyond the turnoff. The paved road passes through town and continues to Playas Cocles and Chiquita and Punta Uva before the pavement peters out at the entrance to the village of Manzanillo. Autotransportes MEPE buses travel from San José four times a day, and hourly throughout the day from Limón and Cahuita. All buses from San José go into Puerto Viejo de Talamanca; most, though not all, Limón-originating buses do as well, but a couple drop you off on the highway. Check if you board in Limón.

A scant three buses per day ply the 15-km (9 mi) paved road between Puerto Viejo and Manzanillo, so unless your schedule meshes exactly with theirs, you're better off biking or taking a taxi to and from the far-flung beaches along the way. Taxis charge $5 to Playas Cocles and Chiquita (as well as north to Playa Negra), $6 to Punta Uva, and $10 to Manzanillo.

Puerto Viejo de Talamanca Essentials

🏧 Bank/ATM **Banco de Costa Rica** ⊠ 50 m south of bridge at entrance to town ☎ 750-0707 ☞ Visa only.

🏧 Pharmacy **Farmacia Amiga** ⊠ Next to Banco de Costa Rica ☎ 750-0698.

🏧 Visitor Information **ATEC** ⊠ Across from Restaurant Tamara 📠 750-0191 ⊕ www.greencoast.com/atec.htm.

Gandoca-Manzanillo National Wildlife Refuge

⓫ The Refugio Nacional de Vida Silvestre Gandoca-Manzanillo stretches along the southeastern coast from the town of Manzanillo to the Panamanian border. Because of weak laws governing the conservation of refuges and the value of coastal land in this area, Gandoca-Manzanillo is less pristine than Cahuita National Park and continues to be developed. However, the refuge still has plenty of rain forest, *orey* (a dark tropical wood) and Jolillo swamps, 10 km (6 mi) of beach where four species of turtles lay their eggs, and almost 3 square km (1 square mi) of *cativo* (a tropical hardwood) forest and coral reef. The Gandoca estuary is a nursery for tarpon and a wallowing spot for crocodiles and caimans.

The easiest way to explore the refuge is to hike along the coast south of Manzanillo. You can hike back out the way you came in, or arrange (in Puerto Viejo de Talamanca) to have a boat pick you up at Punta Mono (Monkey Point), a three- to four-hour walk from Manzanillo, where you find secluded beaches hidden by tall cliffs of fossilized coral. The mangroves of Gandoca, with abundant caimans, iguanas, and waterfowl, lie six to eight hours away. Park administrators can tell you more and recommend a local guide; inquire when you enter Manzanillo village and the locals will point you toward them. ☎ *750–0398 (ATEC)* ☉ *Daily 7–4.*

Outdoor Activities

A guide can help you get the most out of this relatively unexplored corner of the country. The **Association of Naturalist Guides of Manzanillo** (⊠ Main rd. ☎ 759–9064 or 843–9122) is consortium of quality, knowledgeable local guides who know the area well and lead a variety of half- and full-day tours. They can take you for a hike in the reserve or out to Monkey Point, with a return trip by boat. They also have horseback riding, bird-, dolphin-, and turtle-watching, and traditional fishing excursions.

DIVING &
SNORKELING

The friendly staff at **Aquamor Talamanca Adventures** (⊠ Main Rd. ☎ 759–0612 ⊕ www.greencoast.com/aquamor2.htm) specializes in land- and ocean-focused tours of the Gandoca-Manzanillo Wildlife

Refuge, and can tend to all your water-sporting needs in these parts, with guided kayaking, snorkeling, and scuba-diving tours, as well as equipment rental. They also offer the complete sequence of PADI-certified diving courses. Companies in Puerto Viejo de Talamanca (⇨ *above*) can arrange boat trips to dive spots and beaches in the refuge as well.

DOLPHIN
WATCHING
The **Talamanca Dolphin Foundation** (⊠Main road, Manzanillo ☎759–9115 ⊕ www.dolphinlink.org) has 2½-hour dolphin observation tours—excellent opportunities to see bottlenose, *tucuxi* (gray), and Atlantic spotted dolphins swimming this section of the coast.

Where to Stay & Eat

¢–$ ✕ **Restaurant Maxi's.** Cooled by sea breezes and shaded by tall, stately palms, this two-story, brightly painted wooden building offers weary travelers cold beer, potent cocktails, and great seafood at unbeatable prices after a day's hike in the refuge. Locals and expatriates alike—and even chefs from Puerto Viejo's fancier restaurants—come here for their lobster fix, and the fresh fish is wonderful, too. Now that the road is paved all the way to Manzanillo, the weekend crowds are getting ever larger. Locals tend to congregate in the rowdy but pleasant downstairs bar, where reggae beats into the wee hours. ⊠ *Main road, Manzanillo* ☎ *759–9073* ⊟ *No credit cards.*

$$ ⊞ **Almonds & Corals Tent Lodge Camp.** Buried in a dark, densely atmospheric beachfront jungle within the Gandoca-Manzanillo Wildlife Refuge, Almonds & Corals takes tent camping to a new level. The "campsites" are freestanding platforms raised on stilts and linked by boardwalks lighted by kerosene lamps. Each safari-style tent is protected by a peaked roof, enclosed in mosquito netting, and has beds, electric lamps, hammocks, and hot water. A fine three-meal restaurant is tucked into the greenery halfway down to the property's exquisite, secluded beach. Rustic camping this is not, but the locale does provide that close-to-nature experience. Your wake-up call is provided by howler monkeys and chatty parrots. ⊠ *Near end of road to Manzanillo* ☎ *759–9056 or 272–2024* 🖷 *272–2220* ⊕ *www.almondsandcorals.com* ✉ *Apdo. 681–2300, San José* ⇝ *25 tent-cabins* ⚲ *Restaurant, fans, whirlpool tub, bar, laundry service, airport shuttle; no a/c, no room phones, no room TVs* ⊟ *AE, DC, MC, V* ¦◎¦ *MAP.*

¢ ⊞ **Cabinas Something Different.** On a quiet street, these shiny, spic-and-span motel-style cabinas are the nicest option in the village of Manzanillo. Each bright tile-floor unit comes with a TV—quite a rarity in these parts—a table, and a small porch. Several sleep up to four people. ⊠ *180 m south of Aquamor, Manzanillo* ☎*759–9014* 🖷*759–9097* ⇝*18 cabins* ⚲*Fans, refrigerators, cable TV; no room phones* ⊟ *No credit cards* ✉ *EP.*

To & from Gandoca-Manzanillo National Wildlife Refuge

15 km/9 mi (20 mins) southeast of Puerto Viejo.

The road from Puerto Viejo de Talamanca ends at the entrance to the village of Manzanillo. Just three buses each day—morning, midday, and late afternoon—connect the two. All taxi drivers in Puerto Viejo charge $10 for the trip here.

Crossing into Panama via Sixaola

Costa Rica's sleepy border post at Sixaola fronts Guabito, Panama's equally quiet border crossing, 44 km (26 mi) south of the turnoff to Puerto Viejo de Talamanca. Both are merely collections of banana-plantation stilt houses and a few stores and bars; neither has any lodging or dining options, but this is a much lower-key crossing into Panama than the busy border post at Paso Canoas on the Pan-American Highway near the Pacific coast. If you've come this far, you're likely headed to **Bocas del Toro,** the real attraction in the northwestern part of Panama. This archipelago of 68 islands continues the Afro-Caribbean and indigenous themes seen on Costa Rica's Atlantic coast, and offers diving, snorkeling, swimming, and wildlife viewing. The larger islands are home to a growing selection of hotels and restaurants, everything from funky to fabulous. Bocas has acquired a cult following among long-term foreign visitors to Costa Rica, who find it a convenient place to travel when their permitted three-month status as a tourist has expired, since a quick 72-hour jaunt out of the country gets you another three months in Costa Rica.

■ TIP➜ **Whatever your destination in Panama, come armed with dollars.** Panama uses U.S. currency, but refers to the dollar as the *balboa.* (It does mint its own coins, all the same size as their U.S. counterparts.) No one anywhere will accept or exchange your Costa Rican colones.

Costa Rican rental vehicles may not leave the country, so crossing into Panama as a tourist is an option only via public transportation. The bus route from San José to Cahuita and Puerto Viejo de Talamanca terminates here at the border approximately six hours after leaving the capital. Disembark and head for the Costa Rican immigration office down a flight of stairs from the west end of a former railroad bridge. Officials place an exit stamp in your passport, after which you walk across the bridge and present your passport to Panamanian immigration. U.S., U.K., and Canadian visitors must also purchase a $5 tourist card for entry into the country; Australian and New Zealand citizens need only their passports. The **Consulate of Panama** (☎ 281–2103) in San José can provide more information. The border crossings are open 7 AM–5 PM (8 AM–6 PM Panamanian time) daily. Set your watch one hour ahead when you enter Panama.

Taxis wait on the Panamanian side to transport you to the small city of Changuinola, the first community of any size inside the country, from which there are bus and air connections for travel farther into Panama. Taxis can also take you to Almirante, where you'll find boat launches to Bocas del Toro.

THE CARIBBEAN ESSENTIALS

Transportation

BY AIR

ARRIVING & You can fly from San José to the airstrip in either Tortuguero (TTQ) or
DEPARTING Barra del Colorado (BCL) via NatureAir or SANSA. At this writing, Na-

tureAir is scheduled to begin landing at the small airport just south of Limón (LIO), with continuing service to Bocas del Toro, Panama (BOC). For more information about air travel between the Caribbean and San José, *see* Air Travel *in* Smart Travel Tips A to Z.

BY BUS

ARRIVING & DEPARTING The transport companies serving this part of the country provide reliable service. London may be retiring its fabled double-decker buses, but you'll ride such vehicles on many of the runs to Limón and Guápiles. Autotransportes MEPE, which has a lock on bus service to the south Caribbean coast, has a reputation for being lackadaisical, but is really quite dependable. Drivers and ticket sellers are accustomed to dealing with foreigners; even if their English is limited, they'll figure out what you want. Bus fares to this region are reasonable. From San José, expect to pay $1.50 to Guápiles, $2.50 to Limón, $5 to Cahuita, $6 to Puerto Viejo de Talamanca, and $7 to Sixaola and the Panamanian border.

All bus service to this part of the country must take alternate routes on those occasions when heavy rains and landslides close the highway through Braulio Carrillo National Park north of San José. The detour passes through Cartago, Paraíso, and Turrialba and rejoins the Caribbean highway at Siquirres. It can add anywhere from one to three hours to your journey. Check before you set out if you travel during the worst of the rainy season.

For more information about bus travel between the Caribbean and San José, *see* Bus Travel *in* Smart Travel Tips A to Z.

GETTING AROUND Buses from San José stop first in Cahuita, then Puerto Viejo de Talamanca before heading to Sixaola. Many buses originate in Limón, traveling to points south. It's the most cost-efficient way to travel.

BY CAR

ARRIVING & DEPARTING The paved two-lane Guápiles Highway continues from Santa Clara southeast to Guápiles, EARTH, Siquirres, and Limón, a total distance from San José to the coast of about 160 km (100 mi). South of Limón, a paved road covers the roughly 40 km (25 mi) to Cahuita, then passes the Cahuita turnoff and proceeds for roughly 16 km (10 mi) toward Puerto Viejo de Talamanca. It is paved as far as the village of Manzanillo. Four-wheel drive is always preferable, but the major roads in this region are generally passable by any car. Just watch for potholes and unpaved sections—they can appear on any road at any time, without marking or warning. The heavier the previous year's rainy season has been, the deeper the *huecos* (potholes, in Costa Rican vernacular), and some years sections are *very* slow going. One-lane bridges appear frequently south of Limón. If the triangular CEDA EL PASO sign faces you, yield first to oncoming traffic.

Road travel to and from this part of the country occasionally becomes more complicated when heavy rains cause landslides blocking the highway near the Zurquí Tunnel in Braulio Carrillo National Park just north of San José. The alternate route is a long, slow journey via Cartago, Paraíso, and Turrialba, rejoining the main route at Siquirres. Check before you set out when traveling during the heaviest of the rainy season.

You cannot drive to Tortuguero or Barra del Colorado; you must fly or take a boat.

■ TIP➜ Several gas stations flank the highway between Guápiles and Limón. South of Limón you'll find just one, Penshurt, north of Cahuita. Fill the tank when you get the chance.

GETTING AROUND
There are no rental agencies in this region. Rent in San José.

BY SHUTTLE VAN

ARRIVING & DEPARTING
If you prefer a more private form of travel, consider taking a shuttle. Gray Line Tourist Bus has daily service that departs from many San José hotels at 6:30 AM for Cahuita and Puerto Viejo de Talamanca. Tickets are $27 and must be reserved at least a day in advance. Comfortable air-conditioned Interbus vans depart from San José hotels daily at 7:50 AM for Guápiles, Siquirres, Limón, Cahuita, and Puerto Viejo de Tala-manca. Reserve tickets ($29) a day in advance.

🚐 Shuttle Van Services **Gray Line Tourist Bus** ☎ 232-3681 or 220-2126 ⊕ www. graylinecostarica.com. **Interbus** ☎ 283-5573 ⊕ www.interbusonline.com.

Contacts & Resources

Banks and emergency contacts are listed at the end of each town entry.

BANKS & EXCHANGING SERVICES

Most larger tourist establishments are prepared to handle credit cards. Banks are sparse in this region. Changing U.S. dollars or traveler's checks is possible at the few offices of Banco Nacional, but lines are long. The Scotiabank and BAC San José in downtown Limón have ATMs that accept Plus- and Cirrus-affiliated cards. The Banco de Costa Rica's ATM in Puerto Viejo de Talamanca accepts only Plus cards. You're best off taking care of getting cash with your ATM card back in San José before venturing here.

7

Ecotourism
Costa Rica–Style

WITH MORE BIRD SPECIES THAN the United States and Canada packed into an area about half the size of Kentucky, and an array of landscapes that run the gamut from lowland rain forest to highland *páramo,* Costa Rica offers nature lovers more interesting stuff than could ever fit in one vacation. The Costa Rican government realized several decades ago that the country's greatest assets were its flora, fauna, and natural beauty, and they set on a course of conservation that has left about a quarter of the national territory in national parks and other protected areas today.

The tourism industry has capitalized on Costa Rica's natural assets and made it one of the easiest places in the world to experience the beauty and complexity of tropical nature. The country has become synonymous with ecotourism, but the term has many interpretations in Costa Rica— from travel that benefits conservation to an abundance of potted plants. Critics note that in Costa Rica, not all that is green is eco. Clearly the importance of nature to the country's most lucrative industry has made Costa Ricans more inclined to protect their natural resources, but as tourism and infrastructure grow, conservationists warn that this kind of development can also be a destructive force. Some wonder just how many parking lots paradise can handle.

Conscientious travelers have plenty of options for ensuring that their Costa Rica vacation contributes to the preservation of the nature they travel so far to see. Nevertheless, the level of eco-hype is such that they could just as easily choose hotels and tour companies that do nothing for nature, or offer little exposure to the country's wild things. Any business can use photos of wildlife in its brochures and on its Web site; providing guests with a quality experience, and ensuring a positive impact on the local environment and culture, are more difficult challenges that not every entrepreneur is willing or able to meet. This section is meant to help concerned travelers do the right thing, and to make their Costa Rica trip as enjoyable, educational, and environmentally friendly as possible.

Where the Wild Things Are

Geography and biology have conspired to endow little Costa Rica with a disproportionate diversity of landscapes and wildlife. From its sultry, coastal mangrove swamps to its cool and precipitous cloud forests, the country holds a mosaic of natural landscapes that are packed with an amazing array of flora and fauna. An explanation of this extraordinary biodiversity is twofold. First is the interaction between its mountainous topography and global weather patterns, which result in an abundance of microclimates and provide the unique conditions for Costa Rica's varied ecosystems. Second is the country's tropical location in a landbridge between two continents—each of which has contributed many plant and animal species. The country is home to South American wildlife such as sloths and toucans, North America creatures such as coyotes and cottonmouths, and a significant number of endemic species such as the volcano junco and Central American squirrel monkey. Add to this the fact that Costa Rica is the seasonal home for hundreds of migrating species— from ruby-throated hummingbirds to hump-backed whales—and you've got a whole lot of wild things out there.

ECO- OR SUSTAINABLE TOURISM

Ecotourism, a relatively recent addition to the English language, has been defined as travel to natural areas to observe and learn about wildlife, tourism that refrains from damaging the environment, or tourism that strengthens conservation and improves the lives of local people. The later two definitions could also apply to sustainable tourism, which has a wider scope than ecotourism and pushes for improvements in everything from city hotels to cruise ships. Whereas proponents of ecotourism believe it has the potential to conserve nature by providing economic opportunities for the rural poor, who are responsible for much of the deforestation in the tropics, sustainable tourism advocates note that all tourism has the potential for negative impacts, and they push for improvement across the entire industry.

If you define ecotourism as tourism that contributes to conservation and community development, then ecotourism is always sustainable tourism. However, not all sustainable tourism is ecotourism, since tourism businesses located far from natural areas can and should implement sustainable practices. The list of hotels certified by the Costa Rican Tourism Board's Sustainable Tourism Certification program, for example, ranges from award-winning eco-lodges to city hotels that have made improvements such as installing sewage treatment systems and switching to energy-saving lightbulbs. For conscientious travelers who are looking for close contact with nature, sustainable may not be enough.

8

What this means for visitors is that a short trip within the country can take them to very diverse landscapes that are home to whole new sets of plants and animals. Each of Costa Rica's regions has its own natural attractions, but somewhere between 60 and 70 percent of the country has been urbanized or converted to agriculture, so if you want to see varied nature, you need to know where to go. The country's renowned national park system holds examples of all of its major ecosystems, and some of its most impressive sights—active volcanoes and flocks of scarlet macaws, for example. There are, however, a growing number of private reserves that protect a significant amount of wilderness. Some of these properties are even better places to see wildlife than the national parks. The government decentralized its national parks system more than a decade ago, grouping the parks and preserves into a series of "conservation areas." For travelers, contemplating the country's protected areas by region is the most practical way to decide what to see.

The Central Valley

Home to more than half of Costa Rica's population, the Central Valley's forests were converted to towns and coffee farms generations ago, but the mountains that tower over it still retain some significant expanses of cloud forest, which can easily be explored on a day trip from San

José. Tapantí National Park, at the eastern end of the valley, is an excellent spot to experience the beauty of the cloud forest, whereas the rain forests of Guayabo National Monument and the private reserve of Rancho Naturalista are more like the protected areas of Caribbean Coast and Northern Plains.

The Northern Plains

Though much of the Northern Plains has been converted to farmland, this vast and verdant region holds some of Costa Rica's best ecological gems. The mountain ranges that define its western and southern borders are topped by lush cloud forest, and the rolling lowlands are dotted with protected rain forests and wetlands, which constitute important ecological oases. The region's principal national parks protect the impressive volcanoes of Poás and Arenal, and the vast wilderness of Braulio Carrillo. It also holds the country's most important private preserves—La Selva Biological Station and the Monteverde Cloud Forest Preserve—two of the best places in the country to see wildlife. Protected areas are complemented by a selection of nature lodges that offer excellent exposure to the region's varied tropical nature. Some of our favorites are Villa Blanca, Laguna del Lagarto Lodge, Chachagua Rain Forest Hotel, Villa Blanca, Valle Escondido, the Selva Verde Lodge, and Rara Avis.

The Northern Pacific

These sweeping plains bordered by dormant volcanoes hold some of the last remnants of Central America's extremely rare tropical dry forest, which changes from a relatively lush wilderness during the rainy season to a desert-like panorama in the dry months (this actually facilitates wildlife watching). The national parks of Santa Rosa, Rincón de la Vieja, Palo Verde, Lomas Barbudal, and Barra Honda all offer exposure to the dry forest, as do the private reserves of Hacienda Guachipelin, Rincón de la Vieja Mountain Lodge, and Los Inocentes Lodges and Reserva Biológica Nosara. Rustic accommodations are available near the wetlands of Palo Verde at the Organization for Tropical Studies' biological station, but a more comfortable way to experience the tropical dry forest is by floating down the Corobicí River on a rafting tour, or on a horseback tour at one of the ecolodges above. This region also holds the important sea turtle nesting beaches of Playa Grande, where the massive leatherback lays its eggs from October to March, and Ostional, where thousands of olive ridley turtles clamber ashore on certain nights from July to January.

The Central Pacific

An ecological transition zone between the dry forests of the North Pacific and the rain forests of the South Pacific, the Central Pacific is home to plants and animals found in both regions. It is one of the few places in the country where you can see such rare animals as the Central American squirrel monkey and the scarlet macaw. It is also probably the easiest place to get a good look at the American crocodile, dozens of which sometimes gather near the bridge over the Tarcoles River, just north of Carara National Park. Carara protects the largest expanse of forest in the region, but the smaller protected areas, such as the Curú National Wildlife Reserve, Manuel Antonio National Park, and Cabo

OSA PENINSULA—ECO HOT SPOT

Though nature seems to work overtime all over the country, Costa Rica's wildest area is the Osa Peninsula, in the South Pacific, much of which is covered by Corcovado National Park. The peninsula's exuberant rain forest is dominated by massive ceiba, espavel, and mahogany trees draped with thick lianas. It is home to scarlet macaws, chestnut mandibled toucans, spider monkeys, and iridescent blue morpho butterflies. It is no coincidence that Corcovado is surrounded by eco-lodges—many of which rank among the country's best—and is visited by dozens of nature cruises every year. Corcovado is an isolated area far from roads, but it can be easily visited via boat from nearby Drake Bay. The coast to the north and south of the park is also backed by thick jungle that holds much of the same wildlife as the park. Most travelers opt for spending a few nights in either the Cabo Matapalo area, near Puerto Jiménez, or Drake Bay.

Blanco Absolute Nature Reserve are excellent places to see wildlife. The private Complejo Ecológico la Catarata, Punta Leona, and Rainmaker reserves protect some impressive scenery and complement the flora and fauna. This region may lack the eco-lodges found in others, but most of Manuel Antonio's hotels are set in the rain forest and offer exposure to nearly all the wildlife found in the nearby national park.

The South Pacific

Costa Rica's wildest corner, and one of the last region's of the country to be settled, the South Pacific has vast expanses of wilderness ranging from the cloud forest and páramo of the Talamanca Mountain Range to the lowland rain forest of Corcovado National Park. This region offers some of the best opportunities to see quetzals and other birds in San Gerardo de Dota, and Scarlet Macaws and countless other critters that abound on the Osa Peninsula. It also has some of the countries most impressive, though least accessible national parks—Chirripó, La Amistad and Corcovado—as well as the greatest concentration of eco-lodges and private preserves. Stunning marine wonders can be found at the Golfo Dulce, the dives spots around Caño Island Biological Reserve, and the seasonal whale migrations that pass between that island and Ballena Marine National Park. The lodges around Drake Bay offer access to the island and, together with the lodges of Carate and Cabo Matapalo (to the east of Corcovado), provide some of the country's best exposure to tropical nature. This region also has the country's most impressive botanical gardens and more than a dozen private reserves, which means it would be quite feasible to spend several weeks exploring its diverse wilderness.

The Caribbean

The lush jungles, beaches, and canals of the Caribbean coast boast the kind of scenery that most people conjure up when they contemplate the tropics—curtains of dense foliage rising up from dark waters, golden

RESPONSIBLE TRAVEL TIPS

The International Ecotourism Society has defined ecotourism as: "responsible travel to natural areas that conserves the environment and improves the well-being of local people." There are plenty of steps that responsible travelers can take to ensure that their trip into the wilderness, or to a rural community, contributes to its preservation. The following are some simple steps that travelers can take to ensure that their trip has a positive impact:

• Stray from the beaten path—by visiting areas that few tourists go to, you can avoid adding to the stress on hot spots and enjoy a more authentic Costa Rican experience.

• Use locally owned lodges, car rental agencies, or tour companies. Eat in local restaurants, shop in local markets, and attend local events. Enrich your experience and support the local economy by hiring local guides.

• Don't be overly aggressive if you bargain for souvenirs and don't short-change local people on payments or tips for services.

• Support conservation by paying entrance fees to parks and protected sites, contributing to local environmental groups.

• Don't litter—pack up all your trash and try to pick up any trash you find.

• Don't remove plants or animals from their natural environment and don't purchase handicrafts that are made from them, such as turtle shell or black coral jewelry.

• Don't feed wildlife or engage in disruptive behavior, making loud noises to scare birds into flight, for example.

• Make sure your tour company or hotel follows sustainable policies, including contributing to conservation, hiring and training locals for most jobs, educating visitors about the local ecology and culture, and taking steps to mitigate negative impacts on the environment.

sand shaded by tall coconut palms, and coral reefs set in turquoise waters. Better still, those settings are animated by nesting sea turtles, howling monkeys, chirping frogs, and the flitting colors of hundreds of bird species. The region's premier natural destination is Tortuguero, where coastal canals and rain forest border a beach where thousands of sea turtles nest each year. Turtle watching is a nocturnal affair that is best from July to October, but the surrounding forest and waterways offer excellent wildlife observation year-round, and all the area's large lodges provide guides and boats for exploring the wilderness. The region's number-two natural destination is Talamanca, in the country's southeast corner. Here, the beach town of Cahuita lies a short walk from the forest, beaches, and coral reef of Cauhuita National Park. Some of the hotels south of Puerto Viejo lie in, or near, the tangled forest of the Gandoca Manzanillo National Wildlife Refuge. Some recommendations include: Cariblue Bungalows, La Costa de Papito, Shawandha Lodge, and the Almonds & Corals Tent Lodge Camp.

Comfort versus Adventure

Though many nature lovers may rough it in Costa Rica, it is easy to enjoy close contact with the country's amazing wildlife without sacrificing any creature comforts. There are lodges that offer first-class accommodations and dining just a stone's throw from the nearest sloth. Some of them also make significant contributions to conservation and community development. Nevertheless, sacrificing a bit of comfort can have its rewards, such as waking up at a biological station as the daily bird chorus begins, or visiting a community tourism project and gaining insight into the local culture. Every traveler knows his or her limit, but if you push yourself beyond what you might normally be inclined to put up with now and then, your vacation can become more of an adventure.

The creature comforts that could be trimmed for the sake of a unique experience include spending a night at La Selva Biological Station, where mediocre food and accommodations are compensated for by mind-boggling wildlife and one of the country's best nature walks. Opt for an overnight rafting trip on the Pacuare River and a hike through the surrounding jungle. Other rough and rewarding options are available at the dozens of community tourism projects throughout the country. They can be booked through the local organizations ACTUAR and COOPRENA. An overnight at one of the country's community lodges can add an interesting cultural aspect to a Costa Rica trip, and will probably make your next night in a nice hotel seem that much more luxurious.

Who Promotes Sustainable Tourism

Various organizations are promoting sustainable tourism to businesses, communities, and travelers, though some are more active in Costa Rica than others. The Rainforest Alliance's sustainable tourism department is based in Costa Rica and has provided training in sustainable practices for dozens of lodges, tour operators, and communities. They have developed a convenient searchable database of sustainable lodges on a conservation portal called the EcoIndex. The International Ecotourism Society, based in Washington, D.C., also works in Costa Rica and its Web site has a database of tour companies, hotels, and other travel services that are committed to sustainable practices. Conservation International promotes sustainable practices to businesses and travelers alike. It has a Web site dedicated to ecotourism that includes a list of links to other eco-organizations. The U.S.-based World Wildlife Fund organizes nature tours to Costa Rica and other countries, the profits of which support conservation. The Global Environment Facility's Small Grants Programme has financed community ecotourism projects in Costa Rica that are represented by the umbrella group/tour booking agency ACTUAR.

The Costa Rican Tourism Board has a rating system for hotels and lodges called the Certification for Sustainable Tourism (CSR), which rates companies on a scale of one to five based on their interaction with the environment and local communities, their policies for sustainability, and the degree to which they encourage clients to support sustainability. However, some of the country's best eco-lodges aren't in the CSR database. Critics claim the program is politicized, but it is also voluntary and suf-

ON THE ROAD TO SUSTAINABILITY

The conservation nonprofit Rainforest Alliance has spent years promoting sustainable tourism in Costa Rica and its efforts have included the publication of a guide to best practices for tourism, and the organizations of dozens of workshops for hotel managers and owners. The following hotels have participated in those sustainable tourism trainings, and some of them have taken significant steps to improve their environmental and social impacts:

The Central Valley: Finca Rosa Blanca Country Inn (Heredia).

The Northern Plains: Villablanca (San Ramón); Chachagua Rainforest Hotel (La Fortuna); Fonda Vela, Sapo Dorado, and Trapp Family Lodge (Monteverde); Selva Verde Lodge (Peruto Viejo de Sarapiquí); and Caño Negro Natural Lodge (Caño Negro National Wildlife Refuge).

The North Pacific: Borinquen Mountain Resort Thermae & Spa, Rincón de al Vieja Mountain Lodge, and Hacienda Guachipelín (Rincón de la Vieja National Park); Villa Del Sueño Hotel (Playa Hermosa); Cala Luna (Playa Langosta); El Jardín del Edén (Tamarindo); El Sueño Tropical, Hotel Belvedere, and Hotel Giada (Samara).

The Central Pacific: Los Mangos Hotel (Montezuma); Hotel Villa Lapas and Villa Caletas (Tárcoles); Costa Verde, Hotel Casitas Eclipse, Hotel Playa Espadilla, and Cabinas Espadilla (Manuel Antonio).

The South Pacific: Savegre Hotel de Montaña (San Gerardo de Dota); Roca Verde, Hacienda Barú, Hotel Diuwak, and Villas Río Mar (Dominical); Villas Gaia (Ballena Marine National Park); Tiskita Jungle Lodge (Playa Pavones); Parrot Bay Village and Villa Corcovado (Puerto Jiménez); Bosque del Cabo and Hotel Lapa Ríos (Cabo Matapalo); Luna Lodge (Carate); Aguila de Osa Inn, Casa Corcovado, Drake Bay Wilderness Resort, Jinetes de Osa, Delfín Amor Eco Lodge, and Punta Mareco Lodge (Drake Bay).

The Caribbean: Evergreen Lodge, Laguna Lodge, Mawamba Lodge, Pachira Lodge (Tortuguero); Cariblue Bungalows, Cabinas Casa Verde, Casa Camarona, Escape Caribeño, La Costa de Papito (Puerto Viejo); and Almendros & Corales (Gandoca-Manzanillo).

fers from underfunding, which led to a long list of hotels awaiting inspections. The program has certified many of the hotels in San José that have taken steps to becoming greener—recycling, installing energy-efficient lightbulbs, and putting signs in rooms asking guests to reuse their towels. The CSR Web site has a searchable database of certified hotels. **🗎 Resources Certification for Sustainable Tourism** (CSR) ⊕ www.turismo-sostenible. co.cr. **ACTUAR** ⊕ www.actuarcostarica.com. **The Ecotourism Society** ⊕ www.ecotourism. org. **Certification for Sustainable Tourism** ⊕ www.turismo-sostenible.co.cr. **Conservation International** ⊕ www.ecotour.org/xp/ecotour. **Rainforest Alliance** ⊕ www. rainforest-alliance.org/programs/tourism and ⊕ eco-indextourism.org/en/home. **World Wildlife Fund** ⊕ www.worldwildlife.org/travel.

COMMUNITY ECOTOURISM

The majority of Costa Rica's tourist lodges belong to foreigners who had the vision, or capital, that most of the locals lacked. Though the true eco-lodges take steps that benefit local communities, many people who live near wild and beautiful areas lack the knowledge and resources needed to get into tourism. Two Costa Rican nonprofit organizations, the Costa Rican Association for Community Rural Tourism (ACTUAR) and the National Ecotourism Network Consortium (COOPRENA), have consequently provided rural communities with the tools and knowledge that they need to run their own tourism businesses, and in the process become better stewards of their natural resources. These umbrella groups run networks that function like travel agencies, offering day trips, overnights, and tour packages to dozens of community lodges and restaurants.

ACTUAR helps more than 20 community-based eco-lodges and tour operations market their offerings. They can book anything from a day trip to a multiday package including meals and transportation. COOPRENA provides a similar service for about a dozen cooperative tourism businesses around the country. Not only do these organizations help rural communities sell their tourism offerings, but they also provide training in areas as granular as kitchen hygiene. Their tours head well off the beaten path, offer exposure to local culture, and serve as incentives for communities to protect their natural resources. They include hiking, horseback, or boat trips up jungle rivers to see waterfalls, rain forest, and much of the same wildlife found in the national parks. They are very inexpensive, but the low-budget nature of the multiday trips might be too slow for many travelers.

The Best Eco-Lodges

The growth of ecotourism over the past decade has left Costa Rica with an overabundance of nature lodges, unevenly distributed through the country. Those lodges range from fairly rustic accommodations with plenty of wildlife, like La Selva Biological Station and the Corcovado Lodge Tent Camp, to more luxurious accommodations like the Lapa Ríos and the Evergreen Lodge. All of them offer close contact with nature, and most have first-rate guides who can help you understand the complexity of tropical ecology and point out things that you might otherwise walk right past. Most of these lodges also protect significant patches of wilderness, benefit local communities, and take steps to decrease their environmental impacts.

The Best Tour Companies

The best thing about having a reputable nature tour operator arrange your trip is that they can set you up with an educated, bilingual guide who will show and teach you about the country's wildlife and ecology. The Costa Rican company Horizontes is known for the quality of its guides (most are biologists) and its commitment to conservation and sus-

ECOTOURISM LODGING

LODGE	LOCATION	ATTRACTIONS
Central Valley		
Rancho Naturalista	Turrialba	*Bird watching*
Northern Plains		
Laguna del Lagarto Lodge	Ciudad Quesada	*Isolated wetlands and rain forests*
Selva Verde Lodge	Puerto Viejo de Sarapiquí	*Set in the rain forest, community projects*
La Selva Biological Station	Puerto Viejo de Sarapiquí	*Amazing wildlife, excellent guides*
North Pacific		
Rincón de la Vieja Mountain Lodge	Rincón de la Vieja National Park	*Forest hikes and horseback tours*
Hacienda Guachipelín	Rincón de la Vieja National Park	*Protected forest, horseback tours*
South Pacific		
Savegre Hotel de Montaña	San Gerardo de Dota	*Birding, hiking, protected forest*
Wilson Botanical Garden	San Vito	*Gardens, guides, protected forest*
Hacienda Barú	Dominical	*Rain-forest tours*
Playa Nicuesa Rainforest Lodge	Golfo Dulce	*Rain forest, hikes*
Tiskitia Jungle Lodge	Playa Pavones	*Rain forest, hikes, bird watching*
Bosque del Cabo	Cabo Matapalo	*Rain forest, wildlife, views, conservation*
Lapa Ríos	Cabo Matapalo	*Great wildlife, hikes, community projects*
Corcovado Lodge Tent Camp	Carate	*Deep in the forest, wildlife, hiking*
Delfin Amor Eco Lodge	Darke Bay	*Rain forest, dolphin and whale watching*
Casa Corcovado	Drake Bay	*Wildlife, hiking*
Caribbean		
Evergreen Lodge	Tortuguero	*Rain forest, wetlands*
Tortuga Lodge	Tortuguero	*Nature tours, turtles*
Almonds & Corals Tent Lodge Camp	Gandoca-Manzanillo	*Set in the rain forest, beach, wildlife*

tainability. Costa Rica Expeditions, the country's original natural-history tour operator, competes with Horizontes to recruit the best guides, but collaborates in contributing to local conservation efforts. Sun Tours, another of the country's original nature specialists, is a smaller company that offers good service and guides. Aventuras Naturales is white-water rafting outfitter with its own lodge and nature reserve on the Pacuare River; they also run bike tours and offer multiday packages. "Soft adventure" travelers are well catered to aboard the 185-foot M.V. *Pacific Explorer,* run by Cruise West, with multiday natural-history cruises that visit the rain forests of Costa Rica's South Pacific coast and Panama. Lindblad Expeditions runs nature cruises to the same area aboard the larger *Sea Voyager.*

The Costa Rican nonprofit organizations ACTUAR and COOPRENA can arrange day trips and overnights to dozens of community lodges and reserves scattered around the country. Those rustic, home-spun adventures take travelers far from the beaten path to expose them to rural Costa Rican life and culture. The Talamanca Ecotourism and Conservation Association (ATEC), in the center of Puerto Viejo de Talamanca, offers many locally run day trips and overnights, from a visit to a Bribri Indian village to dolphin-watching excursions.

ACTUAR ☎ 228-5695 ⊕ www.actuarcostarica.com. **ATEC** ☎ 750-0191 ⊕ www. greencoast.com/atec.htm. **Aventuras Naturales** ☎ 225-3939, 800/514-0411 in North America ⊕ www.toenjoynature.com. **COOPRENA** ☎ 248-2538 ⊕ www.turismoruralcr. com. **Costa Rica Expeditions** ☎ 222-0333 ⊕ www.costaricaexpeditions.com. **Cruise West** ☎ 800/203-8306 ⊕ www.cruisewest.com.

Horizontes ☎ 222-2022 ⊕ www.horizontes.com. **Lindblad Expeditions** ☎ 212/765-7740, 800/397-3348 in North America ⊕ www.lindblad.com. **Sun Tours** ☎ 296-7757 ⊕ www.crsuntours.com.

Volunteer & Learning Vacations

The Earthwatch Institute, of Massachusetts, runs expeditions to Costa Rica that allow travelers to participate in research and conservation of sea turtles, monkeys, and other creatures. Elderhostel runs excellent educational programs to Costa Rica, though younger travelers might feel a bit out of place on them. Globe Aware arranges volunteer vacations at a community conservation project near Carara National Park, in the Central Pacific. United Planet offers short-term volunteer programs all over Costa Rica, most of which involve supporting rural ecotourism and conservation efforts.

Earthwatch ☎ 800/776-0188 ⊕ www.earthwatch.org.

Elderhostel ☎ 800-776-0188 ⊕ www.elderhostel.org.

Globe Aware ☎ 877/588-4562 ⊕ www.globeaware.org.

United Planet ☎ 800/292-2316 ⊕ www.unitedplanet.org/2006/quest.html.

8

UNDERSTANDING COSTA RICA

COSTA RICA AT A GLANCE

A BRIEF HISTORY

WILDLIFE & PLANT GLOSSARY

MENU GUIDE

VOCABULARY

COSTA RICA AT A GLANCE

Fast Facts

Capital: San José
Type of government: Democratic republic
Independence: September 15, 1821 (from Spain)
Population: 4,248,508
Population density: 82 persons per square km (204 persons per square mi)
Literacy: 95%

Language: Spanish (official); English spoken by most in the tourism industry
Ethnic groups: White (including mestizo) 94%, black 3%, Amerindian 1%, Asian 1%, other 1%
Religion: Roman Catholic 76%, Evangelical Protestant 15%, other 6%, none 3%

Geography & Environment

Land area: 51,100 square km (19,730 square mi); slightly smaller than the U.S. state of West Virginia)
Coastline: 1,290 km (802 mi)
Terrain: Rugged central range with 112 volcanic craters that separates the eastern and western coastal plains
Natural resources: Hydroelectric power, forest products, fisheries products
Natural hazards: Droughts, flash floods, thunderstorms, earthquakes, hurricanes, landslides

Flora: 9,000 species, including 1,200 orchid species and 800 fern species; tidal mangrove swamps, tropical rain forest, subalpine forest
Fauna: 36,518 species, including 34,000 species of insects and 2,000 species of butterflies
Environmental issues: Deforestation, rapid industrialization and urbanization, air and water pollution, soil degradation, plastic waste

Economy

Currency: Colón, (*pl.*) colones
GDP: $37.97 billion
Per capita income: $4,670
Unemployment: 6.6%
Major industries: Tourism, microprocessors, food processing, textiles and clothing, construction materials, fertilizer, plastic products
Agricultural products: Bananas, coffee, pineapples, sugar cane, corn, rice, beans, potatoes, beef
Exports: $6.2 billion

Major export products: Bananas, coffee, pineapples, electronic components, sugar, textiles, electricity
Export partners: (in order of volume) U.S., Holland, Guatemala, Canada, Malaysia, Nicaragua, Germany
Imports: $7.84 billion
Major import products: Chemicals, consumer goods, electronic components, machinery, petroleum products, vehicles
Import partners: U.S.(46.1%), Japan (5.9%), Mexico (5.1%), Brazil (4.2%)

Did You Know?

- Tourism earns more foreign exchange than bananas and coffee combined.

- Costa Rica did away with its military in 1949.

- Five percent of the world's identified plant and animal species are found in this country.

- Costa Rica is the home of five active volcanoes—including Volcán Arenal, the second-largest active volcano in the world.

A BRIEF HISTORY

First Encounters

In mid-September 1502, on his fourth and last voyage to the New World, Christopher Columbus was sailing along the Caribbean coast of Central America when his ships were caught in a violent tropical storm. He found sanctuary in a bay protected by a small island; ashore, he encountered native people wearing heavy gold disks who spoke of great amounts of gold in the area. Sailing farther south, Columbus encountered more natives wearing gold. He was convinced that he had discovered a land of great wealth. Some say this is why Columbus named the land Costa Rica, the "Rich Coast." Others believe the name referred to the lush greenery of the land itself.

The Spanish Colonial Era

The first few attempts by the Spanish to conquer Costa Rica, beginning in 1506, were unsuccessful owing to sickness and starvation among the Spanish troops, hearty resistance by the indigenous population, and rivalries between various expeditions. By 1560, almost 60 years after its discovery, no permanent Spanish settlement existed in Costa Rica and early settlers were largely left to their own devices. But that all changed in 1563 when explorer Juan Vásquez de Coronado—a "good Coronado" as Ticos are fond of saying, to distinguish him from other pillaging conquistadors named Coronado—founded the colonial capital of Cartago.

Costa Rica remained the smallest and poorest of Spain's Central American colonies, producing little wealth for the empire. Unlike other mineral-rich colonies around it, Costa Rica was largely ignored in terms of conquest. Costa Rican settlers and native peoples endured the difficult living conditions of an agriculture-based existence in exchange for Spain's lack of interest. The population stayed at fewer than 20,000 for centuries and was mainly confined to small, isolated farms in the highland Central Valley and the Pacific lowlands. By the end of the 18th century, however, Costa Rica began to emerge from isolation. Some trade with neighboring Spanish colonies was carried out and the population began to expand across the Central Valley.

When Napoléon defeated and removed King Charles IV in 1808 and installed his brother Joseph on the Spanish throne, Costa Rica pledged support for the old regime, even sending troops to Nicaragua in 1811 to help suppress a rebellion against Spain. By 1821, though, sentiment favoring independence from Spain was prevalent throughout Central America, and a declaration of independence for all of Central America was issued by Guatemala on September 15 of that year. Costa Rica then became part of the Mexican empire until 1826, when it became part of the United Provinces of Central America. Costa Rica declared its independence as a sovereign nation in 1838.

The only major threat to that sovereignty took place in 1856, when the mercenary army of U.S. adventurer William Walker invaded the country from Nicaragua, which it had conquered the year before. Walker's plan to turn the Central American nations into slave states was cut short by Costa Rican president Juan Rafael Mora, who raised a volunteer army and repelled the invaders, pursuing them into Nicaragua and joining troops from various Central American nations to defeat the mercenaries. This conflict produced national hero Juan Santamaría, a young drummer boy from a poor family (⇨ CloseUp "A National Hero" *in* chapter 2).

Foundations of Democracy

For the major part of the 19th century the country was ruled by a succession of wealthy families. Coffee was introduced to the country in the 1820s and bananas in the 1870s, and these crops became the country's major sources of foreign exchange. The government spent profits from the coffee trade on improving roads and ports, and other civic projects that included San José's Teatro Nacional.

In 1889 the first free popular election was held, characterized by full freedom of the press, frank debates by rival candidates, an honest tabulation of the vote, and the first peaceful transition of power from a ruling group to the opposition. This provided the foundation of political stability that Costa Rica enjoys to this day.

Booming exports were cut short by the arrival of World War I, followed by the Great Depression and World War II. Poverty soared and a social revolution threatened in the late 1930s, as the popular Communist Party threatened strikes and violence. Costa Rica's version of the New Deal came in 1940, when conservative president Rafael Angel Calderón Guardia allied with the Catholic Church and implemented many of the Communist Party's demands, leading to a system of socialized medicine, minimum-wage laws, low-cost housing, and worker-protection laws.

The success of Calderón's social reforms was tainted by accusations of corruption, which resulted in a civil uprising in 1948, led by the still-revered José "Don Pepe" Figueres Ferrer, who had been exiled by Calderón as the political leader of the opposition. After a few months of armed conflict, a compromise was reached—Figueres would respect Calderón's social guarantees and preside over an interim government for 18 months. In 1949 Figueres abolished Costa Rica's military and created a national police force, nationalized the banking system and public utilities, and implemented health and education reforms. He stepped down after 18 months, only to be reelected twice in free elections.

The Modern Era

During the 1950s and 1960s, insurance, telecommunications, the railroad system (now defunct), ports, and other industries were nationalized. The state-led economic model, although increasingly inefficient, led to a rising standard of living until the early 1970s, when an economic crisis introduced Costa Ricans to hyperinflation. By mid-1980s Costa Rica had begun pulling out of its economic slump, in part thanks to efforts to diversify the economy. By the mid-1990s, tourism had surpassed bananas as the country's largest earner of foreign exchange, and high-tech companies such as Intel and Motorola opened plants and service centers in Costa Rica, providing good-paying jobs for educated professionals.

Recent years have seen the continued growth of the tourism industry, and the establishment of a thriving but controversial Internet-based gambling industry tied to U.S. sporting events. The economy continues to bedevil Costa Rica: inflation hovers around 10% annually and the country's currency continues to be devalued on a regular basis. Attempts to privatize state-owned industries have been unsuccessful, and the process of negotiating a Central American free-trade agreement with the United States (and its mandated opening of state enterprises to competition) continues to generate heated debate.

Today the challenge facing Costa Rica is how to conserve its natural resources while still permitting modern development. The government has been unable or unwilling to control illegal logging, an industry that threatens to destroy the country's old-growth forests. Urban sprawl in the Central Valley and the development of megaresorts along the Pacific coast threaten forests, wildlife, and the slow pace of life that makes Costa Rica so enjoyable for visitors. Although tourism provides a much-needed injection of foreign exchange into the economy, the government has not fully decided which direction it should take. The buzzwords now are "ecotourism" and "sustainable development," and it is hoped that Costa Rica will find it possible to continue down these roads.

WILDLIFE & PLANT GLOSSARY

Here is a rundown of some of the most common and attention-grabbing mammals, birds, reptiles, amphibians, plants, and even a few insects that you might encounter. We give the common Costa Rican names, so you can understand the local lingo, followed by the latest scientific terms.

Fauna

Agouti (*guatusa*; *Dasyprocta punctata*): A 20-inch, tail-less rodent with small ears and a large muzzle, the agouti is reddish brown on the Pacific side, more of a tawny orange on the Caribbean slope. It sits on its haunches to eat large seeds and fruit and resembles a large rabbit without the long ears.

Anteater (*oso hormiguero*): Three species of anteater inhabit Costa Rica—the very rare giant (*Myrmecophaga tridactyla*), the nocturnal silky (*Cyclopes didactylus*), and the Collared, or Vested (*Tamandua mexicana*). Only the last is commonly seen, and too often as roadkill. This medium-size anteater, 30 inches long with an 18-inch tail, laps up ants and termites with its long, sticky tongue and has long, sharp claws for ripping into insect nests.

Armadillo (*cusuco*; *Dasypus novemcinctus*): The nine-banded armadillo is widespread in Costa Rica and also found in the southern United States. This nocturnal and solitary edentate roots in soil with a long muzzle for a varied diet of insects, small animals, and plant material.

Baird's Tapir (*danta*; *Tapirus bairdii*): The largest land mammal in Costa Rica (to 6½ feet), Baird's Tapir is something like a small rhinoceros without armor. Adapted to a wide range of habitats, it's nocturnal, seldom seen, but said to defecate and sometimes sleep in water. Tapirs are herbivorous and use their prehensile snouts to harvest vegetation. The best opportunities for viewing wild tapirs are in Corcovado National Park.

Bat (*murciélogo*): With more than 100 species, Costa Rica's bats can be found eating fruit, insects, fish, small vertebrates, nectar, and even blood, in the case of the infamous vampire bat (*vampiro, Desmodus rotundus*), which far prefers cattle blood to that of any tourist. As a group, bats are extremely important ecologically, and are essential to seed dispersal, pollination, and controlling insect populations.

Butterfly (*mariposa*): Estimates of the number of butterfly species in Costa Rica vary, but all range in the thousands. The growing number of butterfly gardens popping up around the country is testament to their popularity among visitors. Three Costa Rican Morpho species—spectacular, large butterflies—have a brilliant-blue upper wing surface, giving them their local nickname of *pedazos de ciel* (pieces of sky). The blue morpho (*Morpho peleides*), arguably the most distinctive, is common in moister areas and has an intense ultraviolet upper surface. Adults feed on fermenting fruit; they never visit flowers.

Caiman (*caiman*): The spectacled caiman (*Caiman crocodilus*) is a small crocodilian (to 7 feet) inhabiting fresh water, subsisting mainly on fish. Most active at night (it has bright-red eye shine), it basks by day. It is distinguished from the American crocodile by a sloping brow and smooth back scales.

Coati (*pizote*; *Nasua narica*): This is a long-nose relative of the raccoon, its long tail often held straight up. Lone males or groups of females with young are active during the day, on the ground, or in trees. Omnivorous coatis feed on fruit, invertebrates, and small vertebrates. Unfortunately, many have learned to beg from tourists, especially in Monteverde and on the roads around Arenal.

Cougar (*puma*; *Felis concolor*): Mountain lions are the largest unspotted cats (to 8 feet, including the tail) in Costa Rica.

Widespread but rare, they live in essentially all-wild habitats and feed on vertebrates ranging from snakes to deer.

Crocodile (*lagarto*; *Crocodylus acutus*): The American crocodile, up to 16 feet in length, is found in most major river systems, particularly the Tempisque and Tárcoles estuaries. It seldom attacks humans, preferring fish and birds. It's distinguished from the caiman by size, a flat head, narrow snout, and spiky scales.

Ctenosaur (*garrobo*; *Ctenosaura similis*): Also known as the black, or spiny-tailed, iguana, this is a large (up to 18 inches long with 18-inch tail) tan lizard with four dark bands on its body and a tail ringed with sharp, curved spines, reminiscent of a dinosaur. Terrestrial and arboreal, it sleeps in burrows or tree hollows. It lives along the coast in the dry northwest and in wetter areas farther south. The fastest known reptile (clocked on land), the ctenosaur has been recorded moving at 21.7 mi per hour.

Dolphin (*delfín*): Several species, including bottlenose dolphins (*Tursiops truncatus*), frolic in Costa Rican waters. Often seen off Pacific shores are spotted dolphins (*Stenella attenuata*), which are small (up to 6 feet), with pale spots on the posterior half of the body; they commonly travel in groups of 20 or more and play around vessels and in bow wakes. Tucuxi dolphins (*Sotalia fluviatilis*) have also been spotted in small groups off the southern Caribbean coast, frequently with bottlenose dolphins.

Frog and Toad (*rana*, frog; *sapo*, toad): Some 120 species of frog exist in Costa Rica; many are nocturnal. The most colorful daytime amphibians are the tiny strawberry poison dart frog (*Dendrobates pumilio*) and green-and-black poison dart frog. The bright coloration of these two species, either red with blue or green hind legs or charcoal black with fluorescent green markings, warns potential predators of their toxicity. The red-eyed leaf frog (*Agalychnis callidryas*) is among the showiest of nocturnal species. The large, brown marine toad (*Bufo marinus*), also called cane toad or giant toad, comes out at night.

Howler Monkey (*mono congo*; *Alouatta palliata*): These dark, chunky-bodied monkeys (to 22 inches long with 24-inch tail) with black faces travel in troops of up to 20. Lethargic mammals, they eat leaves, fruits, and flowers. The males' deep, resounding howls sound like lions roaring, but actually serve as communication among and between troops.

Hummingbird (*Trochilidae*): Weighing just a fraction of an ounce, hummingbirds are nonetheless some of the most notable residents of tropical forests. At least 50 varieties can be found in Costa Rica, visiting typically red, tubular flowers in their seemingly endless search for energy-rich nectar. Because of their assortment of iridescent colors and bizarre bills and tail shapes, watching them can be a spectator sport. Best bets are hummingbird feeders and anywhere with great numbers of flowers.

Iguana (*iguana*): Mostly arboreal but good at swimming, the iguana is Costa Rica's largest lizard: males can grow to 10 feet, including tail. Only young green iguanas (*Iguana iguana*) are bright green; adults are much duller, females dark grayish, and males olive (with orangish heads in breeding season). All have round cheek scales and smooth tails.

Jaguar (*tigre*; *Panthera onca*): The largest New World feline (to 6 feet, with 2-foot tail), this top-of-the-line predator is exceedingly rare but lives in a wide variety of habitats, from dry forest to cloud forest. It's most common in the vast Amistad Biosphere Reserve, but it is almost never seen in the wild.

Jesus Christ Lizard (*gallego*): Flaps of skin on long toes enable this spectacular lizard to run across water. Costa Rica has three species of this lizard, which is more properly called the basilisk: lineated (*Basilis-*

cus basiliscus) on the Pacific side is brown with pale lateral stripes; in the Caribbean, emerald (*Basiliscus plumifrons*) is marked with turquoise and black on a green body; and striped (*Basiliscus vittatus*), also on the Caribbean side, resembling the lineated basilisk. Adult males grow to 3 feet (mostly tail), with crests on the head, back, and base of the tail.

Leaf-Cutter Ant (*zompopas*; *Atta* spp.): Found in all lowland habitats, these are the most commonly noticed neotropical ants, and one of the country's most fascinating animal phenomena. Columns of ants carrying bits of leaves twice their size sometimes extend for several hundred yards from an underground nest to plants being harvested. The ants don't eat the leaves; their food is a fungus they cultivate on the leaves.

Macaw (*lapas*): Costa Rica's two species are the scarlet macaw (*Ara macao*), on the Pacific side (Osa Peninsula and Carara Biological Reserve), and the severely threatened great green macaw (*Ara ambigua*), on the Caribbean side. These are huge, raucous parrots with long tails; their immense bills are used to rip fruit apart to reach the seeds. They nest in hollow trees and are victimized by pet-trade poachers and deforestation.

Magnificent Frigatebird (*tijereta del mar*; *Fregata magnificens*): A large, black soaring bird with slender wings and forked tail, this is one of the most effortless and agile flyers in the avian world. More common on the Pacific coast, it doesn't dive or swim but swoops to pluck its food, often from the mouths of other birds.

Manatee (*manatí*; *Trichechus manatus*): Although endangered throughout its range, the West Indian manatee can be spotted in Tortuguero, meandering along in shallow water, browsing on submerged vegetation. The moniker "sea cow" is apt, as they spend nearly all their time resting or feeding. Their large, somewhat amorphous bodies won't win any beauty contests, but they do appear quite graceful.

Margay (*caucel*; *Felis wiedii*): Fairly small, this spotted nocturnal cat (22 inches long, with an 18-inch tail) is similar to the ocelot but has a longer tail and is far more arboreal: mobile ankle joints allow it to climb down trunks head first. It eats small vertebrates.

Motmot (*pájaro bobo*): These handsome, turquoise-and-rufous birds of the understory have racket-shape tails. Nesting in burrows, they sit patiently while scanning for large insect prey or small vertebrates. Costa Rica has six species.

Northern Jacana (*gallito de agua*; *Jacana spinosa*): These birds are sometimes called "lily trotters" because their long toes allow them to walk on floating vegetation. Feeding on aquatic organisms and plants, they're found in almost any body of water. They expose yellow wing feathers in flight. Sex roles are reversed; "liberated" females are larger and compete for mates (often more than one), whereas the males tend to the nest and care for the young.

Ocelot (*manigordo*; *Felis pardalis*): Mostly terrestrial, this medium-size spotted cat (33 inches long, with a 16-inch tail) is active night and day, and feeds on rodents and other vertebrates. Forepaws are rather large in relation to the body, hence the local name, *manigordo*, which means "fat hand."

Opossum (*zorro pelón*; *Didelphis marsupialis*): Like the kangaroo, the common opossum belongs to that rare breed of mammals known as marsupials, distinguished by their brief gestation period and completion of development and nourishment following birth in the mother's pouch. The Costa Rican incarnation does not "play possum," and will bite if cornered rather than pretend to be dead.

Oropendola (*oropéndola*; *Psarocolius* spp.): These crow-size birds in the oriole family have a bright-yellow tail and nest in colonies, in pendulous nests (up to 6 feet long) built by females in isolated trees. The Montezuma species has an orange beak and blue cheeks, the chestnut-headed has a yellow beak. Males make an unmistakable, loud, gurgling liquid call. The bird is far more numerous on the Caribbean side.

Parakeet and Parrot (*pericos,* parakeets; *loros,* parrots): There are 15 species in Costa Rica (plus two macaws), all clad in green, most with a splash of a primary color or two on the head or wings. They travel in boisterous flocks, prey on immature seeds, and nest in cavities.

Peccary: Piglike animals with thin legs and thick necks, peccaries travel in small groups (larger where the population is still numerous); root in soil for fruit, seeds, and small creatures; and have a strong musk odor. You'll usually smell them before you see them. Costa Rica has two species: the collared peccary (*saíno, Tayassu tajacu*) and the white-lipped peccary (*chancho de monte, Tayassu pecari*). The latter is now nearly extinct.

Pelican (*pelícano*): Large size, a big bill, and a throat pouch make the brown pelican (*Pelecanus occidentalis*) unmistakable in coastal areas (it's far more abundant on the Pacific side). Pelicans often fly in V formations and dive for fish.

Quetzal: One of the world's most exquisite birds, the resplendent quetzal (*Pharomachrus mocinno*) was revered by the Maya. Glittering green plumage and the male's long tail coverts draw thousands of people to highland cloud forests for sightings from February to April.

Roseate Spoonbill (*garza rosada; Ajaja ajaja*): Pink plumage and a spatulate bill set this wader apart from all other wetland birds; it feeds by swishing its bill back and forth in water while using its feet to stir up bottom-dwelling creatures. Spoonbills are most common around Palo Verde and Caño Negro.

Sloth (*perezoso*): Costa Rica is home to the brown-throated, three-toed sloth (*Bradypus variegatus*) and Hoffmann's two-toed sloth (*Choloepus hoffmanni*). Both grow to 2 feet, but two-toed (check forelegs) sloths often look bigger because of longer fur and are the only species in the highlands. Sloths are herbivorous, accustomed to a low-energy diet, and well camouflaged.

Snake (*culebra*): Costa Rica's serpents can be found in trees, above and below ground, and even in the sea on the Pacific coast. Most of the more than 125 species are harmless, but are best appreciated from a distance. Notable members of this group include Costa Rica's largest snake, the boa constrictor (*Boa constrictor*), reaching up to 15 feet, and the fer-de-lance (*terciopelo, Bothrops asper*), which is a much smaller (up to 6 feet) but far more dangerous viper.

Spider Monkey (*mono colorado, mono araña*): Lanky and long-tailed, the black-handed spider monkey (*Ateles geoffroyi*) is the largest monkey in Costa Rica (to 24 inches, with 32-inch tail). Moving in groups of two to four, they eat ripe fruit, leaves, and flowers. Incredible aerialists, they can swing effortlessly through branches using long arms and legs and prehensile tails. They are quite aggressive and will challenge on-lookers and often throw down branches. Caribbean and southern Pacific populations are dark reddish brown; northwesterners are blond.

Squirrel Monkey (*mono titi*): The smallest of four Costa Rican monkeys (11 inches, with 15-inch tail), the red-backed squirrel monkey (*Saimiri oerstedii*) has a distinctive facial pattern (black cap and muzzle, white mask) and gold-orange coloration on its back. It is the only Costa Rican monkey without a prehensile tail. The species travels in noisy, active groups of 20 or more, feeding on fruit and insects. Numbers of this endangered species have been estimated between 2,000 and 4,000 individuals. Most squirrel monkeys in Costa Rica are found in Manuel Antonio National Park, in parts of the Osa Peninsula, and around the Golfo Dulce.

Three-Wattled Bellbird (*pájaro campana;*

Procnias tricarunculata): Although endangered, the bellbird can be readily identified in cloud forests (around Monteverde, for example), where it breeds by its extraordinary call, a bold and aggressive "bonk," unlike any other creature in the forest. If you spot a male calling, look for the three pendulous wattles at the base of its beak.

Toucan (*tucán, tucancillo*): The keel-billed toucan (*Ramphastos sulfuratus*) with the rainbow-colored beak is familiar to anyone who's seen a box of Froot Loops cereal. Chestnut-mandibled toucans (*Ramphastos swainsonii*) are the largest (18 inches and 22 inches); as the name implies, their lower beaks are brown. The smaller, stouter emerald toucanet (*Aulacorhynchus prasinus*) and yellow-eared toucanet (*Selenidera spectabilis*) are aptly named. Aracaris (*Pteroglossus Spp.*) are similar to toucans, but colored orange-and-yellow with the trademark toucan bill.

Turtles (*tortuga*): Observing the nesting rituals of the five species of marine turtles here is one of those truly memorable Costa Rican experiences. Each species has its own nesting season and locale. The olive ridley (*lora; Lepidochelys olivacea*) is the smallest of the sea turtles (average carapace, or hardback shell, is 21–29 inches) and the least shy. Thousands engage in nighttime group nesting rituals on the North Pacific's Ostional. At the other extreme, but only slightly farther north on Playa Grande, nests the leatherback (*baula; Dermochelys coriacea*) with its five-foot-long shell. On the north Caribbean coast, Tortuguero hosts four of them: the leatherback, the hawksbill (*carey; Eretmochelys imbricata*), the loggerhead (*caguama; Caretta caretta*), and the green (*tortuga verde; Chelonia mydas*), with its long nesting season (June–October) that draws the most visitors and researchers.

Whales (*ballena*): Humpback whales (*Megaptera novaeanglia*) appear off the Pacific coast between November and February; they migrate from California and as far as Hawaii. You can also spot Sey whales, Bryde's whales, and farther out to sea, Blue whales and Sperm whales. On the Caribbean side, there are smaller (12 to 14 feet) Koiga whales.

White-Faced Capuchin Monkey (*mono cara blanca; Cebus capuchinus*): Medium-size and omnivorous, this monkey (to 18 inches, with 20-inch tail) has black fur and a pink face surrounded by a whitish bib. Extremely active foragers, they move singly or in groups of up to 20, examining the environment closely and even coming to the ground. It's the most commonly seen monkey in Costa Rica. It's also the most often fed by visitors, to the point where some monkey populations now have elevated cholesterol levels.

White-Tailed Deer (*venado; Odocoileus virginianus*): Bambi would feel at home in Costa Rica, although his counterparts here are slightly smaller. As befits the name, these animals possess the distinctive white underside to their tail (and to their bellies). They are seen in drier parts of the country, especially in the northwest province of Guanacaste.

White-Throated Magpie-jay (*urraca; Calocitta formosa*): This southern relative of the blue jay, with a long tail and distinctive topknot (crest of forward-curved feathers), is found in the dry northwest. Bold and inquisitive, with amazingly varied vocalizations, these birds travel in noisy groups of four or more.

Flora

Ant-acacia (*acacia; Acacia* spp.): If you'll be in the tropical dry forest of Guanacaste, learn to avoid this plant. As if its sharp thorns weren't enough, acacias exhibit an intense symbiosis with various ant species (*Pseudomyrmex* spp.) that will attack anything—herbivores, other plants, and unaware human visitors that come in contact with the tree. The ants and the acacias have an intriguing relationship, though, so do look, but don't touch.

Bromeliad (*piña silvestre*): Members of the

family Bromeliaceae are *epiphytes,* living on the trunk and branches of trees. They are not parasitic, however, and so have adapted to acquire all the necessary water and nutrients from what falls into the central "tank" formed by the leaf structure. Amphibians and insects also use the water held in bromeliads to reproduce, forming small aquatic communities perched atop tree branches. In especially wet areas, small bromeliads can even be found on power lines. Their spectacular, colorful efflorescences popular—and expensive— houseplants in northern climes.

Heliconia (*helicónia; Heliconia* spp.): It's hard to miss these stunning plants, many of which have huge inflorescences of red, orange, and yellow, sometimes shaped like lobster claws, and leaves very much the size and shape of a banana plant. With luck, you'll catch a visiting hummingbird with a beak specially designed to delve into a heliconia flower—truly a visual treat.

Mangroves (*manglares*): Taken together, this handful of salt-tolerant trees with tangled, above-ground roots make up their own distinct ecosystem. Buttressing the land against the sea, they serve as nurseries for countless species of fish, crabs and other marine animals and provide roosting habitat for marine birds. Mangroves are found on the coast in protected areas such as bays and estuaries.

Naked Indian Tree (*indio desnudo; Bursera simaruba*): This tree can be found in forests throughout Costa Rica, often forming living fences, and is instantly identifiable by its orange bark that continually sloughs off, giving rise to another common name, the sunburnt tourist tree. One theory suggests that the shedding of its bark aids in removing parasites from the tree's exterior.

Orchid (*orquídea*): The huge Orchidaceae family has more than 1,200 representatives in Costa Rica alone, with nearly 90% percent living as epiphytes on other plants. The great diversity of the group includes not only examples of great beauty but exquisite adaptations between flowers and their insect pollinators. With a combination of rewards (nectar) and trickery (visual and chemical cues), orchids exhibit myriad ways of enticing insects to cooperate.

Strangler Fig (*Matapalo; Ficus spp.*): Starting as seedlings high in the canopy, these aggressive plants grow both up toward the light, and down to the soil, slowly taking over the host tree. Eventually they encircle and appear to "strangle" the host, actually killing it by hogging all the available sunlight, leaving a ring of fig trunk around an empty interior. Figs with ripe fruit are excellent places for wildlife spotting, as they attract monkeys, birds, and an assortment of other creatures.

MENU GUIDE

Rice and beans are the heart of Costa Rica's *comida típica* (typical food). It's possible to order everything from sushi to crepes in and around San José, but most Ticos have a simple diet built around rice, beans, and the myriad fruits and vegetables that flourish here. Costa Rican food isn't spicy, and many dishes are seasoned with the same five ingredients—onion, salt, garlic, cilantro, and red bell pepper.

Spanish	English

General Dining

Spanish	English
Almuerzo	Lunch
Bocas	Appetizers or snacks (literally "mouthfuls") served with drinks in the tradition of Spanish tapas.
Casado	Heaping plate of rice, beans, fried plantains, cabbage salad, tomatoes, *macarrones* (noodles), and fish, chicken, or meat—or any variation thereof; *casado* and *plato del día* are often used interchangeably
Cena	Dinner
Desayuno	Breakfast
Plato del día	Plate of the day
Soda	An inexpensive café; casados are always found at sodas

Especialidades (Specialties)

Spanish	English
Arreglados	Sandwiches or meat and vegetable puff pastry
Arroz con mariscos	Fried rice with fish, shrimp, octopus, and clams, or whatever's fresh that day
Arroz con pollo	Chicken with rice
Camarones	Shrimp
Ceviche	Chilled, raw seafood marinated in lime juice, served with chopped onion and garlic
Chilaquiles	Meat-stuffed tortillas
Chorreados	Corn pancakes, served with *natilla* (sour cream)
Corvina	Sea bass
Empanadas	Savory or sweet pastry turnover filled with fruit or meat and vegetables
Empanaditas	Small empanadas
Gallo pinto	Rice sautéed with black beans (literally, "spotted rooster"), often served for breakfast
Langosta	Lobster
Langostino	Prawns
Olla de carne	Soup of beef, chayote squash, corn, yuca

	(a tuber), and potatoes
Palmitos	Hearts of palm, served in salads or as a side dish
Pejibaye	A nutty, orange-colored palm fruit eaten in salads, soups, and as a snack
Pescado ahumado	Smoked marlin
Picadillo	Chayote squash, potatoes, carrots, or other vegetables chopped into small cubes and combined with onions, garlic, and ground beef
Pozol	Corn soup
Salsa caribeño	A combination of tomatoes, onions, and spices that accompanies most fish dishes on the Caribbean coast

Postres (Desserts) & Dulces (Sweets)

Cajeta de coco peel	Fudge made with coconut and orange
Cajeta	Molasses-flavored fudge
Dulce de leche	Thick syrup of boiled milk and sugar
Flan	Caramel-topped egg custard
Mazamorra	Cornstarch pudding
Pan de maiz	Sweet corn bread
Torta chilena	Flaky, multilayered cake with dulce de leche filling
Tres leches cake	"Three milks" cake, made with condensed and evaporated milk and cream

Frutas (Fruits)

Aguacate	Avocado
Anon	Sugar apple; sweet white flesh; resembles an artichoke with a thick rind
Banano	Banana
Bilimbi	Looks like a miniature cucumber crossed with a star fruit; ground into a savory relish
Fresa	Strawberry
Cas	A smaller guava
Granadilla	Passion fruit
Guanábana	Soursop; large, spiky yellow fruit with white flesh and a musky taste
Guayaba	Guava
Mamon chino	Rambutan; red spiky ball protecting a white fruit similar to a lychee
Mango	Many varieties, from sour green to succulently sweet Oro (golden); March is the height of mango season
Manzana de agua	Water apple, shaped like a pear; juicy but not very sweet
Marañon	Cashew fruit; used in juices

Melon	Canteloupe
Mora	Blackberry
Palmito	Heart of palm
Piña	Pineapple
Papaya	One of the most popular and ubiquitous fruits
Pipa	Green coconut; sold at roadside stands with ends chopped off and straws stuck inside
Sandia	Watermelon
Carambola	Star fruit

Bebidas (Beverages)

Agua dulce	Hot water sweetened with raw sugarcane
Batido	Fruit shake made with milk (con leche) or water (con agua)
Café con leche	Coffee with hot milk
Café negro	Black coffee
Fresco natural	Fresh-squeezed juice
Guaro	Harsh, clear spirit distilled from fermented sugarcane
Horchata	Cinnamon-flavored rice drink
Refrescos	Tropical fruit smoothie with ice and sugar

VOCABULARY

	English	Spanish	Pronunciation
Basics			
	Yes/no	Sí/no	see/no
	OK	De acuerdo	de a-**kwer**-doe
	Please	Por favor	pore fah-**vore**
	May I?	¿Me permite?	may pair-**mee**-tay
	Thank you (very much)	(Muchas) gracias	(**moo**-chas) **grah**-see-as
	You're welcome	Con mucho gusto	con **moo**-cho **goose**-toe
	Excuse me	Con permiso	con pair-**mee**-so
	Pardon me	¿Perdón?	pair-**dohn**
	Could you tell me?	¿Podría decirme?	po-dree-ah deh-**seer**-meh
	I'm sorry	Disculpe	Dee-**skool**-peh
	Good morning!	¡Buenos días!	**bway**-nohs **dee**-ahs
	Good afternoon!	¡Buenas tardes!	**bway**-nahs **tar**-dess
	Good evening!	¡Buenas noches!	**bway**-nahs **no**-chess
	Goodbye!	¡Adiós!/¡Hasta luego!	ah-dee-**ohss**/**ah**-stah-**lwe**-go
	Mr./Mrs.	Señor/Señora	sen-**yor**/sen-**yohr**-ah
	Miss	Señorita	sen-yo-**ree**-tah
	Pleased to meet you	Mucho gusto	**moo**-cho **goose**-toe
	How are you?	¿Cómo está usted?	**ko**-mo es-**tah** oo-**sted**
	Very well, thank you.	Muy bien, gracias.	**moo**-ee bee-**en**, **grah**-see-as
	And you?	¿Y usted?	ee oos-**ted**
Days of the Week			
	Sunday	domingo	doe-**meen**-goh
	Monday	lunes	**loo**-ness
	Tuesday	martes	**mahr**-tess
	Wednesday	miércoles	me-**air**-koh-less
	Thursday	jueves	hoo-**ev**-ess
	Friday	viernes	vee-**air**-ness
	Saturday	sábado	**sah**-bah-doh

Months

January	enero	eh-**neh**-roh
February	febrero	feh-**breh**-roh
March	marzo	**mahr**-soh
April	abril	ah-**breel**
May	mayo	**my**-oh
June	junio	**hoo**-nee-oh
July	julio	**hoo**-lee-yoh
August	agosto	ah-**ghost**-toh
September	septiembre	sep-tee-**em**-breh
October	octubre	oak-**too**-breh
November	noviembre	no-vee-**em**-breh
December	diciembre	dee-see-**em**-breh

Useful Phrases

Do you speak English?	¿Habla usted inglés?	**ah**-blah oos-**ted** in-**glehs**
I don't speak Spanish	No hablo español	no **ah**-bloh es-pahn-**yol**
I don't understand (you)	No entiendo	no en-tee-**en**-doh
I understand (you)	Entiendo	en-tee-**en**-doh
I don't know	No sé	no seh
I am American/ British	Soy americano (americana)/ inglés(a)	soy ah-meh-ree-**kah**-no (ah-meh-ree-**kah**-nah)/ in-**glehs (ah)**
What's your name?	¿Cómo se llama usted?	koh-mo seh **yah**-mah oos-**ted**
My name is . . .	Me llamo . . .	may **yah**-moh
What time is it?	¿Qué hora es?	keh **o**-rah es
It is one, two, three . . . o'clock.	Es la una. . . . Son las dos, tres	es la **oo**-nah/sohn lahs dohs, tress
How?	¿Cómo?	**koh**-mo
When?	¿Cuándo?	**kwahn**-doh
This/Next week	Esta semana/ la semana que entra	**es**-teh seh-**mah**-nah/lah seh-**mah**-nah keh **en**-trah
This/Next month	Este mes/el próximo mes	**es**-teh mehs/el **proke**-see-mo mehs
This/Next year	Este año/el año que viene	**es**-teh **ahn**-yo/el **ahn**-yo keh vee-**yen**-ay

Yesterday/today/ tomorrow	Ayer/hoy/mañana	ah-**yehr**/oy/mahn-**yah**-nah
This morning/ afternoon	Esta mañana/ tarde	es-tah mahn-**yah**-nah/**tar**-deh
Tonight	Esta noche	es-tah **no**-cheh
What?	¿Qué?	keh
What is it?	¿Qué es esto?	keh es **es**-toh
Why?	¿Por qué?	pore **keh**
Who?	¿Quién?	kee-**yen**
Where is . . . ?	¿Dónde está . . . ?	**dohn**-deh es-**tah**
the bus stop?	la parada del autobus?	la pah-**rah**-dah del oh-toh-**boos**
the post office?	la oficina de correos?	la oh-fee-**see**-nah deh koh-**reh**-os
the museum?	el museo?	el moo-**seh**-oh
the hospital?	el hospital?	el ohss-pee-**tal**
the bathroom?	el baño?	el **bahn**-yoh
Here/there	Aquí/allá	ah-**key**/ah-**yah**
Open/closed	Abierto/cerrado	ah-bee-**er**-toh/ ser-**ah**-doh
Left/right	Izquierda/derecha	iss-key-**er**-dah/ dare-**eh**-chah
Straight ahead	Derecho	dare-**eh**-choh
Is it near/far?	¿Está cerca/lejos?	es-**tah** **sehr**-kah/ **leh**-hoss
I'd like . . .	Quisiera . . .	kee-see-ehr-ah
a room	un cuarto/una habitación	oon **kwahr**-toh/ **oo**-nah ah-bee-tah-see-**on**
the key	la llave	lah **yah**-veh
a newspaper	un periódico	oon pehr-ee-**oh**-dee-koh
a stamp	la estampilla	lah es-stahm-**pee**-yah
I'd like to buy . . .	Quisiera comprar . . .	kee-see-**ehr**-ah kohm-**prahr**
a dictionary	un diccionario	oon deek-see-oh-**nah**-ree-oh
soap	jabón	hah-**bohn**
suntan lotion	loción bronceadora	loh-see-**ohn** brohn-seh-ah-**do**-rah
a map	un mapa	oon **mah**-pah
a magazine	una revista	**oon**-ah reh-**veess**-tah
a postcard	una tarjeta postal	**oon**-ah tar-**het**-ah post-**ahl**

How much is it?	¿Cuánto cuesta?	**kwahn**-toh **kwes**-tah
Telephone	Teléfono	tel-**ef**-oh-no
Help!	¡Auxilio! ¡Ayuda! ¡Socorro!	owk-**see**-lee-oh/ ah-**yoo**-dah/ soh-**kohr**-roh
Fire!	¡Incendio!	en-**sen**-dee-oo
Caution!/Look out!	¡Cuidado!	kwee-**dah**-doh

Salud (Health)

I am ill	Estoy enfermo(a)	es-**toy** en-**fehr**-moh(mah)
Please call a doctor	Por favor llame a un médico	pohr fah-**vor ya**-meh ah oon **med**-ee-koh
acetaminophen	acetaminofen	a-say-ta-**mee**-no-fen
ambulance	ambulancia	ahm-boo-**lahn**-see-a
antibiotic	antibiótico	ahn-tee-bee-**oh**-tee-co
aspirin	aspirina	ah-spi-**ree**-na
capsule	cápsula	**cahp**-soo-la
clinic	clínica	**clee**-nee-ca
cold	resfriado	rays-free-**ah**-do
cough	tos	toess
diarrhea	diarrea	dee-ah-**ray**-a
fever	fiebre	fee-**ay**-bray
flu	Gripe	**gree**-pay
headache	dolor de cabeza	doh-**lor** day cah-**bay**-sa
hospital	hospital	oh-spee-**tahl**
medication	medicamento	meh-dee-cah-**men**-to
pain	dolor	doh-**lor**
pharmacy	farmacia	fahr-**mah**-see-a
physician	médico	**meh**-dee-co
prescription	receta	ray-**say**-ta
stomach ache	dolor de estómago	doh-**lor** day eh-**sto**-mah-go

SMART TRAVEL TIPS

Consult the Essentials sections that end each chapter for information as it relates to specific regions.

AIR TRAVEL

ARRIVING & DEPARTING

If you are visiting several regions of the country, flying into San José's Juan Santamaria Airport, in the center of the country, is the best option. Flying into Liberia's Daniel Oduber Airport makes sense if you are planning to spend your vacation in Guanacaste. Bus travel time between the Liberia airport and most of the resorts is less than two hours.

Most travelers fly into the larger San José airport, the transportation hub to nearly every point in the country. Rarely does an international flight get into San José early enough to make a domestic connection, as the weather for flying is typically clear until about noon only. So you'll likely end up spending your first night in or near the city, and leave for your domestic destination the next morning out of the SANSA terminal next to the international airport or via NatureAir out of tiny Tobias Bolaños Airport.

Heavy rains in the afternoons and evenings during the May-to-November rainy season sometimes cause flights coming into San José to be rerouted to Panama City, where you may be forced to spend the night. ■ TIP➜ In the rainy season, always book a flight with the earliest arrival time available.

Once in Costa Rica, some airlines recommend calling the San José office about three days before your return flight to reconfirm; others, such as TACA, explicitly say it's not necessary. It's always a good idea to call the local office the day before you are scheduled to return home to make sure your flight time hasn't changed.

From the United States: Miami has the highest number of direct flights, but nonstop flights are also available from New York, Houston, Dallas, Atlanta, Chicago, Phoenix, Washington, D.C., Charlotte, and Los Angeles. Continental, American, America West, Delta, US Airways, and

Addresses
Air Travel
Airports
Bus Travel
Cameras & Film
Car Travel
Children in Costa Rica
Consumer Protection
Customs & Duties
Disabilities & Accessibility
Discounts & Deals
Eating & Drinking
Electricity
Emergencies
Etiquette & Behavior
Gay & Lesbian Travel
Health
Holidays
Insurance for Your Trip
Internet
Language
Lodging
Mail & Shipping
Money Matters
Packing
Passports & Visas
Restrooms
Safety
Senior-Citizen Travel
Shopping
Students in Costa Rica
Taxis
Telephones
Time
Tours & Packages
Travel Agencies
Visitor Information
Volunteer & Educational Travel
Web Sites We Like
Women Travelers

United are the major U.S. carriers with nonstop service to Costa Rica. Martinair has nonstop flights from Orlando and Miami. From New York, flights to San José are 5½ hours nonstop or 6 to 7 hours via Miami. From Los Angeles, flights are about 6 to 7 hours nonstop or 8½ hours via Mexico; from Houston, 3½ hours nonstop; from Miami, 3 hours; from Charlotte, 4 hours; and from Chicago, 5½ hours. In general, nonstop flights aren't that much more expensive.

Other than obvious considerations such as price and scheduling, a regional airline like Mexicana and TACA (a Central American airline) is a good choice if you're visiting more than one Central American country; major U.S. airlines don't serve routes such as Costa Rica–Honduras.

From elsewhere in Central America: International flights to Costa Rica tend to be cheaper than those to Nicaragua or Panama, so if you're doing two or three countries, it makes sense, budget-wise, to start in Costa Rica. Copa, TACA, and Lacsa fly between Panama City and San José and between Managua, Nicaragua, and San José. NatureAir flies between Granada, Nicaragua, and Liberia or San José, and between Bocas del Toro, Panama, and San José.

🛪 Major Airlines **Air Canada** ☎ 888/247-2262 in Canada, 506/243-1860 in Costa Rica ⊕ www.aircanada.com. **America West** ☎ 800/327-7810 in U.S., 0800-011-0888 in Costa Rica, ⊕ www.americawest.com. **American Airlines** ☎ 800/433-7300 in U.S., 506/257-1266 in Costa Rica ⊕ www.aa.com. **Continental** ☎ 800/231-0856 in U.S. and Canada, 0800/044-0005 in Costa Rica ⊕ www.continental.com. **Delta** ☎ 800/241-4141 in U.S. and Canada, 506/257-4141 in Costa Rica. **United Airlines** ☎ 800/241-6522 in U.S.,. **US Airways** ☎ 800/622-1015 in U.S. and Canada, 430-6690 in Costa Rica ⊕ www.usairways.com.

CHECK-IN & BOARDING

Always **find out your carrier's check-in policy.** Plan to arrive at the airport about two hours before your scheduled departure time for domestic flights and 2½ to 3 hours before international flights. You may need to arrive earlier if you're flying from one of the busier airports or during peak air-traffic times. To avoid delays at airport-security checkpoints, try not to wear any metal. Jewelry, belt and other buckles, steel-toe shoes, barrettes, and underwire bras are among the items that can set off detectors.

Always **bring a government-issued photo ID** to the airport; even when it's not required, a passport is best.

GETTING AROUND

Given Costa Rica's often difficult driving conditions, distances that appear short on a map can represent hours of driving on dirt roads pocked with craters; buses can be a slow and uncomfortable way to travel. Domestic flights are a desirable and practical option. And because 4WD rental rates can be steep, flying is often cheaper than driving. Most major destinations are served by daily domestic flights.

The informality of domestic air service—"airports" outside of Liberia and San José usually consist of simply an airstrip with no central building at which to buy tickets—means you might want to purchase your domestic airplane tickets in advance (by phone or online), although you can buy them at the San José or Liberia airports or at travel agencies once you're in the country. In theory, you can purchase tickets up to two hours before the flight is set to go. This is a potentially viable option in the May–October low season, but we recommend grabbing a seat as soon as you know your itinerary.

There are two major domestic commercial airlines: SANSA and NatureAir. Most NatureAir and SANSA flights leave from the San José area (⇨ Airports); NatureAir's Quepos-Palmar Sur route is the only interdestinational commercial flight that skips San José. Commercial planes are small—holding between 6 and 19 passengers; some San José–Liberia flights hold up to 45 passengers. Charter company Macaw Air flies its five-passenger Cessna 206 out of Liberia, allowing you to bypass San José altogether; it also offers one daily commercial flight between Tamarindo and Liberia. Domestic flights are nonstop, with the exception of some flights to the far south, where you might stop in Drake Bay

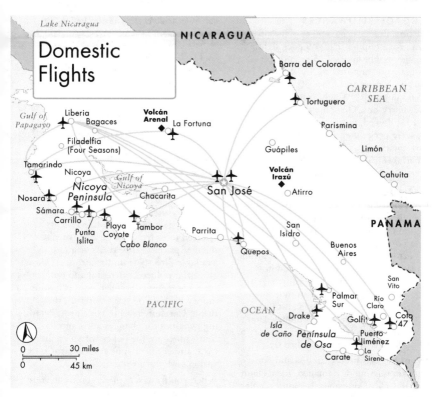

Domestic Flights

first, then continue on to Puerto Jiménez, for example. You can buy SANSA and NatureAir tickets online, over the phone, and at most travel agencies in Costa Rica. Buy Macaw Air tickets online or by phone.

■ TIP→ **SANSA air passes—$199 for one week and $249 for two weeks—can be a good deal. NatureAir's Adventure Pass, available April 21 to November 30, offers unlimited domestic flights for one ($249) or two ($299) weeks.**

Charter flights within Costa Rica are not as expensive as one might think, and can be an especially good deal if you are traveling with a group of four to eight people. If a group this size charters a small plane, the price per person will be only slightly more than taking a regularly scheduled domestic flight, and you can set your own departure time. The country has dozens of airstrips that are accessible only by charter planes. Unlike NatureAir or SANSA, the

charter companies listed here do not have English-speaking staff, though some allow online booking. Charter planes are most often booked through tour operators, travel agents, or remote lodges. Most charter planes are smaller than domestic commercial planes—with Macaw, you might even end up on a tiny four-passenger supply plane with no copilot.

⚠ **Don't book a domestic flight on the day you arrive in or leave Costa Rica**; connections will be extremely tight, if possible at all, and you'll be at the mercy of temperamental weather and delays.

🔲 Domestic & Charter Airlines **Aerobell Air Charter** ☎ 506/290-0000 ⊕ www.aerobell.com. **Macaw Air** ☎ 506/653-1362 ⊕ www.macawair. com. **NatureAir** ☎ 800/235-9272 in the U.S. or Canada, 506/299-6000 in Costa Rica ⊕ www. natureair.com. **SANSA** ☎ 506/221-9414 or 506/442-9385 ⊕ www.flysansa.com.

BAGGAGE ALLOWANCES

The tiny, domestic passenger planes in Costa Rica require that you pack light. A luggage weight limit of 25 pounds (11.3 kilograms) is imposed by SANSA and Macaw; NatureAir allows 30 pounds (13.6 kilograms). Weight restrictions include carry-ons. On some flights extra luggage is allowed, but is charged about 50¢–55¢ per pound. Heavy packers can leave their surplus for free in a locked area at NatureAir's terminal. SANSA no longer offers extra baggage storage.

LOST LUGGAGE

If you arrive in Costa Rica and your baggage doesn't, the first thing you should do is go to the baggage claims counter and file an official report with your specific contact information. Then call your airline to find out if they can track it and how long you have to wait—generally bags are located within two days. Continue on your trip as you can; bags can be sent to you just about anywhere in the country. Don't expect too much from local officials; try to get updates from the airline directly.

If your bag has been searched and contents are missing or damaged, file a claim with the TSA Consumer Response Center as soon as possible. If your bags arrive damaged or fail to arrive at all, file a written report with the airline before leaving the airport.

HOW TO COMPLAIN

If your baggage goes astray or your flight goes awry, complain right away. Most carriers require that you **file a claim immediately.** The Aviation Consumer Protection Division of the Department of Transportation publishes *Fly-Rights,* which discusses airlines and consumer issues and is available online. You can also find articles and information on mytravelrights.com, the Web site of the nonprofit Consumer Travel Rights Center.

Complaints

U.S. Transportation Security Administration Contact Center (☎ 866/289–9673 ⊕ www.tsa.gov).

🚺 Airline Complaints **Aviation Consumer Protection Division** ☎ 202/366–2220 ⊕ airconsumer.ost.

dot.gov. **Federal Aviation Administration Consumer Hotline** ☎ 866/835–5322 ⊕ www.faa.gov.

CUTTING COSTS

It's smart to call a number of airlines and check the Internet; when you are quoted a good price, book it on the spot—the same fare may not be available the next day, or even the next hour. Always check different routings and look into using alternate airports. Also, price off-peak flights and red-eye, which may be significantly less expensive than others. Travel agents, especially low-fare specialists (⇨ Discounts & Deals), are helpful.

Consolidators are another good source. They buy tickets for scheduled flights at reduced rates from the airlines, then sell them at prices that beat the best fare available directly from the airlines. (Many also offer reduced car-rental and hotel rates.) Sometimes you can even get your money back if you need to return the ticket. Carefully read the fine print detailing penalties for changes and cancellations, purchase the ticket with a credit card, and confirm your consolidator reservation with the airline.

When you fly as a courier, you trade your checked-luggage space for a ticket deeply subsidized by a courier service. There are restrictions on when you can book and how long you can stay. Some courier companies list with membership organizations, such as the Air Courier Association and the International Association of Air Travel Couriers; these require you to become a member before you can book a flight.

Many airlines, singly or in collaboration, offer discount air passes that allow foreigners to travel economically in a particular country or region. These visitor passes usually must be reserved and purchased before you leave home. Information about passes often can be found on most airlines' international Web pages, which tend to be aimed at travelers from outside the carrier's home country. Also, try typing the name of the pass into a search engine, or search for "pass" within the carrier's Web site.

🚺 Online Consolidators **AirlineConsolidator.com** ⊕ www.airlineconsolidator.com; for international tickets. **Best Fares** ⊕ www.bestfares.com; $59.90

annual membership. **Cheap Tickets** ⊕ www. cheaptickets.com. **Expedia** ⊕ www.expedia.com. **Hotwire** ⊕ www.hotwire.com. **lastminute.com** ⊕ www.lastminute.com specializes in last-minute travel; the main site is for the U.K., but it has a link to a U.S. site. **Luxury Link** ⊕ www.luxurylink.com has auctions (surprisingly good deals) as well as offers at the high-end side of travel. **Onetravel.com** ⊕ www.onetravel.com. **Orbitz** ⊕ www.orbitz.com. **Priceline.com** ⊕ www.priceline.com. **Travelocity** ⊕ www.travelocity.com.

AIRPORTS

Costa Rica has two international airports. Juan Santamaría International Airport (SJO) is the country's main airport. It's about 24 km (15 mi), or 30 minutes by car, northwest of downtown San José, just outside the city of Alajuela. The SANSA terminal for domestic flights is here. The country's other international airport is Daniel Oduber International Airport (LIR), a small airport near Liberia, in the North Pacific, the hub for domestic charter airline Macaw Air. Only five airlines fly to Liberia: United Airlines, from Chicago; American Airlines, from Miami; Delta, from Atlanta; Continental, from Houston; and US Airways from Charlotte, NC. The tiny Tobias Bolaños airport, in the San José suburb of Pavas (west of the city), serves domestic airline NatureAir, domestic charter companies, and a handful of private planes.

Other places where planes land in Costa Rica aren't exactly airports. They more resemble a carport with a landing strip, at which an airline representative arrives just minutes before a plane is due to land or take off.

Prepare yourself for long waits at immigration and customs, and for check-in and security checkpoints, especially at Juan Santamaría, where you need to get to the airport three hours before your flight. This may change for the better; at this writing, work was resuming on infrastructure renovations that had been stalled for three years. Most North American flights arrive at this airport in the evening and depart early in the morning, which are the busiest times.

Liberia is a tiny airport, so check-in times are usually shorter. However, infrastructure hasn't quite caught up to the exponential increase in flights, so we recommend that you arrive at least two hours before international departures.

Juan Santamaría is a full-service airport with many arrivals and departures each day, so if you miss your flight or have some other unexpected mishap, you're better off there. Fares are usually lower to San José than to Liberia.

GROUND TRANSPORTATION FROM JUAN SANTAMARÍA AIRPORT

You exit the airport into a fume-filled parking area flanked by hordes of taxis and tour vans. If you're with a tour, you need only look for a representative of your tour company with a sign that bears your name. If you need a taxi, first buy a voucher at a kiosk just outside the arrivals exit, then present it to the driver of one of the orange Taxis Unidos cabs (no other taxis are allowed in the arrival area). Rates are standardized to the various parts of town; most areas of San José are $12–$15. Avoid *collectivos,* or minivans—they're almost the same price as a taxi, but the van is often crammed with other passengers, and you'll have to make stops at their hotels, making your transfer another journey in itself.

DEPARTURE TAXES

When you fly out of Costa Rica, you'll have to pay a $26 airport departure tax in colones or with a Visa credit card. You can pay the tax upon arrival or departure at the Bancrédito counter in the airport, or at any Bancrédito or Banco de Costa Rica branch in Costa Rica during your trip. Lines are long, so don't leave it until the last minute. The Four Seasons, Punta Islita, the Hotel Marriott in Belén, Hotel Presidente in the capital, and Fiesta Resorts allow you to pay for the tax on your hotel bill and give you the receipt for the airport. If you're staying at an upscale hotel, ask—the program is catching on fast.

DUTY-FREE SHOPPING

■ TIP→ **San José's Juan Santamaría International Airport is a good place to buy sou-**

venirs, including Costa Rican coffee, wood and leather crafts, bottled sauces for cooking, and T-shirts. Prices in the airport are higher than at other souvenir shops, but the extra money may be worth it to avoid carrying souvenirs around during your vacation. Unlike many Latin American countries, Costa Rica does not have a large artisan community and doesn't produce spectacular crafts. The types and quality of souvenirs you find in the airport are generally the same as the products you find elsewhere in the country.

🖪 Airport Information **Aeropuerto Internacional Daniel Oduber (LIR)** ✉ 17 km/11 mi west of Liberia ☎ 506/668-1010. **Aeropuerto Internacional Juan Santamaría (SJO)** ✉ 16 km/10 mi northwest of downtown San José, just outside Alajuela ☎ 506/437-2626 (departure and arrival info) or 506/443-1737. **Aeropuerto Internacional Tobías Bolaños** ✉ 3 km/2 mi west of San José, Pavas ☎ 506/232-2820.

BUS TRAVEL

ARRIVING & DEPARTING

Tica Bus has daily runs between Costa Rica and Panama or Nicaragua; Transnica has daily service between Costa Rica and Granada and Managua. We recommend choosing Tica Bus if at all possible, but Transnica is acceptable in a pinch. Tica Bus offers an "executive" service on some of its green-season Managua–Costa Rica runs, which means for about $3 more you'll get breakfast. Both companies have comfortable, air-conditioned coaches with videos and on-board toilets, and make it easy to cross the border. For border-crossing details, see Chapters 3, 6, and 7.

🖪 Bus Companies **Tica Bus** ✉ C. 9 and Avda. 4, San José ☎ 221-8954 ⊕ www.ticabus.com. **Transnica** ✉ C. 22, between Avdas. 3 and 5, San José ☎ 223-4920 ✉ Hotel Guanacaste, Liberia ☎ 666-0085.

GETTING AROUND

All Costa Rican towns are connected by regular bus service. Bus service in Costa Rica is reliable, comprehensive, and inexpensive; fares for long-distance routes are usually $3–$10 one-way. Buses between major cities are modern and air-conditioned, but once you get into the rural areas, you may get a converted school bus

without air-conditioning. The kind of bus you get is the luck of the draw (no upgrades here). Bus travel in Costa Rica is formal, meaning no pigs or chickens inside and no people or luggage on the roof. On longer routes, buses stop midway at modest restaurants. Near the ends of their runs many nonexpress buses turn into large taxis, dropping passengers off one by one at their destinations; to save time, take a *directo* (express) bus. Be prepared for bus-company employees and bus drivers to speak Spanish only.

The main inconvenience of buses is that you usually have to return to San José to travel between outlying regions and that long-distance service is much slower than flying. For example, a bus from San José to the Osa Peninsula is 9 hours or more, whereas the flight is 1 hour. Shorter distances are more negligible—the bus to Quepos is 3½ hours and the flight 30 minutes—and in those cases the huge price difference might be worth the extra hours of travel. There is no main bus station in San José; buses leave from a variety of departure points.

⚠ **Don't put your belongings in the overhead bin unless you have to, and if you do, keep your eye on them. If anyone—even someone who looks like a bus employee—offers to put your luggage on the bus or in the luggage compartment underneath for you, politely decline. If you must put your luggage underneath the bus, get off quickly when you arrive to retrieve it.**

Many visitors take the more convenient (but more expensive) alternative of booking a private shuttle van (⇨ Shuttle Van Services, *below*) or hiring a private driver (⇨ Car Travel). Both options are still cheaper than flying in most cases.

FARES & SCHEDULES

Bus companies don't have printed bus schedules to give out, although departure times may be printed on a sign at the bus company's office and ticket window. Bus-line phones are usually busy or go unanswered. The schedules and prices we list are accurate at this writing, but can change frequently. ■ TIP➡ **For up-to-date information, go to the bus station a day be-**

fore your departure, or get a schedule from an ICT tourist office (⇨ Visitor Information). Hotel employees can usually give you the information you need.

Buses usually depart and arrive on time; they may even leave a few minutes before the scheduled departure time.

TICKETS & RESERVATIONS

Tickets are sold at bus stations and on the buses themselves; reservations aren't accepted, and you must pay in person with cash. If you pay on the bus, be sure to have loose change handy, though the driver will accept bills of 1,000 colones. Buses to popular beach and mountain destinations often sell out on weekends and the days before and after a holiday. It's also difficult to get tickets back to San José on Sunday afternoon. Some companies won't sell you a return ticket from the departure point; especially during the peak season, make sure the first thing you do upon arrival is buy your ticket back. Sometimes tickets include seat numbers, which are usually printed on the tops of the chairs. Smoking is not permitted on buses.

SHUTTLE VAN SERVICES

Two private bus companies, Gray Line Tours Fantasy Bus and Interbus, travel to the most popular tourist destinations in modern, air-conditioned vans. Interbus vans seat 8 to 16 people; Gray Line vans seat 14 to 28 people. Be sure to double-check information that is listed on the Web site—published prices may not be accurate and routes are not always running. This service costs about $20–$55 one-way, but can take hours off your trip. Hotel-to-hotel service is offered as long as your lodging is on the route; if you're heading off the beaten track, it's a hotel-to-nearest-hotel service.

🚐 Shuttle Van Companies **Gray Line Tourist Bus** ☎ 232-3681 or 220-2126 ⊕ www. graylinecostarica.com. **Interbus** ☎ 283-5573 ⊕ www.interbusonline.com.

🚐 Photo Help **Kodak Information Center** ☎ 800/ 242-2424 ⊕ www.kodak.com.

CAR TRAVEL

■ TIP➜ If you're planning to go to only one or two major areas, taking a shuttle van or a domestic flight is usually a better and cheaper option than driving. Renting is a good choice if you're destination hopping, staying at a hotel that's a trek to town, or going well off the beaten path. Car trips to northern Guanacaste from San José can take an entire day, so flying is probably better if you don't have long to spend in the country. Flying is definitely better than driving for visiting the South Pacific.

Many travelers shy away from renting a car in Costa Rica, if only for fear of the road conditions, acknowledged as a crisis by the government in 2005. Indeed, this is not an ideal place to drive: in San José traffic is bad and car theft is rampant (look for guarded parking lots or hotels with lots); in rural areas roads are often unpaved or potholed—and tires aren't usually covered by the basic insurance. And Ticos are reckless drivers—with one of the highest accident rates in the world. But while driving can be a challenge, it's a great way to explore certain regions, especially Guanacaste, the Northern Plains, and the Caribbean coast (apart from Tortuguero and Barra del Colorado). Keep in mind that mountains and poor road conditions make most trips longer than you'd normally expect.

A standard vehicle is fine for most destinations, but a *doble-tracción* (4WD) is often essential to reach the remoter parts of the country, especially during the rainy season. Even in the dry season, you must have a 4WD vehicle to reach Monteverde and some destinations in Guanacaste. The big 4WD vehicles can cost roughly twice as much as an economy car, but compact 4WDs, such as the Daihatsu Terios, are more reasonable, and should be booked well in advance. Agencies may try to bump you up a category—stay firm. Most cars in Costa Rica have manual transmissions.

■ TIP➜ Specify when making the reservation if you want an automatic transmission; it usually costs about $5 more per day, but some companies such as Avis and Hertz don't charge extra. Larger, more expensive automatic Montero and Sorrento models are also available. If you plan to rent any kind of vehicle between December 15 and

January 3, or during Holy Week (the week leading up to Easter)—when most Costa Ricans are on vacation—reserve several months ahead of time.

Costa Rica has around 30 car-rental firms. Most local firms are affiliated with international car-rental chains and offer the same guarantees and services as their branches abroad. At least a dozen rental offices line San José's Paseo Colón; most large hotels and Juan Santamaría Airport have representatives. Renting in or near San José is by far the easiest way to go. It's feasible to rent in Liberia, Manuel Antonio, and Tamarindo. In most other places across the country it's either impossible or very difficult and expensive to rent a car.

EMERGENCIES

Costa Rica has no highway emergency service organization. In Costa Rica 911 is the nationwide number for accidents. Traffic police are scattered around the country, but Costa Ricans are very good about stopping for people with car trouble. Whatever happens, don't move the car after an accident, even if a monstrous traffic jam ensues. Call 911 first if the accident is serious (nearly everyone has a cell phone here and it's almost a given that someone will offer to help). Also be sure to call the emergency number your car-rental agency has given you. For fender benders, contact the Traffic Police, who will try to locate a person to assist you in English—but don't count on it. If you don't speak Spanish, you may want to contact the rental agency before trying the police.

🚨 Emergency Services **Ambulance and Police** ☎ 911. **Traffic Police** ☎ 222-9245.

GASOLINE

There is no self-service gas in Costa Rica; 24-hour stations are generally available only in San José or on the Pan-American Highway. Most other stations are open from about 7 to 7, some until midnight.

Try to fill your tank in cities—gas is more expensive in rural areas and gas stations can be few and far between. Major credit cards are widely accepted. Ask the attendant if you want a *factura* (receipt). Regular unleaded gasoline is called *regular* and high-octane unleaded is called *super*. Gas is sold by the liter. The cost at this writing is 81¢ per liter ($3.08 per gallon) for regular and 85¢ per liter ($3.23 per gallon) for super.

HIRING A DRIVER

Hiring a car with a driver makes the most sense for sightseeing in and or around San José. You can also usually hire a taxi driver to ferry you around for about $10 an hour. At $50–$75 per day plus the driver's food, hiring a driver for areas outside the San José area costs almost the same as renting a 4WD, but is more expensive for multiday trips, when you'll also have to pay for the driver's room. Some drivers are also knowledgeable guides; others just drive. Unless they're driving large passenger vans for established companies, it's doubtful that drivers have any special training or licensing. Hotels can usually direct you to trusted drivers; but *The Tico Times*, available at supermarkets, souvenir shops, bookstores, and hotels, also has ads for drivers. Counter staff at Economy (⇨ *below*) can recommend experienced drivers. Alternatively, Alamo (⇨ *below*) provides professional car-and-driver services for minimum three-day rentals (available May–November only). You pay $60 on top of the rental fee, plus the driver's food and lodging, or a flat $100 that includes the driver's expenses.

INSURANCE

If you have a major credit card or auto insurance at home, you may not have to pay the mandatory collision insurance ($12–$25 per day, depending on the agency or the kind of car). Before you rent, see what coverage you already have. Deductibles are usually $1,000–$2,000. Third-party injury insurance is generally not covered by credit cards; it costs about $10 per day in addition to the collision insurance, with a 20% deductible; some agencies provide additional insurance to eliminate the deductible.

INTERNATIONAL DRIVING PERMITS

International driving permits (IDPs) are not necessary in Costa Rica. Your own driver's license is good for the length of your initial tourist visa. You must carry your passport, or a copy of it with the entry stamp, to prove when you entered the country.

RATES

High-season rates in San José begin at $45 a day and $300 a week for an economy car with air-conditioning, manual transmission, unlimited mileage, and obligatory insurance; but rates fluctuate considerably according to demand, season, and company. Rates for a 4WD vehicle during high season are $70–$90 a day and $450–$550 per week. Often companies will also require a $1,000 deposit, payable by credit card. It's getting easier to rent a vehicle with automatic transmission, but some companies still charge about $5 more per day; reserve well in advance and know that options are more limited.

Cars picked up at or returned to Juan Santamaría Airport incur a 12% surcharge. Arrangements can be made to pick up cars directly at the Liberia airport, but a range of firms have offices nearby and transport you from the airport free of charge—and with no surcharge to rent. Check cars thoroughly for damage before you sign the rental contract. Even tough-looking 4WD vehicles should be coddled. ⚠ **The charges levied by rental companies for damage—no matter how minor—are outrageous even by U.S. or European standards.**

One-way service surcharges are $50–$150, depending on the drop-off point. To avoid a hefty refueling fee, fill the tank just before you turn in the car, but be aware that gas stations near the rental outlet may overcharge. It's almost never a deal to buy the tank of gas that's in the car when you rent it; the understanding is that you'll return it empty, but some fuel usually remains. Car seats cost about $5 per day. Additional drivers are about $5–$10 per day if there is any charge at all. Almost all agencies have cell-phone rental; prices range between $2 and $6 per day, with national per-minute costs between 50¢ and $2.

REQUIREMENTS & RESTRICTIONS

Car seats are compulsory for children under four years old, and can be rented for about $5 per day; reserve in advance. Rental cars may not be driven across borders to Nicaragua and Panama. Seat-belt use is compulsory in the front seat. Fuel-efficiency measures restrict certain cars from the city center once a week, according to the final license-plate number (e.g., plates that end in 9 are restricted on Fridays). However, this does not apply to rental cars; if you are stopped, do not pay a bribe. To rent a car, you need a driver's license, a valid passport, and a credit card. The minimum renter age varies; agencies such as Hertz, Budget, and Alamo rent to anyone over 21; Avis sets the limit at 23. Though it's rare, some agencies have a maximum age limit.

ROAD CONDITIONS

San José is terribly congested during weekday morning and afternoon rush hours (7–9 AM and 4–6 PM). Avoid returning to the city on Sunday evening, when traffic to San José from the Pacific coast beaches backs up for hours. Look out for potholes, even in the smoothest sections of the best roads, whether you're in San José or in the countryside. Also watch for unmarked speed bumps where you'd least expect them, particularly on rural main thoroughfares. During the rainy season, roads are in much worse shape. Check with your destination before setting out; roads, especially in Limón Province, are prone to wash-outs and landslides.

San José has many one-way streets and traffic circles. Streets in the capital are narrow. Pedestrians are supposed to have the right of way but do not in reality, so be alert when walking. The local driving style is erratic and aggressive but not fast, because road conditions don't permit too much speed. Frequent fender benders tie up traffic. Keep your windows rolled up in the center of the city, because thieves may reach into your car at stoplights and snatch your purse, jewelry, and so on.

Outside of San José you'll run into long stretches of unpaved road. Frequent hazards in the countryside are potholes, landslides during the rainy season, and cattle on the roads. Drunk drivers are a hazard throughout the country on weekend nights. Driving at night is not recommended anyway, since roads are poorly lighted and many don't have painted center lines or shoulder lines.

🔢 **Online Maps Amazon** ⊕ www.amazon.com, www.amazon.ca, www.amazon.co.uk. **Fishpond** ⊕ www.fishpond.co.nz. **Less10** ⊕ www.less10.com.

RULES OF THE ROAD

Driving is on the right side of the road in Costa Rica. The highway speed limit is usually 90 kph (54 mph), which drops to 60 kph (36 mph) in residential areas. In towns limits range from 30 to 50 kph (18 to 31 mph). Speed limits are rigorously enforced in all regions of the country. Seat belts are required, and an awareness campaign has increased enforcement. *Alto* means "stop" and *ceda* means "yield." Right turns on red are permitted except where signs indicate otherwise, but in San José this is usually not possible because of one-way streets and pedestrian crossings.

Signage is notoriously bad, but improving. Watch carefully for *No Hay Paso* (Do Not Enter) signs; one-way streets are common, both in small towns as well as in San José, and it's not unusual for a street to transform from a two-way to a one-way, forcing a not-so-obvious turn. Streetlights are often out of service and key signs missing or knocked down because of accidents.

Local drunk driving laws are strict. You'll get nailed with a 10,000-colón fine if you're caught driving in a "predrunk" state (blood alcohol levels of 0.049%–0.099%). If your level is higher than that, you'll pay 20,000 colones, the car will be confiscated, and your license taken away. Policemen who stop drivers for speeding and drunk driving are often looking for payment on the spot—essentially a bribe. Whether you're guilty or not, you'll get a ticket if you don't give in. Asking for a ticket instead of paying the bribe discourages corruption and does not compromise your safety. You can generally pay the ticket at your car-rental company; it will remit it on your behalf.

Car seats are required for children ages four and under, but car-seat laws are not rigorously enforced. Many Tico babies and children ride on their parents' laps. Children over 10 are allowed in the front seat. Drivers are prohibited from using hand-held cell phones, but this is almost never enforced, and distracted chatters are the rule.

⚠ **There are plenty of questionable drivers on Costa Rican highways; be prepared for harebrained passing on blind corners, tailgating, and failing to signal.** Watch, too, for two-lane roads that feed into one-lane bridges with specified rights-of-way.

There's not always a method to the driving madness, but locals use two tactics that are surprisingly effective. Stick your left hand out the window and wave slightly if you want to merge left (get your passenger to do it to maneuver to the right), and flick your lights if you want oncoming traffic to slow down so you can turn left. Hone your reflexes: drivers behind you will honk at you a millisecond before the light turns green. Green traffic lights flash just before turning to yellow; always look carefully, as drivers regularly speed through lights that have long since turned red.

🔢 **Major Agencies Alamo** ☎ 800/522-9696 in the U.S., 800/462-5266 or 506/233-7733 in Costa Rica ⊕ www.alamocostarica.com. **Avis** ☎ 800/331-1084, 800/272-5871 in Canada, 0870/606-0100 in the U.K., 02/9353-9000 in Australia, 09/526-2847 in New Zealand, 506/232-9922 in Costa Rica ⊕ www.avis.co.cr. **Budget** ☎ 800/527-0700 in the U.S. and Canada, 0870/156-5656 in the U.K., 300/794-344 in Australia, 0800/283-438 in New Zealand, 506/436-2000 in Costa Rica ⊕ www.budget.co.cr. **Dollar** ☎ 866/746-7765 in the U.S. and Canada, 0800/085-4578 in the U.K., 506/443-2950 in Costa Rica ⊕ www.dollarcostarica.com. **Economy** ☎ 877/326-7368 in the U.S. and Canada, 506/231-5410 in Costa Rica ⊕ www.economyrentacar.com. **Hertz** ☎ 800/654-3001, 800/263-0600 in Canada, 0870/844-8844 in the U.K., 02/9669-2444 in Australia, 09/256-8690 in New Zealand, 506/221-1818 in Costa Rica ⊕ www.costaricarentacar.net. **National Car Rental** ☎ 800/227-7368, 506/290-8787 in Costa Rica ⊕ www.natcar.com.

SAFETY & PRECAUTIONS

- If you are renting a car, don't forget to arrange for a car seat in advance.
- Riptides are a force to be reckoned with. Ask locals to point out safe places to swim and never let a child swim unattended in the ocean or go deeper than his or her waist.
- Sunburn and dehydration can be serious in Costa Rica. Slather on the sunscreen and make sure kids swim in T-shirts and wear hats. (Even waterproof sunscreen can wear off quickly.) Give kids lots of water or juice. If you're taking bus trips, which can be extremely hot, schedule them for early in the morning or late afternoon.
- Kids are more prone to stomach problems from contaminated water, so avoid tap water and ice.
- Wild animals aren't pets; explain how harmful it is to feed the monkeys, no matter how cute and tame they seem.
- On hikes, make sure a nature-aware adult walks in front of children to watch for camouflaged snakes or fireant burrows.

🖪 BBBs **Council of Better Business Bureaus** ☎ 703/276-0100.

CUSTOMS & DUTIES

When shopping in Costa Rica, keep receipts for all purchases. Be ready to show customs officials what you've bought. Pack purchases together in an easily accessible place. If you think a duty is incorrect, appeal the assessment. If you object to the way your clearance was handled, note the inspector's badge number. In either case, first ask to see a supervisor. If the problem isn't resolved, write to the appropriate authorities, beginning with the port director at your point of entry. It usually takes about 10–30 minutes to clear customs when arriving in Costa Rica.

IN COSTA RICA

Visitors entering Costa Rica may bring in 500 grams of tobacco, 5 liters of wine or spirits, 2 kilograms of sweets and chocolates, and the equivalent of $500 worth of merchandise. One camera and one video camera, six rolls of film, binoculars, and electrical items for personal use only are also allowed. Customs officials at San José's international airport rarely examine tourists' luggage, but if you enter by land, they'll probably look through your bags. Officers at the airport generally speak English.

IN THE U.S.

U.S. residents who have been out of the country for at least 48 hours may bring home $600 worth of foreign goods dutyfree, as long as they have not used the $600 allowance or any part of it in the past 30 days. This allowance, lower than the standard $800 exemption, applies to the 24 countries in the Caribbean Basin Initiative (CBI)—including Costa Rica. If you visit a CBI country and a non-CBI country, you may bring in $800 worth of goods duty-free, but no more than $600 may be from a CBI country.

🖪 **U.S. Customs and Border Protection** ⊕ www.cbp.gov ☎ 877/227-5551, 202/354-1000.

DISCOUNTS & DEALS

DISCOUNT RESERVATIONS

To save money, look into discount reservations services with Web sites and tollfree numbers, which use their buying power to get a better price on hotels, airline tickets (⇨ Air Travel), even car rentals. When booking a room, always **call the hotel's local toll-free number** (if one is available) rather than the central reservations number—you'll often get a better price. Always ask about special packages or corporate rates.

When shopping for the best deal on hotels and car rentals, look for guaranteed exchange rates, which protect you against a falling dollar. With your rate locked in, you won't pay more, even if the price goes up in the local currency.

DISCOUNT RESERVATIONS

🖪 Hotel Rooms **Accommodations Express** ☎ 800/444-7666 or 800/277-1064. **Hotels.com** ☎ 800/219-4606 or 800/364-0291 ⊕ www.hotels.com. **Turbotrip.com** ☎ 800/473-7829 ⊕ w3.turbotrip.com.

PACKAGE DEALS

Don't confuse packages and guided tours. When you buy a package, you travel on your own, just as though you had planned the trip yourself. Fly/drive packages, which combine airfare and car rental, are often a good deal. In cities, ask the local visitor's bureau about hotel and local transportation packages that include tickets to major museum exhibits or other special events.

EATING & DRINKING

In San José and surrounding cities, *sodas* (informal eateries) are usually open daily 7 AM to 7 or 9 PM, though some close on Sunday. Other restaurants are usually open 11 AM–9 PM. In rural areas restaurants are usually closed on Sunday, except around resorts. In resort areas some restaurants may be open late. Most all-night restaurants are in downtown San José casinos. However, Nuestra Tierra and Manolos are both good 24-hour options, and for late-night cravings the doors at Denny's at the Best Western Irazú just north of San José are always open. Normal dining hours in Costa Rica are noon–3 and 6–9. **Unless otherwise noted, the restaurants listed in this guide are open daily for lunch and dinner.** *Desayuno* (breakfast) is served at most sodas and hotels.

Except for those in hotels, most restaurants close between Christmas and New Year's Day and during Holy Week (Palm Sunday to Easter Sunday). Call before heading out. Those that do stay open may not sell alcohol between Holy Thursday and Easter Sunday. Even if you keep your base in San José, consider venturing to the Central Valley towns for a meal or two.

WHAT IT COSTS AT DINNER				
$$$$	$$$	$$	$	¢
over $25	$20–$25	$10–$20	$5–$10	under $5

Prices are per-person for a main course, excluding 13% tax and 10% service fee.

The restaurants we list are the cream of the crop in each price category. Properties indicated by a ✕🏠 are lodging establishments whose restaurant warrants a special trip.

PAYING

■ **TIP→** Credit cards are not accepted at most restaurants in rural areas. Always ask before you order to find out if your credit card will be accepted. Visa and Master-Card are the most commonly accepted cards; American Express and Diners Club are less widely accepted. ■ **TIP→** Remember that 23% is added to all menu prices: 13% for tax and 10% for service. Because a gratuity is included, there's no need to tip, but if your service is good, it's nice to add a little money to the obligatory 10%.

RESERVATIONS & DRESS

Reservations are always a good idea; we mention them only when they're essential or not accepted. Book as far ahead as you can, and reconfirm as soon as you arrive. (Large parties should always call ahead to check the reservations policy.) We mention dress only when men are required to wear a jacket or a jacket and tie.

Costa Ricans generally dress more formally than North Americans. For dinner, long pants and closed-toed shoes are standard for men except for beach locations, and women tend to wear dressy clothes that show off their figures, with high heels. Shorts, flip-flops, and tank tops are not acceptable, except at inexpensive restaurants in beach towns.

ELECTRICITY

North American appliances are compatible with Costa Rica's electrical system (110 volts) and outlets (parallel two-prong). Australian and European appliances require a two-prong adapter and a 220-volt to 110-volt transformer. Most laptops operate equally well on 110 and 220 volts and so require only an adapter, but you should bring a surge protector for your computer. Never use an outlet that specifically warns against using higher-voltage appliances without a transformer. Dual-voltage appliances (which are usually designed especially for travel) need only a two-prong adapter.

EMERGENCIES

Dial 911 for an ambulance, the fire department, or the police. Costa Ricans are usually quick to respond to emergencies.

In a hotel or restaurant, the staff will usually offer immediate assistance, and in a public area passersby can be counted on to stop and help.

For emergencies ranging from health problems to lost passports, contact your embassy. (Citizens of Australia and New Zealand should contact the British Embassy.)

🔢 **Emergency Contacts Ambulance (Cruz Roja), Fire, Police** ☎ 911. **Traffic Police** ☎ 222–9330.

🔢 **Foreign Embassies British Embassy** (Embajada Británica) ✉ 11th fl., Centro Colón, between Cs. 38 and 40, Paseo Colón, San José ☎ 506/258–2025 ⊕ www.embajadabritanica.com. **Canadian Embassy** (Embajada Canadiense) ✉ Sabana Sur, Oficentro Ejecutivo La Sabana, Torre No. 5, 3rd fl., behind the Controlaría building, San José ☎ 506/242–4400 ⊕ www.dfait-maeci.gc.ca/latin-america/sanjose. **United States Embassy** (Embajada de los Estados Unidos) ✉ C. 120 and Avda. 0, Pavas, San José ☎ 506/519–2000 or 506/220–3127 for after-hours emergencies ⊕ www.usembassy.or.cr.

ETIQUETTE & BEHAVIOR

If invited to someone's home, take a hostess gift such as flowers or a bottle of wine or some trinket from your home country. If offered food at someone's home, accept it and eat it even if you aren't hungry. You will be offered coffee and should accept, although it's not necessary to finish the whole cup. Know that Costa Ricans don't like to say no, and will often avoid answering a question or simply say *gracias* when they really mean no.

On the whole, Costa Ricans are extremely polite, quick to shake hands and place a kiss on the right cheek (meaning you need to bear left when going in for the peck). Ticos tend to use formal Spanish, preferring, for example, *con mucho gusto* (with much pleasure) instead of *de nada* for "you're welcome." At the same time, a large number of Costa Rican men make a habit of ogling or making gratuitous comments when young women pass on the street. Women should wear a bra at all times. Family is very important in Costa Rica. It is considered polite to ask about one's marital status and family—don't confuse this with prying.

As you would anywhere, dress and behave respectfully when visiting churches. In churches men and women should not wear shorts, sleeveless shirts, or sandals; women should wear skirts below the knee.

HEALTH

Malaria is not a problem in Costa Rica except in some remote northern Caribbean areas near the Nicaraguan border. Poisonous snakes, scorpions, and other pests pose a small (often overrated) threat. The CDC marks Costa Rica as an area infested by the *Aedes aegypti* (dengue-carrier) mosquito, but not as an epidemic region. A few thousand cases in locals are recorded each year; on average, the numbers have been dropping, with the exception of a spike in 2005. Cases of fatal hemorrhagic dengue are rare. The highest-risk area is the Caribbean, and the rainy season is peak dengue season elsewhere. You're unlikely to be felled by this disease, but you can't take its prevention too seriously: *Repelente* (insect repellent spray) and *espirales* (mosquito coils) are sold in supermarkets and small country stores. U.S. insect repellent brands with DEET are sold in pharmacies and supermarkets. Mosquito nets are available in some remote lodges; you can buy them in camping stores in San José. ■ **TIP→ Mild insect repellents, like the ones in some skin softeners, are no match for the intense mosquito activity in the hot, humid regions of the Caribbean, Osa Peninsula, and Southern Pacific. Repellants made with DEET or picaridin are the most effective.** Perfume, aftershave, and other lotions and potions can actually attract mosquitoes.

While it's unlikely you will contract malaria or dengue, if you start suffering from high fever, the shakes, or joint pain, make sure you ask to be tested for these diseases when you go to the local clinic. On the off chance you do have them, it's more likely doctors here will be able to provide an accurate diagnosis and treatment. Your embassy can provide you with a list of recommended doctors and dentists.

Government facilities—the so-called "Caja" hospitals (short for Caja Costarricense de Seguro Social, or Costa Rican Social Security System)—and clinics are of acceptable quality, but notoriously over-burdened, a common complaint in social-ized-medicine systems anywhere. Private hospitals are more accustomed to serving foreigners. They include Hospital CIMA, Clínica Bíblica, and Clínica Católica, which all have 24-hour pharmacies. The long-established and ubiquitous Fischel pharmacies are great places for your pre-scription needs. Antibiotics and psy-chotropic medications (for sleep, anxiety, or pain) require prescriptions in Costa Rica. Little else does. But plan ahead and bring an adequate supply with you from home; matches may not be exact.

For specific clinic, hospital, and pharmacy listings, *see* Chapters 1 through 7.

DIVERS' ALERT
Do not fly within 24 hours of scuba diving.

FOOD & DRINK
Most food and water is sanitary in Costa Rica. In rural areas you run a mild risk of encountering drinking water, fresh fruit, and vegetables contaminated by fecal mat-ter, which in most cases causes a bit of *turista* (traveler's diarrhea) but can cause leptospirosis (which can be treated by an-tibiotics if detected early). Although it may not be necessary, you can stay on the safe side by avoiding uncooked food, unpas-teurized milk (including milk products), and ice—ask for drinks *sin hielo* (without ice)—and by drinking bottled water. Mild cases of turista may respond to Imodium (known generically as loperamide) or Pepto-Bismol (not as strong), both of which can be purchased over the counter. Drink plenty of purified water or tea; chamomile (*manzanilla* in Spanish) is a good folk remedy. In severe cases, rehy-drate yourself with a salt-sugar solution (½ teaspoon salt and 4 tablespoons sugar per quart of water).

Ceviche, raw fish cured in lemon juice—a favorite appetizer, especially at seaside re-sorts—is generally safe to eat. ■ TIP➔ **Buy organic foods whenever possible; chemicals, many of which have been banned elsewhere, are sprayed freely here without regulation.**

OTHER HAZARDS
Heat stroke and dehydration are real dan-gers, especially for hikers, so drink lots of water. Take at least 1 liter per person for every hour you plan to be on the trail. Sunburn is the most common traveler's health problem. Use sunscreen with SPF 30 or higher. Most pharmacies and super-markets carry sunscreen in a wide range of SPFs, though it is relatively pricey.

The greatest danger to your person actu-ally lies off Costa Rica's popular beaches—riptides are common wherever there are waves, and tourists run into seri-ous difficulties in them every year. If you see waves, ask the locals where it's safe to swim; and if you're uncertain, don't go in deeper than your waist. If you get caught in a rip current, swim parallel to the beach until you're free of it, and then swim back to shore. ⚠ **Avoid swimming where a town's main river opens up to the sea. Sep-tic tanks aren't common.**

SHOTS & MEDICATIONS
Most travelers to Costa Rica do not get any vaccinations or take any special medi-cations. However, according to the U.S. Centers for Disease Control, travel to Costa Rica poses some risk of malaria, hepatitis A and B, dengue fever, typhoid fever, rabies, Chagas' disease, and *E. coli.* The CDC recommends getting vaccines for hepatitis A and typhoid fever, especially if you are going to be in remote areas or plan to stay for more than six weeks.

Check with the CDC for detailed health advisories and recommended vaccinations. In areas with malaria and dengue, both of which are carried by mosquitoes, bring mosquito nets, wear clothing that covers your body, and apply repellent containing DEET in living and sleeping areas. There are some pockets of malaria near the Nicaraguan border on the Caribbean coast. You probably won't need to take malaria pills before your trip unless you are staying for a prolonged period in the north, camping on northern coasts, or crossing the border into Nicaragua or Panama. You should discuss the option with your doctor. Children traveling to

Central America should have current inoculations against measles, mumps, rubella, and polio.

PHARMACIES

Farmacia is Spanish for "pharmacy," and the names for common drugs *aspirina,* Tylenol, and *ibuprofen* are basically the same as they are in English. Pepto-Bismol is widely available. Many drugs for which you need a prescription back home are sold over the counter in Costa Rica. Pharmacies throughout the country are generally open from 8 to 8, though it's best to consult with your hotel's staff to be sure. Some pharmacies in San José affiliated with clinics stay open 24 hours.

MEDICAL PLANS

No one plans to get sick while traveling, but it happens, so consider signing up with a medical-assistance company. Members get doctor referrals, emergency evacuation or repatriation, hotlines for medical consultation, cash for emergencies, and other assistance. SOS Assistance is one such company. Prices are around $60 to $90 per person for a one-week trip, including cancellation insurance.

🔁 Medical-Assistance Companies **International SOS Assistance** ⊕ www.internationalsos.com ✉ 3600 Horizon Blvd., Suite 300, Trevose, PA 19053 ☎ 215/942-8000 or 800/523-6586 ✉ Landmark House, Hammersmith Bridge Rd., 6th floor, London, W6 9DP ☎ 20/8762-8008 ✉ 12 Chemin Riant-bosson, 1217 Meyrin 1, Geneva, Switzerland ☎ 22/785-6464 ✉ 331 N. Bridge Rd., 17-00, Odeon Towers, Singapore 188720 ☎ 6338-7800.

🔁 Health Warnings **National Centers for Disease Control and Prevention** (CDC) ☎ 877/394-8747 international travelers' health line, 800/311-3435 other inquiries, 404/498-1600 Division of Quarantine and international health information ⊕ www.cdc.gov/travel. **Travel Health Online** ⊕ tripprep.com. **World Health Organization** (WHO) ⊕ www.who.int.

HOLIDAYS

January 1:	First day of the year
April 11:	Juan Santamaría Day, a national hero
Easter Week:	Thursday and Good Friday, religious activities
May 1:	International Labor Day
July 25:	Anniversary of the Annexation of Guanacaste Province
September 15:	Independence Day
August 2:	Day of the Virgin of Los Angeles (patron saint of Costa Rica)
August 15:	Mothers' Day
December 25:	Christmas Day

INSURANCE FOR YOUR TRIP

The most useful travel-insurance plan is a comprehensive policy that includes coverage for trip cancellation and interruption, default, trip delay, and medical expenses (with a waiver for preexisting conditions).

Without insurance you'll lose all or most of your money if you cancel your trip, regardless of the reason. Default insurance covers you if your tour operator, airline, or cruise line goes out of business—the chances of which have been increasing. Trip-delay covers expenses that arise because of bad weather or mechanical delays. Study the fine print when comparing policies.

If you're traveling internationally, a key component of travel insurance is coverage for medical bills incurred if you get sick on the road. Such expenses aren't generally covered by Medicare or private policies. U.K. residents can buy a travel-insurance policy valid for most vacations taken during the year in which it's purchased (but check preexisting-condition coverage). British and Australian citizens need extra medical coverage when traveling overseas. Check the policy carefully, and make sure it covers the adventure sports, such as canopies or white-water rafting, that you'll be engaging in in Costa Rica.

Always **buy travel policies directly from the insurance company**; if you buy them from a cruise line, airline, or tour operator that goes out of business you probably won't be covered for the agency or operator's default, a major risk. Before making any purchase, review your existing health and home-owner's policies to find what they cover away from home.

🔁 Travel Insurers In the U.S.: **Access America** ☎ 800/729-6021 ⊕ www.accessamerica.com.

Travel Guard International ☎ 715/345-1041 or 800/826-4919 ⊕ www.travelguard.com.

🔲 In the U.K.: **Association of British Insurers** ☎ 020/7600-3333 ⊕ www.abi.org.uk. In Canada: **RBC Insurance** ☎ 800/565-3129 ⊕ www.rbcinsurance.com. In Australia: **Insurance Council of Australia** ☎ 02/9253-5100 ⊕ www.ica.com.au. In New Zealand: **Insurance Council of New Zealand** ☎ 04/472-5230 ⊕ www.icnz.org.nz.

LANGUAGE

Spanish is the official language, although many tour guides and locals in heavily touristed areas speak English. You'll have a better time if you learn some basic Spanish before you go and if you bring a phrase book with you. At the very least, learn the rudiments of polite conversation—niceties such as *por favor* (please) and *gracias* (thank you) will be warmly appreciated. For more words and phrases, *see* the Spanish glossary *in* the Understanding Costa Rica chapter.

In the Caribbean province of Limón a creole English called Mekatelyu is widely spoken by older generations. English is understood by most everyone in these parts.

LANGUAGES FOR TRAVELERS

A phrase book and language-tape set can help get you started. *Fodor's Spanish for Travelers* (available at bookstores everywhere) is excellent.

LODGING

A number of Web sites help you through the lodging search. **Budget** options can be found through Costa Rican Hostelling International (⇨ Students in Costa Rica, *below*). **Low-end** alternatives are often referred to as *cabinas* whether they offer a cement cigar-box motel or free-standing rustic rooms. Most have private rooms, cold-water cement showers, fans instead of air-conditioning, limited—if any—secure parking or storage, and may share bathrooms. Owners tend to be Costa Rican. Often without Web sites, e-mail, or links to major agencies, these hotels tend to follow a first-come, first-served booking policy. They may have room during peak seasons when mid- or upper-end options are booked solid.

Mid-range options include boutique hotels, tasteful bungalows, bed-and-breakfasts, and downtown casino hotels. Those in the hotter beach areas may not have hot-water showers. Many have pools, Internet access, and meal options. They tend to be foreign-owned and, with the exception of the casinos, have personalized service. Because they're generally small, you may have to book one or two months ahead, and up to six months in the high season. Booking through an association or agency can significantly reduce the time you spend scanning the Internet, but you can often get a better deal and negotiate longer-stay or low-season discounts. Costa Rica Innkeepers is a good resource.

High-end accommodations can be found almost everywhere. They range from luxury tents to exquisite hotels and villa rentals, and are often more secluded. You'll find all the amenities you expect at such areas, with one notable exception: the roads and routes to even five-star villas can be atrocious. This category is sometimes booked up to a year in advance for Christmas, and during this season you may only be able to book through agents or central reservations offices. **Resorts** are generally one of two options: luxurious privileged gateways to the best of the country (such as Punta Islita) or generic budget all-inclusives (such as the Barceló) that probably run counter to what you're coming to Costa Rica for. General local consensus is that the Four Seasons hotel is in a category unto itself, unmatched in pomp and price anywhere in the country.

Several **chain hotels** have franchises in the Costa Rica, leaning toward generic and all-inclusive (⇨ Chain Hotels, *below*). The upside is that they are rarely booked solid, so you can always fall back on one in a worst-case scenario, and they often have member discounts.

Nature lodges and hotels in the South Pacific (where restaurants aren't an option) may be less expensive than they initially appear, as the price of a room usually includes three hearty meals a day, and sometimes guided hikes. These, and other remote accommodations, may not have daily Internet access even though they have a Web site: be patient if you're attempting to book directly. Since many of the hotels are remote and have an eco-friendly approach (even to luxury), air-conditioning, in-room telephones, and TVs are exceptions to the rule. Consider how isolated you want to be; some rural and eco-lodges are miles from neighbors and other services and have few rainy-day diversions.

⚠ Most hotels, especially those in San José, require that you reconfirm your reservation 24 to 48 hours before you arrive. If you don't reconfirm, you may find yourself without a room. Travel Web Costa Rica and the ICT both provide hotel lists, searchable by star category.

The lodgings we list are Costa Rica's cream of the crop in each price category. We always list the facilities that are available, but we don't specify whether they cost extra; when pricing accommodations, always ask what's included and what costs extra. Properties are assigned price categories based on the range from the least-expensive standard double room at high season (excluding holidays) to the most expensive. **Keep in mind that hotel prices we list exclude 16.4% service and tax.**

WHAT IT COSTS FOR 2 PEOPLE				
$$$$	$$$	$$	$	¢
over $200	$125–$200	$75–$125	$35–$75	under $35

Prices are for two people in a standard double room in high season, excluding service and tax (16.4%).

🏠 Lodging Resources **Costa Rican Hotel Association** ☎ 506/248-0990 ⊕ www.costaricanhotels. com. **Costa Rica Innkeepers** ☎ 506/441-1157 ⊕ www.costaricainnkeepers.com. **Instituto Costarricense de Turismo (ICT)** ☎ 866/267-8274 in the U.S. and Canada, 506/299-5800 in Costa Rica ⊕ www.visitcostarica.com. **Travel Web Costa Rica** ☎ 800/788-7857 in the U.S. and Canada, 506/256-3222 in Costa Rica ⊕ www.crica.com.

RESERVATIONS

At Costa Rica's popular beach and mountain resorts reserve well in advance for the dry season (mid-December–April everywhere except the Caribbean, which has a short September–October "dry" season).

During the rainy season (May–mid-December except on the Caribbean coast, where it's almost always rainy) most hotels drop their rates considerably, which sometimes sends them into a lower price category than the one we indicate.

■ TIP→ **If you're having trouble finding a hotel that isn't completely booked, consider contacting a tour operator who can arrange your entire trip (⇨ Tours & Packages). Since they reserve blocks of rooms far in advance, you might have better luck.**

APARTMENT, CONDO & VILLA RENTALS

Furnished rentals accommodate a crowd or a family, often for less and at a higher comfort level. Knowledgeable Costa Rican Vacations handles bookings for upscale condos and villas in Manuel Antonio, Dominical, and several hotspots in Guanacaste. Nosara Home Page lists apartments and villas on the Nicoya Peninsula; Villas International has an extensive list of properties in Quepos and Tamarindo. The House of Rentals, a Century 21 affiliate, arranges houses and condos in the Flamingo and Tamarindo areas.

🏠 **Costa Rican Vacations** ☎ 800/606-1860 in the U.S. and Canada, 506/296-7715 in Costa Rica ⊕ www.vacationscostarica.com. **Century 21/House of Rentals** ☎ 506/654-5161 ⊕ www. houseofrentalscostarica.com. **Nosara Home Page** ⊕ www.nosara.com. **Villas and Apartments Abroad** ☎ 212/213-6435 or 800/433-3020 ⊕ www. vaanyc.com. **Villas International** ☎ 415/499-9490 or 800/221-2260 ⊕ www.villasintl.com.

🏠 International Agents **Hideaways International** ☎ 603/430-4433 or 800/843-4433 ⊕ www. hideaways.com, annual membership $185. **Vacation Home Rentals Worldwide** ☎ 201/767-9393 or 800/633-3284 ⊕ www.vhrww.com. **Villas and Apartments Abroad** ☎ 212/213-6435 or 800/433-3020 ⊕ www.vaanyc.com. **Villas International** ☎ 415/499-9490 or 800/221-2260 ⊕ www.villasintl.com.

CAMPING

One of the cheapest ways to spend the night in this region is to camp; as long as you have your own tent, it's easy to set up house almost anywhere. Most official campgrounds are cement swaths crammed with cranked stereos; the exceptions, and really, the only camping we would highly recommend, are the national-park camping areas. It's illegal and somewhat dicey to camp outside of campgrounds, but many landowners in rural areas will allow you to camp on their land. Do not pitch your tent without getting permission first. Don't ever leave your belongings or a campfire unattended.

HOME EXCHANGES

A handful of home exchanges are available; this involves an initial small registration fee and you'll have to plan farther ahead. It's an excellent way to immerse yourself in true Costa Rica, particularly if you've been here before and aren't relying so heavily on tourism support that hotels can offer. Drawbacks include restricted options and dates. Many companies list home exchanges, but we've found Home-Link International, which lists a handful of jazzy houses in Costa Rica, and Intervac, which as of this writing only listed one house, to be the most reliable.

🏠 Exchange Clubs **HomeLink USA** ☎ 954/566-2687 or 800/638-3841 ⊕ www.homelink.org; $75 yearly for a listing and online access; $45 additional to receive directories. **Intervac U.S.** ☎ 800/756-4663 ⊕ www.intervacus.com; $140 yearly for a listing, online access, and a catalog; $95 without catalog.

MEAL PLANS

In every hotel review, we specify whether a meal plan is included in the base price of a room by using the following acronyms:

EP: European Plan (no meals)

CP: Continental Plan (Continental breakfast)

BP: Breakfast Plan (full breakfast)

MAP: Modified American Plan (breakfast and dinner)

FAP: Full American Plan (breakfast, lunch, and dinner)

AI: All Inclusive (all meals, drinks, and most activities)

🏠 Online Resources **Hotels.com** ☎ 800/246-8357 in U.S. ⊕ www.hotels.com. **lastminute.com** ⊕ www.lastminute.com. **Zuji** ⊕ www.zuji.com.au.

MAIL & SHIPPING

The Spanish word for post office is *correos*. Mail from the United States, Canada, or Europe can take up to two to three weeks to arrive in Costa Rica, a couple of weeks more from Australia or New Zealand (occasionally it never arrives at all). Within the country, mail service is even less reliable. Outgoing mail is marginally quicker, with delivery to North America in five to ten days, to Europe in two weeks, and to Australia and New Zealand in about three weeks, especially when sent from San José. All overseas cards and letters will automatically be sent airmail. Mail theft is a chronic problem, so do not mail checks, cash, or anything else of value.

Minimum postage for postcards and letters from Costa Rica to the United States and Canada costs the equivalent of U.S. 24¢; to the United Kingdom, 28¢; and to Australia or New Zealand, 38¢.

You can have mail sent poste restante (*lista de correos*) to any Costa Rican post office (specify Correo Central to make sure it goes to the main downtown office). In written addresses, *apartado*, abbreviated *apdo.*, indicates a post office box. The American Express office in San José does not hold mail, even for those with AE cards or traveler's checks.

Post offices are generally open weekdays 8–5:30, and on Saturdays 8–noon. Stamps can be purchased at post offices and some souvenir shops. These vendors will also accept the mail you wish to send; mailboxes do not exist in Costa Rica. Always check with your hotel, which may sell stamps and post your letters for you.

EXPRESS SERVICES

UPS has offices in San José, Tamarindo, Jacó, Manuel Antonio, Sarchí, Arenal, and Limón. DHL has dropoffs in San José (Rohrmoser, Paseo Colón), Curridabat, Heredia, Liberia, Limón, Ciudad Quesada, Jacó, Quepos, and San Isidro. Both have central information numbers with English-speaking staff to direct you to the nearest office. FedEx has offices in San José only. Prices are about 10 times what you'd pay at the post office, but packages arrive in a matter of days. ("Overnight" is usually a misnomer—shipments to most North American cities take two days, to Britain three, and to Australia and New Zealand four or five.)

🚹 **Express-Service Main Offices** DHL ✉ 600 meters northeast of the Real Cariari Mall, La Aurora Heredia ☎ 506/209-6000 ☞ Call for other locations. **Federal Express** ✉ Zona Franca Metropolitana, Ciudad Barreal de Heredia, Local 1B, Heredia ✉ Centro de Servicio Mundial, Paseo Colón, 100 m east of León Cortés statue, San José ☎ 0800/052-1090. **United Parcel Service** (UPS) ✉ 50 meters east of Pizza Hut, Paseo Colón, San José ☎ 506/290-2828 ☞ Call for other locations.

SHIPPING PACKAGES

Shipping parcels through the post office is not for those in a hurry, because packages to the United States and Canada can take weeks; to the United Kingdom, Australia, and New Zealand, months. Also, packages may be pilfered. However, post-office shipping is the cheapest way to go, with rates at $6–$12 per kilogram.

Some stores offer shipping, but it is usually quite expensive. If you can, carry your packages home with you.

MONEY MATTERS

In general, Costa Rica is cheaper than North America or Europe, but travelers looking for dirt-cheap developing-nation deals may find it's more expensive than they bargained for—and prices are rising as more foreigners visit and relocate here. Food in modest restaurants and public transportation are inexpensive. A 1-mi taxi ride costs about $1. Here are some sample prices to give you an idea of the cost of living in Costa Rica: 2-liter bottle of Coca-Cola, $1.40–$1.60; cup of coffee, 50¢–95¢; bottle of beer, $1–$1.50; sandwich, $2–$3.

The Costa Rican currency, the colón (plural: colones), is subject to continual, small devaluations. At this writing, the colón is 497 to the U.S. dollar, 602 to the Euro, 425 to the Canadian dollar, 877 to the pound sterling, 376 to the Australian dollar, and 345 to the New Zealand dollar.

Substantially reduced fees are almost always available for children and students.

FREQUENTLY USED CONVERSIONS

In most cases we've rounded to the nearest dollar or euro.

COLONES	U.S. DOLLARS	EUROS
100	20¢	17¢
500	$1	83¢
1,000	$2	€2
5,000	$10	€8
10,000	$20	€17
25,000	$50	€42

ATMS & BANKS

Lines at San José banks would try the patience of a saint; instead, get your spending money at a *cajero automático* (ATM). If you do use the bank, remember that Mondays, Fridays, and the first and last days of the month are the busiest days.

Although they are springing up at a healthy rate, don't count on using an ATM outside of San José. While not exhaustive, the A Todas Horas (ATH) company Web site lists locations of its cash machines, and notes which ones offer colones, dollars, or both; click on *búsqueda de cajeros* to see the lists by region.

All ATMs are 24-hour; in addition to banks, you'll find them in major grocery stores, some hotels, gas stations, and even a few McDonald's. ATH, Red Total, and Scotiabank machines supposedly accept both Cirrus (a partner with MasterCard) and Plus (a partner with Visa) cards, but often don't. If you'll be spending time away from major tourist centers, particularly in the Caribbean, get most or all of the cash you need in San José and carry a few U.S. dollars in case you run out of colones. It's helpful to have both a Visa and a MasterCard—even in San José—as many machines accept only one or the other. Both companies have sites with fairly comprehensive lists of accessible ATMs around the world (*see below*).

ATMs are sometimes out of order and sometimes run out of cash on weekends.

■ TIP→ PIN numbers with more than four digits are not recognized at some ATMs in Costa Rica, such as those at Banco Nacional or Banco de Costa Rica. If you have a five-digit PIN, change it with your bank before

you travel, or use only cash machines marked ATH.

In San José the main Banco Popular, which accepts Plus cards, is at Avda. 2 and C. 1, near the National Theater. The Credomatic office, housed in the Banco de San José central offices on C. Central between Avdas. 3 and 5, is the local representative for most major credit cards; get cash advances there, or at any bank (Banco Nacional and Banco San José are good for MasterCard; Banex, Banco Popular, and Banco Cuscatlan always accept Visa).

State banks are open weekdays 9–5, and some are open Saturday morning. Several branches of Banco Nacional are open until 6, or occasionally 7. Private banks—Scotiabank, Banco Banex, and Banco de San José—tend to keep longer hours and are usually the best places to change U.S. dollars and traveler's checks. The Banco de San José in Juan Santamaría International Airport is open every day 5 AM–10 PM.

Though it might seem counterintuitive, ■ TIP➔ **whenever possible, use ATMs only during bank business hours.** ATMs here have been known to "eat" cards, and are frequently out of cash. When the bank is open, you can go in to retrieve your card or get cash from a teller. As a safety precaution, look for a machine in a bank with a guard nearby.

🔢 Resources **A Todas Horas (ATH)** ⊕ www.ath.fi. cr. **MasterCard** ⊕ www.mastercard.com/atmlocator/ index.jsp. **Visa** ⊕ www.visalatam.com/e_index.jsp.

CREDIT CARDS

All major credit cards (except Discover) are accepted at most major hotels and restaurants in this book. As the phone system improves and expands, many budget hotels, restaurants, and other properties have begun to accept plastic; but plenty of properties still require payment in cash. Don't count on using your credit card outside of San José. ■ TIP➔ **Carry enough cash to patronize the many businesses without credit-card capability.** Note that some hotels, restaurants, tour companies, and other businesses add a surcharge (around 5%) to the bill if you pay with a credit card, or give you a 5%–10% discount if you pay in cash. It's always a good idea to pay for large purchase with a major credit card if possible, so you can cancel payment or get reimbursed if there's a problem.

At this writing, Costa Rica does not have the technology to accept the prepaid American Express card.

Throughout this guide, the following abbreviations are used: **AE**, American Express; **DC**, Diners Club; **MC**, MasterCard; and **V**, Visa.

CURRENCY EXCHANGE

All non-U.S. currency must be exchanged in banks; Australian and New Zealand dollars cannot be exchanged anywhere, even in banks.

Although ATM transaction fees may be higher here than at home, ATM rates are excellent because they're based on wholesale rates offered only by major banks. You won't do as well at exchange booths in airports, in hotels, in restaurants, or in stores.

Costa Rican colones are sold abroad at terrible rates, so you should wait until you arrive in Costa Rica to get local currency. Residents of Australia, Canada, New Zealand, and the U.K. should bring U.S. dollars to exchange. Private banks—Scotiabank, Banco Banex, and Banco de San José—are the best places to change U.S. dollars and traveler's checks. There is a branch of the Banco de San José in the airport (open daily 5 AM–10 PM) where you can exchange money when you arrive—it's a much better deal than the Global Exchange counter. Taxi and van drivers who pick up at the airport accept U.S. dollars.

Avoid people on the city streets who offer to change money. San José's outdoor money changers are notorious for shortchanging people and passing counterfeit bills.

🔢 Exchange Services **International Currency Express** 🕿 888/278-6628 orders ⊕ www. foreignmoney.com. **Travel Ex Currency Services** 🕿 800/287-7362 orders and retail locations ⊕ www.travelex.com.

TAXES

All Costa Rican businesses charge a 13% sales tax. Hotels charge a 16.4% fee covering service and tax. Restaurants add 13% tax and 10% service fee to meals. Tourists are not refunded for taxes paid in Costa Rica.

TIPPING

Costa Rica doesn't have a tipping culture, but positive reinforcement goes a long way to fostering a culture of good service, which is hit and miss. Tip only for good service. Taxi drivers aren't tipped, but it's common courtesy to leave an extra 200–300 colones if they've helped you navigate a complicated set of directions. ■ TIP→ **Do not use U.S. coins to tip, because there is no way for locals to exchange them.**

Chambermaids get 1,000–1,500 colones per day; for great service try to leave up to 10% of your room bill. Concierges are usually not tipped. Room-service waiters should be tipped about 500 colones, as should bellhops (more in the most expensive hotels).

Restaurant bills include a 13% tax and 10% service charge—sometimes these amounts are included in prices on the menu, and sometimes they aren't. If the menu doesn't indicate whether service is included, ask. An additional gratuity is not expected, especially in cheap restaurants, but people often leave something extra when service is good. Leave a tip of about 200 colones per drink for bartenders, too.

At some point on a trip, most visitors to Costa Rica are in the care of a naturalist guide, who can show them the sloths and special hiking trails they'd never find on their own. Give $10 (or 5,000 colones) per day per person to guides if they've transported and guided you individually or in small groups, and about 10% of the rental to a hired driver of a small car. Give less to guides or drivers on bigger tours. For tour guides, it's okay to pay with U.S. dollars.

TRAVELER'S CHECKS

Vendors and tour operators are becoming more familiar with traveler's checks, and usually accept them; for security, it's a good idea to bring some money in this form. If you have an American Express card and can draw on a U.S. checking ac-

count, you can buy U.S.-dollar traveler's checks at the American Express office in San José for a 1% service charge.

PACKING

Travel light, and make sure you can carry your luggage without assistance. Even if you're planning to stay only in luxury resorts, odds are at least once you'll have to haul your stuff a distance from bus stops, the shuttle drop-off, or the airport. Another incentive to pack light: domestic airlines have tight weight restrictions (at this writing 25–30 pounds [11.3 to 13 kilograms]) and not all buses have luggage compartments.

It's a good idea to ■ TIP→ **pack essentials in one bag and extras in another, so you can leave one bag at your hotel in San José (most hotels allow this if you are staying with them again before your departure flight) or with NatureAir (⇨ Air Travel) if you exceed weight restrictions.** Frameless backpacks and duffel bags can be squeezed into tight spaces and are less conspicuous than fancier luggage.

Bring comfortable, hand-washable clothing. T-shirts and shorts are acceptable near the beach and in tourist areas; long-sleeve shirts and pants protect your skin from ferocious sun and, in some regions, mosquitoes. Leave your jeans behind—they take forever to dry and can't be worn out in the evenings. Pack a waterproof, lightweight jacket and a light sweater for cool nights, early mornings, and trips up volcanoes; you'll need even warmer clothes for trips to Chirripó National Park or Cerro de la Muerte and overnight stays in San Gerardo de Dota or on the slopes of Poás Volcano. Bring at least one good (and wrinkle-free) outfit for going out at night.

Women might have a tough time finding tampons, so bring your own. For almost all toiletries, including contact lens supplies, a pharmacy is your best bet. Don't forget sunblock, and expect to sweat it off and reapply regularly in the high humidity. Definitely bring sufficient film and batteries, since they're extremely expensive here.

Snorkelers staying at budget hotels should consider bringing their own equipment;

otherwise, you can rent gear at most beach resorts.

In your carry-on luggage, pack an extra pair of eyeglasses or contact lenses and enough of any medication you take to last a few days longer than the entire trip. You may also ask your doctor to write a spare prescription using the drug's generic name, as brand names may vary from country to country. In luggage to be checked, **never pack prescription drugs, valuables, or undeveloped film.** And don't forget to carry with you the addresses of offices that handle refunds of lost traveler's checks. Check *Fodor's How to Pack* (available at online retailers and bookstores everywhere) for more tips.

To avoid customs and security delays, carry medications in their original packaging. Don't pack any sharp objects in your carry-on luggage, including knives of any size or material, scissors, nail clippers, and corkscrews, or anything else that might arouse suspicion.

To avoid having your checked luggage chosen for hand inspection, don't cram bags full. The U.S. Transportation Security Administration suggests packing shoes on top and placing personal items you don't want touched in clear plastic bags.

Check *Fodor's How to Pack* (available at online retailers and bookstores everywhere) for more tips.

PACKING FOR ADVENTURE

You have to get down and dirty—well, more like wet and muddy—to see many of the country's natural wonders. This packing list is not comprehensive; instead, it's a guide to some of the things you might not think to bring. For your main piece of luggage, a sturdy internal-frame backpack is great, but a duffel bag works, too. You can get by with a rolling suitcase, but then bring a smaller backpack as well.

- Quick-drying synthetic-fiber shirts and socks

- Hiking boots or shoes that can get muddy and wet

- Waterproof sport sandals (especially in the Osa Peninsula, where most transportation is by boat, and often there are no docks)

- Knee-high socks for the rubber boots that are supplied at many lodges

- A pair of lightweight pants (fire ants, mosquitoes, and other pests make covering yourself a necessity on deep-forest hikes)

- Pants for horseback riding (if that's on your itinerary)

- Waterproof, lightweight jacket, windbreaker, or poncho

- Day pack for hikes

- Sweater for cool nights and early mornings

- Swimsuit

- Insect repellant (with DEET, for forested areas and especially on the Caribbean coast, where there are pockets of malaria)

- Flashlight with spare batteries (for occasional power outages or inadequately lighted walkways at lodges)

- Sunscreen with a minimum of SPF 30 (waterproof sunscreens are best; even if you're not swimming, you might be swimming in perspiration)

- Large, portable water bottle

- Hat and/or bandannas (not only do they provide shade, but they prevent perspiration from dripping down your face)

- Binoculars (with carrying strap)

- Camera (waterproof, or with a waterproof case or dry bag, sold in outdoor shops)

- Film (film in Costa Rica can be expired and is expensive)

- Imodium and Pepto-Bismol (tablet form is best)

- Swiss Army knife (and remember to pack it in your *checked* luggage, never your carry-on—even on domestic flights in Costa Rica)

- Zip-lock bags (they always come in handy)

- Travel alarm clock or watch with an alarm (don't count on wake-up calls)

- Nonelectric shaving utensils

- Toilet paper (rarely provided in public bathrooms)

PASSPORTS & VISAS

Canadians, U.S. citizens, and citizens of the U.K. need only a passport to enter Costa Rica for stays of up to 90 days. Make sure it's up-to-date—you'll be refused entry if the passport is due to expire in less than six months. You are presented with a 30-day tourist visa when you arrive. Once you're here, you can go to the *Migración* office in La Uruca and extend the visa to 90 days. In practice, dealing with local immigration is frustrating and time-consuming. It's easier and more fun to spend a weekend in Nicaragua or Panama—but don't expect to do that undetected more than a couple of times.

Due to high rates of passport theft, travelers in Costa Rica are no longer required to carry their original documents with them at all times, although you must have easy access to them. Photocopies of the data page and your entry stamp are sufficient.

■ TIP→ **For easy retrieval in the event of a lost or stolen passport, before you leave scan your passport into a portable storage device (like an iPod) that you're carrying with you or e-mail the scanned image to yourself.**

LOST PASSPORTS

If your passport is lost or stolen, first call the police—having the police report can make replacement easier—and then call your embassy (⇨ Emergencies, *above*). Australians and New Zealanders can get assistance at the U.K. embassy; the Canadian embassy is also an option for Australians. You'll get a temporary Emergency Travel Document that will need to be replaced once you return home. Fees vary according to how fast you need the passport; in some cases the fee covers your permanent replacement as well. The new document will not have your entry stamps; ask if your embassy takes care of this, or whether it's your responsibility to get the necessary immigration authorization.

U.S. Citizens **National Passport Information Center** ☎ 877/487-2778, 888/874-7793 TDD/TTY ⊕ travel.state.gov.

RESTROOMS

Toilet paper is not discarded into the toilet in Costa Rica, but rather in a trash bin beside it. Septic systems are delicate and the paper will clog the toilet. At some public restrooms you might have to pay 50¢ or so for a few sheets of toilet paper. At others, there may not be any toilet paper. It's always a good idea to have some tissues at the ready.

SAFETY

Violent crime is not a serious problem in Costa Rica, but thieves can easily prey on tourists, so be alert. Crimes against property are rife in San José. In rural areas theft is on the rise. For many English-speaking tourists, standing out like a sore thumb can't be avoided in Costa Rica. But there are some precautions you can take:

- Don't bring anything you can't stand to lose.

- Don't wear expensive jewelry or watches.

- In cities, don't carry expensive cameras or lots of cash.

- Carry backpacks on your front; thieves can slit your backpack and run away with its contents before you notice.

- Don't wear a waist pack, because thieves can cut the strap.

- Distribute your cash and any valuables (including credit cards and passport) among a deep front pocket, an inside jacket or vest pocket, and a hidden money belt. (If you use a money belt, carry some cash in your purse or wallet so you don't have to reach for the hidden pouch in public.)

- Keep your hand on your wallet if you are in a crowd or on a crowded bus.

- Don't let your purse just dangle from your shoulder; always hold on to it with your hand for added security. If you cross the strap over your body, you run the risk of being dragged with your bag if you're mugged.

- Keep car windows rolled up and car doors locked at all times in cities; elsewhere, roll up windows and lock doors whenever you leave your car.

- Park in designated parking lots, or if that's not possible, accept the offer of the *guachimán* (a term adopted from English, pronounced "watchie man")— men or boys who watch your car while you're gone. Give them the equivalent of a dollar per hour when you return.

- Never leave valuables visible in a car, even in an attended parking lot: take them inside with you whenever possible, or lock them in the trunk.

- Padlock your luggage.

- Talk with locals or your hotel staff about crime in the area. They will be able to tell you if it's safe to walk around after dark and what to avoid.

- Never walk in a narrow space between a building and a car parked on the street close to it; a prime hiding spot for thieves.

- Do not walk in parks at night.

- Men should be suspicious of overly friendly or sexually aggressive females. At best they are probably prostitutes; at worst they have targeted you for a scam.

- Never leave a drink unattended in a club or bar: scams involving date-rape drugs have been reported in the past few years, targeting both men and women.

- Never leave your belongings unattended anywhere, including at the beach or in a tent.

- If your hotel room has a safe, use it, even if it's an extra charge. If your room doesn't have one, ask the manager to put your valuables in the hotel safe and ask him or her to sign a list of what you are storing there.

- If you are involved in an altercation with a mugger, immediately surrender your possessions and walk away quickly.

If the worst happens, at the risk of sounding cynical, we wouldn't recommend making a police report, unless your passport was stolen. You'll wait hours for an English-speaking officer, hours to give your statement, and probably the rest of your life to ever see justice done. Call your credit-card company using the numbers we provide (⇨ Credit Cards *in* Money Matters).

LOCAL SCAMS

Scams are common in San José, where a drug addict may tell tales of having recently been robbed, then ask you for donations; a distraction artist might squirt you with something, or spill something on you, then try to clean you off while his partner steals your backpack; pickpockets and bag slashers work buses and crowds; and street money changers pass off counterfeit bills. To top it all off, car theft is rampant. Beware of anyone who seems overly friendly, aggressively helpful, or disrespectful of your personal space.

Don't believe taxi drivers when they say the hotel is closed, unless you've personally gotten out and checked it yourself. Many want to take you somewhere else to earn a commission. If a taxi driver says he does not have change and the amount is substantial, ask him to drive to a store or gas station where you can get change. This might be enough to prompt him to suddenly "find" the difference to give you. Avoid paying with large bills to prevent this.

A number of tourists have been hit with the slashed-tire scam: someone punctures the tires of your rental car (often right at the airport, when you arrive) and then comes to your "aid" when you pull off to the side of the road and robs you blind. Forget about the rims: always drive to the nearest open gas station or service center if you get a flat.

TIPS FOR WOMEN TRAVELERS

Lone women travelers will get a fair amount of attention from men, but in general should be safe. Women should not hitchhike alone or in pairs. Blondes and redheads will get more grief than brunettes. To avoid hassles, avoid wearing short shorts, short skirts, or sleeveless tops. On the bus, try to take a seat next to a woman. Women should not walk alone in San José at night or venture into dangerous areas of the city at all. Ask at your hotel which neighborhoods to avoid. Ignore unwanted comments. If you are being harassed on a bus, at a restaurant, or in some other public place, tell the manager. In taxis, sit in the back seat. If you want to fend off an earnest but decent admirer in a bar, you can politely say *"Por favor, necesito un tiempo a solas."* (I'd like some time on my own, please.) Stronger is *"Por favor, no moleste."* (Please stop bothering me.), and for real pests the simple *"Váyase!"* (Go away!) is usually effective. Costa Rican men often fancy themselves Latin lovers and profess adoration before the first drink has even arrived; they lean toward machismo and can be persistent, even overaggressive.

TAXIS

Your hotel can usually call you a reputable taxi or private car service, and when you're out to dinner or on the town, the restaurant or disco can just as easily call you a cab—it's much easier than trying to hail one on the street in the wee hours, and safer, too.

■ TIP➔ Taxi drivers are infamous for "not having change." If it's just a few hundred colones, it's probably not worth your time. If it's a lot, ask them to drive to a store or gas station where you can make change. They'll often miraculously come up with the difference, or wait patiently while you get it. To avoid this situation, never use a 10,000-colón bill in a taxi, and avoid paying with 5,000-colón bills unless you've run up almost that much in fares.

It's illegal, but taxis charge up to double

for hotel pickups or fares that take them out of the province (such as San José to Alajuela or vice versa). Ask the manager at your hotel about the going rate for the destination to which you're heading. Drivers have a fairly standard list of both legal and illegal fares.

TELEPHONES

The country code for Costa Rica is 506. Local telephone numbers have seven digits. The Costa Rican phone system is very good by the standards of other developing countries. However, phone numbers change often and are handed out willy-nilly.

Domestic and international calls (aside from those to an operator) from almost all public phones require phone cards (⇨ *below*). Coin-operated phones exist, but are scarce.

CALLING WITHIN COSTA RICA

You can make local calls from any phone with a domestic calling card (⇨ Phone Cards, *below*). First dial 197, then the PIN on the back of your card (revealed after scratching off a protective coating), then the phone number. Some phones have a card reader on the right-hand side; swiping the card through once you've dialed 197 saves tedious keying, but the readers are hit-and-miss. There are no area codes in Costa Rica, so you only need dial a seven-digit number; without the 506 country code. Fewer and farther between are the gray coin-operated phones; posted on each are the coins accepted (it varies from phone to phone).

Dial 113 for domestic directory inquiries and ☎ 110 for domestic collect calls, usually your only option if you don't have a phone card.

CALLING OUTSIDE COSTA RICA

The cheapest way to call internationally is to call from a pay phone using an international phone card (⇨ Phone Cards, *below*); you can also call from a pay phone using your own long-distance calling card; or call from a telephone office. Dialing directly from a hotel room is very expensive, as is recruiting an international operator to connect you. ⚠ WATCH OUT FOR

PAY PHONES MARKED CALL USA/CANADA WITH A CREDIT CARD. THEY ARE *WILDLY* EXPENSIVE.

To call overseas directly, dial 00, then the country code, the area code, and the number. You can make international calls from almost any phone with an international calling card purchased in Costa Rica. First dial 199, then the PIN on the back of your card (revealed after scratching off a protective coating), then dial the phone number as you would a direct long-distance call.

When requesting a calling card from your phone provider, ask specifically about calls from Costa Rica. Most 800-number cards don't work in Costa Rica. Callingcards. com is a great resource for prepaid international calling cards. At this writing, it lists at least one calling-card company with rates of 1¢ per minute for calls to the U.S.

You may find the local access number blocked in many hotel rooms. First ask the hotel operator to connect you. If the hotel operator balks, ask for an international operator, or dial the international operator yourself. To reach an English-speaking operator, you'll have more luck dialing the international operator (☎ 175 or 116). One way to improve your odds of getting connected to your long-distance carrier is to sign up with more than one company: a hotel may block Sprint, for example, but not MCI. If all else fails, call from a pay phone.

AT&T, MCI, and Sprint access codes make calling long-distance relatively convenient but can be very expensive.

To make a collect call from any phone, dial 09 (instead of 00 for a regular call), the country code for the country you're calling, and then the number.

Calls to the United States and Canada are 27¢ per minute; calls to the United Kingdom, Australia, and New Zealand are 52¢) per minute.

CALLING HOME: COUNTRY CODES	
Australia	61
Canada	001
New Zealand	64
United Kingdom	44
United States	001

☒ Access Codes **AT&T Direct** ☎ 0800/011-4114. **British Telecom** ☎ 0800/044-1044. **Canada Direct** ☎ 0800/015-1161. **MCI WorldPhone** ☎ 0800/012-2222. **Sprint International Access** ☎ 0800/013-0123. ☒ Telephone Resources **Callingcards.com** ⊕ www.callingcards.com. **International information** ☎ 124. **International operator** ☎ 175 or 116.

CELL PHONES

If your cell phone or pager company has service to Costa Rica, you theoretically can use it here, but expect reception to be impossible in many areas of this mountainous country.

Most car-rental agencies have good deals on cell phones, often better than the companies that specialize in cell-phone rental. If you're not renting a car, a number of companies will rent TDMA or GSM phones; remember, coverage is spotty. Rates range from $7–$10 per day, plus varying rates for local or international coverage and minimum usage charges. You'll need your ID, a credit card, and a deposit, which varies per phone and service but averages $350–$400; some rent only to those over 21. The deposit then drops significantly with companies that can hook you up with a rented local chip for your own phone.

Brusque but professional, Cell Phones Costa Rica will get you hooked up, whether you fly into San José or Liberia. Cellular Telephone Rentals Costa Rica has higher daily rates but free local calls.

☒ Cellular Phone Rentals **Cell Phones Costa Rica** ☎ 877/268-2918 in U.S. and Canada, 506/293-5892 in Costa Rica ⊕ www.cellularphonescr.com. **Cellular Telephone Rentals Costa Rica** ☎ 800/769-7137 in the U.S., 506/845-4427 in Costa Rica ⊕ www. cellulartelephonerentals.com.

PHONE CARDS

Most public phones require phone cards (for local or international calls), but phone cards can also be used from any nonrotary telephone in Costa Rica, including residential phones, cell phones, and hotel phones. It's rare to be charged a per-minute rate for the mere use of the phone in a hotel.

Phone cards are sold in an array of shops, including Más X Menos supermarkets, post offices, offices of the Costa Rican

Electricity Institute (ICE), and at any business displaying the gold-and-blue TARJETAS TELEFÓNICAS sign. International cards tend to be easier to find in downtown San José and in tourism areas.

With *tarjetas para llamadas nacionales* (domestic calling cards), cards are available in denominations of 500 colones and 1,000 colones. Phone-card rates are standard throughout the country, about 2¢ per minute; a 500-colón card provides about 50 minutes of landline calls. This decreases sharply if calling a cell phone; rates vary. *Tarjetas para llamadas internacionales* (international calling cards) are sold in $10, $20, 3,000-colón, and 10,000-colón amounts (denominations are inexplicably split between dollars and colones). It's harder to find the 10,000-colón cards; your best bet is to try a Fischel pharmacy or an ICE office.

Some public phones accept *tarjetas chip* ("chip" cards), which record what you spend, though they're a dying breed. ■ TIP➡ **Avoid buying chip cards: they malfunction, you can use them only at the few-and-far-between chip phones, and they are sold in small denominations that are not sufficient for international calls.**

TIME
Costa Rica does not observe daylight saving time, so from November to April it's six hours behind GMT, the equivalent of Central Time in the U.S. (one hour behind New York). The rest of the year, it is seven hours behind GMT, the equivalent of Mountain Time in the U.S. (two hours behind New York).

TOURS & PACKAGES
Because everything is prearranged on a prepackaged tour or independent vacation, you spend less time planning—and often get it all at a good price.

As Costa Rica's tourism community becomes more Web-savvy, more and more travelers to the country are booking their own trips. But getting a package tour—some of which can be custom-organized to fit what you want to do and can be private, with just you and your companions—is an easier, quicker way to go. You can also benefit from the experience of the tour company, which (theoretically) knows the best local guides, hotels, and outfitters, and provides one convenient point person to answer all of your questions. Travel agents are another quick and easy option (⇨ Travel Agencies).

The best Costa Rican packages are with companies that combine sun and sand with nature and adventure, and do it all responsibly. For ecotour companies and tips on choosing a sustainable eco-vacation, *see* the Ecotourism Costa Rica–Style chapter. Several major international and specialty-tour package companies sell Costa Rica all-inclusive and custom itineraries direct.

■ TIP➡ **Some of the best general package-tour companies are ecotour specialists. For information on these companies, *see* Ecotours, *below.*** Costa Rica Expeditions has built a rock-solid reputation for adventure tours, and books Abercrombie & Kent packages for travelers from the U.S. Horizontes is an industry leader known for its excellent service and sophisticated, educational, hiking-pace nature immersions; it handles the U.K. and Australian Abercrombie & Kent bookings. Swiss Travel works primarily with cruise ships, and is the best equipped for large groups. TAM Travel is another longtime Costa Rican agency that organizes excellent independent traveler vacations. Budget-minded travelers who don't mind groups of 30 to 40 people will find reliable Caravan the most accessible.

Conservationists, particularly those into bird-watching, should check out Costa Rica Sun Tours: the founding Aspinall family is renowned in Costa Rica for long-term efforts to preserve the country's wild spaces. U.S.-based companies include Nature Expeditions International, which runs upscale trips to Costa Rica year-round, with flexible dates and itineraries tailored but not limited to travelers 40 and over. Austin-Lehman Adventures provides mid- to upscale adventure and family packages focused on sustainable tourism; its Costa Rica Family Adventure is designed for families with children ages 5 and up. Canada-based Butterfield & Robinson flies you to the most luxurious hotels on its high-end nature package tour.

Unless they are specifically marked as private tours, you will be included in a larger group. Ideally you won't want to be sharing the rain forest with more than 12 people at a time.

BOOKING WITH AN AGENT

Travel agents are excellent resources. But it's a good idea to collect brochures from several agencies, as some agents' suggestions may be influenced by relationships with tour and package firms that reward them for volume sales. If you have a special interest, find an agent with expertise in that area. The American Society of Travel Agents (ASTA) has a database of specialists worldwide; you can log on to the group's Web site to find one near you.

Make sure your travel agent knows the accommodations and other services of the place being recommended. Ask about the hotel's location, room size, beds, and whether it has a pool, room service, or programs for children, if you care about these. Has your agent been there in person or sent others whom you can contact?

Do some homework on your own, too: local tourism boards can provide information about lesser-known and small-niche operators, some of which may sell only direct.

🖪 Recommended Package-Tour Companies **Abercrombie & Kent** ☎ 800/554−7094 in the U.S. 630/954−2944 direct ⊕ www.abercrombiekent.com. **Austin-Lehman Adventures** ☎ 800/575−1540 in the U.S. and Canada, 406/655−4591 worldwide ⊕ www.austinlehman.com. **Butterfield & Robinson** ☎ 800/678−1147 in North America or 416/864−1354 ⊕ www.butterfield.com. **Caravan** ☎ 800/227−2826 or 312/321−9800 in the U.S. ⊕ www.caravantours.com. **Costa Rica Expeditions** ☎ 506/257−0766 ⊕ www.costaricaexpeditions.com. **Costa Rica Sun Tours** ☎ 506/296−7757 in Costa Rica ⊕ www.crsuntours.com. **Nature Expeditions International** ☎ 800/869−0639 in the U.S. or 954/693−8852 ⊕ www.naturexp.com. **Swiss Travel** ☎ 506/282−4898 ⊕ www.swisstravelcr.com. **TAM Travel** ☎ 506/256−0203 ⊕ www.tamtravel.com.

BUYER BEWARE

Each year consumers are stranded or lose their money when tour operators—even

large ones with excellent reputations—go out of business. So check out the operator. Ask several travel agents about its reputation, and try to **book with a company that has a consumer-protection program.** (Look for information in the company's brochure.) In the United States, members of the United States Tour Operators Association are required to set aside funds (up to $1 million) to help eligible customers cover payments and travel arrangements in the event that the company defaults. It's also a good idea to choose a company that participates in the American Society of Travel Agents' Tour Operator Program; ASTA will act as mediator in any disputes between you and your tour operator.

Remember that the more your package or tour includes, the better you can predict the ultimate cost of your vacation. Make sure you know exactly what is covered, and beware of hidden costs. Are taxes, tips, and transfers included? Entertainment and excursions? These can add up.

🖪 Tour-Operator Recommendations **American Society of Travel Agents** (⇨ Travel Agencies). **CrossSphere−The Global Association for Packaged Travel** ☎ 859/226−4444 or 800/682−8886 ⊕ www.CrossSphere.com. **United States Tour Operators Association** (USTOA) ☎ 212/599−6599 ⊕ www.ustoa.com.

BIKING TOURS

Costa Rica is mountainous and rough around the edges. It's a rare bird that attempts a road-biking tour here. But the payoff for the ungroomed, tire-munching terrain is uncrowded, wildly beautiful off-road routes. Most bike-tour operators want to make sure you're in moderately good shape and do some biking at home. Others, such as Coast-to-Coast, have easier two-day jaunts. Veteran rider Norman List offers a Volcano tour for mid- to upper-level riders that's mainly BYOB (Bring Your Own Bike), although a handful of rentals are available. Knowledgeable Kevin Hill at BiCostaRica runs top-notch tours, and will also help set up rides for people who want to go it alone. Lava Tours offers great technical and downhill riding. Operators generally provide top-notch equipment, including bikes, helmets, water bottles, and so forth, but welcome serious bikers who bring their own ride. Leave the hybrids at home—this is mountain-biking territory. Operators usually meet you at the airport and take care of all logistics. All companies can design custom tours for extreme cyclists if requested.

The red-clay trails around Lake Arenal in the Northern Zone are a popular draw for tour groups, but become impassible rivers of mud when it rains. The rolling hills, valley views, and proximity to San José make the Orosí Valley a favorite for more Sunday-style riders. If you're hardcore, look into Jungle Man Adventures' Pacific-to-Caribbean journey that takes about a week, following the infamous *Ruta de los Conquistadores* (Route of the Conquistadors), along which a gruelling three-day race takes place each year.

Topographical maps (not biking maps per se) are generally provided as part of the tour, and include unpaved roads that are often perfect for mountain biking. If you're striking out on your own, these maps can usually be found at the San José bookstore Lehmann for about $3. Some basic Spanish is highly recommended if you're going to do it yourself—your chances of finding an English speaker on the jungle trail are limited.

Airlines do have policies on bikes, but veterans say it really comes down to whom you talk to—call twice, get names and details, and have them handy when you check in. Most airlines accommodate bikes as luggage, provided they are dismantled and boxed. ■ TIP→ **Check with individual airlines about packing requirements and blackouts—more than one eager tour participant has been turned away because of high-season bike bans.** Some airlines sell bike boxes, also sold at bike shops, for about $15. International travelers often can substitute a bike for a piece of checked luggage at no charge (if the box conforms to regular baggage dimensions); otherwise, U.S. and Canadian airlines charge $100–$200 each way.

🄵 Operators **BiCosta Rica** 🚲🚲 506/446–7585 or 380-3844 ⊕ www.bruncas.com/bicostarica.html. **Coast to Coast Adventures** ☎ 506/280-8054

⊕ www.ctocadventures.com. **Jungle Man Adventures** ☎ 506/225-7306 ⊕ www.adventurerace.com. **Lava Tours** ☎ 506/278-2558, 888/862-2424 in the U.S. and Canada ⊕ www.lava-tours.com. **Norman List** ☎ 506/692-2062 or 391-4892 ⊕ www.rockriverlodge.com.

🄵 Bike Maps **Lehmann** ⊠ Avda. Central, between Cs. 1 and 3, San José ☎ 223-1212.

BIRD-WATCHING TOURS

You will almost definitely get more out of your time in Costa Rica by taking a tour rather than trying to find birds on your own. Bring your own binoculars but don't worry about a spotting scope; if you go with a tour company that specializes in birding tours, your guide will have one. Expect to see about 300 species during a weeklong tour. Many U.S. travel companies that offer bird-watching tours subcontract with the Costa Rican tour operators listed below. By arranging your tour directly with the Costa Rican companies, you avoid the middleman and save money. Avian Adventures, based out of the U.K., uses local guides.

🄵 Operators **Avian Adventures** ☎ 01384/372-013 ⊕ www.avianadventures.co.uk. **Costa Rica Expeditions** ☎ 506/222-0333. **Horizontes** ☎ 506/222-2022.

DIVING TOURS

Costa Rica's Cocos Island—one of the best dive spots in the world—can be visited only on a 10-day scuba safari on the *Okeanos Aggressor* or *Undersea Hunter*. But Guanacaste, the South Pacific, and to a lesser extent, the Caribbean, offer some respectable underwater adventures. Bill Beard's Costa Rica in the Gulf of Papagayo, Guanacaste, is a diving-tour pioneer and has country-wide options. Diving Safaris, in Playa Hermosa, has trips to dive sites in Guanacaste. In the South Pacific, Costa Rica Adventure Divers in Drake Bay and Quepos arranges five-day trips. In this same area, Caño Island is a good alternative if you can't afford the money or time for Cocos Island, particularly in the rainy season, when dive sites closer to shore are clouded by river runoff.

🄵 **Bill Beard's Costa Rica** ☎ 954/453-5044, 877/853-0538 in the U.S. ⊕ www.billbeardcostarica.

com. **Costa Rica Adventure Divers** ☎ 506/236-5637, 800/317-0333 in the U.S. ⊕ www.costaricadiving.com. **Diving Safaris** ☎ 506/672-0012 ⊕ www.costaricadiving.net. *Okeanos Agressor* ☎ 506/289-2261, 866/653-2667 in the U.S. and Canada ⊕ www.agressor.com. *Undersea Hunter* ☎ 506/228-6613, 800/203-2120 in the U.S. and Canada ⊕ www.underseahunter.com.

FISHING TOURS

If fishing is your primary objective in Costa Rica, you are better off booking a package. During peak season you may not even be able to find a hotel room in the hot fishing area, let alone one of the top boats and skippers. The major fish populations move along the Pacific coast through the year, and tarpon and snook fishing on the Caribbean is subject to the vagaries of seasonal wind and weather, but viable year-round. San José–based Costa Rica Outdoors has been in business since 1995, arranging fishing packages; it is one of the best bets for full service and honest advice about where to go, and works with the widest range of operators around the country. More than 100 outfits have high-quality, regionally based services. Anglers in the know recommend Kingfisher Sportfishing in Playa Carrillo, Guanacaste; J.P. Sportfishing Tours in Quepos; Roy's Zancudo Lodge near Golfito; and Río Colorado Lodge on the northern Caribbean coast. While fishing is hit or miss, when booking a holiday, get it on record from your tour operator that it's the traditional season for the type of fishing you'd like to do.

☛ **Blue Fin Sport Fishing** ☎ 506/777-1676 ⊕ www.bluefinsportfishing.com. **Costa Rica Outdoors** ☎ 506/231-0306, 800/308-3394 in the U.S. ⊕ www.costaricaoutdoors.com. **J.P. Sportfishing Tours** ☎ 506/244-6361, 866/620-4188 in the U.S. ⊕ www.jpsportfishing.com. **Kingfisher Sportfishing** ☎ 506/656-0091 ⊕ www.costaricabillfishing.com. **Río Colorado Lodge** ☎ 506/232-4063, 800/243-9777 in the U.S. and Canada ⊕ www.riocoloradolodge.com. **Roy's Zancudo Lodge** ☎ 506/776-0008, 877/529-6980 in the U.S. ⊕ www.royszancudolodge.com.

FLIGHTSEEING

San José–based pilot Jenner Rojas will take you anywhere in Costa Rica for flightseeing and picture taking. The rate is $320 (for up to three people) per hour, with discounts for longer trips. Skyline Nature Ultralight Flying Tours, based in Bahía Ballena on the South Pacific, gives bird's-eye ultralight tours of the area's mangroves and national park; only one passenger per trip. Rides are $150 per hour, but you can also do a $65 20-minute pass over the mangroves. Macaw Air sends people into the North-Pacific sunset for $170 (maximum 4 passengers), and has picture-taking trips on the Pacific Coast.

☛ **Jenner Rojas** ☎ 506/385-5425 or 506/296-7241 ✉ bluebird@costarricense.cr. **Macaw Air** ☎ 506/653-1362 ⊕ www.macawair.com. **Skyline Nature Ultralight Flying Tours** ☎ 506/743-8037 ⊕ www.fly-ultralight.com.

HIKING TOURS

Most nature tour companies include hiking as part of their itineraries, but these hikes may be short and not strenuous enough for serious hikers. Let the tour operator know what you expect from a hike. Ask a lot of questions about hike lengths and difficulty levels before booking the tour or you may be disappointed with the amount of time you get to spend on the trails. The following companies cater to both moderate and serious hikers.

☛ **Gap Adventures** ☎ 800/708-7761 in the U.S. and Canada, 0870/999-0141 in the U.K. ⊕ www.gapadventures.com. **Serendipity Adventures** ☎ 877/507-1358 in the U.S. and Canada, 506/558-1000 in Costa Rica ⊕ www.serendipityadventures.com. **The Walking Connection** ☎ 602/978-1887, 800/295-9255 in the U.S. and Canada ⊕ www.walkingconnection.com.

TRAVEL AGENCIES

A good travel agent puts your needs first. Look for an agency that has been in business at least five years, emphasizes customer service, and has someone on staff who specializes in your destination. In addition, **make sure the agency belongs to a professional trade organization.** The American Society of Travel Agents (ASTA) has more than 10,000 members in some 140 countries, enforces a strict code of ethics, and will step in to mediate agent-client disputes involving ASTA members.

ASTA also maintains a directory of agents on its Web site; ASTA's TravelSense.org, a trip planning and travel advice site, can also help to locate a travel agent who caters to your needs. (If a travel agency is also acting as your tour operator, *see* Buyer Beware *in* Tours & Packages.)

Percentage-wise, in Costa Rica do-it-your-selfers are gaining on travel agents in terms of airline-ticket purchases and hotel bookings. But if you want someone else to do the heavy lifting of finding a hotel, arranging reservations with tour operators, etc., consider using a travel agent. Travel agents and planners can often hook you up with guides and operators that know the area inside out, and will help get you to the right place at the right time to see a quetzal or rural cultural event. They also give you a person to call if things go wrong.

■ TIP➔ Travel agents are excellent resources, and if you run into trouble with hotels or operators, you stand a much better chance of getting the situation resolved. It is otherwise very difficult to hold people accountable in Costa Rica. Some local agents confirm at least three times after definitively booking a hotel for a client; legwork that you may not be aware is necessary and probably something you'd rather leave to someone else.

Beware of some bigger agents, who may steer you to tour companies and large hotels that reward them for volume sales. This is less of a concern in smaller, independent agencies. If you have a special interest, find an agent with expertise in that area. While the American Society of Travel Agents (ASTA) has a database of specialists worldwide, most "specialists" list almost every country and kind of tourism available; those who are clearly specialists in Latin America are your best bet. Log on to the group's Web site to find an ASTA travel agent in your neighborhood.

Make sure your travel agent knows the accommodations and other services of the place being recommended—easier said than done in Costa Rica, where even the most renowned hotels can be notoriously inconsistent with their info. Ask about the hotel's location, room size, beds, and whether it has a pool, room service, or programs for children, if important. Has your agent been there in person or sent others whom you can contact? Improved Internet access has nurtured the growth of reputable online, Costa Rica–based tour agencies. Not only are they truly experts in Costa Rica, but they provide welcome in-country assistance should glitches pop up.

Do some homework on your own, too: local rural tourism organizations can provide information about lesser-known and small-niche operators, some of which may sell only directly. Confirm that the agency belongs to a professional trade organization, like ASTA. For more information on precautions to take when choosing a travel agent, *see* Buyer Beware *in* Tours & Packages.

▨ Costa Rica Travel Agents **Lynch Travel** ☎ 506/777-1170 or 506/777-0161 from Costa Rica ⊕ www.lynchtravel.com. **Travel Store** ☎ 506/279-8927 ⊕ www.allcostaricatravel.com. **Intertur** ☎ 800/468-3788, 506/290-0761 in Costa Rica ⊕ www.interturcr.com.

▨ Local Agent Referrals **American Society of Travel Agents (ASTA)** ☎ 703/739-2782 or 800/965-2782 24-hr hotline ⊕ www.astanet.com and www.travelsense.org. **Association of British Travel Agents** ☎ 0901/201-5050 ⊕ www.abta.com. **Association of Canadian Travel Agencies** ☎ 613/237-3657 ⊕ www.acta.ca. **Australian Federation of Travel Agents** ☎ 02/9264-3299 or 1300/363-416 ⊕ www.afta.com.au. **Travel Agents' Association of New Zealand** ☎ 04/499-0104 ⊕ www.taanz.org.nz.

VISITOR INFORMATION

Learn more about foreign destinations by checking government-issued travel advisories and country information. For a broader picture, consider information from more than one country.

The official tourism board, the Instituto Costarricense de Turismo (ICT), has free maps, bus schedules, and brochures. However, these folks could do better with the information they provide. Arrive armed with specific questions and know that they will not recommend hotels. Visitor information is provided by the Costa Rica Tourist Board in Canada and in the United States

▨ Tourist Information **Costa Rican Embassy in the U.K.** ✉ Flat 1, 14 Lancaster Gate, London W2

3LH 🕾 020/7706-8844 ⊕ http://costarica. embassyhomepage.com. **Instituto Costarricense de Turismo** (ICT) 🕾 866/267-8274 in the U.S. and Canada, 506/299-5800 in Costa Rica ⊕ www. visitcostarica.com ✉ Plaza de la Cultura, C. 5, between Avdas Central and 2 🕾 506/222-1090 ✉ Juan Santamaría Airport 🕾 506/443-1535. 🛂 Government Advisories **U.S. Department of State** 🕾 888/407-4747 or 202/501-4444 from overseas ⊕ www.travel.state.gov. **Consular Affairs Bureau of Canada** 🕾 800/267-6788 or 613/944-6788 from overseas ⊕ www.voyage.gc.ca. **U.K. Foreign and Commonwealth Office** 🕾 0845/850-2829 or 020/7008-1500 ⊕ www.fco.gov.uk/travel. **Australian Department of Foreign Affairs and Trade** 🕾 300/139-281 travel advisories, 02/6261-3305 Consular Travel Advice ⊕ www.smartraveller.gov.au. **New Zealand Ministry of Foreign Affairs and Trade** 🕾 04/439-8000 ⊕ www.mft.govt.nz.

VOLUNTEER & EDUCATIONAL TRAVEL

Costa Rica has an abundance of volunteer opportunities for diverse interests. You can tag sea turtles as part of a research project, build trails in a national park, or volunteer at an orphanage. Many of the organizations require at least rudimentary Spanish. Most of the programs for volunteers who don't speak Spanish charge a daily fee for room and board. The Institute for Central American Development Studies (ICADS) is a nonprofit social justice institute that runs a language school and arranges internships and field study (college credit is available); some programs are available only to college students. ICADS places you with local social service organizations, environmental groups, and other organizations, depending on your interests. The Costa Rica Rainforest Outward Bound School offers two adult programs that combine self-exploration with a truly rural learning experience. Mesoamerica, a nonprofit organization devoted to peace and social justice, has three- and six-month newswriting internships for young journalists.
🛂 **Costa Rica Rainforest Outward Bound School** 🕾 506/278-6058, 800/676-2018 in the U.S. ⊕ www.crrobs.org. **Costa Rican Humanitarian Foundation** 🕾 506/390-4192 or 506/282-6358 ⊕ www.crhf.org. **Institute for Central American Development Studies** (ICADS) 🕾 506/225-0508

⊕ www.icadscr.com. **Mesoamerica** 🕾 506/253-3195 ⊕ www.mesoamericaonline.net.

SPANISH-LANGUAGE PROGRAMS

Thousands of people travel to Costa Rica every year to study Spanish. Dozens of schools in and around San José offer professional instruction and home stays, and there are several smaller schools outside the capital. Conversa has schools off Paseo Colón, and in Santa Ana, west of the capital; offering hourly classes as well as a "Super Intense" program (5½ hours per day). On the east side of town, ILISA provides cultural immersion in San Pedro. Mesoamerica is a low-cost language school that is part of a nonprofit organization devoted to peace and social justice. La Escuela D'Amore is in beautiful Manuel Antonio. Arco Iris Spanish School (⇨ Gay & Lesbian Travel) is a unique gay-friendly option. Language programs at the Institute for Central American Development Studies include optional academic seminars in English about Central America's political, social, and economic conditions.
🛂 **Conversa** 🕾 506/221-7649, 800/367-7726 in North America ⊕ www.conversa.net. **ILISA** 🕾 506/280-0700, 800/280-0700 in the U.S. ⊕ www.ilisa.com. **Institute for Central American Development Studies** (ICADS) 🕾 506/225-0508 ⊕ www.icadscr.com. **La Escuela D'Amore** 🕾 506/777-1143, 310/435-9897 in the U.S. ⊕ www.escueladamore.com. **Mesoamerica** 🕾 506/253-3195 ⊕ www.mesoamericaonline.net.

VOLUNTEER PROGRAMS

In recent years more and more Costa Ricans have realized the need to preserve their country's precious biodiversity. Both Ticos and far-flung environmentalists have founded volunteer and educational concerns to this end.

Caribbean Conservation Corporation (CCC) is devoted to the preservation of sea turtles. Earthwatch Institute leads science-based trips studying octopi, turtles, or the rain forest. The Talamancan Association of Ecotourism and Conservation (ATEC), as well as designing short group and individual outings centered on Costa Rican wildlife and indigenous culture, keeps an updated list of up to 30 local organizations that welcome volunteers. Beach cleanups, recycling, and some wildlife projects don't require proficiency in Spanish.

🔲 **Caribbean Conservation Corporation** ☎ 506/297-5510, 352/373-6441 in the U.S. ⊕ www.cccturtle.org. **Earthwatch Institute** ☎ 978/461-0081, 800/776-0188 in the U.S. and Canada, 44/01865-318838 in the U.K., 61/03-9682-6828 in Australia ⊕ www.earthwatch.org. **Talamancan Association of Ecotourism and Conservation (ATEC)** ☎ 506/750-0191 ⊕ www.greencoast.com/atec.htm.

WEB SITES WE LIKE

- We wouldn't be doing our job if we didn't mention Fodors.com (⊕ www.fodors.com), a complete travel-planning site. In addition to researching prices and booking plane tickets, hotel rooms, rental cars, and vacation packages, you can post your pressing questions on the Talk forum and read hotel, restaurant, and sights ratings by fellow travelers. Other planning tools include a currency converter and weather reports, and there are loads of links to travel resources.

- Info Costa Rica (⊕ www.infocostarica.com) has a Web site with maps, photos, news articles, links to local artist sites, and chat rooms.

- For tide info, real estate, news, and travel information, Costa Rica.com (⊕ www.costarica.com) is a good bet.

- For current events, check out the English-language newspaper *The Tico Times* (⊕ www.ticotimes.net).

- Horizontes (⊕ www.horizontes.com) is a tour operator that offers nature vacations but also has extensive general information on its Web site.

- Similar, but slightly less user friendly, is the site by competing nature tour company Costa Rica Expeditions (⊕ www.expeditions.co.cr), which offers ecologically minded trips.

- The U.S. Embassy's comprehensive site (⊕ www.usembassy.or.cr) has health information, travel warnings, links to great sites, and much more.

- The Boomers Abroad Costa Rica page (⊕ www.boomersabroad.com/costarica.html) has links to just about everything you'd want to know about the region.

- The Real Costa Rica (⊕ www.therealcostarica.com) slips in a bit of attitude with its information, but scores high marks for overall accuracy.

INDEX

A

Afro-Caribbean heritage, *403*
AgriTour Pineapple Tour, *373*
Air travel, *445–450*
  Caribbean, *411–412*
  Central Pacific, *305*
  Central Valley, *109*
  North Pacific, *243–244*
  Northern Plains, *166*
  San José , *63*
  South Pacific, *364*
Airports, *449*
Alajuela, *82–89*
Alta ✕ ▦ , *80*
Amimodo ✕ , *404*
Apartments, condos, and villa rentals, *461*
Aquas Termales, *320*
Arco Iris Lodge ▦ , *149*
Arenal Rain Forest Reserve, *140*
Arenal Volcano National Park, *127*
Art galleries, *56*
Atenas, *267–268*
ATMs, *463–464*
ATV Tours, *236, 260, 275, 277*
Azul Profundo, *217*

B

Bahía Salinas, *183*
Bajo del Tigre trail, *145–146*
Bakea ✕ , *45*
Ballena Marine National Park, *331–334*
Balneario, *99*
Banks
  Caribbean, *377, 389, 411, 413*
  Central Pacific, *266, 269, 303*
  Central Valley, *82, 88, 94, 96, 108*
  North Pacific, *187–188, 238, 242, 245*
  Northern Plains, *122, 135, 151, 154, 166–167*
  San José, *64–65*
  South Pacific, *317, 325, 334, 364*
Barba Roja (Bar), *303*
Barra del Colorado, *388–389*
Barra Honda National Park, *240–241*
Barrantes, Victor, *383*
Barva de Heredia, *94*
Barva Volcano, *158–159*

Basilica de Nuestra Señora de los Angeles, *96*
Beaches, *16, 19–22*
  Central Pacific, *256–257, 270–285, 290, 292*
  North Pacific, *170, 180–181, 183, 189–192, 195–234*
  South Pacific, *326, 331–332, 336, 340–345*
Bicycling, *134, 161, 288, 399, 472–473*
Billy's Beach Karolas ✕ , *298–299*
Bird-watching, *16, 473*
  Central Valley, *68, 106–107*
  North Pacific, *228, 239*
  Northern Valley, *144*
  South Pacific, *310, 313–315, 318, 323, 346–347, 358*
Blue Jay Lodge ▦ , *265*
Boat and ferry travel, *196, 199, 206–207, 211–213, 270*
Bosque del Cabo ▦ , *353*
Bosque del Rio Tigre Lodge, *346–347*
Bosque Eterno de los Niños, *145*
Brasilito, *209*
Braulio Carrillo National Park, *17, 157–159*
Bread and Chocolate ✕ , *404–405*
Bungee jumping, *116*
Bus travel, *450–451*
  Caribbean, *412*
  Central Pacific, *305*
  Central Valley, *109*
  North Pacific, *244*
  Northern Plains, *166*
  San José, *63*
  South Pacific, *364–365*
Butterfly Farm, *83, 85*
Butterfly Garden, *402*

C

Cabinas Arenas ▦ , *302*
Cabinas Casa Verde ▦ , *405–406*
Cabinas Ramirez ▦ , *303*
Cabo Blanco Absolute Nature Preserve, *263*
Cabo Matapalo, *352–354*
Cachí, *101*
Café Britt, *91*
Café del Teatro Nacional ✕ , *37*

Café Mundo ✕ , *41*
Café Rainforest ✕ , *125*
Cahuita, *394–398*
Cahuita Butterfly Garden, *395*
Cahuita National Park, *398–400*
Camping, *461–462*
Caño Island Biological Reserve, *361*
Caño Negro National Wildlife Refuge, *152–154*
Caño Negro Wildlife Refuge, *16, 19*
Canoeing, *277*
Canopy tours
  Central Pacific, *264, 271, 277, 283, 288, 296*
  North Pacific, *175, 193, 232*
  Northern Plains, *138–141, 162*
Car travel, *451–455*
  Caribbean, *412–413*
  Central Pacific, *305–306*
  Central Valley, *109*
  North Pacific, *244–245*
  Northern Plains, *166*
  San José, *63–64*
  South Pacific, *365*
Carara Biological Reserve, *16, 268–269*
Carate, *354–355*
Caribbean, *9, 367–413*
  children's activities, *395, 402*
  coastal Talamanca, *389–411*
  contacts and resources, *413*
  ecotourism, *373, 379–382, 402–403, 419–420*
  hotels, *371–372, 384–386, 388–389, 392, 397, 405–407, 410*
  nightlife, *397–398, 407–408*
  North Coast, *377–389*
  Northern Lowlands, *372–377*
  outdoor activities, *370, 376–377, 379–383, 388, 391, 395–396, 399–400, 402–404, 409–410*
  price categories, *371*
  restaurants, *371, 383–384, 392, 396–397, 404–405, 410*
  shopping, *386, 392, 408–409*
  tours and packages, *371, 383, 402–403*
  transportation, *386–387, 411–413*
Caribbean Conservation Corporation (CCC), *379*
Cariblue Hotel ▦ , *405*

Carnaval, *391*
Cartago, *94–95*
Casa Corcovado 🏨 , *356, 362*
Casa del Sonador, *100*
Casa Luisa ✕ , *48*
Casa Marbella 🏨 , *386*
Casa Orquideas, *336–337*
Casa Turire 🏨 , *107–108*
Casinos, *58–59*
Casita Romántica 🏨 , *230*
Catalina Islands, *205*
Cataratas de la Fortuna, *125*
Cataratas de Nauyaca, *326*
Catedral (Alajuela), *83*
Catedral Metropolitana, *28*
Caving, *240–241*
Cell phones, *470*
Cemeteries, *391*
Central Highlands, *312–317*
Central Pacific, *8, 19, 247–306*
  beaches, *256–257, 270–285, 290, 292*
  children's activities, *253, 256, 258–259, 265–266, 272, 279–281, 285, 290, 300–302*
  Coast, *270–304*
  contacts and resources, *306*
  ecotourism, *194, 418–419*
  hotels, *258, 260–262, 265–266, 268, 272–274, 279–281, 284–285, 288–289, 299–303*
  Inland, *266–269*
  nightlife and the arts, *262, 281–282, 289, 303*
  outdoor activities, *248, 250, 256, 259–260, 264, 267, 270–272, 274–279, 283, 286, 288, 294, 296–297*
  price categories, *251*
  restaurants, *252–253, 257–258, 260, 264–265, 267, 272–274, 279, 284, 288, 298–299*
  shopping, *282, 304*
  Southern Nicoya tip, *252–266*
  tours and packages, *251, 296*
  transportation, *305–306*
Central Valley, *7, 67–110*
  children's activities, *81–83, 85, 89*
  ecotourism in, *194*
  hotels, *77–78, 80, 85–90, 93, 107–108*
  nightlife and the arts, *78*
  North of San José, *81–94*
  outdoor activities and sports, *107*
  price categories, *71*

  restaurants, *76–77, 79–80, 85–86, 89–93, 96, 101–103, 107*
  shopping, *78–79, 80*
  transportation, *109–110*
  Turrialba region, *103–109*
  West of San José, *72–81*
Centro Agronómico Tropical de Investigación y Ensenanza, *106*
Centro Nacional de la Cultura, *28–29*
Cerámica Las Palomas, *80*
Cerro de La Muerte, *16*
Cerro de la Muerte, *315*
Cha Cha Chá ✕ , *396*
Chalet Nicholas 🏨 , *133*
Children's activities
  Caribbean, *395, 402*
  Central Pacific, *253, 256, 258–259, 265–266, 272, 279–281, 285, 290, 300–302*
  Central Valley, *81–83, 85, 89*
  North Pacific, *180–181, 193, 202, 207, 213, 217, 224–225, 235–236, 239*
  Northern Plains, *116, 125, 137, 143, 145, 163–164*
  San José, *33, 39–40*
  South Pacific, *317–318, 320–321, 325–329, 332–334, 338, 344, 347–348, 350, 353, 355, 362–364*
Chirripó National Park, *321–322*
Chocolate Tour, *402*
Chorotegan pottery, *241*
Chubascos ✕ , *156*
Church of San Blas, *241*
Church of San Juan Bosco, *125*
Churches
  Central Valley, *83, 91, 96*
  North Pacific, *241*
  Northern Plains, *116, 120–121, 125*
  Orosi Valley, *99*
  San José, *28–29*
Cinco Hormigas Rojas 🏨 , *53–54*
Ciudad Neily, *324*
Ciudad Quesada (San Carlos), *122–123*
Clarion Hotel Amón 🏨 , *52*
Climate, *15, 243*
Cloud forests, *135–136, 319,* ⇨ *Also* Rain forests
Cloudbridge Reserve, *320*
Club del Mar ✕ 🏨 , *279–280*

Cóbano, *256*
Coastal Talamanca, *389–411*
Coffee industry, *12*
  Central Valley, *61, 68, 85, 91–92*
  Northern Plains, *143*
Coope-Tortillas ✕ , *240*
Coral reefs, *399*
Corcovado Lodge Tent Camp 🏨 , *355*
Corcovado National Park, *16–17, 357–361*
Correos de Costa Rica (Post Office), *29, 32*
Costa Flores, *372*
Costa Verde 🏨 , *300*
Crafts, *60–62*
  Caribbean, *408*
  Central Valley, *78, 80*
  South Pacific, *352*
Credit cards, *464*
Cristal Ballena Hotel Resort 🏨 , *333*
Cruises, *390*
Currency exchange, *463–464*
Curú National Wildlife Refuge, *253, 256*
Customs and duties, *455*

D

Desafio Adventures, *127–129, 146*
Discounts and deals, *455–456*
Diving, *21*
Docelunas ✕ 🏨 , *280*
Doka Estate, *85*
Dolphin-watching, *410*
Dominical, *16, 278, 325–331*
Dragonfly Bar & Grill ✕ , *214*
Drake Bay, *356, 362–364*

E

EARTH (Escuela de Agricultura de la Región Tropical Húmeda), *373*
Earthquakes, *39*
Ecocentro Danaus, *125*
Ecotourism, *415–425*
  Caribbean, *373, 379–382, 402–403, 419–420*
  Central Pacific, *194, 418–419*
  Central Valley, *194, 417–418*
  North Pacific, *192–194, 198, 227, 241–242, 418*
  Northern Plains, *121, 125, 143, 145–146, 418*
  South Pacific, *194, 353–354, 357–361, 419*
El Cafetal Inn 🏨 , *268*

El Chorro waterfall, *260*
El Encanto Bed & Breakfast
⌂ , *397*
El Gran Escape ✕ , *288*
El Loco Natural ✕ , *404*
El Mango Moon ⌂ , *301*
El Mundo de la Tortuga, *218*
El Restaurante Jade Luna ✕ ,
348–349
El Sol ⌂ , *149*
El Sol y La Luna ✕ , *200*
Electricity, *456*
Emergencies, *452, 456–457*
Caribbean, 377, 389, 411, 413
Central Pacific, 266, 269, 303
Central Valley, 82, 88–89, 94,
96, 108
North Pacific, 187–188, 238,
242, 245
Northern Plains, 122, 135, 151,
154, 166–167
San José, 65
South Pacific, 317, 325, 334,
364
Escazú, *74–79, 72*
Etiquette and behavior, *457*
Evergreen Lodge ⌂ , *384*
Express services, *462–463*

F

Fábrica de Carretas Chaverri,
120
Festivals, *12–13*
Finca Ecológica, *143,*
145–146
Finca La Isla Botanical
Garden, *402*
Finca Rosa Blanca Country Inn
⌂ , *93*
Fincas Naturales, *290*
Fishing, *335*
Caribbean, 370, 383, 388
Central Pacific, 248, 250, 257,
288
North Pacific, 172, 196, 199,
202, 207, 213, 236
Northern Plains, 128
South Pacific, 310, 327, 332,
337, 340–341, 347, 353
tours, 474
Fonda Vela ✕ ⌂ , *148*
Fortín, *91*

G

Gandoca-Manzanillo National
Wildlife Refuge, *409–410*
Gay and lesbian travel, *57, 59*
Gecko's Restaurant/Bar ✕ ,
209

Giacomín ✕ , *40*
Giardino Tropical Restaurant
Pizzeria ✕ , *229*
Ginger Restaurant Bar ✕ ,
196
Golf, *21, 209, 213*
Golfito, *336–340*
Grecia, *116–117*
Guápiles, *372–373*
Guacamaya Lodge ⌂ , *225*
Guanacaste National Park,
182
Guanacaste Province, ⇨ *See*
Northern Zone
Guayabo National Monument,
106

H

Hacienda Barú, *325–326*
Hacienda Guachipelín ⌂ ,
178
Hacienda La Casona, *180*
Hacienda Pozo Azul, *161*
Hang gliding, *277*
Hanging bridges, *141*
Health, *457–458*
Heliconia Island, *161*
Heredia, *90–94*
Hiking
Caribbean, 399
Central Pacific, 256, 260,
271–272, 288, 292, 296
North Pacific, 175, 180, 202,
241–242
Northern Plains, 145–146,
157–159
South Pacific, 310, 315, 318,
320, 347, 360–361
tours, 474
History of Costa Rica,
430–431
Holidays, ⇨ *See* Festivals and
seasonal events
Home exchanges, *462*
Horseback riding
Central Pacific, 260, 277, 283,
296
North Pacific, 175, 224, 228
Northern Plains, 128–129, 146,
156, 159, 161
South Pacific, 327, 341, 347
Hot springs, *127, 174–175*
Hotel Bougainvillea ✕ ⌂ ,
89–90
Hotel Bula Bula ✕ ⌂ , *219*
Hotel Canciones del Mar ⌂ ,
280
Hotel Casitas Eclipse ⌂ ,
300–301

Hotel Don Carlos ⌂ , *52*
Hotel El Velero ⌂ , *196–197*
Hotel Fleur de Lys ⌂ , *49*
Hotel Giada ⌂ , *234*
Hotel Inn on the Park ⌂ ,
301
Hotel le Bergerac ⌂ , *55*
Hotel Los Almendros ⌂ , *303*
Hotel Manuel Antonio ⌂ ,
303
Hotel Playa Negra ⌂ ,
223–224
Hotel Poseidon Restaurant ✕ ,
279
Hotel Punta Islita ⌂ , *237*
Hotel Punta Leona ⌂ , *273*
Hotel Santo Tomás ⌂ , *52*
Hotel Sí Como No ⌂ , *300*
Hotel Vela Bar Restaurant ✕
⌂ , *299*
Hotel Villa Casa Blanca ⌂ ,
203
Hotel Villa Lapas, *272*
Hotel Villabosque ⌂ , *302*
Hotels, *460–461*
Caribbean, 371–372, 384–386,
388–389, 392, 397, 405–407,
410
Central Pacific, 258, 260–262,
265–266, 268, 272–274,
279–281, 284–285, 288–289,
299–303
Central Valley, 77–78, 80–82,
77–78, 80, 85–90, 93,
107–108
meal plans, 462
North Pacific, 173, 175,
178–182, 184, 186–187, 193,
196–197, 200–201, 203–207,
210, 214–215, 219–221, 223,
225–226, 229–231, 233–234,
236–240, 242
Northern Plains, 115, 117, 121,
123, 127, 130–135, 148–150,
152–153, 156–157, 160,
162–163, 165–166
price categories, 71, 115, 173,
251, 311, 371
South Pacific, 312–313,
315–316, 318–321, 323–324,
328–330, 333–334, 338–339,
341–342, 344, 349–350,
353–356, 362–364

I

Iglesia de la Inmaculada
Concepción, *91*
Iglesia de San Ramón,
120–121

Iglesia de las Mercedas, *116*
Iglesia de San José de Orosi, *99*
Iglesia de Ujarrás, *101*
Iguana Lodge ⊡, *349*
INBioparque, *89*
Inland (Central Pacific), *266–269*
Insurance, *459–460*
Irazú, *18, 96, 103*
Isla Tortuga, *258–259*

J

Jacó, *17, 275–283*
Jardín Botánico Lankester, *98*
Jardín de Mariposas (Monteverde), *145*
Jardín de Mariposas Spyrogyra, *39–40*
Jardín de Orquídeas, *145*
Jazz Café, *57*
John H. Phipps Biological Field Station, *379*

K

Kaltak Artesanías, *61*
Kap's Place ⊡, *51*
Karen Mogensen Fischer Museum, *259*
Kayaking, *129, 211–213, 232, 236, 277, 286, 294, 297, 332, 341, 347–348*
Kitesurfing, *134, 183–184*

L

L'Ile de France ✕, *46*
La Amistad National Park, *325*
La Casona del Cafetal, *100–102*
La Cocina de Leña ✕, *44*
La Cruz, *181–182*
La Fortuna, *18, 123–133*
La Garita, *85*
La Lechería, *145*
La Mariposa ⊡, *300*
La Merced National Wildlife Refuge, *332*
La Negrita festival, *95*
La Paloma Lodge ⊡, *362*
La Paz Waterfall Gardens, *155*
La Pecora Nera ✕, *404*
La Posada ⊡, *302*
La Puesta del Sol ✕, *225*
La Ruta de los Santos, *312*
La Selva Biological Station, *16–17, 164–165*

La Selva Zoo & Bromeliad Garden, *235–236*
La Vela Latina, *235*
Lagarta Lodge ⊡, *230–231*
Laguna del Cocodrilo Bistro ✕, *213–214*
Laguna del Lagarto Lodge ⊡, *123*
Lake Arenal, *133*
Languages, *460, 476*
Lapa Ríos, *353–354*
Las Baulas Marine National Park, *218*
Las Cruces Biological Station, *322*
Las Horquetas, *165*
Las Pumas rescue shelter, *238*
Las Quebradas Biological Center, *317*
Las Ruinas, *95*
Lava tours, *101*
Liberia, *184–188*
Limón, *390–393*
Llanos de Cortés, *238*
Los Cusingos Neotropical Bird Sanctuary, *317*
Los Inocentes Lodge ⊡, *180–181*
Loth, Daryl, *383*
Luluberlu, *408*
Luna Azul ⊡, *230*

M

Más X Menos, *61*
Machu Picchu ✕, *47*
Magellan Inn ✕ ⊡, *397*
Mail and shipping, *462*
Malpaís, *16, 263–266, 278*
Manantial de Agua Viva Waterfall, *270*
Mangrove forests, *319*
Manuel Antonio National Park, *17, 19–20, 290–304*
Maria Bonita Restaurant ✕, *221*
Marie's Restaurant ✕, *207*
Marriage laws, *298*
Marriott Costa Rica Hotel ⊡, *81–82*
Marriott Los Sueños Ocean and Golf Resort ✕ ⊡, *274*
Massage and yoga, *227*
Matapalo, *278*
Mawamba Lodge ⊡, *385*
Mercado Artesania, *339*
Mercado Central (San José), *32*
Mercado Viejo (Heredia), *91*

Moin, *394*
Money, *463–464*
Monkeys, *293*
Montaña de Fuego ⊡, *131*
Monteverde, *143, 145–151, 137*
Monteverde Cloud Forest Biological Reserve, *17, 135–137*
Monteverde Coffee Tour, *143*
Monteverde Lodge ⊡, *148–149*
Montezuma, *259–262*
Mountain biking, *134, 161, 288*
Mundo de las Serpientes, *116*
Museo de Arte Costarricense, *38*
Museo de Arte y Diseño Contemporáneo, *32–33*
Museo de Cultura Popular, *91*
Museo de Culturas Indigenas Doctora María Eugenia Bozzoli, *161*
Museo de Formas, Espacios y Sonidos, *33*
Museo de los Niños, *40*
Museo del Oro Precolombino, *34*
Museo Filatélico, *32*
Museo Juan Santamaría, *83*
Museo Nacional, *34*
Museo para la Paz, *34*
Museums
   Central Pacific, 259
   Central Valley, 83, 91
   Northern Plains, 161
   San José, 23, 32–34, 38, 40

N

National parks, *16, 20–22*
   Caribbean, 380–382, 398–400
   North Pacific, 175–182, 218, 238–242
   Northern Plains, 127, 154–159
   South Pacific, 321–322, 325, 331–334, 336
Nature Lodge Finca los Caballos ⊡, *261*
Necochea Inn ⊡, *330*
Nicaraguan border, *183, 389*
Nicoya coast, *241–242*
Nightlife and the arts
   Caribbean, 397–398, 407–408
   Central Pacific, 262, 281–282, 289, 303
   Central Valley, 78

North Pacific, 197, 201, 203, 208, 210, 216–217, 231, 234–235
Northern Plains, 132, 150–151
San José, 23, 56–60
South Pacific, 330–331, 339, 342, 345, 350–351, 364
North Caribbean Coast, 377–389
North Pacific, 8, 169–245
children's activities, 180–181, 193, 202, 207, 213, 217, 224–225, 235–236, 239
contacts and resources, 245
ecotourism, 192–194, 198, 227, 241–242, 418
Far Northern Guanacaste, 174–188
hotels, 173, 175, 178–182, 184, 186–187, 193, 196–197, 200–201, 203–207, 210, 214–215, 219–221, 223, 225–226, 229–231, 233–234, 236–240, 242
Nicoya Coast, 188–238
nightlife, 197, 201, 203, 208, 210, 216–217, 231, 234–235
outdoor activities, 170, 172, 174–175, 180, 183–184, 193, 195–196, 199–200, 202, 204–207, 209, 211–213, 219, 220, 222–224, 228, 232–233, 236, 239, 241–242
price categories, 173
restaurants, 173, 186, 196, 200, 202, 205, 207, 209–210, 213–214, 219, 221, 223, 225, 228–229, 233, 236–237, 242
shopping, 197–198, 201, 217, 226, 231, 235
Tempisque River Basin, 238–242
transportation, 243–245
Northern Lowlands, 372–377
Northern Plains, 7–8, 114–167
Arenal Volcano area, 122–135
Caño Negro Refuge Area, 152–154
children's activities, 116, 125, 137, 143, 145, 163–164
contacts and resources, 167
ecotourism in, 121, 125, 143, 145–146, 418
hotels, 115, 117, 121, 123, 127, 130–135, 148–150, 152–153, 156–157, 160, 162–163, 165–166

Monteverde Cloud Forest Area, 135–151
nightlife and the arts, 132, 150–151
Northwest of San José, 116–122
outdoor activities and sports, 116, 128–129, 134, 152–154, 156, 162
Puerto Viejo Loop, 154–166
restaurants, 115, 121, 129–130, 147–148, 156
shopping, 120, 132, 150
transportation, 166–167
Nosara, 226–232
Nosara Yoga Institute, 227
Nuevo Arenal, 133–134

O

Ollie's Point, 180, 199
Original Canopy Tour, 140
Orosi Valley, 68
Orosi Valley Loop, 97–102
Osa Peninsula, 345–364, 419
Ostional National Wildlife Refuge, 227
Outdoor activities, 18
Caribbean, 370, 376–377, 379–383, 388, 391, 395–396, 399–400, 402–404, 409–410
Central Pacific, 248, 250, 256, 259–260, 264, 267, 270–272, 274–279, 283, 286, 288, 294, 296–297
Central Valley, 68, 104, 107
North Pacific, 170, 172, 174–175, 180, 183–184, 193, 195–196, 199–200, 202, 204–207, 209, 211–213, 219, 220, 222–224, 228, 232–233, 236, 239, 241–242
Northern Plains, 114, 127–129, 157–159, 116, 128–129, 134, 152–154, 156, 162
South Pacific, 310, 313–315, 316, 320, 323, 326–327, 332–333, 337, 340–341, 346–348, 353, 354, 356–361, 363
Oxcarts, 13–14, 72, 117, 120

P

Pachanga ✕ *, 214*
Pachira Lodge 🏨 *, 385*
Pacific Edge 🏨 *, 330*

Packing tips, 465–467
Pacuare River, 68
Palo Verde National Park, 21, 238–240
Panama border, 411
Papagayo Peninsula, 188
Paquera, 253
Paraíso, 101
Parasailing, 297
Parque Central (Alajuela), *83*
Parque Central (Barve de Heredia), *94*
Parque Central (Heredia), *90–91*
Parque Central (San José), *34–35*
Parque España, 35
Parque Juan Santamaría, 83
Parque Metropolitano La Sabana, 38
Parque Morazán, 35
Parque Nacional, 35
Parque Reptilandia, 326
Parque Zoológico Simón Bolívar, 40
Paso Real, 324
Passports and visas, 467
Pavones, 17, 278
Peace Lodge 🏨 *, 156–157*
Peñas Blancas, 183
Pharmacies, 459
Phone cards, 470–471
Pico Blanco, 72
Piedras Blancas National Park, 336
Pizza & Pasta a Go-Go ✕ *, 233*
Pizzeria El Jardin Tortuga ✕ *, 333*
Pizzeria Liliana ✕ *, 323*
Playa Avellanas, 222–223
Playa Bahía Junquillal, 181
Playa Ballena, 332
Playa Cacao, 336
Playa Carillo, 235–237
Playa Cocles, 278
Playa Conchal, 208–211
Playa Copal, 183
Playa de los Artistas ✕ *, 260*
Playa Dominical, 326
Playa Dominicalito, 326
Playa Escondido, 292
Playa Espadilla, 290
Playa Espadilla Sur, 292
Playa Flamingo, 16, 206–208
Playa Grande, 16, 218–220
Playa Guiones, 227

Playa Hermosa, 21, 195–198, 278, 283–285
Playa Herradura, 274–275
Playa Jobo, 183
Playa Junquillal, 224–226
Playa La Pita, 272–273
Playa Langosta, 220–222
Playa Manuel Antonio, 292
Playa Nancite, 180
Playa Naranjo, 180
Playa Negra, 223–224, 278
Playa Nicuesa Rainforest Lodge 🏨, 338
Playa Ocotal, 202–203
Playa Pan de Azúcar, 203–204
Playa Pavones, 16, 343–345
Playa Piñuela, 332
Playa Playita, 292
Playa Potrero, 204–206
Playa Rajada, 183
Playa Tambor, 256–257
Playa Uvita, 331–332
Playa Ventanas, 332
Playa Zancudo, 340–341
Playas del Coco, 198–202
Plaza de la Cultura, 35–36
Plaza de la Democracia, 36–37
Plaza del Banco Central, 37
Poás volcano, 19, 154–157
Pop's ✕, 32
Pozo Azul, 326
Price categories
Caribbean, 371
Central Pacific, 251
Central Valley, 71
hotels, 71, 115, 173, 251, 311, 371
North Pacific, 173
Northern Plains, 115
restaurants, 71, 115, 173, 251, 311, 371
San José, 27
South Pacific, 311
Prostitution, 257
Puerto Jiménez, 345–352
Puerto Viejo de Sarapiquí, 18, 160–164
Puerto Viejo de Talamanca, 400–409, F17
Punta Catedral, 292
Punta Islita, 237–238
Punta Serrucho, 292
Punta Uva, 16
Puntarenas, 252–253

Q

Quepos, 18, 285–289

R

Rain forests, 17, 19–22
Caribbean, 319
Northern Plains, 114
Rainmaker nature reserve, 286
Ranario de Monteverde, 143
Rancho Santa Alicia, 186
Rappelling, 129, 162
Rara Avis, 165–166
Reserva Biológica Nosara, 227
Resort Florblanca ✕ 🏨, 265
Restaurants, 456
Caribbean, 371, 383–384, 392, 396–397, 404–405, 410
Central Pacific, 252–253, 257–258, 260, 264–265, 267, 272–274, 279, 284, 288, 298–299
Central Valley, 76–77, 79–80, 85–86, 89–93, 96, 101–103, 107, 76–77, 79–81
health issues, 458
menu guide, 438–440
North Pacific, 173, 186, 196, 200, 202, 205, 207, 209–210, 213–214, 219, 221, 223, 225, 228–229, 233, 236–237, 242
Northern Plains, 115, 121, 129–130, 147–148, 156
price categories, 71, 115, 173, 251, 311, 371
San José, 23, 40–49, 58
South Pacific, 312, 315, 318, 323, 327–328, 333, 337–338, 341, 343, 348–349
Restrooms, 467
Río Pacuare, 104
Río Reventazón, 104
Rincón de la Vieja National Park, 170, 174–179
Rincón de la Vieja Volcano, 18, 21
Rio Savegre, 315
Riptides, 279
Rock River Lodge 🏨, 134

S

Sámara, 232–235, 278
Safety, 455, 467–469
Sailing, 22
Salsa Brava, 278
San Antonio de Belén, 81–82
San Antonio de Escazú, 72
San Gerard de Rivas, 320–321
San Gerardo de Dota, 313–317
San Isidro, 317–320
San José, 7, 18–20, 23–65
Barrios Amón and Otoya, 23, 52–54
children's activities, 33, 39–40
contacts and resources, 64–65
downtown, 28–37
emergencies, 65
hotels, 49–56
nightlife and the arts, 24, 56–60
North and East of downtown, 38–39, 54–55
price categories, 27
restaurants, 24, 40–49, 58
shopping, 60–62
transportation, 63–64
West of downtown, 37–38, 54
San Miguel, 72
San Rafael de Heredia, 159
San Ramón, 120–122
San Vito, 322–324
Sanchiri Mirador, 98, 101
Santa Ana, 79–81
Santa Elena, 143, 145–151, 137
Santa Elena Reserve, 137, 146
Santa Rosa National Park, 179–181
Santa Teresa, 263–266
Santamaría, Juan, 82
Santo Domingo, 89–90
Sarchí, 117, 120
Savegre Hotel de Montaña 🏨, 315–316
Scuba diving
Caribbean, 370, 409–410
Central Pacific, 271
health issues, 458
North Pacific, 170, 172, 196, 199, 202, 206, 232
South Pacific, 310, 332
tours, 473–474
Selvatura, 137
Sendero Botello trail, 159
Sendero Tranquilo Reserve, 143, 146
Serpentario Monteverde, 143
Shawandha Lodge 🏨, 405
Shopping
Caribbean, 386, 392, 408–409
Central Pacific, 282, 304
Central Valley, 78–79, 80
North Pacific, 197–198, 201, 217, 226, 231, 235
Northern Plains, 120, 132, 150

San José, 61–62
South Pacific, 313, 324,
    330–331, 334, 339, 344–345,
    352
Shuttle vans, 451
Caribbean, 413
Central Pacific, 306
Central Valley, 109–110
North Pacific, 245
Northern Plains, 167
South Pacific, 365
Siquirres, 373, 376–377
Snorkeling
Caribbean, 370, 399–400,
    409–410
Central Pacific, 248, 250, 294,
    297
North Pacific, 196, 199, 202,
    232
South Pacific, 310, 332, 363
Soma ✕, 264
South Pacific, 9, 307–365
beaches, 326, 331–332, 336,
    340–345
Central highlands, 312–317
children's activities, 317–318,
    320–321, 325–329, 332–334,
    338, 344, 347–348, 350,
    353, 355, 362–364
Coast, 325–334
contacts and resources, 365
ecotourism, 194, 353–354,
    357–361, 419
Golfo Dulce, 334–345
hotels, 312–313, 315–316,
    318–321, 323–324, 328–330,
    333–334, 338–339, 341–342,
    344, 349–350, 353–356,
    362–364
nightlife, 330–331, 339, 342,
    345, 350–351, 364
Osa Peninsula, 345–364
outdoor activities, 310,
    313–315, 316, 320, 323,
    326–327, 332–333, 337,
    340–341, 346–348, 353, 354,
    356–361, 363
price categories, 311
restaurants, 312, 315, 318, 323,
    327–328, 333, 337–338, 341,
    343, 348–349
shopping, 313, 324, 330–331,
    334, 339, 344–345, 352
transportation, 364–365
Valle de El General region,
    317–325
Southern Nicoya tip,
    252–266
Sueño del Mar ▨, 221

Surfing, 17, 278
Caribbean, 370, 403
Central Pacific, 248, 264,
    277–279, 283–284
North Pacific, 170, 172, 180,
    199, 213, 219, 222–223,
    228, 232–233
South Pacific, 310, 327, 343,
    353
Swimming, 279, 294, 297

T

Tárcoles, 270–272
Tabacón Hot Springs, 19
Tabacón Resort ▨, 130
Taller Eloy Alfaro eHijos, 120
Tamarindo, 17, 211–218, 278
Tamarindo Wildlife Refuge,
    218
Tambor Tropical ▨, 258
Tapantí National Park, 97,
    99–100, 102
Taxes, 464–465
Taxis, 469
Central Valley, 110
San José, 65
Teatro Nacional, 36
Teatro Popular Melico Salazar,
    37
Telephones, 469–470
Tempisque River Basin,
    238–242
Terciopelo Cave, 240–241
Termales del Bosque, 123
Tilarán, 134–135
Time zones, 471
Tin Jo ✕, 47
Tipping, 465
Tirimba Rainforest Center, 161
Tiskita Jungle Lodge ▨, 344
Toad Hall, 132
Tortuga Lodge ▨, 385–386
Tortuguero, 379, 383–387
Tortuguero National Park, 16,
    380–382
Tours and packages,
    455–456, 471–474
Caribbean, 371, 383, 402–403,
    371
Central Valley, 71
ecotours, 423–425
North Pacific, 173
Northern Plains, 115, 127,
    140–141
Train travel, 393
Trams, 141
Transportation
Caribbean, 386–387, 411–413

Central Pacific, 305–306
Central Valley, 109–110
North Pacific, 243–245
Northern Plains, 166–167
San José, 63–64
South Pacific, 364–365
Travel agencies, 474–475
Traveler's checks, 465
Tropical dry forests, 319
Tropical Garden Hotel ▨,
    281
Turrialba, 18, 104–109
Turtle watching
Caribbean, 370, 380–383
North Pacific, 170, 172, 180,
    213, 218–219

U

Ultralight flights, 233, 277,
    297, 333

V

Venado Caverns, 128
Villa Alegre ▨, 221
Villa Decary ▨, 133
Villablanca ▨, 121–122
Villas de la Selva ▨, 301
Villas Rio Mar ▨, 329
Visas, 467
Visitor information, 475–476
Vista del Valle Plantation Inn
    ▨, 117
Vocabulary, 441–444
Volcán Arenal, 18, 126–127
Volcán Irazú, 96, 103
Volcán Turrialba, 105–106
Volcanoes, F18–22
Cartago and Irazú volcanos,
    95–103
Central Valley, 68, 94–103,
    105–106
North Pacific, 170, 172,
    175–179
Northern Plains, 126–127,
    154–159
Volunteer programs,
    476–477

W

Waterfalls, 125, 248, 260,
    270, 315, 326
Watson, Modest, 394
Websites, 477
Whale-watching, 310, 333
White-water rafting, 18
Caribbean, 370, 376–377, 403
Central Pacific, 286

Central Valley, 68, 104
North Pacific, 239
Northern Plains, 129, 162
Wildlife and plant glossary,
432–437
Wildlife watching, 238–239,
248, 250, 293–295, 297,
310, 323, 351, 358–360,
370

Wilson Botanical Garden,
322–323
Windsurfing, 134, 183–184
Witch's Rock, 180, 199
Women travelers, tips for, 469

X

Xandari Resort Hotel & Spa
🖼, 87

Y

Ylang-Ylang Beach Resort 🖼,
261
Yoga, 250

Z

Zarcero, 122
Zona de Los Santos, 312–313
Zoo Ave, 83

PHOTO CREDITS

Cover Photo (red-eyed tree frog): Turco. 5, *Punta Islita Ocean Resort.* 8, *Michael Javorka/viestiphoto.com.* 9 (left), *Jenny K. Frost.* 9 (right), *Juan Amighetti/Costa Rica Tourist Board (ICT).* 12, *Ken Ross/viestiphoto.com.* 13, *Ken Ross/viestiphoto.com.* 14, *Philip Coblentz/Brand X Pictures.* 16, *Jenny K. Frost.* 17, *Ken Ross/viestiphoto.com.* 18, *Jenny K. Frost.* **Chapter 1: San José:** 23, *Costa Rica Tourist Board (ICT).* 24 (top), *Ken Ross/viestiphoto.com.* 24 (bottom left), *Ken Ross/viestiphoto.com.* 24 (bottom right), *José Fuste Raga/age fotostock.* 25, *CostaRicaPhotos.com.* 26, *Ken Ross/viestiphoto.com.* 27 (left), *Ken Ross/viestiphoto.com.* 27 (right), *Dan Peha/viestiphoto.com.* **Chapter 2: Central Valley:** 67, *Juan Amighetti/Costa Rica Tourist Board (ICT).* 68 (top), *Ken Ross/viestiphoto.com.* 68 (bottom left), *Costa Rica Consulate.* 68 (bottom right), *Costa Rica Tourist Board (ICT).* 69 (left), *G. Cozzi /age fotostock.* 69 (right), *Rios Tropicales.* 71 (top), *Rancho Naturalista.* 71 (bottom), *Dan Peha/viestiphoto.com.* 97 (top), *Ken Ross/viestiphoto.com.* 97 (bottom), *Philip Coblentz/Brand X Pictures.* 99, *Costa Rica Tourist Board (ICT).* 100, *Kevin Schafer/age fotostock.* 101, *Ken Ross/viestiphoto.com.* **Chapter 3: The Northern Plains:** 111, *Ken Ross/viestiphoto.com.* 112 (top), *Ken Ross/viestiphoto.com.* 112 (bottom), *Ken Ross/viestiphoto.com.* 113 (top), *Ken Ross/viestiphoto.com.* 113 (bottom left), *Ken Ross/viestiphoto.com.* 113 (bottom right), *Ken Ross/viestiphoto.com.* 114, *Ken Ross/viestiphoto.com.* 126, *Ken Welsh/age fotostock.* 127, *Ken Ross/viestiphoto.com.* 138 (top), *Ken Ross/viestiphoto.com.* 138 (bottom), *Sky Walk, Monteverde.* 139 (top), *Sky Walk, Monteverde.* 139 (bottom), *Jenny K. Frost.* 140, *Ken Ross/viestiphoto.com.* **Chapter 4: The North Pacific:** 169, *Costa Rica Tourist Board (ICT).* 170 (top), *CostaRicaPhotos.com.* 170 (bottom), *Juan Amighetti/Costa Rica Tourist Board (ICT).* 171 (top), *Costa Rica Tourist Board (ICT).* 171 (center), *Alvaro Leiva/age fotostock.* 171 (bottom), *Ken Ross/viestiphoto.com.* 173, *Ken Ross/viestiphoto.com.* 189 (top), *Ken Ross/viestiphoto.com.* 189 (bottom), *Joe Viesti/viestiphoto.com.* 190, *Ken Ross/viestiphoto.com.* 191 (top), *© age fotostock.* 191 (center), *Hotel Luna Azul.* 191 (bottom), *Punta Islita Ocean Resort.* 192 (top), *Ken Ross/viestiphoto.com.* 192 (bottom), *Ken Ross/viestiphoto.com.* **Chapter 5: The Central Pacific:** 247, *Scott West/viestiphoto.com.* 248 (top), *CostaRicaPhotos.com.* 248 (bottom), *Ken Ross/viestiphoto.com.* 249 (top), *Juan Amighetti/Costa Rica Tourist Board (ICT).* 249 (center), *Ken Ross/viestiphoto.com.* 249 (bottom), *Jenny K. Frost.* 251, *Ken Ross/viestiphoto.com.* 291, *Philip Coblentz/Brand X Pictures.* 292, *Alvaro Leiva/age fotostock.* 293, *SuperStock/age fotostock.* 294, *Alison Skrabek.* 295, *Ken Ross/viestiphoto.com.* **Chapter 6: South Pacific:** 307, *Ken Ross/viestiphoto.com.* 308 (top), *Ken Ross/viestiphoto.com.* 308 (bottom left), *Ken Ross/viestiphoto.com.* 308 (bottom right), *Ken Ross/viestiphoto.com.* 309 (top), *Costa Rica Tourist Board (ICT).* 309 (bottom), *Ken Ross/viestiphoto.com.* 310, *Ken Ross/viestiphoto.com.* 311 (top), *Costa Rica Tourist Board (ICT).* 311 (bottom), *Costa Rica Consulate.* 357, *Ken Ross/viestiphoto.com.* 359 (first row left), *Ken Ross/viestiphoto.com.* 359 (first row center), *Philip Coblentz/Brand X Pictures.* 359 (first row right), *SuperStock/age fotostock.* 359 (second row left), *Robert Winslow/viestiphoto.com.* 359 (second row center), *Bill Terry/viestiphoto.com.* 359 (second row right), *Bill Terry/viestiphoto.com.* 359 (third row left), *Ken Ross/viestiphoto.com.* 359 (third row center), *Mary Clay/viestiphoto.com.* 359 (third row right), *Bill Terry/viestiphoto.com.* 359 (fourth row left), *Eric Horan/age fotostock.* 359 (fourth row center), *Kevin Schafer/age fotostock.* 359 (fourth row right), *Morales/age fotostock.* 359 (bottom), *Kevin Schafer/age fotostock.* **Chapter 7: The Caribbean Coast:** 367, *Alfredo Maiquez/age fotostock.* 368 (top), *Costa Rica Tourist Board (ICT).* 368 (bottom left), *Ken Ross/viestiphoto.com.* 368 (bottom right), *Alison Skrabek.* 369 (top), *Costa Rica Tourist Board (ICT).* 369 (bottom), *Costa Rica Tourist Board (ICT).* 370, *Ken Ross/viestiphoto.com.* 371, *Robert Winslow/viestiphoto.com.* 380, *Joe Viesti/viestiphoto.com.* 381, *Ken Ross/viestiphoto.com.* 382 (top), *Ken Ross/viestiphoto.com.* 382 (bottom), *Caribbean Conservation Corporation.* **Color Section:** View of Arenal Volcano on a clear day: *Ken Ross/viestiphoto.com.* Manuel Antonio National Park coastline: *Robert Winslow/viestiphoto.com.* Tica dancer performs at a cultural festival in San José: *Ken Ross/viestiphoto.com.* White-faced capuchin: *Philip Coblentz/Brand X Pictures.* Digging into Class-IV rapids on the Pacuáre River: *Dan Peha/viestiphoto.com.* Sky Walk's hanging-bridge hike in Monteverde Cloud Forest: *Ken Ross/viestiphoto.com.* A scarlet macaw and blue-and-gold macaw: *Kurt Ramseyer/viestiphoto.com.* Sun-seekers at Espadilla Beach, in Manuel Antonio National Park: *Alvaro Leiva/age fotostock.* Black river turtles hang out in Tortuguero: *Ken Ross/viestiphoto.com.* Coffee beans: *Michael Javorka/viestiphoto.com.* Painted oxcart: *Brand X Pictures.* The clear-blue crater lake at Poás Volcano: *Ken Ross/viestiphoto.com.* San José's Pre-Columbian Gold Museum: *Costa Rica Tourist Board.* Heliconia: *S. Murphy-Larronde/age fotostock.*

NOTES

NOTES

NOTES

NOTES

NOTES

NOTES

NOTES

NOTES

NOTES

NOTES

ABOUT OUR WRITERS

Freelance writer David Dudenhoefer has spent the better part of the past two decades in Costa Rica. He first arrived in 1986 as an exchange student at the Universidad de Costa Rica, where he concentrated on tropical biology and surfing. In the ensuing years he wrote for dozens of publications, guided nature tours, and contributed to seven other Fodor's guides. He has written extensively on ecotourism in Costa Rica and elsewhere and has worked for organizations that promote sustainable tourism, such as the Rainforest Alliance and United Nations Development Programme. David is convinced that straying from the beaten path and spending time with the locals is an excellent way to spice up any vacation. This year he wrote the chapter on ecotourism.

Yolanda Hernandez, our Central Pacific writer, arrived in Costa Rica in 2002 to write for a nonprofit housing organization. Based in the San José area, she's now a freelance writer, editor, translator, and theater student. She travels throughout Latin America and the Caribbean.

Brian Kluepfel lives in the suburbs of New York and ekes out a living as a freelance writer when his cats are not pestering him. He has traveled and worked in Central and South America and is the former editor of the *Bolivian Times*. He has also updated the Fodor's Guides to Peru, Chile, Alaska, Guatemala and South America, and is the author of one children's book.

World traveler and seasoned journalist Dorothy MacKinnon arrived in Costa Rica in 1999, promptly fell in love with the country, and took up a post in San José to contribute stories to *The Tico Times* on ecotourism—and to write the North Pacific and South Pacific chapters of this guide. Along the way, she has learned passable Spanish and become a passionate birder and enthusiastic nature-lover. In her past life, she was a reporter and copy editor for *The Financial Post* in Canada and *The Washington Post*.

Joy Rothke is a freelance journalist who lived in the Northern Lowlands of Costa Rica for three years, where she learned to love birds and ignore insects. Joy has been published in many print and online newspapers and journals, including the *Chicago Tribune, San Francisco Chronicle, The New York Times* syndicate, *The Tico Times* (in Costa Rica), *Diablo* magazine, and *San Francisco Focus* magazine (where she also served as an editor), Salon.com, Women.com, and MSN Sidewalk.com.

Biologist and naturalist Ryan Sarsfield travels extensively in Central and South America, but considers Costa Rica his first home away from home. He has studied insect dung in Guanacaste, Costa Rica; birds in Pohnpei, Micronesia; and rattlesnakes in Sonora, Mexico. He has also taught Spanish on a Japanese cruise ship and English in Brazil; and led tours in Brazil and Venezuela. Ryan revised the Central Valley chapter and wrote the wildlife glossary.

Suzanna Starcevic came to Costa Rica in 2000 on a whim, and is mildly surprised (and somewhat pleased) to find herself still there. A journalist by trade, she has worked her way across Canada as a writer and editor, and spent three years as Weekend Editor at *The Tico Times*. She currently works as a translator and freelance writer. Suzanna revised the Central Valley and Smart Travel Tips A to Z chapters.

San José–based freelance writer and pharmacist Jeffrey Van Fleet has spent the last decade enjoying Costa Rica's long rainy seasons and Wisconsin's cold winters. (Most people would try to do it the other way around.) He saw his first resplendent quetzal, that bird-watcher's Holy Grail, while researching this guide. Jeff is a regular contributor to Costa Rica's English-language newspaper, *The Tico Times,* and has written for Fodor's guides to Chile, Argentina, Peru, and Central and South America. Jeff updated the San José, Caribbean, and Northern Plains chapters for this edition.